The Student Handbook to
THE APPRAISAL OF REAL ESTATE

14th Edition

Readers of this text may also be interested in the following publications from the Appraisal Institute:

- *The Appraisal of Real Estate*, 14th edition
- *Capitalization Theory and Techniques Study Guide*, 3rd edition
- *The Dictionary of Real Estate Appraisal*, 5th edition
- *Market Analysis for Real Estate*
- *Valuation by Comparison: Residential Analysis and Logic*

Appraisal
Institute®

*Professionals Providing
Real Estate Solutions*

The Student Handbook to
THE APPRAISAL OF REAL ESTATE

14th Edition

By Mark R. Rattermann, MAI, SRA

Appraisal Institute • 200 W. Madison • Suite 1500 • Chicago, IL 60606 • www.appraisalinstitute.org

The Appraisal Institute advances global standards, methodologies, and practices through the professional development of property economics worldwide.

Reviewer (current edition): Peter D. Bowes, MAI
Reviewers (earlier editions): Don M. Emerson, MAI, SRA
Frank E. Harrison, MAI, SRA
John A. Schwartz, MAI

Chief Executive Officer: Frederick H. Grubbe
Director of Communications: Ken Chitester
Senior Manager, Publications: Stephanie Shea-Joyce
Senior Book Editor/Technical Writer: Michael McKinley
Technical Book Editor: Emily Ruzich
Manager, Book Design/Production: Michael Landis

For Educational Purposes Only

The materials presented in this text represent the opinions and views of the developers and reviewers. Although these materials may have been reviewed by members of the Appraisal Institute, the views and opinions expressed herein are not endorsed or approved by the Appraisal Institute as policy unless adopted by the Board of Directors pursuant to the Bylaws of the Appraisal Institute. While substantial care has been taken to provide accurate and current data and information, the Appraisal Institute does not warrant the accuracy or timeliness of the data and information contained herein. Further, any principles and conclusions presented in this textbook are subject to court decisions and to local, state, and federal laws and regulations and any revisions of such laws and regulations.

This book is sold for educational and informational purposes only with the understanding that the Appraisal Institute is not engaged in rendering legal, accounting, or other professional advice or services. Nothing in these materials is to be construed as the offering of such advice or services. If expert advice or services are required, readers are responsible for obtaining such advice or services from appropriate professionals.

Nondiscrimination Policy

The Appraisal Institute advocates equal opportunity and nondiscrimination in the appraisal profession and conducts its activities in accordance with applicable federal, state, and local laws.

Library of Congress Cataloging-in-Publication Data
Rattermann, Mark, 1951-
   The student handbook to The appraisal of real estate, 14th edition / by Mark R. Rattermann, MAI, SRA.
      pages cm
   "This student handbook is designed to be used as a supplement to the 14th edition of The Appraisal of Real Estate."
   ISBN 978-1-935328-50-6
1. Real property--Valuation--United States--Handbooks, manuals, etc. 2. Personal property--Valuation--United States--Handbooks, manuals, etc. I. Appraisal of real estate. II. Title.
   HD1389.5.U6R89 2014
   333.33'2--dc23

2013042233

Table of Contents

About the Author

Mark R. Rattermann, MAI, SRA, has been a real estate appraiser and broker in Indianapolis since 1979. He initially worked as a residential broker only but soon moved to focus on real estate appraisals. He has written eight books about real estate and appraisals with a focus on both residential and nonresidential topics.

Additionally, Mr. Rattermann has written courses and seminars for the Appraisal Institute and has been a teacher of appraisal courses and seminars for 30 years. He has lectured in 40 states and four foreign countries and has written over 20 seminars for both online and classroom presentation. He has been published many times in *The Appraisal Journal.*

Mr. Rattermann lives in the Indianapolis area with his wife of 29 years, Jeanine. They have four grandchildren who all live in the area.

Mr. Rattermann's contact information is listed on the Appraisal Institute website (www.appraisalinstitute.org) and can be located by clicking on "Find an Appraiser."

Foreword

The Student Handbook to THE APPRAISAL OF REAL ESTATE, 14TH EDITION complements the latest edition of the Appraisal Institute's classic text, highlighting key concepts and providing supplementary examples and exercises for classroom use or self-study. Together, the textbook and handbook provide a solid foundation for beginning appraisers to develop a sound understanding of the profession, prepare for the state licensing examination, and make a strong start in their appraisal careers.

The 14th edition of *The Appraisal of Real Estate* contains significant updates to keep up with important changes in the appraisal industry while remaining firmly rooted in essential appraisal principles. The textbook has been reorganized into three major components: the introductory chapters that cover real estate and appraisal, the core set of chapters that mirror the organization of the valuation process, and the concluding chapters that cover appraisal practice specialties such as appraisal review and consulting. The 14th edition also includes more discussion of important topics such as scope of work, statistics, appraisal review, consulting, valuation for financial reporting, and green building.

The *Student Handbook* has been updated to reflect revisions in the textbook and to provide easy-to-follow discussions of the topics covered. This handbook does not replace the textbook. Rather, it helps explain the essential concepts of valuation theory using examples based on situations that appraisers commonly face. The handbook walks readers through every chapter of the 14th edition of *The Appraisal of Real Estate*, summarizing key concepts, identifying important terms, and providing additional examples. Each chapter of the *Student Handbook* ends with a set of review exercises for readers to work through and test the knowledge they have acquired. Suggested solutions to these exercises are provided for classroom discussion or further study.

The author of this handbook, Mark R. Rattermann, MAI, SRA, a long-time fellow colleague in the Appraisal Institute's Hoosier State Chapter, is widely recognized as an experienced and respected real estate educator with firsthand knowledge of what students need to know and how they learn best. Like other Appraisal Institute handbooks, this student handbook contains practical, valuable instructional material for the well-rounded appraiser. In tandem with *The Appraisal of Real Estate*, 14th edition, the *Student Handbook* is a useful resource to help beginning appraisers understand essential appraisal principles and procedures and achieve their career goals. An appraiser new to the profession—or any real estate professional in a related discipline interested in valuation—will find that the *Student Handbook* provides the shortest route to appraisal competence. I truly wish such a handbook had been available to me 35 years ago when I entered the profession and am thrilled that the Appraisal Institute has made this material available to professional valuers, in addition to those interested in valuation, from around the world.

Richard L. Borges II, MAI, SRA
2013 President
Appraisal Institute

How to Use This Book

This student handbook is designed to be used as a supplement to the 14th edition of *The Appraisal of Real Estate* textbook and can serve as a student manual for education providers engaged in qualifying education for beginning real estate appraisal students. The material in this handbook may not be sufficient to meet all educational requirements in every state, so check with your state agency for specific state certification requirements.

The *Student Handbook* expands upon and provides alternative explanations of topics covered in *The Appraisal of Real Estate*, 14th edition. The theoretical foundation of appraisal and the mechanics of the valuation process are summarized, but students seeking further clarification should consult the textbook.

Each chapter of this handbook includes a list of the key words that well-informed appraisers should be familiar with. Key words are defined in the current editions of the textbook and *The Dictionary of Real Estate Appraisal*. When necessary, additional explanation of frequently encountered and often confused terms is provided in this text.

This handbook also includes review exercises at the end of each chapter to reinforce the topics presented and provide additional problems to solve. The solutions to the review exercises are not designed to replace the conclusions presented in the textbook, but rather to elaborate on that material. Suggested solutions to the review exercises appear at the end of each chapter. Many of the solutions include references to corresponding pages in *The Appraisal of Real Estate*, 14th edition, and readers are advised to consult the textbook for additional discussion of the topics covered.

Suggested Study Habits

- Read the textbook material and the associated chapters in the handbook. If the handbook is used in a classroom setting, do your reading before class begins. Rereading the material again after the class lecture may be necessary for students with limited real estate experience.
- Highlight the text and take notes in the margins. Use one highlighter color for the material you do not understand, one for the material you want to go over again, and another for the material that is likely to be on the examination (if applicable).
- Scan the material before sitting down to read it closely. Set a goal for each reading session. Create a schedule that will get you to your goal in the allotted time. A realistic and achievable timetable for reading the textbook is essential.
- After reading a section, take some time to think about what you have just read. It is important to review the material so that it sticks with you.
- Try to answer the questions at the end of each chapter, even if you did not feel you understood everything you read. Mark your answers with a pencil so you can correct any incorrect answers later.
- Review the key words highlighted at the beginning of each chapter so that you know the new terms to look for. Test developers focus on these terms because professional competency requires a clear understanding of the technical language used in the profession.
- Have a dictionary available when you read. The most current edition of *The Dictionary of Real Estate Appraisal* is the best reference for appraisal-related terminology, but a standard English dictionary is better than none at all.
- Have a calculator available at all times. The best calculator for solving the problems in this handbook is the Hewlett-Packard HP-12C, but other financial calculators will also work. Note that the HP-12C is usually required in advanced real estate appraisal and mortgage courses.

Introduction

The Appraisal Profession

Most state governments did not regulate appraisers before 1990, and the states that did had only limited rules with few professional educational requirements. Many people were considered to be appraisers just because they said they were. The only way to identify full-time, professional appraisers was through their designations from trade associations, which was similar to hiring an accountant with a CPA certification. The public did not generally know what the designations meant or what was required to earn them, and some lesser-quality designations were developed and promoted, diminishing the credibility of the designations from the larger organizations.

Two of the largest and most well-known real estate appraisal organizations, the Society of Real Estate Appraisers and the American Institute of Real Estate Appraisers (AIREA), unified to establish the Appraisal Institute in 1991. These organizations had been independent of each other since they each got their start in the 1930s. The Society of Real Estate Appraisers was established primarily as an organization for residential appraisers. The Society had ties to the savings and loan community. The American Institute of Real Estate Appraisers was set up under the banner of the National Association of Real Estate Boards, which is now the National Association of Realtors. When the Society and the AIREA unified, that affiliation with the Realtors ceased. The merger also simplified the designations for appraisers and clients alike. Only two designations are now awarded–the MAI and the SRA. The other designations from the Society and AIREA still exist, but no new designations are currently given. All the designations still have meaning in the marketplace, but state licensing and certification of appraisers has changed the perception of appraisal credentials for clients.

In the wake of the Savings and Loan Crisis of the late 1980s, the Federal Financial Institutions Reform, Recovery, and Enforcement Act (FIRREA) of 1989 restricted appraisals of *federally related transactions* (FRTs) to state-licensed or state-certified appraisers. Each state was charged with setting up an agency to regulate the licensing of the profession. While FIRREA only required appraisers to be licensed or certified to do federally related transactions, many state agencies used the new licensing requirements as the standard for all appraisals.

Two of the largest and most well-known real estate appraisal organizations, the Society of Real Estate Appraisers and the American Institute of Real Estate Appraisers, unified to establish the Appraisal Institute in 1991.

---

federally related transaction (FRT)
Under Title XI of the Financial Institutions Reform, Recovery and Enforcement Act (FIRREA), any real estate-related financial transaction that a Federal Financial Institutions Regulatory Agency (FFIRA) engages in, contracts for, or regulates, and that requires the services of an appraiser.

KEY TERMS	
advocacy	certification
appraisal	client
The Appraisal Foundation	client pressure
appraisal report	federally related transaction
Appraisal Subcommittee	licensing
appraiser	

FIRREA established The Appraisal Foundation (TAF) to set the appraisal rules and minimum qualifications for the state programs. The non-profit organization is directed by a board of trustees and has two boards charged with the most important duties:

- The Appraiser Qualifications Board (AQB) establishes the minimum amount of education and experience required for licensing or certification. The AQB also establishes the exam content outline that states use to set educational goals for their programs and to guide curriculum development. A significant overhaul of the AQB's educational curriculum and experience requirements went into effect in 2008.
- The Appraisal Standards Board (ASB) writes, edits, and amends the Uniform Standards of Professional Appraisal Practice (USPAP), the document stipulated by FIRREA as "the rules" for appraisers. By itself, USPAP carries no legal authority. However, it becomes the law of the land through adoption by state, local, and federal agencies. In many states, USPAP rules have been adopted for all appraisals regardless of the involvement of the federal government in a transaction.

FIRREA also named the Appraisal Subcommittee of the Federal Financial Institutions Examination Council (FFIEC) as the governmental regulating arm to ensure that all the state programs were in compliance with federal requirements. The Appraisal Subcommittee of the FFIEC audits each state every few years to ensure that state programs comply with the law. If the programs do not comply, they can be decertified and would not be acceptable to federally regulated lenders and others. So although states have their own independent programs, the federal government maintains a supervisory role in the process.

In many states, the types of appraisal licenses offered include the following:

- Trainee, Registered, or Associate Appraiser
- Licensed Residential Appraiser
- Certified Residential Appraiser
- Certified General Appraiser

Trainee, Registered, or Associate Appraiser

The trainee classification usually includes some sort of apprenticeship period. In some states these appraisers can do all types of work, but in other states they are limited to certain tasks. Most states allow trainees to focus on residential or non-residential properties, depending on the focus and license of the supervisor. In many states, the trainee can serve the apprenticeship and then apply for the Certified General license, skipping what are sometimes considered interim steps to the top level.

Licensed Residential Appraiser

Licensed Residential Appraisers are usually limited to one- to four-unit properties with loans of less than $1 million (transaction value). In most states, these licensees can also do work that does not involve federal transactions, which includes but is not limited to divorce settlements, estate settlements, and right of way condemnation projects.

Certified Residential Appraiser

Certified Residential Appraisers are usually limited to one- to four-unit properties but have no limits on transaction value. In most states, these individuals can also do work that does not involve federal transactions. In a few states, a Certified Residential Appraiser can also do non-residential work on non-federally related transactions.

Certified General Appraiser

Certified General Appraisers are usually licensed to appraise any type of property. It should be noted that having the license or certification that is approved to a certain level does not automatically bring competency. A Certified General Appraiser may not be competent in appraising a particular type or size of property or a property in a specific location despite meeting all the requirements of certification. These licensees can also do work that does not involve federally related transactions.

The worksheet on the following page provides a list of state licensing and certification requirements for you to research in your state.

Common Appraisal Designations Before FIRREA	
Conferring Body	**Designations**
American Institute of Real Estate Appraisers	MAI, RM
Society of Real Estate Appraisers	SRA, SRPA, SREA
American Society of Appraisers	ASA
Independent Fee Appraisers Association	IFA

State Licensing and Certification Requirements

Investigate the requirements for your state and fill in the following worksheet:

Requirements for Trainee, Registered, or Associate Appraiser's License

Educational requirements: _____

Experience requirements: _____

Testing: _____

Fees: _____

Other requirements: _____

Requirements for Licensed Residential Appraisers

Educational requirements: _____

Experience requirements: _____

Testing: _____

Fees: _____

Other requirements: _____

Requirements for Certified Residential Appraisers

Educational requirements: _____

Experience requirements: _____

Testing: _____

Fees: _____

Other requirements: _____

Requirements for Certified General Appraisers

Educational requirements: _____

Experience requirements: _____

Testing: _____

Fees: _____

Other requirements: _____

Helpful hint: Check www.appraisalinstitute.org/education/regagncs.asp for an updated listing of state regulatory agencies.

Ethics for Appraisers

Some professions require that practitioners be advocates for the client's position, while others prohibit it. Attorneys and real estate brokers are commonly required to be advocates. Because appraisers, like accountants, have additional obligations to the intended users of their work, they are required to be disinterested third parties and treat the client and intended users of an appraisal service with fairness and ethical behavior.

An accountant often does work in which the client and intended user are on completely different sides of the issue. In the first few years of the twenty-first century, some large accounting firms were scrutinized because they prepared audits that were considered by many to be misleading. As a result, investors put money into companies that had substantial losses that went unreported. When an accountant or appraiser takes an assignment, the customer is not always right. If a client asks you to prepare an appraisal report with a specific conclusion, you must decline that assignment. The appraisal profession suffers from some of the same client pressures as the accounting industry. Clients ask appraisers to hide the negatives and highlight the positives in their reports, but professional ethics require appraisers to be disinterested third parties. Sometimes that requires you to say no when asked to mislead the reader of the report to a conclusion other than the truth.

For many appraisers, the first days spent on the job set the tone for the remainder of their careers. If you get a reputation for doing unethical things, clients who are looking for an unethical appraiser will call you, while clients who want truthful and unbiased appraisals will stay away because they cannot afford to use an appraiser with a bad reputation.

To promote ethical behavior in the profession, appraisers should be compensated in a manner that avoids any incentive or the appearance of an incentive for deceptive practices. Most appraisers are paid by the hour or on a flat-fee basis, which provides little incentive to mislead a client or intended user. You should not structure assignments so that your payment is subject to a lender making a loan, a deal closing, or any subsequent event. For example, some appraisers accept fee arrangements in which they are paid if a mortgage loan closes. In this case, the loan may be declined if the appraisal process unearths negative information, so the appraiser would not be paid if that information were reported. This gives the appraiser an incentive to not report the negative data, which is clearly unethical.

Appraisers may not accept appraisal assignments in which they have a bias toward the property or parties involved or a monetary incentive to provide a predetermined or biased opinion of value. For example, accepting appraisal assignments from a spouse who is a loan originator paid on commission is unethical. Because the family income would be increased by the approval of loans and the loans would be approved partially on the basis of the outcome of the appraisal, that conflict of interest would make any such arrangement unacceptable.

Types of Properties Being Appraised

Residential

Residential properties include one- to four-unit homes. Properties with more than four units are considered multifamily and are classified as income-producing properties. Appraising multifamily residential properties requires extra training and experience. (Characteristics of one-unit, condominium, and two-unit homes are defined and discussed further in the chapters dealing with building description and highest and best use analysis.)

Agricultural

In some states, the largest land use is agricultural. Agricultural properties involve substantial amounts of an area's income and employment base. Appraisals of agricultural properties often require specialized knowledge of soil productivity, water rights, livestock support, and other complicated valuation criteria.

In some areas, agricultural properties are interim uses until land developers can build homes, offices, retail buildings, or other types of properties on the site. In those areas, other specialized training may be necessary to establish the depth of the market, the soil type required for construction, the availability of utilities, the absorption

---

advocacy
Representing the cause or interest of another, even if that cause or interest does not necessarily coincide with one's own beliefs, opinions, conclusions, or recommendations.

client pressure
Influence exerted by clients to force appraisers to perform their professional duties in unethical ways, e.g., returning a predetermined value for the subject of an appraisal.

---

rates for the sale of one-unit residential lots, and other valuation criteria.

Industrial
Industrial properties are involved in industry–in other words, the manufacturing, warehousing, and distribution of goods.

Commercial
The goods that are produced in industrial properties are bought and sold in commercial properties, e.g., office buildings, shopping centers, and freestanding retail properties. In other words, the business of commerce is conducted on commercial real estate.

Special-Purpose
Special-purpose properties include churches, schools, golf courses, funeral homes, railroad corridors, and automobile dealerships (which could also be considered as commercial properties). Special-purpose properties are restricted to only certain uses because of their design or configuration and often have a limited market. In some markets these unique properties can be difficult to appraise because they often raise the questions "Who would buy this, and how much would they pay?" without providing market sales data of comparable properties or other evidence to support an estimate of market value. In an appraisal of market value, there must be a market for there to be market value.

Common Mistakes in Property Classification

Industrial properties are sometimes erroneously classified as commercial properties by inexperienced appraisers. Similarly, the term *commercial property* is often used incorrectly to describe apartments, schools, churches, and other special-purpose, income-producing properties.

Clients Served

Attorneys
Attorneys will hire appraisers for divorce, estate, trust, and other legal matters that require an estimation of the value of an asset. This type of work can make up a large portion of an appraiser's practice and can provide exposure to a diverse range of property types. Litigation is common in contemporary American society, and appraisers who are skilled in presenting expert testimony can be very successful as litigation work specialists.

Lenders
All sorts of lending institutions–banks, savings banks (including trust departments), mortgage companies, and mortgage brokers–hire appraisers. Traditionally, lenders have been the largest client base for most appraisers. This tends to change over time, however, because changes in interest rates greatly affect this type of work. When rates go down, many loans are made for refinancing debt and purchasing new properties. When rates go up, first mortgage loans are fewer but second mortgage financing picks up.

Corporate Relocation Companies
Many large corporations and some government agencies transfer employees around the world on an everyday basis. Sometimes the transferring agency or corporation will offer to buy the employee's old home so that the employee can move to the new location without having to worry about it. In many markets, corporate relocation generates a large amount of appraisal work. These assignments require you to be very detailed and precise because these types of clients do not want to know what a residential property will sell for in case they have to foreclose. Rather, they want to know what a property is worth because they intend to buy it for immediate resale on the open market.

Government Agencies
When a state, city, town, or even a school district needs to acquire real estate, an appraisal must be performed before a deal can be made. Even if the government agency has an agreeable seller, two or three appraisals may be required. If the seller is not agreeable and the government agency must use its power of eminent domain, several more appraisals may need to be ordered–e.g., the condemning authority can order another appraisal, the judge may order one, two, or three more appraisals, and the property owner may order one or more appraisals.

Eminent domain and condemnation work requires specialized training and expertise, but some appraisers focus on this type of work exclusively because it allows for a much more stable practice without the common problems of collecting fees and dealing with client pressure to report a specific value. Some appraisers do nothing but easement acquisition appraisals for utility companies or utility departments in local government, although working exclusively for one agency can raise questions about objectivity and advocacy. In recent years, this has become a larger portion of many appraisers' workloads.

Private Individuals

Private individuals make up a large portion of the workloads of some appraisers, but serving these clients requires better "people skills" than working for government and financial institutions. Reporting the market value of a property could be a disappointment if the client is the owner and may even result in non-payment of the fee. To remain a disinterested third party, you should collect the fee up front and never promise a specific result on the appraisal.

Individuals Involved in Real Estate Transactions

The significant players in most real estate markets are

· buyers and sellers
· brokers and salespeople
· banks and mortgage lenders
· title insurance companies
· surveyors
· appraisers
· developers, builders, and entrepreneurs

Type of Work Requested

Appraisal

An appraisal is not a physical object but a process through which an appraiser develops an opinion of value. To complete an appraisal, you must perform all the required research and analysis, but reporting the results of the appraisal on paper may not necessarily be a part of the assignment. An appraisal report is the communication of an opinion of value with supporting information. It can be considered the *product* of the appraisal process.

Appraisal reports can be delivered in oral or written form. Oral reports are sometimes used in court situations and for zoning hearings and are often used when property owners seek advice from appraisers. Although oral reports are generally brief, standards of professional practice require appraisers to retain large workfiles of data supporting the reported conclusions along with a signed certification page, which must all be available for review upon request.

A form appraisal report is the most common written reporting format for residential properties. Form reports are seldom used for nonresidential

properties, even though nonresidential forms are available. A form report is often used as a checklist of required items and to communicate a value opinion. An appraisal form limits an appraiser's ability to communicate when a client needs a wide variety of information about the property or when the property is not a type commonly appraised. Forms are often supplemented with additional pages of comments and data.

Narrative appraisal reports are written reports that can convey an opinion of value with a much wider range of supporting information on property types, real estate interests, and specific client needs than is found in form reports. Narrative reports do not always follow a specific presentation outline like residential reports, but many appraisers do follow a format based on standards requirements. (Note that appraisal reports are covered in more detail in Chapter 31.)

Appraisal Review and Consulting

The services that appraisers provide often fall outside the strict definition of an appraisal. The most common of these services are appraisal review and consulting.

Appraisal review is the process of developing an opinion of the quality of another appraiser's work. Banks have traditionally employed appraisal reviewers to make sure that the appraisal reports they receive are complete and credible. Governmental agencies also employ appraisal reviewers to look at appraisals submitted in condemnation proceedings and other situations in which the value of real estate is at issue.

Consulting is a broader category, encompassing a variety of appraisal-related services that may involve developing an opinion of value. However, the opinion of value is not the focus of the assignment in consulting work. For example, a developer may ask an appraiser to research supply and demand levels for industrial space in the market and make a recommendation for the size and amenities of a proposed industrial park. From the appraiser's perspective, the research would focus on the feasibility of various land use options, not on the ultimate value of the real estate under investigation.

Both appraisal review and consulting assignments may involve reporting the conclusions of an appraiser's analyses. Professional standards still apply to those reports, but they differ from the standards related to appraisal reports. Appraisal review is discussed in more detail in Chapter 32, and consulting is discussed in Chapter 33.

Basic Mathematics and Analytical Skills for Appraisers

Order of Operations

1. If grouping symbols such as parentheses ( ), brackets | |, and braces { } are present, the expressions within those symbols are simplified first starting with the innermost grouping of symbols.

2. Powers and roots, if they occur, should be performed first.

3. Multiplication and division are performed in the order that they appear from left to right.

4. Addition and subtraction are then performed in the order that they appear from left to right.

In some appraisal analyses, the problems may be written using the standard order of operations, which means that analysts must know the rules. Most problems are expressed using parentheses, brackets, and braces to show the order of operations.

Exponents

The use of exponents makes it easier to write certain expressions involving repetitive multiplication:

$$K \times K \times K \times K \times K \times K \times K \times K \times K = K^9$$

Note that the exponent (9) specifies the number of times the base (K) is used as a factor rather than the number of times multipli-cation is performed (8). Understanding the use of exponents is important in the appraisal analysis of income properties because the time value of money tables and formulas are based on the mathematical expression $(1 \cdot I)^N$.

Percentage of Change

The percentage of change, delta (Δ), is used in several calculations for the income capitalization techniques. The formula for delta is

$$\Delta = \frac{\text{final value} - \text{starting value}}{\text{starting value}}$$

Example: What percentage of change occurs if a property purchased for $90,000 sells for $72,000?

Answer: $\dfrac{\$72,000 - \$90,000}{\$90,000} = \dfrac{-\$18,000}{\$90,000} = -0.20 = -20\%$

Example: What percentage of change occurs if a property purchased for $75,000 sells for $165,000?

Answer: $\dfrac{\$165,000 - \$75,000}{\$75,000} = \dfrac{\$90,000}{\$75,000} = 1.20 = 120\%$

Basic Math Skills

1. Solve the following problem.

   $2 \times 5 / 7 + 4 / 5 = ?$

   a) 0.1818

   b) 2.229

   c) 0.80

   d) 0.75

2. Solve the following problem.

   $-16 / -4 - 9 = ?$

   a) -5

   b) +16

   c) 1.2308

   d) -13

3. If a residential property sold for $96,500 in January 2009 and resold in March 2013 for $103,500, what was the annual (straight-line) increase in the sale prices?

   a) 7.25%

   b) 5.5%

   c) 1.74% per year

   d) 17.4%

4. What is the acreage of the following site?

   (Note: 1 acre = 43,560 square feet)

   250.3'

   925.335'

   a) 2,351.27 sq. ft.

   b) 11,782.83 sq. ft.

   c) 5.317 acres

   d) 21.095 acres

5. If you purchased a property for $125,000 one year ago and sold it today for $123,500, what would be the percent change on a straight-line basis?

   a) 1.21%

   b) -1.21%

   c) -1.20%

   d) 1.20%

6. Solve the following problem.

   $12 \times 11 + 5 / 7 - 6 = ?$

   a) 13.57

   b) 111.11

   c) 126.71

   d) 132.56

7. What is the area of the following circle?

   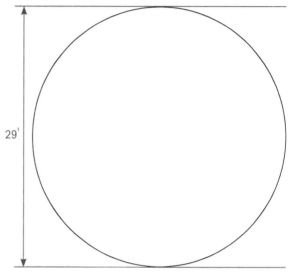

   29'

   a) 29 feet

   b) 660.52 square feet

   c) 841.00 square feet

   d) 2,642 square feet

8. If a residential property has a lot measuring 150 feet by 250 feet,

   a) The site size is 25,000 square feet.

   b) The site size is 37,000 square feet.

   c) The site size is 12 acres.

   d) The site size is 0.86 acres.

9. What is the volume of a box measuring 9 feet by 9 feet by 15 feet?

   a) 40 square yards

   b) 45 cubic yards

   c) 45 cubic feet

   d) 50 cubic yards

10. What is the square root of 144?
    a) 10
    b) 11
    c) 12
    d) 14

11. What is the area of the following triangle?

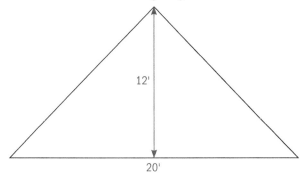

12'
20'

    a) 100 square feet
    b) 110 square feet
    c) 120 square feet
    d) 130 square feet

12. What is the annual rate of increase indicated by the sale of a property at $135,000 four years ago and a resale today at $144,500? Use the annual straight-line method. Round your answer to the nearest percentage point.
    a) 2%
    b) 4%
    c) 7%
    d) 9%

13. A nearby property sold for $125,000 and included a finished basement. The subject property is almost identical except that it does not include a basement. What does this tell you about the subject?
    a) The subject is worth $125,000.
    b) The subject is worth more than $125,000.
    c) The subject is worth less than $125,000.
    d) This information does not give any indication of value.

14. What is the area of the following drawing?

6' 9"
12' 8"

    a) 82.0 square feet
    b) 85.5 square feet
    c) 88.32 square feet
    d) 90.32 square feet

15. If a property is increasing in value by 3.5% per year on a straight-line basis, what is the value of a property that was purchased 22 months ago for $155,000? Round your answer.
    a) $160,000
    b) $165,000
    c) $170,000
    d) $175,000

16. A property just sold for $1 million, and the gross income was $235,000 per year. The operating expenses were $100,000. What can you say about this property?
    a) The ratio of gross income to sale price is 23.5%.
    b) The ratio of sale price to gross income is 425%.
    c) The ratio of net income to sale price is 13.5%.
    d) All of the above

17. The subject house has the following characteristics:

Finish Type	Size	Cost of Const.
Living area	1,200 sq. ft.	$85.00
Garage	550 sq. ft.	$25.00
Basement	1,200 sq. ft.	$25.00
Screened porch	450 sq. ft.	$25.00

    What is the cost to build this home?
    a) $34,000
    b) $85,000
    c) $145,750
    d) $157,000

18. You are selling a property for $104,450. You must pay a 6% real estate brokerage fee, a $600 title insurance expense, a $300 expense for a survey, and a $100 closing fee. What will you net at the closing?

a) $97,000

b) $98,000

c) $99,000

d) $100,000

19. A lender has quoted an interest rate of 5.5% per year with three points on a 75% loan for a property selling for $125,000. What will the expense be for the lender points?

a) $2,812.50

b) $3,750.00

c) $5,156.25

d) $6,875.00

20. A lender has quoted an interest rate of 5.5% per annum with monthly payments. What is the interest payment in the first month for a $100,000 mortgage amount? Round your answer to the nearest $100.

a) $400

b) $500

c) $600

d) $700

1. **b) 2.229**

    $([2 \times 5]/7) + (4/5)$

    $(10/7) + (4/5)$

    $1.4286 + 0.800 = 2.2286$, rounded to 2.229

2. **a) -5**

    $(-16/-4) - 9$

    $4 - 9 = -5$

3. **c) 1.74% per year**

    $103,500 - 96,500 = 7,000$

    $7,000/96,500 = 0.0725$

    $7.25388/50$ (months) $= 0.0014507$

    0.0014507 (rate/mo.) $\times 12 = 0.0174$

4. **c) 5.317 acres**

    $250.3 \times 925.335 = 231,611$ square feet

    $231,611/43,560 = 5.317$ acres

5. **c) -1.20%**

    $(123,500 - 125,000) / 125,000 = -1.20\%$

6. **c) 126.71**

    $(12 \times 11) + (5/7) - 6$

    $132 + 0.7143 - 6 = 126.71$

7. **b) 660.52 square feet**

    $29/2 = 14.5$ feet

    $14.5^2 \times 3.1416 = 660.52$ square feet

8. **d) The site size is 0.86 acres.**

    $150 \times 250 = 37,500$ square feet

    $37,500/43,560 = 0.86$ acres

9. **b) 45 cubic yards**

    $9 \times 9 \times 15 = 1,215$ cubic feet

    $1,215/27 = 45$ cubic yards

10. **c) 12**

    $12 \times 12 = 144$

11. **c) 120 square feet**

    $12 \times 20 \times 0.5 = 120$ square feet

12. **a) 2%**

    $144,500 - 135,000 = 9,500$

    $9,500/135,000 = 0.07037$

    $0.07037/4 = 0.0175925$, rounded to 2%

13. **c) The subject is worth less than $125,000.**

14. **b) 85.5 square feet**

15. **b) $165,000**

    $0.035/12 = 0.00291667$

    $0.00291667 \times 22 = 0.064167$

    $1.064167 \times 155,000 = 164,946$

16. **d) All of the above**

17. **d) $157,000**

Finish Type	Size	Cost of Const.	Total Cost
Living area	1,200 sq. ft.	$85.00	$102,000
Garage	550 sq. ft.	$25.00	$13,750
Basement	1,200 sq. ft.	$25.00	$30,000
Screened porch	450 sq. ft.	$25.00	$11,250
Total reproduction cost of improvements			$157,000

18. **a) $97,000**

Sale price	$104,450
$104,450 \times 0.06$ –	$6,267
Title insurance –	$600
Survey –	$300
Closing –	$100
	$97,183

19. **a) $2,812.50**

Sale price	$125,000
×	0.75
	$93,750
×	0.03
	$2,812.50

20. **b) $500**

0.055 / 12 × 100,000 = 458.33, rounded to $500

1

Introduction to Appraisal

What Is an Appraisal?

An *appraisal* is the act or process of developing an opinion of value. In other words, an appraisal is not the written report but an analytical process. The appraiser defines the subject of the appraisal, decides what is needed to answer the question put forth by the client, and then performs the research and analysis necessary to answer the question.

Before entering into a contract, the client and the appraiser may discuss the appraisal services to be performed. However, the appraiser, not the client, ultimately determines how much work is needed to competently and credibly answer the client's question, given the nature of the subject property and the requirements of the assignment under standards of professional appraisal practice. Likewise, the appraiser and the client will usually discuss how the conclusions of the appraiser's research and analyses are to be communicated, but the appraiser must decide how to report those conclusions so that the information presented conforms to professional standards.

What Is Real Property?

The formal definition of real estate describes the physical thing, not the rights in realty. You can

real estate
An identified parcel or tract of land, including improvements, if any.

real property
The interests, benefits, and rights inherent in the ownership of real estate.

touch real estate but you cannot buy it or sell it. When you buy land and buildings, the real estate is conveyed through the exchange of real property rights. In other words, ownership is realized by a deed that transfers the rights of the current owner to the new owner.

The formal definition of *real property* describes the rights in realty. Appraisers do not appraise real estate; they appraise real property, which is an important distinction. The bundle of rights theory, which holds that the rights in realty can be broken down into smaller parts, is important in many appraisals.

The Bundle of Rights

Ownership of real estate is commonly described as the *bundle of rights*. Ownership can be divided into smaller entities (usually represented as sticks tied in a bundle) that can be retained or sold off individually. The "sticks" include

- the right to sell a property (or property components, if divided–such as an oil well, a water well, sand, and gravel)
- the right to occupy real estate
- the right to lease a property
- the right to mortgage a property
- the right to create a life estate

Appraisers value the rights in realty rather than the physical, tangible items. The physical items form the basis of the value, but the rights are what are conveyed from buyer to seller and what make real estate valuable. Real estate

KEY TERMS	
easement	personal property
eminent domain	police power
escheat	real estate
fee simple estate	real property
intangible property	taxation

> Note that that some of these concepts related to rights are common law and some are codified, but all are subject to interpretation by the courts. Appraisers are often required to seek the advice of competent real estate attorneys to confirm the local laws that might apply to the subject property. A common source of advice is an attorney working for a title insurance or abstract agency. These attorneys are focused on the relevant issues and usually have a greater depth of knowledge than other real estate attorneys.

ownership is not usually established by occupying or using the site, but by the name on the deed recorded at the county recorder or auditor's office.

Most people are not familiar with the process of acquiring real estate for public ownership, which is a significant part of the real estate appraisal business. Most municipal agencies cannot buy real estate without seeking out a third-party opinion of value. As a result, considerable appraisal work is available from government agencies.

Buyers of real estate for private ownership make decisions based on the available alternatives, so they place less emphasis on appraisals and more on their own perceptions and subjective investment options. Many new appraisers think real estate buyers are going to be their best customers only to find that buyers are seldom willing to pay for a value opinion when they already feel they know the market.

Public Restrictions on Ownership

The definition of fee simple estate as stated in *The Dictionary of Real Estate Appraisal*, 5th ed.– "absolute ownership unencumbered by any other interest or estate, subject only to the limitations imposed by the governmental powers of taxation, eminent domain, police power, and escheat"– describes the absolute ownership of real estate rights. The owners of a fee simple interest can do almost anything they want on that property, but they are still subject to the limitations imposed by the four powers of government:

- taxation
- eminent domain
- police power
- escheat

Exercising these powers of government, a state, county, or municipal government can

- levy taxes against rights in realty and force the sale of a property if taxes are not paid in a timely manner
- take private property for public use, such as a road-widening project or a new school or park, if the owner is paid a fair amount in return
- restrict a private owner's use of real estate through zoning, building codes, traffic regulations, and other forms of police power
- take possession of privately owned real estate if the owner dies without a will or identifiable heirs

Eminent domain is a source of a lot of appraisal work because governments are required to establish just compensation when taking private property through condemnation. Even with just compensation, real estate owners are often very upset by the condemnation process, so eminent domain proceedings are probably the most contentious application of the powers of government.

Unlike eminent domain, which singles out specific parcels for government action, police power usually applies limitations to ownership such as zoning in a broader fashion, across specific areas rather than on specific properties. If a governmental body downzones a single parcel and that change results in a diminution of value, the property owner could argue that the property has been taken through condemnation, and just compensation would have to be paid.

> **taxation**
> The right of government to raise revenue through assessments on valuable goods, products, and rights.
>
> **eminent domain**
> The right of government to take private property for public use upon the payment of just compensation. The Fifth Amendment of the US Constitution, also known as the *takings clause*, guarantees payment of just compensation upon appropriation of private property.
>
> **police power**
> The inherent power of government to regulate property in order to protect public health, safety, and general welfare.
>
> **escheat**
> The right of government that gives the state titular ownership of a property when its owner dies without a will or any ascertainable heirs.

> Condemnation is the act or process through which government exercises its right of eminent domain.

Private Restrictions on Ownership
Easements are non-possessory interests in real property that convey the right to use, but not own, a portion of real estate from the fee owner to the easement owner. Easements are held by individuals, corporations, utility companies, governments, and adjacent property owners. Certain easements allow someone to do a specific action on another person's property. For example, easements may be required to run sewer and water lines and telephone, electric, and cable television wires through privately owned land. These easements must be purchased by the procuring agency. When platted, most subdivisions include easements to provide access for utility companies to do maintenance.

Types of Easements	
affirmative easement	easement by prescription
appurtenant easement	easements in gross
conservation easement	negative easement
easement by necessity	preservation easement

Personal Property and Intangible Assets

If an item is classified as *personal property*, it may or may not be included in the appraisal. Personal property is classified and valued differently than real property. Many lenders will not invest in personal property because, if the real property goes through foreclosure, the personal property could leave the premises with the borrower. Most personal property also has a shorter life span than real estate, which means lenders are cautious about loaning for 30 years on an item that will only be around for five years.

A new kitchen sink is personal property when it is in the showroom or boxed up on the floor of a house before installation, but as soon as it is installed in a countertop and the plumbing is attached, that sink becomes a fixture and part of the real estate. This is an important distinction in real estate sales, mortgages, and litigation. If an item is considered real estate, it is included in the sale of the rights in realty (unless specifically excluded) and must be left behind when the sellers leave or the mortgage is foreclosed. If an item is considered personal property, the sellers can take it with them. Many arguments occur over what is or is not real estate, and sometimes the courts have to make the ultimate decision.

> **personal property**
> Identifiable tangible objects that are considered by the general public as being "personal"—for example, furnishings, artwork, antiques, gems and jewelry, collectibles, machinery and equipment; all tangible property that is not classified as real estate.
>
> **intangible property**
> Nonphysical assets, including, but not limited to, contracts, franchises, trademarks, copyrights, and goodwill items such as a valuable trade name and a trained workforce.

While real property and personal property make up the tangible asset class and personal property includes all tangible property that is not classified as real property, intangible property consists of nonphysical assets such as contracts, franchises, trademarks, copyrights, and goodwill items. Intangible property is also sometimes known as *intangible assets.* The valuation of intangible property will be discussed in more detail in Chapter 35. For now, it is important to remember that the appraiser must identify which of these types of property are to be valued in each appraisal assignment before deciding whether to accept the assignment. This is necessary for the appraiser to properly ascertain if he or she has the professional competency required to adequately complete the assignment.

Why Appraisals Are Needed

Appraisals are needed for all property types (residential, agricultural, industrial, commercial, and special-purpose). Appraisals are requested by many different types of clients (attorneys, lenders, corporate relocation companies, government agencies, and private individuals) in many different types of situations (ownership transfers, credit and financing, litigation, and investment counseling, decision making, and accounting).Significant financial decisions are often involved, and appraisals are often required by law. Mortgage lending appraisals have historically been the most common type of appraisals. Regardless of the specific circumstances, providing a sound, objective value opinion and maintaining professional integrity should be the primary objectives of any appraisal assignment.

The Purpose of an Appraisal

In every appraisal, the appraiser needs to indicate the definition of the value being developed and reported to the client. While the public and most real estate owners define value as the amount the seller could sell the property for if exposed on the market today, variations may affect a value opinion. For example, if you define *value* as something other than a cash-equivalent amount, the appraisal report must indicate the impact of any special financing on the value conclusion because of the extraordinary conditions assumed in the value definition.

The intended use of the appraisal is also a significant piece of information in any appraisal report. If the intended use is for mortgage lending purposes and the potential investors (i.e., the intended users) will be reading the conclusions, the appraiser is responsible for making sure that those investors are not misled to erroneous conclusions. In many lending situations, the appraisal report will have to familiarize the reader with the subject property and its location. If the intended use is to assist a seller in the pricing of a property for sale, most owners already know the location and property very well, so the requirements of the appraisal and report would be very different.

1. Appraisal is
   a) The act or process of telling the client the market value of the real estate
   b) The act or process of developing an opinion of value
   c) The report conveyed to the client
   d) A lucrative profession

2. Real estate is
   a) The rights in realty
   b) The physical land and appurtenances affixed to the land
   c) What transfers on the day of closing
   d) The "bundle of rights"

3. Real property includes
   a) Any and all buildings on the subject site
   b) All interests, benefits, and rights inherent in the ownership of real estate
   c) The physical land and appurtenances affixed to the land
   d) Property that is not artificial

4. The manner in which a client employs the information contained in the appraisal report is called
   a) The intended use
   b) The purpose of an appraisal
   c) The base of an appraisal
   d) The appraisal premise

5. Real property consists of
   a) Rights in realty
   b) Land and all improvements thereon
   c) The right to use or occupy real estate
   d) One-unit residences

6. Appraisals are always used
   a) To make residential mortgages
   b) To settle divorces
   c) To settle lawsuits
   d) To solve problems that involve real estate valuation

7. An appraiser is appraising a small residential property and observes that it has a clothes washer and dryer. Should these items be included in the appraisal?
   a) The appraiser should not include these items because they are personal property.
   b) The appraiser should include these items, but they should be identified as such and their contributory value should be estimated.
   c) The appraiser should not include these items because they could be taken out when the current owners leave.
   d) The appraiser should include these items because they were intended to be left with the property.

8. Items that are built to be permanent and intended to be included with real property are
   a) Trade fixtures
   b) Real estate
   c) Personal property
   d) Chattel fixtures

9. An appraiser
   a) Determines value
   b) Determines price
   c) Measures and develops an opinion of value
   d) Measures price

10. Easements are another division of property rights. They usually give a party the right
    a) To cross over another person's property without permission
    b) To access the property to perform a specific service
    c) To use the property during the term of the lease to a tenant
    d) To reenter the property if the payments are not made to the lender on time

11. The Fifth Amendment to the US Constitution
    a) Requires the government to pay just compensation for land taken for the common good
    b) Prohibits the consumption of alcoholic beverages
    c) Limits the terms of the President
    d) Is called the "Bill of Rights"

12. Suppose that you have owned a 40-acre parcel of land for the last 25 years. You paid the taxes on the real estate for the first 20 years but have not paid them for the last five. Which of the following statements is true?

    a) The state will get the taxes when the property is sold since the buyer will insist that the taxes be paid prior to closing.

    b) The state has the right to sell the real estate to pay the back taxes.

    c) The state is powerless to collect these taxes.

    d) The state will sue you, and the courts will garnish your wages to get paid.

13. Suppose that you own a house and five acres just outside the town of Monticello. This home is adjacent to Route 23, which has been a small two-lane highway for many years. Last year, the state decided to widen this road to six lanes to accommodate all the future traffic that will be created by a new riverboat casino. To facilitate this expansion, the state will need about 50 feet off the front of your homestead. The state will

    a) Just take the property and use it

    b) Pay whatever you ask to keep you from suing them

    c) Pay you a fair and equitable amount based on the estimated property value before the taking and another valuation after the taking

    d) Take this property from you and replace it with some land in another area of the same county

14. A fee simple interest in real property is limited only by

    a) Taxation, eminent domain, police power, and easements

    b) Taxation, eminent domain, police power, and escheat

    c) Eminent domain, police power, leases, and escheat

    d) Eminent domain, police power, zoning, and escheat

15. A deed should be recorded because

    a) Recording gives public notice of the transaction and sets the priority

    b) It is required by law

    c) The title does not pass until the deed is recorded

    d) Recording makes the deed a legal document

16. Zoning and environmental protection regulations are examples of

    a) Clouds on title

    b) Public use

    c) Escheat

    d) Police power

Note: Unless otherwise noted, italicized references indicate the pages in *The Appraisal of Real Estate*, 14th edition, that readers should consult for additional discussion of these topics.

1. b) The act or process of developing an opinion of value
    Page 2

2. b) The physical land and appurtenances affixed to the land
    Page 4

3. b) All interests, benefits, and rights inherent in the ownership of real estate
    Page 4

4. a) The intended use
    This student handbook

5. a) Rights in realty
    Page 4

6. d) To solve problems that involve real estate valuation
    Page 8

7. b) The appraiser should include these items, but they should be identified as such and their contributory value should be estimated.

8. b) Real estate
    Page 7

9. c) Measures and develops an opinion of value
    Page 2

10. b) To access the property to perform a specific service
    This student handbook

11. a) Requires the government to pay just compensation for land taken for the common good
    Page 6

12. b) The state has the right to sell the real estate to pay the back taxes.
    Page 6

13. c) Pay you a fair and equitable amount based on the estimated property value before the taking and another valuation after the taking
    Page 6

14. b) Taxation, eminent domain, police power, and escheat
    Page 6

15. a) Recording gives public notice of the transaction and sets the priority
    This student handbook

16. d) Police power
    Page 6

2

Land, Real Estate, and Ownership of Real Property

The appraisal of real estate begins with land. There cannot be real estate without the land underneath the buildings. Land provides wealth as the site of income-generating activities or as the source of natural resources. Land is a physical commodity, but in the United States the sale and purchase of the physical commodity is accomplished through the exchange of real property rights associated with the land, not by a physical exchange of the land itself.

Concepts of Land

Land is ultimately many things to many different people, and the appraiser's job is to understand how various parties view and value it.

Geographic and Environmental

Each parcel of land is unique because it occupies a different physical space than any other parcel of land. Land can be used for a variety of activities, so its highest and best use will be determined by its location, zoning, traffic count, topography, access to utilities, surrounding land uses, and many other factors. The types and availability of soils, water, and vegetation differ with each parcel. These factors will have an effect on most property uses and may even be the most important factors.

Legal

Land use regulations (most commonly, zoning) limit the utility of a site, and that utility is what creates value. Therefore, land use regulations are important, and sometimes controversial, elements of the valuation process. Developers may spend many thousands of dollars to guide projects through a multitude of zoning laws, land use regulations, and landscape regulations, especially when nearby property owners are resistant to new development.

Land use regulations can make the appraisal of real estate very challenging. Every appraiser

doing market value appraisals must research land use regulations to ensure that the highest and best use is compliant with current zoning rules or, if not, that the owner is likely to obtain a change or variance in zoning regulations.

Economic

In capitalist societies like the United States, improved and unimproved real estate can be a major source of wealth creation. The owner of an acre of land can rent it out, sell it, develop it by building on it, and in some cases mine it or remove other assets from it. Many land owners also grow plants or crops on their land, including grains, fruits, trees, or sometimes just grass. Individuals can invest in real property (i.e., the rights to land and the improvements upon it) as an alternative to the stock market, the bond market, or a simple bank savings account. Real estate investments can carry more risk than other investments and may be more difficult to liquidate than stocks or bonds.

Social

Because the amount of dry land is relatively fixed, competition for that limited amount of space has a direct influence on the intensity of land use in different areas. If the population density is only one family per square mile, land use and safety regulations are not needed much. However, if the density is 300 families per square mile, social controls over the behavior of local residents are more important.

Some property owners do not believe it is the government's duty to control land use. They believe instead that the market should do this. Others believe society needs to control land uses to ensure that incompatible uses do not appear next to each other. The extent of public control over privately owned land is a controversial and often political issue in some areas, and appraisers must consider zoning and land use regulations in nearly all appraisals. In some appraisals, the probable uses of land will not be clear, and you will have to support your opinion of highest and best use under the existing zoning or after an expected change in zoning.

Forms of Real Property Ownership

The first major distinction in real property ownership is private versus public ownership. Most public property ownership is designed to meet the needs of the community. Publicly owned property includes streets, utility systems, and public facilities such as schools and parks. The use of public property is regulated by police power.

Most appraisal assignments involve privately owned property. The ownership of private property may take the following forms:

- individual ownership

- concurrent ownership, which may take the form of joint tenancy, tenancy by the entirety, or tenancy in common
- ownership by legal entities, including land trusts, corporations, partnerships, and syndications

Regardless of the form of real property ownership, the appraiser must clearly identify the interest to be valued in each appraisal assignment according to professional standards. The interest appraised is determined by the appraisal's intended use and the client's needs, not necessarily by what type of property ownership is currently in place. The forms of ownership will be discussed in more detail in Chapter 7.

1. Land is unique because
   a) No two parcels have the same soil composition
   b) No two parcels have the same owners
   c) No two parcels have the same tax levies
   d) No two parcels can occupy the same space on the face of the earth

2. The supply of land is
   a) Increasing all the time
   b) Established by the surveyors
   c) Infinite
   d) Finite

3. The concepts of land are
   a) Immobile, durable, finite, and useful
   b) Legal, geographic and environmental, economic, and social
   c) Land, labor, capital, and entrepreneurialism
   d) Leasehold, leased fee, and fee simple

4. An example of a governmental force that affects real estate value would be
   a) Market demand for mortgage loans
   b) Population changes in the market
   c) Changes in decorating styles
   d) Changes in local building codes

5. Zoning and environmental protection regulations are examples of
   a) Clouds on a title
   b) Public use
   c) Escheat
   d) Police power

6. Which of the following is not a way to hold title or deed to real estate?
   a) Joint tenancy
   b) Tenancy at will
   c) Tenancy in common
   d) Tenancy by the entirety

7. A parcel of land was owned by Ms. Long, who offered it for sale or lease. Short Development Co., a retail developer, obtained control of the real estate and then improved it with a retail building. The listing agent said that Long and Short split the real estate and that Long owns the land but Short owns the building. Which of the following statements is correct?
   a) This is a classic situation in which the land is owned by one party and the building is owned by another party.
   b) This is most likely a situation in which the owner leased the property to the developer, who improved the property. The terms of the lease must be researched.
   c) This is likely to be a situation in which the rights in realty were split. The owner retained the subsurface rights, and the developer owns the supersurface rights.
   d) This situation is not possible. One person must own all the rights in realty, and the rights cannot be split.

Note: Unless otherwise noted, italicized references indicate the pages in *The Appraisal of Real Estate*, 14th edition, that readers should consult for additional discussion of these topics.

1. d) No two parcels can occupy the same space on the face of the earth
    Pages 11-12

2. d) Finite
    Page 12

3. b) Legal, geographic and environmental, economic, and social
    Pages 12-15

4. d) Changes in local building codes
    Page 16

5. d) Police power
    Page 16

6. b) Tenancy at will
    Page 17

7. b) This is most likely a situation in which the owner leased the property to the developer, who improved the property. The terms of the lease must be researched.
    Pages 16-17

The Nature of Value

Value can be a complex concept, encompassing many varied but related influences. Real estate appraisers think of value in specific terms, defining particular types of value in relation to the needs and desires of the market participants involved.

The History of Value Theory

Studying the reasons why some commodities have value and others do not is not a recent phenomenon. Various schools of economic thought have contributed to the development of modern value theory. The classical school represented by Adam Smith departed from mercantilist theory by attributing value to the cost of production. The labor theory of value, set forth by Karl Marx, and the opposing concept of marginal utility, which linked value to demand, challenged the classical theory of value. The neoclassical economics of Alfred Marshall combined classical supply-cost considerations with the demand-price theory of the marginal utility school.

In mid-eighteenth century Europe, a group of political economists known as *physiocrats* put forth the idea of agriculture as a main source of wealth and land as a major productive agent. This opposed mercantilism, the prevalent theory of the time, which focused on trade as a major means of accumulating wealth. The physiocrats provided the foundation for classical value theory.

The Classical School

The economic thinkers of the classical school were the first to identify the four agents of production and look at the factors that create value, supply, and demand. The economist Adam Smith is responsible for forming the basic ideas of this school of thought:

- Capital, land, and labor are the primary agents of production.
- Value is created when the agents of production produce a useful item.
- The price of an item reflects how much it cost to produce that item. (This idea influenced the cost approach.)

Smith also considered the role of utility and scarcity in value.

Other classical economists developed a theory of rent based on the concept of marginal land and the law of diminishing returns, which were forerunners of highest and best use analysis and the land residual technique, and defined the relationship between interest and value in use.

Challenges to Classical Value Theory

The two major challengers of classical theory were the labor theory of value and the Austrian school of thought, which focused on marginal utility. Karl Marx advocated the labor theory, which claimed that all value is the result of labor. Meanwhile, the Austrian school regarded value as a function of demand and utility as its main principle. Marginal utility formed the basis for the concept of contribution.

The Neoclassical Synthesis

In the late nineteenth and early twentieth century, the neoclassical school merged the classical school with the Austrian school. Specifically, the supply-cost considerations of the classical school were combined with the demand-price theory of marginal utility. Alfred Marshall was the main force behind this movement, which formed the

KEY TERMS	
anticipation	law of decreasing returns
change	law of increasing returns
competition (among properties)	progression
	regression
entrepreneurial coordination	supply and demand

basis for modern appraisal theory. Marshall is responsible for identifying the three approaches to value, while the American economist Irving Fisher developed the income theory of value, an early forerunner of the income capitalization approach.

Modern Appraisal Theory
In the 1920s and 1930s, land economics became an established field of study. Also during this time, the first authoritative texts on real estate appraisal were published. This led to more appraisal writings being published. These early writings linked value theory to valuation theory, translated economic theory into appraisal theory, explained the use of capitalization rates, emphasized the three approaches to value, and set forth procedures for applying these approaches.

Agents of Production
A marketable property is the result of the combination of four agents of production:

- land
- labor
- capital
- entrepreneurial coordination

Obviously, the underlying *land* is required to produce marketable real estate. The term *labor* refers not only to the work required to build a structure but also the hard materials used in the construction process. *Capital* includes the equipment (machinery and tools), buildings, and infrastructure necessary to produce other goods. *Entrepreneurial coordination* refers to the required return expected by a property buyer. The related term *entrepreneurial incentive* refers to the amount of money a developer expects to make, while *entrepreneurial profit* refers to the amount of money the developer actually receives. Most developers go into a proposed project expecting a profit and often net much less than expected, but they would not enter a deal at all if they expected to lose money.

Factors of Value
Four qualities of a commodity interact to create value:

1. Utility
2. Scarcity
3. Desire
4. Effective purchasing power

Utility
With few exceptions, an item will have value only if it is useful. Real estate that performs no useful function will usually have no value. The function of land may be subtle and sometimes it is noneconomic. For example, sometimes the only utility a plot of land can claim is its ability to provide insulation from other properties and uses, for which many buyers will pay good money. If a parcel of land in an agricultural area is too wet to plow, it may have little value. On the other hand, if it is too wet to plow but grows grass well, it may be perfect grazing land.

Scarcity
Scarcity is the basis of demand. If an item is plentiful, it will have less value than it would if it were scarce. Iron ore and gold both have utility. However, one is worth a lot more than the other, primarily because of its relative scarcity. Air is an absolute necessity, but it is so plentiful that it has no value. The same substance can be much more scarce, and much more valuable as a result, in some markets as compared to others. For example, water is nearly free in some parts of the country but must be trucked in to other areas.

Desire
To have value, an item must be desired by potential purchasers. If a feature of a property has utility and scarcity and is desired by the market, it will have value. If there is no desire, there is no value. For example, a house is put up for sale, and it is the only house in the neighborhood with a swimming pool. That pool has utility and is scarce in that market, but it will only add value to the real estate if potential buyers want it. Home buyers in Minnesota would probably have less desire for a swimming pool than home buyers in Georgia.

Effective Purchasing Power
The entire population of a county may want to buy a $1 million home, but only a few people may be able to pay for one. To have value, an item must appeal to a market that can afford to buy it. If a $1 million house is built in an area where the highest per family income is only $50,000 per year, it is doubtful that anyone could afford to buy the property, and as a result it would not sell for the anticipated price.

Supply and Demand
The four factors of value create demand. Entrepreneurs create the supply of an item to satisfy

that demand. When demand increases, supply increases to satisfy demand in the long run. Prices may increase because of the scarcity of the item in the short run, but the potential profit will eventually entice new providers to come to the market or existing providers to produce more.

Measuring supply and demand is important for informational reasons. If 75 homes of similar ages in the same market area go up for sale at asking prices ranging from $100,000 to $125,000 and only 15 sales occurred in the same market segment the previous year, this probably implies an oversupplied market and a variety of other problems.

If you use the cost approach to develop an opinion of value, it is important to understand the supply and demand factors of the subject's market. When you apply the income capitalization and sales comparison approaches, any oversupply should already be reflected in the sale prices or lease rates of the recent comparables, and no adjustment is needed.

Distinctions Among Price, Cost, and Value

Appraisers today carefully define the terms *price*, *cost*, and *value* and distinguish the differences between the three concepts.

Price

Price is the amount of money agreed upon by buyers and sellers for the transfer of real estate. A sale price is a *fact*, not an opinion like market value. *Prices* are set in the *marketplace.*

Cost

As used by appraisers, *cost* represents the dollar amount required to reproduce, build, or assemble an improvement. The total cost of a building is the sum of the amounts needed to pay for the building components, labor, a competitive profit for the builder or developer, and other expenses. An improved property may be worth less than the cost to build it due to depreciation caused by age, wear and tear, functional problems, and problems outside the property. Properties can sell for more than they cost to build (with a reasonable profit) in the short run, but competition will push prices back down in the long run. The old saying "excess profit breeds ruinous competition" still holds true.

Value

Value is used to describe worth. In the appraisal profession, the word *value* is never used alone; it always appears with a modifier as in *market value, insurable value*, and so on.

Anticipation and Change

All goods and services can be valued at the present worth of future benefits. A refrigerator has value to you because you think the appliance will keep food fresh for a period of time in the future. If you think the refrigerator will only function as a kitchen appliance for a year, you will pay much less for it than if it is expected to function for a decade. The anticipation of future benefits creates demand and value. In real estate, anticipation of the benefits of ownership (such as appreciation in value in the future, the right of occupancy, and tax benefits) makes a buyer willing to spend capital.

Change is inevitable in any market. Real estate markets are constantly changing because of increases or decreases in interest rates, employment levels, or demographics. All appraisers must be able to recognize change in real estate markets because that is a basic requirement of market analysis.

Supply and Demand, Substitution, Balance, and Externalities

Supply and Demand

The supply and demand of real estate controls the price. In periods of high demand, prices increase in the short run, and supply increases to meet demand in the long run. In a real estate market, supply is much slower to change than demand. Changes in employment, interest rates, and demographics can cause demand to rise or fall quickly, but real estate improvements take a long time to build, which means supply will be slow to adjust.

Supply and Demand in Overbuilt Markets

When too many new homes are being built, developers cannot sell them or can only sell them at a discount. If the discounts are severe, the developers may not make any profit, which would tend to discourage them from building more "spec" properties. If they lose money, other builders will not be likely to enter the market because of the poor prospects.

If the market is hot and buyers cannot find many buildings to buy, prices will increase and developers will find that they can build a property and sell it for the cost of construction plus a reasonable profit. When builders find they can make a lot of money on new properties, they increase production to maximize profits. Once the builders are making excessive profits, subcontractors and other entrepreneurs will become builders until too many properties are being built and the market becomes oversupplied.

Competition

The level of competition between potential buyers for an item is the source of the item's value. If there was no potential competition for a product, a buyer could simply wait until the sellers were desperate to sell and then lower the price to unreasonable levels. Because of the fear that some other buyer will get it first, buyers cannot just wait the sellers out. Competition between sellers to find a buyer causes them to lower their prices to attract buyers away from equally desirable properties. Builders cannot charge any price they want for a new property because they have competition too. Competition keeps sellers from charging too much and buyers from paying too little.

Substitution

A buyer will pay no more for goods and services than the cost of obtaining substitute goods or services. The substitution of one product for another is needed for a competitive open market. This is an important concept for appraisers to understand because the prices of real estate can only increase when the alternatives available to buyers will allow it. An owner of a one-year-old property can sell that property for no more than the cost of building a new structure that could serve as a substitute (assuming that used improvements are worth less than new ones). Therefore, a one-year-old building is limited by the cost of a new building.

Balance

Property value is created and sustained when interacting elements are in a state of equilibrium. When a $1 million property produces $100,000 in net income, investors will be attracted to it. If the property costs $1 million but only produces

$10,000 in net income per year, which is a net return of 1% on the investment, the elements are out of balance and no new buildings will be brought to market until productivity returns.

The principle of diminishing marginal productivity—which is also known as the *law of diminishing returns*—says that too much of a good thing is bad. A 2,000-sq.-ft. house will sell for a fair price in a neighborhood where most homes have 1,500 to 2,500 square feet of living area. If a home of 4,000 square feet is in the same neighborhood as 1,500- to 2,000-sq.-ft. homes, it will not sell for an amount equal to its physically depreciated cost.

Contribution

According to the principle of contribution, any component's value must be measured as the difference between what the property is worth with and without that item or feature. Some components add value commensurate with their cost, and others fall short. If an item adds more value than its cost, the excess demand will be filled by more production. This issue arises when appraisers are asked to adjust sale prices of comparable properties for dissimilarities between the subject and comparable sales. Appraisers almost always have to make adjustments in the sales comparison approach, and the principle of contribution is the basis of that process. What is the value of a two-car attached garage on a property that is selling for $75,000? Is it the same as it would be on a $350,000 home? Measuring the contribution of an item often requires you to find a property sale with the item and a nearly identical property sale that does not have the feature in question.

Surplus Productivity

Surplus productivity is the net income to the land remaining after the other costs have been satisfied. If the property value is greater than the cost of production, the surplus productivity goes to the land. In the short run, some properties will have greater value than the production costs. In the long run, supply will meet the excess demand.

Conformity

The principle of conformity holds that optimum value will be achieved when a property conforms to the demands of the widest market. A property that substantially deviates from market demands will not sell for its optimum price. There is a common saying in real estate: "By definition, a unique property means that no one else will want to buy it." While this may not be true in all cases, a property that is truly different from all others probably does not have a popular design. It is also possible, but less likely, that the property is a trendsetter. If it is a trendsetter, many more properties like it will be seen in the near future. If it is just an unusual property, it may be difficult to sell without substantial alterations.

Externalities

According to the principle of externalities, real estate values can be affected by the following conditions outside the property:

- changing interest rates
- changes in tax laws
- overproduction

Because real estate is not movable, the actions of market participants in the area, or sometimes outside the area, will affect its value. For example, if the local city council is promoting jobs, it may rezone sections of a metropolitan area to industrial uses. If the city rezones a large amount of land for industrial use, there could be a glut of industrial land, which will cause existing industrial property values to fall.

If the local school board votes to build a large and elaborate new high school, the property taxes for an area may increase to pay for it. As a result, the tax burden may be detrimental to the value of a residence in a submarket where few people have children in school. If, on the other hand, the house is in a submarket where buyers seek out the newest and best schools, the new high school may have a positive effect on values.

1. When real property is sold by one person to another, the amount of money used to compensate the seller is called
   a) The *cost* of the real property
   b) The *value* of the real property
   c) The *price* of the real property
   d) The *income* of the real property

2. A cash-equivalent price
   a) Reflects what a seller would accept as if he or she received cash at the closing
   b) Includes the seller paying no more than 5 points (5%)
   c) Indicates that the rights in realty can only be fee simple
   d) Assumes that the buyer did not have to get a mortgage

3. A good's capacity to satisfy human desires or needs is known as
   a) Creative demand
   b) Utility
   c) Functional obsolescence
   d) Effective demand

4. The city planning department has indicated that a vacant residential lot located in a flood zone cannot be given a building permit. This site
   a) Has lost nearly all utility
   b) Has become scarce
   c) Has lost all desirability
   d) Has lost any effective purchasing power

5. Demand for real estate may be affected by
   a) Increasing population and employment
   b) The availability of mortgage financing
   c) Increases in purchasing power
   d) All of the above

6. The four agents of production are
   a) Land, labor, capital, and improvements
   b) Land, labor, capital, and entrepreneurship
   c) Land, labor, capital, and money
   d) Land, improvements, labor, and materials

7. Real property has value because it
   a) Is nearby
   b) Is popular
   c) Is desirable
   d) Provides future benefits

8. The supply of one-unit residential properties is most affected by
   a) An increase in employment in the area
   b) A decrease in mortgage interest rates
   c) An increase in the number of apartments built
   d) An increase in the number of homes built

9. Two homes in the same addition have the same size, location, amenities, and features. One is priced at $100,000, and the other is priced at $110,000. Which of the following statements is the most accurate?
   a) The lower-priced home will require a longer marketing time.
   b) The lower-priced home will attract more demand.
   c) The lower-priced home will get fewer showings.
   d) The lower-priced home will always sell for more than the full list price.

10. When a property is put up for sale, the seller is forced to reduce the price when
    a) The buyers tell him or her to do so
    b) The broker tells him or her to do so
    c) The listing expires and a new broker insists on a lower price
    d) The seller decides that a price reduction is needed to facilitate a sale

11. In a high-demand market, the cost of building a new property will increase substantially until
    a) It becomes impossible for prices to go higher
    b) The supply increases because new builders get into the market
    c) The charges from suppliers and subcontractors go down
    d) The Federal Reserve System increases interest rates

12. A one-unit homeowner who builds a new and unique structure will commonly find that

   a) The structure's uniqueness will cause the market to like it and pay more for it

   b) Properties that do not conform to popular designs will sell for more

   c) Generally, fewer people desire unique structures

   d) The market will pay as much for this property as any other because of its unique nature

13. Externalities are

   a) Factors outside the property that can affect the property value

   b) Losses in value due to design and changes in building standards

   c) Increases in value due to changes in land value

   d) Losses in value due to changes in buyer preferences

14. When demand for housing increases, the supply

   a) Increases immediately

   b) Increases slowly

   c) Is unaffected

   d) Will diminish

15. The overproduction of new homes

   a) Causes oversupply and lower prices

   b) Causes increases in demand

   c) Causes prices to increase

   d) Causes the market to move toward a state of equilibrium

16. A buyer invests in a small strip mall because she believes the property will net $25,000 per year. This is an example of

   a) Anticipation

   b) Change

   c) Competition

   d) Substitution

17. As an agent of production, *capital* is

   a) The necessary equipment, buildings, and infrastructure for development

   b) The location of the center of government

   c) A death sentence

   d) The building in which a legislative body meets

18. The statement "property values are created and sustained when the characteristics of a property conform to the demand of its market" refers to

   a) Use value

   b) Contribution

   c) Conformity

   d) Supply and demand analysis

Note: Unless otherwise noted, italicized references indicate the pages in *The Appraisal of Real Estate*, 14th edition, that readers should consult for additional discussion of these topics.

1. c) The *price* of the real property
    Page 26

2. a) Reflects what a seller would accept as if he or she received cash at the closing

3. b) Utility
    Page 24

4. a) Has lost nearly all utility
    Pages 24-25

5. d) All of the above
    Pages 25-26

6. b) Land, labor, capital, and entrepreneurship
    Page 23

7. d) Provides future benefits
    Page 27

8. d) An increase in the number of homes built
    Pages 25-26

9. b) The lower-priced home will attract more demand.
    Pages 25-26

10. d) The seller decides that a price reduction is needed to facilitate a sale
    Page 28

11. b) The supply increases because new builders get into the market
    Pages 25-26

12. c) Generally, fewer people desire unique structures
    This student handbook

13. a) Factors outside the property that can affect the property value
    Page 33

14. b) Increases slowly
    Pages 25-26

15. a) Causes oversupply and lower prices
    Pages 25-26

16. a) Anticipation
    Page 27

17. a) The necessary equipment, buildings, and infrastructure for development
    This student handbook

18. c) Conformity
    This student handbook

4

The Valuation Process

The valuation process is the blueprint for the appraisal. It begins with the questions an appraiser asks the client when the initial phone call, fax, or e-mail comes in and ends with writing and delivering the appraisal report to the client and sending the invoice. Some of the steps in this process are self-explanatory and need little discussion, but others require substantial thought and inquiry.

Identification of the Appraisal Problem

The first step in the valuation process requires you to determine who you are working for (the client), what the client is asking for, the effective date of valuation, the subject of the appraisal, and whether there are any extraordinary assumptions, hypothetical conditions, or other relevant assignment conditions to consider. This information is needed to show the reader of the appraisal report why certain elements of the appraisal are emphasized and others are ignored. It also shows the reader what limiting conditions, hypothetical conditions, or extraordinary assumptions you have placed on the value opinion.

For example, it is common for appraisers to estimate the value of a property assuming that a building will be built on the site, the zoning will be changed, or access to sewers is available. All of these are legitimate assumptions that would affect the value significantly if they were not true. Most appraisals include certain standard assumptions, such as that there are no significant subsurface soil conditions that would affect the subject property's value.

Scope of Work Determination

The determination of the scope of work is an important part of any appraisal because it shows the reader of an appraisal report what type of inspection was done, what research was done, and how the value opinion was prepared. The scope of work statement will explain why something was done and sometimes why something else was not done in the appraisal. An appraiser cannot be all things to all people. As a result, the scope of work discussion limits the expectations of the client and intended users of the report.

Planning the Appraisal

Since all appraisals are research projects, a plan is absolutely necessary. Researching sales or rental data can be time-consuming and should usually be started immediately upon accepting an assignment. Getting phone calls returned may take several days. Start the research early so that data is on hand when the report is due.

Scope Creep
The term scope creep has recently found its way into usage in the appraisal profession. It refers to a shift in the focus of a given assignment or role, which usually results in the appraiser doing more work for little or no extra compensation. The best way for an appraiser to prevent scope creep is to ensure that there is mutual understanding as to what the client expects at the outset of an assignment and to provide a clear statement of the expected scope of work in the engagement letter or preliminary agreement.

KEY TERMS	
cost approach	reconciliation
final opinion of value	sales comparison approach
income capitalization approach	valuation process

Data Collection and Property Description

The analysis portion of the valuation process begins with the data collection and property description. To develop an opinion of value, you must decide who the typical buyers are and how much they will pay for the property. To estimate what a buyer will pay, most appraisers research what buyers paid before for similar real estate, which should tell them what buyers will pay again.

Relevance should be the first consideration for all the data you use in an appraisal. Some appraisers are notorious for including excessive amounts of irrelevant data in appraisal reports to increase the number of pages and make the reports look credible when they are not. While large quantities of relevant data are impressive, large quantities of irrelevant data are a waste of time and paper and can be misleading.

Data Analysis

Finding the data is important, but knowing how to analyze it is even more important. Just having data is of little consequence unless you can show how it leads to a value conclusion. Some appraisers do an excellent job of getting information but do not really know what to do with it once they have it. Others are good at analysis but do not do a good job of research.

Some Questions to Ask about Comparable Properties

- Is the property that is listed, sold, leased, or offered for lease comparable to the subject property?
- Is the highest and best use of the comparable consistent with the highest and best use of the subject?
- What property interest was sold? Is it the same as the interest in the property being appraised?
- What improvements were in place on the date of the sale or lease?

Market Analysis

Market analysis can help you address changes in the subject's market. Nearly all appraisals require some level of market analysis, and this step in the process is critical for the analysis of proposed improvements when the subject will add additional units to the supply. Less attentive appraisers often skip market analysis, ignoring current market conditions and relying instead on historic sales data. If they are up-to-date, sales comparables can only show if the market has changed. Old sales

---

Some Questions Answered by Market Analysis

- What market will the subject compete in?
- How much supply is in place, coming, or going?
- What is the current and future demand for properties in the same market?

---

will tell you what the market was like when those sales were negotiated but may not represent the market on the effective date of analysis.

Highest and Best Use Analysis

Highest and best use analysis involves the consideration of two scenarios:

- the highest and best use of the site as though vacant
- the highest and best use of the property as improved

Highest and Best Use of the Site As Though Vacant

To ensure an appropriate opinion of market value, you must first analyze the highest and best use of the land as though vacant. In other words, you must decide what use would be appropriate for a site if it were vacant, which is often a hypothetical condition. Even when improvements are in place, you must assume that the land is vacant so the value of the land on its own can be estimated, which may lead you to the conclusion that the improved property has less value than the vacant land. Of course, when estimating if the land is worth more as vacant than as improved, you must consider the cost of removing the existing building improvements. The cost of removing the improvements is not considered in the land valuation because the land is assumed to be vacant in that analysis. The cost of demolition will be considered in the analysis of the value of the improved property and the highest and best use.

Highest and Best Use of the Property As Improved

In the second part of highest and best use analysis, the appraiser analyzes the property as improved. This analysis will tell you if the property is worth more with or without improvements and if the existing improvements should be retained, altered, or razed and the site be redeveloped. The analysis of the highest and best use of the property as improved will also tell you if there will be any losses in value due to functional obsolescence. If a home has only two bedrooms in a market that demands four bedrooms, the highest and best use analysis would include a discussion of the cost of correcting the problem or the loss in value if the correction is not financially feasible. Highest and best use analysis is one of the most important steps in market value appraisals for properties in transition or properties with designs that are not conducive to economic use (e.g., special-purpose properties).

Land Value Opinion

In most appraisal assignments, the subject property's site must be valued as though vacant. Several techniques are available to value vacant land:

- sales comparison
- allocation
- extraction
- subdivision development analysis
- land residual technique
- ground rent capitalization

Land valuation is discussed at length in Chapter 17, but the various techniques are summarized below.

Sales Comparison Approach

In land valuation, the sales comparison approach may be considered a study of historical market activity. An opinion of the market value of the subject's site can be supported by the analysis of historical sales of similar sites plus or minus minor adjustments for differences. This technique follows straightforward logic: "If the sellers of that property were able to achieve a sale price of $X, then this property ought to be worth $X plus or minus the applicable adjustments."

Allocation

The allocation technique is a ratio analysis in which the appraiser researches and develops a ratio of land value to property value in an area where vacant land sales are available to support the land value. After developing an estimate of the ratio of land value to property value, you then apply that ratio to the subject property's area to develop an opinion of land value. You can use this approach when there are no comparable vacant land sales in the area. Allocation is not a useful technique if the existing improvements do not represent the highest and best use of the site as though vacant.

Extraction

To apply the extraction technique, an appraiser researches comparable sales of improved properties in the subject's area, estimates the value of the building and site improvements of the properties (usually through the cost approach), and then subtracts those amounts from the sale prices. The remaining values are the extracted land values. Extraction can be used when there are no comparable vacant land sales. Like allocation, extraction is not a good technique if the subject improvements do not represent the highest and best use of the site as though vacant.

Income Capitalization Techniques

Subdivision Development

Appraisers use the subdivision development technique when the highest and best use of the subject property is to develop the site but there are few comparable sales of vacant tracts that were later developed into subdivisions. If there is demand for subdivision acreage, land has usually been sold for development and sales of undeveloped land will be available for analysis. In areas where this is not the case, however, subdivision development analysis can be a useful tool.

Land Residual Technique

The land residual technique converts the income a property can command into a value opinion for the land and the building. This technique is rarely used in most markets because of the difficulty in separating income to the building from income to the land.

Ground Rent Capitalization

Ground rent capitalization is a great technique for valuing land leases. It is used widely in markets in which the subject property is subject to a land lease that has a long term remaining and the income is limited by the lease. If a vacant land property is leased to a tenant on a long-term basis, the only benefits accrued by the lessor (i.e., the leased fee owner) are the cash flows and property reversion, which may only be received a long time in the future. If a tenant builds significant improvements on long-term leased land, the holder of the leased fee interest (commonly referred to as the *ground owner*) has much less risk in the beginning of the lease term because the landlord gets the new building if the tenant defaults. For some appraisals, ground rent capitalization is the only relevant methodology for valuing real property rights.

A lease based on vacant land that was not intended to be improved is not really comparable to a lease of a vacant site on which the lessee intended to build substantial improvements. The risk is much different, and therefore the capitalization rates will also be significantly different.

Application of the Three Approaches to Value

The three approaches to value do not apply in all situations, but some or all are used in most appraisals. (Substantial discussion of each of the approaches to value is presented in Chapters 18 through 29.) The approaches to value reflect the three options for property buyers or renters:

- buy an existing property (sales comparison approach)
- rent a property (income capitalization approach)
- buy land and build a new building (cost approach)

Sales Comparison Approach

The sales comparison approach to value is based on the premise that if you paid a certain amount for a property that is similar to the subject property, you would pay that same amount for the subject property. Also, looking at comparable listings (not sales) should reveal what the subject will not sell for. The sales comparison approach is used in almost all appraisals. If a market value opinion is sought, sales comparison analysis is usually a primary technique, especially in residential appraisals.

Most residential appraisal clients and intended users have rules, guidelines, and procedures in place to ensure that the appraiser does the sales comparison analysis correctly.

Sales Comparison Approach Procedure

1. Collect data on recent sales, current listings, and even pending sales (sold but not closed) that are comparable to the subject property.
2. Verify the information by confirming that the data obtained is factually accurate and the sales transactions reflect arm's-length market considerations.
3. Select the most relevant units of comparison in the market (e.g., price per acre, price per square foot, price per front foot) and develop a comparative analysis for each unit.
4. Adjust the sale price of each comparable property to reflect how it differs from the subject property.
5. Reconcile the various value indications produced from the analysis of comparable sales to a value bracket or a single value indication. Comparable sales will give indications of value, but comparable listings will usually show what the current competition is and what the subject *cannot* sell for.

Income Capitalization Approach

The income capitalization approach is based on the premise that some properties sell to investors interested in the income potential of the properties. For some property types (such as one-unit residential properties), the income capitalization approach is not the primary approach to value. For many others, this is the only truly persuasive approach to value because the typical buyers are investors who compare the real estate investment to alternatives in the stock or bond markets. Any appraisal of a property type that is primarily purchased by investors who base their decisions on net cash flows should include this approach to value.

The conversion of annual income into a market value is made through a direct capitalization rate calculation or a discounted cash flow (DCF) analysis. For example, if a property sold for $1 million and the annual net income was $91,000, you could say that the property sold for 10.99 times its annual income. You could also say that its annual income was 9.1% (0.0910) of its sale price. These mathematical relationships are the basis of the direct capitalization of a single year's income into an estimate of market value.

As another example, consider a property with an estimated net income of $69,000 per year in a market in which similar properties have an annual income of 9.1% of the sale price. An appraiser could make the following calculation to estimate the value of the property:

$$\$69,000/0.091 = \$758,242$$

You can also value real property by adding up the present worth of its future benefits (discounted cash flow analysis). For example, if a property is projected to make $25,000 per year for the next 10 years and then will sell for $200,000, you can estimate value by adding up the *present value* of each year's cash flows plus the *present value* of the probable resale price. A dollar in the future is worth less than a dollar today (because of the time value of money), so the present worth of future benefits decreases when the income is to be received further in the future. (The concept of the time value of money is discussed more fully in Chapters 21 and 25.)

Cost Approach

The cost approach is based on the theory of substitution. Obviously, no well-informed investor would pay more for an existing property than the cost of building a new structure with the same

Income Capitalization Approach Procedure
1. Research the income and expense data for the subject and comparable properties.
2. Estimate the potential gross income of the property by adding the projected rental income and any other potential income.
3. Estimate the vacancy and collection loss.
4. Subtract the vacancy and collection loss from the total potential gross income to arrive at the effective gross income of the subject property.
5. Estimate the total operating expenses for the subject by adding fixed expenses, variable expenses, and a replacement allowance (when applicable).
6. Subtract the estimate of total operating expenses from the estimate of effective gross income to arrive at net operating income.
7. Apply the direct capitalization or yield capitalization technique to this data.

Cost Approach Procedure
1. Estimate the value of the site as though vacant and available to be developed to its highest and best use.
2. Determine whether reproduction cost or replacement cost is most applicable to the assignment.
3. Estimate the direct and indirect improvement costs as of the effective appraisal date.
4. Estimate the entrepreneurial incentive or profit based on market analysis.
5. Add the estimated direct and indirect costs as well as the entrepreneurial incentive or profit to yield the total cost of the improvements.
6. Estimate the depreciation. If necessary, allocate it among physical deterioration, functional obsolescence, and external obsolescence.
7. Deduct the estimated depreciation from the total cost of the improvements.
8. Estimate how much any site improvements that were not considered as part of the direct costs contribute to value.
9. Add the land value to the total depreciated cost of the improvements to yield the property's market value.
10. Make adjustments for any personal property or intangible assets included.
11. Adjust the value conclusion for the property interest being appraised to yield the value of the specified property interest.

utility. While the cost approach is most persuasive in the appraisal of new or nearly new properties (e.g., a new building is a direct competitor of a building less than five years old), you can also use it in the analysis of older properties by subtracting a reasonable amount to compensate for the age of improvements and other losses in value.

How much more will a new home sell for as compared to an identical two-year-old home? Appraisers can study market data and extract how much less buyers pay for two-year-old homes than for new ones. This amount is called *depreciation*. When buildings are newer, depreciation is usually minimal. As the improvements get older, they suffer more losses. When this happens, depreciation becomes more significant and less easy to estimate.

Final Reconciliation of Value Indications

The next-to-last component of the valuation process brings the value indications from the various techniques and procedures used into a single value opinion or range of values. For example, if the value estimates are $198,000 from the cost approach, $202,000 from the sales comparison approach, and $203,000 from the income capitalization approach, then the final value opinion might be $200,000, depending on the relative importance placed on the different approaches to value in that assignment.

The appraiser's job often includes interpreting conflicting data for the client. Sometimes the data source is wrong. Sometimes the motivations of buyers and sellers do not meet the requirements of the definition of *market value*. Sometimes there are errors in the logic and presentation of data. You must present enough data to ensure that the credibility of the results is not in question. The quality and quantity of data is always a concern.

Report of Defined Value

The report of the defined value is usually the last step in the process and often the most time-consuming part of any appraisal assignment. After you have done all the research and analysis of the subject property and its market, you will typically write a report document to be delivered to the client. Many appraisal reports are highly structured and you will essentially fill out a form, but others are not structured at all and you must decide what and how much to write.

1. The three approaches to value are
   a) Market analysis, market consensus of opinion, and market research
   b) Sales extraction, cost replication, and income multiplication
   c) Sales comparison, cost, and income capitalization
   d) Graphic analysis, linear regression, and statistical analysis

2. Highest and best use
   a) Is specified by the client
   b) Must be considered in all appraisals
   c) Includes two parts when the property is improved: the highest and best use as though vacant and the highest and best use as improved
   d) Assumes demand for the property within the existing or proposed use

3. Land valuation techniques include
   a) Subdivision development, depreciated cost, and consensus
   b) Sales comparison approach, consensus, and extraction
   c) Sales comparison approach, allocation, and extraction
   d) Assessment multipliers, assessor's opinions, and multiple regression multipliers

4. The valuation technique in which land and building are valued separately is
   a) The income capitalization approach
   b) The sales comparison approach
   c) Linear regression
   d) The cost approach

5. The valuation technique in which the income a property earns is considered is
   a) The income capitalization approach
   b) The sales comparison approach
   c) The cost approach
   d) None of the above

6. In the valuation process, defining the value estimated is included in the
   a) Identification of the appraisal problem
   b) Preliminary analysis and data selection and collection
   c) Highest and best use analysis
   d) Land value opinion

7. One reason to estimate the highest and best use "as though vacant" and "as improved" is
   a) To increase the size of the report, which increases the fee
   b) Because it necessitates a land value estimate for analytical purposes
   c) To allow for estimating physical depreciation
   d) To recognize when the improvements should be razed

8. Land value can be estimated using all of the following techniques except
   a) The sales comparison method
   b) The cost method
   c) The income method
   d) The allocation method

9. There are three approaches to estimating market value because
   a) Purchasers have three alternative options available
   b) USPAP indicates that all appraisals must use all three approaches to value
   c) There are three ways to look at anything
   d) It is required for good statistical significance

10. One activity that is not part of defining the appraisal problem is
    a) Identifying the fee with the client
    b) Identifying the property rights to be appraised
    c) Identifying the type of value to be estimated
    d) Identifying the valuation date

11. What is the final step of the valuation process?
    a) Final reconciliation and estimation of the single value estimate
    b) Final reconciliation and determination of the range or single estimate
    c) Completion of a report with the defined value
    d) Application of the three approaches to value

Note: Unless otherwise noted, italicized references indicate the pages in *The Appraisal of Real Estate*, 14th edition, that readers should consult for additional discussion of these topics.

1. c) Sales comparison, cost, and income capitalization
   Page 36

2. c) Includes two parts when the property is improved: the highest and best use as though vacant and the highest and best use as improved
   Pages 42-43

3. c) Sales comparison approach, allocation, and extraction
   Page 44

4. d) The cost approach
   Page 47

5. a) The income capitalization approach
   Pages 46-47

6. a) Identification of the appraisal problem
   Page 38

7. d) To recognize when the improvements should be razed
   Pages 42-43

8. b) The cost method
   Pages 43-44

9. a) Purchasers have three alternative options available
   Page 36

10. a) Identifying the fee with the client
    Page 38

11. c) Completion of a report with the defined value
    Page 48

5

Elements of the Assignment

This chapter will discuss the significant elements of appraisal assignments:

- the client
- the intended use and intended users of the appraisal
- the purpose of the assignment (including the type and definition of value)
- the effective date of the value opinion
- the relevant property characteristics
- the assignment conditions

This will prepare you to focus more closely on two important and complex appraisal concepts:

1. the type and definition of value
2. the rights being appraised

Client

The decision to accept an assignment begins with the identification of the client and the intended users of an appraisal. Sometimes the appraiser who is initially approached does not have the appropriate qualifications for the assignment. A client may ask an appraiser to do something unethical or produce a value target. If you take all the work that comes to your door, regardless of what and where it is, you may sometimes find yourself on thin ice. Many appraisers limit their work to areas in which they are comfortable, competent, and efficient. Many appraisers will also reject a certain client's work because they know the assignments will be problematic.

Intended Use and Intended Users

You must know going into an assignment how the appraisal report will be used. Identifying the intended use may require you to do one type of analysis instead of another. For example, suppose a curbside appraisal (also known as a *drive-by appraisal*) was ordered by a mortgage lender with the expressed intended use as a documentation of value for loan underwriting. The appraisal and report were developed and delivered to the client, who later gave a copy of the report to the property owners. A year later, the property owners presented the appraisal report as evidence in a condemnation court proceeding for a right-of-way taking by the city. The appraiser was criticized by an attorney for not developing an opinion of market value for the subject for both before and after the taking, although the intended use of the appraisal had been for mortgage underwriting rather than condemnation proceedings. A separate appraisal with a different intended use would have to be conducted for use in the court proceeding.

Defining the intended use of an appraisal is an important step in the process that ties directly into defining the type of value to be used.

Type of Value and Its Definition

You must also know and be able to describe the type of value (such as market value or use value) to be developed in the appraisal. This process is similar to identifying the intended use because it requires you to know why you are doing the appraisal and the appropriate type of research and analysis necessary. The type of value to be developed in the appraisal must be consistent with the intended use.

Effective Date of the Opinion of Value

The effective date of the value opinion can be before, after, or on the date of inspection. Retrospec-

KEY TERMS	
definition of value	intended use of the appraisal
extraordinary assumption	prospective opinion of value
hypothetical condition	retrospective value opinion

tive value opinions backdate the appraisal into the past. Prospective value opinions value the property at some future point in time. Some appraisers never use a date other than the date of inspection, but others work with prospective and especially retrospective effective dates all the time. In a retrospective appraisal, you have the advantage of knowing what happened after the date of appraisal, but the value opinion should only reflect what buyers would decide on that date based on the data available at that time. Prospective appraisals involve looking into the future, which is always difficult. Determining a valid value opinion reflecting market conditions a few months in the future is not difficult in most cases, but forecasting value a few years ahead with any accuracy can be much more difficult. Most prospective values involve new construction that needs to be valued when the property is completed or when occupancy is stabilized at some point in the future.

Relevant Property Characteristics

The important characteristics of a property include the legal rights, the physical property (land and buildings), the location, and other items to be valued. Identifying property characteristics is accomplished using maps, photographs, narratives, checklists, and other methods. The level of detail in the description of the real estate will vary with the reporting option used.

An important characteristic in one appraisal may not be important in another, as shown in the following examples:

- The analysis of a written lease on the subject property would be very important in an appraisal of the leased fee interest in an office building with a long-term lease, but the analysis of the lease would not be nearly as important in an appraisal of the fee simple interest of that same property.
- The size and species of the trees in the front yard of a one-unit residential property would not be nearly as important to describe in a mortgage appraisal report as they would be in a condemnation case in which the trees were part of the real estate acquired by the governmental body.

Assignment Conditions

Extraordinary Assumptions and Hypothetical Conditions

Appraisers often need to assume some condition is true even when it is not known to be true or even

possible or when it is known to be false but will be assumed to be true for the purposes of the analysis.

Extraordinary assumptions have many applications in appraisal, but all require you to draw conclusions as if some fact were true even though you do not actually know whether it is. Examples of extraordinary assumptions include the following:

- An appraisal analysis and opinion of market value are subject to the completion of the construction of a 2,000-sq.-ft. house on a vacant lot as described in the blueprints on a date six months from now. This is an extraordinary assumption with a prospective value. That is, you should assume that the property will be built on the site as of the future date, although you cannot know whether that will actually occur.
- An appraisal is subject to the owner obtaining the right and ability to connect to the sewer and water utilities.
- An appraisal is subject to the kitchen being remodeled according to the plans and specifications provided as of a date in the future.

Many extraordinary assumptions require you to draw conclusions about a property assuming something is in place at a certain time when you cannot be sure that it would be, such as in the case of proposed construction.

In contrast, a hypothetical condition deals with a fact that is known to be false but is assumed to be true for the purposes of the analysis. Examples of hypothetical conditions include the following:

- You are appraising a one-unit home on the corner of two busy streets as of today. The subject property is zoned R-4 Residential, but there is ample evidence to support a possible change in zoning. The commercial land value is much higher than the improved residential value. The appraisal is subject to changing the zoning from R-4 to C-5 Commercial. This is a hypothetical condition because the property is not zoned C-5 as of today and the zoning change may or may not be granted at a future date, but you perform the appraisal as if the zoning change was already granted.
- An appraisal is subject to construction of the proposed residence on a vacant site as of today. This is different than the prior example because building a house in six months is possible, but building a house in one day is not. In residential appraisals, it is common to

specify the condition that the value is estimated assuming construction of the home as of the date of the inspection when the lot is vacant. This is a hypothetical condition because it is known not to be true but is assumed to be true for the purposes of the appraisal.

Like extraordinary assumptions and hypothetical conditions, general limiting conditions are often required because of limitations in the extent of the inspection, data research, and other areas. The assumptions required in most appraisals are defined and listed in the initial phase of the valuation process.

Jurisdictional Exceptions

A jurisdictional exception is invoked in the rare instance when a relevant law or regulation provides an exception to the applicable professional standards. For example, a federal, state, or local law may be required to stand instead of an appraisal standards rule. Only the portion of the professional standards that conflicts with the regulation is affected by a jurisdictional exception, and the remainder of the professional standards still applies. Because jurisdictional exceptions may affect the results of the appraisal, they must be identified at the outset of an assignment and clearly disclosed in the appraisal report.

Distinctions Between Examples of Extraordinary Assumptions and Hypothetical Conditions

extraordinary assumption: For the purposes of the appraisal assignment, you assume a commercial property has no environmental problems when you really do not know this to be true.

hypothetical condition: For the purposes of the appraisal assignment, you assume a commercial property has no environmental problems when you know it does have contamination problems.

An assignment involving such a hypothetical condition could be misleading unless the report indicates very clearly the existence of environmental problems and there is a legitimate reason for making the assumption that no such problems exist. Examples of legitimate reasons include:

· The appraisal report is being prepared for use in litigation having to do with the environmental problem.

· A highest and best use study is conducted in which the cost of curing the problem is compared to the "clean" value of the property to decide on the property's use.

---

1. The date of the value opinion is
   a) The first date the appraiser was on site
   b) The last date the appraiser was on site (the inspection date)
   c) The date stipulated by the client
   d) The date the appraiser received the order

2. An appraisal is made as of a specified date to
   a) Establish the due date of the fee
   b) Prove that the appraiser inspected the property
   c) Satisfy the requirements of the client
   d) Indicate the date when the buyer agreed to purchase the property

3. Data requirements for an appraisal assignment are determined by the
   a) Client
   b) Appraiser
   c) Nature of the problem
   d) Type of property

4. The value to be estimated is determined by the
   a) Property type
   b) Client's problem
   c) Highest and best use
   d) Existing zoning classification

5. An appraiser found that the subject has a septic system in the front yard. The appraiser could not tell if the system was working, so she assumed it was operational. The appraiser has made a(n)
   a) Extraordinary assumption
   b) Hypothetical condition
   c) Standard assumption that is assumed in all appraisals
   d) Error in judgment

6. An appraiser was asked to appraise the fee simple interest in a 0.24-acre site improved with a 24-year-old residence. The appraiser stated in the report that "It is clear that the roof covering is not in marketable condition. It is a condition of this appraisal and the value opinion that the roof shingles be replaced." This would be an example of a(n)
   a) Extraordinary assumption
   b) Hypothetical condition
   c) Ordinary assumption
   d) Ordinary limiting condition

7. In an appraisal assignment, a jurisdictional exception is applicable when
   a) An attorney says it is applicable.
   b) That part of USPAP does not seem to fit the assignment.
   c) The client says it is applicable.
   d) The state or local laws or regulations are contrary to a part or parts of USPAP.

8. An appraiser inspected the subject property and found termite damage on the floor joists in the crawl space. The client told him to assume that it was repaired and condition the value on the repair. This is an example of a(n)
   a) Extraordinary assumption
   b) Hypothetical condition
   c) Unethical request
   d) Request that is common, ethical, and part of the standard limiting conditions found in most appraisal reports

9. An appraiser was asked to appraise the fee simple interest in a 0.24-acre site improved with a 24-year-old residence in February. The ground and the roof of the house were covered with 10 inches of snow. The appraiser stated in the report that "It is assumed that the roof covering is in marketable condition." This would be an example of
   a) An extraordinary assumption
   b) A hypothetical condition
   c) An ordinary assumption
   d) An ordinary limiting condition

10. An appraiser states the following in an appraisal report: "This appraisal assumes that there are no negative subsurface conditions that will impact the market's reaction to this property, such as subsidence or the existence of toxic waste or soft substrata that is incapable of supporting a building foundation." This is an example of a(n)
    a) Extraordinary assumption
    b) Hypothetical condition
    c) Ordinary assumption
    d) Ordinary limiting condition

Note: Unless otherwise noted, italicized references indicate the pages in *The Appraisal of Real Estate*, 14th edition, that readers should consult for additional discussion of these topics.

1. c) The date stipulated by the client
    Page 52

2. c) Satisfy the requirements of the client
    Page 52

3. c) Nature of the problem

4. b) Client's problem
    Page 51

5. a) Extraordinary assumption
    Page 53

6. b) Hypothetical condition
    Pages 53-54

7. d) The state or local laws or regulations are contrary to a part or parts of USPAP.
    Pages 54-55

8. b) Hypothetical condition
    Pages 53-54

9. a) An extraordinary assumption
    Page 53

10. c) Ordinary assumption
    Pages 52-55

Identifying the Type of Value and Its Definition

Appraisers rarely use the term *value* on its own, as this can be misleading or vague in an appraisal report. Instead, they refer to a particular type of value, which helps clarify the terms used in the appraisal assignment for the benefit of the intended users. As a result, identifying and defining the type of value that will be the focus of the appraisal assignment is an important part of the first step in the valuation process, i.e., identifying the assignment elements. The type of value should be mutually understood and agreed upon by the client and appraiser at the outset of an assignment, and the type and definition of value must be included in the appraisal report, according to professional standards.

Most appraisal assignments deal with one of the more common types of value such as market value or use value, but all sorts of modifiers can be used with the word *value*. The definition of value helps answer the question "What is being valued?" and thereby makes the task of clearly identifying the type and definition of value an essential task in the valuation process.

Market Value

The meaning of the term *market value* has been debated by many appraisers. To most people, *market value* means the amount the subject property would sell for if the owner offered it for sale as of the date of appraisal, and in most cases it is as simple as that. If the subject were exposed to the market via a competent broker (or some other marketing system), what would be an acceptable offer?

Remember that analysis of market value assumes that a market exists. If there are no buyers,

there is no market and therefore no market value. If a property does not have a viable market in its current use, a change in use will be required.

In a market value appraisal, you should apply the definition of *market value* to every comparable sale to see if the sale price in that transaction represents the market value of that property. If the comparable sale does not comply with the definition of *market value*, you should assess if that sale gives an indication of the subject's market value. In many appraisals, the defined value is the crucial issue. For example, special-purpose properties must have a market to have market value. Many appraisers lose sight of this fact when they appraise unusual properties. If there is no viable market, a change in use is likely.

Many definitions of *market value* are in use today, and there are many exceptions and caveats to the definitions in various situations. The common thread in all the definitions is that the value opinion is the amount that the buyer would pay for the property under fair sale conditions.

Types of Value	
disposition value	public interest value
fair value	retrospective value
insurable value	salvage value
investment value	scrap value
liquidation value	use value
market value	value of the going concern
prospective value	

KEY TERMS	
assessed value	liquidation value
disposition value	market value
fair value	use value
insurable value	value of the going concern
investment value	

Other Types of Value

Even though market value is the most commonly asked-for type of value in real estate appraisal, other types of value might be the focus of an assignment. Other types of value are often associated with appraisals performed for financial reporting purposes or appraisals of real estate with business components, which can be more complex assignments than appraisals for lending purposes.

Fair Value

Accountants and appraisers both deal with questions of value, and the evolving definition of *fair value* reflects the overlap of their professional practices. The Sarbanes-Oxley Act as well as changes made to the Financial Accounting Standards Board's approach to reporting corporate assets for tax purposes and in financial reports have both made the traditional accounting definition of *fair value* more like the appraiser's definition of *market value*–i.e., a measure of value in exchange. Current thinking on fair value assumes that the asset (which may be real estate) is valued at its highest and best use, either through its use in combination with other assets or on its own. Again, the underlying premise of fair value is that the property must have a viable market on the date of appraisal.

Use Value

To develop an estimate of use value, an appraiser assumes the use stipulated by the client. In a use value appraisal, the use of the property is usually not the same as the highest and best use in a market value appraisal. The use value is often much higher than market value would be. For example, assume that you own a factory with specialized design and equipment and ask an appraiser to determine what the factory is worth to your corporation, which has use for these special features.

The use value estimate could be the same as the market value if there is a resale market for the special features, meaning that other buyers in the market would be willing to pay for the features when they are associated with the subject real estate. The use value opinion will be much higher than market value if there are no buyers who will pay a premium for the features, i.e., the market value is low because no market exists. The most common way to estimate use value is the cost approach, which allows for segregating and deducting physical depreciation.

Investment Value

The term *investment value* describes a value estimate for which the client, rather than the market, stipulates the rate of return. For example, assume a client asks you to value a property "based on a 10% return," when evidence indicates that the market rate of return is only 8%. This is a legitimate service to perform because potential investors may only be willing to invest when the market is favoring their position. This value is commonly used in appraisals of investment-grade, nonresidential properties.

Value of the Going Concern

The term *value of the going concern* refers to a value opinion that takes income from both the real estate and the associated business into account. Appraisals involving the value of a going concern are commonly used when the market values of the real estate and business are difficult to segregate, such as in appraisals of bowling alleys, funeral homes, hotels, and automobile dealerships. It is difficult to conceive of selling a hotel without selling the business along with the real estate. Some restaurants will also include non-realty components when they change hands, which means that the value indicated by the sale price of the restaurant would be greater than the underlying value of the real estate.

Limited-Market and Special-Purpose Properties

Some properties do not have very deep markets—meaning that there are few sellers and few buyers—which makes estimating market value difficult. If there is no evidence of any market activity, you may have to use an alternative "economic" use as the basis of a market value opinion.

If there really is no market for a property, the cost approach to value is not going to tell you what the subject would sell for on the open market unless you include a deduction for a change in use. If there are very few buyers available, you must decide who would buy the property and what that party would pay.

A broad, gray line separates situations in which appraisers estimate the value of a going concern from those in which they estimate the market value of the real estate alone. As appraisers use the term, *market value of the going concern* (or *business value* or *business enterprise value*) applies to the types of real estate for which there is a premium for the business income over the rental income. *Market value* of real estate applies to the types of real estate for which rental income (and the eventual reversion) is the sole economic benefit of ownership.

The "key employee" can be a major issue in an estimate of the value of a going concern. If a business is built up around the skills and expertise of a single person, the value of the total assets of the business is diminished when that person leaves. For example, consider a restaurant that has exceptional food and attracts a long line of customers each night. The value of the business could drop quickly if the chef responsible for the menu leaves and the regular customers follow that person to a different restaurant. The value of a going concern can be less durable than real estate value because it is often based on intangible assets.

Public Interest Value

Appraisers are occasionally called on to analyze non-economic uses of land. Non-economic uses include usage as public parks, endangered species habitats, or other similar uses that are not usually the highest and best use of the land. *Market value* may not be an appropriate type of value for these situations. Instead, what is known as *public interest value* is the type of value that clients want appraised. These terms may not be interchanged, nor should the value to the public be considered in a market value appraisal.

When appraisals of public properties are prepared, it is important to find out what the intended use is and to be sure that the value opinion is not misleading. Remember that market value assumes a market. If the appraiser cannot find any sales, buyers, or sellers for a property in that use, the appraiser should be careful when using the term *market value*.

Assessed Value

Assessed value is the value of the real estate for taxation purposes. The assessed value can be a percentage of the market value or a ratio of cost to value. Assessed value is a direct function of the as-sessor's best estimate of a property's market value in some states, while in others it has little to do with value but is only a function of equitable taxation. An assessor's opinion of assessed value can be converted into an opinion of market value in some states but not in others. Assessors in some states are required to estimate use value, not market value, because some large and very expensive improved properties have a great deal of value to the owner but much less value on the market.

Insurable Value

Insurable value is the portion of value covered by casualty insurance. This is often set in the insurance contract rather than through the real estate market, although insurance rates themselves may be affected by competition among insurers. State law, which varies by state, may also affect insurable value.

Liquidation Value and Disposition Value

When a property can only be exposed to the market for a limited time for some reason, the type of value being appraised is often liquidation value or disposition value rather than market value. Common examples include foreclosures, short sales, or other situations in which a property is not offered on the market in a manner that fits the definition of market value.

For example, a lender who wants to get a nonperforming loan off the books might set the amount of time that the foreclosed property can be marketed before a sale needs to be made. In this case, an appraiser could develop an opinion of disposition value for the property given the atypical marketing effort. To estimate market value, the appraiser would likely need to make a large adjustment for the conditions of sale (e.g., the brief exposure time), and that sort of adjustment can be difficult to support.

1. The value of a property to a particular user is known as
   a) Market value
   b) Value in exchange
   c) Use value
   d) Leasehold value

2. *Market value* is
   a) Always equal to cost
   b) Always equal to sale price
   c) The amount of money a property should sell for on the open market
   d) A fact that can be reported by the appraiser

3. The mayor of a small town recently hired you to estimate the value of a new one-story, three-bay fire station. The fire station was built last year at a cost of $2.5 million (land and buildings). Similar-sized, one-year-old commercial buildings in comparable locations are selling for $2 million. If you appraise this building for approximately $2.5 million, you probably have conveyed an opinion of
   a) Market value
   b) Investment value
   c) Use value
   d) Value in transition

4. Investment value is
   a) The value of a specific property to anyone
   b) The value of a property within a specific use
   c) The value of a property to a specific buyer with specific investment criteria
   d) The value on which lenders will base loans

5. *Market value* can be described as
   a) The price a person paid for real property
   b) The cost of the land plus the cost of the building
   c) The present worth of future benefits
   d) Whatever someone will pay for something

6. You were recently asked to appraise a local hotel. The bank asked you to value the property for lending purposes. The comparable sales you used in this analysis were all sales of the entire operation. The income used in your calculation was based on the rental rate of each sleeping room and the sales at the restaurant and bar. You are most likely appraising the
   a) Market value of the fee simple interest
   b) Market value of the leased fee interest
   c) Value of the going concern
   d) Value in use

7. Which of the following is *not* a part of the definition of *market value* used by federal financial institutions?
   a) Buyer and seller are typically motivated
   b) The property sells in 90 to 120 days
   c) Payment is made in cash or cash-equivalent terms
   d) Both parties are well informed

8. Investment value is best measured by
   a) Market price to a specific investor
   b) Market value to a specific investor
   c) The cost of acquiring a competitive substitute property with the same utility to a typical purchaser
   d) The present worth of anticipated future benefits to a specific investor

9. Estimating market value for federal financial institutions requires identification of the desires and priorities of
   a) Well-informed buyers and sellers
   b) A fully informed seller
   c) A typically informed purchaser
   d) A typically informed seller

10. *Market value* is
    a) Equal to market price
    b) An estimate of a price that would have been negotiated for a sale today
    c) A measure of value in use
    d) Equal to replacement cost

11. Dennis hired an appraiser for an assignment involving a commercial property. Dennis asked the appraiser to provide an opinion of value for him using his investment criteria, which included an overall capitalization rate of 12%. The market capitalization rate for this type of investment would normally be 10%. The opinion of value that the appraiser provides would be the

a) Investment value

b) Exchange value

c) Market value

d) Use value

12. A client asked an appraiser to value the ABC industrial property based on the assumptions that

· the consummation of the sale occurred within a short time period

· the seller was under extreme compulsion to sell

· the exposure time was short

· there was no special financing

This value is best described as

a) Market value

b) Liquidation value

c) Sheriff's value

d) Value in use

13. The local government levies taxes based on a defined value of the real estate. A local government official develops an opinion of the value according to state regulations. The local government official is developing the

a) Market value

b) Value in use

c) Assessed value

d) Insurable value

14. The owner of a small manufacturing plant recently sold the plant for $1,900,000. This amount includes the real estate, the equipment, the name of the company, and the client list. This $1,900,000 amount would be considered the

a) Assessed value

b) Insurable value

c) Value in use

d) Value of the going concern

Note: Unless otherwise noted, italicized references indicate the pages in *The Appraisal of Real Estate*, 14th edition, that readers should consult for additional discussion of these topics.

1. c) Use value
    Page 62

2. c) The amount of money a property should sell for on the open market
    Pages 58-60

3. c) Use value
    Page 62

4. c) The value of a property to a specific buyer with specific investment criteria
    Page 63

5. c) The present worth of future benefits
    Pages 58-60

6. c) Value of the going concern
    Pages 63-64

7. b) The property sells in 90 to 120 days
    Pages 58-60

8. d) The present worth of anticipated future benefits to a specific investor
    Page 63

9. a) Well-informed buyers and sellers
    Pages 58-60

10. b) An estimate of a price that would have been negotiated for a sale today
    Pages 58-60

11. a) Investment value
    Page 63

12. b) Liquidation value
    Pages 65-67

13. c) Assessed value
    Pages 64-65

14. d) Value of the going concern
    Pages 63-64

7

Identifying the Rights to Be Appraised

Because property rights rather than real estate itself are the commodity traded in the real estate marketplace, identifying the property rights that are relevant to an appraisal assignment helps answer the question, "What is being appraised?" The appraiser and client must have a mutual understanding of whether the full bundle of rights or some particular set of sticks from that bundle is the focus of the assignment at the outset.

Partial Interests in Real Property

The most complete form of real estate ownership, the fee simple estate, can be broken down into several general groups of property interests:

- economic interests such as leased fee and leasehold interests
- legal interests such as life estates and easements
- physical interests such as air and subsurface rights
- financial interests (debt and equity)

Note that debt and equity are discussed in greater detail in Chapter 10. Various types of partial interests are described in this chapter.

Economic Interests

Lease Interests

When a lease is signed, the landlord conveys the right to occupy a parcel or portions of a parcel to a tenant for a specified period of time, which means that the fee simple interest has been divided into leased fee and leasehold interests. The rental rates and lease terms will affect the values of the various interests. The lease term will have a large effect on its estate's value. A lease that has 60 years to run at a specific rate will affect the value greatly, but a lease at the same rate with only 60 days to run will usually have a minimal effect on the value.

Leased Fee Interests

When the lessor has contractually transferred the rights of possession to another party, the leased fee interest represents the landlord's rights. The lease rate, term, and other conditions stipulated in the lease document affect this interest greatly. When

> Appraisers can and often do appraise partial interests in real estate.

> A *gross lease* is a lease in which the landlord pays nearly all expenses associated with the operation of the real estate. A *net lease* is the opposite of a gross lease in the sense that the tenant pays nearly all the expenses. In most cases, the landlord will try to structure the leases so that the tenant pays the expenses whenever possible. When the leases are structured so that the expenses are paid by the landlord, the property is much less efficient. A variety of techniques are available to help properties become more efficient, but most involve passing some of the expenses on to the tenant.

KEY TERMS

air rights	general partnership	littoral rights	sandwich lease
condominium ownership	joint tenancy	partnership	stock corporation
conservation easement	land trust	party wall	sublease
cooperative ownership	leased fee interest	preservation easement	subsurface rights
easement	leasehold interest	remainderman	syndication
easement appurtenant	life tenant timesharing	right of way	tenancy
easement in gross	limited partnership	riparian rights	transferable development right (TDR)

While it is not really possible to sell the land and building separately, it is possible to sell the leased fee interest (which can be very close to the value of the land) and the leasehold interest (which can be very close to the value of the building).

A lease creates a division of the fee simple interest, and sometimes lenders must make mortgages on less-than-fee-simple interests. Lenders want to protect their interest or at least quantify the risks of foreclosure. It is legally permissible for a party with a higher interest in the priority of liens to subordinate its interest to another. This is often done to facilitate a land lease in which the tenant will be building a substantial building on the leased land. It is possible to mortgage any interest in real estate, but the liquidity of the interest is a major consideration. A lender has to determine if a buyer for the specified interest can be found. The partial interest may have value on paper (based on the terms of the lease) but not an achievable value in the market because no buyer would pay the indicated amount for the less-than-fee interest, especially if the lease involved had only a few months or a year left to run.

a property is sold, any existing leases run with the land. A new owner must adhere to the terms of the leases in place, and the value of the leased fee interest may be limited by those leases. In some cases, the value of the leased fee interest is purely a function of the lease income plus the reversion. If a property is leased for a specific term at a specific rate, the buyer of that property is limited to those benefits and the resale price at reversion.

Leasehold Interests

Sometimes a tenant will pay lease rates that are lower than the market rate for that space. When this occurs, the tenant has an interest to protect, which is known as a *positive leasehold interest.* Unless prohibited in the lease, the tenant could sublease the property for a profit, pocketing the difference between the market rate paid by the sublessee and the below-market rate in the original lease. A tenant who cannot sublease the space still enjoys the discount while occupying the space, which is worth something to the tenant.

A substantial leasehold interest can occur when market rental rates increase but the lease has a fixed rate. It is more common to find a substantial leasehold interest when the tenant spends money on the leased property, such as when the tenant constructs the building on leased land or does all the interior finishing in a leased space. If the subject property is leased based on lease rates for vacant land and the tenant builds the improvements, which could command higher rental rates, a large leasehold interest value would be created.

For example, if a land owner leases a plot for 99 years to a tenant who builds a building on the site, the tenant's interest must be considered because the lease does not extinguish upon sale. The new owner of the leased fee interest will receive the periodic income and the the real estate at the end of the lease. The owner of the leasehold interest will retain the use of the property for 99 years. In these situations, appraisers may see an improved property during the site visit and mistakenly conclude that the lease rate is far too low for the intensity of the land use, failing to recognize that the lease rate was based on the land value alone.

Subleasehold or Sandwich Interests

Another type of interest is created by subleasing the property. A *subleasehold interest,* also known as a *sandwich interest,* is created when there are two leases on the same space at the same time. In cases like this, a tenant has leased all or part of the leased space to another party, the sublessee. The original tenant usually no longer needs the space, but the lease term has not expired. A subleasehold interest is also created when a building is developed on leased land (technically a leased fee interest) and the building or a portion of it is leased to another party. These interests are often valued based on a comparison of the market rent for the property and the rate paid by the tenant. The sandwich interest (Exhibit 7.1) belongs to the original tenant or the person who is between the holders of the leased fee and subleasehold interests.

Exhibit 7.1   Sandwich Interest

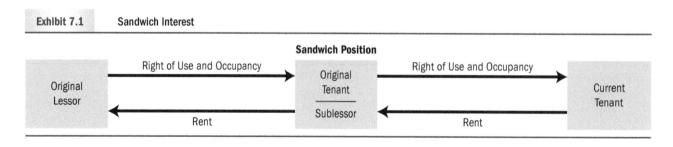

Legal Interests

Life Estates

Life estates are conveyed by the property owner to another person for the length of that person's life. The rights conveyed are twofold:

1. The right to occupy the real estate for the life of a person known as the *life tenant*
2. The right to own the real estate in fee simple after the life tenant dies, which is held by the *remainderman*

> If a person receives a life estate based on someone else's life, it is called a *pur autre vie* life estate, i.e., "for another life." An example of this type of life estate would be giving your daughter-in-law a life estate for as long as your son lives.

Both interests are marketable, and the life tenant does not have to live on the property. The life tenant's estate cannot be inherited because it is based on one person's lifetime.

A *determinable fee* or *defeasible estate* is similar to a life estate in that the rights in realty are transferred subject to some other action or event, but the rights are not necessarily tied to the life of a person. A life estate, determinable fee, or defeasible estate is usually granted by someone who wants to ensure that another person has a place to live and will not be able to give or will the property to another.

Easements

Assisting in the transfer of the rights to easements can be a great source of work for appraisers. To value an easement, an appraiser usually develops an opinion of value of the subject property without the easement and then again with the easement in place, making a "before and after" analysis. The difference in the value indications is the amount offered to the property owner for the easement. This amount can obviously be a source of great debate, and sometimes both the condemning authority and the property owner will commission two or three appraisals.

Explained another way, an easement does not transfer the fee simple interest in a property, so the value of an easement will usually be an estimate of the lack of utility of the property caused by the presence of the easement (and the loss of rights to the property owner). For example, an easement for a pipeline located in the building setback section of a lot is much different than the same easement running through the buildable portion of a residential site. One easement will not prevent construction of an improvement (because additional construction is already prohibited by the setback provision), but the other probably will.

Transferable Development Rights

Transferable development rights (TDRs) are used in some areas to influence development by allowing property owners to sell off their development rights to others. For example, suppose that a community limits each property owner to building only one house per acre of land. A farmer with 100 acres of land could sell off the rights to build 100 houses on this land to another person with a different 100 acres. The person buying the rights could build 200 houses on the land, and the seller would no longer have the right to build any houses on the other plot.

The use of TDRs promotes development in and around urban areas while sustaining farmland or other natural resource land in rural areas. TDRs can also increase the value of land away from the development and decrease the value of land closer to development. That is, owners of land away from a development would have some-

> An *affirmative easement* gives an individual the right to access a portion of another person's real estate for a specific task. An affirmative easement may also be called the *dominant tenement* or *dominant estate*.
>
> A *negative easement* describes real estate burdened by an easement, and it can also be called the *servient tenement* or *servient estate*.

> **easement**
> A conveyance, in law, of certain rights held by one person in land owned by another. Easements convey the right to cross a property but little else. They are commonly used to ensure access to a property via another person's property, or to ensure that utility companies have access to their lines, pipes, and structures. Common easement types include appurtenant easements, avigation easements, conservation easements, and utility easements.
>
> **right of way**
> The right to cross the land of another; for example, the right to build a highway across private land. This term is generically used to refer to the public's right to cross land belonging to another, but it can also refer to railroad right of way, pipeline right of way, etc.
>
> **party wall**
> A common wall erected on the boundary between two adjoining properties, buildings, or units.

thing to sell to developers, but would not have anything to sell without the TDRs.

As another example, a municipality may allow owners of property in a CBD historic district to sell TDRs for development elsewhere. This allows for the preservation of the historic improvements and growth outside the district while the property owners can sell the development rights to make up for the lost economic potential caused by the imposition of redevelopment restrictions within the historic district.

Physical Interests

Unrestricted ownership of real estate extends from the center of the earth to the heavens. Real estate is usually identified by the space on the face of the earth described in the legal description of the land. Land includes the ground and everything attached to it, meaning the things under and above the surface. In other words, a land owner can dig down into the land or build up from it into the air above.

Examples of situations involving physical interests include the following:

- Some states restrict mineral rights when the asset is spread under more than one parcel of land.
- Underground water can be drawn from under a parcel of land from a well on another owner's land. State laws may differ in this respect.
- Avigation easements can be acquired by federal, state, and local governments to allow aircraft to use air space at low altitudes to approach airfields.

Vertical Interests

The holder of the full bundle of rights may be able to sell off the airspace above the land's surface or the ground below it. This technique allows a prop-erty owner to maintain an operation or use on the surface of the land but sell off the higher elevations to different users. Selling off above-surface rights requires preparing a legal description of the elevations in question in the deed. A common example is the acquisition of the right to develop a building above train tracks, allowing trains to still operate underneath the improvements constructed in the airspace above.

Subsurface rights can also be sold off. Mineral rights commonly change hands. Water, sand and gravel, oil drilling, and coal mining companies are always looking for mineral rights to purchase from land owners. Different contractual arrangements can specify when, where, and how the minerals are extracted.

Water Rights

Water rights can be a significant factor in the valuation of some real estate, especially in areas where access to clean water is limited or controlled by others. Properties with access to a water supply can have much greater value than properties with little access or properties for which water has to be trucked in.

Ownership of water and adjacent land is determined by doctrines of *riparian* and *littoral rights*. Some states recognize common-law riparian rights of owners of land bordering a river or stream, giving those owners use of the water that passes over or adjacent to their land as long as they do not inhibit the riparian rights of others. Littoral rights are held by the owners of properties that are adjacent to large navigable bodies of water, such as lakes and oceans. These property owners possess the land up to the high water mark, and the government owns all the land under the water (See Exhibit 7.2). Riparian and

Exhibit 7.2   Water Rights in Navigable Waters

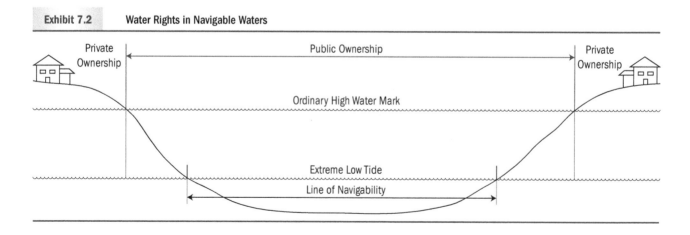

The term *accretion* is used to describe additional dry land that is created when deposits are left by a river or stream, which increases the size of the owner's land. In the process of *reliction*, dry land is created by the receding water line. Land can also be lost to *erosion*, which is the passage of water over the banks. Some legal descriptions incorporate rivers and streams into the defining lines, so these issues can cause legal arguments if inconsistencies arise.

littoral rights run with the land and cannot be separated from the fee interest.

Financial Interests

In the breakdown of ownership interests in real estate, financial interests are the financial divisions of ownership such as mortgage and equity, sale with leaseback provisions, senior and subordinate debt, and equity syndications. Mortgage investments have a great impact on real property value and equity yield rates.

Forms of Ownership

An important distinction should be made between partial interests and forms of ownership. Interests relate to *what* is owned, whereas forms of ownership relate to *who* owns the interest.

Concurrent Ownership of Real Property

More than one person or entity can have a nondivisible interest in real estate. Dividing concurrently owned real estate can complicate the valuation process because minority positions may or may not sell for a proportionate percentage of the sale price. For example, a 30% share of ownership may not sell for 30% of the price of the whole property.

As another example, suppose a farmer dies and leaves his farm to all of his four children in equal percentages as tenants in common. One of the heirs could sell this 25% interest on the open market to someone outside the family for 25% of the real estate's value as a whole. In this case, the

buyer would be a non-family owner with a minority interest in a family-owned parcel.

Legal Entity Ownership of Real Property

In addition to ownership by individuals, real estate can be owned by land trusts, partnerships, corporations, and syndications, i.e., groups of people in various configurations with individuals holding various rights.

Land Trusts

Like all trusts, a land trust is simply a vehicle to hold an interest in real estate on behalf of another party. The public often cannot tell who the owner is. Only the trustee will know. Ownership by a land trust can be used to acquire and maintain property ownership by a professional management company. This technique is used widely in some markets, while in other markets it is not used at all.

Partnerships

Partnerships are a great technique for putting together money to purchase real estate. Any piece of real estate is affordable if enough partners can be found. There are many different partnership arrangements and legal entities, but they are usually organized by the percentage of equity input at the time of purchase.

In a general partnership, all parties are responsible for partnership issues and obligations. In a limited partnership, the general partners are responsible for the debt. The limited partners are only responsible for an amount equal to their equity input, so they can lose their investments but nothing more.

Stock Corporations

Stock is both a form of corporate ownership and a shareholder's financial interest in a property. Large corporations commonly own real estate, and it is also common to divide the rights in realty based on a shareholder's percentage of ownership. Some US Securities and Exchange Commission (SEC) filings are required if too many partners or shareowners are included.

Real estate can be owned by a small number of partners who put their interests into a corporation. The interests may be divided into uneven percentages of the whole. By incorporating, the partners can sell their interests to one or more people. They may or may not still be liable for the mortgage amount, depending on the lender, but they can be less liable for the problems that could arise from real estate ownership (e.g., environmental contamination). A great deal of nonresidential real estate is owned by corporations or limited liability companies (LLCs).

Appraisers are commonly asked to value a partial interest in a piece of real estate in a closely held corporation. The corporation shares are not openly traded, and the interest may not be marketable to anyone other than family members or friends. This is a difficult type of appraisal assignment because little data is available for partial interest sales. Shares in closely held corporations may be difficult to liquidate because the interest is too large to be widely distributed and too small to control the property. Minority owners who want to liquidate their interests may not be able to find buyers at a price equal to their interest.

For example, consider a small corporation created to buy a parcel of real estate. The corporation has four partners with ownerships of 17%, 17%, 17%, and 49%. These percentages were carefully adjusted to ensure that no single person controls the business. None of the partners has a majority ownership, so none of them could put relatives on the payroll, withdraw money as a "management fee," or sell the property to a friend at a discounted price without the consent of one or more of the other partners. However, can the owners sell their minority interests on the open market for the percentages listed?

In some markets, this type of partnership is quite marketable, but in many others it is not. An appraiser would have to judge whether a minority interest would be marketable. Most appraisers would hire a CPA or attorney to assist in this determination, especially if an allocation is being done for IRS reporting purposes. CPAs and attorneys who specialize in this area may have applicable data and court rulings on this type of issue.

Syndications

Real estate equity syndications were once a popular method of holding real estate. They are much less popular now because of changes made to the tax code in 1986, which gave them less preferable tax treatment. The same issues of liquidity and control that apply to stock corporations are important in the valuation of syndications.

Special Forms of Ownership

Condominium Ownership

Condominiums are a modern form of property ownership in which the rights to residential, com-

> The definition of *condominium* depends on the state in which the property is located.
>
> **Helpful Hint**
> An Internet search of the phrase *condominium law* will usually generate a list of websites that provide information on the applicable laws for each state.

mercial, industrial, or special-purpose real estate are conveyed using a method other than standard vertical rights in realty. Condominiums are legal entities in most states. In some states, all condominiums are classified on deeds as *horizontal property regimes*, while in other states the word *condominium* must appear in the legal description of the property. In most circumstances, condominium ownership indicates that the rights in realty are limited both vertically and horizontally, and the owner can neither dig down under the ground nor build up.

Condominium ownership was originally used to allow owners to sell off upper-floor apartments and still obtain individual mortgage loans. As an example, the ownership of a condominium unit in a project with 50 units would typically be conveyed as "unit #__ and a 1/50th interest in the common elements." Condominiums are easily mortgaged, and their value is only minimally dependent on the other units in the project.

Because each state defines a condominium differently, appraisers must research their state laws. Most states have current state laws on condominiums posted on the Internet. If it is difficult to ascertain the definition of a condominium in a particular state, contact a real estate title insurance attorney. These professionals are usually well schooled in the law regarding condominium ownership.

> In some markets, less than 50% of the homes that are called "condominiums" meet the legal definition of the term. It is common for developers to call projects "condominiums" but plat the units as one-unit attached homes with high homeowners' association dues. *Condominium* is a legal term, and you should not confuse this type of property ownership with other properties that are commonly referred to as condominiums by nonprofessionals.

Cooperative Ownership

Prior to the popularity of the modern condominium, cooperative ownership was one of the favorite techniques of developers in urban areas such as New York City. A cooperative is created by a developer who purchases an apartment complex in a corporate name and then sells shares of stock in the corporation to prospective residents. The shares of stock are usually accompanied by a proprietary lease that allows shareholders to live in a unit as long as they pay their pro rata share of the expenses, including their share of the master mortgage payment on the loan the developer used to buy the property. Physically similar units in one cooperative apartment building are probably not comparable to units in another building because of the variance in the mortgage indebtedness.

For example, if a subject property has an 80% master mortgage and an otherwise similar property has a 40% master mortgage, sales of units in the latter property will not serve as useful comparables without a large adjustment for financing terms. The mortgage payment in the project with a 40% mortgage will be much lower than the property with the 80% mortgage, which results in lower monthly fees and higher prices. The project with 80% indebtedness will have a higher mortgage payment, which would cause a lower value and lower price. The two properties may look identical from the street, but they would not be considered comparable because of their different financial structures.

Timesharing

Timesharing is a modern way of dividing the rights in realty over time. With timesharing, an owner buys an interest in a condominium that is limited to a specific week of the year or some other period of time. Timeshares are popular in resort areas and can be traded freely for a different time period or a time period in a different project. This type of property division was created during the advent of condominium ownership and became popular because owners could put the maintenance burden on another entity or person.

1. Life estates
   a) Are not salable and therefore are never appraised
   b) Represent the full bundle of rights limited by the life of a person
   c) Are not legal in most states
   d) Cannot be used for income property

2. Suppose that you are a man who owns a small rental house with two acres, and you marry a woman who has a son from a previous marriage. To provide for your new stepson, you give him a life estate in the small house. When your stepson turns 18, he can
   a) Mortgage his interest
   b) Rent the property out
   c) Sell the life estate to someone else who will rent the property
   d) All of the above

3. A lease
   a) Must be for at least one year
   b) Conveys the right of occupancy to another
   c) Must include the landlord paying the taxes
   d) Does not affect the appraisal since it does not affect the salable interest

4. Air rights are
   a) The rights to adequate ventilation of leased property
   b) The rights to use and control space above a specific parcel of land (as defined on the surface)
   c) The right to have air above the subject property
   d) Similar to a cooperative

5. Suppose that you buy a single-story home that is attached on two sides and has the following characteristics:
   · A slab floor
   · A common maintenance agreement for exterior repairs
   · Common snow plowing and street maintenance
   · A common swimming pool, clubhouse, and tennis courts
   You have to pay a $100-per-month fee for maintenance, and you were told by the broker that the property is a "condo." The assessor says that you have a 4,000-sq.-ft. lot, and the legal description is "Lot 12 in the Calgary Addition." You probably own
   a) An attached home on a small lot with a mandatory fee
   b) A condominium
   c) A townhouse
   d) A zero lot line

Use the following data to solve Review Exercises 6 through 8.

Suppose that you own a one-acre parcel in downtown Cleveland. This parcel was vacant when you leased it three years ago to the Cleveland Development Company for 99 years. The 99-year lease specified a rent of $30,000 per year net to the owner. The Cleveland Development Company built a 15-story office building on this parcel and leased the building space to 31 different tenants, including two whole floors to Amalgamated Products.

6. Amalgamated Products holds
   a) The fee simple interest
   b) The leased fee interest
   c) The leasehold interest
   d) A subleasehold interest

7. You hold
   a) The leased fee interest
   b) The leasehold interest
   c) A subleasehold interest
   d) A subleased fee interest

8. What happens to the building at the end of the 99-year lease?
   a) Any buildings on this land belong to you and/or your successors.
   b) The Cleveland Development Company can remove the building before the lease ends.
   c) The building still belongs to the Cleveland Development Company because that company built it.
   d) You will probably have to sell this property long before the 99 years is up, which will void the lease.

9. A project with units that are limited both vertically and horizontally and have a percentage ownership in the common elements is a
   a) Condominium
   b) PUD
   c) Cooperative
   d) Timeshare

10. A real property interest held by a lessee and conveying the right of use and occupancy for a stated term under certain conditions is called the
    a) Leasehold estate
    b) Fee simple estate
    c) Leased fee estate
    d) Determinable fee estate

11. Which of the following is not a way to hold title to realty?
    a) Joint tenancy
    b) Tenancy at will
    c) Tenancy in common
    d) Tenancy by the entirety

12. The highest and fullest estate in land is the
    a) Fee for service
    b) Fee simple
    c) Fee simple determinable
    d) Life estate

13. Ownership of real property by two or more parties with an undivided interest is called
    a) Joint tenancy
    b) Tenancy by the entirety
    c) Sole proprietorship
    d) Tenancy in common

14. TDRs are
    a) Topical development restrictions
    b) Transferable development rights
    c) Temporary development rights
    d) Tailored developments—residential

15. Suppose that you bought a fee simple interest in a parcel of real estate last year. Six months later, you leased the vacant land to John for 50 years, and he built a four-story office building on it. The salable rights are as follows:
    a) You have the fee simple, and John has the leased fee.
    b) You have the leased fee, and John has the leasehold.
    c) You have the leasehold, and John has the leased fee.
    d) You have the leased fee, and John has the fee simple.

16. A leased fee interest is
    a) The ownership interest of the tenant when a lease is in effect
    b) The ownership interest of the landlord when a lease is in effect
    c) The ownership interest of the mortgage holder when a lease is in effect
    d) The ownership interest of the sublessor when a lease is in effect

17. Bob owned a 100-acre farm in Hamilton County. When he died, he had no heirs, no friends, and no will. Which of the following statements is true?
    a) The land will be in Bob's name forever because he died without heirs.
    b) The land will pass to the adjacent owners equally.
    c) The land will pass to the first person to occupy the land for seven years (i.e., squatter's rights).
    d) The state will take the property and sell it.

Note: Unless otherwise noted, italicized references indicate the pages in *The Appraisal of Real Estate*, 14th edition, that readers should consult for additional discussion of these topics.

1. b) Represent the full bundle of rights limited by the life of a person
    Page 74

2. d) All of the above
    Page 74

3. b) Conveys the right of occupancy to another
    Page 70

4. b) The rights to use and control space above a specific parcel of land (as defined on the surface)
    Page 78

5. a) An attached home on a small lot with a mandatory fee
    Pages 83-86

6. d) A subleasehold interest
    Pages 73-74

7. a) The leased fee interest
    Page 72

8. a) Any buildings on this land belong to you and/or your successors.
    Page 72

9. a) Condominium
    Pages 83-84

10. a) Leasehold estate
    Page 72

11. b) Tenancy at will
    This student handbook

12. b) Fee simple
    Page 69

13. d) Tenancy in common
    Page 80

14. b) Transferable development rights
    Page 76

15. b) You have the leased fee, and John has the leasehold.
    Page 72

16. b) The ownership interest of the landlord when a lease is in effect
    Page 72

17. d) The state will take the property and sell it.
    Page 6

8

Scope of Work

The scope of work of an appraisal assignment is the type and extent of work necessary to solve the client's valuation problem in a manner consistent with professional standards. The valuation process described in Chapter 4 serves as a core overview of what all appraisals must contain, but the scope of work of an assignment describes the amount of work necessary to produce a credible appraisal. One size definitely does not fit all in appraisal practice, so you must consider the elements of the assignment relevant to each appraisal performed.

The scope of work of an assignment applies to the actions involved in the valuation process for that assignment. For example, an appraisal that only requires a simple drive-by inspection (or no inspection at all) has a different scope of work than one in which a site visit in the company of the property manager and building engineer along with a complete measurement of the premises is called for. Similarly, the amount of market data required to support the value opinion of a house in an active and stable market will likely be less than the amount of market data needed in an appraisal of a more complex property type or a property in a less healthy market. It is important to remember that the scope of work of an appraisal must not be so limited that the appraisal results in an opinion of value that is not credible.

Appraisers have flexibility in determining the scope of work of an assignment based on the specific assignment conditions involved, but they are still responsible for producing credible opinions of value. In that way, the scope of work decision helps appraisers customize their services to the client's informational needs. It also prevents appraisers from doing less than what is necessary or wasting time and money doing more than what is necessary and producing results that are not credible.

Likewise, scope of work can be a moving target if the appraiser learns midway through an assignment that more data than originally anticipated will be needed. Appraisers routinely revise the scope of work as new information comes to light. For example, the property being appraised is a one-acre site improved with a 50-year-old, single-unit residence. The appraiser was asked to prepare a standard residential form report, but the property was zoned commercial and the highest and best use is to remove the house and sell the property as a commercial building site. The appraiser started out researching single-unit residential comparables but ended up researching commercial land sales.

Problem Solving

Determining the scope of work of an appraisal assignment is part of an exercise in problem solving. The process of solving any problem can be divided into three parts:

1. Identifying the problem
2. Determining the solution
3. Applying the solution

Identifying the Problem

An appraisal problem involves an opinion of value of a particular set of property rights in a unique piece of real estate as of a certain date. All the elements of the assignment identified in the first step of the valuation process (see Chapter 5) are essential considerations in the determination of scope of work. For example, an assignment involving an opinion of market value will have a different scope of work than an assignment involving use value because of the informational demands involved in supporting a type of value other than market value. Simply explaining the difference between the definitions of *market value* and *use value* to the client and intended users of the use value appraisal would add to the complexity and intensity of that assignment.

Determining the Solution

The determination of the scope of work of an assignment is at the center of the problem-solving process. An appraiser can take many routes through the valuation process to get to an opinion of value. One route may be more effective and efficient than all the others, however, which is why the determination of the scope of work of an assignment is a practical business consideration in appraisal practice, not simply a prescribed practice of appraisal standards. An appraiser who does a good job determining the appropriate scope of work for an assignment can finish that assignment as quickly as possible and then move on to other paying work–i.e., an appraiser with a good plan of work will be more productive than an appraiser who does not understand the scope of work rules and does more than what is needed.

The solution that an appraiser decides on for a given problem obviously has to be acceptable to people who would want an appraisal in a similar situation (i.e., clients), but the scope of work should also be considered appropriate for the situation by the appraiser's peers. The flexibility of scope of work is limited by the community standards of the appraisal profession, or what other appraisers would consider a credible solution to be. In the single-unit residential market, appraisers often perform curbside inspections of the subject property and comparable sales, or both exterior and interior inspections of the subject but only exterior inspections of the comparable sales. In some cases, however, appraisers perform no physical inspection of the subject or comparable properties. It is important for appraisers to make sure that the appraisal report is not misleading and that the results of the assignment remain credible considering the intended use.

Applying the Solution

The natural completion of the problem-solving process is achieved by acting on the scope of work decision. This entails data collection and analysis, application of the approaches to value, the final reconciliation of value, and communicating the opinion of value in an appraisal report. The scope of work serves as the plan for all those activities.

Disclosure of Scope of Work

Determining the appropriate scope of work for a specific appraisal assignment is only half the battle. You must also communicate the scope of work to the client so that he or she understands the services you will be (and will not be) providing.

Just as the level of intensity of the appraisal activities performed depends on the complexity of the assignment, the level of detail you should disclose to the client depends on that person's sophistication. For example, an experienced local lender who knows the housing market and just needs a form report for lending purposes does not need much explanation about what the appraiser did to complete the assignment. On the other hand, a narrative appraisal report of a proposed office building in an expanding market would probably include a lengthy account of the extraordinary assumptions and hypothetical conditions that apply when proposed construction is appraised, how much market data was collected to support conclusions about the leasing period and other market phenomena, and what approaches to value the appraiser considered in the appraisal (and why).

The manner in which scope of work is disclosed is as flexible as scope of work itself. A discussion of scope of work can be included as a separate section in a written appraisal report or worked into each section of the report (e.g., the scope of work for each approach to value and so on). Alternatively, the disclosure of scope of work could be explained in a conversation with the client if the results of the appraisal are going to be delivered as an oral report.

1. The scope of work in an appraisal report is acceptable
   a) If the client approves it
   b) If the secondary market approves it
   c) If it meets or exceeds the expectations of parties who are regularly intended users for similar assignments and what the appraiser's peers' actions would be in performing the same or a similar assignment
   d) If the client approves, the appraiser thinks it is not misleading, and the state appraiser board has given explicit approval

2. The scope of work decision
   a) Is established and cannot be changed after the assignment is accepted
   b) Is an ongoing process that can change as the appraisal process proceeds
   c) Is established solely by the client
   d) Is established by the Appraisal Subcommittee (ASC)

3. The scope of work of an appraisal
   a) Must always include an inspection of the subject and all comparable sales
   b) Must always include an interior and exterior inspection of the subject property
   c) Must always include an inspection of the subject, at least on the exterior
   d) May or may not include an inspection of the subject or comparable sales

4. Scope of work
   a) Is a term that is unique to the appraisal profession
   b) Defines the level of detail of the appraisal report
   c) Defines the extent of research and analyses of the appraisal process
   d) Is not used in appraisal

Note: Unless otherwise noted, italicized references indicate the pages in *The Appraisal of Real Estate*, 14th edition, that readers should consult for additional discussion of these topics.

1. c) If it meets or exceeds the expectations of parties who are regularly intended users for similar assignments and what the appraiser's peers' actions would be in performing the same or a similar assignment
    Page 89

2. b) Is an ongoing process that can change as the appraisal process proceeds
    Page 92

3. d) May or may not include an inspection of the subject or comparable sales
    Pages 87-91

4. c) Defines the extent of research and analyses of the appraisal process
    Page 87

9

Data Collection

Nearly every appraisal is a research assignment with a specific goal—an opinion of value supported by market evidence. An important part of the valuation process is collecting data. To produce a supportable appraisal and a credible solution, you must formally identify the problem the client is asking you to solve and decide what work is necessary to solve that problem. Then you need to design a research plan and collect the necessary data so you can analyze the data and see what it tells you.

It is important to keep in mind that your appraisal conclusions are only as good as the data used to arrive at those conclusions, and you are ultimately responsible for the quality of the data you use.

Data Fundamentals

In the past, simply finding data was a common challenge for real estate appraisers. The ever-increasing sophistication of data technology has made collecting information easier than ever. Today, the major challenge lies in filtering through the glut of information to select the most appropriate and useful data for the task at hand and confirming the accuracy of the data. Clients are aware of the amount of information available to appraisers, and they often explicitly require appraisers to use only the most relevant data in their analyses.

Data Collection in the Scope of Work

Before beginning to collect information, the appraiser must determine the different types of data needed to answer the client's question. The appraiser determines the type of data to be collected based on

- the scope of the assignment
- the subject's property type
- the subject's market area conditions

The appraisal report should include a discussion of what data was used (and often what data was *not* used) in the appraisal analyses.

Data Sampling

Even in the most data-rich environments, appraisers are unlikely to have access to all the available information. Generally, appraisers analyze a sample from the entire population to support their conclusions. When the data used by an appraiser is carefully selected for comparability, the conclusions drawn from that data can be just as credible—if not more so—than conclusions drawn from a larger set of data with less comparable properties and transactions.

Data Standards

Data standards make it possible for quality data to be shared and used consistently in the real estate community. The consistent use of terms in shared databases helps ensure that the data transferred will work in any compatible system, thereby improving efficiency. Before the lending crisis that began in 2007, the use of electronic data interchange (EDI) by the mortgage industry paved the way for efforts to develop real estate data standards by such groups as the Mortgage Industry Standards Maintenance Organization (MISMO) and the Open Standards Consortium for Real Estate (OSCRE). MISMO's main focus has been standardizing data specific to mortgages and real property reporting, while OSCRE's scope encompasses business process standards.

> Some of the most serious complaints against appraisers' work involve appraisers who do an incompetent job of researching market data or who analyze the data incorrectly. This may be interpreted as laziness, but it may really be a lack of the necessary skill set.

KEY TERMS		
household	listing	offering

After the housing crisis began, Fannie Mae developed a system that required lenders to deliver appraisal reports electronically. A larger initiative for both Fannie Mae and Freddie Mac was then developed, which led to the 2011 introduction of the Uniform Appraisal Dataset (UAD) as a requirement for appraisal assignments pertaining to conventional mortgage loans sold to government-sponsored enterprises (GSEs). The UAD system converted data that was previously only read and interpreted by human eyes to data with specific terms in specific locations on the forms so it could be easily compiled as electronic data.

However, the standardization of data in real estate has not been implemented as quickly as it has in other industries. Appraisal clients' demands for consistency and transparency are encouraging further movement toward uniform data standards, which are becoming more important as appraisers increasingly move into global markets.

Types of Data Used in Real Estate Appraisal

Macro-Level Data

Macro-level data (also sometimes known as *general data*) relates to the four forces that affect real property values:

- social
- economic
- governmental
- environmental

This type of data is usually not specific to the subject property but is applicable in many assignments of similar types of properties. Appraisers who work in their hometowns usually do not have to research macro-level data, while appraisers who work in unfamiliar locations have to research general market data for every appraisal assignment.

Economic Trends

Appraisers must understand when economic trends are changing and which way they are heading. (Chapter 10 discusses economic trends in more detail.) Needless to say, real estate lenders want to know the value as of today as well as the direction in which the appraiser thinks the value is going. If the value is going down, lenders will be more conservative in underwriting loans. If the value is rising, the underwriting criteria may be more liberal. It is common for trends in the market for detached one-unit residential properties to be different than the trends in the multi-

family market in the same area. It is also common for the industrial market to show one value trend while the retail market shows another.

The information on economic trends that appraisers gather can be broken down into various geographic sectors:

- international economic trends
- national economic trends
- local economic considerations
- trends affecting rural land

Gathering data on foreign investments may or may not be significant in any given appraisal. In some metropolitan areas, you may find significant changes in the real estate market because a company that was once locally owned and managed has sold out to or merged with an international company headquartered elsewhere. When some companies merge, they leave the production and management in the same location; others move one function out of town and leave a large hole in the local or regional real estate market. Conversely, foreign investment in plants within the United States has created many jobs and much development because of the international firms' desire to manufacture and sell products here. Jobs drive population growth, and population drives housing demand and real estate prices.

National economic trends will obviously affect local retail, industrial, and special-purpose properties and will influence residential markets, although most residential appraisers do not research this data extensively. An area tied to a particular industry that is suffering, for whatever reason, will probably see local property values diminish. In a recession, sales of big ticket items such as automobiles fall, so a city or region that is heavily invested in that industry will suffer also. Jobs drive population migrations, and population growth or loss causes demand for housing to change.

Sometimes a particularly hard winter or a long and bitter labor battle will cause a shift in economic trends with repercussions for the local real estate market. Incentives in another part of the country can cause a shift in jobs from one region to another. Appraisers need to be aware of and understand these issues.

Like politics, real estate is local. While appraisers need to keep track of national and regional issues, local trends are usually more significant. Many tools are available to analyze local trends, including statistics on housing starts,

Many decisions that affect real estate trends, values, and economic viability are made by foreign owners and managers of companies in the United States. Needless to say, it is important to read newspapers, watch television news programs, and surf the Internet for news from around the world. If a major employer announces that a new manufacturing plant will be built in a small city, the new jobs will create population movement into the area and demand for new housing, commercial properties, and even industrial support services. Conversely, if another major employer sells out to an international company with headquarters overseas, the top jobs may be moved to that location, again affecting housing demand.

When employees who have lost their jobs try to sell their homes, there may be no buyers to replace them if the local economic base in that market is limited to a single ailing industry. Conversely, job expansion in a market will bring many new employees to an area, and most need housing of one sort or another. With high demand and stable supply, prices should rise in the short run.

Appraisers often assume that a market is moving in one direction or another and then find out that the statistics do not confirm the conclusion. Many appraisers have their own biases regarding valuation trends and issues because they are often influenced by the last person they talked to. Appraisers who rely on word of mouth or a consensus of opinion to develop their own opinions are usually not going to be paid well for their services. Why hire appraisers for an opinion if they are only asking others for their opinions? In most cases, the assignment is researching the data and developing your own opinion of value rather than calling several knowledgeable sources and reconciling their opinions.

---

population changes, job gains or losses, unemployment, and resale property price trends.

Development trends, farming methods, and crop yields affect property values in rural areas. Farmers cannot buy additional acreage for expansion if they are not making a profit on the land they already have. Farmland is sometimes converted to development land as urban areas expand into rural areas.

In many areas of the United States, development trends follow utility lines (sewer and water). While the absence of sewers can mean that there is no development in an area, in other areas the absence of a public water supply could be the major factor that impedes development. Development trends are easy to research by asking the staff of the local zoning department or managers at utility companies where sewer and water lines are available. Don't forget to ask about a line's capacity.

Having a pipe next to the subject property may not be adequate if the pipe is half the size it needs to be and upsizing it requires replacing 10 miles of pipe. The cost of installing new sewer lines or upsizing has decreased substantially in recent years because of new technology like "pipe bursting" and directional drilling. Pipe bursting is a process in which a new and larger pipe is forced into an older and smaller pipe, allowing the new and larger pipe to be installed without digging up the old pipe. Directional drilling allows contractors to install sewer and water pipes in the ground without having to disturb the surface, which can cut costs by two-thirds in some applications. Directional drilling is also used to lay new power lines without disturbing the surface.

Demographics (Social Trends)

Demographic trends are just as important as economic trends in the analysis of real estate supply and demand, especially in the appraisal of proposed properties when there is no occupancy history. A new apartment complex may or may not be absorbed into the market in a reasonable period of time, depending on the number of occupants expected to move in or out of the market area. Asking who lives in an area, who works there, and who shops there will often indicate why a market works the way it does. However, fair lending rules may preclude you from reporting some of this data. Because it is so difficult to define a "family," "household," or any other grouping of residents and stay within fair housing regulations, many real estate analysts use "mail drops" as the defined grouping.

In most residential appraisal reports, you should avoid offering any unsupported conclusions regarding the people who live in an area as well as making any representations that would lead a reader to conclude that a certain type of person should live or does live in a certain area. It is also unwise for you to make supported but prejudicial remarks about who should live in certain areas.

Helpful Hint

More discussion about fair housing regulations can be found in the Conduct section of the Ethics Rule of the Uniform Standards of Professional Appraisal Practice (USPAP) and USPAP's Advisory Opinion 16 (AO-16).

Governmental Regulations

Government zoning regulations may change the way the market behaves as much as social attitudes and trends do. An area with high demand may be zoned in a way that precludes development. In fact, it is not unusual for the areas with the most land use controls to have the highest demand. In some regions, land use regulations and zoning are very controversial, contentious, and strictly enforced, while in other areas of the country these rules are relaxed because creating new jobs or expanding the property tax base is of paramount importance. Competing constituencies may claim that "we need jobs" and "we need to protect our neighborhoods," but in many markets it is difficult to do both.

Understanding the underlying philosophies of the decision makers in a community will allow you to judge who will be able to get a property rezoned and for what purpose. In some cases, it may indicate who will never be able to get a property rezoned. The ability to change the zoning of a property could mean the difference between a very low and a very high property value.

The economic policies of state government can also affect real estate values. One state may raise property taxes or business taxes higher than an adjacent state and cause some business owners along the borders to move in one direction or the other. One state may have a personal property tax and another may not, which can coax manufacturers to move. When a state is engaged in a plan to create more jobs of a certain type, various types of real estate may be affected. For example, industrial real estate may be affected if new manufacturing jobs are created, while commercial real estate may be affected if new service jobs are created.

Trends in Building Activity

The rate of construction starts changes with demand, but the response time can be very slow. Overbuilding or underbuilding will result in the short run. Demand changes rapidly because of increases or decreases in employment, changes in interest rates, population trends, and limitations on development in other areas. Supply is much slower to respond because of the lead time required to plan, design, and build improvements. In the short run, if supply is fixed and demand increases, the price of real estate increases. In the long run, the supply will increase and prices should go back down.

Most appraisers track the cost of new construction fairly closely. As costs increase, the value of existing improved properties will often increase as well. If depreciation rates are 2% per year and building costs increase at a similar rate, the net effect will be no change in value. When the cost of a new home goes up more than the rate of depreciation in the market, the replacement cost of an existing home will also go up despite the fact that the existing improvements are older. Suppose local builders charge the same amount to build a building as they did the previous year. If land values do not change, the values of real estate must go down because the buildings get older each year.

Taxes

States, counties, townships, cities, and towns usually levy taxes based on the following year's budgets for various agencies and departments. The tax levy is an important piece of information when comparing properties from different taxing districts because the methods of taxation will vary from one market to another. In some markets, all properties are assessed based on market value. In other markets, residential properties are valued at market value and nonresidential properties are valued "in use." In some areas, assessed value is based on value "in use" all the time. Use value and market value opinions can vary widely.

In some markets, arguing about tax burdens can be a major part of an appraiser's business. Appraisers who work as real estate tax consultants face some ethical issues. Appraisers are required to be disinterested third parties, but many people doing tax appeal work are paid based on the work's success. Appraisers should not be paid based on any subsequent event and especially not based on the success of the client's financial goals. Clearly, as an appraiser you cannot serve as the tax agent, the listing agent, or even the auctioneer on a property you appraised if you are paid a commission or fee based on the percentage of value or the subsequent closing of the loan. If your pay depends on whether or not the deal closes, you would obviously want to remove any obstacles to closing the sale, which would just as obviously cause bias in the value opinion–i.e., you would be tempted to assign a lower value to ensure that the sale proceeds.

> In some areas, the tax rate is called the *millage rate*. A mill is $0.001, which is one-tenth of one cent. Fifty mills equals a nickel.

Financing

Because real estate is so expensive, buyers in most markets need financing as a condition of purchase. The terms and underwriting criteria for loans may affect the buyer's ability to get financing and buy property. If interest rates go down and apartment dwellers are able to buy a house, both the multifamily and one-unit residential markets will be affected. If underwriting criteria change and some people no longer qualify to buy, this will also affect the market. If foreclosure rates are up in an area and lenders leave a market, competition based on rates will diminish and rates will increase.

> Insufficient diligence in collecting data and the collection of incorrect data are common reasons for complaints against appraisers.

Micro-Level Data

Micro-level data (also sometimes known as *specific data*) includes data on the subject property, comparable sales, leases, and other market phenomena. This data is usually secondhand but not third- or fourth-hand. Appraisers usually obtain micro-level data from observation or from multiple listing services and government databases. The reliability of this data is critical to each step in the valuation process. In the sales comparison approach, sales and listing data are researched. In the cost approach, vacant land comparables, reproduction cost comparables, and depreciation comparables are researched. In the income capitalization approach, leases and capitalization rate comparables are researched and analyzed.

Competitive Supply Inventory

Multiple listing service (MLS) systems can provide a list of current listings for one-unit residential, condominium, and small multifamily properties. Various associations and organizations should be able to provide the number of competing commercial and industrial properties.

Demand Study

An MLS system can also provide a historical sales rate for similar properties to illustrate demand. For example, if 65 homes in a particular market area were sold for between $175,000 and $200,000 in the last 12 months and there are currently only 14 listings for sale, this would imply that there is an undersupply of homes in the market because

there is only a 2½-month supply left at the current rate of sale.

$$14/(65/12) - 2.5846$$

To reach the conclusion that this market is oversupplied, a benchmark level of inventory needs to be established. In other words, you would need to determine if a two-month supply or a six-month supply would be normal. This type of inventory analysis is used in many industries to establish market trends.

Data Sources and Verification

In every market value appraisal, you will need to research the current taxes on the subject property, zoning, market conditions, and comparable sales and leases. Much of this data can be obtained from the local MLS service, but some will only be available from government agencies or through primary research. The Internet has become a significant asset in researching most types of data. Every day, more and more data is made available on the Internet if the owner of the data wants it to be.

Public Records

Some assessor's offices publish deeds with sale prices, some only make physical data accessible, and others publish very little data for appraisers to use. While many appraisers rely on MLS data as their primary source, most appraisers will try to confirm data in the public record to ensure that any review appraiser checking their work will not find something they missed. It is always embarrassing when a review appraiser finds the sale of the house next door that closed a month before the appraisal was done and the original appraiser did not use this sale. It looks bad, even if it is an honest mistake.

Listings and Offerings

For some appraisals, comparable sales are difficult to find or are in limited supply, so appraisers will also include one or more comparable listings (current offerings). These listings are of properties that are currently on the market but do not have an accepted offer yet. This data is easy to find because the property usually has a "for sale" sign on it and the information is disseminated to as many people as possible by the agent. Because the property has not yet sold, however, the listing can only tell one side of the story. In the case of a comparable sale, the price is the amount the buyer was willing to pay and the seller was willing to accept. In the case of a listing, the list price is only the price the seller is willing to accept. This data can only indicate what a property will *not* sell for. It is illogical to assume that sellers will get more than what they are asking for (assuming the property has been on the market for a while); it is more reasonable to conclude that a list price denotes the ceiling of value. This is not an absolute rule because some properties are listed for sale at prices below where they should be. In most cases, properties that are listed too low sell in a short time.

For example, a one-unit residential property is currently offered for sale at a list price of $249,000. This listing has been on the market for 90 days and is in a market in which homes usually sell in 30 days. It was originally offered for sale at $269,900 and the price was reduced twice; it is now $249,000. This home, which has averaged two showings per week since the broker first obtained the listing, is nearly identical to the subject of your appraisal. What can you conclude from this data? It is illogical to claim that a property is worth more than what an identical property could not be sold for. Absent any extenuating circumstances, you can conclude that the subject property will not sell for $249,000, either.

> USPAP requires all appraisers to indicate the current list price of the subject property if it is currently offered for sale.

Multiple Listing Services

A multiple listing service (MLS) is the most common data source for residential appraisers to find local property listing and some sale data, and commercial MLS systems are becoming more widespread. While property descriptions and broker information are usually accurate in MLS systems, MLS data can be unreliable in some markets because the listing broker has complete control of the data that is input. The listing broker can intentionally or unintentionally mislead appraisers to believe that a property sold for more or less, was in better or worse condition, or did or did not have favorable terms.

Today, the state of MLS databases is undergoing a transition, as the control of data by local MLS organizations is being challenged. Some MLS mergers have occurred, and a few national databases have formed. However, concerns

regarding competition, poor data quality, and misuse of confidential data have limited widespread mergers. Privacy requirements regarding shared confidential data are constantly changing.

You are responsible for the quality of the data in your appraisal reports. If you use data that is incorrect and a review appraiser uncovers the flaws, your opinion of value loses credibility, just as if you had used fraudulent data. There are two common schools of thought regarding data confirmation:

- If you put data on the page, it has to be absolutely correct, and any error is a big problem. Appraisers who subscribe to these high standards tend to use less data, and they spend most of their time confirming the data. For a residential appraisal, this type of appraiser would use only three comparable sales but would call the brokers on all three sales to confirm the property condition, terms, and other relevant data.
- Other appraisers believe that there will always be errors, miscommunications, and other unknown issues that can never be uncovered regardless of the amount of research done. These appraisers use much more data but spend less time trying to confirm the details. For a residential appraisal, this type of appraiser will use six to nine comparable sales from the MLS and not confirm them other than to correct obvious errors. If an appraiser uses nine comparable sales with errors, it is less likely that any one error will affect the analysis significantly. This technique tends to be more like statistical analysis in which larger amounts of data are used.

In either case, your goal is to present a supportable opinion of value that will stand the scrutiny of an appraisal reviewer and your client. If your data is weak, the reviewer will find that out or will find better data. All appraisers should assume that a reviewer will be looking over their work soon after they send it to the client.

National Property Databases

Data storage and retrieval has become a less tedious task as technology has become more sophisticated. Some organizations compile and then resell comparable data to subscribers. In most cases, the data is entered by the subscribers who pay a fee to subsidize the administration of the database. These databases are like MLS systems for comparable sales and leases. In a small market, all the data may be entered by a single subscriber and re-

"I will pay any price for any real estate if you name the price but I name the terms."

—real estate adage

trieved by the same subscriber, which offers little advantage to that person. The Real Estate Transaction Standard (RETS) is making it easier for data to be entered in national property databases.

Published News

Local newspapers and business trade publications can be useful sources of real estate data. Generally, these should not be the only sources you use, but news sources can give you leads and often provide names of brokers, buyers, and sellers to help you confirm transaction data. Sometimes people will tell a newspaper reporter something completely different than what they would tell an appraiser.

Market Participants

The best firsthand source of information on what happened in a market transaction is a party who was involved. Sometimes these people will give tainted information, but at least the data does not suffer from mistranslation. A buyer may say he bought a house for $100,000, but the seller says she sold it for $105,000. The difference could be accounted for by the $5,000 allowance the seller gave for repairs as part of the price, or $105,000 could have been the list price and $100,000 was the sale price.

A good appraiser focuses on the terms of the transaction as much as the price. If a broker says the buyer paid $100,000 for the property but the seller paid the buyer a $25,000 allowance for repairs, then the true market price is $75,000 for the property in "as is" condition. A reported sale price of $100,000 for a property worth $50,000 seems inappropriate on the surface but may be reasonable if a seller-paid

decorating allowance of $50,000 is included. When interpreting the information received from market participants, always ask yourself, "What does this indicate the value of the subject property to be?"

Sources of Competitive Supply and Demand Data

The most common data sources for competitive supply and demand data are the MLS system for residential properties and national databases for nonresidential properties. Some areas have MLS systems for nonresidential properties, while in other areas data is found almost entirely in public records.

Appraisers use competitive supply and demand data to tell their clients what economic conditions exist at the time of appraisal. Unfortunately, many underwriters and investors make the mistake of only wanting to put money into markets have increasing prices. They forget that a good market can have a long way to drop, but a fair or poor market may be ready to turn the corner.

Geographic Information Systems and TIGER Data

The development of geographic information systems (GIS) has provided business decision makers with an important analytical tool. Harnessing the increasing affordability of computing power in the digital age, GIS users have converted formerly static databases of economic and demographic information into dynamic archives of geographically encoded data that can be analyzed, manipulated, mapped, and displayed with relative ease.

The TIGER acronym, which stands for "topographical integrated geographic encoding and referencing," describes a database that integrates census and geographical data in a GIS environment. The TIGER system was created by the US Department of the Census, and the census data and maps used by the TIGER system are available through the department's website (www.census.gov). This database is very relevant because it shows useful demographic data on properties, neighborhoods, and regions.

Selecting Comparable Data and Establishing Comparability

The choices you make in selecting comparable sales or listings are critical to an accurate analysis of the market. Your decisions regarding what is comparable influence how much data is needed, how far back to go for comparables, which similar property features are required, and which others can be adjusted for.

In an appraisal report, you cannot possibly discuss all the possible reasons buyers choose one property over another. Every market and market participant will be different, so it is important to choose comparable transactions in which the deciding factors are as similar as possible. In one residential market, the number of bedrooms may be the most important factor to buyers who would be attracted to the subject property, while the tax burden on the real estate may be the most crucial issue in another market. In yet another market, the age of the improvements or the garage size could be most important. You can investigate the important property features by interviewing market participants, but that may not always be possible or fruitful.

In most markets, appraisers interview brokers more often than they interview buyers and sellers. Real estate brokers may have biases, but interviewing them gives you an informed opinion of why one property sells for more than another from people who see more transactions than anyone else in the market. Talking to brokers can also lead you to additional data. You can learn about the terms of the sale, the price, and the motivations of buyers and sellers. Brokers also speak the language of real estate and are aware of contemporary issues that may or may not have affected the sale. Although most real estate brokers are fairly tight-lipped when a sale is pending, they are usually quite helpful when the deal is closed. They have some ethical issues to deal with if they give pending prices to appraisers, so most brokers will only discuss sensitive data about a sale after it has closed. Real estate brokers are on the front lines of most real estate deals, whereas appraisers are researchers trying to find out what really happened in the sale after the fact.

Verification

Appraisers should try to verify any secondary and informal sales data they have collected to ensure that those sales occurred under conditions that match the definition of value used in the appraisal assignment. Appraisers most commonly verify data obtained through public record databases by conducting interviews with the relevant market players. Because different clients have different data verification requirements, the degree of verification that needs to be undertaken should be investigated when determining the scope of work for each particular assignment.

When verifying data, appraisers seek to ensure that the data is complete and correct and that it conforms to the relevant standards and requirements. Appraisers also determine if the sales or rentals used were arm's-length transactions, if they were affected by any specific conditions, and whether any contingencies or concessions were involved.

Data Organization

Researching significant amounts of data is almost useless unless a system for organizing that data is available. The most commonly used organizational tool is an adjustment grid similar to the grids used in residential appraisal forms. Other methods for organizing data can be equally effective, but few are better. In most appraisals, data is arrayed in a spreadsheet similar to the format of modern computer software like Microsoft Excel, Lotus 123, and Quattro Pro. Spreadsheet analysis allows a user to view large quantities of data on a single page and compare data without flipping between pages.

Units of Comparison

When raw data does not seem to be comparable, appraisers often break down sales or lease information into a unit of comparison like the price per square foot of gross building area, the price per acre, the price per front foot, or other units recognized in the market. (Appraisers also convert data to a unit of comparison for consistency with market thinking.) This method allows you to make somewhat logical comparisons between a $1 million farm sale with 200 acres and a $100,000 sale with only 18 acres. Units of comparison are used in nearly all markets and provide a significant analytical tool.

Certification

On nearly all residential appraisal report forms, you sign your name to a certification page that indicates that the comparable sales used are the most similar, proximate, and recent available. In appraiser fraud or civil liability cases, the certification is often brought up by the opposing attorney. If you sign your name to a document saying the comparable sales you included are the most similar, proximate, and recent available when in fact they are not and the appraisal is significantly inflated, you could be held liable for this misleading statement. Always assume that an appraisal reviewer will be reading the document as soon as you turn it in. Never assume that the document will be put in some file and never read.

---

1. Improvement cost data can be obtained from
    a) Builders
    b) Marshall & Swift and other cost services
    c) Sales of new homes
    d) All of the above

2. Demand for housing is affected when
    a) Builders cannot find enough building materials to complete the job
    b) A new factory opens and several hundred new employees are hired
    c) Zoning laws restrict new construction to the point that not enough homes are built
    d) The builders do not recognize a downturn in the market

3. Competitive supply sources for housing include
    a) Rental units
    b) Houses for sale
    c) Houses that will be for sale
    d) All of the above

4. If the subject property is 10% superior to Comparable Sale 1 and the comparable sold for $100,000, what is the indicated value of the subject?
    a) $100,000 \times 1.10 = $110,000
    b) $100,000/0.90 = $111,111
    c) $100,000 \times 0.90 = $90,000
    d) $100,000/1.10 = $90,909

5. If a comparable property is 10% superior to the subject property and the comparable sold for $100,000, what is the indicated value of the subject?
    a) $100,000 \times 1.10 = $110,000
    b) $100,000/0.90 = $111,111
    c) $100,000 \times 0.90 = $90,000
    d) $100,000/1.10 = $90,909

6. The assessment ratio is
    a) The ratio of assessed value to market value
    b) The ratio of assessed value to the average value for properties in the same district
    c) The ratio of the assessor's salary to the total property value in that jurisdiction
    d) Used in non-residential appraisals because it is simple and easy to understand

7. Ten mills equals
    a) 0.1000
    b) 0.0100
    c) 0.0010
    d) 0.0001

8. If a property has a market value of $56,000 in a city that charges a millage rate of 75 mills and applies an assessment ratio of 25%, what are the annual real estate taxes for this property?
    a) $1,050
    b) $4,200
    c) $10,500
    d) $3,150

9. If the assessment ratio is 25% and the millage rate is 120 mills, what is the tax rate?
    a) 3.6%
    b) 3.0%
    c) 0.30%
    d) 0.36%

10. In the appraisal of a one-unit residence, a significant attribute is
    a) The availability of rail siding access
    b) The amount of road frontage
    c) The size and age of the house
    d) The depth of the crawl space area

11. If a comparable sold for $100,000 and is identical to the subject property except that the subject has more living area,

   a) The comparable is worth less than $100,000.

   b) The subject is worth more than $100,000.

   c) The subject is worth the same as the comparable.

   d) The subject should be worth more than $100,000 if the extra area is recognized in the market as adding more value.

12. *Macro-level data* is

   a) Data about the subject property

   b) The sale prices of the comparables

   c) Items of information on value influences that derive from social, economic, governmental, and environmental forces and originate outside the property being appraised

   d) The comparable rentals

13. In the sale of residential properties, the amount of property taxes is

   a) Irrelevant because buyers don't care about taxes; they only care about the payment amount

   b) Important because the ability to qualify for a mortgage loan includes principal, interest, taxes, and insurance (PITI); lenders compare the buyers' income amounts with the required payment, including taxes and insurance

   c) Significant but only if it is above the market standard

   d) Not included in any calculation or consideration in the mortgage approval process

14. For appraisal purposes, a *household* is best described as

   a) All persons who live in one multi-unit apartment building

   b) All persons related to each other who occupy one housing unit

   c) A married couple and their dependent children

   d) All persons, related or unrelated, who occupy one housing unit

Note: Unless otherwise noted, italicized references indicate the pages in *The Appraisal of Real Estate*, 14th edition, that readers should consult for additional discussion of these topics.

1. **d) All of the above**
    Pages 116-117

2. **b) A new factory opens and several hundred new employees are hired**
    Pages 25-26

3. **d) All of the above**
    Pages 110-111

4. **a) $100,000 × 1.10 = $110,000**
    Confirmation of the calculation

Comparable sale	$100,000
Factor	× 1.10
Value of the subject	$110,000

5. **d) $100,000/1.10 = $90,909**
    Confirmation of the calculation

Subject value	$90,909
Factor	× 1.10
Sale price of comparable	$100,000

6. **a) The ratio of assessed value to market value**
    Page 108

7. **b) 0.0100**
    This student handbook

8. **a) $1,050**
    $56,000 \times 0.25 = 14,000$
    $14,000 \times 0.075 = 1,050$

9. **b) 3.0%**
    $0.25 \times 0.120 = 0.03$
    $0.03 = 3\%$

10. **c) The size and age of the house**
    This student handbook

11. **d) The subject should be worth more than $100,000 if the extra area is recognized in the market as adding more value.**
    This student handbook

12. **c) Items of information on value influences that derive from social, economic, governmental, and environmental forces and originate outside the property being appraised**
    Page 102

13. **b) Important because the ability to qualify for a mortgage loan includes principal, interest, taxes, and insurance (PITI); lenders compare the buyers' income amounts with the required payment, including taxes and insurance**
    Page 108

14. **d) All persons, related or unrelated, who occupy one housing unit**
    Page 105

10

Economic Trends in Real Estate Markets and Capital Markets

Capital markets have a huge impact on real estate markets. Most types of financial investment compete with other investments such as real property, so a change in the supply and demand for one type will cause a change in others. For example, if bond market yields rise, mortgages will be affected because they are essentially long-term bonds backed by real estate. If stock market yields are high, the mortgage market must compete to attract money or there will be a shortage of funds for real estate mortgages. Most real estate is financed, so the rates for financing real estate will directly affect its value by expanding or restricting the ability of investors to participate in the real estate market. Buyers cannot buy if they do not have enough money on hand and cannot borrow the money they need.

In the valuation process, the analysis of economic trends is an ongoing investigation of the market fundamentals of the area that an appraiser works in and an awareness of the influence of broader capital market trends on local real estate markets. The dearth of real estate sales activity when credit dried up following the financial crisis of 2007-2008 is the most recent dramatic example of the codependent relationship that real estate and capital markets can have.

Real Estate Markets

Some property types have deep markets with many buyers and sellers, while others have markets with only a few participants. If a real estate market has many participants, such as the market for one-unit homes, it tends to be refined, which

means that there is more consistency in the prices paid for properties. If a market has few participants, such as the market for specialized industrial buildings, it can be erratic, which makes identifying market patterns difficult.

Real estate markets are not always well organized or well defined, and in some cases trends and consistency can be difficult to find. Efficient markets offer low prices, fast response times, and predictable values. Most real estate markets have none of these characteristics. (See Exhibit 10.1.)

Cycles in Real Estate Markets

Real property values tend to go up and down based on supply and demand in the short run, but values are tied more to building cost increases in the long run. Supply and demand tend to change as interest rates change. Other influential factors include overbuilding, employment increases, and the movement of the workforce. In the long run, an old building should not be worth more than a new one. Therefore, the amount of appreciation a property enjoys will be limited to the rate of increases in building costs plus any increase in land value. There will be short-term losses and gains above the rate of inflation or depreciation, but in the long run the theory of substitution will prevail and new construction prices will hold the existing property values down.

Because improvements take so long to build and the permitting process may take months or years to complete, a developer may start the process but not actually break ground for a year or more. In these cases, new competition may arrive on the scene without current developers knowing about it. This

KEY TERMS	
bond	mortgage
debt	nonrecourse loan
deed of trust	recourse debt
equity	secondary mortgage market
inflation	security
land contract	stock

Exhibit 10.1   Efficient Markets Versus Real Estate Markets

Efficient Markets	Real Estate Markets
Goods and services are very similar and can be substituted for one another. **Examples:** gasoline, shares of company stock, a bottle of any brand-name soft drink, paper clips	Real or perceived differences in location, school systems, proximity to services, and other issues make real estate too unique to be easily compared for pricing purposes. Comparisons may be easier in some residential markets.
The quality of goods is standardized or similar. **Examples:** a loaf of bread, a bottle of milk	The quality of improvements on real estate varies from a cardboard shack to a mansion. Differences in quality make direct comparisons difficult.
There are many buyers and sellers, which prevents any one person from influencing the market too much. **Examples:** the New York Stock Exchange, an automobile auction	There are many buyers and sellers for popularly priced homes, but there are only a few players for regional shopping centers, mobile home parks, funeral homes, and sand and gravel mines. As a result, prices may vary from transaction to transaction. Many market participants give buyers and sellers more options.
Efficient markets are self-regulating because there are market participants. Market behavior is hard to hide. **Example:** gasoline sales	Real estate is highly regulated, as is evidenced by the licensing of certain buyers and sellers. Real estate fraud is common in many markets. Even the most professional real estate appraisers and brokers can be tempted because they see so many people getting wealthy from unethical practices. In the long run, the "bad guys" get their just desserts.
Supply and demand are never too far out of balance because there are so many buyers and sellers. When supply is too high and prices fall, bargain hunters come in to absorb the excess inventory. When prices are too low, the supply is absorbed and sellers can raise prices.	In real estate, supply and demand are constantly out of balance. The demand for frontage property on a busy commercial street may be extremely high and the supply is limited. If new homes are in short supply in a residential market, builders cannot just throw a unit up. It takes months and sometimes years to satisfy the demand for some types of real estate.
Buyers are knowledgeable and fully informed about market conditions. **Examples:** the gasoline market, a grocery store	In many real estate markets, the only knowledgeable people in the transaction are the brokers and, after the sale, the appraiser. Because buyers are sometimes misled, many mistakes can be made.
Buyers and sellers are brought together in a formal system to facilitate the sale **Example:** the New York Stock Exchange	The closest thing to a formal system for bringing real estate buyers and sellers together is the Realtors' MLS system. The Internet might replace this system in the future by bringing buyers and sellers together directly.
Goods are readily consumed and easily transported. If they are difficult to transport, market demand in one area cannot be used to satisfy oversupply in another. For example, the market for 75-ft. boats will never be efficient because they are too hard to move from one place to another. In some markets, the cost of transportation will inhibit shopping in another area.	Real estate is one of the most durable commodities in American society. Some people buy a new home at age 25 and never buy any more real estate until they are 65. Property is fixed in location. If the price of real estate is too high in one location, you cannot pick it up and move it to a better area. Some real estate is so specialized in design that there is no active resale market for it.

can create too much supply, which will cause prices to go down until the demand absorbs the oversupply and prices increase enough to sustain new construction. Overbuilding forces prices down so that builders have to halt new construction. Too much demand allows prices to go higher, which causes profit margins to be excessive. After that, "excess profits breed ruinous competition" until prices drop again.

The Life Cycle of Real Estate Markets

The four life stages of market areas are

- growth
- stability
- decline
- revitalization

Growth

In growing areas, improvements are newer, there is new construction, and the prices of improved real property tend to approximate the cost of new construction less depreciation. A market area in the growth stage is competing well with other market areas. For example, new home buyers are often active in growing areas.

Stability

A stable market area is holding its own, and property values are stable or increasing slightly, depending on maintenance levels. Stable market areas are well placed, and the prices of real estate are very dependent on maintenance levels. Potential home buyers are no longer looking for new construction, but they don't really want to rehabilitate old homes yet because prices are too high.

Decline

Property values in declining areas are stable at best or decreasing at worst. Because sellers outnumber buyers, prices must fall to attract more demand. At this stage, vacancies increase and some building improvements become deteriorated or may even be razed. Deferred maintenance becomes more apparent as the market declines. Most properties in declining areas need some work but not so much as to make them unusable.

Revitalization

A market area in revitalization recognizes the need for monetary input. Revitalization is the time for restoration and remodeling. Some structures are torn down to the framing and redeveloped into new structures. The latter is very common in historic districts where large sums of money will be spent to make a property like new. Historic areas can be popular with investors who hope to make larger profits than they might elsewhere by rehabilitating properties in declining areas that have the potential to turn around.

Capital Markets

Because real estate is so expensive, large sums of borrowed money are usually required in any market transaction. The usual places to get money for real estate purchases are bonds, stocks, mortgage loans, and deeds of trust. These all have their advantages and disadvantages, depending on the needs of the lender or borrower.

Bonds

Bonds are capital market instruments with fixed interest rates for a term of one year or more. The mortgage interest rates compete directly with corporate bonds because both represent long-term investments with some level of risk. To pay for capital projects, many counties, cities, and other government agencies offer municipal bonds. These offer the advantage of being tax-free on a federal basis. As a result, yields are much lower than corporate bonds, which carry more risk.

Stocks

Shares of stock are an investment in a company like the money the investor put in to start the company. A share of any corporation is a claim on its assets and the ability to vote for a board of directors that will run the company. Some stocks that are listed on stock exchanges are *liquid*, meaning that they are convertible to cash. Other stocks that represent closely held corporations or are not traded openly are not liquid.

Mortgages

A mortgage is the pledge of collateral for a loan on real estate. The mortgage is not the loan document but the document that pledges the real estate for repayment. A mortgage "note" is the document that says, "I promise to pay back the money I borrowed." The mortgage document says, "If I don't repay the loan, you can take the real estate."

A mortgage gives the lender the right to repossess the collateral if the borrower does not honor the contractual commitment. It is possible to have multiple mortgages on a property, so the order in which the documents are recorded will determine who gets repaid first. It is not unusual for a property worth $200,000 to have $250,000 in mortgage loans against it. In a foreclosure, each lender does not get a prorated share. Instead, the priority of each mortgage establishes who gets what. Second and third mortgages are recorded and repaid after the first mortgage.

Exhibit 10.2 lists various types of mortgage arrangements.

Deeds of Trust and Land Contracts

In some states, the lender will require that the deed be transferred to a third party for safekeeping rather than file a mortgage lien against a property. In these cases, the third party will hold the deed until both sides of the mortgage agree that it is paid off. If there is any disagreement about the mortgage, a judge decides the matter.

Monetary Policy

The Federal Reserve System, which controls monetary policy in the United States, is not directly tied to any legislative or executive body. The leaders are appointed by the president and confirmed by the Senate, which makes it a quasi-governmental body. This system of central banking prevents the politicization of monetary policy, which is much more efficient than letting Congress or the president set interest rates.

Money Market Instruments

Money markets set the price of borrowing money—i.e., the *interest*. It may be better to think of interest as the cost of renting capital for a period of time. Money market instruments, such as Treasury bills, Treasury notes, other government securities, certificates of deposit, commercial paper, and Eurodollars are bought and sold based on their future yield. An instrument with a 10% interest rate will sell for more than an instrument yielding only 8%. Therefore, if interest rates go

up, older existing instruments with lower interest rates go down in value.

Rate Relationships

Investment yield rates for different investments vary. The difference in the rates charged for mortgage loans, real estate investments, government bonds, and other investments will depend on the alternatives available at the time, the risk of not getting your money back, and the risk associated with not being able to use your money for more profitable investments at a later date. The inability to get your money back quickly is an important factor in a mortgage loan, which may tie up the capital for 30 years. The higher the risk, the higher the interest rate.

Like many other observers of money market trends, appraisers make a habit of tracking economic indicators like conventional mortgage rates, Treasury bill yields, and similar information reported in the financial press.

Sources of Capital for Real Estate

Because most real estate is financed, the sources of financing are of paramount importance. When mortgage money is tight, the sale of real estate is stifled. When mortgage money is plentiful, real estate can sell to buyers who would not otherwise qualify for loans. Of course, recent financial events have illustrated the risk involved to real estate markets when mortgage money becomes too plentiful.

Equity

It is possible, although not common, for real estate to sell without financing. With 100% equity, the market interest rates have a minimal effect on sales. In some markets, it is common for real es-

---

Federal Reserve System

Since the 1800s, the central banking system has been composed of member banks from all over the United States. The Federal Reserve System influences the supply of money through

· reserve requirements
· the federal discount rate
· the activities of the Federal Open Market Committee

A bank's reserve requirement is the ratio of deposits to the total amount of money loaned out. The higher the reserve requirements, the less money financial institutions have available to lend but the more solvent the financial institution is.

The federal discount rate is the interest rate on loans made from the Federal Reserve to its member banks. This rate is often the benchmark for many other loan rates.

The Federal Open Market Committee (FOMC) buys or sells securities to increase or decrease the money supply. When the FOMC sells securities from the Fed's portfolio, it pulls money into the Fed and out of circulation, which slows down the economy. The opposite is also true.

Exhibit 10.2   Mortgage Types, Terms, and Definitions

Blanket mortgage	Covers more than one property; common in subdivision development and situations in which the equity in one property is insufficient to satisfy the loan policy. Individual properties are usually released from the blanket mortgage as they are sold, and part of the balance of the blanket mortgage is paid off.
Interest-only mortgage	The borrower only pays the interest. The periodic payments do not lower the principal amount at all during the term of the loan. The balance on the first day will also be the balance on the last day, i.e., no amortization.
Direct reduction mortgage loan	The principal repayment starts out slow but gets larger as the loan gets older and the interest charges diminish; the most commonly used mortgage type.
Adjustable rate mortgage (ARM)	The interest rate is not fixed over the full term, which enables the lending institution to increase its yield if the rates go up. While the payment may be fixed for a few years, it can change when the rate changes.
Wraparound mortgage loan	The lender assumes an existing mortgage and then adds some new money to make the principal amount large enough for most buyers to assume. Because the lender is blending the older (and presumably lower) interest rate with a newer (and presumably higher) interest rate, the borrower enjoys a rate that is lower than would normally be possible.
Participation mortgage loan	The lender receives a payment that includes a share of the periodic income and sometimes the increase in the resale value of the property; sometimes used for nonresidential properties to allow the lender to retain more of the ownership interest.
Shared appreciation mortgage loan	The lender agrees to give a lower interest rate in return for a portion of the increase in the appreciation of the real estate (if any); applicable only to some properties. This was based on the concept that real estate prices always increase. This was shown to be flawed thinking.
Convertible mortgage	Instead of receiving a principal payment each period, the lender may take an ownership interest in the property. The lender becomes one of the owners over the life of the mortgage loan.
Graduated payment mortgage loan	Payments are less than what is required to pay off the loan in the beginning and increase in later years. These loans were thought to be a good tool because a borrower's income usually increases in later years when a larger payment is more affordable. These loans have higher risk because the loan amount gets bigger in the first few years, and if there is no appreciation in property values, the borrower owes more than what the property is worth. Again, this was based on the assumption that real estate values would always increase.
Zero coupon mortgage loan	Debt with no interest or principal payments being made. The interest accrues against the real estate, which means that the balance gets higher as the loan gets older. This type of loan is very risky unless there is substantial equity.
Reverse annuity mortgage loan	A lender's tool used to slowly extract equity from a property to supplement a person's income. Property owners who owe little or nothing on a property can borrow the same amount of money each month on a schedule. The interest and principal get bigger each month. However, the borrowers don't care because they are looking for periodic income rather than resale at the end of the term, when they are presumed to be too old to need the property.
Conditional sales contract	Not really a mortgage, but a signed contract in which the seller agrees that the title will pass to the buyer when the buyer pays off the loan on the property. The seller holds the deed while the monthly payments are made, until the debt is repaid.
Purchase money mortgage	Another seller-financing contract in which the title is transferred to the buyer like a standard mortgage, with the lender as the prior owner. This tool allows sellers to make the deal work but to keep the paper and maintain the right to foreclose.

tate to sell for cash. In other markets, it is common for sales to require 95% financing. In the wake of the financial crisis, lenders have tended to require more of an equity investment from potential home borrowers to mitigate the inherent risk of lending.

Real Estate Investment Trusts

Trusts are a tool for assembling money needed for real estate investments. Real estate investment trusts (REITs) are a popular contemporary method of purchasing real estate. REIT financing is commonly used for large office projects, industrial developments, shopping centers, and trophy office towers, particularly when funds from traditional sources are scarce.

Partnerships

Partnerships have long been a common method of assembling money for real estate purchases. Partnerships involve two or more people and can be arranged in many ways. In the 1980s and 1990s, it was popular to assemble investors into limited partnerships. These partnerships sometimes netted considerable profit for the general partners and little if any profit for the limited partners. The structure of a partnership helps diversify both the risk and the reward of an investment.

If the partners are actively involved in the management of a property, they may contribute to value by adding good ideas at critical points during the property's holding period. Some small partnerships can be quite successful because the partners are watching over the investments and are all easily accessible and able to make quick decisions as a group. Larger partnerships do not offer this benefit.

Joint Ventures

Joint ventures are put together to pool funds for the purchase of a specific piece of real estate. Some of the largest properties are owned by joint ventures, with a financial institution such as a life insurance company or pension trust working with an entrepreneurial development organization.

Pension Funds

Pension funds collect large amounts of money for future liabilities. The excess funds need to be invested in some entity that returns fairly good yields. Pension funds sometimes buy real estate outright, or they may invest in mortgages for the properties often through the secondary mortgage market. Many pension funds are not subject to government regulation of investments and can invest in properties that other trusts cannot.

Life Insurance Companies

Like pension funds, life insurance companies accumulate large amounts of money for future liabilities, and they will invest in the mortgage market or as equity investors in real estate. Traditionally, life insurance companies have invested in some of the largest projects in the country.

Hedge Funds

In recent years, hedge funds emerged as players in real estate investment, buying distressed properties and real estate securities that have a significant potential upside. As private funds, these institutions are not subject to many of the restrictions of public equity funds and therefore can make more aggressive investments.

International Equity Capital

International investors seeking higher yields have come to the United States and invested in both mortgages and equity positions in real estate. Some of these projects have been very large investments and many have been unprofitable. In the 1980s and 1990s, real estate prices were often pushed up by off-shore money, which proved to be disastrous for many foreign investors. In the first decade of the twenty-first century, the decline in the value of the dollar made investment in US real estate (through the securitized mortgage market or through direct investment) attractive until the sub-prime mortgage crisis hit. Sovereign wealth funds have since emerged as significant equity investors in real estate markets, either through direct investment or through investment in other funds.

Debt

Most real estate purchases involve debt, and most debt is structured with both interest (yield) and principal (equity) payments. Part of the typical amortized mortgage payment covers renting the money, and part repays the debt over the holding period.

Commercial Banks

Commercial banks have traditionally served as lenders of construction and development financing. In the past, they made most of their loans under variable-rate contracts and did not suffer significant losses when interest rates increased. However, commercial banks did lose a lot of money when Congress changed the tax laws in the mid-1980s and removed many of the tax benefits of owning real estate. This change caused a rapid and severe drop in commercial property values, which caused many banks to foreclose on those properties. Today large commercial banks have become a source of permanent financing for certain nonresidential property types and some in small communities also provide home loans to their customers as part of the financial services they offer. Many banks (large and small) originate the mortgage loans and then sell them on the secondary market when it is thought to be most profitable or when they need to convert them into cash.

Community Banks

Although individually community banks are smaller than commercial banks, the loan portfolios of community banks tend to hold a much higher proportion of commercial real estate debt than the portfolios of commercial banks do. Community banks focus on construction and development lending for local clients.

Life Insurance Companies

Most mortgages made by life insurance companies are on large shopping centers or large industrial buildings. Before these projects began being financed in the stock market (through REITs), life insurance companies were the major source of permanent financing for these types of large real estate developments.

Mutual Savings Banks

Mutual savings banks are similar to savings and loans with more regulatory leeway to invest in real estate, although those real estate investments have to compete with investments in government and corporate bonds and stock.

Junior Mortgage Originators

Junior mortgages on real estate are offered by lending institutions other than the primary lender and include a variety of lending products and seller-financing vehicles. Because senior liens are repaid first, junior mortgages have higher interest rates to account for the higher risk in those investments.

Securitization and Real Estate Investment Markets

Mortgage-backed securities come in a variety of structures, contracts, and participation levels. The goal of securitizing real estate debt is to bring a broader base of investors into the mortgage market, which reduces the chance of great losses by banks and financial institutions when they are the sole lenders. Because this type of investment is yield-driven, it is possible that the value of the mortgage and equity will not equal the value of the real estate and, in fact, there could be considerable business income influencing the deal. For example, it is not very unusual for an investor to pay more than the cost of production of the improved real estate if the owner increases the yield by paying over market rent or by including more than real estate in the income stream (e.g., the lease). This makes the real estate value indication from that sale less definite.

The subprime lending crisis of 2007 and 2008 was the result of many factors, including ag-

---

Secondary Mortgage Market

The major players in the secondary mortgage market include governmental and quasi-governmental entities set up by the federal government to ensure that adequate capital is available in the residential mortgage market. In the wake of the housing bubble, the US federal government took receivership of the two largest government-sponsored entities, Fannie Mae and Freddie Mac.

Fannie Mae has historically been one of the largest buyers of mortgages. Fannie Mae's willingness to buy mortgages from mortgage companies opened that part of the business to many lending institutions other than banks, which created competition for mortgages, especially in small towns. Because of Fannie Mae's dominance in the mortgage business, many competitors quote its rules and guidelines as if they were appraisal rules that appraisers must follow. Under its new conservatorship, Fannie Mae's mission remains to increase the availability of mortgage finance.

Like Fannie Mae, Freddie Mac was bought out by the US Treasury Department in 2008 and put into a conservatorship to ensure that the organization's mission of increasing the availability of mortgage finance could continue despite the financial losses suffered by the organization. Fannie Mae and Freddie Mac are expected to operate as usual but with stronger backing for holders of the securities issued by the organizations.

Other GSEs are significant participants in the secondary mortgage market. *Ginnie Mae* is a HUD agency that generates funds for the mortgage market and special programs by subsidizing residential mortgage-backed securities. This agency was the result of a split from Fannie Mae in 1968. The Federal Agricultural Mortgage Corporation, or *Farmer Mac*, is the agricultural equivalent of Fannie Mae. It is a quasi-governmental entity serving rural property owners. Farmer Mac has not been as big a player as Fannie Mae.

Banks, savings and loan institutions, Fannie Mae, and Freddie Mac generate or buy most residential mortgages, but many mortgages are generated and bought by individuals or companies. For example, it is not unusual for parents or grandparents to make a mortgage loan to their children when a traditional lender would not, which in effect functions as a secondary market for mortgage funds.

gressive underwriting by lenders competing for opportunities to get money out the door and then securitize the loans and sell them to hedge funds, the secondary market, or other investors. The combination of predatory lending practices and insufficient oversight of the securitized mortgage market was a volatile mixture that forced the federal government to step in to bail out various investment banks and government-sponsored enterprises as well as to increase scrutiny of the trade in collateralized debt obligations (CDOs). Client pressure to inflate appraisals and inadequate analysis of the loan pools by the ratings agencies contributed to excessive lending to unqualified borrowers on property with inflated values, which later proved to be a significant problem and eventually led to the nationwide credit crunch. Mortgage loans were often originated by mortgage brokers with little invested in the process and few penalties for processing weak loan portfolios. These loans were easily sold to banks and other investors who also sold them as investments on the stock market to other institutions and even to Fannie Mae and Freddie Mac. Quality control was a severe problem.

Risk
A variety of types of risk may affect an investment in real property, from the simple market risk of shifts in supply and demand for the type of real estate being analyzed to risks related to external forces such as inflation's effect on purchasing power, changes in tax laws affecting operating expenses, or new zoning regulations affecting potential land uses. The different varieties of risk (market risk, financial risk, environmental risk, and so on) can affect the value of a property alone or in combination with other types of risk. The higher the risk, the higher the required yield to attract investors. The higher the required yield, the lower the price paid for the investment. For income-producing property, the higher the risk, the higher the capitalization rate. The higher the capitalization rate, the lower the value.

Debt and Equity Relationships

All else being equal (i.e., risk), investment money flows toward the option with the greatest yield potential. The capital markets provide investors with more information about risk and reward than real estate markets do, although appraisers do have tools such as reports from ratings services to help them compare potential returns from investment options.

For nonresidential real estate, the mortgage yield rates will give an indication of the required yield for the equity return. If mortgage lenders are willing to loan at 8% per year and are in the most secure position (i.e., the first to get money at a sheriff's sale), the equity position with greater risk would expect to see a higher return. Equity investors stand to lose their entire investment and in some cases more than that if they sign personally. For nearly all properties with mortgages, the investor or owner is in a much riskier position than the lender whose interest is first in line in a foreclosure sale.

Investment Yields

An amount loaned may be different than the amount stipulated as the loan amount on mortgage documents, for example, because of up-front points paid by the borrower. The lender's yield is affected by the amount of points paid. If the lender charges five points on the loan, the yield will be higher than stipulated on the document because the investor is paying less for the loan ($95,000) than its face amount ($100,000). A lender's yield is always calculated based on the amount of the periodic payments compared to the amount loaned or, in many cases, the amount shown on the loan documents.

Leverage

The term *leverage* describes the increase or decrease in yield to a property owner through which the borrower is able to secure a mortgage with an interest rate that is lower or higher than the yield rate on the property. For example, if a property has a cash flow rate of 12% per year (i.e., you paid $100,000 for the property and it pays out $12,000 per year) but the mortgage interest rate is 10%, then you are making 12% on all the money you invested and 2% on all the money the lender invested.

Financial leverage has made many real estate owners much more money than would normally be possible. However, remember that in a foreclosure sale the owner is in the second position and could lose all the capital invested if the property does not sell for much at the sheriff's sale. There is usually much higher risk associated with highly leveraged investments. If you own an eight-unit apartment complex with 25% debt and four of the units become vacant because interest rates went down and those tenants moved out to buy homes of their own, you can probably still make the payments. If you have 95% debt, the financial burden is much greater. If the four units go vacant, the cash flows will be less than the mortgage payment and the owner must "feed the investment." Leverage is a double-edged sword; it can make you a lot of money but can also drag you down quickly.

Mortgage Exhibit 1

Mortgage payments can be calculated easily on most financial calculators. As an exercise in calculating a mortgage payment directly, use the following formula. In this mortgage loan calculation formula, I = the periodic interest rate and N = the number of payments. The resulting amount should be multiplied by the amount loaned to get the periodic payment.

The formula for calculating a monthly mortgage payment is

$$\frac{I}{1 - \left(\dfrac{1}{(1 + I)^N}\right)}$$

What is the monthly payment for a 7%, 30-year mortgage with an initial amount of $100,000?

$$I / 12 = 0.00583333$$
$$N = 360 \ (30 \times 12)$$
$$I / [1 - (1 / (1 + I)^N)] = \text{payment factor}$$
$$0.00583333 / [1 - (1 / (1 + 0.00583333)^{360})] =$$
$$0.00583333 / [1 - (1 / 8.11640064)] = 0.00583333 / [1 - 0.12320732]$$
$$0.00583333 / 0.875679268 = 0.006653303$$
$$0.006653303 \times \$100,000 = \$665.30$$

The following table and graphs show an amortization schedule for a small mortgage. Notice the direction of the change in interest and principal in the trend lines. The loan is amortized on a monthly basis.

Principal amount: $25,000
Interest rate: 7.00% per annum

Mortgage term: 60 months
Payment: $495.03

	Balance	Payment	Interest	Principal	Balance
1	$25,000.00	$495.03	$145.83	$349.20	$24,650.80
2	$24,650.80	$495.03	$143.80	$351.23	$24,299.57
3	$24,299.57	$495.03	$141.75	$353.28	$23,946.29
4	$23,946.29	$495.03	$139.69	$355.34	$23,590.94
5	$23,590.94	$495.03	$137.61	$357.42	$23,233.53
6	$23,233.53	$495.03	$135.53	$359.50	$22,874.03
7	$22,874.03	$495.03	$133.43	$361.60	$22,512.43
8	$22,512.43	$495.03	$131.32	$363.71	$22,148.72
9	$22,148.72	$495.03	$129.20	$365.83	$21,782.89
10	$21,782.89	$495.03	$127.07	$367.96	$21,414.93
11	$21,414.93	$495.03	$124.92	$370.11	$21,044.82
12	$21,044.82	$495.03	$122.76	$372.27	$20,672.55
13	$20,672.55	$495.03	$120.59	$374.44	$20,298.11
14	$20,298.11	$495.03	$118.41	$376.62	$19,921.49
15	$19,921.49	$495.03	$116.21	$378.82	$19,542.66
16	$19,542.66	$495.03	$114.00	$381.03	$19,161.63
17	$19,161.63	$495.03	$111.78	$383.25	$18,778.38
18	$18,778.38	$495.03	$109.54	$385.49	$18,392.89
19	$18,392.89	$495.03	$107.29	$387.74	$18,005.15
20	$18,005.15	$495.03	$105.03	$390.00	$17,615.15
21	$17,615.15	$495.03	$102.76	$392.27	$17,222.88
22	$17,222.88	$495.03	$100.47	$394.56	$16,828.31
23	$16,828.31	$495.03	$98.17	$396.86	$16,431.45
24	$16,431.45	$495.03	$95.85	$399.18	$16,032.27
25	$16,032.27	$495.03	$93.52	$401.51	$15,630.76
26	$15,630.76	$495.03	$91.18	$403.85	$15,226.91
27	$15,226.91	$495.03	$88.82	$406.21	$14,820.70
28	$14,820.70	$495.03	$86.45	$408.58	$14,412.13
29	$14,412.13	$495.03	$84.07	$410.96	$14,001.17
30	$14,001.17	$495.03	$81.67	$413.36	$13,587.81
31	$13,587.81	$495.03	$79.26	$415.77	$13,172.04
32	$13,172.04	$495.03	$76.84	$418.19	$12,753.85
33	$12,753.85	$495.03	$74.40	$420.63	$12,333.22
34	$12,333.22	$495.03	$71.94	$423.09	$11,910.13
35	$11,910.13	$495.03	$69.48	$425.55	$11,484.58
36	$11,484.58	$495.03	$66.99	$428.04	$11,056.54
37	$11,056.54	$495.03	$64.50	$430.53	$10,626.01
38	$10,626.01	$495.03	$61.99	$433.04	$10,192.96
39	$10,192.96	$495.03	$59.46	$435.57	$9,757.39
40	$9,757.39	$495.03	$56.92	$438.11	$9,319.28
41	$9,319.28	$495.03	$54.36	$440.67	$8,878.61
42	$8,878.61	$495.03	$51.79	$443.24	$8,435.37
43	$8,435.37	$495.03	$49.21	$445.82	$7,989.55
44	$7,989.55	$495.03	$46.61	$448.42	$7,541.13
45	$7,541.13	$495.03	$43.99	$451.04	$7,090.09
46	$7,090.09	$495.03	$41.36	$453.67	$6,636.42
47	$6,636.42	$495.03	$38.71	$456.32	$6,180.10
48	$6,180.10	$495.03	$36.05	$458.98	$5,721.12
49	$5,721.12	$495.03	$33.37	$461.66	$5,259.46
50	$5,259.46	$495.03	$30.68	$464.35	$4,795.11
51	$4,795.11	$495.03	$27.97	$467.06	$4,328.05
52	$4,328.05	$495.03	$25.25	$469.78	$3,858.27
53	$3,858.27	$495.03	$22.51	$472.52	$3,385.75
54	$3,385.75	$495.03	$19.75	$475.28	$2,910.47
55	$2,910.47	$495.03	$16.98	$478.05	$2,432.42
56	$2,432.42	$495.03	$14.19	$480.84	$1,951.57
57	$1,951.57	$495.03	$11.38	$483.65	$1,467.93
58	$1,467.93	$495.03	$8.56	$486.47	$981.46
59	$981.46	$495.03	$5.73	$489.30	$492.16
60	$492.16	$495.03	$2.87	$492.16	$(0.00)

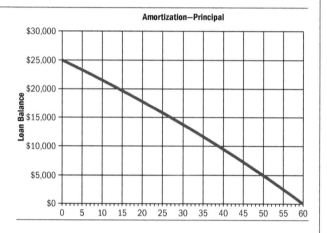

Amortization—Principal

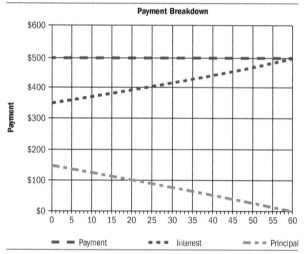

Payment Breakdown

— — Payment   · · · Interest   — · — Principal

1. Market area life cycles include
    a) Growth, stability, decline, and revitalization
    b) Growth, stability, decline, and gentrification
    c) Growth, stability, appreciation, and decline
    d) Growth, level off, appreciation, and decline

2. You buy a one-unit home for $100,000 and put down 20% as equity on the deal. How much is the mortgage?
    a) $120,000
    b) $100,000
    c) $80,000
    d) $60,000

3. You purchase a one-unit home for $100,000 and put 25% down. The lender charges three points to get the mortgage. How much do the points cost you?
    a) $4,000
    b) $2,250
    c) $1,000
    d) $0

4. You have a first mortgage of $75,000 and a second mortgage of $35,000 on your home, and the property value is $100,000. What is your equity?
    a) $65,000
    b) $25,000
    c) $10,000
    d) -$10,000

5. A *land contract*, also known as a *conditional sales contract* or an *installment sales contract*, is
    a) A sale of real property with the seller financing the sale and transferring the rights in realty
    b) A sale of real estate with the seller financing the sale but retaining the deed until the loan is paid off
    c) A purchase agreement with many conditions on it
    d) A sales contract with a mortgage loan

6. The Federal Reserve System
    a) Was established and is now controlled by Congress
    b) Was established by Congress but is now independent of it
    c) Was established and is controlled by the president of the United States
    d) Was established and is controlled by the national banks in the United States

7. Commercial paper is
    a) Loans made by commercial banks
    b) Loans made by the Federal Reserve Bank to its members
    c) A corporation's short-term notes
    d) A corporation's long-term notes

8. The secondary mortgage market
    a) Is where second mortgages are bought and sold
    b) Has historically been dominated by investors like Fannie Mae and Freddie Mac who buy and sell mortgage loans
    c) Is in Chicago
    d) Is where inferior credit (B paper) loans are bought and sold

9. Stocks are
    a) A punishment for bad appraisers
    b) A lending instrument
    c) A low-risk, high-yield investment
    d) An ownership interest in a company (i.e., shares)

10. A mortgage is a
    a) Document that makes a borrower promise to repay money
    b) Document that indicates the interest rate and terms of a loan
    c) Pledge of collateral for a real estate loan
    d) Pledge of collateral for a car loan

11. If a 9% annual rate mortgage has quarterly payments, the effective interest rate is
    a) 9% per annum
    b) 0.75% per month
    c) 2.25% per quarter
    d) 3.50% per half

12. A deed of trust is
    a) A document that makes a third party responsible for the money
    b) A document that gives a third party the deed until the mortgage loan is paid off
    c) A deed given by a prisoner who has behaved for many years
    d) Used as a tool to make foreclosure more efficient

13. Which of the following can serve as evidence that a neighborhood is in the growth cycle?

   a) Abandoned automobiles on site

   b) Several newspapers on front porches

   c) Older structures being remodeled

   d) New construction of buildings

Note: A financial calculator is needed to solve Review Exercises 14 through 17 and 19 through 21.

14. What is the periodic payment of a fully amortized mortgage with *quarterly* payments, an initial loan amount of $125,000, a loan term of 25 years, and an interest rate of 9.75% per year?

   a) $3,348.11

   b) $1,113.92

   c) $13,507.12

   d) $12,187.50

15. What is the periodic payment of a fully amortized mortgage with *annual* payments, an initial loan amount of $125,000, a loan term of 25 years, and an interest rate of 9.75% per year?

   a) $3,348.11

   b) $1,113.92

   c) $13,507.12

   d) $12,187.50

16. What is the future value in two years of a single cash payment of $1,000 received today at 10% interest per year? Assume annual accounting.

   a) $1,210.00

   b) $826.45

   c) $1,000.00

   d) $900.00

17. What is the present value of a cash payment of $1,000 that will not be received for two years at 10% per year? Assume annual accounting.

   a) $1,210.00

   b) $826.45

   c) $1,011.12

   d) $901.33

18. An appraiser doing market research found a comparable sale in which the seller took back a mortgage with a 20% down payment at 8% per year with monthly payments based on a 30-year amortization but with a five-year balloon payment. The sale price was $104,500. The current market rate for mortgages is 10% for 30 years. A week after the closing, the seller sold the mortgage for $75,000 to a local real estate broker. What is the cash-equivalent sale price of this comparable sale?

   a) $79,602.85

   b) $95,900.00

   c) $100,502.85

   d) $104,500.00

19. What is the periodic payment of a fully amortized mortgage with *monthly* payments, an initial loan amount of $125,000, a loan term of 25 years, and an interest rate of 9.75% per year?

   a) $3,348.11

   b) $1,113.92

   c) $13,507.12

   d) $12,187.50

20. What is the balance in five years of a mortgage with *monthly* payments, an initial loan amount of $125,000, a loan term of 25 years, and an interest rate of 9.75% per year?

   a) $117,438

   b) $125,000

   c) $113,507

   d) $121,875

21. What is the new payment on a 25-year, monthly payment, adjustable-rate mortgage after five years if the interest rate changes from 9.75% to 8.75%? The original amount of the loan was $125,000, the original term was 25 years, and there are 20 years left on the mortgage. Round your answer.

   a) $1,000

   b) $1,050

   c) $1,100

   d) $1,150

Note: Unless otherwise noted, italicized references indicate the pages in *The Appraisal of Real Estate*, 14th edition, that readers should consult for additional discussion of these topics.

1. a) **Growth, stability, decline, and revitalization**
    Page 136

2. c) **$80,000**
    $100,000 \times 0.80 = 80,000$

3. b) **$2,250**
    $100,000 \times 0.75 = 75,000$
    $75,000 \times 0.03 = 2,250$

4. d) **-$10,000**
    $75,000 + 35,000 = 110,000$
    $100,000 - 110,000 = -10,000$

5. b) **A sale of real estate with the seller financing the sale but retaining the deed until the loan is paid off**
    Page 141

6. b) **Was established by Congress but is now independent of it**
    Page 142

7. c) **A corporation's short-term notes**
    Page 144

8. b) **Has historically been dominated by investors like Fannie Mae and Freddie Mac who buy and sell mortgage loans**
    Page 152

9. d) **An ownership interest in a company (i.e., shares)**
    Page 138

10. c) **Pledge of collateral for a real estate loan**
    Page 138

11. c) **2.25% per quarter**
    This student handbook

12. b) **A document that gives a third party the deed until the mortgage loan is paid off**
    Page 140

13. d) **New construction of buildings**
    Pages 106-107

14. a) **$3,348.11**

Term is 4 × 25:	100 [n]
Interest rate is 9.75 / 4	2.4375 [i]
Amount loaned:	125,000 [CHS] [PV]
Balloon payment:	0 [FV]
Solve for [PMT] =	3,348.11

15. c) **$13,507.12**

Term is one per year:	25 [n]
Interest rate is 9.75 / 1:	9.75 [i]
Amount loaned:	125,000 [CHS] [PV]
Balloon payment:	0 [FV]
Solve for [PMT] =	13,507.12

16. a) **$1,210.00**

Term:	2 [n]
Interest rate is 10%:	10 [i]
Amount loaned:	1,000 [CHS] [PV]
Periodic payment:	0 [PMT]
Solve for balloon payment ([FV]) =	1,210

17. b) **$826.45**

Term:	2 [n]
Interest rate is 10%:	10 [i]
Future payment:	1,000 [FV]
Periodic payment:	0 [PMI]
Solve for [PV] =	-826.45

18. **b) $95,900.00**

The cash equivalency of a sale can be obtained by adding together the amount of the equity to the value of the mortgage ($V_M + V_E = V_O$). Therefore, if the down payment was $20,900 and the mortgage was worth $104,500 (assuming it sold for its value), then 20,900 + 75,000 = 95,900.

19. **b) $1,113.92**

Term is 12 × 25:	300 [n] or 25 [g] [n]
Interest rate is 9.75 / 12:	0.8125 [i] or 9.75 [g] [i]
Amount loaned:	125,000 [CHS] [PV]
Balloon payment:	0 [FV]
Solve for [PMT] =	1,113.92

20. **a) $117,438**

Term is 12 × 25:	300 [n] or 25 [g] [n]
Interest rate is 9.75 / 12:	0.8125 [i] or 9.75 [g] [i]
Amount loaned:	125,000 [CHS] [PV]
Balloon payment:	0 [FV]
Solve for [PMT] =	1,113.92
Change term to payments made (5 × 12):	60 [n] or 5 [g] [n]
Solve for [FV] =	117,438.27

21. **b) $1,050**

Term is 12 × 25:	300 [n] or 25 [g] [n]
Interest rate is 9.75 / 12:	0.8125 [i] or 9.75 [g] [i]
Amount loaned:	125,000 [CHS] [PV]
Balloon payment:	0 [FV]
Solve for [PMT] =	1,113.92
Change N to PMTs made (5 × 12):	60 [n] or 5 [g] [n]
Solve for [FV] =	117,438.27
Put the balance in Year 5 in [PV]:	[CHS] [PV]
Change the term to 20 years (20 × 12):	240 [n] or 20 [g] [n]
Change the interest rate (8.75 / 12):	0.7292 [i] or 8.75 [g] [i]
Change the future value to 0:	0 [FV]
Solve for [PMT] =	1,037.81

11

Neighborhoods, Districts, and Market Areas

A *neighborhood* is a group of complementary land uses. A *district* is a type of neighborhood characterized by homogenous land use; it is also known as an *area of influence*. Neighborhoods tend to be defined differently by their inhabitants as well as by individual appraisers. One neighborhood can include residential, commercial, and industrial properties. Neighborhoods do not have to be limited to platted subdivisions or certain city blocks. Neighborhoods are usually delineated geographically in relation to major roads, natural geographic features, and political boundaries (such as school systems or city limits).

A *market area* can include several districts and often includes more than one neighborhood. The term refers to the area in which market participants live and work. A market area is generally broader than a neighborhood. For many years, appraisers have focused on neighborhoods as the basis of locational analysis. More recently, however, appraisers have recognized that home buyers and especially investors in nonresidential properties do not limit their options to a single neighborhood. Market studies complement neighborhood analysis because the latter is focused narrowly and the former allows broader analysis of supply and demand issues.

Segmentation and Delineation of Real Estate Markets

Many people have some role in the transactions that occur in real estate markets, from buyers and sellers to lenders, developers, and property managers. Market participants are motivated by different desires. A seller wants the highest price and the fewest concessions in the transaction, while an investor looks for a certain level of return on the investment at an acceptable level of risk. Despite the different motivations of the market participants, they are brought together in activities relating to a specific segment of a real estate market, such as low-rise suburban office properties or mid-sized, investment-grade apartment buildings.

The defining characteristics of a submarket include

- property type
- property features (occupancy, customer base, quality of construction, design, and amenities)
- market area (location and boundaries)
- supply of substitute properties
- proximity of complementary properties (support facilities)

Defining Geographical Boundaries

One of the easiest ways to establish the boundaries of a market area is to ask local real estate brokers what parameters potential buyers of the subject property will use when searching for competitive listings. In other words, if a buyer says "Show me properties in this township or that taxing district," the data from that area will be representative of the competition for properties similar to the subject property.

> While neighborhood analysis gives the reader of an appraisal report an impression of the subject property's immediate environment, the process can also lead appraisers to make prejudicial or prohibited statements regarding the subject neighborhood. If you do appraisals for residential lending purposes, you must be very careful to ensure you comply with fair lending rules in this part of the appraisal report. Many publications and seminars are available to help you expand your knowledge of this sensitive issue.

KEY TERMS	
central business district (CBD)	submarket
disaggregation	trade area
market segmentation	

For most people, neighborhood boundaries are more difficult to delineate than market area boundaries. Most residential lenders insist that appraisers delineate the neighborhood in their reports. While the formal definition of the term *neighborhood* refers to "a group of complementary land uses," that wording is not as clear as it could be. Many appraisers define a neighborhood by the price range of homes, which is not entirely correct because it more closely resembles a grouping of similar land uses. Some appraisers use only natural geographic boundaries, which makes some neighborhoods very large and others very small. Some appraisers look for observable differences in maintenance, quality of construction, or age of improvements to define a neighborhood. Again, these criteria are more likely to identify a defined district than a neighborhood.

A neighborhood should be defined geographically, so it is best illustrated using a map such as a zoning map on which the client can see likely land uses and geographic boundaries. Neighborhoods often include several different types of uses. If you use a zoning map to delineate the neighborhood, your client can see the other uses by classification. Defining the geographic boundaries of a district is usually much easier because they are usually shown on the local zoning map. A zoning map is one of the best exhibits an appraiser can include because it helps the reader of the report visualize the surrounding land uses.

Neighborhoods are sometimes considered to be as large as a 10-square-mile area, while at other times they may extend only a few blocks in each direction. Do not confuse neighborhood delineations with a market area. A neighborhood can have many different land uses. A market area will normally be much larger and include competing properties.

Value Influences in Real Estate Markets

Four forces affect value:

1. Social trends such as demographics
2. Economic circumstances such as employment or supply and demand factors
3. Governmental controls and regulations such as zoning, services, and fiscal policies
4. Environmental conditions such as climate and other environmental and geographic issues

These forces continuously cause changes in the market for any good or service.

Consider the following examples:

- In an area with demand for new development, land may be worth 10 times more than it was a few years earlier when there was no demand for development. As area populations increase, property values change. Developers and entrepreneurs will pay more for prime land if the demographics suit the proposed use. If the land is subprime, the development may not ultimately be viable. During 2007-2009, prices of farmland increased significantly, but prices of residential development land fell a great deal. This led to developments being "unplatted" and returned to farmland.

- A multitenant office building in a metropolitan area may be worth a lot of money in a market that is in balance, but it may be worth much less when a few more developers build new office buildings in that area and the additional space cannot be absorbed. Excess space for lease causes prices to stabilize or decline, which lowers the net operating income and in turn lowers the value.

- A commercial property that has value today may not have value tomorrow if nearby highway traffic is diverted to another street by government action.

- A property may be worth little in a neighborhood lacking public sewer access but could be worth much more if sewers were available.

- If a city is adjacent to a large body of water, real estate next to the water may be expensive because of the view. It may also mean that expansion in all four directions is not possible and development is forced to go in three directions, which increases commuting times and affects prices. In areas where there are geographic limitations to development, prices for land may be so high that the construction of taller buildings is feasible.

- All real estate in a defined area may lose or gain value if the Federal Reserve raises or lowers interest rates.

Social Forces

As the population of an area increases, the need for new housing units increases substantially, translating into more apartments, condominiums, mobile homes, or one-unit detached homes. As the demographics change, the supply and demand of housing will change. Likewise, an increase in population drives the demand for retail uses of

Exhibit 11.1   Zoning Map

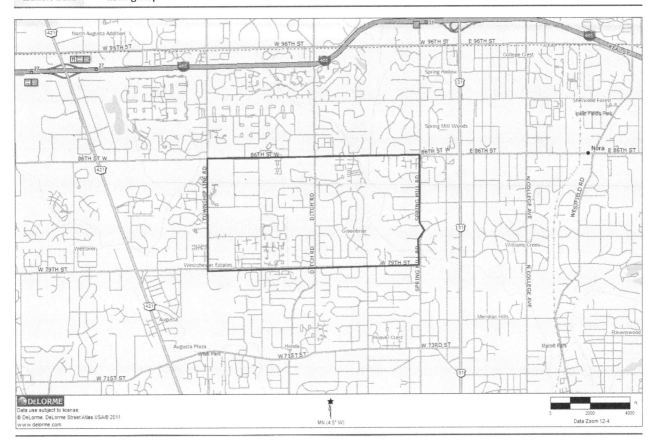

land in an area. For retail properties, "rooftops means retail." For other words, it takes population to support retail stores.

Economic Forces

It is common for one market to have more or less of a particular type of property than another. It is also not unusual for one area to have substantial poverty because of a historical, community-wide reliance on a single industry that has left town, consolidated with another business, or downsized. Few industries are immune to changes in business or economic trends, which also affect the land and buildings those businesses occupy. Even medical and funeral businesses are affected negatively if the population declines.

Governmental Forces

If a community has no zoning in place, the value of a property can be diminished because of an adverse land use that was not prohibited by regulations. Conversely, a community that has restrictive land use regulations may have difficulty attracting new jobs and the real estate development that accompanies

economic growth. In other words, many people want to attract new jobs to an area until a manufacturing plant is proposed to be built next to their homes--the classic case of "NIMBY," or "not in my back yard."

Environmental Forces

An open field in a farm community that is too hilly to be farmed may be usable only as pasture. If a similar parcel is located in an area where hilly land is popular for residential sites, the topography could have a positive effect on value. Rolling land can be more difficult to build on than level land, so level land often commands a higher price.

A parcel of residential land next to an interstate highway may command no value premium, and sometimes a value impediment, due to traffic noise. On the other hand, a commercial site next to an interstate highway interchange may bring a substantial premium. Both parcels may be valued the same if there is no population in the area to support commercial or residential uses.

More broadly, climate change may affect the desirability of a location if the characteristics of the local climate that once attracted residents and businesses—e.g., a dry, hot climate or ample snow for skiing in the winter—are altered dramatically over time, although the effect is likely to be marketwide.

Analyzing Value Influences

While fair lending regulations may prohibit reporting specific demographic information in some cases, appraisers must be able to identify who the prospective buyers of a property are and why they would buy it. In one market segment, a home with only two bedrooms may sell at a deep discount, while in a nearby neighborhood with many residents of a different age group, the same two-bedroom home might sell at a premium. It is not your job to explain to the reader of the appraisal report the reasons why buyers purchase specific properties if it violates fair housing laws; your job is to understand the forces at work in the market.

Social Influences

Home buyers want a neighborhood that provides for healthy social interactions (i.e., friendly neighbors) and is safe, clean, free of crime, and close to public services and employment. Safety issues are the most significant in some residential neighborhoods, while in other neighborhoods the access to utilities may be more significant.

Economic Influences

In general, residential property buyers want neighboring homes to be of similar quality, condition, and value. Land-to-building value ratios in most neighborhoods show that the value of the homes will cause the value of the location to increase or decrease accordingly.

Governmental Influences

A lack of zoning controls can create an atmosphere in which buyers do not want to buy or build a home because they fear offensive uses will be built nearby. An excessive tax burden can directly affect a buyer's ability to afford a property. Real estate taxes are directly factored into the qualification ratios that nearly all lenders use. Excessively high taxes will lower the amount of mortgage a buyer can qualify for.

Environmental Influences

Location

Access to services is important, but the quality, size, and condition of surrounding properties is most important and will make one location viable and profitable while another is not. This is true for residential and nonresidential properties alike. Brokers often say that the three most important things in real estate are "location, location, and location, not necessarily in that order." A new home built in an area with substantial crime may not sell for a price equal to its cost of construction. However, the same home will sell for top dollar if it is built in a popular area with no safety concerns. It is also possible that a property in an area with some safety concerns is quite salable with four bedrooms but not salable at all if it has two bedrooms. As an appraiser, you must know the potential buyers for the subject property and their requirements.

Linkages

The time and distance relationship between a particular land use and supporting facilities can play as large a role as location. In the housing market, the proximity of schools, interstate highways, and shopping is important. For industrial properties, utilities, access to interstate highways, and surrounding land uses are important. Different property types have different needs. Linkages to modern conveniences are crucial to many buyers and especially to decision makers.

Characteristics of Real Estate Districts

Districts are greatly affected by the availability and pricing of public water and sewer services. Zoning is used to make districts compact and compatible. Other factors that affect value differ depending on the district.

One-Unit Residential Districts

One-unit residential districts are usually found in many parts of urban areas. The design of residential districts has changed over the last century. Many cities that developed in the later 1800s and early 1900s were not planned well—they just "happened." From the 1950s on, city governments have made great efforts to plan their environments. Today they create very restrictive zoning ordinances to limit land use to specific activities.

Modern urban planners try to avoid putting industrial uses next to residential uses unless a buffer separates them. Sometimes modern urban planners will draw planning maps to put one-unit detached homes on large lots next to homes on smaller lots, next to condominiums, next to apartments, next to office buildings, and down the chain to light industrial uses. While that progression sounds ideal, it seldom works because of the haphazard way developments are proposed. Homeowners are usually voters, so policy makers must listen to existing landowners while still keeping their eyes on job growth and the tax burden.

The age of a one-unit residential district can be estimated by identifying the predominant architectural style. Before the Great Depression, most new subdivisions were built with narrow lots and alleys in the rear. Some homes had carriage houses, but most did not have garages. The alley would allow vehicles or carriages access to the rear of the property. Later in the twentieth century, lots grew wider and driveways were built alongside the houses, leading to the detached garage. In the 1960s, many developers began to build houses with attached garages. Houses were also built closer to the street during this time. House styles became more similar, and construction was regulated by the government much more aggressively through building codes. As the twentieth century turned into the twenty-first, Internet and computer usage began to influence housing design. Some modern homes include data line hookups, electronic thermostats, and other computerized equipment throughout the house. Most houses today have attached garages and on-site parking.

Included in the one-unit home classification are condominiums and attached one-unit homes. In many communities, higher-density residential districts provide a buffer between commercial or industrial uses and lower-density, one-unit residential uses.

The overbuilding in the suburbs that took place before the financial crisis of 2007-2008 contributed to suburban sprawl but also renewed efforts to increase residential density in some areas. While the commuting time to central business districts (CBDs) does influence the value of homes in outlying suburbs, some suburban areas are developing their own commercial districts as employers move further from the CBDs and closer to employees. Looking at metropolitan migratory patterns over time can help appraisers determine possible patterns for the future.

The recent growth of telecommuting has also made more outlying areas into feasible residential communities. Looking at an area's demographics can help you determine if telecommuting has an influence on housing supply and demand.

Multifamily Districts

Apartments and small residential income properties are an important part of the housing inventory. Apartments are designed to fit many price levels and tenant profiles, and they range substantially in quality and condition. Providing municipal services and keeping the peace can be a problem in small areas with high occupancy. Many of the same value influences for one-unit residential districts also affect multifamily districts, but the higher density levels of multifamily districts can be a distinguishing factor.

Because most apartment buildings are investor-owned, appraisers of these properties need to analyze the behavior of investors, who usually focus on the three Rs:

- risk
- return
- recovery or recapture

If an investment is risky, most investors require a higher rate of return. Smart investors compare investment options and put more money in the one that returns the most. The return on an investment is usually accomplished through a series of periodic payments, like the monthly lease payments for an apartment complex. Most investments involve a lump-sum capital return at the end. Investors in apartments will consider whether they will get all their investment back, more than their investment back, or less than their investment back at the end of the holding period. If the property is declining in value over the holding period, then the periodic payments will have to be higher to recoup the investment in increments (like a mortgage loan) or the price paid going into the investment must be less.

Appraisers may be able to access published data on apartment supply, rent levels, and vacancy rates, or they may have to gather data through primary research.

Commercial Districts

Most cities, towns, and villages have some sort of central commercial district. In rural areas, commercial districts are commonly at the crossroads of two highways or sometimes next to the home of an entrepreneur. A commercial district can be loosely defined as a group of offices or stores. Included in this definition are retail districts/shopping centers, CBDs, and highway commercial districts, which are strategically located near auto transportation routes. A primary influence on value for commercial districts is the surrounding trade area that is served by the district.

Office Districts

Office districts are also known as *office parks, business parks*, or *business centers*. They may be planned or strip developments and are often surrounded by residential districts that supply the labor force.

Office districts are commonly found in larger cities where enough business is conducted to maintain an area of low-intensity commercial uses. In small towns and villages, there may only be one or two business zoning classifications, and office uses will be mingled with retail uses. In larger cities, offices are clustered into districts to provide buffers from more intense retail uses.

Some office properties are owner-occupied, such as insurance and real estate sales agencies or doctor's and stockbroker's offices, and some are occupied by tenants. Office districts may consist of small or large buildings inhabited by small or large companies. Many office properties are multitenant buildings owned by investors interested in the return on and return of the investment. Industrial users often choose to locate in office districts rather than CBDs because office districts often offer better options in terms of location, utility, and cost. Office districts usually require large amounts of parking in suburban areas and accessible pay lots in urban settings. Parking can be a big issue in the appraisal of office properties.

Retail Districts

A retail district is an area where consumer goods are sold, such as a strip mall, a collection of retail stores, or an enclosed regional mall. These properties are sometimes owner-occupied, but many are multitenanted. The investor's criteria will be the most important factor in valuing multitenant properties.

Retail districts are highly reliant on their local trade areas. Neighborhood and strip retail centers serve small local neighborhoods, while community shopping centers serve larger trade areas. Regional and super-regional shopping centers, including specialty centers such as outlet malls and warehouse clubs, serve an even larger customer base determined by transportation routes.

Shopping centers may be anchored by a big-box store or large movie theater that serves as a main attraction. The recent growth of online sales has affected the sales potential of retail districts, and e-commerce is expected to continue growing and affecting the demand for retail space.

Central Business Districts

Central business districts (CBDs) are areas in larger towns and cities that contain the most intense commercial or office uses, i.e., the centralized location that businesses gravitate to. CBDs often include several different types of land use, commonly a combination of office, retail, financial, and recreational uses. When land values get too high, the CBD becomes unaffordable for many retail users, and only the most profitable can locate there. With high land costs, office developers tend to build up rather than out, which creates an even greater demand for parking, public transportation, and other amenities required for workers (such as restaurants, dry cleaners, and day care).

Over the past 25 years, some CBDs have declined because of a lack of available land, redevelopment restrictions, high levels of crime, and the development of suburban commercial centers. Other CBDs have grown and succeeded because of factors such as a high concentration of flourishing companies, improved public transportation access and parking areas, sales promotions, and the addition or revitalization of housing stock. If a downtown area is popular as a residential location, the support businesses will follow.

Industrial Districts

Industrial districts contain concentrations of the land uses that are often the most unwelcome, but necessary, in many communities. Because industry drives economic growth, economic development efforts often focus on encouraging the growth of industrial jobs in an area. In well-planned areas, zoning laws can help control noise, pollution, and other undesirable by-products of industrial areas. Environmental contamination is a greater risk in industrial districts than in other types of districts.

Industrial districts include

- flex space
- warehouse and distribution centers
- manufacturing districts

Industrial districts range from those that house assembly, distribution, and similar types of light operations to more heavy operations such as steel plants and foundries. Older industrial districts are characterized by limited parking and multistory buildings, while newer districts often house one-story buildings with higher ceilings. Industrial operations near residential developments often face pressure from their neighbors to cease operations. Getting a building permit to expand a business can be very difficult if the nearby residents (i.e., the voters) are strongly opposed to it.

Flex Space

Industrial districts with large portions of office space and a small percentage of industrial uses are known as *flex industrial districts*. In some areas it is difficult to differentiate flex space from one-story office use. Users of these properties include

- appliance distributors with repair facilities
- HVAC contractors with combined office and repair facilities
- commercial and industrial tire stores (institutional sales only)
- carpet and floor covering distributors
- wholesale distributors of other products

Flex space tenants are usually looking for an area with some visibility where industrial uses are allowed. Occasionally, you may even find a church in a flex industrial district.

Warehouse and Distribution Centers

Access to interstate highways or airports is a prerequisite for a modern warehouse district. Buildings in these districts require specially configured lots to allow large semitrailers to be maneuvered on site, but they usually do not need much employee parking. Some appraisers put miniware-

house properties in this category, but those buildings are slightly different because they almost always are sold to investors whereas industrial buildings are often sold to owner-users.

Manufacturing Districts

Manufacturing districts represent the most intensive land uses in many areas. Zoning classifications often break down industrial uses into subcategories based on factors such as

- location (urban or suburban)
- size and height of building
- outside storage of materials
- railroad siding

Planners usually isolate manufacturing districts away from residential districts. Sometimes a manufacturing district develops in a remote area only to see the city build up around it. Homeowner complaints are common as residential areas encroach on manufacturing areas.

Agricultural Districts

The sizes of agricultural districts vary widely. Agricultural land uses are seldom discussed in large urban areas but are a primary focus in rural areas. The growth of urban areas and suburban sprawl have led to encroachment on agricultural areas, and government efforts to limit this encroachment have had limited effects.

Farmers deal with all kinds of impediments to profitability, including

- domestic and foreign competition
- environmental pollution
- weather problems
- lack of available capital
- the high cost of fuel and mechanical equipment

The valuation of properties in agricultural districts can be tricky because the value of farmland usually depends on profitability. If there is little profit, there is little incentive for a farmer to buy more land to increase the size of the business.

Another factor in the valuation of farmland is the potential for development. Most farms in the United States will not be developed for nonagricultural use in the next 100 years, but some may be developed into residential or commercial uses within the next 10 years. As an appraiser, you must be able to identify parcels of land that are being farmed temporarily while zoning changes are pending or utilities are being made available so that the land can be developed for some other use. It is not unusual for an agricultural parcel with no potential for development to sell at one-tenth of the price of another agricultural parcel that is next to an urbanized area with utilities, good linkages, and a highest and best use as the future site of commercial or multifamily development.

Value influences in agricultural districts often relate to individual properties and depend on what resources the farms are producing. However, agricultural districts generally rely on roads and transportation routes, the availability of public utilities, and other government services such as schools.

Specialty Districts

A specialty district is an area where a certain type of business is concentrated. Specialty districts sometimes come about by design or because several companies in the same business moved to an area, causing it to develop a reputation as being a home to that industry. Historic districts are a bit different from other specialty districts in that they are often tied to tax incentives for remodeling old buildings to their original use and condition. Most specialty districts have government land use approval, and the value influences of these types of districts depend on the type of business or activity that is conducted there.

Medical Districts

A major hospital can slowly transform the surrounding area into a medical district as doctors and other practitioners locate their facilities nearby. Office buildings eventually convert to medical space, and industrial buildings switch to hospital suppliers. Even surrounding condominiums and apartments may be built or converted to appeal to employees of the major medical institution.

Medical districts are often characterized by suburban locations, proximity to highways, spacious settings with attractive landscaping, and high demand for land. The value of medical properties is influenced by the demographics of the surrounding population, particularly in terms of age, as well as the general economic climate and the state of the national healthcare industry. Utilities are particularly important to healthcare facilities, and waste disposal is also a specific concern. Appraisers usually focus on assessing the financial status and physical condition of the hospital that serves as the economic center of the medical district. The appraisal of medical facilities is a specialized area of appraisal with a required knowledge of the

current medical demand and payment systems available–i.e., medicare, health insurance, etc.

Research and Development Parks

In research and development (R&D) parks, also known as *science parks,* one industry usually gets a foothold first and others soon join in. Companies will often cluster together so they can share expertise. Properties in R&D parks may have to be compared to other property sales in R&D parks to ensure locational similarity.

R&D parks usually include office and industrial uses. Older science parks are characterized by single-story warehouses, while newer parks often house several-story office buildings. Science parks are often sponsored by universities.

High-Technology Parks

High-tech parks are similar to R&D parks and have the same characteristics. These districts are often developed near universities because many of their employees come from academia. In some cases, an office or industrial park will be labeled "high-tech" in the expectation that it can be adapted to that use by the time high-tech tenants are actually found. Developers or the local government may offer special benefits in an attempt to attract that sort of tenant. Computer and electronics companies often dominate high-tech parks.

Education Districts

Education districts are usually focused around a large school. Land uses around the institution (such as apartments, restaurants, bookstores, and computer stores) support that use. In some cities, special zoning classifications will be delineated around a campus to ensure that there is adequate student housing and few distractions for the students. Institutions of higher education provide the main economic base for some cities and towns, and students and educators often contribute to the economic and cultural landscape of the larger community.

Historic Districts

In older cities, certain homes and commercial buildings are classified as historic buildings. A historic district is classified as such by state or local governments, which limit development in those areas to approved projects only. Once a historic district meets the requirements to become federally or locally certified, financial benefits such as property tax incentives are made available to property owners, developers, investors, and renovators by the local and national government.

1. A neighborhood is
   a) A residential subdivision
   b) An area with similar zoning and density
   c) A group of complementary land uses
   d) An area with homes of the same price

2. A district is
   a) An area within a neighborhood where all the properties are vacant
   b) A type of neighborhood that is characterized by homogeneous land use
   c) The delineation of zoning classifications
   d) An area where city attorneys reside

3. Neighborhood social influences include all of the following except
   a) Population density
   b) Occupant skill levels
   c) Occupant age levels
   d) Vacancy rates

4. Economic influences include all of the following except
   a) Occupant income levels
   b) Crime levels
   c) Property rent levels
   d) Property value levels

5. Governmental influences include all of the following except
   a) Tax burdens
   b) Special assessments
   c) Zoning, building, and housing codes
   d) Changes in property use

6. *Linkages* are
   a) The devices used to change a property from one use to another
   b) The relationships between a buyer and seller in a real estate deal
   c) Time-distance relationships between a property use and the supporting facilities
   d) The tools necessary to market real estate

7. A *trade area* is
   a) An area where property owners trade rather than sell the properties
   b) A geographic area from which a retail center will draw its customers
   c) An area where the owners-inhabitants are generally employed
   d) An area where an office building owner will trade tenants with other office building owners

8. The value of improved residential real estate is most influenced by
   a) The passage of time
   b) The brokers' opinions of the property values
   c) Changes in shopping patterns for consumers of goods and services
   d) Construction cost increases

9. The four forces that influence real estate values are
   a) Social, economic, governmental, and environmental
   b) Land, labor, capital, and green space
   c) Eminent domain, police power, escheat, and taxation
   d) Governmental, social, taxation, and economic conditions

Note: Unless otherwise noted, italicized references indicate the pages in *The Appraisal of Real Estate*, 14th edition, that readers should consult for additional discussion of these topics.

1. c) A group of complementary land uses
    Page 172

2. b) A type of neighborhood that is characterized by homogeneous land use
    This student handbook

3. d) Vacancy rates
    Pages 166-167

4. b) Crime levels
    Pages 167-168

5. d) Changes in property use
    Pages 168-169

6. c) Time-distance relationships between a property use and the supporting facilities
    Page 171

7. b) A geographic area from which a retail center will draw its customers
    Page 174

8. d) Construction cost increases
    Pages 166-171

9. a) Social, economic, governmental, and environmental
    Page 166

12

Land and Site Description

Real estate appraisers develop opinions of value for the rights in realty, meaning the space on the face of the earth as defined in the legal description. The utility of land gives it value. If a parcel of land is located in an identified flood hazard area and the local zoning ordinance will not allow development (which is likely and logical), the utility of that land may be limited. If the property is located at the corner of two busy streets, many commercial uses may be possible, and the property may have an extremely high value. However, if a property is located in a popular area with high demand for commercial uses but the soil is not stable, the value may be negligible. Similarly, a parcel of land in a high demand location that has been polluted by a gas station with leaking underground storage tanks may not have any value or may even have a negative value.

Raw land that has been improved with utilities, adjacent streets, drainage plans, and other amenities is called a *site*. There is a big difference between a farmer's field and a site ready for a new office building and a big difference in cost to the builder or owner.

Legal Descriptions of Land

Appraisers should know how to read legal descriptions of land. Identification of the subject is required by USPAP, and often only the legal description fully identifies the subject real estate. Less experienced real estate brokers and appraisers may think that the subject property can be identified by its address, but addresses are not usually definitive or even permanent. While the description of the real estate may refer to a parcel number or other identifying number, the underlying method of identifying the property should be the legal description. You cannot appraise a property if you do not know what it includes.

The function of a legal description is to uniquely differentiate one parcel of land from another. The legal description of a parcel is the same regardless of the improvements on it. Although the parcel may be improved, the application of the cost approach and highest and best use analysis will still require the development of an opinion of land value (of the site as though vacant).

Techniques used to describe land have evolved over the years, but all are still based on landmarks that are placed to give surveyors a common starting point. Modern surveying techniques include the use of lasers, Global Positioning System (GPS) receivers, and other electronic devices. Most of these tools are recent developments. Land has been described for years without them, so discrepancies between older and newer legal descriptions are likely. Some discrepancies are resolved easily but others require court action.

Metes and Bounds

The metes and bounds system is used in states that were part of the original American colonies, and

KEY TERMS	
assemblage	plottage
base line	principal meridian
corner influence	raw land
excess land	rectangular (government) survey system
floodplain	
frontage	site
legal description	stigma
lot and block system	surplus land
metes and bounds system	

the system has been integrated into legal descriptions to some degree in other areas. This method is based on a series of distances and directions from one monument to another. Monuments are natural features such as creeks, rivers, big trees, and rocks. Monuments can also be man-made items such as fences, roads, and utility poles. The basic technique probably evolved from one owner simply telling a prospective buyer something like, "I own the land from that tree to that shrub to that creek." Unfortunately, landmarks may not be fixed in location. If a landmark is fixed, the system works well, but if the creek in the owner's simple description drifts or the shrub dies, the description is not useful.

Each metes and bounds description must begin at a specific place, which is called the *point of beginning*. The point of beginning must be specific, or the rest of the description could be incorrect. A point of beginning must be either a known point (such as a monument) or a point in an adjoining survey. Starting from the point of beginning, a property's boundary lines, or *calls*, are described by the course (direction) and distance of the boundary line. The course is the direction in which the boundary line travels, and the distance is the length of the boundary line. Surveyors can use angles to measure the direction of a boundary line instead of or in addition to bearings. An angle runs from the last described direction.

A metes and bounds description must close, meaning that the beginning and ending point must be the same. The legal description starts at a geographic point, follows each boundary line by course and distance, and ultimately ends back at the point of beginning. If a legal description does not close, it is not usable because buyers, sellers, lenders, title companies, and courts will not know what to include in the land parcel.

Rectangular Survey System

When the United States was very young, the original colonies were already using the metes and bounds system. Thomas Jefferson headed a committee that devised a new method of describing land in deeds, plats, and other legal documents that was based on an idea brought to the United States by the British soldier Colonel Henry Bouquet. The new system, the rectangular survey system, which divides land into a series of rectangles, was adopted by Congress in 1785 and was first used as the standard system of land description for the Louisiana Purchase.

The rectangular survey system (also known as the *government survey system*) is based on a set of intersecting lines that form squares. Principal

The *rectangular survey system* is used to describe land in the following states:

Alabama	Iowa	New Mexico
Alaska	Kansas	North Dakota
Arizona	Louisiana	Ohio
Arkansas	Michigan	Oklahoma
California	Minnesota	Oregon
Colorado	Mississippi	South Dakota
Florida	Missouri	Utah
Idaho	Montana	Washington
Illinois	Nebraska	Wisconsin
Indiana	Nevada	Wyoming

Metes and Bounds Legal Description

Tract No. 1: Situated in the County of Hamilton, in the State of Ohio, and in the Township of Brown, and bounded and described as follows:

Being on the waters of the East Fork of the Big Chicago River, and being part of A. Billford's Survey No. 97, and a part of A. McKel's Survey No. 30. Beginning at a point between a black and white oak stump, N.E. corner of Asa Pimberton's Survey No. 19; thence North 45¼ degrees East 46.54 poles to a stone in a county road; thence with the line of said road North 36 degrees West 46.7 poles to a stone corner to a lot formerly owned by E. Thomas; thence with this line North 46½ degrees East 65¼ poles to a stone corner to Alexander Northam's tract of land; thence with Alexander Northam's lines South 44 degrees East 94.6 poles to a stone near a hickory, corner to graveyard lot; thence with the line of said lot South 44 degrees West 16 poles to a stone corner to said lot; thence with another of said lines South 44 degrees East 41.9 poles to a stone corner to a lot sold to E.J. Dalon by said Alexander, thence with this line South 45¾ degrees West 25.88 poles to a stone corner to said lot; thence South 74 degrees West 73 poles to a stone in the west side of the East Fork of the Big Chicago River; thence South 5 degrees West 21 poles to a stone in the west side of the new state road; thence with the middle of said road South 85 degrees West 47½ poles to a stone in the east boundary line of Asa Pimberton's Survey No. 19; thence with said line North 56¼ poles to the beginning, *containing eighty-six and one-half acres of land (86.5 acres), be the same more or less.*

Saving and excepting there from the following tracts: *Four acres* sold to Woodrow Lindon and *two and one-half acres* sold to Leroy Lewis.

meridians run north and south. Base lines run east and west. These lines divide a state into areas that are easily described. Because of the difficulty of describing small parcels in this system, land descriptions often make use of the metes and bounds system as well. The rectangular survey system is also hard to apply to areas with difficult terrain.

Township and Range Lines

While the rectangular survey system is precise, the area of land created by intersecting principal meridians and base lines under the grid system is still too large for most property owners. Township and range lines are necessary to describe smaller parcels. Township lines run east and west at six-mile intervals parallel to base lines. Land on either side of the principal meridians is also divided into six-mile strips by north and south lines called range lines. The intersecting township lines and range lines make up a grid pattern. Each square within the grid has about six miles on each side. These squares, called townships, make up the basic units of the rectangular survey system. Because of the curvature of the earth, not all townships are perfectly configured.

Correction Lines and Guide Meridians

Because the earth is round, range lines converge on each other and ultimately meet at the North Pole. As a result, the northern boundary line of a well-surveyed township should be about 50 feet shorter than its southern boundary line. In the case of the fourth township north of the base line, the difference is four times as great, or about 200 feet. The rectangular survey system has correction lines to compensate for these anomalies. Each fourth township line (24 miles) north and south of a base line is designated as a correction line. Each correction line is a new base line for townships that lie between it and the next correction line.

Sections

The six-by-six-mile township square is further subdivided into 36 sections; each section is one mile square and contains about 640 acres. The sections are numbered consecutively from 1 to 36, starting on the northeast corner of the township and proceeding west to east and back again in a serpentine manner, ending in the southeast corner with the number 36. Sections are subdivided further into quarter sections, and quarter sections can be divided into halves or quarters (see Exhibit 12.1).

A government survey description is read backwards. That is, when trying to find the parcel

principal meridians
A principal meridian runs due north and south through a particular area or state. Principal meridians are identified by the distance in degrees, minutes, and seconds west of the Greenwich meridian.

base lines
A base line runs east and west and is identified as "so many degrees north of the equator."

on a map, you read from the end of the description to the beginning to determine the location and size of the property.

Lot and Block System

The lot and block system is commonly used in urban settings where lots are small and the developer of an area has an opportunity to draw and file a plat. This system allows the developer to write a long legal description of the plat and record the plat with the recorder's office. The developer's description then serves as a reference in all future legal descriptions. A deed can just say "Lot 4 in Pleasant Acres Addition" rather than include a half page of distances and directions. Exhibit 12.2 shows an example of a legal description using the lot and block system.

Title and Record Data

In addition to ensuring that the subject property is the correct one, appraisers must research historical market activity in the subject's market area. It is always embarrassing to turn in a well-written, comprehensive, detailed, well-supported appraisal report on the wrong property. Title and record data is very important. The client needs to help the appraiser identify the real property and real estate to be appraised, but you should make every effort to make sure the data is accurate. You may still get paid if you appraise the wrong property as long as the client told you to appraise that particular property. However, if you did not require the client to be specific, you can only blame yourself for the mistake.

Ownership Information

In most states, you can obtain ownership information from county records of the auditor or assessor. This data can also be obtained directly from property owners by asking to see their title insurance policy or deed abstract. You may be surprised to find there are some limitations on the rights in realty that you did not know about but could have

Exhibit 12.1   Subdivision of a Section in the Rectangular Survey System

5,280 feet

1,320 feet 20 chains	1,320 feet 80 rods	2,640 feet 40 chains = 160 rods	
W ½ of NW ¼ 80 acres	E ½ of NW ¼ 80 acres	NE ¼ 160 acres	2,640 feet

		N ½ of NW ¼ of SE ¼ 20 acres		W ½ of NE ¼ of SE ¼	
NW ¼ of SW ¼ 40 acres	NE ¼ of SW ¼ 40 acres			20 acres	20 acres
		20 acres		1 furlong	

		10 acres	10 acres	5 acres	5 acres	5 acres
SW ¼ of SW ¼ 40 acres	40 acres			5 acres		
					SE ¼ of SE ¼ of SE ¼	
80 rods	440 yards	660'	660'		10 acres	

Exhibit 12.2   Survey of Platted Land

PROPERTY ADDRESS: 1424 Emerald Court Carmel, Indiana 46030

PROPERTY DESCRIPTION: Lot 4 in PLEASANT ACRES, Block 1, an Addition to Hamilton County, Indiana, as per Plat thereof Recorded as Instrument No. 9956337 Cabinet No. 2 Slide No. 549, in the Office of the Recorder of Hamilton County, Indiana

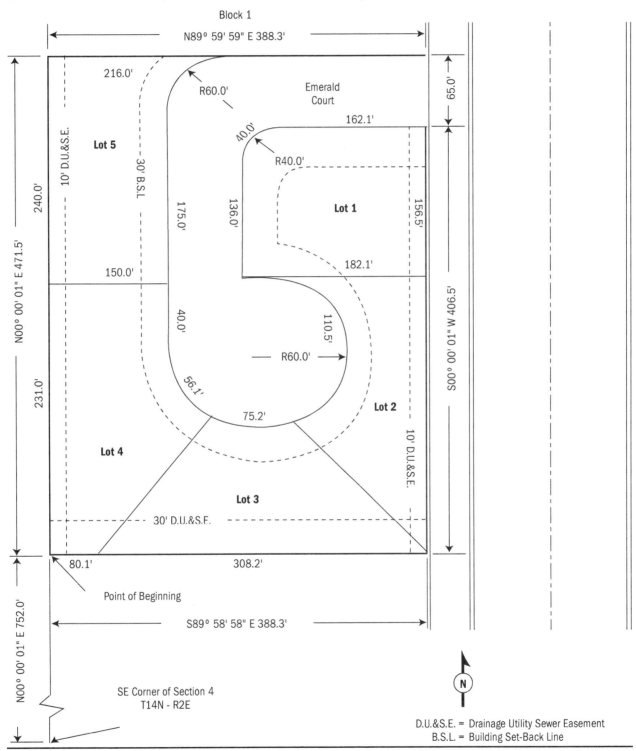

TITLE COMPANY: Acme Title Insurance Corporation

known by just asking to see the title insurance policy. Data gathered in this research includes

- the history of ownership or recent sales, listings, or options
- leases in place as of the effective date of appraisal
- easements and rights of way that may cover a portion of the subject
- deed or plat restrictions on the subject
- subsurface rights or mineral extraction licenses

Zoning and Land Use Information

Zoning and land use information is usually available from local planning or zoning departments and is easily confirmed. Inexperienced appraisers often fail to investigate the details and requirements of the actual zoning classification. You may need assistance from planning and zoning staff members to help you understand the effects of zoning regulations. It is every appraiser's duty and responsibility to thoroughly check zoning and land use regulations applicable to the subject, which include but are not limited to

- minimum lot size
- utility availability
- minimum building size
- minimum road frontage
- minimum side yard requirements

Compliance with zoning and land use regulations may fall into two categories:

1. Legal land use
   Researching the allowable uses may be simple or complicated.
2. Development standards
   If the parcel is being used in compliance with zoning requirements but the lot size is too small, the side yards are too small, or there is a building in the setback area, the problem areas will commonly be considered as non-compliant with development standards rather than as illegal land uses. Development standards are sizes, distances, and other configuration definitions outside the use of the land.

Before a plat is filed, a surveyor prepares a plat drawing showing the dimensions, directions, references, easements, and locational attributes of the parcel. This document is then recorded in the county in which the land is located.

In some appraisals, the appraiser must consider the likelihood of a zoning change. Considering probable changes in zoning regulations is just as important as looking at the current zoning regulations in place in those situations. To do this, appraisers consider the appropriateness of the current zoning, analyze past zoning change patterns, and possibly interview planning and zoning staff and prepare land development forecasts.

Assessment and Tax Information

Like zoning information, assessment and tax information is available in various county or township offices. The subject property's tax burden may disqualify a potential buyer from purchasing the (residential) property. The taxes on income properties are annual expenses that directly affect the bottom line and therefore the property value. Even when property taxes are passed through to the tenant, the tenant may avoid a property with high tax levies in favor of a property with lower taxes. This can affect value and therefore net income.

Physical Characteristics of Land

Size and Shape

Size and shape affect value in many ways. A parcel that has no frontage on a road may not be suitable for building. A commercial parcel with limited frontage will sell for much less than another parcel with abundant road frontage. A 10,000-sq.-ft. parcel may be adequate for a $300,000 home but too small for a $600,000 home.

Corner Influence

While corner lots are highly desirable for commercial users, they are often discounted by residential users. Corner lots offer greater visibility and access for commercial property owners but afford less privacy and require more sidewalks to be maintained or built by residential owners. Commercial uses–such as gas stations, fast-food restaurants, and drug stores–require visibility for signage and access to attract convenience-oriented buyers.

Plottage Potential

Two parcels with a less intense use may experience an incremental increase in value when

A surveyor measures distances parallel with sea level. Surveyors indicate property sizes as if the land were flat. For example, a surveyor would not measure up the side of the hill.

combined into a single parcel with a more intense use. For example, two small parcels may only have value as residential building sites when considered separately, but they have commercial value when assembled. The act of putting two parcels together to create a larger, more valuable site is known as *assemblage*. *Plottage* is the term given to the additional value that accrues when two or more parcels are assembled.

Excess Land and Surplus Land

Excess and surplus land are both forms of extra land that is not needed for the highest and best use of the property as improved. Excess land can be separated and sold off for another use, but surplus land cannot. Excess land has a separate highest and best use, but surplus land has a highest and best use as part of the original tract. Exhibit 12.3 shows an industrial parcel with excess land in the first drawing and surplus land in the second.

Topography

Topography is sometimes overlooked in appraisal assignments when it should be of primary concern. Some parcels of land may be unbuildable

A subject site may sometimes be usable as a building site if the topography is adequate, and sometimes it may not be. A topographic map will tell the reader if the slope of the earth is very steep.

due to the steepness of the site. (Construction costs may be 50% higher because of the difficulty of building on a rolling or steep lot.) Other parcels may be poor building sites because of a lack of adequate drainage. Some commercial properties are valued much lower because they are below the grade level of adjacent roads, which impacts visibility, or discounted because they are too high and the potential customer only sees the landscaping. You must consider and analyze the topography of the site in any valuation of real estate. In addition to physically inspecting a site, you can obtain copies of topographical surveys and other useful maps to obtain topographical data.

Geodetic Survey Program

The National Geodetic Survey (www.ngs.noaa.gov) is a government-sponsored topography mapping system that grew out of the original Survey of the

Exhibit 12.3	Excess and Surplus Land

Example of Excess Land

Under the zoning, the minimum lot size is 43,560 square feet and the minimum frontage is 175 feet. The market requires only one acre for this parcel to be marketable and will not pay as much per square foot for land over the one-acre required amount. This parcel can legally be divided into two parcels.

Example of Surplus Land

The minimum lot size is 43,560 square feet and the minimum frontage is 175 feet. Again, the market requires only one acre for this parcel to be marketable and will not pay as much per square foot for land over the one acre required amount. Because this is not a corner site, it does not have enough frontage to sell off as another parcel.

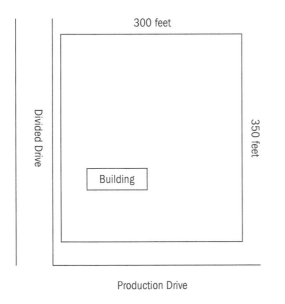

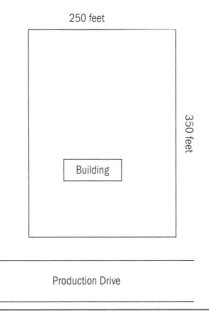

Coast conducted in 1807. The survey is a primary source of topographical maps and data. These maps may be found in a variety of government offices and sometimes even on computer disk.

Soil Analysis

In the valuation of agricultural properties, soil types may be of primary importance to the typical buyer and appraiser. In the valuation of a residential lot, the soil type may preclude building certain structures or may require the use of additional support. To adequately analyze soils, appraisers use the maps prepared by government agencies. Reviewing these maps may help in analyzing the highest and best use of a site. In many cases, finding out information on soil types, uses, and suitability can be as easy as asking the owner the right questions.

Engineers or geologists may also be hired to ascertain if a soil type is suitable for a proposed use. For example, if a property owner is considering installing a septic system as a substitute for a costly connection to the public sewer system, the soil may not accept this use. If a property owner is considering building a home on a parcel, that owner may need to install extra drainage because the soil will not allow absorption and runoff water will be a concern.

Floodplain and Wetlands Analysis

Designation as a federal floodplain or wetland will inhibit and may preclude any development on certain parcels. Appraisers are often asked by their clients to indicate if the subject property is located in a flood hazard area. If so, building permits may not be issued. Keep in mind that some properties mapped in the identified flood hazard areas may be later identified as above that elevation. Properties in flood areas may also be elevated to bring them out of the flood zone. It is also important to note that in many markets building a septic system in a FEMA-identified flood hazard area is not permitted. This can also include

> It is usually necessary for appraisers to come to a conclusion regarding flood hazards for proposed improvements or in highest and best use analysis, but it is probably best to avoid stating definitively that a property is or is not in a flood hazard area. Instead, indicate to your client where the property lies on the map. However, the determination of a flood hazard has more to do with topography than maps, which is why you should not indicate if a property is located in a hazard area but rather if it is *mapped* as being in a hazard area.

replacing an existing system. It is important for an appraiser to know where the septic system is in relation to the flood hazard area.

Wetland designation is a major factor in all appraisals of large vacant parcels because it affects highest and best use. A property that is designated a wetland by state or federal agencies will usually have fairly significant limitations on development. If a parcel of land is designated a wetland, adding fill dirt or dredging the land to dry it out is not permitted. These regulations would also impede or prohibit a proposed use of a wetland parcel as a site for any improvements, which reduces the value of the land significantly. Mapping of wetlands is done at the US Fish and Wildlife Service of the US Department of the Interior.

Utilities

Researching the availability and capacities of utilities may be the most significant part of an appraisal of vacant land. Without electric service or available clean water, most development is prohibited. Development trends often follow public water and sewer lines. The typical buyer for a home with well water and a septic tank may be completely different than the typical buyer for a home in the same price range with public utilities. Out-of-town buyers are often apprehensive about buying homes with septic systems for fear of failure in the future. In some appraisals, the subject property may have utilities nearby, but they may not be of sufficient size or capacity to serve the property.

Site Improvements

Site improvements are sometimes included in appraisals as an afterthought despite their major impact on value. For some properties, the site improvements may represent more than 50% of a property's value. Common site improvements include

- on-site utilities
- fences
- driveways
- landscaping
- other growing assets

Some appraisers include in-ground swimming pools and other non-building structures in the site improvements. Because many site improvements are growing assets, it is difficult to apply standard age-life depreciation schedules to them. For example, grass that is one year old is often worth more than new grass.

Accessibility

Access and visibility are major factors for many buyers of commercial properties. The two attributes are often classified under the single term *location*, which is an oversimplification of the issue. Good access is important to a commercial user but may not have any positive impact on a residential property. In many markets, corner lots will sell for much more because they give a commercial property the best access and visibility. A business that has many competitors will not do as well without ease of access. For example, a car dealership can be successful without an excellent access point because most buyers will not ignore that type of business even if it takes extra effort to get there. On the other hand, the value of a fast food restaurant will be affected greatly by its inaccessibility.

Environment

Climate and natural resources affect values greatly. The availability of resources like ground water can change the highest and best use and control the value of vacant land in many cases. On the other hand, even an unsubstantiated allegation about an environmental problem is enough to ruin a property's reputation and diminish its value in an unsophisticated market.

Contamination and Environmental Risk Issues

Since the 1960s, federal and state governments have taken on the responsibility of regulating land use to reduce the contamination of the water and air supply. Landowners are held responsible for water and air pollution caused by activities on their sites. Buyers can be made liable for the cost of cleaning up sites and other related expenses if they are in the chain of ownership when contamination is found.

Appraisers cannot possibly be aware of all potential environmental hazards, but it is reasonable to assume that appraisers are able to recognize situations in which contamination is likely to have occurred. One common limiting condition of an appraisal is that the opinion of value is subject to a clean environmental report from an environmental engineering firm. This condition is used when an appraiser feels there could be a problem. The analysis of environmental contamination can be a complex appraisal problem, and professional competency issues are discussed in USPAP's Advisory Opinion 9: The Appraisal of Real Property That May Be Impacted by Environmental Contamination.

Environmental contamination issues are more commonly encountered by appraisers now than they were in the past. While appraisers are not expected to detect environmental contaminants or measure the remediation costs, they are expected to be able to estimate the effect of contamination on property values. In the past, appraisers most commonly focused on sites that were sources of the contamination. Recently, that focus has shifted to non-source sites that are near or adjacent to contaminated sites.

Special Characteristics of Rural, Agricultural, or Resource Land

The ability to grow a crop translates into value. Soil type, water rights, drainage, irrigation, climate, labor, and the availability of capital all influence the ability of a farmer to bring in a crop

Common and Significant Environmental Problems	
Industrial plant pollution into a nearby river	Can affect property values but more commonly will cause the polluter to pay for all related expenses, including legal expenses.
Industrial plant pollution into the water table	May go on undetected for many years, and then some time later the owners or previous owners are required to pay to clean up the mess.
Gas stations leaking fuel into the ground or water table from underground fuel storage tanks that have rusted through	A fairly common type of contamination and a fairly expensive type of problem to fix. Any gas station or property where petroleum products were sold or used can be a risky property.
Farms that have underground oil or gasoline storage tanks	It is also common for some farms to have old cars, trucks, and tractors buried on site, which can rust away and contaminate the soil.
One-unit homes that have underground oil storage tanks	Tanks in the ground can leak for years without being noticed, and then the contaminant can come to the surface with serious consequences.
Commercial users polluting the ground with chemicals from commercial processes	Dry cleaning businesses create an environmental problem if they dump into a cistern. Another common problem is car dealerships with in-ground automobile lifts that leak into the ground.

on a given plot of land. Environmental controls are also important on farm properties. Gas and oil storage tanks, the use of chemicals, and environmental issues may influence property values.

Mineral rights are a significant issue with some properties. Some rural properties are mined for their sand, gravel, rock, stones, oil, and natural gas. Water is an even more important resource. It is easy to fail to recognize mineral extraction as the highest and best use of a site, and something as basic as water can be the most important part of the highest and best use analysis. In some markets, land with minerals to extract does not sell for more than other nearby land, but in other markets it sells at significantly higher prices.

Other special considerations for agricultural land include special tax provisions, recreational potential, proximity to more densely populated areas, wildlife habitats, and "hidden" environmental contamination. Rural properties may appear to be green and clean but may suffer contamination from fertilizers, pesticides, or aging underground gasoline storage tanks. It was not unusual for some land owners to use low spots on a parcel as trash dumps. These can be 2 feet under the surface or 40 feet down. This is a difficult thing for an appraiser to know.

1. A site is
   a) A platted subdivision lot
   b) A telescope on a gun barrel
   c) Land underneath buildings
   d) Land that is improved so that it is ready to be used for a specific purpose

2. Which of the following statements is correct?
   a) Land and sites can be created by people.
   b) Sites can be created, but land is fixed in amount.
   c) Land can be created and destroyed, but sites are fixed in amount.
   d) Neither land nor sites can be created or destroyed because both are fixed in amount.

3. An example of a rectangular survey legal description is
   a) Part of the Northwest Quarter of Section 25, Township 17N, Range 3E
   b) Lot 27 in Pleasant View Acres
   c) A parcel of land beginning at the oak tree in Bill Jones's farm, then southwest 123 feet to the center of the creek next to the bridge over US Highway 35
   d) Unit 27, in Mark's Horizontal Property Regime

4. Which of the following statements about zoning is correct?
   a) Zoning controls land use.
   b) Zoning controls building construction.
   c) Zoning is controlled and regulated by the federal government.
   d) Zoning is only used in cities and metropolitan areas.

5. *Plottage* is
   a) The process by which large parcels of land are divided into lots and recorded in county offices
   b) The assemblage of two or more parcels of land
   c) The name of the discount given when larger parcels sell for more per acre than smaller ones
   d) An incremental increase in value that results when two or more sites are combined to produce greater utility

6. *Excess land* is
   a) Land that is not needed to support the subject's primary highest and best use or not needed to support existing improvements
   b) Land that is not needed according to zoning requirements
   c) Land included with the subject that is above the lender's limits
   d) Land value that is above the assessor's estimate of value

7. A rectangular site measures 125 feet (frontage) by 256 feet (depth), of which 26 feet is in the public right of way. What is the gross and net site area?
   a) 0.66 acre gross and 0.73 acre net
   b) 35,100 square feet gross area and 32,000 square feet net area
   c) 38,656 square feet gross area and 32,000 square feet net area
   d) 32,000 square feet gross area and 28,750 square feet net area

8. A full section of land usually
   a) Measures 5,000 feet by 5,000 feet
   b) Measures 2,640 feet by 2,640 feet
   c) Includes 27,878,400 square feet
   d) Is 600 acres

9. An acre of land includes
   a) 43,560 square feet
   b) 320 acres
   c) 180 acres
   d) 27 hectares

10. Flood maps are published by
    a) The Army Corps of Engineers
    b) FHA/HUD
    c) The Federal Emergency Management Agency
    d) The Federal Land Bank

Note: Unless otherwise noted, italicized references indicate the pages in *The Appraisal of Real Estate*, 14th edition, that readers should consult for additional discussion of these topics.

1. d) Land that is improved so that it is ready to be used for a specific purpose
   Page 189

2. b) Sites can be created, but land is fixed in amount.
   This student handbook

3. a) Part of the Northwest Quarter of Section 25, Township 17N, Range 3E
   Page 192

4. a) Zoning controls land use.
   Pages 195-196

5. d) An incremental increase in value that results when two or more sites are combined to produce greater utility
   Page 199

6. a) Land that is not needed to support the subject's primary highest and best use or not needed to support existing improvements
   Page 200

7. d) 32,000 square feet gross area and 28,750 square feet net area
   This student handbook

8. c) Includes 27,878,400 square feet
   This student handbook

9. a) 43,560 square feet
   This student handbook

10. c) The Federal Emergency Management Agency
    Page 205

13

Building Description

Most appraisal reports are made to support an opinion of the market value of an improved property—i.e., land with a building (or buildings) on it. The building improvements on a site usually account for at least 50% of the total property value, and they may represent more than 75% of the total value in many cases. Clearly, the improvements are a major part of what makes properties valuable, and you must know which improvements are good, which are bad, and which are irrelevant to the typical buyer in the subject property's market area.

Analyzing the quality of construction, architectural style, and functional utility of the building improvements is a core skill of real estate appraisers, and communicating your conclusions about the contribution of the improvements to the value of the property in a meaningful way is the function of the building description in an appraisal. The building description is the process by which the appraiser identifies the improvements on the site, their condition, and how they compete with the improvements of other properties in the same market. Depending on the scope of work and the level of detail required in the report, this process could be as simple as providing a photograph of the improvements or as detailed as providing a comprehensive description of the building along with many photographs documenting the state of the exterior and interior finishes, condition, and amenities.

Architectural styles change over time. Appraisers must be mindful of how building design relates to functional utility, which is the ability of a property or building to be useful and perform the function for which it was intended. In assessing the functional utility of building improvements, an appraiser answers the question "Does the building do what it was designed to do?" In many markets, curb appeal is a major determinant of whether a property gets a second look. The appeal of an architectural style is subjective, and one buyer's desired design may be rejected by another buyer. Appraisers must stay contemporary—i.e., they must know what is hot and what is not. The popular designs will vary with the region, price point, and buyer's demographic.

Site Visit

The intensity of an appraiser's site visit can vary greatly depending on the nature of the appraisal assignment. Some appraisers routinely perform inspections from the front seats of their cars parked at the curb, while others walk through the building and note nearly every construction detail and its condition.

The site visit is the most "visible" part of the appraisal process, and for many consumers it is the only time the client can see the appraiser at work actively examining the property. Lackadaisical inspections and the reporting errors that result are the source of a lot of litigation against appraisers. A roof that starts leaking after the new owner moves in may cause a client to look for someone to blame, which can result in a lawsuit against the appraiser.

Appraisal clients may confuse the scope of work involved in an inspection done for an appraisal (performed by an appraiser) and a complete property inspection prior to purchase (performed by a home inspector or building engineer). This has led many appraisers to avoid calling the process of collecting data on the subject property an "inspection." What appraisers once called a "property inspection" may now be called a "viewing," "walk-through inspection," or "subject property data collection," among other terms, and is referred to in the 14th edition of *The Appraisal of Real Estate* and in Appraisal Institute educational materials as a *site visit*.

KEY TERMS	
architectural style	green building
building description	long-lived items
formal architecture	short-lived items
functional inutility	vernacular architecture
functional utility	

Elements of a Building Description

In most appraisal assignments, the appraiser is expected to provide a description of the building improvements that meets the expectations of the intended user. If the client is a lender, the building description may have to be adequate to describe the building to someone who has not seen it and never will. If the intended user of the report is the owner of the property who already knows the improvements well, the building description may be very brief.

Typical property buyers have strong opinions about what building features are important, and appraisers must understand those preferences to estimate value. You need to know how big a building is, how old it is, what condition it is in, and other relevant details such as the presence of any deferred maintenance or deficiencies that may cause future problems. You should also take note of the use of the building on the date of inspection. Zoning and building codes may become an issue later in the analysis, and you will have to consider an alternative use if the current property use or even the structure itself is prohibited by zoning.

If buyers think a building feature is incidental, it will be insignificant in the valuation of that property. If buyers take note of an amenity or construction detail, you should also. Remember that in most resales of existing homes, a buyer may first view the property for only 10 to 45 minutes. Most residential brokers schedule two or three appointments per hour to show homes to prospective buyers. Given the drive time, this pace limits the inspection time for each property to only a few minutes. This is a significant issue for appraisers; property owners often give appraisers long lists of features and details to check during the inspection because they assume those features will contribute to value. However, many of these features will be easily forgotten after a long day of house shopping. The features that contribute value are those that buyers take note of when they are on site and remember when they are making purchase decisions.

You can describe building improvements using words or pictures. Photographs tend to be easier for readers of an appraisal report to deal with, but they cannot describe the importance of many details of construction. Therefore, you will need to prepare some narrative description in some cases and add pictures as needed to keep the property description in line with the scope of work.

Most clients are very interested in how well-maintained a property is, so appraisers should note any items of deferred maintenance or any deficiencies that can cause future problems. Lenders also worry about large, expensive repairs that would cause buyers to have deferred maintenance and additional repairs due to lack of cash. For example, a buyer for a small owner-occupied office building spends all of her cash on the down payment. A year after purchase, the heating, ventilation, and air-conditioning (HVAC) system fails with a cost of repair of $75,000. The owner cannot borrow any additional funds for the repairs. She now cannot operate her business because of cold temperatures. The business fails and the loan payments stop. This foreclosure was due to an unforeseen or perhaps unnoticed capital repair.

Use Classification and Building Codes and Ordinances

Building design is tied to the use of the property—e.g., residential, commercial, industrial, agricultural, governmental, or special-purpose. Zoning laws limit use and consequently affect design; this is an important part of many highest and best use analyses. If the zoning does not allow a proposed use, that use probably does not meet the requirements of highest and best use in a market value appraisal (i.e., it is not legally permissible).

Similarly, a land use that is not legal because of building codes must be excluded from consideration as the highest and best use in a market value appraisal. You should be knowledgeable about local codes in order to correctly analyze construction requirements and, most importantly, assess safety issues. Some appraisers take classes or study local building codes to decrease liability, but unfortunately many do not. In most states, zoning is a local control issue, and the zoning laws and regulations will vary from city to city, which means an appraiser must research the details of many jurisdictions in a practice that covers many municipalities. Changes in zoning controls are not normally retroactive, so the possibility of legal but not conforming uses exists in many appraisal assignments. This also requires a great deal of research and knowledge of the zoning and land use codes.

Size

The size of a building is one of the most significant valuation factors for all property types, so appraisers must measure and report the size of buildings in a consistent manner. The marketplace recognizes several standards for measuring buildings. Most buildings are measured from the exterior, and the amount of area includes the walls. Some properties like office buildings are measured from the exterior but are valued based on leasable (or rentable) area. For residential properties, most appraisers, lenders, and many assessors follow the standards for measuring residences published by the American National Standards Institute (ANSI).

Format

The format used to describe building improvements in an appraisal report varies substantially from one assignment to the next. In each case, the format depends on the needs of the intended user of the report. One client may require substantial details of construction, while the next client may not even understand what the appraiser is referring to when describing certain details of construction. The outline shown in Exhibit 13.1 illustrates a common method of organizing a building description.

Description of Exterior Materials and Design

The exterior description of the property usually includes discussion of the substructure (or foundation) and the superstructure.

Exhibit 13.1	Elements of a Building Description

A. Substructure
1. Footings
2. Slabs
3. Piles
4. Columns
5. Piers
6. Beams
7. Foundation walls

B. Superstructure
1. Framing
2. Insulation
   a. Home Energy Rating System (HERS)
   b. Other third-party rating system
3. Ventilation
4. Exterior walls
5. Exterior doors
6. Windows, storm windows, and screens
7. Facade
8. Roof and drain system
9. Chimneys, stacks, and vents
10. Special features

C. Interior description
1. Interior walls, partitions, and doors
2. Division of space
   a. Storage areas
   b. Stairs, ramps, elevators, escalators, and hoists
3. Interior supports
   a. Beams, columns, and trusses
   b. Flooring system (subflooring)
   c. Ceilings

4. Painting, decorating, and finishing
   a. Basements
   b. Floor coverings
   c. Walls, partitions, and ceilings
   d. Molding and baseboards
   e. Fireplaces
5. Protection against decay and insect damage
6. Miscellaneous and special features
7. Personal property
   a. Furniture
   b. Fixtures
   c. Trade fixtures
   d. Equipment

D. Mechanical systems
1. Plumbing system
   a. Piping
   b. Fixtures
   c. Hot water system
2. Heating, ventilation, and air-conditioning systems
   a. Heating systems
      1) Warm or hot air
      2) Hot water
      3) Steam
      4) Electric
   b. Air-conditioning and ventilation systems
3. Electrical systems
4. Miscellaneous equipment
   a. Fire protection
   b. Elevators, escalators, and speed ramps
   c. Signals, alarms, and call systems
   d. Loading facilities
   e. Attached equipment (process-related)

Assessors, appraisers, and brokers all measure buildings so they can describe the improvements to other real estate professionals, but they do not all use the same methods. While it is important for all real estate professionals to use the same terminology, it is even more important to maintain the consistency of the data within appraisals. If the assessors in the market area follow a different set of rules than appraisers and the assessor's measurement of gross living area is the only source available for that data, you should adjust the assessor's measurements to compensate for any differences from the calculations used by other appraisers in the market. In other words, be sure to always compare "apples to apples." If the assessor's numbers have to be adjusted, you must explain the rationale to avoid being accused of altering the facts to the client's advantage. Remember that if an appraisal reviewer reads the report with assessor's numbers that have been adjusted, the reviewer may not know why that was done or may assume something nefarious. It is important to note any adjustments to ensure the reviewer understands.

The following measures are commonly used throughout the real estate industry:

- gross living area
- gross building area
- gross leasable area

Gross living area (GLA) is commonly used to describe the size of residential properties. This measurement is made by measuring the outside walls of the dwelling with a tape measure. GLA only includes the floors that are completely above the grade level of the site.

In most cases, any part of the floor area that is below grade is considered basement area. This rule causes much consternation among brokers, owners, and casual market observers because they want to consider finished basements in the above-grade area. In most markets, a finished basement costs less to build than above-grade living area; this doesn't necessarily mean that a finished basement is worthless, just that it is not as valuable as the above-grade area. Some appraisers are pressured to make their reports conform to a set of standard guidelines and are reluctant to adjust an adequate amount for basements. As a result, they undervalue this feature to stay within perceived "guidelines."

For example, an appraiser working for a residential lender adjusts more than 15% on a net basis or 25% on a gross (absolute numbers) basis. The appraiser is likely to be asked to explain why the adjustment is so large. An appraiser expecting a query for an adjustment of that size may erroneously underestimate the value of basements to avoid conflict with the lender's guidelines.

Gross living area is always finished area and is heated and cooled in most markets. To be included in gross living area, finished living area must have a ceiling height of at least 7 feet except in the following areas:

- areas under ceiling beams, HVAC duct work, and other obstructions (with an absolute minimum of at least 6 feet 4 inches)
- areas under stairways
- areas in rooms where the ceiling is sloped

At least one-half of the finished area in that room must have a vertical ceiling height of at least 7 feet, and no portion of the finished area that has a height of less than 5 feet may be included in this finished square footage. This exception applies to areas in which the ceiling slopes down to the floor. Only part of this area is usable and recognized by the market, so it must be treated differently.

Areas that cannot be included in GLA include the following:

- openings to the floor below (except for the area of both stair treads and landings proceeding to the floor below included in the finished area.)
- garages and other unfinished areas
- porches, patios, decks, and other similar areas that are not enclosed or suitable for year-round occupancy

Gross building area (GBA) is used in commercial, industrial, and multifamily properties. In most markets, GBA is the total building area including the walls, but the method used to calculate this amount can vary from market to market.

A common method of calculating gross building area in office buildings is to measure to the outside finished surface of the permanent outer building walls without any deductions. Unlike gross living area, which does not include below-grade living area, all enclosed floors of the building—including basements, mechanical equipment floors, penthouses, and the like—are included in the gross building area measurement of office buildings. Parking spaces and parking garages are generally excluded. Again, that does not mean parking areas have no value, simply that they are classified differently.

Gross leasable area (GLA) is used in shopping centers and in some markets for office buildings to measure the total floor area for which tenants pay rent. In some office buildings, GLA includes a pro rata share of common areas, which allows a landlord to lease the hallways and common areas when the building is leased to several tenants on the same floor. GLA can include basements and mezzanines, and it is commonly measured from the center of interior partitioning to outside wall surfaces.

Context is usually sufficient to indicate whether the acronym *GLA* refers to gross living area or gross leasable area.

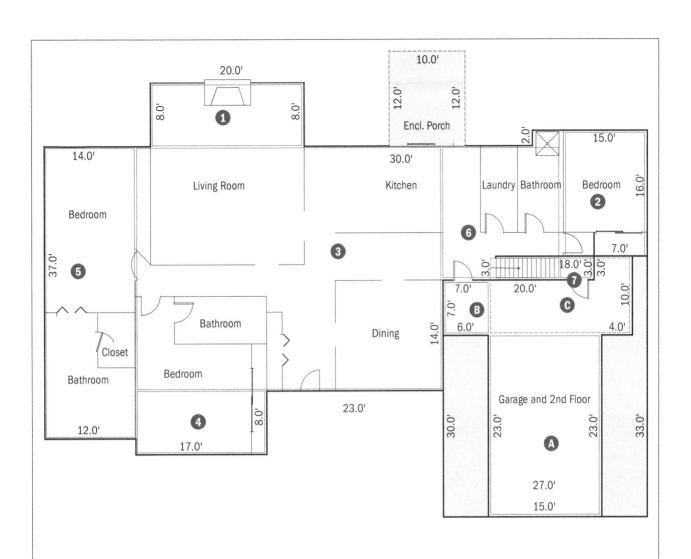

Area Calculation Summary

Code	Description	Size
GLA1	First Floor	2448.00
GLA2	Second Floor	574.00
P / P	Porch	120.00
GAR	Garage	831.00
	TOTAL LIVABLE (rounded)	3022

Living Area Breakdown

Breakdown				Subtotal
First Floor				
①	8.0	×	20.0	160.00
②	15.0	×	16.0	240.00
③	31.0	×	40.0	1240.00
④	8.0	×	17.0	136.00
⑤	12.0	×	37.0	444.00
⑥	12.0	×	17.0	204.00
⑦	3.0	×	8.0	24.00
Second Floor				
Ⓐ	15.0	×	23.0	345.00
Ⓑ	7.0	×	7.0	49.00
Ⓒ	10.0	×	18.0	180.00

Substructure

The substructure is the part of the building that is below ground level and supports the remainder of the improvements above ground level. Weather and soil conditions in different geographical regions affect the type of substructure construction. From an appraiser's perspective, this part of the building is difficult to inspect because it is all underground. If the structure has a basement, the substructure may be visible from the interior.

The typical substructure of a building can be very different from one area of the country to another. It is common for buildings to have basements with concrete walls in some areas while monolithic slabs are much more common in other areas. In some parts of the country, wood foundations are found, and still others may have houses built up on pedestals. Many foundation walls create a barrier from cold air to keep plumbing lines located below the first floor from freezing. In other words, these buildings are not on pedestals because of their plumbing.

Superstructure

The superstructure is the part of the building that is above ground level, and it is the area of emphasis in the building description of most appraisals.

Framing

Framing commonly refers to the structural portion of the building; it can be concrete block, brick, structural steel, wood frame, or some other material. Wood framing is the most popular construction method for houses, and steel beams are used in most nonresidential buildings. However, wood framing may not be practical in some areas because of termites. Local codes rather than owner preferences may regulate what can be built.

Insulation and Ventilation

Energy costs add significantly to the cost of property ownership. Modern builders focus on making building improvements more energy-efficient than they were in the past when energy costs were lower. Sealing up a building tightly promotes energy efficiency, but it can create new challenges

A building's substructure is visible during construction but hidden after construction is completed. The interior of a basement is usually the only portion visible to an appraiser on a site visit.

Light-gauge steel framing is lighter and more dimensionally stable than wood framing, but it conducts more heat and requires more energy to manufacture. Prepunched holes allow piping, wiring, and bridging straps to pass through the framing members.

such as ventilation problems, mold growth, and rot of structural members. Adding insulation is usually a straightforward procedure, but it too can be problematic in certain types of construction.

Because many people visit commercial, industrial, and other types of buildings over the course of a day, good ventilation is important. Hotel banquet and meeting rooms may accommodate hundreds or even thousands of people in a single room, so air must be changed fairly briskly. Most large meeting rooms have high ceilings to increase the air volume for that reason. Commercial buildings with completely closed air systems can have many serious problems including sick building syndrome and rot. Mold has also become a major issue in recent years. Correcting mold problems can be costly and complicated.

Exterior Walls and Doors
The high cost of energy has made well-insulated and draft-free doors and walls an important part of the energy equation. Air locks, which are two sets of doors, are commonly seen in commercial

buildings and some residential structures. Air locks are designed to limit the amount of cold air flowing into the building during the winter. Revolving doors in commercial buildings serve the same purpose. In hurricane-prone areas, door standards include a minimum requirement for withstanding the impact of high winds.

Windows, Storm Windows, and Screens
Again, energy efficiency dictates that modern windows have two or three panes of glass and tight sealing mechanisms for opening and closing. Some older structures can be made more energy-efficient by adding exterior mounted storm windows over older single-pane glass. Windows are fixed in most nonresidential properties for security purposes and to prevent outside air from entering in cases such as an employee forgetting to close a window and leaving it open overnight.

Facade
A building's facade is an external wall covering of construction material (e.g., brick, stone, vinyl) or

a veneer that is usually nonstructural. A decorative facade, such as synthetic stucco, is often used to update old buildings.

Roof and Drainage System

Most properties need a drainage plan to remove rainwater efficiently. It is an important part of an appraiser's job to recognize a drainage problem relating to a building and, more importantly, a site. Appraisers often find drainage problems next to a property's foundation because the soil has settled in the area that was excavated to build the structure. Drainage problems can cause or aggravate wet basements or crawl spaces and can be seen when the ground, driveway, or parking area tapers toward the structure rather than away from it.

An example of a designed drainage system is the roof on the structure itself. A residence with a steep roof pitch will have great drainage while a roof with a low pitch will drain more slowly. A steep roof is more expensive to build and has been recognized in most markets as a design attribute. The weight of snow is a factor for all roof designs in many markets where snowfall is appreciable.

Roofing on nonresidential buildings varies from asphalt shingles to a slightly elevated mopped asphalt surface. Steel, aluminum, or other materials are used to cover roofs.

Chimneys, Stacks, and Vents

Many new homes have gas-fueled fireplaces with metal-lined flues instead of masonry chimneys. Roof vents are required in most modern homes and buildings to allow the heat and humidity buildup to escape in attic areas. In some climates, attics have moisture problems so severe that they require power ventilation. Also, ventilation can be an issue for office buidlings because the population density can be significant in some intense uses.

Description of Interior Materials and Design

Interior descriptions can be more important than exterior descriptions to clients who will occupy the property or rent space to tenants whose first concern is interior finishes. The condition of the walls, floor coverings, and trim are significant factors to many buyers and renters because they are most noticeable.

Interior Walls, Partitions, and Doors

Walls, partitions, and doors are similar in most houses, but in nonresidential properties they can vary substantially depending on use, building codes, and other requirements. The least expensive finish in a building is an open room. The most expensive finish is substantial partitioning with many doors and windows. Interior finishes of wallpaper, wood paneling, and other materials can also influence value.

Interior Supports

In many appraisals assignments, the client may propose moving interior walls, which may not be physically possible or financially feasible. If a wall supports an upper level or roof structure, moving it can be very expensive. In commercial buildings, especially in office markets where open floor plans are popular, the ability to move interior walls can be critical to a property's marketability. For example, an old school building with concrete block load-bearing walls will probably not sell for as much as one convertible to an open-span layout because of the lack of flexibility. As another example, a racquetball facility with 10 courts may or may not be feasible for other uses depending on the ability to move the demising walls.

Beams, Columns, and Trusses

Beams, columns, and trusses are interior support features that allow buildings to be clear span or have required interior supports. In many properties, the location of the columns is a major design factor and inhibits some uses.

Flooring System

Flooring systems vary by construction type. Some flooring systems are wood over 2-by-10s, but many structures have steel or wood trusses. Buildings can also have a concrete-over-steel floor structure or poured concrete over gravel on grade.

Ceilings

Ceilings come in various styles, finishes, and construction quality levels. Some retail properties have unfinished ceilings but others have extensive ceiling finishes. In houses, ceilings can cover a myriad of systems and features. In commercial properties, the space between the finished ceiling and the floor above may also house the air returns for the HVAC system. The quality of ceiling finishes affects value.

Stairs, Ramps, Elevators, Escalators, and Hoists

Stairs, ramps, elevators, escalators, and hoists are used to make multistory structures efficient. In some markets, buildings with more than a certain number of floors must have elevators. In other markets, buildings without elevators are not worth much less than those with elevators. An offsetting cost of maintenance is associated with these assets. The cost of maintaining an elevator can be thousands of dollars per year. Older elevators can also have Americans with Disabilities Act (ADA) issues.

Painting, Decorating, and Finishing
Painting, decorating, and finishing may be the least expensive items of construction, but they can have the most significant impact on value. In many cases, decorating and interior finishing may be the most memorable part of the buyer's inspection process and therefore the most significant part of that party's decision-making process. The wrong color paint on a wall may displease a buyer and inhibit a sale despite the relatively low cost of changing the color.

Protection Against Decay and Insect Damage
Some properties are susceptible to insect or rodent infestation, which can cause serious damage. In some markets, appraisers are asked to comment on the existence of termite infestation and damage. Appraisers who do not find or report these problems expose themselves to civil lawsuits. (This is not to say that an appraiser need be a qualified expert in finding insect infestation and damage but only that an appraiser should report it if it is seen.) Unfortunately, some properties that are especially susceptible to termite damage are the most difficult to inspect. Wood floor joists in a house with a short crawl space may be very close to the soil and thereby much more prone to termite damage. Inspecting the floor joists in a short crawl space can be difficult or impossible if access is limited and lighting is poor. Buildings with basements are usually easier to inspect for termites unless the basement has permanent interior finishing, which can make it impossible to inspect the substructure without causing damage. Like doctors, appraisers try to "do no harm" when conducting site visits.

Miscellaneous and Special Features
All buildings have unique features, and some special features can set a property apart from its competition. In houses, these features may include central vacuum systems, in-home stereo systems, wireless Internet capability, special kitchen appliances, and cabinetry. Commercial properties may have extra HVAC or security equipment. Special handlers, rail siding, cooler or freezer space, and overhead doors may be found in industrial properties.

In markets where the typical buyer is an owner-occupant, a special feature may contribute substantially to value, but in a slightly different market where the owners are investors, the same feature may be worthless. For example, a private bathroom in an industrial building may be valuable in a market where the typical buyer of that type of facility is the owner of the company that would occupy the building, but a private bath-

---

Green Building and Sustainability

The green building movement has gained momentum and flourished despite the economic downturn that began in 2008. Perhaps one reason for the movement's popularity is its focus not only on reducing the unnecessary usage of environmental resources such as water and the harmful byproducts of certain forms of power generation but also on cutting operating expenses, which is of immediate benefit to property owners.

Because real estate has such a large effect on the economy, the concept of *sustainability* has become important in the industry. As the term applies to real estate, *sustainability* generally refers to development that meets current needs without compromising the ability to meet future needs. Green building is the most widely recognized way to further the goal of sustainability. The concepts of *green building* and *sustainability* are still relatively new to real estate appraisers, and the terms do not have definitions that are universally agreed upon. However, professional standards for green building like the Leadership in Energy and Environmental Design (LEED) standards developed by the US Green Building Council are seen increasingly in new construction.

Measuring the effectiveness of green or sustainable building efforts and describing the effect of new building materials and construction techniques can be challenging. The six most common and significant green building practices relate to the site, water, energy efficiency, indoor air quality, materials, and operations and maintenance, and those areas are often the focus of an appraiser's investigation of the effect of green building principles on value.

Energy Efficiency and the Whole Building Approach
An important part of the green building movement is the "whole building approach," which looks at all the functional components of a building as a single system. This improves on the traditional approach of separately installed mechanical systems in a building that operate independently of, and sometimes counterproductively to, each other. Two important design concepts of the whole building approach are *front-end loading*, which involves preconstruction planning and teamwork, and *end-use/least-cost considerations*, which focus on creating the desired end use of a product at the lowest possible cost to the involved parties as well as to the environment.

room would not be of much additional value in a market where the typical industrial real estate owner is an investor leasing the property to a real estate manager of a large corporation.

Personal Property

Any non-realty components of the subject property, also classified as furniture, fixtures, and equipment (or FF&E), should be identified by the appraiser during the site visit, and the appraisal report should specify if personal property is included in the ownership interest being valued. In some situations involving litigation, case and statutory laws may apply to personal property.

Some property types are more likely to include personal property. For example, a bakery's ovens, a restaurant's refrigerators and freezers, or a gym's exercise machines would all fall under the category of personal property.

Some property that would normally be considered "fixed" in design and therefore classified as real estate might be considered trade fixtures in leased property and therefore not included in an appraisal of the leased fee interest. It is important to clarify what is included in the appraisal and what class of asset best describes it--real estate, personal property, intangible asset, or trade fixture. This is a large issue now for lenders who do not want to make a loan for 20 years on an asset that may be portable and may not be part of the property in the event of foreclosure.

Equipment and Mechanical Systems

Plumbing System

Plumbing systems can vary in quality and quantity from property to property. The quality of plumbing can be a significant indication of the overall quality of the improvement. Some property owners spend 20% of the total cost of construction on plumbing lines and fixtures. In some properties, plumbing can be added easily, such as when a structure is built over a crawl space. However, structures on slab floors may need substantial alterations for installing new discharge lines, which are usually installed below the floors. New plumbing systems installed in buildings today can facilitate repairs and inflow controls much better.

Heating, Ventilation, and Air-Conditioning Systems

Heating, ventilation, and air-conditioning (HVAC) systems differ from property to property and can vary greatly in cost. In low-cost industrial buildings, hanging space heaters may suffice. Some expensive commercial buildings and homes may have constant recirculating hot water systems with forced-air cooling, but in some low-cost homes HVAC is limited. Typically, more expensive systems yield more efficient outputs. When analyzing HVAC systems, you should take into account the trade-off between the cost of the item and the cost of operation.

Electrical Systems

The necessary capacity of an electrical system depends largely on the use of the property. Modern buildings have extensive electrical connections. Appraisers are often asked to comment on electrical capacity (amperage) and the adequacy and condition of electrical service, especially in residential properties. Giving this kind of advice can

The electrical system can be one of the most complicated components in a structure. Appraisers may need special training to be able to identify potential problems in an electrical system. Determining the adequacy of a building's electrical service may require more than simply inspecting the panelboard in the basement.

be risky for an appraiser who has only minimal training in this area of construction.

The most significant issue for electrical systems in older buildings is the lack of capacity. An older building may have a 300-ampere service, but the uses require an 800-ampere service. Tenants may use or install systems that draw 20 amperes for a single circuit, which will overload a 15-amp system, causing the circuit breaker to open and turn the power off. Installing additional power lines is usually a complicated process.

Miscellaneous Equipment

Specialized equipment can take many forms, from central vacuum systems in houses to special alarms and security systems in commercial properties. When evaluating a property with special equipment, you must decide if the feature will be fully recognized in the market. A low-cost residential property with a five-car garage is not likely to return the replacement cost of the over-sized garage upon resale. The amount returned to the seller depends on the typical buyer's market expectations. Property owners always assume that because they liked some feature enough to buy it, others will be willing to pay for it as well.

Analysis of Architectural Style and Functional Utility

Style and design that are considered acceptable today may not be acceptable tomorrow. A building design can be functional but not acceptable in the market because of changing architectural fashions. On the other hand, some designs are attractive but not buildable. Architects are responsible for designing buildings that are not only attractive but also use space efficiently and have reasonably low maintenance and construction costs. The best designs are a combination of the efforts of the architect, builder, broker, and owner because each person gives valuable input into the final product.

Architectural Style

The wide range of architectural styles can be classified into two distinct types:

1. Formal architecture, which follows historical patterns and is easily identified by people with formal training
2. Vernacular architecture, which is local in style and emphasizes function over form

Vernacular architectural styles are characteristic of low-cost and sometimes low-quality improvements such as the house on the left. Efficient construction techniques and broad appeal in the marketplace drive the development of vernacular building. Formal architecture, on the other hand, tends to be evident in more expensive properties such as the house on the right. In formal architecture, aesthetic concerns tend to outweigh efficiency, particularly when architectural detail is a defining characteristic of the desired building style.

Functional Utility

Functional utility is the ability of a building to be used for its intended purpose. The use must be acceptable to the market for the property to be functionally efficient. A property can be designed well for a non-market use and still have functional obsolescence because there is no market for it. For example, a racquetball club facility may be perfectly designed for that use, but the resale market for that use is likely to be negligible if the business cannot turn a profit. The building may not be usable for anything but storage because of the fixed walls in small intervals.

Design and Functional Utility by Property Type

Residential

Functional utility in residential properties is a moving target. What is popular today will most likely not be popular in a decade. Designers are always trying to move standards in one direction or another. Lifestyles change, and housing adapts to these trends. In many markets, a new house with a one-car garage may have been marketable 30 years ago, but it is probably not marketable now. A house without air-conditioning in the southern part of the United States would have been marketable 40 years ago, but not now. The best way to research market preferences is to interview local brokers, builders, buyers, and especially salespeople involved with model homes. Salespeople of model homes are actually seeing firsthand what people want and more importantly what they are willing to pay for. Often, the easiest way to stay in touch with the preferences of buyers is to join and participate in a local real estate board or association.

Because housing standards differ depending on region and consumer income levels, appraisers must analyze standard expectations for each particular market. However, residences have generally improved over time. Abundant closet space, appliances such as dishwashers and garbage disposals, larger and more elaborately furnished kitchens and baths, and master bedrooms with spa tubs are popular in new housing. Multiple bathrooms are also popular, even in smaller apartments and condominium units.

Commercial

Functional utility for commercial properties is best measured against new construction designs. If you want to know what the market wants, you generally need only look at what is currently being built. Market requirements for different types of commercial properties vary with use. Overall, the efficiency of commercial construction has increased greatly over time. This is evident in new building materials and methods, structural improvements, and increased total enclosed areas, which leads to higher rental income.

Functional utility in shopping centers may include issues like parking adequacy and design, common area design, support by anchor stores, access points, and common area draw. Visibility, access, and attractiveness are significant considerations. A parking lot configuration that leads all the tenants to the anchor is good for the anchor but inhibits other tenants. A well-trained security force may be very expensive but required to obtain the desired customers. In some areas, auto theft at malls is common.

Trends in shopping centers are constantly changing. Some popular trends today are retail centers anchored by big-box stores with a larger number of smaller anchors and lifestyle centers aimed at attracting high-income customers.

Office buildings have completely different requirements. In most offices, visibility and easy access are less important than office efficiency issues such as elevators, security, parking, and the amount of bathrooms and windows. Office buildings can also have HVAC issues because of the increasing heat load created by computers and other electronic equipment. Although changes in trends for office buildings occur more slowly than for other types of commercial properties, flexibility has generally become an important factor in an office building's desirability. Older buildings must be able to accommodate updates in heating, cooling, and wiring to stay competitive, and newer buildings do better in the market if they are able to accommodate tenants' needs for expansion.

Hotels are sensitive to changes in the market standards of both commercial and residential properties. Hotels used to be open to the outside, but in recent years most owners have enclosed external walkways so guests can check in without going outside. ADA compliance and room size are significant issues for older hotels. Many hotels also offer food and beverage service and some have meeting rooms, which bring in another set of design criteria. Some new hotels are attached to shopping malls and chain restaurants, and some are even part of office plazas or tech parks.

Appraisers need to consider the mix of uses when analyzing a hotel's functional utility.

A hotel must be oriented to the needs of its particular set of patrons. Resort hotels must provide options for entertainment and recreation, while motels need only cater to the needs of guests who spend most of their time elsewhere. Extended-stay hotels offer more private space and amenities, while conference centers have larger lobbies, restaurants, and meeting spaces.

Industrial

Industrial properties have unique requirements. Manufacturing plants have significant issues with building designs because different operations require different building configurations. A manufacturer of snow shovels will have different plant requirements than a manufacturer of computers. In some cases, refrigerator or freezer space is important, while manufacturing operations, electrical capacity, or natural gas service may be the most important factor in other cases.

The appraiser is more concerned about the desirability of a feature to the potential buyer than its importance to the current owner. For example, a manufacturer of injection-molded plastic products needs many overhead conveyors, but there is no resale market for this facility to another manufacturer of similar products, which are no longer being manufactured in the area. The appraiser thinks this building will have a highest and best use as storage, in which case the existence of the conveyor system, although significant to the current owner, adds nothing to the market value. In fact, removal of the conveyor system might be a significant expense affecting market value.

Warehousing, storage, and distribution facilities have different requirements than manufacturing facilities because the former are focused on the movement of finished goods in and out of the facility. Easy access to tractor-trailers or railroad cars is much more important than the interior process. Ceiling heights may be a big issue for buyers of this type of property because of storage needs.

When appraising any improved industrial property, you must ask, "Is there going to be a market for this property in this configuration, or will it have to be adapted to a broader market in order to find a buyer?" The highest and best use of a manufacturing plant built around specialized equipment may be to remove all the specialized equipment because there is no resale market for the improvements as is.

Generally, newer one-story, square-shaped buildings with high ceilings are the most flexible, efficient, cost-effective, and therefore most desirable type of industrial building. Buildings and plants with specialized designs and uses have fewer potential users, while buildings used for light manufacturing and processing are more desirable in the wider market. Good access is a primary locational consideration for all types of industrial buildings.

Buildings on Agricultural Properties

Buildings on agricultural properties can also require special design features and have significant functional utility issues when their specialized equipment is not marketable. Special wiring and plumbing may be required for milking processes, and special troughs or plumbing may be required for confined feeding operations.

In many markets, the modern farm no longer conforms to the stereotype of a large tract of land with big, open buildings. The current trend in farming has been moving away from larger numbers of small, family-owned farms and moving toward smaller numbers of larger, business-owned farms with increasingly specialized operations and equipment needs. The number of agricultural buildings per acre of land and the contribution of farm buildings to total farm value have also decreased.

Special-Purpose Buildings

Special-purpose buildings are found in all markets. Facilities like car dealerships, funeral homes, schools, churches, breweries, and bowling alleys have specialized designs and limited markets. Some special-purpose properties have a resale market, but many times the appraiser must identify another use. Buyers will be able to use some special-purpose properties "as is." However, in many markets these buildings must be reconfigured to make them marketable, and appraisers must compensate for that cost. Because conversion to another use is not always economically feasible, the highest and best use of many special-purpose properties (such as sports stadiums) may be to remove the improvements.

The appraiser must consider if there is still demand for the use for which the property was originally constructed, and if so, whether the property can compete with other properties designed for that same use. Overall attractiveness and structural support are also important considerations.

The adaptive-use movement works to preserve nonfunctional, special-purpose buildings that are architecturally significant and possibly find new uses for them. For example, Dearborn Station, a now-defunct historic train depot in downtown Chicago, currently houses retail uses, including a restaurant and bar.

Mixed-Use Buildings
Mixed-use buildings have a combination of two or more uses on one site or in one building, such as apartments above a retail store or a branch bank inside an office building. These properties also beg the question, "Will there be a market for this property with this combination of uses?" Depending on the situation, mixed-use properties may or may not be marketable, profitable, or attractive to buyers.

Mixed-use properties require extensive planning in order to successfully combine compatible uses. Because each intended use comes with its own design criteria, appraisers must analyze the separate uses individually and consider the structure as a whole to determine if the uses have been integrated successfully. Mixed-use buildings are often characterized by multiple stories connected by escalators and elevators, multiple entranceways, central courtyards or galleries, and interconnecting pedestrian thoroughfares that provide access to parking facilities.

Quality and Condition Survey
Appraisers use the term *quality* to describe the cost, durability, and efficiency of an element of construction or the entire property. The term is almost always applied in comparisons of properties that compete with the subject property. This means that a building is not compared to all buildings in a community, only to buildings it competes for buyers with. A manufactured home that competes with other manufactured homes would have "average" construction quality within that market segment. Similarly, if a mansion with top-quality features and appointments competes in a market with other homes of similar quality, it is considered to be of "average" quality within its market segment.

Appraisers use the term *condition* to describe the amount of wear and tear a property has endured. Condition is also a relative term. It is quite possible for a good-quality home to be in fair or poor condition or a fair-quality home to be in good condition. A 75-year-old building that has had typical maintenance for its market segment but still needs a little work is considered to be in "average" condition because it is the same as most homes it competes with. A home that has

had impeccable maintenance levels and meets the standards of its high-end market is also considered to be in "average" condition. The ratings are relative, so most appraisers compare the condition of the subject property to the properties it competes with.

Fannie Mae and Freddie Mac have instituted a new system of rating quality and condition. The UAD standard no longer compares the subject property with competing properties, which results in many properties being labeled *average*. The new system compares the subject improvement to all residential properties with a detailed description of the ratings Q1 to Q5 and C1 to C5, as shown in Exhibit 13.2.

Items in Need of Immediate Repair
Items in need of immediate repair are often factored into sale prices. These are treated differently in the sales comparison approach because in the minds of buyers these problems are not examples of deferred maintenance but have to be addressed immediately to make the property marketable.

Many appraisers mistakenly label items or properties as "good" quality or being in "good" condition when in fact those items are comparable to competing properties and therefore should be rated only "average" for that market. Keep in mind that if most properties in a market area are well-maintained, then a property with no obvious deferred maintenance is in average condition for that market.

Green Building Documentation

In valuation analyses for green properties, appraisers may want to include special documentation of the quality of green construction from sources such as

· third-party ratings and certifications (from LEED, ENERGY STAR, the EPA, etc.)

· commissioning reports

· indoor air quality assessments

· site evaluations of ecosystem health, functionality, and services

· lease agreements and other documentation of income adjustments

· incentives, including tax abatements, that may offset additional "green" costs

· modeled operating data (for proposed buildings)

· post-occupancy evaluations (for properties that are at least one year old)

· technical specifications of the benefits of particular systems and their cost estimates (for existing or proposed buildings)

C1: The improvements have been recently constructed and have not been previously occupied. The entire structure and all components are new and the dwelling features no physical depreciation.

> Note: Newly constructed improvements that feature recycled or previously used materials and/or components can be considered new dwellings provided that the dwelling is placed on a 100 percent new foundation and the recycled materials and the recycled components have been rehabilitated/remanufactured into like-new condition. Improvements that have not been previously occupied are not considered "new" if they have any significant physical depreciation (that is, newly constructed dwellings that have been vacant for an extended period of time without adequate maintenance or upkeep).

C2: The improvements feature no deferred maintenance, little or no physical depreciation, and require no repairs. Virtually all building components are new or have been recently repaired, refinished, or rehabilitated. All outdated components and finishes have been updated and/or replaced with components that meet current standards. Dwellings in this category are either almost new or have been recently completely renovated and are similar in condition to new construction.

> Note: The improvements represent a relatively new property that is well maintained with no deferred maintenance and little or no physical depreciation, or an older property that has been recently completely renovated.

C3: The improvements are well maintained and feature limited physical depreciation due to normal wear and tear. Some components, but not every major building component, may be updated or recently rehabilitated. The structure has been well maintained.

> Note: The improvement is in its first-cycle of replacing short-lived building components (appliances, floor coverings, HVAC, etc.) and is being well maintained. Its estimated effective age is less than its actual age. It also may reflect a property in which the majority of short-lived building components have been replaced but not to the level of a complete renovation.

C4: The improvements feature some minor deferred maintenance and physical deterioration due to normal wear and tear. The dwelling has been adequately maintained and requires only minimal repairs to building components/mechanical systems and cosmetic repairs. All major building components have been adequately maintained and are functionally adequate.

> Note: The estimated effective age may be close to or equal to its actual age. It reflects a property in which some of the short-lived building components have been replaced, and some short-lived building components are at or near the end of their physical life expectancy; however, they still function adequately. Most minor repairs have been addressed on an ongoing basis resulting in an adequately maintained property.

C5: The improvements feature obvious deferred maintenance and are in need of some significant repairs. Some building components need repairs, rehabilitation, or updating. The functional utility and overall livability are somewhat diminished due to condition, but the dwelling remains useable and functional as a residence.

> Note: Some significant repairs are needed to the improvements due to the lack of adequate maintenance. It reflects a property in which many of its short-lived building components are at the end of or have exceeded their physical life expectancy but remain functional.

C6: The improvements have substantial damage or deferred maintenance with deficiencies or defects that are severe enough to affect the safety, soundness, or structural integrity of the improvements. The improvements are in need of substantial repairs and rehabilitation, including many or most major components.

> Note: Substantial repairs are needed to the improvements due to the lack of adequate maintenance or property damage. It reflects a property with conditions severe enough to affect the safety, soundness, or structural integrity of the improvements.

Quality Ratings and Definitions

Q1: Dwellings with this quality rating are usually unique structures that are individually designed by an architect for a specified user. Such residences typically are constructed from detailed architectural plans and specifications and feature an exceptionally high level of workmanship and exceptionally high-grade materials throughout the interior and exterior of the structure. The design features exceptionally high-quality exterior refinements and ornamentation, and exceptionally high-quality interior refinements. The workmanship, materials, and finishes throughout the dwelling are of exceptionally high quality.

Q2: Dwellings with this quality rating are often custom designed for construction on an individual property owner's site. However, dwellings in this quality grade are also found in high-quality tract developments featuring residences constructed from individual plans or from highly modified or upgraded plans. The design features detailed, high-quality exterior ornamentation, high-quality interior refinements, and detail. The workmanship, materials, and finishes throughout the dwelling are generally of high or very high quality.

Q3: Dwellings with this quality rating are residences of higher quality built from individual or readily available designer plans in above-standard residential tract developments or on an individual property owner's site. The design includes significant exterior ornamentation and interiors that are well finished. The workmanship exceeds acceptable standards and many materials and finishes throughout the dwelling have been upgraded from "stock" standards.

Q4: Dwellings with this quality rating meet or exceed the requirements of applicable building codes. Standard or modified standard building plans are utilized and the design includes adequate fenestration and some exterior ornamentation and interior refinements. Materials, workmanship, finish, and equipment are of stock or builder grade and may feature some upgrades.

Q5: Dwellings with this quality rating feature economy of construction and basic functionality as main considerations. Such dwellings feature a plain design using readily available or basic floor plans featuring minimal fenestration and basic finishes with minimal exterior ornamentation and limited interior detail. These dwellings meet minimum building codes and are constructed with inexpensive, stock materials with limited refinements and upgrades.

Q6: Dwellings with this quality rating are of basic quality and lower cost; some may not be suitable for year-round occupancy. Such dwellings are often built with simple plans or without plans, often utilizing the lowest quality building materials. Such dwellings are often built or expanded by persons who are professionally unskilled or possess only minimal construction skills. Electrical, plumbing, and other mechanical systems and equipment may be minimal or non-existent. Older dwellings may feature one or more substandard or non-conforming additions to the original structure.

Definitions of Not Updated, Updated, and Remodeled

Not Updated

Little or no updating or modernization. This description includes, but is not limited to, new homes.

Residential properties of fifteen years of age or less often reflect an original condition with no updating, if no major components have been replaced or updated. Those over fifteen years of age are also considered not updated if the appliances, fixtures, and finishes are predominantly dated. An area that is 'Not Updated' may still be well maintained and fully functional, and this rating does not necessarily imply deferred maintenance or physical/functional deterioration.

Updated

The area of the home has been modified to meet current market expectations. These modifications are limited in terms of both scope and cost.

An updated area of the home should have an improved look and feel, or functional utility. Changes that constitute updates include refurbishment and/or replacing components to meet existing market expectations. Updates do *not* include significant alterations to the existing structure.

Remodeled

Significant finish and/or structural changes have been made that increase utility and appeal through complete replacement and/or expansion.

A remodeled area reflects fundamental changes that include multiple alterations. These alterations may include some or all of the following: replacement of a major component (cabinet(s), bathtub, or bathroom tile), relocation of plumbing/gas fixtures/appliances, significant structural alterations (relocating walls, and/or the addition of square footage). This would include a complete gutting and rebuild.

Source: UAD Field-Specific Standardization Requirements (Document Version 1.4), pp. 35-37. Available online at https://www.fanniemae.com/content/technology_requirements/ uad standardization-requirements.pdf/.

Short-lived Items

Some items of deferred maintenance may be curable (i.e., repairable), but the repairs may not be financially feasible on the date of appraisal. In other words, the items may still have value at the present time and do not need to be replaced just yet. A property owner would expect to replace a short-lived item at least once over the course of the building's life. The appraiser can estimate whether a short-lived item needs to be replaced by comparing the cost of any repairs with the possible increase in value. For example, carpeting in an office building might exhibit some wear and tear but may still have a few years of life left, and replacing the carpet at the present time may not add more value (through higher rental rates or a higher sale price) than the cost of installing the carpet.

Long-lived Items

In contrast to short-lived items, long-lived items are expected to last the full life of the building, so they are not likely to be repaired or replaced unless some major defect is present. Again, the appraiser may determine that the necessary repairs to correct damage to a long-lived item may not be financially feasible. This would be an example of incurable physical deterioration, which is discussed in Chapter 29.

1. *Gross leasable area* is
   a) Commonly used in retail centers
   b) Commonly used in residential properties
   c) Commonly used in industrial properties
   d) Commonly used in apartments

2. *Terra-cotta* is
   a) Hard-burned unglazed clay, usually molded into shapes for the ornamentation of structures
   b) A foundation built of locally mined stone
   c) A type of electrical service
   d) A green mold that forms on the top of chimneys

3. What is the size of the building shown here?

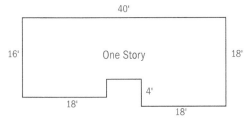

   a) 485 square feet
   b) 668 square feet
   c) 672 square feet
   d) 725 square feet

4. What is the size of the area shown here?

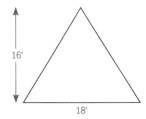

   a) 288 square feet
   b) 144 square feet
   c) 576 square feet
   d) 725 square feet

5. *Gunite* is
   a) Pneumatically placed concrete usually associated with in-ground pools
   b) A type of insulating material
   c) A type of roof shingle
   d) Part of a staircase

6. *Romex* is
   a) A type of window blind
   b) A type of wiring
   c) A type of asphalt
   d) A type of tile

7. A *jalousie* is
   a) A type of window with several window panes
   b) A type of furnace
   c) A type of wood framing
   d) A type of earthen dam

8. *Gross living area* is
   a) Commonly used in retail centers
   b) Commonly used in residential properties
   c) Commonly used in industrial properties
   d) Commonly used in apartments

9. *Superstructure* refers to
   a) The area of a building above grade
   b) The area of a building that is not needed to meet minimum standards
   c) Land that is not needed to support the existing improvement
   d) An overimprovement

10. Short-lived items do *not* include
    a) Interior paint
    b) Roof covering
    c) Water heater
    d) Structural steel

11. *Footings* are
    a) The layout of a building's ground floor
    b) Below the frost line in most buildings
    c) The foundation walls of a structure
    d) Usually the same thickness as the framing walls

12. *Gutters* are
    a) Construction workers specializing in demolition
    b) Designed to trap water on the roof to keep if off the heads of the property's inhabitants
    c) Only needed in special-purpose properties
    d) Designed to channel water away from the building's foundation

13. *Eaves* are
    a) The portion of a roof projecting beyond the vertical wall of the building
    b) The part of the floor system that is under the framing
    c) The lowest part of the foundation
    d) The top of the roof at its highest point

14. *HVAC* is an acronym for
    a) High, vacant, and cold
    b) Heating, ventilation, and air-conditioning
    c) Hot, vertical, and cramped
    d) Heating, ventilation, and cooling

15. *Functional inutility* is
    a) A weak market segment
    b) An impairment of the functional capacity of a property or building
    c) The lack of a utility room in a house
    d) A weak market due to the oversupply of homes

16. A *baluster* is
    a) A railed platform that projects from the face of a building above the ground level
    b) One of the closely spaced vertical members in a stairway or balcony
    c) The fabric top in a curtain that is usually located on kitchen windows
    d) A weak or insignificant performance by an appraiser or other real estate professional

17. A *casement window* is
    a) A vertically hinged window that opens like a door
    b) A horizontally hinged window that opens from the bottom to shed water
    c) A shaded window that is designed to prevent criminals from "casing the joint"
    d) A window that does not open at all

18. *Ceiling joists* are
    a) The structural members that the ceiling is attached to
    b) The structural members that the roof shingles and underlayment are attached to
    c) The boards that the gutters are attached to
    d) The steel supports for the first floor that run to the basement

19. *Clapboard* is
    a) A type of wood siding
    b) A place to put dishes and other kitchen utensils
    c) A place in a house where the ironing board is usually stored
    d) A type of roofing material

20. *Brick* is
    a) A natural material that is used only in building houses
    b) Made of clay and baked
    c) A natural material found in the earth that is cut into small pieces
    d) A construction item that holds up the residence and is used for structural strength in modern housing

21. *Coping* is
    a) A type of power saw used to crosscut logs
    b) A small run of caulk around the front door
    c) The space between bricks that is filled with mortar
    d) The masonry cap put on a wall to provide for watershed

22. A small building used to manufacture saw blades is an example of
    a) Commercial land use
    b) Industrial land use
    c) Residential land use
    d) Special-purpose land use

Note: Unless otherwise noted, italicized references indicate the pages In *The Appraisal of Real Estate*, 14th edition, that readers should consult for additional discussion of these topics.

1. a) **Commonly used in retail centers**
    Page 225

2. a) **Hard-burned unglazed clay, usually molded into shapes for the ornamentation of structures**

3. b) **668 square feet**

4. b) **144 square feet**

5. a) **Pneumatically placed concrete usually associated with in-ground pools**

6. b) **A type of wiring**

7. a) **A type of window with several window panes**
    Page 233

8. b) **Commonly used in residential properties**
    Page 225

9. a) **The area of a building above grade**
    Page 229

10. d) **Structural steel**
    Pages 272-274

11. b) **Below the frost line in most buildings**
    Page 229

12. d) **Designed to channel water away from the building's foundation**
    Page 237

13. a) **The portion of a roof projecting beyond the vertical wall of the building**
    Page 237

14. b) **Heating, ventilating, and air-conditioning**
    Page 248

15. b) **An impairment of the functional capacity of a property or building**
    Page 259

16. b) **One of the closely spaced vertical members in a stairway or balcony**

17. a) **A vertically hinged window that opens like a door**
    Page 236

18. a) **The structural members that the ceiling is attached to**

19. a) **A type of wood siding**

20. b) **Made of clay and baked**

21. d) **The masonry cap put on a wall to provide for watershed**

22. b) **Industrial land use**
    Pages 223-224

14

Statistical Analysis in Appraisal

Once upon a time, data was difficult to compile, analyze, and present. However, the unstoppable advance of information technology has changed this. Data is uniformly stored electronically now and computers and software are inexpensive. Statistical analysis of large amounts of data is used as a tool in many professions, from medicine to rocket science and beyond. Like any tool, statistical analysis works best in the hands of a trained professional who knows how to use the tool properly.

In appraisal, statistical analysis is the process of transforming raw data into information that helps an appraiser solve a problem related to value. The use of statistical analysis in a specific assignment is often a function of the scope of work. In other words, the problem the appraiser is trying to solve can often determine the type of statistical analysis that needs to be used. A complex appraisal assignment may require complex statistical analysis such as regression modeling in contrast to the straightforward data gathering and basic analysis of a typical appraisal for mortgage lending.

What Is Data?

From the legal description and other identifying characteristics of the subject property provided by the client to the market information about transactions involving comparable properties collected by an appraiser, the data appraisers routinely deal with in the appraisal process comes in many flavors. In the broadest terms, data is either qualitative or quantitative in nature. That is, it describes or it measures (although it can also do both).

Data can be placed in a hierarchy as follows:

1. Nominal
2. Ordinal
3. Interval
4. Ratio

Nominal data simply provides a name for some phenomenon. For example, architectural styles like *Georgian, Victorian,* or *Prairie Style* are all labels that distinguish between various properties but serve no other function on their own. However, ordinal data, such as ratings of construction quality like *poor, fair, average,* or *good,* can be ordered. That data both labels the construction quality and provides an ordered comparison or relative quality. Interval data, on the other hand, is ordinal with intervals that are mathematically meaningful, like the dates of construction of comparable properties. A building completed in 2010 is three years older than a building completed in

KEY TERMS	
automated valuation model (AVM)	normal curve
	parameter
central limit theorem	qualitative data
coefficient of variation	quantitative data
confidence interval	range
descriptive statistics	regression analysis
geometric mean	sample
inferential statistics	skewness
interquartile range	standard deviation
mean	statistics
median	variance
mode	

2013. Ratio data is the most useful in statistical applications because it is meaningful on its own. That is, interval data like a building's completion date of 2011 is only meaningful when compared with other interval data (e.g., another property's completion date of 2009). On the other hand, ratio data like a gross building area of 100,000 square feet is relevant because its scale starts at 0 square feet with each square foot traveled along that scale differentiating the size of the building by a measurable amount from the 0 point.

Appraisers use data of all four levels in their analyses, and in that way statistics permeates the familiar valuation process.

Populations and Samples

In statistics, the term *population* refers to all possible items that could be included in a data set, while *sample* refers to the finite group of items that actually are a part of a data set. For example, if an appraiser is interested in the market value of 100,000-sq.-ft. warehouses in Akron, Ohio, then all of the 100,000-sq.-ft. warehouses in Akron would make up the population. However, if the appraiser only has access to a dozen 100,000-sq.-ft. warehouses in that market, then those dozen warehouses would make up the sample.

A *parameter* describes a characteristic of the population, such as the mean value of all 100,000-sq.-ft. warehouses in Akron. Sometimes it is feasible to research a population parameter (such as the mean market value of all the 100,000-sq.-ft. warehouses in Akron) and sometimes it is not (such as the mean market value of all the 100,000-sq.-ft. warehouses in North America). When the population parameter is not known, it is estimated. In contrast to a population parameter, a *statistic* describes the characteristics of a sample data set and is therefore a known and verifiable measure.

Descriptive statistics are used to describe overall patterns in the data, such as the average of the data, the exact middle of the range of numbers, or the most frequent number. These are called *measures of central tendency*. Descriptive statistics are not used to draw any conclusions about future trends in the data or in other data sets. Descriptive statistics simply make the patterns in the data easier to understand. In other words, descriptive statistics *describe* the data rather than analyze it.

Inferential statistics, in contrast, involve the use of mathematical analyses, many based on probability theory, to make "inferences" or educated guesses about unknown trends or patterns in the data. For example, if an appraiser uses statistical software to examine a data sample of 100,000 houses in North America, that appraiser can calculate the average or mean price for the houses in that data set. The mean describes the data. Based on the sample and its implicit relationship to the larger population, the appraiser can then *infer* a mean value for all houses in North America, applying the descriptive statistics from the sample to the analysis of the population as a whole.

Measures of Central Tendency

The ability to draw conclusions from large quantities of data can make inferences more credible, but this predictive power does not come without problems. It is important to know what the assets and liabilities of the basic statistical measures are.

Median

The *median* is the middle value in a data set that has been organized as an ordered array from highest to lowest or vice versa. The median can be meaningful if the data set has extreme values that would affect the relevance of the other measures of central tendency as a description of the data set.

Arithmetic Mean

The arithmetic mean is the most commonly cited measure of central tendency. The mean is the sum of the values divided by the number of observations, or what most people consider the "simple average."

One problem with the mean is that it is influenced by extreme values in the data set. In those situations, the median is a better indicator of central tendency. For example, the mean of the data presented in Exhibit 14.1 is nearly $218,000, but the median is $213,000. In this case, the median is a more accurate description of the data set. When the "outlier" value of $265,000 is taken out of the calculation, the mean of the sample is approximately $215,000. This is closer to the median than the mean because the median only counts the $265,000 as one more piece of data.

Geometric Mean

The geometric mean is simply a different approach to calculating an average, i.e., the nth root of the product of n data elements rather than the sum of n data elements divided by n. As an example, the geometric mean of the data set in Exhibit 14.1 is $217,198, close to the arithmetic mean. This measure is often useful when analyzing amounts that are compounded over time, such as financial returns. The geometric mean of the data set {2, 4, 6, 8} is 4.426728 because $\sqrt[4]{(2 \times 4 \times 6 \times 8)} = 4.26728$, or $2 \times 4 \times 6 \times 8 = 384$ and then $384^{1/4} = 4.26728$.

Mode

The *mode* is the most frequent value in the data set. A data set can have more than one mode because two (or more) different values may have the same number of occurrences. The mode may be meaningful in some applications, but it is not often a relevant measure of central tendency in real estate analysis in which the individual values within a data set may be correlated to some factor other than central tendency (see Exhibit 14.2).

Measures of Dispersion

Measures of dispersion describe how much variation there is between elements of a data set. They include

- standard deviation
- variance
- coefficient of variation
- range

If data is graphed with each value along the horizontal axis and the frequency with which it occurs in the data set along the vertical axis and the data values cluster closely around the mean,

then there is little variability in the data (see Exhibit 14.3). If, in contrast, the data points are spread out away from the mean, there is a high degree of variability in the data (see Exhibit 14.4).

Exhibits 14.3 and 14.4 are both examples of normally distributed data in which the mean, median, and mode are all the same value. In this case, the value is 10. The difference between the two graphs is the variance, or the degree to which the data is spread out. In Exhibit 14.3, the data is distributed between the values of 5 and 15, while in Exhibit 14.4 the data is distributed between the values of 0 and 20. The wide distribution in the latter flattens the curve and spreads out the data.

Standard Deviation and Variance

The variance of a data set is a mathematical formula that calculates how large the differences between the values are. Standard deviation and variance are closely related. This relationship between the standard deviation and the variance is largely a matter of mathematical convenience. In order to have a positive value for the variance (which is necessary for some of the more complicated statistical tests), the differences between the values in the data set are squared to calculate the variance. However, in order to make this measure of dispersion more useful, the square root of the variance (the standard deviation) is used more often because it is directly comparable to the mean.

Exhibit 14.1	Measures of Central Tendency	
1	$199,900	
2	$200,000	
3	$205,000	
4	$205,000	
5	$206,800	
6	$209,000	
7	$211,000	
8	$213,000	← Median
9	$215,900	
10	$220,000	
11	$225,000	
12	$228,000	
13	$231,000	
14	$232,000	
15	$265,000	
	$217,773	← Mean
	$205,000	← Mode

Exhibit 14.2	Bimodal Data Set	
1	$356,900	
2	$400,000	
3	$420,000	
4	$420,000	
5	$427,200	
6	$436,000	
7	$444,000	
8	$452,000	← Median
9	$463,600	
10	$480,000	
11	$500,000	
12	$500,000	
13	$524,000	
14	$528,000	
15	$660,000	
	$467,447	← Mean
	$420,000	← Mode
	$500,000	←

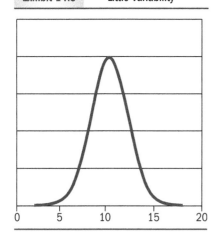

Exhibit 14.3   Little Variability

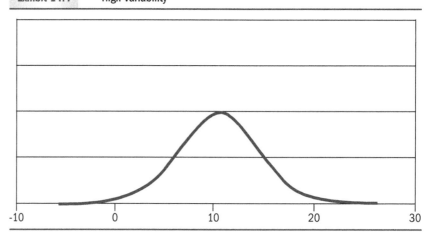

Exhibit 14.4   High Variability

Exhibit 14.5 lists some comparable sales taken from a retail market. Some of the details of the sales are listed, and the data is arrayed in order of price. The standard deviation of the sample data is $102,864, with a mean sale price of $1,078,887.

When data is normally distributed, such as in Exhibits 14.3 and 14.4, 67% of the data falls within one standard deviation either above or below the mean. In Exhibit 14.5, the prices of 67% of the properties fall between $976,023 and $1,181,751.

Coefficient of Variation

The coefficient of variation helps determine what data is relevant and what data is not. In the sale price distribution table, the mean value line on its own does not describe which unit of comparison the market is using. In the standard deviation line, the dollar value is not conclusive because it has to be compared to the value of the mean. That is, looking at the standard deviation does not usually show the unit of comparison that is most closely aligned with the mean.

Dividing the standard deviation by the mean results in a percentage that makes standard deviation proportional and therefore meaningful. The coefficient of variation (COV) line in Exhibit 14.5 suggests that the price per square foot of gross leasable area may be the best statistical indicator of what the market is doing because it follows the pattern so well.

Range

The concept of the *range* of a data set is quite simple. The range is simply the difference between the largest and the smallest data values. In Exhibit 14.5, the sale prices range from $925,000 to $1,325,000. While there is a very obvious relationship between the amount of variability and the range of a data

set, keep in mind that one "outlier," or extreme data value, can artificially inflate the range of a data set and make this value particularly misleading.

Interquartile Range

A range is often divided into quarters. The first quartile is the midpoint between the smallest data value and the median. Logically, the second quartile is the median itself. Finally, the third quartile is the value that is the midpoint between the median and the largest data value.

The data between the first and third quartile is the closest to the median. If an analyst said that the range from the first and third quartile was $1,001,250 to $1,154,000, this would describe the range of data closest to the median. The range between the first and third quartile is called the *interquartile range* or the *midspread,* and it is also a measure of statistical dispersion.

Measures of Shape

To use inferential statistics, a set of assumptions needs to be made about the data, the most crucial of which is the normality assumption. Statisticians have found that if a data set violates this assumption, any inferences drawn from statistical analysis of that data is likely to be unreliable. A *normal curve* is a symmetrical distribution in which the mean and median are the same. Exhibits 14.3 and 14.4 shown earlier in this chapter are examples of normal curves.

The normal distribution is found in many different fields of science. Because of its ubiquity, many statistical procedures assume that the normal distribution is the underlying distribution of the data set being analyzed by that statistic. In

the median (Q2)
the upper quartile (Q3)
the largest observation (Q4)

Exhibit 14.5	Sale Price Distribution		
Sale	Sale Price	Gross Leasable Area	Price/Sq. Ft. GLA
1	$925,000	10,500	$88.10
2	$936,500	10,605	$88.31
3	$950,000	10,710	$88.70
4	$959,500	10,815	$88.72
5	$967,000	10,925	$88.51
6	$975,000	10,925	$89.24
7	$983,500	11,035	$89.13
8	$1,000,000	11,145	$89.73
9	$1,002,500	11,150	$89.91
10	$1,008,000	11,255	$89.56
11	$1,013,500	11,155	$90.86
12	$1,020,000	11,245	$90.71
13	$1,035,000	10,450	$99.04
14	$1,045,000	10,775	$96.98
15	$1,058,500	11,000	$96.23
16	$1,065,000	11,045	$96.42
17	$1,068,500	11,250	$94.98
18	$1,075,000	11,955	$89.92
19	$1,100,000	12,075	$91.10
20	$1,111,500	12,195	$91.14
21	$1,125,000	12,315	$91.35
22	$1,145,000	12,250	$93.47
23	$1,153,000	12,565	$91.76
24	$1,155,000	12,500	$92.40
25	$1,181,500	12,815	$92.20
26	$1,192,000	13,150	$90.65
27	$1,200,000	12,945	$92.70
28	$1,205,000	13,005	$92.66
29	$1,215,000	13,075	$92.93
30	$1,250,000	13,205	$94.66
31	$1,325,000	13,995	$94.68
Mean	$1,078,887	11,743	$91.83
Std. Dev.	102863.964	989.6479	2.848513
COV	9.53%	8.427625%	3.10%
SD of Pop.	101191.268	973.555	2.802193

Using the data in Exhibit 14.5, the box and whisker plot shows

- the mean: $1,078,887
- the median: $1,065,000
- the minimum: $925,000
- the maximum: $1,325,000
- Quartile 1: $1,001,250
- Quartile 3: $1,154,000

The first piece of information available from a box plot is the position of the mean and median in relation to each other. Recall that in a normal distribution, the mean and the median are the same value. In Exhibit 14.6, the mean is slightly larger than the median, which may be problematic for the assumption of normality. The range of data can be seen by looking at the two endpoints of the whiskers, which also gives a clue as to the extent of the range in the data.

Finally, a box and whisker plot indicates if the data is skewed or if there is more data at either the left or right end of the distribution than would be expected in a normal distribution. In Exhibit 14.6, the data skews slightly to the right. This skewness is shown by two characteristics of the graphic:

1. The mean is greater than (i.e., to the right of) the median.
2. The difference between the maximum value and the third quartile ($34,400) is considerably greater than the difference between the minimum value and the first quartile ($15,000).

fact, almost any large data set is likely to form a normal distribution when graphed.

One useful graphic is a *box and whisker plot,* which is a graphical representation of the variability in the data. Whether or not data is normally distributed can be determined by using the five-number summary of a box and whisker plot, which includes

- the smallest observation
- the first quartile (Q1)

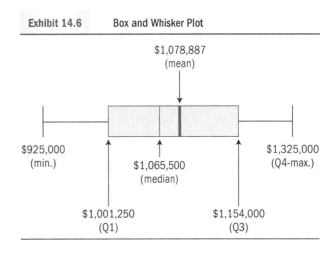

Exhibit 14.6   Box and Whisker Plot

$1,078,887
(mean)

$925,000
(min.)

$1,065,500
(median)

$1,325,000
(Q4-max.)

$1,001,250
(Q1)

$1,154,000
(Q3)

There is a possibility that the data is not normally distributed, and appropriate statistical tests need to be performed to determine if the data is normal.

Frequency and Percentage Distributions

Box and whisker plots are a useful way to determine the distribution of data. They can be drawn quickly by hand and do not require any complex calculations. However, an alternative and sometimes more informative way to determine the shape of a distribution is to plot the data in a histogram. To draw a histogram, the numerical data is converted into categorical data at the desired level of detail, and categories defined by ranges of values are set up.

Exhibit 14.7 shows a data set of property prices that range from $180,000 to $250,000. This data can be categorized in $10,000 increments, counting the number of homes within each range. The price ranges are then presented as a histogram (Exhibit 14.8).

The shape of the histogram approximates the "bell curve" characteristics of the normal distribution. As previously noted, skewed data occurs when there are more data points at either the left or right

Exhibit 14.7	Categories	
Price	Number of Properties	Proportion of Total Observations
$180,000 to $190,000	1	0.04
$190,000 to $200,000	2	0.08
$200,000 to $210,000	5	0.20
$210,000 to $220,000	8	0.32
$220,000 to $230,000	5	0.20
$230,000 to $240,000	3	0.12
$240,000 to $250,000	1	0.04

Exhibit 14.8 Histogram

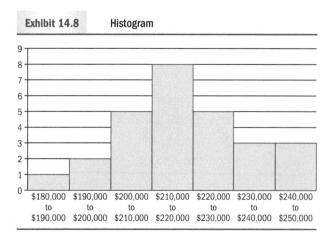

> *Kurtosis* refers to the "peakedness" of the data distribution. The normal distribution has a kurtosis of 3 (usually calculated by statistical software, rarely calculated by hand) and is moderately peaked. A distribution with a kurtosis higher than 3 is leptokurtic, and one with a kurtosis less than 3 is platykurtic. While skewness in data can be a real problem for statistical analysis, kurtosis is not usually a problem.

end of the distribution than would be expected in a normal distribution. On a histogram, skewed data looks lopsided, with either the left or the right side of the bell being elongated or distorted.

Skewness is also detectable using a descriptive statistic that takes into consideration the number of observations (n), the amount of variability (S), and the differences between the mean of the sample and each individual observation ($x_i - \bar{x}$):

$$Skewness = \frac{n}{(n-1)(n-2)} \sum \left(\frac{x_i - \bar{x}}{S} \right)^3$$

If the value obtained from the skewness calculation is close to zero, the data is not skewed. If the value is negative, the data is left (or negatively) skewed; if the value is positive, the data is right (or positively) skewed.

Central Limit Theorem and Inference

The central limit theorem states that regardless of the shape of the underlying population distribution, the distribution of a set of sample means drawn from a population will be approximately normal when the sample size is at least 30. In other words, even if the underlying population distribution is not "normal," a sufficiently large *sampling distribution of sample means* (i.e., computing a series of mean values calculated from samples taken from that population and then graphing those means) is normally distributed.

In most situations, 30 observations serve as a sufficiently large sample, and if the underlying distribution is symmetrical, a sample of 15 will do. There are several things to keep in mind, however, when considering the central limit theorem. First of all, to be as confident as possible about the inferences made, a sample of 30 is not always enough. The larger the sample size, the more confidence you can have in the inferences based on that sample. Second, sampling *from more than one population* is necessary in many situations, and the central limit theorem suggests that at least 30 observations from each population should be taken to form your sample. For instance, if you want to use statistical analysis to compare the sale prices of apartment buildings with a lake view to the prices of apartment buildings in the same city that are not near a lake, you would need a sample of 30 observations from each population, or at least 60 transactions.

Confidence Intervals and Sample Size

A *confidence interval* defines the degree of uncertainty associated with an inference. Confidence intervals make two assertions about the data:

1. The true value of a population measure falls within the range of values provided.
2. The degree of confidence in the first assertion can be set at a desired level.

The most common use of confidence intervals relates to the mean of a population, so that is used in the analysis of the data in Exhibit 14.9.

The sample mean for the sale price is $742,917 and the standard deviation of the population (as calculated using Microsoft Excel) is $63,921. Recall that the figures computed, while they are descriptive of the sample, are also used to make inferences about the underlying population. The calculation of the confidence interval involves the standard deviation, the sample size, and the desired level of confidence expressed as a percentage.

$$\text{Confidence Interval} = \bar{x} \pm t_{n-1}\frac{s}{\sqrt{n}}$$

Adding and subtracting that value from the sample mean creates a "window" that you can be confident the population mean falls within. For example, the 90% confidence interval (again, as calculated using Excel) around the mean price would be from $723,720.79 to $762,112.61, or a value of $19,195.91. (When the standard deviation of the population is not known, as is often the case, the calculations may involve statistics from what is known as the *student's t distribution,* which invokes the central limit theorem's assumption of normality.)

To increase the level of confidence (to 95%, for example), the confidence interval must be widened. In this example, the 95% confidence interval (22,873.34) yields a range from $720,043.36 to $765,790.04. Note that what is gained in "confidence" is lost in precision. The interval is getting larger and less useful as it becomes more certain that the population mean is in the "window." The dilemma then becomes how you can have a great deal of confidence that a population mean is in the interval without making the interval so wide that it is useless.

Exhibit 14.9	Confidence Interval	
Sale	Sale Price	GLA
1	$600,000	6,500
2	$650,000	7,000
3	$650,000	5,500
4	$660,000	6,000
5	$690,000	7,000
6	$700,000	7,500
7	$700,000	8,750
8	$700,000	7,750
9	$700,000	11,000
10	$710,000	8,500
11	$710,000	11,500
12	$720,000	9,000
13	$720,000	9,500
14	$720,000	9,000
15	$735,000	9,000
16	$745,000	10,000
17	$750,000	10,000
18	$750,000	9,500
19	$752,500	10,000
20	$760,000	10,250
21	$760,000	10,500
22	$790,000	12,000
23	$795,000	12,000
24	$800,000	13,000
25	$810,000	13,000
26	$810,000	12,000
27	$840,000	13,500
28	$850,000	15,500
29	$850,000	15,000
30	$860,000	14,500
Mean	$742,916.70	10,141.67
Std. dev.	$65,013.54	2,664.165
COV	8.75%	26.27%
Std. dev. of pop.	63,920.8	2,619.386
90% Con. Int.	19,195.91	786.6219

Increasing the number of observations in a sample will increase confidence without increasing the interval. Given a desired confidence level, you can calculate the number of observations that should be taken from the population in order to meet these criteria. However, one thing to keep in mind when calculating sample size is that the more variability there is in a population (i.e., the more the data is dispersed), the more observations will be needed in the sample. If it is known that the population is variable, it is best to err on the safe side and use as large a sample as possible.

Regression Analysis

The most common statistical technique used in the analysis of real estate markets is regression analysis. The ability of regression analysis to account for single or multiple value influences in an equation makes it a flexible tool for a variety of valuation applications when an adequate amount of data is available.

Simple Linear Regression

One of the most useful statistical relationships is a *correlation*. Simply put, a correlation is a linear relationship between two variables. It is possible to graph the relationship between the variables with a straight line and, if the correlation is high, make predictions about other unknown data points based on that line. For example, one straightforward and simple relationship in real estate appraisal is that sale price often increases in a linear fashion as the gross leasable area (GLA) of a property increases. Given enough data, you can compute the correlation between the size of a set of properties and their sale prices and then graph that relationship.

Suppose you need to know approximately how much an office property with 10,500 square feet of GLA is worth. Using Exhibit 14.10 (which contains data from Exhibit 14.7), locate 10,500 on the *x*-axis

Exhibit 14.10   Regression Line

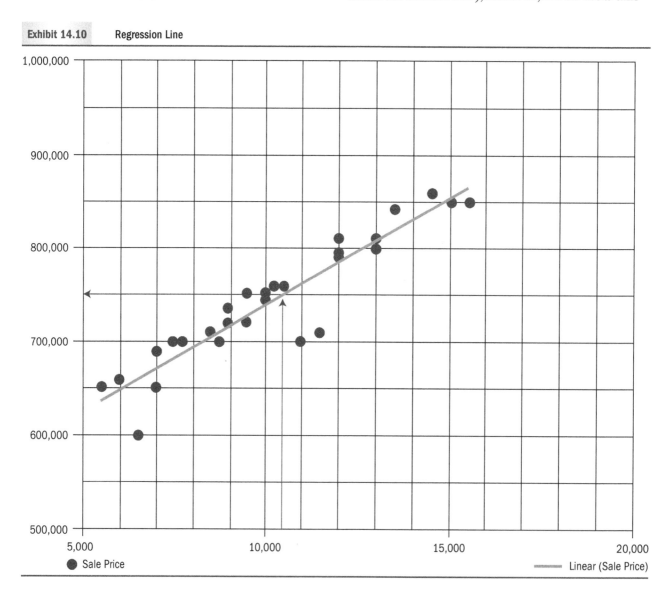

● Sale Price   ━━━━ Linear (Sale Price)

and then find the point on the correlation line where 10,500 falls. Run a line from the point of intersection to the y-axis to find the accompanying sale price. This graph suggests that an office property of this size would be worth approximately $750,000.

The formula for simple linear regression is

$$Y = a + b x + e$$

where Y is the monetary value of the property, or the dependent variable. The coefficient b is the slope of the regression line. The slope of a line is a numerical reflection of the linear relationship between the independent and dependent variables. The variable x in the equation is the independent variable (in this case, a gross leasable area of 10,500 square feet), and a is the y-intercept of the regression line. Finally, e is an error term reflecting the amount of variability in the regression line, which can be seen in the vertical distance between the data points and the regression line as it is drawn.

In many cases, simply plotting the data will give a good idea of whether or not a correlational relationship exists between two variables. If the points on a scatter plot are clustered together roughly forming a line, a significant correlation probably exists. Sometimes, however, the plotted data looks like a cloud of random dots with any number of possible regression lines of differing slopes, all of which look more or less reasonable. In these instances, you are better served using a statistical program such as Minitab, the Statistical Package for the Social Sciences (SPSS), or Statistical Analysis Software (SAS) to make predictions. These programs will give you a t-statistic that indicates whether the line drawn by the statistical package is a reliable description of the relationship between the two variables. In most cases, a t-value over 2 is good, but it is always best to consult a statistics textbook or similar resource to see if the value obtained is significant.

Exhibit 14.11	Regression Analysis Output

Regression Analysis: C2 versus C1

The regression equation is

C2 = 512694 + 22.7 C1

Predictor	Coef	SE Coef	T	P
Constant	512694	17725	28.92	0.000
C1	22.701	1.692	13.41	0.000
S = 24278.7		R-Sq = 86.5%	R-Sq(adj) = 86.1%	

Multiple Linear Regression

A linear relationship between two variables such as gross leasable area and sale price is easy to understand and work with. However, many different variables could affect the price of a property, such as an urban versus a suburban location, access to a major road, or the presence (or absence) of an amenity such as a desirable view. If the value question requires more detailed analysis of specific value influences, it would be useful to include other variables in a statistical test like multiple linear regression that can sort out the relative contributions of each variable.

In many cases, the variables of interest are not continuous variables that can be expressed numerically (such as price, size, etc.). Instead, they are categorical variables that are expressed by categorical labels (such as "view" or "no view," "urban" or "suburban"). In these instances, appraisers use "dummy" variables, assigning numerical values to each variable (such as 1 = urban and 0 = suburban), so that a regression analysis can be performed. In this way, many variables that would have been left out of the statistical analysis can be included.

Multiple linear regression analysis involves large, complex statistical calculations. No one performs these calculations by hand. Fortunately, SAS, SPSS, and Minitab all have statistical applications that handle linear regression with ease. (Some forms of regression analysis are possible using Excel, but these applications require significant expertise in both statistical analysis and Excel.) Using these programs is easier than interpreting the output. In most cases, a series of t-statistics for each of the variables included in the regression is reported.

Statistical Applications in Appraisal Practice

Automated Valuation Models

Property tax assessors developed mass appraisal techniques to improve productivity given the large number of properties they needed to value and to ensure equitable taxation of those properties. Automated valuation models (AVMs) grew out of those mass appraisal practices, combining the use of neural network and expert knowledge with regression models.

Regression-based AVMs apply multiple regression models to produce a variety of measures including value-estimation equations, value estimates, adjustment coefficients, or a combination of these outputs. Although the appraisal community initially feared that AVMs would replace human appraisers by automating the valuation process, the most dire predictions have not come to pass. Currently, AVMs are most often used as underwriting devices and tools designed to assist human appraisers.

Custom Valuation Models

Custom valuation models make it possible for appraisers with statistical knowledge to use large data sets to model customized, unique valuation questions. Custom valuation models are difficult and expensive to set up, and appraisers should not try to design models outside of their areas of expertise and experience.

1. Extreme values in a data set have the greatest effect on
   a) The mean
   b) The median
   c) The mode
   d) The confidence interval

2. A statistic that describes a characteristic of a population is a
   a) Sample
   b) Variable
   c) Parameter
   d) Mean

3. Which of the following is *not* a measure of central tendency?
   a) Variance
   b) Mean
   c) Median
   d) Mode

4. Under which of the following circumstances is the mean most amenable to statistical inference?
   a) When the sample data includes values at each extreme
   b) When the sample data includes values at one extreme
   c) When the sample data for values cannot be estimated reliably
   d) When the sample data for values is quite large

Note: Review Exercises 5-9 refer to the same data.

5. Which of the following series of property values represents an ordered array of data?
   a) $375,000; $355,000; $350,000; $325,000; $319,000; $310,000
   b) $310,000; $319,000; $325,000; $350,000; $355,000; $375,000
   c) Both a and b
   d) Neither a nor b

6. Based on the sample data set of property prices shown in Question 5, which of the following prices would be the mean?
   a) $340,000
   b) $350,000
   c) $337,500
   d) $339,000

7. Based on the same sample data set of property prices, which of the following would be the median?
   a) $337,500
   b) $342,500
   c) $325,000
   d) $340,000

8. The mode for the sample of property prices cannot be determined for which of the following reasons?
   a) There are not enough observation values in the data set.
   b) No value occurs more than once in the array.
   c) It cannot be derived from an even number of observation values.
   d) It is never used as a measure of central tendency relating to property prices.

9. The *range* for this data set of property prices is
   a) $50,000
   b) $56,000
   c) $65,000
   d) $75,000

10. Which of the following is *not* an illustration of the distribution of a data set?
    a) Scatter diagram
    b) Box and whisker plot
    c) Bell curve
    d) Histogram

11. A normally distributed population that shows no skewness would be represented best as a(n)
    a) Bell curve
    b) Measure of central tendency
    c) Scatter diagram
    d) Automated valuation model

12. Appraisers might use custom valuation models to apply statistics to each of the following situations *except*
    a) To perform property tax assessment and equity studies
    b) For price or rent trend analysis
    c) To produce and review descriptive statistics by user-defined property characteristics
    d) To prepare value estimates for litigation

13. What is the difference between descriptive statistics and inferential statistics?

    a) Descriptive statistics are always reported in graphic form while inferential statistics are always reported in tabular form.

    b) Inferential statistics support conclusions about the population data while descriptive statistics only reflect the characteristics of the sample data set.

    c) Unlike descriptive statistics, inferential statistics cannot be used in the analysis of historical data.

    d) Descriptive statistics include the measures of central tendency and variance, while inferential statistics include linear regression coefficients and *t*-statistics.

14. What are the mean, median, and modes of the data sample?

    a) Mean: $123,500   Median: $122,500   Mode: $122,000

    b) Mean: $123,143   Median: $122,500   Mode: $122,500

    c) Mean: $123,143   Median: $123,250   Mode: $122,500

    d) Mean: $123,500   Median: $123,250   Mode: $122,500

15. What is the standard deviation of the sample?

    a) 2,423

    b) 2,657

    c) 2,870

    d) 2,515

16. Which measure of central tendency best represents the most probable selling price of the subject property?

    a) Mean

    b) Median

    c) Mode

    d) None of the above

17. What are the mean, median, and mode sale price?

    a) Mean: $345,499   Median: $344,250   Mode: $338,000

    b) Mean: $336,700   Median: $342,250   Mode: $338,000

    c) Mean: $345,595   Median: $345,595   Mode: $338,000

    d) Mean: $346,181   Median: $346,000   Mode: $338,000

18. What is the sample standard deviation of sale price?

    a) 9,941

    b) 10,604

    c) 9,610

    d) 10,111

Review Exercises 14-16 refer to the following data.

A two-bedroom condominium unit located in a large, established residential development is offered for sale on the open market. The two-bedroom units in the development are all similar and subject to the same common area charges. In this development, 14 two-bedroom units have been resold recently or placed under agreement for resale at prices ranging from $120,000 to $127,000. Arranged in an array, the sale prices are as follows:

$120,000
$120,000
$120,000
$120,500
$122,500
$122,500
$122,500
$122,500
$124,000
$124,000
$126,000
$126,000
$126,500
$127,000

Price variance is generally attributed to interior finish and fixtures. The subject property is considered typical.

Review Exercises 17-19 refer to the following data.

In the Southern Hills market area, 12 small office properties sold in the past year. Sale prices were

Sale Price	Date
$335,400	9 months ago
$357,200	3 months ago
$338,000	12 months ago
$329,990	10 months ago
$358,500	4 months ago
$342,500	8 months ago
$346,000	7 months ago
$336,400	9 months ago
$361,200	2 months ago
$354,300	4 months ago
$348,500	5 months ago
$338,000	7 months ago

19. What is the range and interquartile range?

    a) Range: 2,600   Interquartile range: 1,300

    b) Range: 31,200   Interquartile range: 15,600

    c) Range: 31,200   Interquartile range: 17,425

    d) Range: 31,200   Interquartile range: 18,550

20. Using simple linear regression, what is the correct equation relating monthly rent to apartment living area in square feet for two-bedroom, two-bath units in complexes of 100 units or more?

    a) $Y = -805 + 3.3\,(x) - 0.01\,(x^2)$

    b) $Y = 750 + 0.24\,(x)$

    c) $Y = 343 + 0.6\,(x)$

    d) $Y = -332 + 1.4\,(x)$

21. Using the regression model, what is the estimated monthly rent for an 840-sq.-ft. apartment in this market?

    a) $829

    b) $839

    c) $845

    d) $850

22. What are the mean and median monthly rents per square foot of living area?

    a) Mean: $835.00   Median: $835.00

    b) Mean: $833.00   Median: $835.00

    c) Mean: $835.50   Median: $837.50

    d) Mean: $835.33   Median: $835.00

23. What is the coefficient of variation of rent per square foot for this rent sample?

    a) 3.84

    b) 30

    c) 21.01

    d) 2.51

24. In statistical terminology, the term *population* refers to

    a) The residents of a community in a given real estate market

    b) The total number of residents responding to a market survey

    c) The complete data set used in the statistical analysis

    d) The complete data set from which the sample data set is derived

Review Exercises 20-24 refer to the following data.

A sample of 30 two-bedroom, two-bath apartment units in complexes containing 100 or more units shows the following monthly rents and unit living areas in square feet.

Rent	GLA in Sq. Ft.
$825	800
$840	850
$830	800
$850	840
$850	860
$820	810
$825	800
$850	855
$850	860
$825	810
$860	850
$875	880
$875	920
$825	810
$850	840
$820	800
$800	790
$855	860
$845	860
$860	880
$840	840
$815	820
$810	820
$810	815
$810	800
$820	810
$820	820
$850	870
$855	860
$800	790

25. Among the factors that affect the accuracy of an inference are
    a) Population size
    b) Sample size and the degree to which the sample reflects the population
    c) The confidence interval of the distribution
    d) The assumption of normality of the data set

26. The median is calculated by
    a) Totaling the values of all observations and dividing the sum by the sample size
    b) Finding the middle value of the ordered array of data values
    c) Adding the lowest and highest values and dividing by 2
    d) Finding the most frequently appearing value in the data set

27. Of the three measures of central tendency, the least practical for making inferences is
    a) The mean
    b) The median
    c) The mode
    d) All three measures are equally practical

28. Which measure of dispersion is the best indicator of which of two data sets is more variable?
    a) The standard deviation
    b) The coefficient of variance
    c) The skewness
    d) The range

29. In a normal distribution, which measures of central tendency are equal?
    a) The mean and median
    b) The mean and mode
    c) The median and mode
    d) All three

30. When a data set is left skewed,
    a) The mean will be greater than the median
    b) The mean will be less than the mode
    c) The range will remain normal
    d) The variance will decrease

31. Automated valuation models (AVMs) are currently perceived as a technology designed to
    a) Replace human appraisers
    b) Help appraisers increase efficiency and cut costs
    c) Help homeowners set listing prices
    d) All of the above

Note: Unless otherwise noted, italicized references indicate the pages in *The Appraisal of Real Estate*, 14th edition, that readers should consult for additional discussion of these topics.

1. a) The mean
    Page 280

2. c) Parameter
    Page 278

3. a) Variance
    Pages 280-283

4. a) When the sample data includes values at each extreme
    Page 280

5. c) Both a and b
    Page 280

6. d) $339,000
    Pages 280-281

7. a) $337,500
    Pages 280-281

8. b) No value occurs more than once in the array.
    Page 281

9. c) $65,000
    Page 286

10. c) Bell curve
    Page 279

11. a) Bell curve
    Page 287

12. c) To produce and review descriptive statistics by user-defined property characteristics
    Page 298

13. b) Inferential statistics support conclusions about the population data while descriptive statistics only reflect the characteristics of the sample data set.
    Page 276

14. b) Mean: $123,143   Median: $122,500   Mode: $122,500

15. d) 2,515

16. a) Mean

17. a) Mean: $345,499   Median: $344,250   Mode: $338,000

18. b) 10,604

19. c) Range: 31,200   Interquartile range: 17,425

20. c) $Y = 343 + 0.6 (x)$

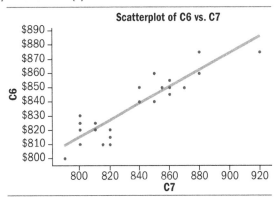

21. **b) $839**

$Y = 343 + 0.59\ (x)$

$ = 343 + 0.59\ (840)$

$ = 838.60$

22. **d) Mean: $835.33**   **Median: $835.00**

23. **d) 2.51**

$COV = [SD\ /\ Mean] \times 100\%$

$ = [21.01/835.33] \times 100\%$

$ = 2.51\%$

24. **d) The complete data set from which the sample data set is derived**

Page 278

25. **b) Sample size and the degree to which the sample reflects the population**

Page 279

26. **b) Finding the middle value of the ordered array of data values**

Page 280

27. **c) The mode**

Page 281

28. **b) The coefficient of variance**

Pages 285-286

29. **a) The mean and median**

Page 287

30. **a) The mean will be greater than the median**

Page 288

31. **b) Help appraisers increase efficiency and cut costs**

Pages 296-298

15

Market Analysis

Market analysis is the portion of the valuation process in which the appraiser develops an opinion about the current and near future supply and demand factors that affect the market for the subject property. Any imbalance in supply and demand should be reflected in comparable sales or leases of existing properties, if they are current. However, if the market has changed recently, older sales will not provide evidence of this change, so market analysis becomes doubly important. New construction may or may not reflect current supply and demand factors because proposed construction affects supply. Adding the purchase price of the land to the cost of constructing a building is not considered a value indication of a comparable sale but could serve as a land comparable and a construction cost comparable.

Market analysis is a necessary first step in highest and best use analysis. You may find a use that will command a higher price than another use. However, if that use is oversupplied and not marketable on the effective date of appraisal, it will not be the highest and best use. An alternative use may be the highest and best use because it is marketable at that time. A higher price in the future may be worth less than a lower price today because money in the future is usually worth less than the same amount of money available today.

Consider a four-acre property located on a busy street with significant redevelopment potential for a commercial-retail use. However, the site is currently improved with a small 16-unit apartment building. The retail market is currently oversupplied and is estimated to remain that way for five more years. The only sales of commercial land in this market are to speculators at about $2 per square foot (174,240 × $2 = $348,480). Prior to the oversupply in this market, land similar to the subject would sell for $10 per square foot (174,240 × $10 = $1,742,400). The apartment complex has 16 units that rent for $1,000 per month on average, there is a 5% vacancy and collection loss, expenses are 32% of effective gross income, and reserves for replacement should be about $10,000 per year.

Market Analysis in the Approaches to Value

Market analysis is used in the cost approach to support any market conditions adjustments to land comparables, estimate any external (economic) obsolescence, and support an estimate of entrepreneurial incentive. If the market is significantly out of balance, external obsolescence (a form of depreciation) will occur. If the market is oversupplied, the property will not sell for as much as it should (based on cost).

In general, an analysis of the current market is needed to explain trends in price levels. More specifically, market analysis is used in the sales comparison approach to support market conditions (time) adjustments. If a market is oversupplied but has corrected itself, the market conditions adjustment may have to be adjusted. Market analysis may also have an influence on estimated marketing time.

Market analysis is used in the income capitalization approach to estimate market rents and expenses and extract capitalization rates from market data. Analysis of the rental market will also help with the estimation of vacancy rate trends.

KEY TERMS

active market	market disequilibrium
basic employment	market equilibrium
buyer's market	marketability study
depressed market	market study
fundamental demand	non-basic or service industries
inferred demand	seller's market
market analysis	weak market

The capitalization rate for an improved property like this is 8%. The taxes and maintenance on the vacant land would be $12,000 per year. The value of the apartments today to an apartment buyer would be $1,425,000, as shown in Exhibit 15.1

Exhibit 15.1	Valuation of Improved Property by the Income Capitalization Approach	
Potential gross income	15 @ $12,000 =	$192,000
Less vacancy and collection loss	-5% × $192,000 =	($9,600)
Effective gross income	=	$182,400
Less operating expenses	-32% × $182,400 =	($58,368
Reserves for capital replacements	=	($10,000)
Net operating income	=	$114,032
Conversion of income to value	$114,032 / 8% =	$1,425,000

At first look, the appraiser may think that the highest and best use is to remove the apartments and sell the land to a retail developer, but that ignores the oversupplied market. The speculators are only paying about $350,000 for land that used to be worth $1,740,000, which implies that they are requiring a 36% yield on the investment for their cost of funds, risk, and entrepreneurial incentive. The values are

Land value today =	$350,000
Improved property value today =	$1,425,000
Land value in the future =	$1,745,000

The highest and best use today is to maintain the apartments with the understanding that the highest and best use could change in the near future.

Market analysis is generally much easier to conduct for residential properties than for nonresidential properties because of the sophistication and organization of the residential data in MLS systems. Using a computer-based MLS system to retrieve the number of current listings, sales (within the past year), or pending sales in a specific market is easy and makes residential market analysis simple, fast, and able to be quite narrowly focused–e.g., four-bedroom homes with two-car garages located in a specific subdivision.

There are two general levels of market analysis within the appraisal profession:

1. A *market study*, which is the study of a broad market that does not focus on a specific property. This is a study of supply and demand for an entire product or service that is not limited to a specific market, price range, or geographic area, such as the study of one-unit homes in Blue Creek County.

2. A *marketability study*, which is the study of market conditions as they relate to a particular property type and price range, such as the study of supply and demand for 20- to 30-year-old, one-unit homes located in Anderson Township in Blue Creek County.

In formal usage, *market analysis* includes both *market studies* and *marketability studies*, while the latter terms are more useful as precise indicators of the nature of particular analyses. Informally, *market analysis* is the more commonly used term to encompass all levels of analysis.

A six-step process can be applied in most market analysis assignments. The scope of each step will vary with the requirements of the assignment, but the six steps shown in Exhibit 15.2 provide a good blueprint to follow for all levels of market analysis.

Foundations of Market Analysis for Real Estate

The meaningful study of real estate markets is impossible without an understanding of some fundamentals about the makeup and mechanics of markets.

Market Definition and Delineation

Markets can be identified in numerous ways:

- by property type (e.g., commercial, residential)
- by property features (e.g., basement, three-car garage)
- by market area (i.e., geographically)
- in terms of substitute properties (e.g., list price from $200,000 to $250,000, 10 to 15 years old)
- in terms of complementary properties (i.e., support facilities)

In every appraisal, you must decide who will buy the subject property, how much they will pay, and what their criteria are. You cannot estimate what a typical buyer will pay unless you know what the typical buyer wants, which means developing an opinion of market criteria for purchase or lease.

Demand

Demand is quick to react to market changes. If mortgage interest rates increase, the residential

Exhibit 15.2   The Six-Step Market Analysis Process

Step 1: Define the Product (Property Productivity Analysis)
First, the analyst surveys the assets of the subject property. Here the appraiser lists the features, attributes, and legal rights that will contribute to value.

Step 2: Market Delineation
Next, the analyst decides who the likely buyers for the subject are and what attributes would attract them. More than one type of buyer could be considered for some properties until the highest and best use is established. Many possible buyers may be considered, but the analyst tries to pinpoint who would ultimately pay the most.

Step 3: Demand Analysis
In the next step, the analyst investigates the current demand for the product. This step can be performed using historical data adjusted for antici-pated new construction and demolitions. Issues to consider include

· changes in population in the market segment

· changes in employment that will cause an influx or exodus of families

· changes in factors that may cause more participation in the market, such as lower interest rates increasing the demand for one-unit homes

Step 4: Supply Analysis (Survey and Forecast of Competition)
Next, the analyst estimates the number and size of properties that are currently competitive with the subject property—both existing and soon to be completed. For example, the number of new building permits filed can give an indication of changes in supply. Also, a review of sales of higher-priced homes can be an indication of a shift in supply. When sales of homes in the $400,000 to $450,000 price range increase, it can cause an increase in the supply of homes for sale in the $350,000 to $400,000 range. Buyers of the higher-priced homes will have to sell their existing houses to buy the nicer ones, putting more lower-priced homes on the market.

Step 5: Analyze the Interaction of Supply and Demand
In the fifth step, the analyst compares supply and demand factors to draw a conclusion about the market for the subject property. If there is excess supply, this step will identify it.

Step 6: Forecast Subject Capture (Market Penetration Concepts)
Finally, the analyst estimates how much of the demand the subject property will satisfy. For example, if the subject property is new construction in an oversupplied market, how will it be received?

real estate market will probably soften within a few weeks. The demand for one-unit homes can be measured by looking at historical sales rates in the same market segment. For example, the value indication from the sales comparison for a property in the Blue Creek subdivision and Hamilton Town-ship school district is $125,000. The 25-year-old improvement includes a basement and a two-car garage. Brokers in the area say the main criterion for buyers is the location in Hamilton Township rather than the subdivision. These brokers also say that home buyers in this market are very conscious of the age of improvements. A review of MLS activ-ity for properties in Hamilton Township shows that there were 27 sales of homes in the $100,000 to $150,000 price range in that township or tax-ing district in the last year, but there are 54 homes for sale now. It is logical to assume that this sales rate would still be valid today. If history is a guide, comparing the number of sales in the last year and the current number of listings indicates that there is a two-year supply of homes for sale in the market; this is an indication of the market's current strength and in many areas may explain why prices are increasing or, in this case, probably decreasing.

It is very important for an appraiser to rec-ognize the factors that will influence demand. Changes in supply are fairly obvious because new construction and demolition activity is usually eas-ily observed. Changes in demand are much more subtle but not usually unexpected for the observant appraiser. For example, an appraiser reads in the newspaper that a large widget manufacturing plant is closing and 400 direct jobs will be lost as well as 500 jobs at suppliers. This plant is located in a town with a population of 25,000 people. What could the appraiser anticipate? Exhibit 15.3 lists some pos-sible repercussions.

Some other factors that should be considered in this scenario include the following:

· Current levels of emigration and immigra-tion. If there was a trend of young people going away to college and not coming back, a population decline would already be in place. If this area was a popular place to retire, some of these issues could be reversed by move-ment to this market for other reasons.

· The age of the current population. An older population may imply a decreasing popula-

Exhibit 15.3   Anticipated Influences on Supply and Demand

Loss in demand for housing	Assuming that 900 jobs are lost, 700 of those workers are too young to retire, and 75% of them live in the subject property's market area, there could be about 500 extra homes for sale because 500 families will have to seek employment in other areas. This assumes that only one person per household works in this industry, which may not be true. Of course, some former widget factory workers will try to find local jobs in other industries, and a few will be successful in their search. Some will commute to other areas for jobs and remain in the same housing market. Some will draw unemployment for a year or two, so this oversupply may not be too bad in the beginning. Many, especially those who work in the skilled trades and management, will have to move to find jobs.
Loss in demand for retail space	A loss of as many as 500 families with 2.5 persons per household would equal a loss in population of 1,250 people. This would not decrease supply but would decrease the demand because the stores in the retail space would have fewer customers, and some stores would not survive this downturn.
Loss in demand for office space	A loss in population means a loss in demand for attorneys, accountants, doctors, dentists, insurance and real estate agents, and, of course, real estate appraisers.
Losses in demand for industrial buildings	One large facility and many small ones will no longer be needed. Absent any new demand and no reduction in supply, the closing of the plant should result in an oversupplied market. Owners of companies building industrial buildings would probably need to shift their focus to other trade areas.

tion due to death and movement to other climates. A younger population may imply growing families and a shift from smaller living units to larger ones.

- Other employment changes. If other plants have recently closed or are planning to close, the downturn could be worse than anticipated, but if new employers are opening new facilities for basic employment, this could decrease or even erase the effect of this plant closing. If the widget manufacturer was paying very high wages (which was perhaps the reason why the plant closed), other manufacturers might have been avoiding the area because they did not want to compete for labor at that price. However, once the widget plant closes, other manufacturers may then fill the void, only at lower wages.

While decreasing demand does not normally reduce supply in the short run, it does reduce supply in the long run. Buildings that are not needed will normally sit vacant or partially leased at reduced rents. This causes net operating income to decrease, which often means insufficient funds for maintenance and capital replacements. This leads to deteriorating conditions, which in turn leads to demolition and a natural reduction in supply.

In addition, it is important to recognize any oversupply or undersupply in the current market. If interest rates are low and the family size in the market is decreasing due to young people moving into their own homes, any oversupply in housing could be absorbed by new demand from shifts in household size.

Also, it is important to note the difference between employment in a basic industry and in service industries. A basic industry brings money into a community from outside the community. In contrast, a service industry serves the population within the community. So a big-box retailer that announces it will be building a new store in this town will not create new wealth in the community but rather will only shift the retail dollars from other places to the new store. There will be a few temporary jobs created for construction of the building.

Finally, it is also important to note that changes in population, housing, jobs, and industry do not happen overnight and often will only be observed months or years after they happen. This means appraisers should be careful about making predictions but should know and report possible changes in demand from significant shifts in the economic base.

Competitive Supply

In an analysis of the entire community, the competitive supply refers to properties that would appeal to a likely buyer of the subject property. Real estate supply typically does not adjust quickly to compensate for increases in demand. It takes a long time to build a new building or house. When demand increases quickly, supply is slow to compensate, and real estate prices will increase in the short run. The analyst needs to decide whether to include all properties in a market or only the properties offered for sale or lease. The former would be compared to the population of family units in that community, but the latter would be compared to the number of buyers or lessees in a market. It is important to remember that *supply* refers to *all* units in a market, not just ones that are for sale. *Demand* refers to demand for all units, not just the number of buyers currently seeking that particular type of real estate.

Market Equilibrium

Over the long run, markets are always moving toward equilibrium. When a market is oversupplied, builders stop building, developers stop developing, and prices stabilize or drop. When a market is undersupplied, builders start working overtime, subcontractors become builders, and laborers become subcontractors. The market for new construction will react when there is profit to be made. The market for existing properties is less reactive to supply and demand because some market participants may need to buy or sell no matter what. Changes in population will have a great impact on this analysis because an oversupply can be absorbed by an increasing population but exacerbated by a decreasing population. You cannot ignore local business and demographic trends.

Trends in Market Activity

Different markets will sometimes react differently to different factors. Houses priced from $200,000 to $300,000 may be affected significantly by an increase in mortgage interest rates, but the market for homes that cost $750,000 to $1 million may not be affected at all if properties in the higher-priced market have lower loan-to-value ratios.

Markets are most efficient when a large number of items are offered for sale and a large number of potential buyers are exposed to the offerings. A seller who has been showing a property for sale ten times a week is unlikely to worry that the first offer received will be the only one. Residential markets are the closest thing to an efficient market found in real estate. The special-purpose property market is probably the least efficient, with few buyers and sellers. The more efficient the market, the more consistent the market behavior will be. Sale prices vary greatly in an inefficient market.

Types and Levels of Market Analysis

Appraisers may use historical or current supply and demand data to research supply and demand factors. Many tools are available for estimating market supply and demand, and the tools that are used in a particular situation will vary with each assignment in each market. For example, if

In a *seller's market*, few properties are available for sale, and there are many buyers. In a *buyer's market*, many competing properties are available for sale, and there are few buyers. In some markets, sellers will put themselves in the shoes of purchasers and therefore decide to take an offer based on the competition and alternatives available to the buyer.

you have found recent comparable sales and the market has been very stable, market analysis may not support an adjustment of the value opinion for market conditions because any changes in market conditions are already reflected in the data and the extracted rates of appreciation or depreciation. On the other hand, if a property is in a volatile market with prices increasing or decreasing in response to changes in demand, market analysis may provide support for a market conditions adjustment to the comparable sales or leases. In other words, if the market has changed since the date of sale, there could be a reason for adjustment.

Market Studies and Marketability Studies

Market studies examine macroeconomic conditions. Appraisers perform market studies to analyze the market for a whole class of properties, not just the subject property. A market study of a nonresidential property type includes a survey of building owners for available space and a survey of brokers for the number of market participants or, more commonly, research on historical absorption rates. For example, if a researcher finds that a total of one million square feet of space is currently available in a market with a 250,000-sq.-ft. absorption rate, this implies that the supply of available space will last four years. In a market with an overall supply of four million square feet, this would imply that construction rates are low and prices are falling. Again, it would be wrong to research all properties in a market and then compare them with the number of buyers in that market. Instead, the correct analysis would be to compare all properties and users for a property or compare all buyers and sellers on a specific date.

In a marketability study, analysts investigate the market for the subject property or properties that compete directly with the subject. For example, if the subject is improved with a building in fair to poor condition and the subject's land value is higher than the improved value, the land value would be the market value of the property. If the subject is zoned for one-unit residential use but could easily be rezoned for multifamily use, which is worth more, the highest and best use would be multifamily. However, if the market for apartments is oversupplied and the land would not sell for apartment development for three years, then the highest and best use may still be a one-unit residential use because of the weak market for apartment land.

Inferred Analysis and Fundamental Analysis

Inferred demand is projected on the basis of current market conditions, rates of change, and absorption patterns—i.e., reading various signs in the market to develop an opinion of demand. The specific sales data used includes the number of days on the market, the list-to-sale-price differential, and broker-supplied information.

Fundamental analysis is a type of investment analysis that investigates basic economic factors and conditions affecting specific sectors and industries. Fundamental analysis is usually primary research conducted by the analyst, studying data directly related to the subject property's market segment. In this process, appraisers research the underlying reasons for demand or lack of it. Rather than simply reading the signs of more or less demand, appraisers research the point in the cycle that the market is at and the reasons why demand will change. This analysis focuses on population trends rather than the number of buyers in the market at any given date.

Levels of Market Analysis

The intensity of market analysis depends on the nature of the appraisal problem to be solved, the needs of the client, the predictability and stability of the real estate markets, and any requirements of professional standards related to the assignment. Certain appraisal assignments require a higher level of market analysis than others. Level A and Level B marketability studies are considered examinations of inferred demand, whereas more intense Level C and Level D studies are considered fundamental analyses. An appraisal of market value rarely requires a Level D marketability study, but a Level C analysis might involve some of the techniques and analyses that are characteristic of a higher-intensity study.

Exhibit 15.4 illustrates the applicability of market and marketability studies for different property types and the factors that appraisers have to consider in those studies.

Exhibit 15.4   Considerations in Market Analysis for Specific Property Types

Residential	Single-unit residential subdivision	The value of a subdivision is directly affected by the absorption rate of the lots. Market analysis cannot be ignored in valuing this property type.
	Apartments	If the sales data for apartments is older, market analysis may help the analyst adjust for market conditions.
	Single-unit	Market analysis is usually only informational for this property type because the sales data is usually so current and comparable that the value opinion does not require adjustment for changes in market conditions. In other words, the value of one-unit homes usually includes very recent comparables that already reflect any changes in property values due to market trends. If this is not true, then market analysis may be more important.
	Two- to four-unit	Like the data for one-unit homes, the market data for two- to four-unit residences is usually so good that market analysis is only informational.
Commercial	Retail	Market analysis may be informational or may be the basis for market condition adjustments made in valuing this property type. Most market analysis is conducted by large brokerage houses or chambers of commerce, therefore it is secondhand data.
	Office	As with retail market analysis, people other than the appraiser often conduct office market analysis. Office markets are sensitive to business trends, which gives market analysis additional importance.
	Hotels and motels	Primary research is fairly difficult to perform, but occupancy rates of comparables will give an indication of the supply side of the equation. Data on the demand for investment sale properties may be more difficult to obtain because national brokers often sell these properties. Market analysis of this property type is often done by brokers who specialize in hotels and motels.
Industrial	Manufacturing	Data on this property type is often old and may require an adjustment for market conditions. Brokers or chambers of commerce usually perform market analyses for manufacturing facilities. This data is usually fairly accurate even though it is secondary data.
	Warehousing	Because warehouse properties are often built speculatively, market analysis is of primary importance in the valuation process for these properties. Warehouse markets are notorious for being undersupplied or oversupplied depending on economic conditions.
	Distribution	The market for distribution space is also often out of balance and requires good market analysis to ensure accurate value opinions.
Agricultural		Market analysis for agricultural properties is often difficult because information from brokers who specialize in this type of property may not be linked via computer, organized in a common database, or accessible to appraisers. Agricultural and resource land markets vary widely depending on the product: · Cash crops (corn, soy beans, tobacco, wheat, etc.) · Livestock (cows, pigs, chickens, etc.) · Mineral extraction (coal, gravel, gas, oil)
Special-Purpose Properties		Again, in some markets market data relating to special-purpose (or *limited-market*) properties is not organized, and market analysis is difficult. Often, these markets are so specialized that there are few buyers and sellers, and market analysis is statistically insignificant because of the lack of data. In many appraisals of special-purpose properties, there is no active resale market, and a change in use is required to develop an opinion of market value. Market analysis will then be focused on the property use that is economically viable and has a resale market. It is important to remember that if there is no market for these properties, there is no market value.

1. Which of the following has the most efficient market?

   a) One-unit residences

   b) Two- to four-family homes

   c) Five- to 50-unit apartments

   d) 51- to 500-unit apartment projects

2. A small town (pop. 2,500) has only two home builders. These two companies have each been building about five houses per year for the last 15 years. The subcontractors they used all came from neighboring towns, but occasionally they would need to import a tradesperson from farther away. The state recently decided to build a new law enforcement academy in the town, which would cause an influx of about 500 people and an increase of about 200 households. There is almost no excess capacity of residences now. What will most likely happen?

   a) The existing builders will gear up to handle the demand, and prices will remain stable.

   b) The existing builders will gear up to handle some of the demand, but some subcontractors will become builders and some workers will become subcontractors. Prices will increase in the short run.

   c) The demand will wait for the supply to catch up, and no new players will enter the business. Prices will remain stable.

   d) The majority of the new households will double up, and demand for housing will not increase. Prices will remain stable.

3. The residential real estate market is much more efficient than the nonresidential real estate market in most cities because

   a) Homes are better designed and thus more efficient

   b) Houses make more economic sense as investments than nonresidential properties

   c) There are more buyers and sellers and the MLS system organizes data

   d) Residential real estate brokers are smarter than nonresidential brokers

4. The current MLS system shows the following data for 5- to 10-year-old homes priced from $100,000 to $125,000: 13 current listings, 4 pending sales (offer accepted but not closed), and 12 sales within the last 12 months. Over the last five years, the same market usually has had about a six-month supply of homes for sale. New home builders and brokers are advertising for the first time in many years. The average number of days on the market is 10% longer than in previous years. Which of the following statements is correct?

   a) This market is oversupplied and prices will be stable at best.

   b) This market is fine and prices will increase slightly.

   c) This market is great and prices will increase rapidly.

   d) This market is weak and prices will be unaffected.

5. Market analysis is included in appraisals

   a) To tell the reader about changes in the neighborhood's economy

   b) To show support for the estimated highest and best use and the existence of a market

   c) To add bulk to the appraisal report and thus raise the fee

   d) To show the reader the direction the market is going

6. A real estate market is

   a) A shopping center office of a realty company

   b) A group of individuals or firms that are in contact with one another for the purpose of conducting real estate transactions

   c) A list of potential buyers for the subject property

   d) A list of potential sellers who have properties similar to the one requested by the buyer

7. Office demand is most affected by

   a) The percentage of owner-occupied residences

   b) The availability of water and sewer services

   c) School taxes

   d) The expansion trends of local businesses

8. Office supply is most affected by
    a) Changes in the population of the subject property's area
    b) Changes in retail buying habits
    c) The conversion or new construction of office buildings
    d) Increases in the regulation of retail construction

9. Retail space demand is affected by
    a) Changes in employment opportunities
    b) Changes in traffic patterns
    c) Increases or decreases in disposable income
    d) All of the above

10. To analyze the market for a one-unit home, an appraiser should investigate
    a) The number of listings and recent sales of homes that would appeal to the same buyer as the subject property
    b) The number of expired listings in the same geographic area as the subject property
    c) The number of listings and recent sales within the subject property's platted subdivision
    d) The number of vacant apartments in the same geographic area as the subject property

11. The economic base is
    a) The lower line in a graph showing the economic output of a community
    b) The ratio of basic industries to technical industries in a community
    c) An inexpensive, large stringed instrument
    d) The economic activity that enables a community to attract income from outside its borders

Note: Unless otherwise noted, italicized references indicate the pages in *The Appraisal of Real Estate*, 14th edition, that readers should consult for additional discussion of these topics.

1. a) One-unit residences
    This student handbook

2. b) The existing builders will gear up to handle some of the demand, but some subcontractors will become builders and some workers will become subcontractors. Prices will increase in the short run.
    Pages 306-307

3. c) There are more buyers and sellers and the MLS system organizes data
    This student handbook

4. a) This market is oversupplied and prices will be stable at best.
    This student handbook

5. b) To show support for the estimated highest and best use and the existence of a market
    Page 300

6. b) A group of individuals or firms that are in contact with one another for the purpose of conducting real estate transactions
    Pages 131-133

7. d) The expansion trends of local businesses
    Pages 319-320

8. c) The conversion or new construction of office buildings
    Page 305

9. d) All of the above
    Pages 319-320

10. a) The number of listings and recent sales of homes that would appeal to the same buyer as the subject property
    Page 309

11. d) The economic activity that enables a community to attract income from outside its borders
    Pages 130-131

Highest and Best Use Analysis

Real estate markets determine highest and best use through the land use decisions that market participants make every day. In market value appraisals, the appraiser's job includes determining the highest and best use, which means estimating what the typical buyer in this market would do with the subject property. In the overwhelming majority of appraisals, this analysis is a routine function. In the remainder, however, determining highest and best use is the most significant and challenging step in the valuation process.

In most appraisals, highest and best use is usually fairly obvious, so appraisers may miss the less obvious highest and best use issues and appraise properties at lower uses when subtle highest and best use issues do arise. For example, an appraiser performs 30 residential appraisals per month and in 29 of them she appraises the property in "as is" condition by subtracting the cost of repairs from the "as repaired" value. Once in a while, the cost of the repairs lowers the market value of the improved property below the value of the "land as though vacant," but the appraiser never thinks about it because of the other 29 appraisals that month in which no such problem occurred. This is why it is necessary for appraisers to develop an opinion of the land value in every market value appraisal. This ensures thar the appraiser notices when a land value is higher than the improved property value.

Sometimes, the appraisal is complete when the highest and best use analysis is conducted because the appraiser needs to develop opinions of value under several different uses and decide which alternative ncts thc highest price to the owner. In most appraisals, this is no more difficult than answering the question "What is the best use for this property today?" However, when highest and best use is not obvious, it can be very controversial. In a few cases, highest and best use analysis may involve estimating the value of the subject under its existing zoning classification and then hypothetically under a different use assuming a change in zoning.

It should be fairly obvious that the value of a parcel of land can be very high or low depending on the potential buyers. For example, assume the subject property is a two-acre site at the corner of two gravel roads in a rural area. The property has traffic counts of 10 cars per day on each street. If you (erroneously) assume that the property has a highest and best use as a fast food restaurant, the value may be estimated as 15 to 20 times higher than if you determine its highest and best use to be as agricultural or residential land. Highest and best use analysis requires the appraiser to consider a great variety of factors.

Fundamentals of Highest and Best Use

In its most straightforward form, *highest and best use* can be defined as

> The reasonably probable use of property that results in the highest value.

To get to the reasonably probable use with the highest value, appraisers must apply four tests to the possible alternative uses:

- legal permissibility
- physical possibility
- financial feasibility
- maximum productivity

Legal permissibility and physical possibility are tested before financial feasibility, and the test of maximum productivity is completed last.

Key Terms	
consistent use	legally nonconforming use
financial feasibility	most probable use
interim use	most profitable use

The definition of *highest and best use* has been simplified over the years. In the past, a commonly used definition included the condition that the property use be "appropriately supported," a vague and much-debated phrase. Other concepts have also been used as alternatives to *highest and best use*. Application of the concept of the *most probable use* by appraisers has significantly decreased in recent years, while the concept of the *most profitable use* is now limited mostly to litigation appraisals.

Highest and best use analysis actually involves two separate analyses:

1. Of the subject property's highest and best use of the site as though vacant
2. Of the highest and best use of the property as improved

First, you consider whether the property is worth more without the existing improvements than with them. Then, you consider possible modifications and changes to the property. These steps follow the thought processes of knowledgeable real estate buyers and owners.

> While estimating highest and best use may sound complicated, it is usually no more difficult than estimating what prudent owners would do with a property to maximize their return. In other words, consider what you would do with the property if you owned it.

Testing Highest and Best Use
Any potential alternative use can be tested for the four criteria of highest and best use. The six-step market analysis process provides the data appraisers need to perform the tests of highest and best use on alternative land uses and helps limit the list of options to a set of reasonably probable uses.

Legally Permissible
Zoning, building codes, setback requirements, leases, deed restrictions, easements, and environmental regulations can all limit land uses, which can be significant in some appraisals. Testing for legal permissibility requires you to have a working knowledge of local zoning ordinances and how to research deeds. It is a common error by some appraisers to assume that the current use is a legal use. This is often not true. For example, suppose the owner of a two-unit residence built 50 years ago converts a detached garage into a third dwelling unit. The appraiser assumes the

third dwelling unit is legal or just does not give it a second thought, but a review appraiser calls the zoning authority because it was a recent conversion and determines that it is, in fact, illegal.

Physically Possible
Any use suggested as the highest and best use must be physically possible. This criterion is usually the easiest to test. The proposed use must fit on the site, the soil must be solid enough to support any improvements, and the topography must be adequate to allow the use. For example, a sit-down fast food restaurant with on-site parking for 30 cars on a quarter-acre site is not physically possible and therefore would not meet this criterion. A one-acre site is generally large enough to build a house on, but that house may not be buildable if 95% of the site in question has a 60-degree slope. It may be impossible to build a house with a basement on a site where the water table is six feet below the surface. There can be an extensive list of reasons why a site cannot support a particular use. It is your job to research these possible limitations.

Financially Feasible
A sensible person would only consider profitable uses of a property, which is the essence of the test of financial feasibility. A parcel of raw land usually has more than one financially feasible use—such as an office building or an industrial facility—if both of those uses are physically possible and legally permitted.

Maximally Productive
Like financial feasibility, the maximum productivity criterion requires that the highest and best use be profitable. The maximally productive use is the one alternative of all possible financially feasible uses that produces the maximum benefit to the owner. For an improved property, this is the use with the highest residual value to the land.

Land As Though Vacant and the Property As Improved
The four tests apply both to the highest and best use of the land as though vacant and of the property as improved. However, applying the tests to the property as improved leads to a conclusion of which of three actions is the best alternative for the existing improvements:

1. Keep the improvements as they are.
2. Modify the improvements in some way.
3. Demolish the improvements and redevelop the land for some other use.

Considerations in Highest and Best Use

Highest and Best Use of Land As Though Vacant

The highest and best use of land as though vacant is not a difficult concept to understand. In nearly all cases, the highest and best use of the land as though vacant is the use that generates the highest land value. Whether the property has building improvements or not, the analytical process is the same. The highest and best use of the land as though vacant assumes that the property is vacant so that the analyst will not make the mistake of valuing the property using improved comparables when the land is worth more vacant.

Legally Permissible Uses of Land As Though Vacant

The analysis of the legal permissibility of the land as though vacant includes looking at the zoning, the probability of a change in zoning, deed restrictions, building codes, historic district rules, and other property legal limitations. In many appraisal assignments, this is the most difficult and time-consuming part of the analysis. Investigating legal permissibility may require research at the local planning and zoning agency, contact with the local recorder's office to find out about covenants and restrictions, or even consulting with an attorney on the legality of a particular land use.

Physically Possible Uses of Land As Though Vacant

Sometimes the shape of the parcel prohibits certain types of buildings and land uses on the site. This determination is usually simple and requires only common sense.

Financially Feasible Uses of Land As Though Vacant

All proposed property uses must cover the cost of construction and generate enough income to support the required rates of return to the equity and mortgage positions. In this step of the analytical

---

Consistent Use

Consistent use can be one of the most significant issues in highest and best use analysis. The principle of consistent use holds that you must analyze the improvements on the basis of their contribution to the value of the site at its highest and best use as though vacant. Appraisers violate this principle when they fail to recognize that a property can have more value without the improvements than with them.

For example, a residential site is improved with a five-year-old, 2,500-sq.-ft. house with a two-car attached garage. Homes like this located in standard platted subdivisions with no commercial potential are selling for $200,000 ($50,000 of which is attributed to the land and $150,000 of which is attributed to the building). The subject property is located at the corner of two busy streets, and the land has significant commercial potential. Zoning is already commercial, but the residential use has remained because of its "grandfathered use" status. Because land is always valued at its highest and best use as though vacant, this property's land value with its commercial highest and best use is $175,000. The market value of the subject property if sold as a residence is $190,000 because it is on a busy street, which is less desirable to a residential buyer.

The property will sell for $190,000 to a residential buyer, but because the value of the land is always estimated "as though vacant," the land value is $175,000. Therefore, the building is only worth the difference between the land value and the improved value, or $15,000.

A mistake some appraisers make is adding the value of the commercial land to the value of the building as a residence, which violates the principle of consistent use. The buyer for this property will not pay the commercial land prices plus the residential improvement value. The residential buyer will think this is a fair to poor location because of the traffic, and the commercial buyer will probably raze the improvements (someday in the future), which implies that the buildings have less and less value as the land value increases.

Probability of a Zoning Change

A property's zoning classification is the primary consideration in the test of the legal permissibility of alternative uses of land as though vacant. Sometimes a change in zoning might allow for a more intense use, and the probability of that zoning change would become an issue for the appraiser along with considerations of the time and expense involved in rezoning the property. This means you may encounter situations in which the zoning in place will have to be ignored because it is probably going to change.

For example, assume that the subject property has been zoned for agricultural use for the last 30 years, but the once-rural area is now urbanized and surrounded by commercial, high-density residential, and special-purpose land uses. All of the surrounding properties were rezoned from agricultural to residential and commercial use recently. The only reason the subject property has not been rezoned is that no one has requested it, and investors and developers active in the market expect this property to be redeveloped for commercial or multifamily use soon. If the property were sold as agricultural land, it would be worth less than 50% of the value if it were sold as commercial land. It is very likely that any buyer would petition for a zoning change immediately.

Given the market dynamics, you would be misleading your client to a false value conclusion if you rely on the existing zoning in your highest and best use analysis, which would be a violation of professional standards.

process, appraisers determine which of the possible uses of the site make financial sense.

Maximum Productivity of Land As Though Vacant

Not only must the proposed use satisfy all the requirements explained earlier, it must also maximize the return. The proposed use must not only be feasible but must also be the most profitable use.

The Ideal Improvement

The ideal improvement maximizes the property value. A two-bedroom home built in a market where three to five bedrooms are standard does not represent the ideal improvement. In highest and best use analysis, you develop an opinion of what should be built on the subject site so you know when the owners do not have it.

The loss in value caused by a difference between the existing improvements (what you have) and the ideal improvement (what you should have) is usually a form of depreciation.

Highest and Best Use of Property As Improved

After analyzing the highest and best use of the land as though vacant, the appraiser identifies the best use for the subject property considering the improvements that are already in place. In other words, you must decide which of the following a prudent owner would do with the existing property:

1. Retain the existing improved use.
2. Modify the existing use (i.e., the improvements) in some way. For example, if the subject property is a residence with two bedrooms in a market where three or four bedrooms are standard, the highest and best use of the property as improved may include adding a third or fourth bedroom to the house.

3. Demolish the existing improvements and redevelop the site for some other use. For example, suppose the subject property is an improved residential site. The site is in a desirable location, the land value (as though vacant) is $400,000, and the value of the property "as is" is $250,000 (ignoring the higher land value). The cost of demolition is $5,000. The highest and best use of the property as improved would be to remove the improvements and redevelop the site because the value of the site less the cost of demolition of the improvements ($400,000 − $5,000 = $395,000) is much higher than the improved value as a residence ($250,000).

The four tests (*physically possible, legally permissible, financially feasible, maximally productive*) are still applicable, but they are performed in the context of the three scenarios relating to the existing use of the property.

Testing Continuation of the Existing Use of the Property As Improved

In a stable and healthy market, the status quo is quite often the highest and best use of the property as improved. The analysis of possible modifications to the existing use has to weigh the advantage of the alterations with their cost to implement along with legal and physical limitations on altering the existing improvements. Clearly, if the renovations would not add more to the market value than they would cost, the renovated improvements would not have a market value higher than that of the existing improvements. Likewise, if there is no probability of a zoning change to allow for a higher use or if the layout of the site and the existing improvements does not allow for modification of the improvements, continuation of the existing use may be the only possible scenario. If the zoning cannot be changed, there are no alternatives available in this analysis.

For example, suppose the subject property is a 20-year-old, 4,000-sq.-ft. fast food restaurant located at the corner of two major streets. The site is a little less than one acre and has two access points, one off each street. The building is situated as far south on the site as possible, and there are two rows of parking along the north end of the site. The number of parking spaces meets the zoning minimums, but there are no extra spaces. The fast food restaurant clearly needs a drive-up window to compete with other fast food restaurants in the market. However, the configuration of the parking lot and the siting of the building do not allow for the addition of a drive-up window. If a drive-up window is built on the side of the building with an open wall, 12 parking spaces would be lost and the improvements would no longer comply with zoning requirements. The highest and best use can no longer be as a fast food restaurant even though it would clearly sell for more than a sit-down restaurant, which is what it would have to be without the drive-up window. The test of physical possibility limited the highest and best use of this property as improved. Note that the highest and best use of this property as thought vacant could still be as a fast food restaurant with a smaller building and less required on-site parking.

As another example, suppose the subject property is a one-acre corner lot improved with a one-unit, three-bedroom residence and a two-car attached garage. The corner lot fronts on a two-lane residential street and a six-lane thoroughfare. The access point is off the residential street with a short fence running along the busy thoroughfare. Market research shows that the property would bring in about $200,000 in the residential market but it could be sold for $250,000 for office building conversion (such as conversion into a real estate office). To convert the house into an office building, access off the thoroughfare would be required, the fence would have to be taken down, and the zoning would have to be changed to commercial. Research into the probability of a zoning change is encouraging, and this change could be obtained with little effort. Obtaining access to the road is less likely.

A visual check of the properties along the thoroughfare indicates that some properties have access to the busy street but most do not. The owner insists that the property is commercial. He is sure access is possible but cannot show any evidence. A review of zoning regulations reveals nothing about access rights. A zoning agency staff person says that she thinks there were some restrictions along the thoroughfare filed by the state highway department. After several phone calls to the wrong people, you talk to a representative of the state highway department, who indicates that the rights to access the thoroughfare were purchased from most of the adjacent property owners 20 years earlier. He adds that if access to the adjacent street were restricted, it would say so on the deed. After a phone call to the owner, you receive

a copy of the deed. The deed clearly states that no access is allowed to the adjacent thoroughfare. The highest and best use is clearly as a residence, and the value is approximately $200,000, not $250,000 as the owner insists. This whole process took more than four days to complete, and most of it was necessary to do a complete appraisal. This is an example of why appraisers should be careful about signing contracts for service when short turnaround times are required and there are no exceptions for issues like this.

Testing Modification of the Existing Use of the Property As Improved

If modifications can be made to the existing improvements to improve the property's market position and generate a higher return (less the cost of modification) than the existing use would, the renovated use would be the highest and best use of the property as improved. As always, to be considered as the most profitable use, any alteration must be physically possible and legally permissible.

For example, consider an aging 50,000-sq.-ft. office/warehouse in an industrial park. When the property was developed 25 years ago, the standard number of dock doors for a distribution facility of this size was five and the building size was adequate for this site, but that is no longer true. The cost of expanding the building by 25,000 square feet and retrofitting the existing space to create five more dock doors, which would make the existing building more competitive in the local market, is estimated to be $250,000. The site has excess land that can accommodate the expansion of the building and the parking area, so the modification of the existing use is physically possible. Since the original development of the building, other buildings in the industrial park have been developed with higher floor area ratios, which suggests that the modification would be allowable under the zoning for the area.

Space in the building currently rents below the market rate because of the property's inferior competitive position in the market. Market analysis suggests that the modification would make the property significantly more attractive, allowing the owner to raise the rent from $8 per square foot to $10 per square foot. In that scenario, the annual potential gross income of the property at full occupancy increases from $400,000 ($8 × 50,000) to $750,000 ($10 × 75,000). The increase of $350,000 more than offsets the $250,000 cost of the modification, so the scenario is financially feasible.

Expenses on a per-square-foot basis are not expected to increase. In fact, the necessary modifications to the existing structure include refurbishing some systems, which would potentially decrease the cost of operating the property on a per-square-foot basis. The increase in potential gross income and the decrease in operating expenses both point to the expansion of the existing improvements as the most productive use and therefore the highest and best use of the property as improved.

Testing Demolition of the Property as Improved and Redevelopment

When the existing improvements contribute nothing to the value of the property as a whole, demolishing the improvements and redeveloping the site—usually to its highest and best use as though vacant—is likely to be the most productive use of the property. Demolition is not necessarily only an option in a depressed market, when property values have fallen enough to attract redevelopers. If land values have risen sharply, the existing improvements may currently account for a smaller and smaller portion of the market value. Many older homes are dubbed "tear downs" in healthy markets because building a new, usually larger residential structure on the site would be more consistent with other new homes in the market and attract buyers in a higher price range.

For example, consider a small family farm and farmhouse on a 10-acre parcel on the southwest corner of two streets that have become increasingly busy over time as development has occurred in the area. The streets have two lanes in each direction and a traffic light at the corner in front of the subject property. Demolition of the existing improvements is estimated to cost $40,000. Utilities and other necessary infrastructure for redevelopment of the site are in place. The parcel has no known physical impediments to the development of a building of almost any size or configuration. A zoning agency staff person indicated there should be no problem rezoning the parcel from agricultural to commercial, multifamily, or special-purpose use.

The area has seen a lot of development recently, including the following:

- The parcel on the northwest corner also has 10 acres and was zoned for agricultural use until a petition to change it to apartment zoning was recently approved and apartments were built on the site. This parcel sold for $65,000 per acre, which is consistent with the apartment market in the area.
- The property on the northeast corner also has 10 acres and was zoned for agricultural use until the owner applied for and received a change in zoning to commercial use. The site was improved with a small strip shopping center immediately after the sale. The raw land sold for $125,000 per acre, which is consistent with the market.
- The parcel on the southeast corner also has 10 acres and was zoned for agricultural use until a new owner applied for and received a change in zoning to special-purpose use for a church. The site was improved with a small church immediately after the sale. The raw land sold for $100,000 per acre, which is consistent with the market.

Similar-sized plots of agricultural land in the area have sold for between $25,000 and $40,000 per acre in recent years. The existing farmhouse and other farm buildings are old and in need of repair, contributing little to the overall property value. It would appear that the highest and best use of the property as improved is to demolish the improvements and redevelop the land for a commercial use because that type of use will command the highest price. It is important to note that not all sites will support redevelopment. If the subject property is improved with an old industrial building that has sat vacant for 25 years, it is possible that no developer would invest the funds to put up a new building in that area for fear of not being able to recoup the investment.

Special Situations in Highest and Best Use Analysis

Excess Land and Surplus Land

Highest and best use considerations are important when a property being appraised includes excess land or surplus land. In fact, whether or not the extra land can be used for some other highest and best use is the main criterion in determining if that extra land is excess land (which may have an independent highest and best use) or surplus land (which can only be used for expansion of the improvements on the other portion of the site).

Proposed Construction

The analysis of the financial feasibility of a proposed improvement is a common consideration in the analysis of a site as though vacant. That is, if a different improvement would be a higher and better use than the existing improvements, that different improvement would have to be built. An extraordinary assumption that the proposed improvements would be completed as planned on the date of value is usually necessary in this situation, along with a clear explanation for the intended user of the appraisal about the timing of the proposed use.

Single Uses

Special-purpose properties designed for a sole use often have to be valued as if they were converted to an alternative economic use. For example, if you are asked to estimate the market value of a fire station building, you must assume a different "market use" because in most communities there would be no buyers for a fire station. There would be buyers, however, for a fire station that is converted into a storefront, a transmission shop, or some other economically feasible use.

Legally Nonconforming Uses

A legally nonconforming use (also known as a *grandfathered use*) is no longer permitted by current zoning or building codes but is allowed to stand until a major change is made to the property. A common grandfathered use is a building located in a flood hazard area. These properties were often built before regulations were put in place restricting new development in the area. Grandfathered uses can be common in areas where zoning ordinances change frequently. In older areas, legal but nonconforming uses may make up 50% or even 75% of the total number of properties. In areas where zoning regulations are less precisely defined, the percentage of legally nonconforming uses may be much smaller. Some lenders do not want to loan money on legally nonconforming uses, but most are not averse.

Because land is always valued as though vacant and parcels with legal nonconforming uses will have a different use if vacant, the value indication of the cost approach will be missing a value increment. That is, if the appraiser adds up the value of the land as though vacant at its highest and best use and the depreciated value of the improvements, the sum will be much less than that indicated by the sales comparison and income capitalization approaches. The reason for this phenomenon is that the land at its highest and best use reflects the current zoning or land use restrictions, but the market recognizes a different (usually more intense) highest and best use, which is only available because of the legal nonconforming use.

Sometimes the difference between a legally nonconforming use and an illegal use is small. The appraiser's job is to know the difference.

For example, the subject property is an office building that was built in a FEMA-identified flood hazard way. The zoning authority made it very clear that the improvements would not be allowed to be built in this area today and could not be rebuilt if destroyed. The land value (V_L) is very low because the site is not developable, but the existing office building is legal but not conforming and has nearly the same value as buildings out of the floodway. That is, the building rents for market rates, so the application of the income capitalization approach suggests that the property is worth the same as other similar properties. The results of the cost approach will be a problem because the land value will be added at flood land prices. If the appraiser correctly values the land at floodway prices but the grandfathered use allows value to be nearly the same as properties outside the floodway, an increment of value will be missing.

Illegal Uses

Unlike legally nonconforming uses, illegal uses are not allowed as an exception to current zoning regulations. If demolition or conversion of the existing improvements is not financially feasible, the property with the illegal use may have no market value or may even be a liability to the current owner. The cost to correct any illegal improvements (such as a building constructed without permits) would have to be accounted for if the property is being valued with an illegal use in place.

Use That Is Not Currently the Highest and Best Use

In some situations, appraisers must analyze the highest and best use of a property as if it were something other than the current use. Appraisals for investment value and use value purposes may require you to consider a use that is not currently the highest and best use. This would be a situation in which an investor says something like, "I don't care about the market value—I want you to consider what I am planning to use the property for and how that compares to my alternatives."

Interim Uses

Appraisers use the label *interim use* to describe a situation in which the current use is only temporary and a higher use is foreseen in the near future. Some appraisers think that all uses are temporary and this label is not needed. Others think this label is useful because in certain circumstances the market recognizes and pays for a future use with the knowledge that the less profitable use will have to persist until market conditions or other factors are right for the conversion. The important consideration in these situations is to value the real estate based on comparables with similar upside potential. A 100-acre farm 15 miles north of the nearest development has potential for development, but perhaps not for another 50 years. Another 100-acre farm 1.5 miles north of sewer lines and other developments is only a year or two away from development. The price of the remote farm would hardly be comparable to that of the farm ready to be developed.

The theory of consistent use is very important in interim use situations because existing improvements may add value as an interim use but add nothing to the later, higher use; they will have to be removed. You should not add value for improvements that a developer is going to raze.

Speculative uses are similar to interim uses in that the land currently has lower market value today but will have higher value in the future. Some appraisers use this label to describe a parcel that a land speculator buys with the intent of holding for a few years while the market improves and then reselling it at a profit.

Mixed Uses

Appraisers often assume that a single parcel has a single highest and best use, which can be a mistake. By definition, mixed-use properties house multiple uses under a single roof. For example, the John Hancock Center in Chicago has many floors of office space, many floors of condominiums, and a restaurant and grocery store along with other retail uses in the building. In many small towns, the buildings on the town square often have apartments above ground-floor retail uses. When faced with a property with mixed uses, you must decide who would buy it and how much they would pay. In many cases, the only buyer is an investor who plans to rent portions of the property out to different users. The potential income is the only important factor to an investor, so the highest and best use analysis should focus on the tests of financial feasibility and maximum productivity.

Special-Purpose Properties

A special-purpose property, such as a chemical processing plant or bowling alley, serves only the function for which it was designed. On these types of properties, special process-related equipment is often installed that cannot be removed without significantly altering the improvements. In the analysis of a special-purpose use, the appraiser determines whether the current special-purpose use remains feasible or if razing the improvements and redeveloping the site would generate a higher return for the property owner. Market analysis of continued demand for the special-purpose use is key. Again, if there is no market for the property in its designed use, there is no market value for that use and another use must be considered.

Conclusions of Highest and Best Use

After testing alternative uses of the land and analyzing the various scenarios for the existing use of the property as improved, the appraiser should be able to communicate the opinion of highest and best use to the intended user of the appraisal. The timing of the highest and best use (i.e., when the use will occur) is as important as the use itself. It is possible for an appraiser to say, for example, that the highest and best use is to continue to farm the land for three to five years and then develop the site with an improved use. Likewise, the potential users and buyers of the highest and best use ought to be identified for the client's benefit, especially if the client is not familiar with the market and the typical market participants.

Reporting Highest and Best Use Conclusions

Every market value appraisal report includes some discussion of the highest and best use of the property being appraised. In assignments concerning residential properties, reporting can be minimized unless the property has unusual circumstances or a change from the existing use to a higher use is suggested. A reader of any appraisal report should be able to follow the appraiser's reasoning. Highest and best use analysis is not an arcane appraisal skill but a logical, common-sense process that follows the steps a typical buyer would take when analyzing the subject property. Most properties are put to their highest and best use because most owners will do what is

- legally permissible
- physically possible
- financially feasible
- maximally productive

In other words, it is not unusual to find that most of the properties in a market are already put to their highest and best use (as improved). However, some properties may not be put to their highest and best use because certain owners may be holding out for a higher use, may not be interested in developing or selling the property, or may be distracted by circumstances that prevent them from making a prudent decision about the use of the property. In some cases, the owners will suggest a change in highest and best use when they market the property but will not change it themselves.

| Exhibit 16.1 | Highest and Best Use Worksheet |

Highest and best use of the land as though vacant and of the property as improved may change depending on the land value of the subject property. Remember that land is always valued as though vacant and available to be put to its highest and best use.

- State Road 47 is a busy thoroughfare with commercial potential. Wagner Street is not a busy street and has no commercial potential.
- The lots along State Road 47 and along Wagner Street are improved with nearly identical homes (by a tract production builder). All the lots are the same size (23,700 square feet).
- All improvements are physically the same in terms of age, condition, quality, etc.
- All sales are current and no sales have financing concessions.
- The properties on the south side of State Road 47 and adjacent to Wagner Street are zoned residential only (commercial not allowed).
- The properties adjacent to and on the north side of State Road 47 are zoned residential/commercial, which allows for both residential and commercial uses.
- It will cost about $3,000 to raze any of these homes.
- The subject property is Lot 4 in the Greenland Addition, a 23,700-sq.-ft. site with the same improvements as all the other lots in both additions. The site is zoned residential/commercial.

Greenland Addition (residential/commercial zoning)

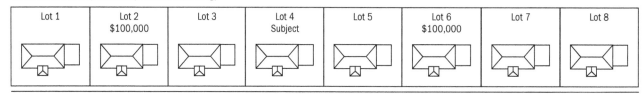

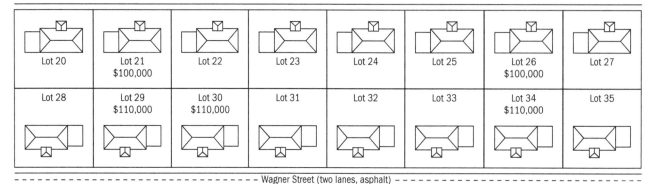

Blue Lake Addition (residential zoning)

Comparable Sales

1. Lot 2 in the Greenland Addition sold for $100,000 to a family that moved in and still lives there.
2. Lot 6 in the Greenland Addition sold for $100,000 to a family that moved in and still lives there.
3. Lot 21 in the Blue Lake Addition sold for $100,000.
4. Lot 29 in the Blue Lake Addition sold for $110,000.
5. Lot 30 in the Blue Lake Addition sold for $110,000.
6. Lot 34 in the Blue Lake Addition sold for $110,000.

Fill in the blanks in the table based on the lot descriptions and the land values given:

Commercial Land Value	Residential Land Value	Land Value of Subject Property	Building Value of Subject Property	Highest and Best Use of Subject Site As Though Vacant	Highest and Best Use of Subject Property As Improved
$1.00 per sq. ft.	$0.50 per sq. ft.	_____	_____	_____	_____
$2.00 per sq. ft.	$0.50 per sq. ft.	_____	_____	_____	_____
$3.00 per sq. ft.	$0.50 per sq. ft.	_____	_____	_____	_____
$4.00 per sq. ft.	$0.50 per sq. ft.	_____	_____	_____	_____
$5.00 per sq. ft.	$0.50 per sq. ft.	_____	_____	_____	_____

See the Suggested Solutions section at the end of this chapter for the correct answers.

1. Highest and best use analysis is required in
   a) All appraisals
   b) Value-in-use appraisals
   c) Investment value appraisals
   d) Market value appraisals

2. Highest and best use analysis requires an estimate of the use as though vacant and as improved to
   a) Estimate the value of the improvements
   b) Ensure that appraisers recognize that the property could be worth more without the buildings than with them
   c) Estimate any functional obsolescence caused by inappropriate improvements
   d) All of the above

3. Highest and best use of the site as though vacant
   a) Is required in all market value appraisals of real property
   b) May require a change in zoning classification, if possible
   c) Assumes the site is vacant or could be made vacant by demolishing the improvements
   d) All of the above

4. Which of the following is *not* a criterion for highest and best use?
   a) Legally permissible
   b) Physically possible
   c) Financially feasible
   d) The maximum size improvement

5. The test of legal permissibility includes all of the following requirements *except*
   a) Deed and plat restrictions
   b) Zoning requirements, building codes, and historic district controls
   c) Compliance with lease provisions
   d) Compliance with supply and demand criteria

6. Common interim uses include
   a) Surface parking lots
   b) High-rise parking lots
   c) Small office buildings with short leases
   d) New car automobile dealerships

7. The concept of consistent use requires an improvement to be valued based on a use that is consistent with the site's highest and best use. In other words, this means that
   a) The highest and best use of the site as though vacant must always consider the improvements thereon
   b) The highest and best use as improved would always be consistent with the "as vacant" analysis
   c) The improvement value must be adjusted down if the land's highest and best use is different than the improved highest and best use
   d) The vacant land value can never exceed the improved value

8. A property includes a one-unit residence on the southeast corner of a five-acre parcel with 467 feet of frontage on each of two roads. The house alone (without land) would be worth $100,000. It was never platted, and there are no deed restrictions. The local zoning ordinance only requires two acres with 200 feet of road frontage. The market for houses with up to five acres is good. Excess land, not required by zoning, sells for only $3,000 per acre. A buildable pad in this market is worth $30,000. The site is far enough from the northern property line to allow an almost perfect split of the parcel in half. What is the highest and best use of the site as though vacant and as improved?
   a) Highest and best use as though vacant = One parcel with five acres.
      Highest and best use as improved = One house on five acres.
   b) Highest and best use as though vacant = Two parcels with ±2.5 acres each.
      Highest and best use as improved = Leave the house and sell off the other site.
   c) Highest and best use as though vacant = One parcel.
      Highest and best use as improved = One house on ±2.5 acres and a vacant lot with ±2.5 acres.
   d) Highest and best use as though vacant = Two parcels with ±2.5 acres.
      Highest and best use as improved = Tear down the house.

9. When a property's highest and best use is likely to change in the near future, the prevailing highest and best use is called a(n)
   a) Pending use
   b) Temporary use
   c) Interim use
   d) Alternative use

10. Land values are never penalized due to the functional problems in existing buildings because
   a) Buildings can be removed or altered
   b) Buildings do not contribute value
   c) Land can change
   d) All of the above

11. A legally nonconforming use is
   a) A use that was legally established and maintained but no longer conforms to existing zoning
   b) A use that was illegally established and maintained
   c) A use that was not legally established and maintained and still does not conform to existing zoning
   d) A use that was not legally established and maintained but for which the government is not enforcing the laws

Use the following data to solve Review Exercises 12 through 14.

The land value of a 5-acre parcel in a prestigious residential area is estimated at $50,000 per acre based on comparable sales right in the area. Improved comparable sales with homes like the subject property show that this property should be worth $225,000 if sold as a house. The demolition cost is $5,000.

12. The value of the land is
   a) $240,000
   b) $245,000
   c) $250,000
   d) $255,000

13. The market value of the fee simple rights for this parcel is
   a) $250,000
   b) $245,000
   c) $230,000
   d) $225,000

14. The market value of the improvement is
   a) $225,000
   b) $175,000
   c) -$25,000
   d) -$5,000

15. If asked to appraise a municipal library, an appraiser
   a) Must find comparable sales of libraries.
   b) Must estimate an alternative use and then find comparables of buildings that are similar to the alternative use.
   c) Must find comparable sales of a library building from one governmental organization to another. The sales must be arm's-length.
   d) Must find comparable sales of adult book stores.

16. An improved residential property has the following characteristics:
   · The land if it were vacant is valued at $85,000
   · The value of the property as it is improved (with the house) is $75,000
   · The cost of removing the house would be $5,000
   What is the market value of the rights to this property?
   a) The property value is $85,000.
   b) The improvement value is -$15,000.
   c) The property value is $80,000.
   d) The property value is $75,000.

17. To be considered the highest and best use, a use must be
   a) Physically possible, legally permissible, financially feasible, and maximally productive
   b) Physically correct and legally possible
   c) Already in existence and legal
   d) Physically possible and appropriate

Note: Unless otherwise noted, italicized references indicate the pages in *The Appraisal of Real Estate*, 14th edition, that readers should consult for additional discussion of these topics.

Exhibit 16.1   Highest and Best Use Worksheet

Commercial Land Value	Residential Land Value	Land Value of Subject Property	Building Value of Subject Property	Highest and Best Use of Subject Site As Though Vacant	Highest and Best Use of Subject Property As Improved
$1.00 per sq. ft.	$0.50 per sq. ft.	$23,700 as commercial and $11,850 as residential = $23,700	$100,000 − 23,700 $76,300	Commercial	Residential
$2.00 per sq. ft.	$0.50 per sq. ft.	$47,400 as commercial and $11,850 as residential = $47,400	$100,000 − 47,400 $52,600	Commercial	Residential
$3.00 per sq. ft.	$0.50 per sq. ft.	$71,100 as commercial and $11,850 as residential = $71,100	$100,000 − 71,100 $28,900	Commercial	Residential
$4.00 per sq. ft.	$0.50 per sq. ft.	$94,800 as commercial and $11,850 as residential = $94,800	$100,000 − 94,800 $5,200	Commercial	Residential
$5.00 per sq. ft.	$0.50 per sq. ft.	$118,500 as commercial and $11,850 as residential = $118,500	$0	Commercial	Commercial (tear down the house)

1. **d) Market value appraisals**
   Page 332

2. **d) All of the above**
   Pages 336-337

3. **d) All of the above**
   Pages 336-337

4. **d) The maximum size improvement**
   Page 332

5. **d) Compliance with supply and demand criteria**
   Page 334

6. **a) Surface parking lots**
   Page 354

7. **c) The improvement value must be adjusted down if the land's highest and best use is different than the improved highest and best use**
   Page 345

8. **b) Highest and best use as though vacant = Two parcels with ±2.5 acres each. Highest and best use as improved = Leave the house and sell off the other site.**

9. **c) Interim use**
   Page 354

10. **a) Buildings can be removed or altered**
    Page 337

11. **a) A use that was legally established and maintained but no longer conforms to existing zoning**
    Pages 349-350

12. **c) $250,000**

13. **b) $245,000**

14. **d) -$5,000**

15. **b) Must estimate an alternative use and then find comparables of buildings that are similar to the alternative use.**
Pages 355-356

16. **c) The property value is $80,000.**

17. **a) Physically possible, legally permissible, financially feasible, and maximally productive**
Page 332

Land and Site Valuation

The amount of space on the face of the earth is finite, so the supply of land is relatively fixed. Prices increase to high levels in some areas because a property's location is also fixed. If land could be physically moved from one location to another, the unique characteristics of different locations would not have such a significant influence on value. For example, commercial land next to a busy street may be very expensive because of the advertising value of the location or ease of access for commuters. Similar sites on a less busy street could not be moved to the busy street and would therefore have less value.

The limitations created by natural boundaries can cause real estate to be more expensive in some areas as compared to others. For example, Chicago has no east side because of its location on Lake Michigan. Los Angeles has natural limitations on its western side where it abuts the Pacific Ocean. Developers in some cities are forced to build multistory buildings rather than single-floor buildings to create space where land is limited. The rights to the space on the face of the earth and the market need for that space, rather than the actual soil, have value.

Value is often created through the subject's location relative to other landmarks. For example, a site on a busy street with access points that create customer traffic will make a fast-food restaurant profitable. On the other hand, a location on a quiet, dead-end street may be the most desirable to residential land buyers.

Relation to Appraisal Principles

Value Concepts and Principles

The anticipation of future benefits is always a consideration in purchasing a property. The value of any item is equal to the present worth of future benefits. Most buyers assume that a parcel purchased today will have resale value in the future and the potential to generate income or other benefits during the holding period when developed to its highest and best use.

Changing economic and physical conditions always affect land value. A new highway adds value to parcels alongside the road if that land can be zoned for commercial use. The change in traffic patterns caused by the new highway may also cause a substantial decline in the value of nearby parcels that are no longer adjacent to the main thoroughfare. This change in market characteristics drives the development of new buildings and the demolition of old ones.

A balance of property types creates optimum value for all. If there is significant demand for residential land but very little land is zoned for residential use, developers are likely to present many petitions to change other zoning classifications to residential. If there is demand for commercial land in an area with no available lots, the prices of existing lots will increase until they reach a point at which it is prudent to tear down existing improvements and redevelop the land.

Mineral, air, and water rights can be significant factors in the analysis of land. Some properties that have available water can be farmed or used for animal grazing while nearby parcels without water may sell for much less. In some areas, a parcel on one side of the road may have abundant water from private wells while owners of a parcel on the other side of the road drill several wells and come up dry every time. A property with water may be farmed or used as a home site, but a dry parcel may have to be put to some other use. In some markets, the residents collect rainwater in ponds, cisterns, or other containers for future use. Appraisers without geographic competency may not know about a water shortage issue.

If the surface of a plot of land is below the flood hazard level and development possibilities are limited, that parcel may still sell for a premium because the buyer knows there are sand and gravel deposits on the site. Sometimes a property appears to have little value because of its limited utility, but it actually has much greater value because of the presence of valuable minerals. For example, what may appear to be nearly worthless land in a flood hazard area that cannot be improved could actually be a valuable sand and gravel mine or a source for underground water. In some markets, water companies are constantly looking for well-head sites, and they are often found in floodplains.

Property Rights and Public Controls

Any analysis of vacant land must include an analysis of zoning, deed, and plat restrictions. In an area of predominantly commercial development, you may find a property on a busy street that is still improved with a one-unit home. In this case, the lot may have a deed restriction that states, "There shall be no commercial land use on any lot in this subdivision." These deed restrictions typically can only be negated by the majority of the property owners or by court order. State, local, and court case laws should be reviewed before assuming a change is possible. Attorneys for title insurance companies or attorneys who specialize in zoning issues may be the best source of advice on these restrictions.

In some states, property owners can sell their rights to develop land to another property owner in the same jurisdiction. These transferable development rights (TDRs) foster higher-density development in urban and suburban areas where utilities are available and infrastructure is in place and preclude development in more remote areas. The development rights of property owners in remote areas have the same value as development rights in areas where utilities and other linkages are present. This doesn't necessarily mean that the properties have the same value, but rather that they have the same component of value attributable to the ability to develop the land. Appraisers working outside their own markets should research zoning carefully to ensure that they understand how these controls will affect value.

A site is a parcel of land that is improved to be used for a specific purpose. A developer creates a site by

· buying raw land
· bringing in utility lines
· adding access points
· moving dirt to provide for drainage

Some real estate is encumbered with easements that preclude certain activities. A conservation easement, a preservation easement, or other agricultural easements may preclude or inhibit certain uses or any development at all.

Physical Characteristics and Site Improvements

The size and shape of a site inhibits certain uses and causes changes in highest and best use. For example, a site next to a major commercial thoroughfare may have diminished value because the parcel is only 30 feet wide and no retailer can use it.

Topography can inhibit certain land uses or at least influence construction costs. A house constructed on the side of a steep hill is much more expensive to build than a house on a level lot. If the residential site on the hill doesn't command a premium in the resale market to offset the additional cost of construction, the vacant parcel may go undeveloped for years until the scarcity of vacant land requires a building or buyer to look at this parcel again. A property at the bottom of a hill may suffer from drainage problems if all the water from above drains down onto the subject site. Drainage problems can be more severe than some appraisers recognize.

View amenities can also affect value. A view of a commercial building may be fine for commercial users, but a residential property owner may have a hard time selling a home that overlooks the same commercial building. Conversely, a residential lot adjacent to a golf course may be worth much more than a parcel across the street that doesn't have the desirable view amenity.

The most important physical factor affecting land value is most likely the availability of public or semipublic utilities. Large areas of vacant land in the path of development may remain undeveloped if the land is not yet connected to public utilities. Many appraisers say that "sewers drive development."

On-site improvements include landscaping, utility hookups, and trees and shrubs. Off-site improvements are not within the property lines but do affect the value of the subject property because of their proximity. For example, new streets, sidewalks, and streetlights in the subject property's neighborhood have a positive effect on value if other competing neighborhoods lack those improvements.

Highest and Best Use

For many years, the Uniform Standards of Professional Appraisal Practice (in Standards Rule

1-3(b)) specified that "[t]he appraiser must recognize that land is appraised as though vacant and available for development to its highest and best use, and that the appraisal of improvements is based on their actual contribution to the site." This language was eventually removed because it was no longer necessary, but the lesson is still valid. Estimating the value of land as though vacant is required so that you can determine whether the building or site improvements need to be razed. When appraising an improved property, appraisers sometimes forget why land is valued as though vacant, which can be a serious problem if they do not recognize that the vacant land can be worth more than the improved property.

Applicability and Limitations of Valuation Techniques

Sales comparison is the preferred method of land valuation, but other methods must often be used. For example, if the subject property is a 90-year-old home in an area of similar older homes, there may not have been a vacant land sale in many years. When market data is scarce, a variety of alternative techniques can be used to estimate land value:

- market extraction
- allocation
- direct capitalization: land residual method
- direct capitalization: ground rent capitalization
- yield capitalization: discounted cash flow analysis

Sales Comparison

The preferred method of land valuation is based on the analysis of historical prices paid for sites similar to the subject by willing buyers and sellers in an open market. If an investigation of historical market data shows that several vacant commercial sites on the subject property's block sold for $5.00 per square foot of usable area, then it would be reasonable to assume that the subject would sell for a similar amount. The sales comparison approach is the simplest to apply and the easiest for appraisal clients, brokers, judges, and juries to understand.

Exhibit 17.1 shows a sales comparison grid in which the subject property is compared to two similar vacant land parcels that were sold in the subject's market area. The sale prices of the comparable sites must be adjusted to account for the differences recognized by the market. The size of the subject site is 0.5 acre and the size of Compa-

rable Site 1 is 0.85 acre. It is reasonable to assume that if the comparable lot was the same size as the subject (i.e., 0.5 acre), it would have sold for less than it did. By subtracting an amount to compensate for the comparable's extra land, the effect of the larger size on the sale price is accounted for. The amount of the adjustment, and sometimes the direction of the adjustment, can be a contentious part of an appraisal when supporting data is spotty. When a large quantity of data is available, more sophisticated statistical analysis can be used in place of the adjustment process.

The sales comparison grid shows some of the most important factors affecting residential sites, and these factors are used to adjust for property differences. In this case, the primary unit of comparison is the "buildable" site. Surplus land, utilities, and other factors are less significant to the property's use. Each market has its own unique issues, however, and other factors could be more important in other markets.

Small adjustments were made for differences in market conditions to compensate for increasing prices over time. The positive adjustments imply that if the comparable properties were sold at the present time, they would sell for more than the recorded gross price in the past. A rolling site appears to be worth more than a level site in this market. However, this is not true in all regions. The grid also indicates that a wooded site is worth more than a site with fewer trees. Again, this is not true in all markets.

Adjustments were made in the grid to compensate for the price range of surrounding homes. Adjustments are made for the price range of improved properties to compensate for the market phenomenon of progression, which means that buyers will pay more for a lot in a higher-priced neighborhood than one in a lower-priced area. Some appraisers make this adjustment by listing one location as superior or inferior to another, but others will try to quantify the adjustment. The use of a percentage adjustment is more precise than using a qualitative method to label one area superior or inferior to another.

In any sales comparison analysis, the adjustment methodology should replicate market reactions to the differences between the subject and comparables as closely as possible. Appraisers sometimes find that percentage adjustments are appropriate, but in other situations they may use dollar adjustments. In many appraisals of nonresi-

Exhibit 17.1   Sales Comparison Grid

	Subject Property	Comparable Sale 1	Adjustment	Comparable Sale 2	Adjustment
Address	8225 Washington Blvd.	1430 E. 82nd Street		1710 E. 80th Street	
Sale price	$0		$79,000		$55,000
Price per sq. ft.	$0	$2.13		$3.61	
Rights transferred	fee simple	fee simple	0.00%	fee simple	0.00%
Subtotal			$79,000		$55,000
Financing	assume cash	contract sale	-5.00%	cash to seller	0.00%
Subtotal			$75,050		$55,000
Conditions of sale*	arm's-length	arm's-length	0.00%	arm's-length	0.00%
Subtotal			$75,050		$55,000
Date of sale	now	5 months ago	1.25%	4 months ago	1.00%
Subtotal			$75,988		$55,550
Topography	rolling	level	5.00%	level	5.00%
Location	cul-de-sac	corner lot	10.00%	cul-de-sac	0.00%
Wooded	10%	50%	-8.00%	50%	-8.00%
Flood area	0.00%	0.00%	0.00%	0.00%	0.00%
Size (square feet)	22,000	37,026		15,246	
Size (acres)†	0.5051	0.8500	-17.25%	0.3500	7.75%
Zoning	residential	residential	0.00%	residential	0.00%
Utilities	public water/sewer	public water/sewer	0.00%	public water/sewer	0.00%
Type (platted)	platted	platted	0.00%	platted	0.00%
Improved property price range‡	$300,000 to $400,000	$450,000 to $550,000	-7.50%	$200,000 to $250,000	6.25%
Other factors	none	none	0.00%	none	0.00%
Net adjustment	N/A		-17.75%		11.00%
Indicated value	N/A		$62,500		$61,661

* Date of sale adjustment = 0.25% per month

† Lot size adjustment = 50% per acre

‡ Price range adjustment = 0.05% per $1,000 in value

dential property, appraisers do not adjust the gross price of comparables. Instead, they adjust a unit of comparison such as price per acre or square foot.

Paired Data Sales Analysis

In paired data sales analysis of land sales, appraisers measure the difference in the sale prices of two properties and explain it by studying differences in the sites. Appraisers normally adjust to a point at which all the bottom-line answers are as close as possible. This is not just luck, it is the method.

For example, assume the subject property is a lot in the middle of the block on Main Street (Lot 15 in Exhibit 17.2). The sale properties are equal to the subject in all other elements of comparison. The process of extracting adjustments from the comparable sales data is shown in Exhibit 17.3.

The first adjustment extracted in the grid is for the date of sale (that is, change in market conditions over time). Comparing the sales of

Lots 2 and 4 shows that the price has increased by $1,000 over the last six months, which implies an appreciation rate of $2,000 per year. Another straightforward example of extraction is between the sales of Lots 20 and 23, for which a $2,000 difference in price occurred over 12 months, again showing an increase of $2,000 per year. Comparing sales of Lots 1 and 6 shows a rate of $2,000 per year as well.

The second adjustment is for street location. Comparing the sale prices of Lots 6 and 12 shows that the market may be paying $1,000 more for lots with frontage on Main Street than for lots with frontage on Market Street. Comparing the sale prices of Lots 14 and 20 further reveals that there seems to be a $1,000 premium for locations on Lake Street over Main Street. Lots 2 and 9 can also be compared to extract a location adjustment after the adjustment for date of sale is made. The

Exhibit 17.2   Lots on Main Street, Market Street, and Lake Street

Market Street 50' R/W -

| Lot 1
Sold $25,000
6 mos. ago | Lot 2
Sold $23,000
12 mos. ago | Lot 3 | Lot 4
Sold $24,000
6 mos. ago | Lot 5 | Lot 6
Sold $26,000
6 days ago |
| Lot 7 | Lot 8 | Lot 9
Sold $26,000
Now | Lot 10 | Lot 11 | Lot 12
Sold $27,000
6 days ago |

Main Street 50' R/W -

| Lot 13
Sold $27,000
Now | Lot 14
Sold $24,000
12 mos. ago | Lot 15
Subject | Lot 16 | Lot 17 | Lot 18 |
| Lot 19
Sold $28,000
Now | Lot 20
Sold $25,000
12 mos. ago | Lot 21 | Lot 22 | Lot 23
Sold $27,000
Now | Lot 24 |

Lake Street 50' R/W -

Exhibit 17.3   Adjustment Grid Using Extracted Rates

	Lot 1	Lot 2	Lot 4	Lot 6	Lot 9	Lot 12	Lot 13	Lot 14	Lot 19	Lot 20	Lot 23
Sale price	$25,000	$23,000	$24,000	$26,000	$26,000	$27,000	$27,000	$24,000	$28,000	$25,000	$27,000
Date of sale	6 mos.	12 mos.	6 mos.	now	now	now	now	12 mos.	now	12 mos.	now
	+1,000	+2,000	+1,000	0	0	0	0	+2,000	0	+2,000	0
Street location	Market	Market	Market	Market	Main	Main	Main	Main	Lake	Lake	Lake
	+1,000	+1,000	+1,000	+1,000	0	0	0	0	−1,000	−1,000	−1,000
Corner	yes	no	no	yes	no	yes	yes	no	yes	no	no
	−1,000			−1,000		−1,000	−1,000		−1,000		
Adjusted price	$26,000	$26,000	$26,000	$26,000	$26,000	$26,000	$26,000	$26,000	$26,000	$26,000	$26,000

sales of Lots 14 and 23 can also be considered to derive an indication of the adjustment for location but only after adjustment for the date of sale. There could also be an adverse locational issue for properties adjacent to or above Market Street; the farther the property is away from that adverse influence, the less its price is affected.

A final adjustment is made for corner influence. This adjustment rate can be extracted from comparable sales of Lots 9 and 12, which imply

that the price of a corner lot is $1,000 more than a property that is not on a corner. Comparing Lots 19 and 23 also supports a $1,000 higher price for the corner lots.

Market Extraction

Market extraction is used to estimate land value when there are few or no comparable land sales in the subject's area or in competing areas. The methodology requires you to research recent

> **The premise behind extraction can be stated as:**
>
> If *X* amount is what the house and land sold for, then what's left over after removing the value of the house from *X* amount must be the value of the land.

comparable sales of improved properties in the subject's area. You then develop an estimate of reproduction cost for each sale property and subtract both the appropriate amount of depreciation and the net value of the site improvements from the gross price. The remainder is the indicated value of the lot. This method can be useful in appraisals in which the land and locational attributes of comparables are very similar to the subject, but extraction of land value is less accurate when the subject and comparables have very different attributes.

Exhibit 17.4 illustrates the extraction method. The comparable property sold for $301,000 (land and buildings). The total cost of the improvements was $253,750. Depreciation from all causes is estimated at 12%, which reduces the indicated value of the building improvements to $223,300. When this amount and the cost of the site improvements ($12,500) are subtracted from the sale price, the net result is the indicated value of the land.

Of course, more than one of these analyses are necessary to support such a conclusion. The extraction technique is not used often because of the number of subjective inputs. It is useful when the subject's site contains an unusual attribute or license and there are no sales of similar vacant land. For example, assume the subject site is located outside a flood hazard area because it is two feet higher than the surrounding ground. All of the comparable sales in the area are in the flood hazard area and do not reflect the subject's use.

Exhibit 17.4	Land Value via Market Extraction		
Gross sale price			$351,000
Cost of residence	2,800 @ $75.00 =	$210,000	
Cost of basement	500 @ $25.00 =	$12,500	
Cost of porches, etc.	500 @ $25.00 =	$12,500	
Cost of garage	750 @ $25.00 =	$18,750	
Total cost of building improvements		$253,750	
Total depreciation (all causes)	12%	− $30,450	
Depreciated value of building improvements			− $223,300
Depreciated value of site improvements			− $12,500
Estimated land value			$115,200

Market extraction can be used if there are sales of improved properties but no land sales. However, it cannot be used to estimate the value of a buildable site for a legally nonconforming use because land is always valued at its highest and best use "as though vacant" and the legal uses of such a property would be lesser uses.

For example, assume the subject property is improved with an older one-unit home on a lot at the corner of two very busy streets. If this property with this house were in an interior location of a subdivision in that market, it would sell for $150,000. Of this $150,000, $35,000 is attributable to the land value, $5,000 is attributable to the site improvements, and $110,000 is attributable to the building value. Because this home is located on a busy street, the property would sell for only $140,000 as a residential property after a discount for the influence of traffic and noise. In this case, the land has a much higher and better use as commercial land and is estimated to be worth $100,000 as commercial land through the analysis of comparable commercial sales. If the extraction method were used, the extracted land value would only be $25,000, calculated as follows:

Overall value	$140,000
Less value of the building	− 110,000
Less value of the site improvements	− 5,000
Land value	$25,000

The house does not contribute the same amount of value on both sites, so this extracted land value is incorrect. In fact, this house is very close to meeting the wrecking ball and the value is much lower. This technique is unreliable when consistent use issues must be addressed.

Allocation

Allocation is another technique used by appraisers when they need an opinion of land value but cannot find any recent land sale comparables. The allocation method is a ratio technique in which improved property sales and vacant land sales in an area that competes with the subject are researched. A ratio of land value to property value is then established and applied to the subject's area. Some appraisers also support the ratio of land value to building value using assessor's records.

Allocation is based on the theory that land value is a function of the entire property value. Also, the subject and comparable properties must be improved to their highest and best use to prevent any loss in value due to an inconsistent use. If the subject is improved to its highest and best use and a comparable is not, the analysis can be skewed. Like extraction, allocation may not be as accurate as sales comparison analysis because of the difficulty in finding persuasive, reliable support for the ratio of land value to property value.

Exhibit 17.5 summarizes the characteristics of four sales of improved properties in areas where land value can easily be estimated. The property in Sale 1 sold for $400,000 and the land is valued at $80,000. The ratio of land value to property value (V_L/V_O) is 20%. This ratio can then be applied to the subject's area to estimate a value range there. If property values in the subject's neighborhood range from $425,000 to $475,000, a reasonable value estimate for the subject's land would be $85,000 to $95,000.

Income Capitalization Procedures

The various income capitalization techniques of land valuation may be the most appropriate methods for the valuation of leased land, especially if a property is under a long-term lease. These techniques may be the primary methods in some situations and not applied at all in others.

In most states, land leases are legally considered leased fee and leasehold interests. If the subject is a vacant parcel leased to a parking lot operator, there is some risk that the operator will not pay the rent. If the subject property is a vacant parcel of land and is leased for a long term to a lessee who built a substantial improvement on it, the land is generally not comparable to the property that is now a surface parking lot. The risk levels are much different because the lessee with the building on the land will lose the rights to the building if there is a default, but the surface parking lot owner usually has little invested.

Direct Capitalization: Land Residual Method

To develop an estimate of land value, the land residual method partitions the income into income attributable to the building and income attribut-

IRV Ratios

The IRV graphic is used to help students and clients understand how to apply direct capitalization techniques using the ratio of income, capitalization rate, and value. To visualize the mathematical relationship between the variables, put your finger over the variable you want to solve for and place that variable on the left side of the equation. With the variable in question covered, the other two variables form a product or quotient that you place on the right side of the equation:

- $I = R/V$
- $R = I/V$
- $V = I/R$

To solve for I, R, or V, you need to know the value of the other two variables on the right side of the equation.

The IRV relationship holds for income, value, and capitalization rates attributable to the entire property or to a property's single component (or combination of components). The ratios do not hold if variables for different elements of the property are mixed. For example, you cannot calculate the total net operating income of the property using a capitalization rate or value to the land.

able to the land. This technique is difficult to apply because it requires data that can be almost impossible to find in many markets. You must know the building value, the building capitalization rate, the net operating income of the property, and the capitalization rate for the land. The land and capitalization rates are further complicated by differences in the risk associated with some leases.

After gross income is estimated and expenses are subtracted, net operating income (I_O) can be divided into land and building components. The overall capitalization rate (R_O) is the ratio of a property's net operating income to the lump-sum value or sale price, so this ratio can be used to estimate the income of a component if the component's value is known. If the capitalization rate to the building (R_B) is 0.10 and the value of the build-

Exhibit 17.5	Land Value via the Allocation Method			
	Sale 1	**Sale 2**	**Sale 3**	**Sale 4**
Sale price	$400,000	$400,000	$420,000	$440,000
Estimated land value	− 80,000	− 80,000	− 84,000	− 88,000
Estimated building value	$320,000	$320,000	$336,000	$352,000
Land/property ratio	20.00%	18.67%	20.45%	20.00%

When the subject of the appraisal is a parcel of leased land, the marketable interest owned by the lessor is the leased fee. When a vacant tract is leased, the landlord's interest is the leased fee. When a large building is built on that leased land by the tenant, the landlord's interest is still the leased fee. The building owner's interest is the leasehold. The "landowner" and the "building owner" are really just the holders of the leased fee and leasehold interests.

ing is known to be $800,000, the income to the building (I_B) can be calculated by multiplying the building value (V_B) by the building capitalization rate (R_B). Once the building income is known, that amount can be subtracted from the overall net operating income to calculate the income to the land (I_L). Once the income to the land is known, the value of the land can be calculated by dividing the income to the land by the capitalization rate to the land. At this point, the land value and building value can be added together to get the overall property value. Exhibit 17.6 shows how to calculate land value using the land residual method.

Keep in mind that the separation of the land and building components for the purposes of analysis is a theoretical division of the real estate because the leased fee and leasehold interests are the actual rights transferred.

Direct Capitalization: Ground Rent Capitalization

Ground rent capitalization is simpler and much more commonly used than the land residual technique described earlier in this chapter. Comparable land sales with similar lease rates and terms are usually difficult to find, so ground rent capitalization may be the only viable technique available to estimate the land value of properties for which the lease income is the most significant attribute. This technique is useful in many land lease situ-

ations and requires few subjective inputs. The direct capitalization of ground rent can be illustrated as follows:

Income to the land (I_L)	$12,000
Capitalization rate for the land (R_L)	÷ 0.12
	$100,000

Some appraisers combine data sources to establish a capitalization rate. They research the sale price of a comparable property that is not leased and the lease rate of a property that has not been sold. Then they combine the lease rate from the property that is leased but has not been sold with the sale price of the property that has been sold but not leased. Combining two different property data sets to get a capitalization rate is less desirable than extracting data directly from the market, but it can be an effective tool in markets where data is limited. The difficulty of combining data like this is that a property with good upside potential will result in a much different sale price than a property with inferior potential, but the lease rates could be exactly the same and the ratio of income to value will be skewed as a result. Combining these data sources should only be done when there is no other way of obtaining the capitalization rate, and it should be checked using other methods to ensure its accuracy. The use of direct capitalization will be the subject of further discussion in later chapters.

Yield Capitalization: Subdivision Development Method (Discounted Cash Flow Analysis)

Subdivision development analysis is based on a discounted cash flow model using the sales of residential, commercial, or industrial lots as the cash flow and the absorption period as the holding period. The value of development land is based

---

Exhibit 17.6	Land Value via the Land Residual Method

The net operating income for the property is $125,000:	$I_O = \$125,000$
The capitalization rate for the land is 10%:	$R_L = 0.10$
The value of the building is $800,000:	$V_B = \$800,000$
The capitalization rate to the building is 12%:	$R_B = 0.12$
Therefore,	
The value of the building multiplied by the capitalization rate to the building equals the income to the building.	$I_B = V_B \times R_B = \$800,000 \times 0.12 = \$96,000$
The income to the building is subtracted from the income overall to determine the income to the land.	$I_L = I_O - I_B = \$125,000 - \$96,000 = \$29,000$
The income to the land is divided by the capitalization rate to the land to estimate land value.	$V_L = \$29,000/0.10 = \$290,000$

on the number of lots that can be developed from it. This technique is applicable in most markets but is complex and therefore used less often when vacant land sales are common and plentiful. This technique requires a large number of calculations, which makes it more cumbersome and less persuasive than direct sales comparison analysis. If comparable sales or listings are available, most appraisers use them in sales comparison analysis rather than apply the more complicated and subjective subdivision development technique.

For example, assume a 40-acre parcel has a highest and best use as a 60-lot residential subdivision. The average lot price is $147,500, the typical buyer is a home builder, and the projection period is over the next 24 months. We can assume the lot prices are stable, but in some cases the discounted cash flow analysis would include small price increases over the holding period. In some markets, development costs are condensed into a shorter period of time, but in others the development costs may start at the end of period one and continue to be paid for all the way into the fourth period. When these costs are incurred can vary in different markets, and the timing may even be different in different price ranges.

In this assignment, you are appraising the raw land, which means the development costs need to be subtracted. The discount rates used in this analysis include a line item for the developer's profit (or entrepreneurial incentive). In some markets, the developer's profit is not considered

> If you can find truly comparable sales of raw land, sales comparison analysis is preferable to the more complicated subdivision development technique.

as a line item but is reflected in a much higher discount rate.

Exhibit 17.7 summarizes the calculations and shows that the indicated land value by the subdivision development method is approximately $3,927,561, which would be rounded to $3.9 million.

The subdivision development method is used widely to value raw land in some areas of the United States but is not used at all in others. In most markets, when the highest and best use of raw land is use as development land for a subdivision, many comparable sales will usually be available because these properties are often located in areas of high development. Comparable sales of development land sometimes have to be analyzed carefully because topographical issues limit the number of lots that can be platted on parcels of the same size. For example, one 100-acre parcel may allow for 50 lots to be built, but another 100-acre parcel that is more level could be developed with 100 lots. The higher-density property is worth more to a developer. In some markets, subdivision development analysis is applied to adjust for differences in zoning ordinances.

While this technique for the valuation of the raw land may have limited applicability in many markets, it is commonly used when clients ask for

Exhibit 17.7   Land Value via Discounted Cash Flow Analysis

Quarter	1	2	3	4	5	6	7	8	Total
Lots per quarter	7.5	7.5	7.5	7.5	7.5	7.5	7.5	7.5	60
Sale price per lot	$147,500	$147,500	$147,500	$147,500	$147,500	$147,500	$147,500	$147,500	
Estimated *PGI*	1,106,250	1,106,250	1,106,250	1,106,250	1,106,250	1,106,250	1,106,250	1,106,250	$8,850,000
Less estimated expenses									
Development costs	$400,000	$400,000	$400,000	$400,000	$0	$0	$0	$0	$1,600,000
Real estate taxes	$4,000	$4,000	$4,000	$4,000	$2,000	$2,000	$2,000	$2,000	$24,000
Sales commission (6%)	$66,375	$66,375	$66,375	$66,375	$66,375	$66,375	$66,375	$66,375	$531,000
Advertising, etc. (4%)	$44,250	$44,250	$44,250	$44,250	$44,250	$44,250	$44,250	$44,250	$354,000
Entrepreneurial incentive (20%)	$221,250	$221,250	$221,250	$221,250	$221,250	$221,250	$221,250	$221,250	$1,770,000
Total expenses	$735,875	$735,875	$735,875	$735,875	$333,875	$333,875	$333,875	$333,875	$4,279,000
Net cash flow	$370,375	$370,375	$370,375	$370,375	$772,375	$772,375	$772,375	$772,375	$4,571,000
Discounted @ 12%	97.09%	94.26%	91.51%	88.85%	86.26%	83.75%	81.31%	78.94%	
Present value	$359,587	$349,114	$338,946	$329,073	$666,257	$646,852	$628,012	$609,720	$3927,561
Present value of land = sum of the present value amounts									$3,927,561

the market value of an existing or proposed project at the point of completion. A lender may ask for the market value of a project when the streets, utilities, and other improvements are in place, and subdivision analysis may be the only tool that can replicate the actions of a typical buyer when there are no comparable sales of completed projects that were sold by the developer to another buyer. In other words, if the lender asks for a market value opinion for the project as raw land and as completed but unsold, this technique may be the only tool available.

1. A *site* is different than *land* because
   a) *Land* represents an improved *site*.
   b) A *site* is improved *land* that is ready to be built upon.
   c) The *land* development method is used to value a *site*.
   d) No difference exists.

2. Land is always valued at
   a) Its current land use as though vacant
   b) Its highest and best use as though vacant
   c) The predominating land uses in the neighborhood
   d) The preferred use of the appraiser's client

3. Sites can be valued by
   a) Sales comparison analysis only
   b) Sales comparison and extraction only
   c) Income capitalization analysis only
   d) Extraction, allocation, and sales comparison

4. In sales comparison analysis, comparable sales are adjusted
   a) To the typical property in the market
   b) To the other sales
   c) To allow for matching up with the other sales
   d) To the subject property

5. When estimating the market value of a site, the appraisal should include
   a) Three comparable site sales transactions
   b) Five to six comparable site sales transactions
   c) Seven to eight comparable site sales transactions
   d) There is no set number of comparable site sales transactions

6. If market value is sought, the sales comparison approach to site valuation is based primarily on an analysis of the market behavior of
   a) Buyers
   b) Sellers
   c) Brokers
   d) Lenders

7. Adjustments to the prices of comparable sites are measured by
   a) Cost to cure any deficiency in the subject property
   b) Front footage
   c) Square footage
   d) The amount a typical buyer will pay more or less for the item

8. In the valuation of land by sales comparison, the order of adjustment should begin with
   a) Property rights transferred
   b) Access and topography
   c) Terms of sale or financing
   d) Location

9. A comparable site sold six months ago for $4,000. It was 10% superior to the subject site with respect to location and 15% inferior to the subject with respect to frontage and shape. The market conditions adjustment is 10% per year. The adjusted sale price of the comparable site (rounded to the nearest $100) is
   a) $4,300
   b) $4,400
   c) $4,500
   d) $4,600

10. A new and improved non-residential property just sold for $235,000. Direct construction costs were $126,000, and indirect costs were 15% of direct costs. Builder's overhead and profit were 25% of total costs. What is the land value by extraction (rounded to the nearest $5,000)?
    a) $50,000
    b) $55,000
    c) $60,000
    d) $65,100

11. The valuation of land with a highest and best use as an industrial subdivision can be estimated using
    a) The summation of the value of all sites
    b) The subdivision development method
    c) The allocation method
    d) The extraction method

12. Use the following instructions to determine the value of the subject property:
   - Assume an appreciation rate of 3% per year.
   - Assume that a rolling site is worth more than a level site.
   - Assume that a wooded site is worth more than a non-wooded site.
   - Assume that a larger site is worth more than a smaller one.
   - Assume that a lot in a higher-priced addition is worth more than a less expensive one.
   - Use percentage adjustments and subtotal after the market conditions adjustments are made.

	Subject Property	Comparable 1	Adjustment	Comparable 2	Adjustment	Comparable 3	Adjustment
Address	1234 W. 87th St	9001 Kissel Road		1112 W. 91st Street		815 W. 86th Street	
Sale price			$45,000		$60,000		$52,000
Rights transferred	fee simple	fee simple	_____	fee simple	_____	fee simple	_____
Subtotal			_____		_____		_____
Financing	assume cash	cash to seller	_____	cash to seller	_____	listing only	_____
Subtotal			_____		_____		_____
Conditions of sale	arm's-length	arm's-length	_____	arm's-length	_____	arm's-length	_____
Subtotal			_____		_____		_____
Market conditions	current	6 months ago	_____	9 months ago	_____	current listing	_____
Subtotal			_____		_____		_____
Topography	rolling	rolling	_____	level	_____	level	_____
Location	River Township	River Township	_____	River Township	_____	River Township	_____
Wooded	75%	25%	_____	75%	_____	25%	_____
Flood area	10.00%	equal	_____	equal	_____	equal	_____
Size (acres)	1.2500	1.0000	_____	1.7500	_____	1.0000	_____
Zoning	Residential R1	Residential R1	_____	Residential R1	_____	Residential R1	_____
Utilities	all public	all public	_____	all public	_____	all public	_____
Type (platted)	platted	platted	_____	platted	_____	platted	_____
Improved property	$200,000	$150,000	_____	$300,000	_____	$300,000	_____
Price range	$300,000	$250,000	_____	$400,000	_____	$400,000	_____
Other factors	none	none	_____	none	_____	none	_____
Net adjustment	N/A		_____		_____		_____
Indicated value	N/A		_____		_____		_____

Note that Comparable 3 is only an offering (i.e., a listing) and has no contract of sale or even a purchase offer.

13. Use the following instructions to determine the value of the subject property:
    - Calculate the price per square foot of land area and use that as the basis of the analysis.
    - Do not use percentage or dollar adjustments. Use qualitative analysis to show if the comparable is superior or inferior to the subject.
    - Assume that prices are increasing.
    - Assume that the East Side of town is inferior to the West Side.
    - Assume that more access points are better than less access points.
    - Assume that higher zoning numbers indicate that the owner has more latitude and greater utility of the site.
    - Assume that in this market, larger parcel sizes mean a lower price per square foot.

Comparable Land Analysis (Qualitative Analysis)					
	Subject	Comparable 1		Comparable 2	
Address	123 Nicole Street	505 Jeanine Drive		123 Eunice Lane	
Data source	N/A	Co-op # 29761		Co-op # 29761	
Sale price	$0		$560,960		$350,000
Price per square foot	$0		$2.61		$3.48
Rights transferred	fee simple	fee simple	_____	fee simple	_____
Financing	assume cash	cash sale	_____	cash sale	_____
Conditions of sale	arm's-length	arm's-length	_____	arm's-length	_____
Date of sale	current	12 months ago	_____	18 months ago	_____
Topography	level	level	_____	level	_____
Location	West Side	East Side	_____	West Side	_____
Access	1 point	2 points	_____	2 points	_____
Visibility	avg./industrial	equal	_____	superior	_____
Flood area	0.00%	0.00%	_____	0.00%	_____
Road frontage	166	341	_____	305	_____
Average depth	981	630	_____	330	_____
Size (square feet)	162,818	215,000	_____	100,500	_____
Size (acres)	3.7378	4.936	_____	2.301	_____
Zoning	Industrial I3S	Industrial I3S	_____	Industrial I4S	_____
Utilities	all public	all public	_____	all public	_____
Other factors	none	none	_____	none	_____
Indicated value per sq. ft.			_____		_____

Note: Unless otherwise noted, italicized references indicate the pages in *The Appraisal of Real Estate*, 14th edition, that readers should consult for additional discussion of these topics.

1. **b) A *site* is improved *land* that is ready to be built upon.**
   Page 189

2. **b) Its highest and best use as though vacant**
   Page 362

3. **d) Extraction, allocation, and sales comparison**
   Page 364

4. **d) To the subject property**
   Pages 364-366

5. **d) There is no set number of comparable site sales transactions**
   Pages 364-368

6. **a) Buyers**
   This student handbook

7. **d) The amount a typical buyer will pay more or less for the item**
   Pages 364-368

8. **a) Property rights transferred**
   Page 368

9. **b) $4,400**
   $4,000 \times 1.05 = 4,200$
   [market conditions adjustment]
   $4,200 \times (1 + -0.10 + 0.15)$
   [adjustments for physical differences]
   $4,200 \times 1.05 = 4,410$

10. **b) $55,000**
    $235,000 - (126,000 \times 1.15 \times 1.25) = 53,875$

11. **b) The subdivision development method**
    Page 372

12. The following is a suggested solution; there is no absolute solution to this problem.

	Subject Property	Comparable 1	Adjustment	Comparable 2	Adjustment	Comparable 3	Adjustment
Address	1234 W. 87th St	9001 Kissel Road		1112 W. 91st Street		815 W. 86th Street	
Sale price			$45,000		$60,000		$52,000
Rights transferred	fee simple	fee simple	_____	fee simple	_____	fee simple	_____
Subtotal			_____		_____		_____
Financing	assume cash	cash to seller	_____	cash to seller	_____	listing only	_____
Subtotal			_____		_____		_____
Conditions of sale	arm's-length	arm's-length	_____	arm's-length	_____	arm's-length	_____
Subtotal			_____		_____		_____
Market conditions	current	6 months ago	+1.5%	9 months ago	+2.25%	current listing	_____
Subtotal			$45,675		61,350		52,000
Topography	rolling	rolling	_____	level	+5%	level	+5%
Location	River Township	River Township	_____	River Township	_____	River Township	_____
Wooded	75%	25%	+5%	75%	_____	25%	+5%
Flood area	10.00%	equal	_____	equal	_____	equal	_____
Size (acres)	1.2500	1.0000	+5%	1.7500	-10%	1.0000	+5%
Zoning	Residential R1	Residential R1	_____	Residential R1	_____	Residential R1	_____
Utilities	all public	all public	_____	all public	_____	all public	_____
Type (platted)	platted	platted	_____	platted	_____	platted	_____
Improved property	$200,000	$150,000	_____	$300,000	_____	$300,000	_____
Price range	$300,000	$250,000	+5%	$400,000	-10%	$400,000	_____
Other factors	none	none	_____	none	_____	none	_____
Net adjustment	N/A		15%		-15%		5%
Indicated value	N/A		52,526		52,148		54,600

13. The following is a suggested solution; there is no absolute solution to this problem.

	Subject	Comparable 1		Comparable 2	
		Comparable Land Analysis (Qualitative Analysis)			
	Subject	**Comparable 1**		**Comparable 2**	
Address	123 Nicole Street	505 Jeanine Drive		123 Eunice Lane	
Data source	N/A	Co-op # 29761		Co-op # 29761	
Sale price	$0		$560,960		$350,000
Price per square foot	$0		$2.61		$3.48
Rights transferred	fee simple	fee simple	_____	fee simple	_____
Financing	assume cash	cash sale	_____	cash sale	_____
Conditions of sale	arm's-length	arm's-length	_____	arm's-length	_____
Date of sale	current	12 months ago	inferior	18 months ago	inferior
Topography	level	level	_____	level	_____
Location	West Side	East Side	inferior	West Side	_____
Access	1 point	2 points	superior	2 points	superior
Visibility	avg./industrial	equal	_____	superior	superior
Flood area	0.00%	0.00%	_____	0.00%	_____
Road frontage	166	341	superior	305	superior
Average depth	981	630	_____	330	_____
Size (square feet)	162,818	215,000	_____	100,500	_____
Size (acres)	3.7378	4.936	inferior	2.301	superior
Zoning	Industrial I3S	Industrial I3S	_____	Industrial I4S	superior
Utilities	all public	all public	_____	all public	_____
Other factors	none	none	_____	none	_____
Indicated value per sq. ft.		A little more than	$2.61	Much less than	$3.48

AKA
Elements of
Comparison
(most common)

Adjustments to sale
↗ price are made

- Quantitative ↗ methodical

✓ vs

- qualitative ↗ intuitive
  adjustments to the sale
  price of comps are not made.
  (- aka - Direct Comparison)
  ex.: C.M.A.

Subject and comparable
Sales are presented on a
Spread sheet that allows
for $ adjustments for individual
line items * Key difference

gross adjustment ⊛ or
- most important
indicated value

4 elements of Comparison

- terms + conditions   - seller pays closing costs - should be deducted from sale
                                                        price dollar for dollar
- Date of Sale
- location of elements
- physical elements

18

The Sales Comparison Approach

The sales comparison approach is the analysis of historical sales, current listings, and even expired listings of similar real properties in a market. This approach can also include the research and analysis of the market history of the subject property. The subject property is valued by comparing similar properties that currently are or recently were on the market or were sold recently. It is usually reasonable to assume that the subject property will sell for an amount similar to the adjusted sale prices of the comparable properties or less than the adjusted list prices of properties on the market or recently off the market.

The sales comparison approach is the most easily understood approach to value and is a direct reflection of market thinking if the comparables used are truly comparable. This approach is not limited to sales that have closed; it is good appraisal practice to analyze current and pending listings of similar properties as well as historical sales.

In addition to the analysis of comparable sales, it is your responsibility to research and reconcile any prior listings or sales of the subject. In every market value appraisal, you must research if the subject was exposed to the market and, if so, at what price. A prior listing of the subject often provides convincing evidence of value. Given competent exposure and a reasonable amount of exposure time, it is illogical to assume that a property would sell for more than the price it was recently listed for if it did not sell.

Relation to Appraisal Principles

Supply and Demand
The best way to analyze market supply and demand factors is to use comparable sales and listings of properties in the same market. An imbalance of supply and demand will be obvious first in the comparable listings and then eventually in the comparable sales. The cost and income capitalization approaches react much less quickly to changes in the market. Many appraisers believe that the first evidence of a declining market can be seen in the comparable listings as list prices are reduced to facilitate sales.

Substitution
The principle of substitution is the basis of the sales comparison approach. A subject property has to be worth less than or as much as the list prices of similar properties in the same market, assuming the comparable properties were priced and marketed adequately. A buyer would always buy a lower-priced substitute if such a property is available and truly comparable. Buyers do not decide how much to pay for real estate based on comparable sales but rather on comparable listings. Comparable listings, rather than properties that have already sold, make up a buyer's options. Appraisers study sales because they need to answer the question of what the eventual sale price of the subject property will be.

Balance
The principle of balance holds that the forces of supply and demand will seek equilibrium. If there is an oversupply of properties for sale in a particular market, the prices of existing properties tend to fall, and builders ideally stop developing new ones. Builders will only start building again once the oversupply is absorbed.

Externalities
Many factors outside the property affect property value. A railroad corridor adjacent to a residential property affects value negatively, while proxim-

KEY TERMS	
arm's-length transaction	sales comparison approach
elements of comparison	units of comparison

ity to conveniences and neighborhood prestige affects values positively. Proximity to an airport may be a very positive attribute for a distribution operation of lightweight products, but proximity to a railroad or shipping lane may be very important to a distributor of large industrial products such as heavy equipment and machinery.

Market Analysis and Highest and Best Use
The selection of comparable sales follows directly from the analyses of the competitive market and the highest and best use of the subject and comparable properties. Highest and best use analysis reveals the property characteristics that the market deems most valuable, which helps appraisers compare meaningful differences in properties that have sold or are currently listed.

Applicability and Limitations
The sales comparison approach is nearly always applicable in market value appraisals. If an appraiser is estimating market value, it stands to reason there should be some market activity to analyze. It is not possible to have market value unless there is a market. Properties rarely have a market (that is, potential buyers) but no comparable sales.

Even when the typical buyers base their decisions on the potential income of a property, sales comparison analysis is valid. This approach also works when the market is weak and there are distressed sales. When the subject improvements do not represent the highest and best use of the site and when prices are going up or down rapidly, the sales comparison approach is the best approach to use.

In addition to the analysis of comparable sales, appraisers can also consider current and expired listings as indications of what the market will bear. If a property was recently offered for sale and did not sell, you can assume that the subject would not sell for the adjusted listing price either. Listings are often used when the data is not very recent or very good.

Prior sales or listings of the subject or the comparable sales used in an appraisal may help to validate the current data. For example, if you find a comparable sale that was reportedly sold for $400,000 this year but a little historical research shows that the same property sold last year for only $200,000, you should investigate what happened to cause this 100% increase in sale price in the span of only one year. In most markets, if

a property sold for $450,000 this year, $380,000 last year, and $345,000 four years earlier (or if the prices had dropped in the same proportion over the same period), appraisers would have little fear that the current data was reported incorrectly.

If you cannot find any recent sales but there are many listings, this may indicate that the market is favoring buyers and penalizing sellers or experiencing decreasing prices. If you find many recent sales and few listings, this may indicate that the market is favoring sellers. In this market, there may be a sharp increase in prices in the short run. In the long run, builders should fill the demand. If you cannot find any similar sales, expired listings, or active listings, highest and best use analysis must come into question.

For example, consider a fire station. There are no sales of comparable properties in the area because there is no market for a fire station as a fire station, because the only possible buyer for that use already owns it. In a market value appraisal, an alternative use is the highest and best use. An appraiser who uses the cost approach to support an opinion of market value for a fire station is actually not doing a market value appraisal but instead appraising use value.

Procedure
The procedure for sales comparison analysis is as follows:

1. *Research the market for information on sales, listings, and offerings.* This step is usually easy for residential appraisers because organized multiple listing service (MLS) systems are computerized and access is relatively inexpensive and convenient. In nonresidential markets, data can often be difficult to find. Sales data is sometimes only obtainable in nonresidential markets by direct research or interviews with buyers or sellers. In many markets, sales data is listed in county records. Some records include the sale details, while others list only the price paid.

2. *Verify the information.* It is the appraiser's responsibility to research data sufficiently to provide support for the value opinion. If the data sources are unreliable, you must research the data further to confirm it or use enough data to ensure that one piece of misinformation will not skew the conclusion. While there is no set standard for confirmation, your

peers can tell you how thoroughly you must check data.

3. *Select the relevant units of comparison.* The price per square foot of gross building area including land is the relevant unit in many markets. In others, the price per square foot of land including buildings is the most relevant. The price may be divided by other price units to find the most relevant rate. Real estate brokers are usually able to tell appraisers what the relevant units of comparison are in a particular market, and statistical tools indicate a market consistency. This will be explored further in the following chapters.

4. *Look for relevant differences in the comparable properties and adjust accordingly.* This step is the analysis of elements of comparison, which are the reasons that real estate prices vary. The selection is usually not a problem, but adjustment amounts for differences can be difficult to extract from the market and support in the appraisal report. Unsupported or illogical adjustments should be avoided.

5. *Reconcile the value conclusions into a single point estimate or range of values.* Collecting, confirming, and analyzing sales data is of little consequence if you cannot reconcile the data into a persuasive, supportable opinion of value.

Researching Transactional Data
Finding data can be the most difficult part of an appraisal assignment. Appraisers of nonresidential property often rely on data from commercial third-party data services such as CoStar. The data source used by most residential appraisers is the local multiple listing service (MLS). Brokers use the MLS system as an advertising technique, and they provide the available market data. The data can be, and often is, tainted by the efforts of brokers to sell properties. Appraisers need to exercise discretion when using MLS data or data from a third-party source exclusively as support for an opinion of value.

To avoid misrepresenting data, you should include enough comparable data to allow for one or more pieces of data to fall out without significantly affecting the analysis. For example, starting with four to six comparable sales would help ensure that at least three of the sales are verifiable and consistent. If this cannot be done, you should verify the data with at least two parties to each transaction. Using minimal amounts of data and not verifying it is unacceptable to most clients,

---

Cascading Errors or Inbreeding Data
When all three approaches to value rely on data from the same statistical population, the independence of the data used in the analyses is compromised. This situation is commonly known as *cascading errors* or *inbreeding data*. In a set of inbred property or transaction data, one unreliable or erroneous data point can have a disproportionate effect on the results of the analysis because that data is used in multiple approaches to value and thereby sabotages the ability of the value indication of one approach to value to provide a check against errors in the others. Verification of property and transaction information is the best way to ensure that the sales data is adequate for the assignment.

state appraiser boards, and courts. Remember that data is not limited to sales. The relevant data can include expired or active listings and prior sales or listings of the subject. Evidence of market activity comes in many shapes and forms.

Verifying Transactional Data
Appraisers are responsible for providing enough evidence of value to support the conclusion. Three comparables may be enough if they are verifiable and give conclusive evidence of the value opinion. If, on the other hand, there is a chance that the data used may be considered inconclusive, additional data should be presented. To support an indication of market value, comparable sales must meet the conditions listed in the definition of value. In a market value appraisal, the sales need to be recent, arm's-length transactions with cash-equivalent terms. If a sale does not meet the defined value criteria, the sale price must be adjusted to account for the difference.

Selecting Units of Comparison
Units of comparison are generally market-specific. For example, it is common for farmland to be broken down into price per acre, commercial land into price per square foot or front foot, and improved commercial or industrial properties into price per square foot of building area including land. Residences are rarely valued by converting the price into a unit of comparison because the data is usually of much better quality.

In appraisals of nonresidential property, it is not unusual to see comparable properties that sold for $200,000 and others that sold for $2 million on the same page of a report. It is difficult to compare $200,000 and $2 million sales in a meaningful way unless the prices are converted into a unit of comparison. This type of comparison is usually found when sales data is poor. However, an appraiser analyzing a $200,000 home sale alongside a $2 million home sale is likely to have the appraisal rejected by many clients. Residential property data is often much more accessible, which allows for analyses based on gross price.

If an appraiser uses a price per acre or perhaps the price per square foot of gross building area including land as the unit of comparison, some thought needs to be given to economies of scale. For example, while the total price of farmland increases with every additional acre, the price per acre starts to decrease at a certain point. In other words, the farmer receives a quantity discount in some markets when the parcel reaches a certain size.

Exhibit 18.1 lists five recent sales of agricultural land in the subject property's market. This gives an example of appraisal data that makes little sense unless it is broken down using a unit of comparison. Envision an appraisal in which this data is presented using only the gross sale prices. Comparing a property with a sale price of $1 million to one with a price of $75,000 would be meaningless unless the prices were broken down into a price per acre. Once this is done, the relative sale prices make much more sense.

Analyzing and Adjusting Comparable Sales

Many different factors affect the sale prices of real estate, and appraisers must investigate and report the reasons prices of comparable properties vary. Adjusting for differences is often the most contentious part of an appraisal. The adjustment amount should reflect the differences recognized by the market.

The adjusted sale price of a comparable is the bottom line. Each comparable sale can provide an indication of value for the subject, but some sellers and buyers may be more or less motivated or the transaction may have unusual circumstances that are not disclosed. As a result, a single sale can often be misleading. Appraisers often consider three sales as a minimum number for analysis, but the minimum varies by property type and the amount of data available in the market. Some properties

clearly require six or seven comparable sales to produce persuasive evidence of value, while others can be valued with three. Some evidence is more convincing than others, and it is up to you to judge how much evidence you need to support your opinion of value. It is natural for appraisers to try to get by with minimal data because it is faster and therefore more profitable, but you should keep in mind that each appraisal report you submit to a client is a reflection of your professional competency.

The number of comparable sales needed often depends on the competitive nature of the market. If a market has many buyers and sellers, it is doubtful that the prices paid for properties will vary much, and three or four comparables may be enough. If the subject property is less popular, there will be fewer comparable properties for analysis and the range in indicated values will be wider. If the sales require large adjustments, the number of comparables needed increases. The more diverse the properties in a market, the more difficult it is to find sale properties that require few adjustments. In most markets, the more data presented, the clearer the value estimate.

If a market has few participants, the range in indicated values may not narrow as more data is analyzed. In those markets, buyers have few alternatives and must choose from a few possible listings. If more listings become available, there is more competition for buyers and more consistency in the market data.

Identification and Measurement of Adjustments

The analysis of elements of comparison can be qualitative or quantitative. Quantitative adjustments are based on gross dollars or percentages. Qualitative analysis places the comparables in a ranking order and identifies adjustments with relative terms like *inferior* or *superior*.

Elements of Comparison

Elements of comparison are the reasons for variations in property prices. For example, adding more square feet of living area to a house usually increases the sale price. As a result, the size of a

Exhibit 18.1	Comparable Land Sales					
	Subject	**Sale 1**	**Sale 2**	**Sale 3**	**Sale 4**	**Sale 5**
Sale price	–	$1,000,000	$750,000	$550,000	$250,000	$75,000
No. of acres	120	175	125	85	35	8
Price per acre	–	$5,714	$6,000	$6,470	$7,142	$9,375

residence is an element of comparison. Similarly, the ceiling height of an industrial property may be an important factor to a buyer. The higher the ceiling, the more a property may be worth, so this would be an element of comparison for industrial properties in that market.

Sequence of Adjustments

There are many classifications of elements of comparison. The first five elements are generally considered to be interrelated and are known as *transactional adjustments*. Adjustments are normally applied to the sale price of comparables in a specific order. These elements of comparison are listed in the suggested order of adjustment in Exhibit 18.2. The second five of the traditional 10 elements of comparison are not usually applied to comparable sales in a particular order. Those elements of comparison are known as *property adjustments*.

Adjustment Grids

Adjustment grids (also called *sales comparison grids*) allow appraisers to replicate the behavior of buyers on a piece of paper. Adjustment grids, which can be developed in a quantitative or qualitative analysis, are best described as a spreadsheet methodology. Many appraisers use common spreadsheet programs to prepare these analyses for their reports. Spreadsheets allow readers to compare and contrast large quantities of data on just a few pages of the report. Exhibit 18.3 shows a grid analysis based on the price per square foot of land including building.

The sample sales comparison grid in Exhibit 18.4 shows how grids are used in many non-residential appraisals. Dollar and percentage adjustments are made to gross sale prices in this case because data is plentiful. When data is poor, the price per square foot of gross building area including land is used more often. If a unit of comparison is used, an adjustment for that item is usually no longer needed. That is, using price per acre eliminates the need to adjust for the number of acres included in the price. Many appraisers adjust for the inverse relationship between size

---

Exhibit 18.2   Suggested Order of Adjustments for Transactional Adjustments

Order	Element of Comparison	Example
1	Real property rights conveyed	Applied to comparable sales that involve different rights trading hands, such as a leased fee interest or a life estate.
2	Financing terms	Compensates for unusual financing terms that were part of a comparable sale. The subject's financing is nearly always considered to be cash or cash-equivalent, as is indicated in the commonly used definition of market value.
3	Conditions of sale	Compensates for more or less motivated sellers or buyers.
4	Expenditures made immediately after purchase	Made at the beginning of the analysis rather than on the condition line because the buyer may have considered the acquisition cost to be the sale price plus the cost of immediate changes. The market conditions adjustment is made to the price adjusted for expenditures made immediately after purchase. This adjustment is important when developing an overall capitalization rate or gross rent multiplier.
5	Market conditions	The adjustment for price changes in the market; used to be known as a *time adjustment*. This adjustment can be positive or negative. In some turbulent markets, sales may be adjusted both up and down in the same analysis.

Note: The five property adjustments—location, physical characteristics, economic characteristics, legal characteristics, and non-realty components of value—do not follow a suggested order. The treatment of property adjustments is discussed more fully in Chapter 19.

Price per Square Foot of Land Including Building

In some appraisals of properties with high land values such as branch banks, fast food restaurants, drugstores, auto service stations, and conveniences stores, the most significant component of value is the land rather than the building. To appraise these properties, appraisers can sometimes obtain reasonable results using a price per square foot of land including building.

Many appraisers have been taught to break down all nonresidential sales comparison analyses into a price per square foot of building area including land, but the analysis of price per square foot of land including building is probably more meaningful when the improvements represent a smaller amount of the property value. The price per square foot of building area including land seems to work better when the building is the most significant asset of the property (such as with office buildings, industrial buildings, or strip malls) but not when the land is most significant.

	Subject	Comparable 1		Comparable 2	
Address	123 Mark Street	211 W. 30th Street		211 W. 25th Street	
Sale price			$425,000		$550,000
Rights transferred	fee simple	fee simple	$0	fee simple	$0
Subtotal			$425,000		$550,000
Financing	cash to seller	cash to seller	$0	cash to seller	$0
Subtotal			$425,000		$550,000
Conditions of sale	arm's-length	arm's-length	$0	arm's-length	$0
Subtotal			$425,000		$550,000
Post-purchase repairs	none	none	$0	none	$0
Subtotal			$425,000		$550,000
Market conditions	current	6 months	2.8%	15 months	7.8%
Current, cash-equivalent price			$436,907		$592,963
Current, cash-equivalent price per sq. ft. of land			$9.93		$10.05
Location	West Side	West Side	$0.00	West Side	$0.00
Land size (sq. ft.)	35,000	44,000	$0.00	59,000	$0.00
Building design	one story/avg.	one story/avg.	$0.00	one story/avg.	$0.00
Construction quality	masonry/avg.	wood frame	$0.10	masonry/avg.	$0.00
Improvement age	21	19	-$0.20	12	-$0.90
Improvement condition	fair	superior	-$0.20	equal	$0.00
Above-ground building area	3,500	2,900	0.30	2,000	$0.75
Basement area (sq. ft.)	0	0	$0.00	0	$0.00
Functional obsolescence	typical only	typical only	$0.00	typical only	$0.00
Other	none	none	$0.00	none	$0.00
Net adjustment			$0.00		-$0.15
Indicated value per sq. ft. of land including building			$9.93		$9.90

and price per acre, which compensates for the common phenomenon that purchasing a larger number of acres lowers the price per acre.

The grid in Exhibit 18.4 is a little unusual in that the attributes of the site of the comparable properties (e.g., access, view, visibility) have been reduced to a land value amount that is compared to the land value of the subject property. The difference is the adjustment rate–e.g., the subject has a $100,000 site and Sale 1 has a $165,000 site. In some markets, this strategy allows appraisers to combine several different attributes that can cancel each other out into a single adjustment. The concept of consistent use should be considered here because it is possible to create an erroneous value conclusion if the land value is based on a use that is not the same as the current improvement. For example, the land value of one of the comparables is based on the price of land

for a commercial use, which is higher than the industrial land values of the subject and other comparable properties. In that case, a comparison of the land values would not provide a consistent result until the property sold for the commercial vacant land use rather than the improved industrial use.

Reconciling Value Indications in the Sales Comparison Approach

After making adjustments to the comparables, appraisers must decide where the data takes them. The reconciliation process allows you to put all the pieces of the puzzle back together and determine a reasonable, supportable opinion of market value.

Reconciliation is the process by which appraisers consider, reevaluate, and reconcile all the data gathered in applying the sales comparison approach to develop an opinion of the subject

Exhibit 18.4   Sales Comparison Grid

	Subject	Comparable 1		Comparable 2		Comparable 3	
	1597 N. Cathy Street	3579 Eunice Street		1593 N. Jeanine Avenue		3571 E. Gina Street	
Sale price			$500,000		$550,000		$400,000
Rights transferred	fee simple	fee simple	$0	fee simple	$0	fee simple	$0
Subtotal			$500,000		$550,000		$400,000
Financing	cash to seller	contract	− $50,000	cash to seller	$0	cash to seller	$0
Subtotal			$450,000		$550,000		$400,000
Conditions of sale	arm's-length	arm's-length	$0	arm's-length	$0	arm's-length	$0
Subtotal			$450,000		$550,000		$400,000
Post-purchase repairs	none needed	none needed	$0	none needed	$0	minor repairs	+ $40,000
Subtotal			$450,000		$550,000		$440,000
Market conditions	now	2 mos.	0.3%	9 mos.	1.3%	3 mos.	0.5%
Current, cash-equivalent price			$451,350		$557,150		$442,200
Location	$100,000	$165,000	− $65,000	$225,000	− $125,000	$78,000	+ $22,000
Adjusted price			$386,350		$432,150		$464,200
Building design	one story/avg.	one story/avg.	$0	one story/avg.	$0	one story/avg.	$0
Const. quality	brick/avg.	brick/avg.	$0	steel/avg.	$0	steel/inferior	$23,210 (5.0%)
Improvement age	8	12	$30,908 (8.0%)	9	$8,643 (2.0%)	5	− $27,852 (− 6.0%)
Improvement condition	average	equal	$0	equal	$0	equal	$0
Abv. gd. bldg. area	5,086	8,000	− $22,408 (− 5.8%)	12,000	− $59,637 (− 13.8%)	10,000	− $45,492 (− 9.8%)
Finished office	25.00%	25.00%	$0	13.95%	$23,768 (5.5%)	25.00%	$0
Freezer/cooler	0	0	$0	0	$0	0	$0
Basement sq. ft.	0	0	$0	0	$0	0	$0
Functional utility	average	average	$0	average	$0	average	$0
Other	none	none	$0	none	$0	none	$0
Net adjustment			$8,500 (+ 2.2%)		− $27,226 (− 6.3%)		− $50,134 (− 10.8%)
			$394,850		$404,924		$414,066

property's value. Appraisers often run through this process too quickly. Sometimes data needs to be reviewed carefully and reconsidered before a conclusion can be reached. Before finalizing a value opinion, you should consider the following:

- the quantity of the comparable sales available
- the quality of the comparable sales available
- the reliability of the data source (or sources)

In some appraisals, analysts have to rely heavily on only three or four pieces of data. In these cases, you have to verify the data much more rigorously because so much is riding on so little. A small error in the reporting will affect the analysis greatly. At other times, comparable sales may be very limited, and you may be forced to use two or three closed sales, a pending offer, and two current listings to arrive at an opinion of value. Lender rules may require three closed comparable sales in a residential appraisal, but that requirement does not mean you cannot give the client three closed sales and three pending comparable sales.

Most appraisers believe that a comparable sale should represent an alternative investment for buyers who would be attracted to the subject property. This does not necessarily mean that the comparable property is currently on the market again, only that buyers looking in the subject's market would put the subject or the comparable property on their short list of alternatives.

Appraisers need to know how reliable sales data is. In nearly every market, there are practitioners who pride themselves on the quality of their data reporting. In these same markets, there are people who do only the minimal reporting and do not always do an accurate job of even that. In some markets, brokers report sale prices in the MLS system that are higher than the actual prices so that they won't have any future problems with appraisers. Furthermore, there are markets with databases that do not provide for reporting the terms of the sale. Knowing only the reported price but not the terms of a comparable sale can make a very large difference in the conclusions presented. Unreliable data is usually useless, and you are responsible for reporting only reliable data.

Some investors place an excessive amount of emphasis on the amount and direction of the adjustments. Logically, the more adjustments made to the sale price of a comparable, the less reliable the final indication of value will be. If the subject property is nearly identical to several recent comparable sales in the same market area, no adjustments are needed.

Units of Comparison and Real Property Interests in the Reconciliation Process

Appraisers sometimes break down sale price into units of comparison to make a more reasonable data analysis. Farm appraisers commonly divide the sale price by the number of acres to calculate the ratio sale price per acre. This process allows appraisers to analyze data that would not otherwise appear to be comparable.

While breaking down sale price into units of comparison is a great system for evaluating real estate, problems may arise when the subject has unusual rights in realty or unusual cash flow characteristics. For example, the subject is a new multitenant office building. Construction is complete, but only 25% of the building is occupied because it is new. The comparable sales found are all new to 10-year-old office buildings with 90% to 100% occupancy. If the analyst compares this new building with 25% occupancy to the older but nearly fully occupied buildings, an adjustment for property rights conveyed or occupancy needs to be made.

If the subject is a parcel of ground that is under lease for 75 years at a specific price, the price per square foot or any other unit of comparison derived from sales with different rights in realty would not give a correct answer. The rights in realty, conditions of sale, and, in some cases, other physical property attributes may be so significant that comparison with a unit of comparison gives an erroneous value conclusion unless the attribute is adjusted for "across the board."

Questions to Ask During Reconciliation in the Sales Comparison Approach
· How much evidence of value is available and how much is included?
· Should comparable listings, pending sales, or even expired listings be considered?
· Should a history of market exposure of the subject property be considered?
· How many of the available comparable sales are truly comparable?
· Do the adjustments to the sales or listings represent the market's reactions?
· Are the comparable properties used legitimate alternatives to the subject property?

1. An opinion of market value via the sales comparison approach is through the eyes of
   a) Well-informed purchasers
   b) Well-informed sellers
   c) Well-informed brokers
   d) Uninformed buyers

2. A major requirement and limitation of the sales comparison approach is that it requires
   a) Several new constructions
   b) An active market of competitive properties
   c) Accurate cost information
   d) Accurate information on investor's expectations

3. Property sale prices
   a) Are negotiated by appraisers
   b) Are negotiated between buyers and sellers
   c) Are set by brokers
   d) Are opinions

4. If the appraisal assignment requires an estimate of market value,
   a) The sales comparison approach is never applicable
   b) The sales comparison approach is usually applicable
   c) The sales comparison approach is not applicable because it represents value in use
   d) The appraiser should always use the cost approach because it represents the most similar buyer's actions

5. In the application of the sales comparison approach in a market value appraisal,
   a) Only closed sales of real property interest can be used
   b) Only current listings and closed sales of real property interests can be used
   c) Only closed comparable sales, listings, and options can be used as indications of value
   d) Closed sales, pending sales, current listings, options to purchase, and refusals can be used as indications of market value

6. Current listings that have been exposed to the market for a reasonable time
   a) Tell the appraiser what the subject's market value cannot exceed
   b) Tell the appraiser what the subject's market value is
   c) Tell the appraiser what the subject's value in use is
   d) Tell the appraiser what the subject's investment value is

7. Units of comparison
   a) Rates are difficult to estimate
   b) Classifications are difficult to estimate
   c) Are items that represent a breakdown of the price based on a significant variable
   d) Are the characteristics that cause the prices paid for real estate to vary

8. Which approach is usually the most applicable for appraising residences?
   a) Cost
   b) Sales comparison
   c) Income capitalization
   d) Cost and income capitalization

Note: Unless otherwise noted, italicized references indicate the pages in *The Appraisal of Real Estate*, 14th edition, that readers should consult for additional discussion of these topics.

1. a) Well-informed purchasers
    Page 378

2. b) An active market of competitive properties
    Pages 380-381

3. b) Are negotiated between buyers and sellers
    Pages 382-384

4. b) The sales comparison approach is usually applicable
    Pages 380-381

5. d) Closed sales, pending sales, current listings, options to purchase, and refusals can be used as indications of market value
    Pages 382-384

6. a) Tell the appraiser what the subject's market value cannot exceed
    This student handbook

7. c) Are items that represent a breakdown of the price based on a significant variable
    Pages 386-388

8. b) Sales comparison
    Pages 380-381

19

Comparative Analysis

The comparative analysis of the subject property and comparable properties encompasses market-supported, quantitative adjustments and additional qualitative analyses of other property or transactional characteristics with differences that cannot be quantified. Generally, quantitative adjustments precede qualitative analysis until all the quantitative adjustments have been made to the comparable sales. In most cases, reconciliation is a qualitative process.

Quantitative Adjustments

Data Analysis Techniques
If the subject and comparables are completely the same, there is no reason to make adjustments to the sale prices of the comparables, but because perfectly comparable sales and listings are seldom found, most appraisals involve some sort of adjustment process. One available technique is paired data analysis, which is very logical and easy to follow. If a property sold for $50,000 more than another property and the higher-priced property was 100 square feet larger, an adjustment of $50 per square foot would appear to be appropriate. What is known as *secondary data analysis* involves the use of third-party statistical research to investigate buyers' behavior and attitudes regarding particular items. Secondary data analysis is less persuasive than paired data analysis.

Paired data analysis (also called *matched pairs analysis*) is popular in markets where there is an adequate quantity of data that appraisers can analyze to explain differences in sale prices. The technique is based on the reasoning that if two properties are essentially the same except for a single characteristic, the difference in price is attributable to the difference in that characteristic. For example, if a single-tenant commercial building sold for $300,000 and an otherwise identical property with 100 more square feet of basement area sold for $301,000, it is reasonable to conclude that the additional $1,000 is attributable to the extra basement area.

Comparative analysis is the general term for the collection of available quantitative and qualitative analytical techniques that appraisers use to analyze comparable sales and listings to derive a value indication in the sales comparison approach.

Types of Adjustments

Dollar adjustments are the most common adjustment type because they are easily understood by the general public and other appraisers. They are used in almost all residential appraisals and some nonresidential analyses as well.

Percentage adjustments are used in many nonresidential appraisal assignments to maintain ratios. Percentage adjustments can be used most appropriately when the method of extraction is very similar to the method of application. Percentage adjustments can be converted to dollar adjustments by a simple mathematical process. Using percentage adjustments is especially useful when the comparisons are not very comparable and large adjustments are warranted.

KEY TERMS	
bracketing	percentage adjustments
comparative analysis	ranking analysis
descriptive statistics	relative comparison analysis
dollar adjustments	scenario analysis
graphic analysis	statistical analysis
inferential statistics	trend analysis
paired data analysis	

While the logic of this technique is excellent, the data is usually not. Paired data analysis is the most commonly quoted but least used technique for extracting adjustment rates from comparisons of residential sales. Most appraisers, even those who cite paired data analysis as their favorite technique, admit that it is nearly impossible to find very similar properties that have just sold and only vary in one respect. Even when this type of data is found, it can lead to a completely different answer than you would expect.

The problems with paired data analysis are the unique qualities of real estate and the lack of recent transfers. By design, one property in a market area is often different from surrounding properties to prevent monotony. Unless the comparable property is in a highly homogeneous area or is an attached building or condominium development, this kind of data does not exist. Finding sales that are comparable in certain specialized nonresidential property markets can be very difficult, and finding sales that are so similar that an adjustment rate can be extracted from the data can be next-to-impossible.

Inaccurate or incomplete data weakens the results of paired data analysis. An appraiser could attribute the difference in the sale prices of two properties to one known characteristic, when the actual cause of the difference may be a difference in some unknown characteristic. Comparing more than one matched pair or multiple combinations of the same data decreases the likelihood of attributing a difference in value to the wrong characteristic because a clear pattern is unlikely to be evident when the wrong characteristic is analyzed.

> Keep in mind that "one sale does not make a market." A single sale can often be found to support or refute just about any position in the real estate market. If more than one sale supports the conclusion, however, the answer may be very different.

Statistical Analysis

In markets with ample data, statistical analysis of recent sales can be used to support adjustments. A linear regression model can be used to extract a rate of adjustment by isolating the contribution of a component. These calculations can be done with many software programs and even with some handheld calculators.

Some appraisers use the common statistical techniques of calculating the mean and median sale prices as support for value conclusions. These techniques can be used when enough data is available, but in most markets they do not offer the precision required by most clients. Calculating the mean (average) sale price or the mean of the price per acre or square foot does not explain why the prices varied within the data set. The value opinion developed by calculating the mean is probably more of a value range than a single-point estimate. A value range is an acceptable result in an appraisal, but it must not be labeled as a precise number. It could be misleading for an appraiser to represent a range of values as a single point estimate. For example, it is possible to select 50 comparable sales on a price-per-acre basis using only higher-value properties and then to simply average the numbers to obtain a mean value conclusion of the higher value sales. The selection of the data parameters is important and can be misused to produce erroneous results in an appraisal. You must be careful to use techniques that are generally acceptable to your peers in the market.

It is very easy to use statistical logic to support true but misleading statements. For example, in a market where a large employer (say, a software development firm) recently closed its doors and left town, a real estate organization published an article in the local newspaper that stated, "The average price of residential properties in town increased by 3% last year. Now is a good time to buy a home before the prices get too high." This statement is true but misleading. In fact, the 100 employees of this company were highly paid software programmers. Their income levels were near the high end of the scale in this town, and nearly all of their homes went on the market at the same time because they were pursuing jobs in other regions. Because most of the workers who lost their jobs were highly paid, the residential market segment most affected was the market for the highest-priced homes in this area. With nearly 100 homes flooding the market at one time, prices were falling quickly. However, because nearly all of the homes for sale were at the high end of the range, the average sale price in this town was actually increasing. The homes at the low end were still selling, but the high-end home sales overwhelmed the low-end sales. The readers of the newspaper were misled to believe that all prices were going up, but most—if not all—were actually going down. The prices of low-end homes were also declining because the reduced prices at the high end pulled buyers up from the lower-priced home market toward the recently discounted higher-end homes.

Graphic Analysis

Graphic analysis is similar to statistical analysis because it allows analysts to isolate an item's contribution to property value by measuring the effect of the item in a trend line. Graphic analysis is best used for properties like agricultural land that are relatively homogeneous and for which the data is relatively poor. Exhibits 19.1 and 19.2 show how tabular data can be converted into a graphic format for graphic analysis.

The graph shows the price per acre declining as the number of acres increases. This phenomenon is common in some markets but unusual in others. Graphic analysis like the example presented here helps clients come to a reasonable conclusion without having to read a lot of an appraisal report, which can be good or bad depending on other conditions.

Cost Analysis/Cost-Related Adjustments

A more logical method of estimating adjustments for physical characteristics is to estimate the depreciated cost of the component. This technique is easy to use and easy for clients outside the real estate community to understand.

Consider the following examples:

- If a screened porch costs $7,500 to build new as of the effective date of appraisal and is only three years old, it is probably worth about $7,000 as an adjustment amount, unless there is market evidence that the item is not in demand.

Area	Size	Cost per sq. ft.	Cost	% Deprec.		$ Deprec.	Net Value	$ per sq. ft.
Screened porch	300	$25.00	$7,500	6%	=	$450	$7,050	$23.50

- If the subject has a 2,000-sq.-ft. basement with 1,000 square feet of finished space, the correct adjustments would reflect the difference between the comparable and the subject for the basement space and then for the finished portion.

Area	Size	Cost per sq. ft.	Cost	% Deprec.		$ Deprec.	Net Value	$ per sq. ft.
Basement	2,000	$25.00	$50,000	15%	=	$7,500	$42,500	$21.25
Finishing	1,000	$30.00	$30,000	25%	=	$7,500	$22,500	$22.50

Obviously, these examples assume there is no functional or external obsolescence. The underlying premise of these calculations is the following appraisal maxim:

Reproduction Cost − Losses from All Causes = Value

Components like basements, porches, and even swimming pools are worth what they cost less de-

---

Exhibit 19.1	Agricultural Land Sales		
Sale	**Price**	**Acres**	**Price per Acre**
1	$400,000	70	$5,714
2	$500,000	90	$5,556
3	$550,000	103	$5,340
4	$600,000	110	$5,455
5	$700,000	135	$5,185
6	$775,000	150	$5,167
7	$805,233	155	$5,195
8	$896,543	175	$5,123
9	$985,700	195	$5,055
10	$1,000,000	200	$5,000
11	$1,256,500	230	$5,463
12	$1,125,890	250	$4,504
13	$1,258,900	285	$4,417
14	$1,358,000	310	$4,381
15	$1,580,000	366	$4,317

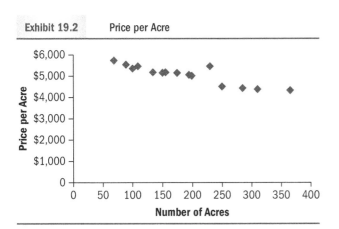

Exhibit 19.2	Price per Acre

If an item is found in a large percentage of the recently improved properties in a market, it would not be reasonable to claim that the item does not contribute value in the market. Many people have obviously paid for the item during construction. If, on the other hand, few properties include this item, its scarcity could be evidence of a lack of demand. For example, it is difficult to support an estimate of functional obsolescence for the superadequacy of an enclosed porch if one out of three homes includes this feature.

preciation from all causes. Of course, depreciation from all causes includes physical, functional, and external forms. A $25,000 in-ground swimming pool behind a $250,000 house in a cold climate probably suffers from a large amount of functional obsolescence. The obsolescence reduces the market value of the item to an amount commensurate with the market's recognition of value. The $25,000 pool may have functional obsolescence of $20,000 in addition to $4,500 in physical deterioration, which means the pool may only be worth $500.

Applying this technique does not suggest that an item is worth $500 if it costs $500. Rather, an item is worth $500 if the market is willing to pay that amount for the item. Basing adjustments on physically depreciated cost usually reflects the market unless the item is functionally wrong for that market or there are external losses.

Capitalization of Income Differences

To use capitalized rent as an adjustment, appraisers find properties with and without the feature in question (as in paired data analysis) and compare the net incomes of the properties. The difference in the net income is then attributable to the item. If the difference can be discerned in the market, that amount can be divided by an appropriate capitalization rate to calculate an adjustment. Of course, the rental difference can also be capitalized using gross rent multiplier analysis, which is discussed in a later chapter.

An example of this would be a multitenant office building where the building rents for $25.00 per square foot per year, except for the tenant on the first floor that has a canopy and drive-up window. This space rents for $30.00 per square foot per year. If no other expenses were associated with this, the extra rent could be attributed to the drive-up window. It should also be noted that some trade fixtures associated with the drive-up

window could affect the rent, depending on who paid for them. If the tenant paid for the conveyor system, the rent should not be affected by that cost, but if the landlord paid for them, the cost would probably be reflected in the rent.

Qualitative Analysis

Three general techniques and many variations are applied in qualitative analysis. The three primary techniques are

- relative comparison analysis
- ranking analysis
- trend analysis

Relative Comparison Analysis

The term *relative comparative analysis* describes the process by which recently sold comparable properties are compared to the subject without any sort of quantitative adjustment to the sale prices. Comparisons are made using relative terms (that is, *superior*, *inferior*, or *equal*) rather than dollar or percentage amounts. This process usually involves only a narrative discussion of the positive and negative attributes of comparables, and that discussion can be hard to follow if the data is extensive or complicated. This technique is essentially a written discussion of why one or more sale properties are better or worse than the subject property—e.g., "This comparable property is *inferior* to the subject, so the subject would sell for a higher price."

Ranking Analysis

In ranking analysis, appraisers research sales, listings, and other data and put the data in an ordered array to facilitate analysis. The subject can then be placed in the array, which provides an indication of value.

It is possible to inspect the subject and then drive by a series of comparable properties and

---

Gross Sale Price

The gross sale price of a comparable sale is the price listed on the closing statement before any deductions are made for real estate brokers' commissions, seller-paid financing concessions, or decorating or repair allowances. The gross sale price is the price as if the buyer paid cash and the seller had no mortgage. In most cases, the gross price is not the amount of money that the seller receives at closing but the amount on the top line of the closing statement. This amount will be adjusted for differences between the terms of the transaction and the criteria in the definition of market value included in the appraisal report. It is possible to list a price with some deductions already made (e.g., for commissions or closing costs), but a long explanation would be necessary to break the custom in this area.

It is important to be accurate. Prices are all numeric, and it is very easy to make a "typo" when reporting prices. Therefore, a review of the sale prices after the appraisal report is printed is strongly recommended. It is easy and understandable for an appraiser to type in the list price by mistake instead of the sale price, which gives a false indication of value. Always review the relevant data after the report is printed. Remember to check your numbers and save yourself the embarrassment of explaining that typo.

estimate if each is better or worse than the subject property. Within a very short time, the appraiser should have a good feeling for the market value of the properties despite the lack of an adjustment grid. For example, Exhibit 19.3 lists 11 comparable sales located in the same subdivision as the subject. The most significant data for these comparable sales is listed in the grid. The subject property is improved with a 2,400-sq.-ft., two-story residence with a two-car attached garage on a 0.35-acre lot. It has an unfinished basement, four bedrooms, and 2½ baths.

If the appraiser places the subject where the data seems to fit the best in the array, it would probably fall between Sales 5 and 6. The subject has a two-car garage, which should pull it down below Sale 4. It has 2,400 square feet, which should push it up above Sale 8. It has a basement, but the basement is not finished, which should put it between Sales 6 and 4. It has four bedrooms, which should keep it below Sale 1 but probably above Sale 8, if not above Sale 6. It appears that the value of the subject should fall between $200,000 and $217,500. Broad ranges such as this are usually unacceptable. In this case, the appraiser has narrowed the value opinion from a range of $167,500 to $245,000 to the much tighter range indicated in the table without the benefit of an adjustment grid or other techniques.

Trend Analysis
Trend analysis is a variant of statistical and graphic analysis that allows appraisers to discern how value is affected by an element of comparison based on visible trends in large amounts of data. Often trend analysis simply indicates the direction of a trend in prices, for example, that

older sales generally had lower prices because the market was improving over time and thus older sales would be considered "inferior" to more recent sales in a qualitative analysis of the data. However, sometimes the technique can be used as a statistical method of quantifying sale price adjustments if the data is conclusive enough to support a precise measure of a trend's effect on sale price. For example, the sale prices of comparable properties were shown to rise at a rate of 1.5% every six months over the last three years as the market recovered from a downturn.

Elements of Comparison
Elements of comparison are the items that cause the prices of real estate to vary. For example, if one house sells for more than another because it is larger, the element of comparison could be the size of the homes. Different property types have different elements of comparison. For industrial warehouse properties, common elements of comparison are ceiling height, amount of office space, and number of docks or overhead doors. In a

	Exhibit 19.3	Ranking Analysis											
	Address	**Bdr.**	**(F/H)**	**Description**	**Acre**	**Garage**	**Levels**	**Bsmt.**	**Fin. Bsmt.**	**GLA sq. ft.**	**Price**	**$ per sq. ft.**
1	773 Coventry Way	5	2/1	Brookshire	0.35	3-car att.	2	yes	yes	2,540	245,000	96.46
2	2429 Windsor Drive	4	2/2	Brookshire	0.38	3-car att.	2	yes	yes	2,584	242,500	93.85
3	2795 Brookshire Parkway	4	3/2	Brookshire	0.35	2-car att.	2	yes	yes	2,254	234,900	104.21
4	2207 Windsor Drive	4	2/1	Brookshire	0.35	3-car att.	2	yes	no	2,677	220,000	82.18
5	888 Duchess Drive	4	3/2	Brookshire	0.38	2-car att.	2	yes	no	2,268	217,500	95.90
6	890 Windsor Drive	3	2/1	Brookshire	0.30	2-car att.	2	yes	no	2,612	200,000	76.57
7	895 Brookshire Court	4	3/2	Brookshire	0.25	2-car att.	2	no	no	2,429	191,000	78.63
8	795 Kent Parkway	4	2/1	Brookshire	0.28	2-car att.	2	no	no	2,156	179,900	83.44
9	795 Hampshire Drive	2	2/1	Brookshire	0.23	2-car att.	1	no	no	2,122	178,000	83.88
10	695 Brookshire Parkway	3	2/1	Brookshire	0.22	2-car att.	1	no	no	1,822	170,000	93.30
11	555 Brookshire Parkway	3	3/2	Brookshire	0.21	2-car att.	1	no	no	2,016	167,500	83.09

one-unit home, common elements of comparison include the size of the house, the location, the lot size, and other common differences.

Several elements of comparison apply to all appraisals, but many apply only to sales of buildings or sales of land. Some elements of comparison apply in one way to an analysis based on unit price but in a completely different way to an analysis based on gross price. For example, the size of a parcel of land must be adjusted to compensate for differences in size if the adjustment is based on the gross price. However, no adjustment or an adjustment in the opposite direction may be needed if the comparative analysis is based on the price per square foot or price per acre.

Sequence of Adjustments

The order in which adjustments are made is irrelevant unless the adjustments mix mathematical operations in a way that affects the magnitude of subsequent adjustments after a subtotal. For example, suppose a property sold for $100,000 and this price is adjusted up 10%, down 10%, up 10%, and then down 10%. The adjusted price would still be $100,000:

$100,000	$100,000	
+ ($100,000 × 0.10)	+ 10,000	Adjustment 1
− ($100,000 × 0.10)	− 10,000	Adjustment 2
+ ($100,000 × 0.10)	+ 10,000	Adjustment 3
− ($100,000 × 0.10)	− 10,000	Adjustment 4
$100,000	$100,000	

If, on the other hand, the price is subtotaled after each upward or downward adjustment is made (i.e., compounded), the adjusted price would be different:

$100,000		
+ ($100,000 × 0.10)	× 1.10	Adjustment 1
$110,000		
− ($110,000 × 0.10)	× 0.90	Adjustment 2
$99,000		
+ ($99,000 × 0.10)	× 1.10	Adjustment 3
$108,900		
− ($108,900 × 0.10)	× 0.90	Adjustment 4
$98,010		

In effect, the 10% adjustments in the additive example above are all based on the $100,000 price. So Adjustment 2 is a 10% downward adjustment of the $100,000 just as Adjustment 4 is. In contrast, the 10% adjustments in the multiplicative example are each based on the immediately preceding adjusted price. That is, the 10% adjustment amount for Adjustment 1 is based on the $100,000 amount, but the 10% adjustment amount for Adjustment 2 is based on the $110,000 amount after the application of Adjustment 1. When using percentage adjustments, appraisers must understand what the basis for each percentage amount is, e.g., is the percentage amount 10% of the $100,000 price before any of Adjustments 1-4 or is it 10% of the $110,000 price after Adjustment 1?

Because multiplication is commutative, the order of adjustments does not change the end result if all the adjustments are done with multiplication alone. For example, the same sales were adjusted up and down with upward adjustments made first.

Adjustment	Adjustment Operation	Adjusted Sale Price
		100,000
1	× 1.10	110,000
3	× 1.10	121,000
2	× 0.90	108,900
4	× 0.90	98,010
Total		98,010

If the downward adjustments are made first, the totals are the same.

Adjustment	Adjustment Operation	Adjusted Sale Price
		100,000
2	× 0.90	90,000
4	× 0.90	81,000
1	× 1.10	89,100
3	× 1.10	98,010
Total		98,010

Some appraisers believe that percentage adjustments should be applied to subtotaled amounts, so the order of adjustments can make a difference to the conclusion. If the sale price of the comparable property includes a premium paid for the property rights conveyed, the market conditions adjustment should be applied to the adjusted price rather than the gross reported price. If the property was purchased with a significant amount of deferred maintenance, the next adjustment–for market conditions–should be applied to the price adjusted up for the deferred maintenance if the typical buyer envisioned the real price to be the reported price plus the needed repairs. As an example, assume a home sold with an artificial $10,000 financing incentive to allow the buyer to avoid the down payment requirements. The adjustment for subsequent differences should be made to a price that is $10,000 lower than the sale price.

The traditional sequence of adjustments is

1. Adjustment for property rights conveyed
2. Adjustment for financing terms
3. Adjustment for conditions of sale
4. Adjustment for expenditures immediately after purchase
5. Adjustment for market conditions
6. Property adjustments—e.g., for location, physical, economic, or legal characteristics, and non-realty components of value

The first five elements of comparison in the sequence of adjustments relate to transactional characteristics of the comparable sales and are known as the *transactional adjustments.*

Many appraisers think the suggested order is a good idea because the extraction of overall capitalization rates (R_o) and income multipliers (*GRM*, *PGIM*, and *EGIM*) should be based on the sale price after the adjustments for property rights, financing terms, conditions of sale, and expenditures immediately after sale. If these are not made prior to the extraction of the capitalization ratios, the resulting value indications would not be equal to the defined value. In other words, a capitalization rate extracted from a comparable sale with financing concessions will result in a capitalized value indication with concessions.

Transactional Adjustments

Real Property Rights Conveyed

A difference in real property rights conveyed is usually the first element of comparison adjusted for, and many appraisers calculate a subtotal after this adjustment. Remember that appraisers value the rights in realty, not the real estate. The value of a life estate cannot be estimated using sales of fee simple interests unless adjustments or qualitative compensations are made for the differences in real property rights conveyed. Likewise, a property that is leased on a long-term basis at a below-market rate cannot be compared to a property with no lease in place unless an adjustment is made. For many properties, the adjustment for property rights can be calculated on a financial calculator by comparing the present value of the

cash flows of the fee simple interest to the present value of the cash flows of the limited interest.

In some areas, mineral and water rights are the most significant factor in the comparative analysis of property rights conveyed. If the subject property is an agricultural property with the rights in realty limited to the surface rights only and all the mineral rights are conveyed to another party, finding comparables may be a significant problem. If the subject property has a long-term lease (such as 99 years) to an oil company, fee simple comparable sales may not be indicative of the value at all. The only way to value such a property may be with the income capitalization approach or by using the sales comparison approach with a significant adjustment for the rights in realty of comparable sales.

In most sales comparison analyses, the adjustment for real property rights conveyed is used to account for differences in the value of leased fee and fee simple estate values, but this type of adjustment can also be used for life estates, easements, encroachments, mineral rights, and other related issues. Adjustments for these items can be estimated using matched pair analysis, cost to cure, or income capitalization methods.

For example, consider a comparable property that was leased for $9 per square foot of gross building area when it sold with a lease in place that has 44 months remaining. The fee simple interest in the subject was being appraised. Expenses associated with both properties (i.e., the comparable and subject properties) were $4 per square foot. Discount (yield) rates in this market were 10%, and market rent is $12 per square foot. There was no difference in vacancy rates or capital replacement requirements. The subject is presumed to be leased at the market rate and the comparable can go to market rental rates in 44 months, so the only difference is the lost net income for 44 months.

Interviews with the parties to the comparable transaction could provide an adjustment for the difference in property rights. Such an adjustment could also be calculated from the market data (using a financial calculator) as follows:

44 [n]

10 [g] [i]   monthly rate

0.25 [PMT]   the difference in net income rates on a monthly basis: ($8 − $5)/12 = 0.25

0 [FV]   no difference in reversions after the lease is over

Solve for [PV] = $9.18 per square foot, which reflects the difference in the subject's and comparable's income for the affected period of time

> In most assignments, the definition of *market value* refers to a "cash-equivalent" sale price, so the effect of financing on value is often a significant consideration.

The rate of $9.18 per square foot can be used as the adjustment for real property rights transferred. This could also be calculated on an annual basis if customary in the subject's market.

Financing Terms

Differences in financing terms are a common element of comparison in markets where sellers must help buyers obtain adequate financing. In this situation, the reported sale price is often inflated because of the financing terms provided by the seller. An adjustment is needed for a comparable sale in which the sale price was increased to cover the additional cost to the seller for the assistance to the buyer. In any given real estate transaction, the price can change by as much as 100%, or more in some cases, because of the terms. An adjustment is made *only* when the financing affects the sale price.

For most appraisal assignments, the relevant definition of *market value* assumes that sellers pay only typical costs, e.g. title insurance, deed preparation, real estate brokerage fees, and similar expenses, but not the cost of the buyer's financing or any other incentive that makes the sellers pay more than they would pay in a cash sale. Therefore, a deal in which the seller pays for the buyer's mortgage is not consistent with the defined value and requires an adjustment.

In some markets, the seller may be asked to provide the financing for the sale. In those cases, it is common for the seller to take the down payment and accept a signed mortgage note for the balance but retain the deed. When the seller is providing the financing, the seller gives the deed to the buyer but then puts a mortgage lien against the property. If the seller takes back a mortgage or sells the property on a conditional sales contract, the seller does not get cash at closing, and some

---

Concessions

In some markets, brokers commonly structure deals with the seller paying decorating, repair, or landscaping allowances that allow the seller to "kick back" money to the buyer for these needed items. These allowances can be bogus if their purpose is to allow the seller to give buyers their down payment. In these cases, the seller simply raises the sale price to reflect the additional cost for the concession.

---

adjustment may be needed. The adjustment for this financing can be estimated by comparing the present value of the contract or mortgage to the cash-equivalent value of the mortgage or contract.

If the financing terms included with the sale of the subject property did not affect the price, no adjustment is needed. A favorable financing condition could possibly be advantageous to both parties and the price would not be affected by it. For example, the seller of a house is financially secure and does not need the proceeds from the sale to live on or to buy another property. She receives an offer for $500,000 with the condition that the seller takes back a purchase-money mortgage for $300,000 with a 30-year amortization and a balloon payment in six years. The proposed interest rate on the mortgage loan held by the seller is 2% below the current mortgage rate but 2% higher than current savings account rates. The seller thinks this is a great deal because she will be getting 2% more interest than she would have received if she put the money in a savings account. The buyer also likes the deal because he will pay a 2% lower mortgage rate. Both sides considered this situation to be favorable to their interests, so the price was probably not affected by the terms and consequently no adjustment is needed. But, if the buyer thought that the deal was favorable because of the financing and thought that he did pay extra for the financing, then the financing terms did impact the price and the sale price would require an adjustment.

A variety of techniques can be used to estimate adjustments for favorable financing terms:

- paired data analysis
- market participant interviews
- cash flow analysis of the mortgage loan using a financial calculator

The preferable method is research and analysis of matched comparables sales. If two properties are identical except for the financing, the difference in the prices paid can be attributed to the financing. For example, assume a small, single-tenant industrial building recently sold for $408,000. This sale was financed by a conditional sales contract at 6% with no money down for 10 years. A week after the sale closed, another property just like it sold for $400,000. This sale was financed with a new mortgage at the market rate. In this situation, the adjustment for financing is obviously $8,000.

Another way to determine the magnitude of a financing adjustment is to interview the parties to the sale. The buyers would be the best people to ask how much value they attributed to the favorable financing. If their responses are honest, the appraiser can use their answer as the adjustment amount. Of course, getting a straight answer from a buyer may be difficult. If the buyers are unavailable or unreliable or the answer seems out of line, the broker representing the buyers may be able to explain the thinking behind the purchase decision. Since no other parties (i.e., seller and seller agents) were involved in the decision process, the process is limited to the buyers and their broker.

The least direct (but easiest) method of calculating a financing adjustment is to use a cash flow analysis with a financial calculator. For example, an appraiser finds a comparable sale of a small storefront with a reported price of $560,000. The seller took back paper (i.e., an interest in the buyer's mortgage) for part of the payment. The down payment was $56,000, so the contract was for $504,000. The purchase-money mortgage was for 10 years, with monthly payments, amortized over 25 years at a rate of 7.5%. The market rate at the time of sale was 9.5%. A financial calculator can be used to calculate the cash-equivalent sale price as follows:

1. Begin by calculating the nominal (stated) amount of the payment for the written mortgage and the balance at the end of Year 10, which is $401,776.25

2. Calculate the value of the mortgage at the market rates, which equals $443,800.76

3. Add back in the down payment of $56,000, which equals $499,800.76

> 25 $\boxed{g}$ $\boxed{n}$ (monthly)
> 7.5 $\boxed{g}$ $\boxed{i}$ (monthly)
> 504,000 $\boxed{PV}$
> 0 $\boxed{FV}$
> Solve for $\boxed{PMT}$ = $3,724.50 (monthly payment)
> 10 $\boxed{g}$ $\boxed{n}$ (change term to Year 10)
> Solve for $\boxed{FV}$ = $401,776.25 (balance at Year 10)
> 9.5 $\boxed{g}$ $\boxed{i}$ (change interest rate)
> Solve for $\boxed{PV}$ = $443,800.76 [present value of mortgage @ 9.5%]

Add back down payment:

> $56,000 $\boxed{+}$ $499,800.76 is the cash-equivalent sale price

The difference between the calculated cash-equivalent sale price and the reported price with the special financing is nearly $60,199.24, which could be used as the adjustment for the financing.

Another similar method of estimating a financing adjustment is through mortgage analysis, comparing the face amount of the mortgage loan with the amount it could be resold for (i.e., the loan's market value). For example, consider a comparable property that sold a week ago for $500,000 with the seller taking back a mortgage of $450,000 at a rate of 6% for 15 years. The week after the sale closed, the privately held mortgage

---

Financing Adjustment Problems

The following problems involve atypical financing situations. Solutions to the problems are shown on page 217, in the Suggested Solutions to Review Exercises at the end of this chapter.

1. A one-unit residential property was reported to have been listed for sale at $359,900 and reportedly sold for $364,500. The fine print of the contract says that the seller paid $13,000 for the buyer's financing costs at the time of closing, which means that the seller agrees to pay a large portion, if not all, of the buyer's costs to obtain a mortgage. What is the cash-equivalent sale price?

2. An office building sold for $1.25 million. The seller took back a conditional sales contract for five years with monthly payments at 6% in a market where the interest rate was 8%. The face amount of the contract was $1 million. The buyer indicated that she thought the financing package available for this property, which was not available for any others, added $25,000 to the price. The seller confirmed that this was a realistic estimate of the cost of financing. What is the cash-equivalent sale price?

3. The buyers of a new home in a platted subdivision paid $425,000 for the property. This home was speculatively built and the builder was having trouble selling it. It was listed in the MLS system for six months at a price of $409,900. To close the sale, the builder agreed to take back a "forgivable second mortgage" from the buyers for $25,000 at 0% interest with the stipulation that the buyers never had to pay it back. What was the cash-equivalent sale price?

4. The buyer of a small farm (175 acres) reportedly paid $700,000 for the property. The seller took back a purchase-money mortgage for $600,000 at 5% in a market where local banks were quoting 8%. The amortization was based on a loan term of 20 years, but there was a Year 5 balloon payment of $500,729. The seller and buyer are not revealing the details of the sale and would not estimate the contribution of the financing. There have been no sales in this area of properties that are similar in size, features, and location, so the appraiser needs to use this comparable sale. What is the contribution of the financing?

was sold to an investor for $400,000. The difference between the sale price of the mortgage note and the nominal amount of the loan is the adjustment. The loan was made for $450,000 but the loan was resold for only $400,000. The cash flow analysis presented above is a variant in which the appraiser estimates what the mortgage loan should sell for rather than what it actually sold for.

Conditions of Sale

The conditions of sale element of comparison describes the variations in the prices paid for real estate due to the motivations of buyers and sellers. This may sound like an easy adjustment to make, but it is very difficult to estimate or even research buyer or seller motivation because of the lack of explanatory, quantitative data and the reticence of buyers and sellers to answer questions candidly. In most cases, when appraisers find transactions with unusual conditions of sale, they move on to other sales to avoid having to make a poorly supported adjustment.

Many appraisers believe that either the buyer or seller is more motivated than the other party in nearly every sale. In other words, the motivations of the buyers and sellers are probably a small factor in nearly all sales and usually do not require an adjustment. Any adjustment in this area should be supported in the appraisal report with additional data providing a standard or average level of motivation. Using more data diminishes the influence of unusual conditions of sale hidden in the sale prices of a few comparables.

Expenditures Made Immediately After Purchase

In comparative analysis, the expenditures made immediately after purchase can be differentiated from deferred maintenance because of the date of the work done. If the repair or improvement is made right after sale, it was assumed to be known to the buyer and was factored into the price. Again, the appraiser makes this adjustment before extracting a capitalization rate, therefore giving a more comparable overall rate.

If the market conditions adjustment is applied to a price that reflects a property in need of immediate repairs, the price would be lower than if it were applied to a price assuming the repairs were completed. By making this adjustment first, the market conditions adjustment is applied to a price for a property that does not have this deferred expense. This adjustment is easy to make because the cost to cure is usually easy to determine. Adjust-

ments can also be made for zoning changes, environmental mitigation, or other capital expenditures.

An adjustment for expenditures made immediately after the sale compensates for the items of deferred maintenance (also known as *curable physical deterioration*) that the buyers considered in need of repair immediately upon taking possession of the real estate. Examples include

- razing a building
- replacing a roof covering
- recarpeting
- repainting

These adjustments are made to the gross sale price before making any percentage adjustments. For example, if a buyer purchased an improved property with the intent of razing the improvement, the cost of razing the improvement would be included in the acquisition cost of the property just as if the buyer had paid for it at closing. If a market conditions adjustment was needed to compensate for increases in prices in this market, it would clearly be applied to the sale price with the cost of demolition added because the buyer factored that cost into the acquisition price.

Market Conditions

An adjustment for the market conditions affecting a transaction is the last of the interrelated elements of comparison. An adjustment for market conditions compensates for changes in the market from the date of the sale of the comparable property to the effective date of the appraisal. If the market has not changed, there is no reason to make an adjustment for the passage of time. This adjustment is usually made on a percentage basis and is applied to the price after adjustment for property rights, financing terms, conditions of sale, and expenditures after the sale. A market conditions adjustment is easily supported by researching sales and resales of the same property over a short time.

As always, the more recent the comparable sales, the better—assuming the effective date of appraisal is current. The date of closing is required for the adjustment grids, but the month and year of the pending sale and the closed sale are preferred because some transfers are pending for a long time. When market conditions adjustments (once known as *time adjustments*) are made, the calculations should be based on the date of the pending sale (i.e., the date of the meeting of the minds) and the effective date of appraisal. The best way to support the rate of change is to find sales and resales of the same property and calculate the difference in value and the rate of change.

The rate of change in market value over time can be calculated in different ways, as shown in the following examples:

- What is the annual rate of change (delta or Δ) on a straight-line basis (Δ/n) for a property that sold in 2009 for $12 million and resold in 2013 for $15 million?

  Divide the difference between the original price ($12 million) and the later price ($15 million) by the original price, and then divide that quotient by the elapsed time:

  $$[(\$15,000,000 - \$12,000,000)/\$12,000,000]/4 = +25\%/4$$
  $$= 6.25\% \text{ per year}$$

  This can also be calculated in a single step on nearly all financial calculators.

- What is the annual rate of change (Δ) on a compound basis for a property that sold in 2009 for $12 million and resold in 2013 for $15 million?

  Using a financial calculator, input the following numbers and solve for i (annual interest rate):

4	n	(years elapsed)
12,000,000	CHS PV	(going-in price)
0	PMT	(no interim payments)
15,000,000	FV	(going-out price)
Solve for	i = 5.74%	

Note that for some financial calculators, the number of payments per year should be set on 1. For HP-12C calculators, this is not necessary.

These calculations are indications of what is happening in those markets, which can be reconciled into an adjustment for the comparable sale. This analysis, like most real estate analyses, is most persuasive when several transactions are used.

The income from the comparable property is usually estimated for the year following the sale, so most appraisers do not make an adjustment for market conditions prior to the extraction of an overall capitalization rate or multiplier because it would negate the ratio of sale price to income. Adjusting the price up to the current date without adjusting the rents would be an "apples to oranges" comparison.

Property Adjustments

In comparative analysis, the five elements of comparison known as the *property adjustments*—lo-

cation, physical characteristics, economic characteristics, legal characteristics, and non-realty components—are generally dealt with after the transactional adjustments. The property adjustments are commonly summed at the end of the analysis. Note that the property adjustments listed above are not the only things that can be adjusted for, but rather these listed elements of comparison are the broader categories in which most items requiring adjustments can be put.

Location

An adjustment for locational differences may be applicable in nearly all appraisals because location affects the value of nearly all types of properties. Locational differences are often the most difficult element of comparison to quantify because appraisers must analyze the buyer's subjective impression of the environment.

Location is important to both residential and nonresidential properties. If comparable properties have similar land value-to-property value ratios, the location adjustment along with the site size, zoning, visibility, and access lines could represent the subject's land value. Support for this adjustment can be as simple as a comparison of the land values of the subject and comparable properties. The difficulty in estimating a location adjustment is sometimes a lack of support. If the subject's land value is $50,000 and the comparable's land value is $60,000, a negative $10,000 adjustment could be made, but some support for both land value estimates may be needed. This logic does not work if the subject or comparables have significantly different land value-to-property value ratios—for example, if a comparable property was in transition when it sold. The principle of consistent use can also cause some confusion in estimating a location adjustment if the estimated land values of the subject and comparables are for different highest and best uses of the land as though vacant.

As an example, assume that the subject property is located in a FEMA flood hazard area. The site can no longer be developed because of the flood area classification, but the existing building on the site is a legally nonconforming use. The land value would be only a fraction of the value of a comparable's land that is not in the flood hazard area—for example, $5,000 for the undevelopable site in the flood area and $50,000 for a comparable site not in the flood hazard area. However, both represent nearly the same utility to the buyer because of the grandfathered use. In this case, the adjustment for location, site, and view would be based on the utility of the land as recognized by the market, not the land value. Remember that land is always valued at its highest and best use as though vacant, but the land value at its highest and best use may not be the way buyers look at it. Buyers are looking at the utility of the land that includes a legally nonconforming use that is not considered in the land valuation.

As a second example, consider a case in which the subject property is an underimprovement, which may cause a problem in estimating a location adjustment based on the land value. In this case, the subject property is a 1,000-sq.-ft. office in a very popular and prestigious office district where most properties are much larger. In this market, it is common for investors in office property to demolish existing improvements so they can build new, much larger, better-quality properties. The subject's land value as a building site is $150,000, and the market value of the improved property is only $160,000, or only about $10,000 away from the wrecking ball. A comparable was found in the area that sold for $150,000. That property has a 2,000-sq.-ft. office building with a basement on a smaller lot valued at only $100,000, or $50,000 away from the wrecking ball. If a location, site, and view adjustment was made based on the land values, it would be possible to add $50,000 for differences in land value and make small adjustments for the size of the property and other factors. This would mean the indicated value for the subject would be overstated by nearly $50,000 because the value of the subject is nearly all land value while the comparable is not.

As another example, assume a new office building was built on a site with a market value of $1 million and improvements that cost $4 million, so the land accounted for 20% of the property value. A year after this building was built, the state widened the highway from two to four lanes, and traffic counts tripled. The land value is now $2 million. The improved property still has a market value of $5 million because the tenants in the building will not pay more rent for highway frontage because they have no signage to take advantage of the traffic. If this property was the subject of an appraisal, it would be inappropriate to compare this land value to the land value of a property on a less valuable site. If an identical comparable sale has a land value of $1 million and sold for $5 million, the comparison of the land values gives a misleading answer because it would lead to a $1 million ad-

justment for an item that was not recognized in the market. The subject's land value would clearly support a different use, such as a fast food restaurant, gas station, or convenience store, but that sort of use will not be developed as long as the improved property is worth more than the land value.

Some appraisers make location adjustments on a dollar basis, others on a percentage basis. If dollar adjustments are made, care should be taken to ensure that the proportion of property value is kept in mind. For example, a $10,000 location adjustment for a $200,000 property would not be as significant as a $10,000 location adjustment for a $75,000 property.

Other ways of supporting location adjustments include

- a comparison of the subject's traffic counts with the comparables, which can show that a commercial site is superior or inferior
- a comparison of the average age of the improvements or the size of the improvements, which can show that a property is in a superior or inferior neighborhood
- a comparison of the distance to the central business district

Residential appraisers often use a comparison of the average prices of homes in one platted subdivision to those in another. For example, if the properties in the subject property's subdivision range in value from $150,000 to $250,000 with an average sale price in the last year of $200,000 but the comparable sales are located in another platted subdivision with prices that range from $200,000 to $300,000 with an average of $250,000, it could be said that the neighborhood of the comparable properties is 25% better than the subject property's neighborhood. Of course, this does not mean that a 25% location adjustment against the sale price is warranted. More likely, a 25% adjustment of land value is appropriate. This tool can be used in a variety of situations to provide support for a location adjustment or to determine lack of support.

Physical Characteristics

The physical characteristics of a property are generally its "sticks and bricks." The differences between the physical characteristics of comparable properties and the subject are often the most significant. These items include

- size
- condition, quality, and age of improvements

- property amenities
- functional utility

When adjusting for differences in physical characteristics, it is important to take the proportion and support of these adjustments into account. For example, a $25,000 condition adjustment to a $500,000 property would be easy to understand, but a $25,000 condition adjustment to a $50,000 property would require an explanation in most cases. Some sort of support is needed for nearly all adjustments. Logic should prevail. An easy way to derive support for an adjustment is to base the adjustment on depreciated cost. Market participants tend to think of cost as a basis for an adjustment for a physical characteristic.

Problems may arise if only physical characteristics are adjusted for because economic considerations are also factors in most markets. Evidence of this can be seen in the market when interest rates change. Physical characteristics of most real estate can be adjusted using paired data analysis or cost analysis as discussed in earlier chapters.

Economic Characteristics

Differences in certain economic characteristics of real property need to be compensated for in the sales comparison approach. For residential properties, the ability to generate income is usually not a factor in the sales comparison approach. In most valuations of income-producing property, however, economic considerations such as the potential income generated by the property must be addressed in all phases of the analysis. For example, a sales comparison grid for an office building should include an adjustment for economic characteristics if a comparable property's long-term rental rate is higher than the subject's. A higher or lower lease rate may have little effect on a price if the term of the lease is short.

The effects of economic characteristics on property values are sometimes accounted for in the sale prices of comparables, e.g., if the subject property has below-market leases and the comparable property does also, no adjustment is needed. Economic factors that affect the value directly can usually be adjusted for and supported by analysis of the property's income stream. Some properties with high real estate taxes become almost unmarketable because of the extra ownership costs, or a property has a very high utility cost due to poor design. These situations increase expenses but not income, and the property values are diminished as a result.

Legal Characteristics

While the zoning classifications and property uses of the subject and comparable properties do not have to be identical, they should be very similar. If a comparable property has a completely different highest and best use than the subject, it is probably not comparable. If the comparable property has a similar highest and best use but the zoning classification is a little more or less intense, then an adjustment is appropriate, but comparisons are probably possible.

Small differences in possible uses or zoning can be quantified by paired data analysis. Large differences in zoning bring into question whether the property is even comparable at all. For example, in an appraisal of industrial land, it is common to use comparable land sales of properties with the same or similar zoning. In many jurisdictions, I-3 zoning may not allow for exterior storage of products or parts, but I-5 zoning does permit this use. Many appraisers will use a comparable sale that is zoned I-5 and a sale that is zoned I-3 for a property that is zoned I-3 or I-5. However, it would not be acceptable in most markets to use comparable sales of land zoned for commercial or residential use in an industrial site appraisal.

Non-Realty Components of Value

Personal property is often included in the sale of certain types of real estate. Furnishings are commonly included in the sale of hotels, restaurants, and other nonresidential properties. In some markets, furniture is typically included in the sale of real estate, and the comparable sales all have some personal property included. It is certainly acceptable to include some personal property in an appraisal, but professional standards may require appraisers to segregate and value this property so underwriters or investors know how much of the appraised value is attributable to this movable property.

In some appraisals, it is also common for other intangible items to be included in the value despite not being considered real property. For example, a buyer of a fast food restaurant may acquire the real estate as well as a franchise license. In the case of an automobile sales showroom, the price paid for the real estate that accompanies the transfer of the franchise can be a third higher than the price of the same property without the franchise. If the subject property does not include that type of intangible asset, an adjustment is needed. If the subject property includes personal property, it is very important to identify this and tell the client how much this personal property contributed to the value opinion.

Adjustments for differences in these items usually require appraisers to estimate the contributory value of the items. These estimates can be based on the depreciated cost of the personal property or the income or expense the item brings to the property. If the item is a used air compressor that is five years old and has a 10-year life, 50% of the cost new is a common value opinion. It is possible that the air compressor could sell for less at an auction or garage sale, but it may or may not have contributed that amount when included with the real estate. Of course, analysts can interview buyers to get their opinions. In many cases, real estate appraisers hire personal property appraisers to estimate the value of those items.

Consideration for Multiple Adjustments

Several methods for extracting and applying adjustments have been presented. Each of these techniques may produce different results. With several legitimate techniques available and several possible answers, the best course of action is to spend the extra time to find the best comparables available and make as few adjustments as possible.

If the data is good, the adjustment process is easy. If the data is weak, appraisers earn their fees.

Remember that you can find yourself at the mercy of the scope of work of an assignment and the data available to support the opinion of value, so you may have to make many adjustments for property differences. If an appraisal report shows many adjustments of large magnitude, the best practice is often to use as much data as is available and apply as many approaches to value as can be reasonably prepared.

1. *Elements of comparison* are
   a) A weatherman's comparison report
   b) The characteristics that cause the prices paid for real estate to vary
   c) Items that represent the breakdown of the price based on a significant variable
   d) Items that represent the bottom-line price after all of the adjustments

2. Adjustments are made
   a) To the subject to make it like the comparables
   b) To the comparables to make them like the subject
   c) To the subject to make it like the market
   d) To the comparables to make them like the market

3. A technique for extracting adjustments directly from the sale prices of comparables based on the contribution of a single feature is called
   a) Grid analysis
   b) Paired data analysis
   c) Cost analysis
   d) Income analysis

4. Adjustments for real property rights conveyed reflect
   a) Physical differences in the subject and the comparables
   b) The differences in the rights in realty transferred between the subject and comparables
   c) The differences in the market on the effective date and the comparables
   d) The differences in the motivations of the sellers and buyers on the date of sale

5. Adjustments for financing terms reflect
   a) The differences in the market on the effective date and the comparables
   b) The differences in the motivations of the sellers and buyers on the date of sale
   c) The differences in sale prices of properties that sold for cash and the ones that sold with financing
   d) The differences in sale prices of properties that sold for cash or market rate financing and the ones that sold with special financing that favors the buyer

6. A conditions of sale adjustment reflects
   a) The differences in the market on the effective date of the appraisal and the dates of sale of the comparables
   b) The differences in sale prices of properties that sold for cash and the ones that sold with financing
   c) The differences between the motivations of the seller and buyer on the date of sale of a comparable and the typical motivations of buyers and sellers as described in the definition of value
   d) The differences in sale prices of properties that sold from non-related parties

7. Graphic analysis is an example of
   a) A quantitative adjustment technique
   b) Qualitative analysis
   c) Computer valuation using a graphics card
   d) A technique used in land valuation only

8. Expenditures made immediately after purchase
   a) Reflect anything paid by the buyer during the warranty period
   b) Reflect anything that the buyers knew they would have to correct and probably factored the cost of into the price paid
   c) Reflect the cost of replacing the decorating to bring the home up to the buyers' standards
   d) Reflect the cost to update the property to the new home market standards

9. *Comparative analysis* is
   a) A general term used to describe the process by which qualitative or quantitative techniques are used to derive a value opinion in the sales comparison approach
   b) The tool used in the cost approach to estimate depreciation to the buildings
   c) A tool used to convert income to value in the income approach
   d) A term used to describe levels that support construction cost

10. Use the price per square foot of gross building area, the price per square foot of land including building, and the price per front foot of land, and select the best unit of comparison for calculating the subject property's value given the comparable data shown.

	Sale Price	Frontage	Lot Depth	Gross Building Area (sq. ft.)	Price per Front Foot	Price per Sq. Ft. of Land	Price per Sq. Ft. of GBA
1	$1,597,530	335	489	45,000	_____	_____	_____
2	$1,358,987	300	410	38,500	_____	_____	_____
3	$1,258,963	400	400	35,000	_____	_____	_____
4	$1,112,598	245	333	32,000	_____	_____	_____
5	$1,000,000	275	405	29,000	_____	_____	_____
6	$987,654	370	415	28,700	_____	_____	_____
Subject		444	455	28,000	_____	_____	_____

What is the value of the subject property based on the data?

a) $800,000

b) $900,000

c) $1,000,000

d) $1,100,000

11. Use the price per square foot of gross building area, the price per square foot of land including building, and the price per front foot of land, and select the best unit of comparison for calculating the subject property's value given the comparable data shown.

	Sale Price	Frontage	Lot Depth	Gross Building Area (sq. ft.)	Price per Front Foot	Price per Sq. Ft. of Land	Price per Sq. Ft. of GBA
1	$125,987	200	246	15,000	_____	_____	_____
2	$135,897	210	250	18,000	_____	_____	_____
3	$145,800	200	285	22,000	_____	_____	_____
4	$99,000	195	200	20,000	_____	_____	_____
5	$128,589	200	255	24,500	_____	_____	_____
6	$175,000	200	339	25,000	_____	_____	_____
Subject		200	275	18,000	_____	_____	_____

What is the value of the subject property based on the data?

a) $100,000

b) $125,000

c) $150,000

d) $175,000

Note: Unless otherwise noted, italicized references indicate the pages in *The Appraisal of Real Estate*, 14th edition, that readers should consult for additional discussion of these topics.

Solutions to Financing Adjustment Problems

1. $364,500 – $13,000 = $351,500

2. $1,250,000 – $25,000 = $1,225,000

3. Clearly, the cash-equivalent price had to be at or less than $400,000. However, it could be argued that these buyers may have paid a premium for this property because the financing package was probably not available from any other seller. In other words, the cash-equivalent price could have been less than $400,000 because the buyer had few choices and paid a premium.

4. Use a financial calculator to solve for the present value of the financing:

20 [g] [n]	Number of periods and payments
5 [g] [i]	Interest rate per period
600,000 [CHS] [PV]	Present value or amount loaned
0 [FV]	Future value or residual or balloon amount
Solve for [PMT] = $3,959.73	
5 [g] [n]	Change n to the number of periods remaining
Solve for [FV] = $500,729.18 (to calculate the mortgage balance)	
8 [g] [i]	Change i to the market rate
Solve for [PV] = -$531,382.55 (to calculate the present value of the mortgage)	

Subtract the present value of the mortgage from the face amount of the mortgage to obtain the contribution of the financing:

600,000 [+] = $68,617.45

---

1. b) The characteristics that cause the prices paid for real estate to vary
   Pages 390-391

2. b) To the comparables to make them like the subject
   Page 388

3. b) Paired data analysis
   Page 398

4. b) The differences in the rights in realty transferred between the subject and comparables
   Pages 405-407

5. d) The differences in sale prices of properties that sold for cash or market rate financing and the ones that sold with special financing that favors the buyer
   Pages 408-410

6. c) The differences between the motivations of the seller and buyer on the date of sale of a comparable and the typical motivations of buyers and sellers as described in the definition of value
   Pages 410-412

7. a) A quantitative adjustment technique
   Page 398

8. b) Reflect anything that the buyers knew they would have to correct and probably factored the cost of into the price paid
   Pages 412-414

9. a) A general term used to describe the process by which qualitative or quantitative techniques are used to derive a value opinion in the sales comparison approach
   Page 397

10. **c) $1,000,000**

Based on the price per square foot of GBA including land:

	Sale Price	Frontage	Lot Depth	Gross Building Area (sq. ft.)	Price per Front Foot	Price per Sq. Ft. of Land	Price per Sq. Ft. of GBA
1	$1,597,530	335	489	45,000	$4,768.75	$9.75	$35.50
2	$1,358,987	300	410	38,500	$4,529.96	$11.05	$35.30
3	$1,258,963	400	400	35,000	$3,147.41	$7.87	$35.97
4	$1,112,598	245	333	32,000	$4,541.22	$13.64	$34.77
5	$1,000,000	275	405	29,000	$3,636.36	$8.98	$34.48
6	$987,654	370	415	28,700	$2,669.34	$6.43	$34.41
Subject		444	455	28,000		Rounded to	$35.00

11. **c) $150,000**

Based on the price per square foot of GBA including land:

	Sale Price	Frontage	Lot Depth	Gross Building Area (sq. ft.)	Price per Front Foot	Price per Sq. Ft. of Land	Price per Sq. Ft. of GBA
1	$125,987	200	246	15,000	$629.94	$2.56	$8.40
2	$135,897	210	250	18,000	$647.13	$2.59	$7.55
3	$145,800	200	285	22,000	$729.00	$2.56	$6.63
4	$99,000	195	200	20,000	$507.69	$2.54	$4.95
5	$128,589	200	255	24,500	$642.95	$2.52	$5.25
6	$175,000	200	339	25,000	$875.00	$2.58	$7.00
Subject		200	275	18,000		Rounded to	$2.55

20

Applications of the Sales Comparison Approach

The application of comparative analysis in the sales comparison approach can be broken down into the distinct but complementary procedures of (a) making quantitative adjustments and (b) applying qualitative analysis to comparable sales data.

Quantitative Adjustments

The magnitude of a quantitative adjustment can be estimated through a trial-and-error process, which will be illustrated using the data in the tables in Exhibits 20.1, 20.2, and 20.3. This process is sometimes called a *sensitivity analysis*. The two comparable sales have been adjusted to account for differences in property rights transferred, financing terms, conditions of sale, expenditures made immediately after the sale, and market conditions. However, if no further adjustment is made in the grid, the current, cash-equivalent prices of the comparable properties range from $389,581 to $565,086. The size of the first floor is the only element of comparison in which there are differences, so paired data analysis would be an appropriate method for making an adjustment and tightening the indicated value range.

Exhibit 20.1 shows an adjustment for more or less above-ground building area of $10 per square foot. This adjustment resulted in a smaller range in indicated values, but this range is not adequate.

In Exhibit 20.2, the adjustment amount is changed to a rate of $40 per square foot. As a result, the low sale becomes the high sale and the high sale becomes the low one.

In Exhibit 20.3, the adjustment amount is revised down to $30 per square foot, and the resulting indication of value from the sale is very close.

To summarize, the adjustment amount for the gross building area (GBA) on the first floor was made at a rate of $10 per square foot in Exhibit 20.1. This adjustment did tighten the range of the indicated values (between $419,581 and $535,086),

but not to a level acceptable to most appraisers or their clients. Exhibit 20.2 shows the results of increasing the adjustment to $40 per square foot of GBA. At this point, most appraisers would see that they went too far and should reduce the adjustment rate a bit. The actual adjustment could have been made by dividing the difference in the current, cash-equivalent prices ($175,505) by the difference in the gross building area of the comparables (6,000), which indicates a rate of $29.25. Exhibit 20.3 shows the results of using a size adjustment of $30 per square foot. After the third set of calculations, a value range that makes sense has been reached. Calculating the proper adjustment rate of $30 per square foot may seem like an exercise in basic mathematics, but you will perform some variation of that process every day and must be comfortable with this sort of analysis.

Qualitative Analysis

Qualitative analysis techniques allow appraisers to apply logic and reason to the value opinion when dollar or percentage adjustments cannot be made. These techniques are used in a variety of assignments, but you must still write a report your client can understand and will want to read. As discussed in earlier chapters, qualitative analysis can be performed more quickly than quantitative calculations, but it often requires much more narrative explanation.

Exhibit 20.4 shows an example of qualitative analysis in grid format. This data should be sufficient for analysts to be able to reach a reasonably accurate conclusion. In the case of low-quality data, however, this technique may leave you without effective support for your answer.

Valuing the subject property with the data in the table and using only "inferior" or "superior" judgments is similar to the analysis required on some old forms used for drive-by appraisals of

Exhibit 20.1 Matched Pair Analysis Using a Sensitivity Analysis for Sales

	Subject	Comparable 1		Comparable 2	
Price		$510,000		$400,000	
Rights transferred	fee simple	fee simple	0.0%	leased fee	-5.0%
Subtotal		$510,000		$380,000	
Financing	cash to seller	cash to seller	$0	cash to seller	$0
Subtotal		$510,000		$380,000	
Conditions of sale	arm's-length	motivated seller	5.0%	arm's-length	0.0%
Subtotal		$535,500		$380,000	
Expenditures after sale	none	minor repairs	5.0%	none	0.0%
Subtotal		$562,275		$380,000	
Market conditions	current	one month ago	0.5%	five months ago	2.5%
Current, cash-equivalent price		$565,086		$389,500	
Location adjustment	Northeast Side	Northeast Side		Northeast Side	
Zoning	Commercial-1	Commercial-1		Commercial-1	
Site size (sq. ft.)	20,000	20,000		20,000	
Building design	one story/avg.	one story/avg.		one story/avg.	
Const. quality	masonry/avg.	masonry/avg.		masonry/avg.	
Improvement age	14 years	14 years		14 years	
Improvement condition	average	average		average	
First floor area (@ $10/sq. ft.)	9,000	12,000	− 30,000	6,000	+ 30,000
Second floor area	0	0		0	
Above-ground building area	9,000	12,000		6,000	
Finished area	75%	75%		75%	
Basement area (sq. ft.)	0	0		0	
Functional obsolescence	typical only	typical only		typical only	
Other	none	none		none	
Net adjustment		− $30,000		+ $30,000	
Indicated value		$535,086		$419,500	

	Subject	Comparable 1		Comparable 2	
Current, cash-equivalent price		$565,086		$389,580	
First floor area (@ $40/sq. ft.)	9,000	12,000	− 120,000	6,000	+ 120,000
Indicated value		$445,086		$509,580	

	Subject	Comparable 1		Comparable 2	
Current, cash-equivalent price		$565,086		$389,580	
First floor area (@ $30/sq. ft.)	9,000	12,000	− 90,000	6,000	+ 90,000
Indicated value		$475,086		$479,580	

residential properties. Based on the given data, a reasonable opinion of market value is $550,000.

The language used in qualitative analysis can confuse clients and appraisers unfamiliar with the process because the sale price of a comparable property with an element of comparison that is labeled *superior* to the same characteristic in the subject property has to be adjusted *downward*, and vice versa for *inferior* characteristics. Some appraisers reverse the labeling to denote that the sub-ject property is *superior* to a comparable property in some way and therefore the sale price of the comparable property should be adjusted upward. Either method of labeling the qualitative differences between elements of comparison is effective as long as the appraiser uses one system consistently and communicates it clearly to the client.

It is also possible to use both quantitative adjustments and qualitative analysis in the same appraisal. For example, Exhibit 20.5 shows a grid

Exhibit 20.4   Qualitative Analysis

	Subject	Comparable 1		Comparable 2		Comparable 3	
Address	597 E. North St.	579 E. Hill St.		593 N. Wcbb Avc.		571 E. Oak St.	
Sale price			$500,000		$550,000		$625,000
Rights transferred	fee simple	fee simple		fee simple		fee simple	
Financing	cash to seller	contract	superior	cash to seller		cash to seller	
Conditions of sale	arm's-length	arm's-length		arm's-length		arm's-length	
Expend. after purch.	none needed	none needed		none needed		minor repairs	inferior
Date of sale	today	July		January		June	
Location/site/view	$80,000 site	$65,000 site	inferior	$80,000 site		$85,000 site	superior
Building design	one story/avg.	one story/avg.		one story/avg.		one story/avg.	
Const. quality	steel/average	brick/equal		frame/inferior	inferior	steel/equal	
Improvement age	8 years	12 years	inferior	9 years	inferior	5 years	superior
Imprv. condition	average	equal		equal		equal	
Abv.-grd. bldg. area	6,086 sq. ft.	5,000 sq. ft.	inferior	6,000 sq. ft.		8,000 sq. ft.	superior
Basement area	3,500 sq. ft.	2,000 sq. ft.	inferior	3,500 sq. ft.		4,500 sq. ft.	superior
Finished basement	2,000 sq. ft.	unfinished	inferior	2,000 sq. ft. finished		2,000 sq. ft. finished	
Functional utility	average	average		average		average	
Garage	2-car att.	2-car att.		2-car att.		2-car att.	
Other	none	none		in-ground pool	superior	none	
Overall comparison		much inferior		nearly equal		much superior	

Exhibit 20.5   Quantitative Adjustment and Quantitative Analysis

	Subject	Sale 1		Sale 2		Sale 3	
Address	12345 N. Main Street	209 S. Main Street		1209 S. Elliot Street		1985 James Street	
Data source	MLS	MLS	9944433	MLS	9934069	MLS	9804039
Gross sale price	$0		$425,000		$458,000		$475,000
Price/sq. ft. & /acre		$3.35	$146,059	$3.59	$156,474	$3.88	$168,919
Rights transferred	fee simple	fee simple	0.0%	fee simple	0.0%	fee simple	0.0%
Subtotal			$146,059		$156,474		$168,919
Financing	assume cash	contract sale	-5.0%	cash sale	0.0%	cash sale	0.0%
Subtotal			$138,756		$156,474		$168,919
Conditions of sale	arm's-length	arm's- length	0.0%	arm's-length	0.0%	arm's-length	0.0%
Subtotal			$138,756		$156,474		$168,919
Expenditures after sale	none assumed	none	0.0%	demolition cost	3.2%	none	0.0%
Subtotal			$138,756		$161,482		$168,919
Date of sale 0.25%	now	4 mos.ago	1.0%	6 mos. ago	1.5%	8 mos. ago	2.0%
Subtotal			$140,144		$163,904		$172,297
Topography	level	level		difficult	inferior	level	
Location	Smallburg	Smallburg		Smallburg		Hensenville	superior
Access	3 points	2 points	inferior	3 points		3 points	
Visibility	avg./industrial	isolated	inferior	equal		highway visibility	superior
Flood area	0.00%	0.00%		0.00%		0.00%	
Road frontage	300	325		300		350	
Average depth	400	390		425		350	
Size (square feet)	130,680	126,750		127,500		122,500	
Size (acres)	3.00	2.91		2.927		2.812	
Zoning	industrial	industrial		industrial		industrial	
Utilities	all public	all public		all public		all public	
Other factors	none	none		rail siding	superior	none	
Indicated value/acre		more than	$140,144 per acre	similar to	$163,904 per acre	less than	$172,297 per acre

used in the valuation of land for a commercial/industrial property.

Notice that the first adjustments were made as percentages (i.e., quantitative adjustments), while the analysis of the property was qualitative. Adjustments were made for special financing to Sale 1, expenditures immediately after sale to Sale 2, and market conditions adjustments to all three comparable sales. The unit of comparison was price per acre rather than the gross price, which indicates that the size of the parcel was compensated for with the unit of comparison.

1. The sales comparison approach requires how many comparisons?

   a) 3

   b) 4

   c) 5

   d) No set minimum number

Use the following data to solve Review Exercises 2 and 3.

The subject property is a small commercial building in a small town. It contains 4,000 square feet of gross building area and was constructed 10 years ago. It has an unfinished basement. The seller has agreed to provide a special financing package worth $4,000. Examination of the market has revealed several sales of competitive properties. It appears that prices in the market are increasing at about 5% per year on a straight-line basis.

  · Comparable 1 has 2,800 square feet of building area. It also has a basement. It was sold approximately one year ago for $275,000 at financing terms that are typical of the market.

  · Comparable 2 has 3,000 square feet of building area without a basement. It sold one year ago for $280,000 at terms generally available in the market.

  · Comparable 3 has 3,000 square feet of building area. It also has a basement. It sold one week ago for $300,000 at financing terms typical of the market.

2. What should be the respective magnitude and sign of the adjustments to Comparables 1, 2, and 3 for financing?

   a) 0, 0, 0

   b) +4,000, +4,000, +4,000

   c) -4,000, -4,000, -4,000

   d) +2,000, +2,000, +2,000

3. What should be the respective magnitude and sign of the adjustments to Comparables 1, 2, and 3 for the basement?

   a) +6,000, +6,000, -6,000

   b) 0, +6,000, 0

   c) -6,000, -6,000, -6,000

   d) 0, +10,000, -10,000

4. What are the indicated values of the comparable sales in the following table? Use any technique considered reasonable.

	Subject	Comparable 1		Comparable 2	
Address	12345 N. Main St.	11232 West St.		1233 East St.	
Price per sq. ft. GBA/price		$163.79	$475,000	$125.00	$525,000
Rights transferred	fee simple	fee simple	0.0%	fee simple	0.0%
Financing	cash to seller	cash to seller	0.0%	cash to seller	0.0%
Conditions of sale	arm's-length	arm's-length	0.0%	arm's-length	0.0%
Post-purchase repairs	none assumed	none reported	0.0%	none reported	0.0%
Date of sale	current	6 months ago	0.0%	9 months ago	0.0%
Current, cash-equivalent price			$475,000		$525,000
Location	Greenleave Addn.	Greenleave Addn.	_____	Greenleave Addn.	_____
Site size (acres)	1.25	1.0	_____	0.75	_____
Site view	golf course	golf course	_____	residential	_____
Building design	2-story/average	2-story/average	_____	2-story/average	_____
Construction quality	wood/frame/avg.	masonry/frame	_____	frame/masonry	_____
Improvement age	23	18	_____	23	_____
Improvement condition	average	average	_____	average	_____
Room count	9/4/2½	11/4/3½	_____	12/4/4½	_____
Above-ground building area	2,943	2,900	_____	4,200	_____
Basement area	756	1,200	_____	1,500	_____
Basement finish area	650	1,000	_____	500	_____
Functional obsolescence	average	average	_____	average	_____
Garage/parking	3-car att. garage	3-car att. garage	_____	4-car att. garage	_____
Miscellaneous	irrigation	equal	_____	equal	_____
Porches, patios, etc.	enclosed porch/deck	none	_____	equal	_____
Features	standard	standard	_____	standard	_____
Fireplaces	1 fireplace	1 fireplace	_____	1 fireplace	_____
Net adjustment			_____		_____
Indicated value			_____		_____

5. The published sale price of a small apartment building was $245,000. The buyer had mostly nonreported income and could not qualify for a standard mortgage. He agreed to purchase the property for $245,000 with the seller taking back a purchase-money mortgage of $175,000 at 7% for 30 years with a balloon payment in six years. The market interest rate for a property like this at the time of sale was at 9% with no points. What is the cash-equivalent sale price using the calculator yield-to-market technique, assuming the buyer would keep the financing in place for six years? (Round your answer to the nearest increment of $25,000.)

a) $250,000

b) $225,000

c) $200,000

d) $175,000

6. The owner of a two-acre commercial site insists that her property has appreciated by at least 5% per year since she bought it four years ago. As the appraiser, you are asked to factor this into the appraisal or refute her contention. Research in this market revealed the following sales and resales of comparable properties:

Sale	Date	Price	Annual Appreciation Rate
1	Price 1 month ago =	$200,000	
	Price 3 years and 1 month ago =	$195,000	_____
2	Price 3 months ago =	$195,000	
	Price 2 years and 4 months ago =	$187,000	_____
3	Price 1 month ago =	$210,000	
	Price 2 years and 4 months ago =	$210,000	_____
4	Sale 2 months ago =	$192,000	
	Sale 1 year ago =	$187,000	_____

What is the annualized reconciled appreciation rate on a straight-line basis? Use annual accounting.

7. The subject property has approximately 6,000 square feet of gross living area, a three-car garage, and a 2,000-sq.-ft. finished basement. The lot is five acres with a creek and small pond on site. This five-year-old house is probably of better quality than 95% of the existing homes in the market and is in similar condition to most houses of this quality in most competing markets. A carefully prepared application of the cost approach with a physical depreciation deduction of 7% resulted in an indication of value of $475,000 (including land). In this market, the highest-priced residential sale price was $225,000 paid five years ago for a one-year-old home that the local bank president built and that one of the two car dealers in the area bought. A review of local professions reveals that only 10 other people in the market could afford the payments for this home (with 20% down). None of the people who qualify to buy a home of this quality are currently looking in the market.

    The highest-priced sales in the last year are listed on the following grid (Comparables 1 and 2). Comparable 3 is located in another small town in the next county to the north. This other town has similar economic conditions, but most area residents think it has a better school system. Comparable 3 is of similar quality as the subject property and is otherwise very comparable to the subject despite the fact that it is in another town.

    The rate of appreciation is 3% per year. The land value is $35,000 for Comparable 1 and $30,000 for Comparable 2. Sale 3 has very similar overall land value, but the value is lower because of the pond in the subject's backyard. The subject property's land sold five years ago (when the house was new) for $45,000.

    What are the indicated values of the comparable properties? Keep in mind that there are no absolute solutions to this exercise. Demonstrate logical analysis in making adjustments and drawing conclusions.

Item	Subject	Comparable 1		Comparable 2		Comparable 3	
Sale price		$200,000		$175,000		$275,000	
Price/AGLA		$80.00	_____	$76.09	_____	$43.65	_____
Date of sale		8 months ago	_____	4 months ago	_____	4 months ago	_____
Location	Salty Creek	Salty Creek	_____	Salty Creek	_____	Johnson Acres	_____
Site	5 acres	1 acre	_____	0.75 acre	_____	5 acres	_____
View	residential/pond	residential	_____	residential	_____	residential	_____
Design/appeal	2-story/avg.	2-story/avg.	_____	2-story/avg.	_____	2-story/avg.	_____
Construction quality	brick/good	brick/average	_____	brick/average	_____	brick/good	_____
Age	5 years old	1 year old	_____	2 years old	_____	12 years old	_____
Condition	average	average	_____	average	_____	average	_____
Room count	10/4/3½	10/4/2½	_____	10/4/2½	_____	11/4/2½	_____
AGLA	6,000	2,500	_____	2,300	_____	6,300	_____
Basement area	2,000	1,200	_____	1,000	_____	2,500	_____
Basement finish	1,500	900	_____	none	_____	1,800	_____
Functional utility	average	average	_____	average	_____	average	_____
HVAC	GFA/cent. AC	GFA/cent. AC	_____	GFA/cent. AC	_____	GFA/cent. AC	_____
Garage/carport	3-car att. garage	2-car att. garage	_____	2-car att. garage	_____	3-car att. garage	_____
Porch/patio	screened porch	screened porch	_____	screened porch	_____	screened porch	_____
Fireplace(s)	2 fireplaces	1 fireplace	_____	1 fireplace	_____	2 fireplaces	_____
Kitchen	standard kitchen	standard kitchen	_____	standard kitchen	_____	standard kitchen	_____
Net adjustment			_____		_____		_____
Indicated value			_____		_____		_____

8. The subject is a 0.3-acre platted residential lot improved with a bilevel house with 1,000 square feet on the upper floor and 1,000 square feet of finished space on the lower level. It has a two-car attached garage and a 500-sq.-ft. wood deck in the back of the house. The 32-year-old home is of average quality for this market and is in average condition. Details of this property are listed in the adjustment grid.

Research in this market did not reveal any bilevel homes that had sold in the last five years. Two sales of homes of different designs were found and are described below. Use these sales to value the subject. Comparable 1 has a traditional home design with an unfinished basement. The basement is almost completely underground. Comparable 2 is a standard 2,000-sq.-ft. residence without a basement. All of the living area of the two-story home is above grade. Use a 3% appreciation rate in this market.

Make the correct adjustments to arrive at indicated values for the comparables.

Item	Subject	Comparable 1		Comparable 2	
Sale price			$80,000		$95,000
Price/AGLA		$80.00	_____	$47.50	_____
Date of sale	–	2 months ago	_____	4 months ago	_____
Location	Palmer's Addition	Palmer's Addition	_____	Palmer's Addition	_____
Site	1/3 acre	1/3 acre	_____	1/3 acre	_____
View	residential	residential	_____	residential	_____
Design/appeal	bilevel/avg.	1-story/avg.	_____	2-story/avg.	_____
Construction quality	brick/average	brick/average	_____	brick/average	_____
Age	32 years old	32 years old	_____	33 years old	_____
Condition	average	average	_____	average	_____
Room count	5/3/2	6/3/2	_____	9/4/2	_____
AGLA	1,000	1,000	_____	2,000	_____
Basement area	1,000 sq. ft.	1,000 sq. ft.	_____	no basement	_____
Basement finish	1,000 sq. ft. w/o	unfinished	_____	no basement	_____
Functional utility	average	average	_____	average	_____
HVAC	GFA/cent. AC	GFA/cent. AC	_____	GFA/cent. AC	_____
Energy efficiency	standard	standard	_____	standard	_____
Garage/carport	2-car att. garage	2-car att. garage	_____	2-car att. garage	_____
Porch/patio	deck	deck	_____	deck	_____
Fireplace(s)	1 fireplace	1 fireplace	_____	1 fireplace	_____
Kitchen	standard kitchen	standard kitchen	_____	standard kitchen	_____
Fence/pool	none	none	_____	none	_____
Net adjustment			_____		_____
Indicated value			_____		_____

9. The subject property is a 2,000-sq.-ft., one-unit home built on 27 acres on a two-lane road in a remote exurban area. The land in this area is rolling, wooded, and generally not tillable because of the topography. Although there is a diverse population in this county, most properties in the immediate area of the subject are remote. They appeal to an "outdoors-type" buyer seeking privacy and limited interaction with neighbors. The following data applies to the subject and comparable properties:

Subject address	1200 W. CR400N
Taxes	$1,427 per half year
Property rights appraised	Fee simple
Sales history	Currently under contract of sale at $175,000 with $5,000 in seller-paid closing costs for the buyer. No other sales or listings have occurred in the last two years.

Neighborhood	
Boundaries	The neighborhood boundaries are considered to be the limits of the Green township in Blue County.
Location	Rural, low-density
Built up	Less than 25%
Growth rate	Slow but stable growth
Property values	Stable, minor increases only
Supply/demand	In balance
Marketing time	6 to 9 months
Predominant occupancy rate	Owner/vacant (0-5%)
Neighborhood price range	$75,000 to $185,000 (predominantly $150,000)
Neighborhood age range	5 to 50 years (predominantly 20 years)
Neighborhood rental range	$500 to $1,000 per month (tenants pay utilities)
Price/rental change	Stable/stable
Present land use	20% one-unit residential, 5% 2- to 4-family residential, 5% church and school, 70% vacant or agricultural
Land use change	Not likely
Market segment	5- to 15-year-old, one-unit homes located in Green township, Blue County, priced from $150,000 to $200,000
	Active listings — 7
	Pending sales = 2
	Closed sales in the last 12 months = 12

Site	
Lot size	27 acres with about 250 feet of road frontage
Zoning	Residential R-1 (conforming)
View	Wooded in the front, a school in the rear
Topography	Rolling, wooded, well drained
Utilities	Well and septic required
Highest and best use (as vacant)	Residential one-unit (little demand for other uses)
Street access	Public, two lanes, asphalt; no sidewalks, curbs, or gutters
Drainage	Rolling topography, well drained
Landscaping/driveway	Minimal landscaping, gravel driveway
FEMA zone	"C" 180500-0025c (6/88)
Easements	No adverse easements or encroachments

Improvements

Improvement type	Detached, one-unit, two-story residence
Improvement age	10 years old, effective age = 10 years
Foundation	Concrete blocks
Roof type	6/12 pitch, standing seam galvanized steel
Construction	Log construction with some interior drywall
Veneer	None—solid wood log home
Gutters and downspouts	Continuous aluminum
Window type	Wood frame, Thermopane glazing
Construction quality	Average as compared to homes in this market
Improvement condition	Average for homes of this age and in this market
Story/style	2-story/log home—simple 2-story Colonial design
Room count	8 rooms, 3 bedrooms, 2 bathrooms
Above-grade area	1,400-sq.-ft. first floor, 600-sq.-ft. second floor
Basement area	1,400-sq.-ft. unfinished basement, concrete walls and floor
Garage (two-car attached)	600-sq.-ft. frame construction, wood veneer, concrete slab floor
HVAC/condition	Gas forced-air heating and central air-conditioning/average
Appliances	Range/oven, dishwasher, hood fan, disposal, refrigerator
Fireplace	Wood-burning, masonry, single opening
Porches, patios	Screened porch, small stoop
Floors	Resilient, hardwood and carpets on tack strips
Walls	Logs and in some areas taped and painted gypsum board
Trim/finish	Colonial wood/average
Bath floor wainscoting	Vinyl (average)/fiberglass (average)
Sump pump	No, gravity flow
Settlement/infestation	None noted
Doors	Wood, six panel, hinged with metal hardware
Attic	Minimal attic area because nearly all of the second floor is finished. Access to the minimal attic is via a scuttle.
Highest and best use as improved	As currently improved (except for functional problems noted)

Cost Approach Data

Reproduction cost	$65.00 per square foot above grade
	$15.00 per square foot basement
	$15.00 per square foot garage
	$7,500 porches
Land value	$27,000 (valued at $1,000 per acre)
Depreciation	10% physical, 5% functional
Site improvements	$4,500 net value

Comparable 1 (data from the MLS system #456789)

Address	1500 W. CR350N
Township	Green
County	Blue
Taxes	$358.00 per half year
List price	$150,900
Sale price	$141,900
Date of sale	6 months ago
Financing	New conventional mortgage, effectively cash-to-seller
Days on market	334 days
Improvement age	6 years actual, 6 years effective
Lot size	12 acres (valued at $18,000)
Topography	Rolling and wooded
Utilities	Well and septic required
Construction	Wood frame, 2 x 4-in. studs, 16-in. O.C.
Veneer	Brick/wood siding
Construction quality	Average for this market
Improvement condition	Average for this market
Story/style	1-story/traditional
Room count	7 rooms, 3 bedrooms, 2 baths
Above-grade area	1,752 square feet
Basement area	No basement—crawl space only
Garage	2-car detached garage (600 square feet)
HVAC	Gas hot water, no AC
Appliances	Range/oven, dishwasher, disposal, refrigerator
Fireplace	One masonry fireplace
Other	Small fenced area, 8-ft. x 10-ft. shed, 8-ft. x 18-ft. raised concrete front porch

Comparable Sale 2 (data from the MLS system #753159)

Address	500 N. CR150W
Township	Green
County	Blue
Taxes	$658.00 per half year
List price	$190,900
Sale price	$189,000
Date of sale	14 months ago
Financing	The seller took back a three-year conditional sales contract at 8% with a 5% down payment from a buyer who did not qualify for a third-party mortgage. The market rate at that time was 8% with 5% to 20% down payment minimums. The buyer indicated she was locked into this property because of the willingness of the seller to take back financing. The buyer indicated she thought she paid 5% extra because of financing.
Days on market	49 days
Improvement age	7 years actual, 7 years effective
Lot size	22 acres (valued at $25,000)
Topography	Rolling and wooded
Utilities	Well and septic required
Construction	Wood frame, 2 x 4-in. studs, 16-in. O.C.
Veneer	Brick/wood veneer
Construction quality	Average for this market
Improvement condition	Average for this market
Story/style	2-story/traditional
Room count	9 rooms, 4 bedrooms, 3 baths
Above-grade area	2,100 square feet
Basement area	1,000-sq.-ft. basement unfinished walk out
Garage	2-car attached garage (600 square feet)
HVAC	Gas forced air heating and central air-conditioning
Appliances	Range/oven, dishwasher, disposal
Fireplace	One masonry fireplace
Other	22-ft. x 24-ft. shed/shop, 12-ft. x 15-ft. screened-in porch

Comparable Sale 3 (data from the MLS system #582987)

Address	150 S. CR50W
Township	Green
County	Blue
Taxes	$458.00 per half year
List price	$169,900
Sale price	$169,000
Date of sale	7 months ago
Financing	The buyer applied for and obtained a mortgage at the market rate. The seller essentially received cash at closing.
Days on market	4 days
Improvement age	9 years actual, 9 years effective
Lot size	8 acres (valued at $12,000)
Topography	Rolling and wooded
Utilities	Well and septic required
Construction	Wood frame 2 x 4-in. studs, 16-in. O.C.
Veneer	Brownstone veneer
Construction quality	Average for this market
Improvement condition	Average for this market
Story/style	2-story/traditional
Room count	8 rooms, 4 bedrooms, 3 baths
Above-grade area	2,300 square feet
Basement area	1,000-sq.-ft. basement unfinished
Garage	2-car attached garage (600 square feet)
HVAC	Gas forced air heating and central air-conditioning
Appliances	Range/oven, dishwasher, disposal
Fireplace	One masonry fireplace
Other	12-ft. x 15-ft. porch

The following grid can be used to value the subject property. The adjustment rates should be supportable. Do not forget that this property is currently under a contract of sale for $175,000 with $5,000 in seller-paid concessions.

Residential Sales Comparison Approach Grid

Item	Subject	Comparable 1		Comparable 2		Comparable 3	
Address	1200 W. 400 N	1500 W. 350 N		500 N. 150 W		150 S. 50 W	
Price	$175,000		$141,900		$189,000		$169,000
Price per GLA	$87.50	$80.99		$90.00		$73.48	
Days on market		334		49		4	
Financing	conventional mortgage	contract sale with conventional mortgage	_____	contract sale	_____	conventional mortgage	_____
Concessions		no concessions	_____	favorable terms	_____	no concessions	_____
Date of sale/time	today	6 months ago	_____	14 months ago	_____	7 months ago	_____
Location	1200 W 400 N	1500 W 350 N	_____	500 N 150 W	_____	150 S 50 W	_____
Leasehold/fee simple	fee simple	fee simple	_____	fee simple	_____	fee simple	_____
Site	27 acres	12 acres	_____	22 acres	_____	8 acres	_____
View	wooded/school	wooded	_____	wooded	_____	wooded	_____
Design and appeal	2-story	1-story	_____	2-story	_____	2-story	_____
Construction quality	log construction	wood frame/ brick	_____	wood frame/ brick	_____	wood frame/ stone	_____
Age	10 years	6 years	_____	7 years	_____	9 years	_____
Condition	average	average	_____	average	_____	average	_____
Room count	8/3/2	7/3/2	_____	9/3/2	_____	8/4/3	_____
Gross living area	2,000	1,752	_____	2,100	_____	2,300	_____
Basement	1,400	no, crawl space	_____	1,000	_____	1,000	_____
Finish	none	none	_____	none WO style	_____	none	_____
Functional utility	average/log	average	_____	average	_____	average	_____
Heating/cooling	GFA/CAC	GHW/no AC	_____	GFA/CAC	_____	GFA/CAC	_____
Energy-efficient items	standard	standard	_____	standard	_____	standard	_____
Garage/carport	2-car att./600	2-car det./600	_____	2-car att./600	_____	2-car att./600	_____
Porches	screened porch	fence, shed, porch	_____	screened porch, 528-sq.-ft. shop	_____	porch	_____
Fireplaces	1 fireplace	1 fireplace	_____	1 fireplace	_____	1 fireplace	_____
Fence, pool, etc.	none	none	_____	none	_____	none	_____
Other	appliances, etc.	equal	_____	equal	_____	equal	_____
Net adjustment			_____		_____		_____
Adjusted sale price of comparable		$ _____		$ _____		$ _____	
GLA Factor	25						

Note: Unless otherwise noted, italicized references indicate the pages in *The Appraisal of Real Estate*, 14th edition, that readers should consult for additional discussion of these topics.

1. **d) No set minimum number**

   This student handbook and page 382

2. **a) 0, 0, 0**

   Note that you may be tempted to choose answer b) to adjust the prices of the comparables to the subject's financing package, but a financing adjustment relates to the definition of value, not the financing package. Would your answer be different if the seller had agreed to $40,000 in concessions, not $4,000?

3. **b) 0, +6,000, 0**

   Note that the correct answer is the only option in which the direction of the adjustments corresponds to the given facts. That is, Comparables 1 and 3 have basements, just like the subject property, so no adjustment for that characteristic is necessary. But Comparable 2 does not have a basement, so its sale price must be adjusted upward to account for that inferior characteristic. After adjusting the sale prices of the comparable properties for market conditions, paired data analysis can be used to support the adjustment amount.

4. The following is one solution, not the only possible solution. Your rationale for an adjustment could be different than that of another appraiser in a different market.

	Subject	Comparable 1		Comparable 2	
Address	12345 N. Main St.	11232 West St.		1233 East St.	
Price per sq. ft. GBA/price		$163.79	$475,000	$125.00	$525,000
Rights transferred	fee simple	fee simple	0.0%	fee simple	0.0%
Financing	cash to seller	cash to seller	0.0%	cash to seller	0.0%
Conditions of sale	arm's-length	arm's-length	0.0%	arm's-length	0.0%
Post-purchase repairs	none assumed	none reported	0.0%	none reported	0.0%
Date of sale	current	6 months ago	0.0%	9 months ago	0.0%
Current, cash-equivalent price			$475,000		$525,000
Location	Greenleave Addn.	Greenleave Addn.		Greenleave Addn.	
Site size (acres)	1.25	1.0	+ 10,000	0.75 acres	+ 15,000
Site view	golf course	golf course		residential	+ 10,000
Building design	2-story/average	2-story/average		2-story/average	
Construction quality	wood/frame/avg.	masonry/frame	– 10,000	frame/masonry	– 10,000
Improvement age	23	18	– 10,000	23	
Improvement condition	average	average		average	
Room count	9/4/2½	11/4/3½	– 5,000	12/4/4½	– 10,000
Abv.-ground building area @45	2,943	2,900		4,200	– 55,000
Basement area @20	756	1,200	– 10,000	1,500	– 15,000
Basement finish area @20	650	1,000	– 5,000	500	+ 5,000
Functional obsolescence	average	average		average	
Garage/parking	3-car att. garage	3-car att. garage		4-car att. garage	– 10,000
Miscellaneous	irrigation	equal		equal	
Porches, patios, etc.	enclosed porch/deck	none	+ 20,000	equal	
Features	standard	standard		standard	
Fireplaces	1 fireplace	1 fireplace		1 fireplace	
Net adjustment			– 10,000		– 70,000
Indicated value			$465,000		$455,000

5. **b) $225,000**

Term is 30:	30 [g] [n]
Interest rate is 7%:	7 [g] [i]
Loan amount is $175,000:	175,000 [CHS] [PV]
Balloon payment:	0 [FV]
Solve for [PMT] =	1,164.28
Change term to payments made (6):	6 [g] [n]
Solve for balance in 6 years ([FV]) =	162,210
Change interest rate to 9%:	9 [g] [i]
Solve for [PV] of mortgage [CHS] =	159,308.93
Add down payment ($245,000 − $175,000 = $70,000) back in:	229,308.93

6.

Sale	Date	Price	Annual Appreciation Rate
1	Price 1 month ago =	$200,000	
	Price 3 years and 1 month ago =	$195,000	0.855%
2	Price 3 months ago =	$195,000	
	Price 2 years and 4 months ago =	$187,000	2.054%
3	Price 1 month ago =	$210,000	
	Price 2 years and 4 months ago =	$210,000	0.000%
4	Sale 2 months ago =	$192,000	
	Sale 1 year ago =	$187,000	3.209%

In this situation, the calculations are straightforward, but the reconciliation is not. Think about when the appreciation occurred, what the dates of the sales data are, and where this will be applied. Is it possible to have a higher rate in the last year than in earlier years?

7. The subject property has overimprovements that must be adjusted for. Note that the price per square foot of GLA and the basement adjustments were very small. These low rates give some consideration to the lack of a deep market for this very large home in a small town. The adjustment rates provided assume the market will not pay a high price for this overimprovement.

Item	Subject	Comparable 1		Comparable 2		Comparable 3	
Sale price			$200,000		$175,000		$275,000
Price/AGLA		$80.00		$76.09		$43.65	
Date of sale		8 months ago	+ 4,000	4 months ago	+ 1,800	4 months ago	+ 2,800
Location	Salty Creek	Salty Creek		Salty Creek		Johnson Acres	
Site	5 acres	1 acre	+ 12,000	0.75 acre	+ 17,000	5 acres	
View	residential/pond	residential	+ 5,000	residential	+ 5,000	residential	+ 5,000
Design/appeal	2-story/avg.	2-story/avg.		2-story/avg.		2-story/avg.	
Const. quality	brick/good	brick/average	+ 5,000	brick/average	+ 5,000	brick/good	
Age	5 years old	1 year old	− 12,000	2 years old	− 9,000	12 years old	+ 21,000
Condition	average	average		average		average	
Room count	10/4/3½	10/4/2½	+ 2,000	10/4/2½	+ 2,000	11/4/2½	+ 2,000
AGLA (20)	6,000	2,500	+ 70,000	2,300	+ 74,000	6,300	− 6,000
Basement area (8)	2,000	1,200	+ 6,400	1,000	+ 8,000	2,500	− 4,000
Basement finish (8)	1,500	900	+ 4,800	none	+ 12,000	1,800	− 2,400
Functional utility	average	average		average		average	
HVAC	GFA/cent. AC	GFA/cent. AC		GFA/cent. AC		GFA/cent. AC	
Garage/carport	3-car att. garage	2-car att. garage	+ 4,000	2-car att. garage	+ 4,000	3-car att. garage	
Porch/patio	screened porch	screened porch		screened porch		screened porch	
Fireplace(s)	2 fireplaces	1 fireplace	+ 1,000	1 fireplace	+ 1,000	2 fireplaces	
Kitchen	standard kitchen	standard kitchen		standard kitchen		standard kitchen	
Net adjustment			+ 102,200		+ 120,800		+ 18,400
Indicated value			$302,200		$295,800		$293,400

8. This problem is much simpler than the previous problem, with fewer adjustments, but the solution will still vary from market to market depending on local practice. The critical issue in this situation is the treatment of the subject property's bilevel or "raised ranch" design. If, for the purposes of comparison, this property is considered a ranch with a finished basement, the analysis is consistent; if it is considered a two-story house, the adjustments would be different.

Item	Subject	Comparable 1		Comparable 2	
Sale price			$80,000		$95,000
Price/AGLA		$80.00		$47.50	
Date of sale		2 months ago	+ 400	4 months ago	+ 1,000
Location	Palmer's Addition	Palmer's Addition		Palmer's Addition	
Site	1/3 acre	1/3 acre		1/3 acre	
View	residential	residential		residential	
Design/appeal	bilevel/avg.	1-story/avg.		2-story/avg.	
Construction quality	brick/average	brick/average		brick/average	
Age	32 years old	32 years old		33 years old	
Condition	average	average		average	
Room count	5/3/2	6/3/2		9/4/2	
AGLA (25)	1,000	1,000		2,000	− 25,000
Basement area (10)	1,000 sq. ft.	1,000 sq. ft.		no basement	+ 10,000
Basement finish (12,000)	1,000 sq. ft. w/o	unfinished	+ 12,000	no basement	+ 12,000
Functional utility	average	average		average	
HVAC	GFA/cent. AC	GFA/cent. AC		GFA/cent. AC	
Energy efficiency	standard	standard		standard	
Garage/carport	2-car att. garage	2-car att. garage		2-car att. garage	
Porch/patio	deck	deck		deck	
Fireplaces	1 fireplace	1 fireplace		1 fireplace	
Kitchen	standard kitchen	standard kitchen		standard kitchen	
Fence/pool	none	none		none	
Net adjustment			+ 12,400		− 2,000
Indicated value			$92,400		$93,000

9.

Residential Sales Comparison Approach Grid

Item	Subject	Comparable 1		Comparable 2		Comparable 3	
Address	1200 W. 400 N	1500 W. 350 N		500 N. 150 W		150 S. 50 W	
Price	$175,000		$141,900		$189,000		$169,000
Price per GLA	$87.50	$80.99		$90.00		$73.48	
Days on market		334		49		4	
Financing	conventional	contract sale with conventional mortgage		contract sale		conventional mortgage	
Concessions		no concessions		favorable terms	− 9,500	no concessions	
Date of sale/time	today	6 months ago		14 months ago		7 months ago	
Location	1200 W 400 N	1500 W 350 N		500 N 150 W		150 S 50 W	
Leasehold/fee simple	fee simple	fee simple		fee simple		fee simple	
Site	27 acres	12 acres	+ 9,000	22 acres	+ 2,000	8 acres	+ 15,000
View	wooded/school	wooded		wooded		wooded	
Design and appeal	2-story	1-story		2-story		2-story	
Construction quality	log construction	wood frame/ brick		wood frame/ brick		wood frame/ stone	
Age	10 years	6 years	− 8,000	7 years	− 6,000	9 years	− 2,000
Condition	average	average		average		average	
Room count	8/3/2	7/3/2		9/3/2		8/4/3	− 2,000
Gross living area	2,000	1,752	+ 6,200	2,100	− 2,500	2,300	− 7,500
Basement	1,400	no, crawl space	+ 16,800	1,000	+ 4,800	1,000	+ 4,800
Finish	none	none		none WO style	− 3,000	none	
Functional utility	average/log	average		average		average	
Heating/cooling	GFA/CAC	GHW/no AC	+ 3,500	GFA/CAC		GFA/CAC	
Energy-efficient items	standard	standard		standard		standard	
Garage/carport	2-car att./600	2-car det./600	+ 1,000	2-car att./600		2-car att./600	
Porches	screened porch	fence, shed, porch	+ 2,000	screened porch, 528-sq.-ft. shop	− 3,500	porch	+ 5,500
Fireplaces	1 fireplace	1 fireplace		1 fireplace		1 fireplace	
Fence, pool, etc.	none	none		none		none	
Other	appliances, etc.	equal		equal		equal	
Net adjustment			+ 30,500		− 17,700		+ 13,800
Adjusted sale price of comparable			$172,400		$171,300		$182,800
GLA Factor	25						

The solution above is not the only possible answer. Many of the adjustments are loosely based on percentages rather than dollar amounts from matched-pair extractions. The site adjustments are based on the site values. The age adjustment is loosely based on an estimate of $2,000 per year, which was extracted as follows:

Item	Comparable 1		Comparable 2		Comparable 3	
Address	1500 W. 350 N		500 N. 150 W		150 S. 50 W	
Price		$141,900		$189,000		$169,000
Financing, etc.			−	$9,500		
Landscaping	−	$5,000	−	$5,000	−	$3,000
Land value	12 acres	− $18,000	22 acres	− $25,000	8 acres	− $12,000
Building value (all components)		$118,900		$149,500		$154,000
Building reproduction cost	1,752 @ $67	$117,384	2,100 @ $65	+ $136,500	2,300 @ $64	+ $147,200
Basement	$0	+ $0	1,000 @ $15	+ $15,000	1,000 @ $15	+ $15,000
Garage	600 @ $15	+ $9,000	600 @ $15	+ $9,000	600 @ $15	+ $9,000
Porches, etc.		+ $3,000		+ $7,000		+ $4,000
Reproduction cost (all components)		$129,384		$167,500		$175,200
Depreciation (building value − reproduction cost)		$10,484		$18,000		$21,200
Age of improvement		6		7		9
$ depreciation per year		$1,747		$2,571		$2,356

Most of the other adjustments were based on depreciated cost new.

21

The Income Capitalization Approach

Relation to Appraisal Principles

Anticipation and Change

All property—real, personal, or intangible—has value equal to the present worth of future benefits of ownership. In real estate, future benefits include interim cash flows or benefits, which are usually cash flows during the holding period and the resale value of the property at the end of the holding period. This axiom is also true when valuing a car, a computer, or something as common as a can of soda.

Because income levels and prices are always changing and because buyers think about their future benefits, which are based on income levels and prices, the income capitalization approach must be forward thinking. The income estimates must take into account future numbers rather than historical ones. Historical income levels are an excellent basis for estimating future cash flows but they must not be the sole source. Likewise, historical expense levels cannot always be relied on to indicate future levels. For example, suppose the subject property has had property taxes of $25,000 each year for the last five years. You might reasonably estimate that the taxes for the next year will also be $25,000, but this may not be the case if the property was reassessed the previous year and the taxes are going to increase to $30,000 per year.

Logically, a buyer would use $30,000 rather than $25,000 in calculations of future benefits.

Supply and Demand

Supply and demand are reflected in income rates, which can be capitalization or yield rates. When the inventory of leased space becomes oversupplied, income rates fall. When the market of income-producing properties for sale becomes oversupplied, the prices of the properties fall, which affects capitalization rates.

Applicability and Limitations

In the income capitalization approach, appraisers convert periodic (usually annual) expected income into a current lump-sum capital value. In other words, appraisers analyze the amount of money a person would pay *today* for an anticipated income *each year* in the future plus the reversion.

The income capitalization approach is applicable when the income potential of the property is a primary consideration of buyers. A one-unit home buyer typically does not consider the property's in-

> To "capitalize" means to convert future income into a lump-sum value amount today.

KEY TERMS		
base rent	investment value	potential gross income (*PGI*)
capital expenses	lease	reconstructed operating statement
contract rent	market rent	replacement allowance
deficit rent	market value	return of capital
effective gross income (*EGI*)	modified gross lease	return on capital
effective rent	net lease	reversion
equity income (I_E)	net operating income (I_O or *NOI*)	revaluation lease
excess rent	operating expenses	step-up (step-down) lease
flat rental lease	overage rent	time value of money
gross lease	overall yield rate (Y_O)	yield rate (*Y*)
income rate	percentage lease	
index lease	percentage rent	

come potential when making a purchase decision, so the income capitalization approach is not normally applicable. On the other hand, the buyer of a shopping center probably considers only income levels when purchasing that type of property, so the income capitalization approach is the most applicable. But, of course, if buyers are focused on earnings, the sales comparison approach must account for that characteristic of property as well. Looking at historical sales of shopping centers normally provides a good indication of value if the economic conditions are similar or can be adjusted for. In other words, the analysis of sales of properties that are bought and sold based on income earned must include considerations of higher or lower earnings in situations where the income capitalization approach is especially applicable.

The income capitalization approach is limited when the income estimates are weak, sales data is not available to extract or confirm capitalization rates, or buyers consider other issues more than the property's income potential.

Definitions

A large variety of specialized technical terms are associated with the income capitalization approach. The following discussion summarizes the most important terms.

Leases

Leases are documents that convey the right to occupy space for a specific period of time and a specific amount of money. Lease income (or *rent*) is the basis of most real estate valuation using the income capitalization approach. Leases can be structured in any legal way the parties agree upon. Exhibit 21.1 describes the most common types of lease structures.

There is an important distinction between a *gross lease* and a *net lease*. The landlord pays all of the expenses associated with the operation of the property in a gross lease situation, while the tenant pays all of the property expenses in a net lease. In a *modified gross lease*, the tenant and landlord share the expenses. The term *net lease* is often used differently or in different variations by real estate professionals, even in the same market. Some brokers call some leases *net leases* and others *net net net* or *triple net leases*. You should ask questions about the "net" label to ensure that the income analysis and the reported expense breakdown are reconciled. As in most cases, labels are not terribly important; rather, how the data is extracted and applied is much more important.

Rent

Rent can take as many forms as leases do, as shown in Exhibit 21.2.

Future Benefits

The future benefits accruing to the owners of real estate are usually periodic cash flows and the reversion (i.e., the resale). For some properties, the cash flows are significant and the resale is minimal, while the situation is reversed for other proper-

---

Interests to Be Valued Worksheet

Appraisers do not appraise "sticks and bricks." Instead, they value the rights in realty for space on the face of the earth (except for condominiums). In the analysis of income-producing properties, this concept is very important because the rights in realty will be split upon the execution of a lease. The right to occupy real estate is conveyed to another when a lease is signed. Depending on the lease terms, the value of an improvement may be held by the tenant (the leasehold interest). In some cases, life estates, easements, mineral rights, and other issues become significant in property valuation.

Remember that although appraisers talk about analyses of "land" and "buildings," these terms do not represent an interest that can be valued. In other words, you can value the land for analytical purposes, but you are really only valuing the interests in realty.

For example, suppose your client owned a commercial parcel of land. His accountant advised him not to sell the land but rather to lease it on a long-term basis. He put a "for lease" sign on the property and received an offer within a few months. The lease he agreed to was for 75 years with payments of $40,000 per year for 50 years and $50,000 per year for the last 25 years. The tenant signed the lease and within hours signed a contract to build a two-story office building on that land. The tenant arranged for a mortgage to finance the construction of the building, which had a reproduction cost of $1,800,000. The lease rate appears to be at the market rate.

1. If the land lease has a 10% capitalization rate, what is the value of the owner's interest in the land (the leased fee interest)?

2. What is the value of the tenant's interest in the building?

3. As the building gets older and closer to the end of the 75-year lease, what will happen?

4. What about the reversion (i.e., the resale of the property) after the lease ends? How much will the building add or subtract from the value?

Note: Check the suggested solutions at the end of this chapter for answers to these questions.

Exhibit 21.1   Common Lease Structures

Type of Lease	Characteristics
Flat rental lease	The tenant pays a flat amount and gets to use the property for a specific time (e.g., most short-term apartment leases). At the end of the lease, the property reverts back to the landlord.
Variable rate lease	The tenant pays one amount now and usually a higher amount later. This is a common condition of long-term leases in which increases are needed in the later years. Increases are commonly made using a Consumer Price Index (CPI) adjustment factor.
Step-up or step-down lease	These leases are scheduled with increases or decreases on certain dates. The rent can increase due to inflation or can be scheduled to go down as the tenant improvement expense is amortized.
Lease with annual increase	This type of lease calls for a standard increase in the rental rate each year. Annual increases are often used in leases of apartments and sometimes in commercial property leases but seldom in leases of industrial facilities.
Revaluation lease	These leases require the rent to be reevaluated (and usually adjusted to the market rate) periodically.
Percentage lease	This type of lease is usually used for retail properties. The tenant pays a flat amount each year plus a percentage of the sales or a percentage of the sales from the first dollar on.

Exhibit 21.2   Common Rent Types

Type of Rent	Characteristics
Market rent	The amount of money the property would command under current market conditions. Market rent can be different from contract rent because it is the amount the property would command ignoring specific leases currently in force.
Contract rent	The amount stipulated in the lease. For leased properties, the contract rent represents the potential gross income. This makes some appraisal assignments easier because the difficulty of estimating the rental income is less relevant.
Effective rent	The rent that considers any concessions offered to tenants to entice them to sign a lease. The contract rent may be much higher than the effective rent if the tenant was given six months of free rent.
Excess rent	The amount of money paid in a lease contract that exceeds the market rate. This is risky income because a tenant who is paying rent in excess of the market rate may try to break or renegotiate the lease.
Deficit rent	The difference between contract rent and the market rate when the contract rent is lower than the market rate. If the deficit is large enough, the landlord may try to get out of the contract.
Percentage rent	The rental income paid by the tenant in a retail building that is tied to the level of sales. This type of income is less reliable than income from flat rental leases and some other types of leases because the income may decrease substantially in a slow economic period. Many appraisers treat this income differently because it is not guaranteed.
Overage rent	The rent paid for the percentage rent over the base rent–i.e., the amount of money that represents the percentage of sales. Percentage leases encourage the owner of the retail center to spend money to promote the business of the tenants because it is in the lessor's best interest for sales to stay above the base amount.

ties. That is, the reversion is more significant if the analysis period is short. For example, the resale of a property at the end of an anticipated holding period of three years is likely a more significant portion of the total proceeds of an investment than the forecast resale value of the same property 10 years out.

While appraisers are not often hired to evaluate the mortgage interest in real estate, these interests are valued in a similar fashion as the future benefits accruing to the owners of real estate. By definition, a standard amortized mortgage starts out at 100% of value and diminishes to 0% over the holding period.

To evaluate the future benefits, appraisers must be able to estimate the gross and net incomes of a property. The standard procedure for estimating income is to start at the gross income and work down to net income. This procedure allows appraisers to analyze the income and expenses and compare them with other properties in the same market. Exhibit 21.3 shows how appraisers deduct the appropriate expenses from gross income,

> Examples of properties with *diminishing assets* are subdivisions, coal mines, and gravel pits. All of these assets, by design, will be worth much less or nothing at the end of the holding period. If everything goes well in a subdivision development, the owner will have no inventory at the end and no reversion. When a coal mine or gravel pit is depleted, the owner usually just owns a hole in the ground.

Exhibit 21.3	Reconstructed Operating Statement		
Potential gross income (PGI)	25,000 sq. ft. @ $19.00	$475,000	
Vacancy and collection loss	5%	(23,750)	
Effective gross income (EGI)		$451,250	
Estimated annual expenses			
Property taxes		$45,000	
Property insurance		8,500	
Repairs		35,000	
Management		22,500	
Utilities		49,000	
Reserve for new roof covering ($25,000 @ 1/20)		1,250	
Reserve for parking lot resurface ($12,000 @ 1/15)		+ 800	
Total expenses		$162,050	(162,050)
Net operating income			$289,200

which results in a net income level that indicates what the investor would receive the next year, assuming the owner has no debt or debt payments.

Potential Gross Income

The starting point in most income analyses of real estate is potential gross income (PGI), the amount of money the property would bring in if it were completely occupied all year long and all tenants paid their rent. This estimate also includes the maximum income from other sources such as parking garages in office buildings and apartments, laundry income in apartments, and vending income in other commercial properties. The initial estimate can be an unrealistic amount because very few properties are full all the time and problems in collecting rent can be common. Because PGI does not represent the amount collected, it is not an amount most owners or buyers calculate. If an appraiser asks an owner, "What is your potential gross income?" the owner will probably give a number that is better described as *effective gross income* (EGI), if an answer is given at all. This figure is usually annual.

Effective Gross Income

Effective gross income (EGI) is the potential gross income less estimated vacancy and collection losses. EGI is best described as the actual amount of money a property owner would expect to collect before paying expenses. If an appraiser calls an owner and asks for the gross income of the property, the EGI is the amount the owner will quote.

Net Operating Income

Net operating income (I_O or NOI) is the effective gross income less *operating expenses* and sometimes less *capital expenses and reserves for replacement*, or the amount of money the real estate owners would expect to put in their pockets after paying expenses but before paying the mortgage payment and income taxes. Net operating income (I_O) is the estimated amount that is divided by the capitalization rate to produce a value estimate in "IRV" ratio analysis.

Equity Income

The term *equity income* (at one time known as the *equity dividend*) describes the cash flow after the debt service has been satisfied. This cash flow is significant because it shows the amount and ratio of the return on investment for the primary investor. To calculate the equity dividend ratio, the income to the equity (after debt service) is divided by the amount of money invested by the equity holder (the down payment):

$$R_E = \frac{I_E}{V_E}$$

In some markets, the equity income is also called the *equity cash flow rate* or the *cash-on-cash return rate*.

Reversion

The term *reversion* refers to the return of the investment at the end of the holding period. For any investment, the return that investment will yield must be considered. If an investor pays $100,000 for a property that returns $10,000 per year for 10 years but does not have a reversion, that investment has a yield of 0% to the investor. However, if an investor pays $100,000 for an investment and receives $10,000 per year for 10 years and a return of $100,000 at the end of the investment period (i.e., reversion), the yield is 10%. If an investment does not have reversion, the periodic cash flows must be larger to compensate.

Operating Expenses

Only expenses that are necessary to maintain the property are considered appropriate to deduct from the gross income estimates. In the application of the income capitalization approach, appraisers usually ask for the property's income and expense history for three to five years to support the projection of future expenses. When reviewing historical income and expenses, some owners include expenses that would not be needed for the subject property maintenance but are nevertheless still paid for income tax purposes, such as extra vehicles, employees, lawn care, fees, or licenses. The only expenses that an appraiser should include in their reconstructed operating estimate are those expenses needed to perpetuate the income stream, including all maintenance, replacements, management expenses, and sometimes capital replacements like roof coverings, furnaces, parking lot resurfacing, and similar items.

Note that debt service is not included as an operating expense. Debt service is hard to consider in this analysis because some investors pay higher or lower interest rates, some pay more money down than others, and some even pay cash. If an expense analysis including debt service is needed, the analysis can be based on standard interest rates with a minimal down payment, which allows appraisers to replicate the steps necessary for the typical buyer to determine if the investment is feasible at a particular price. The property yield after debt service depends on the level of debt. The use of debt to increase the owner's yield is called *leverage.*

Fixed Expenses

Fixed expenses typically do not vary with occupancy. The most common fixed expenses are real estate taxes and property insurance. These expenses are ongoing regardless of the occupancy level. Some appraisers argue that other expenses like HVAC operating costs are fixed because it is not possible to heat and cool only part of a multitenant building. Keep in mind that expenses need to be accurately estimated regardless of the label placed on them.

Variable Expenses

As the term implies, *variable expenses* fluctuate with occupancy levels and other factors. Examples include utilities, janitorial service, repairs and maintenance, and property management. These costs may make a large difference in the value of an income-producing property. Some property owners insist that the appraiser remove the management expense for an owner-occupied property, but this would be incorrect because it

suggests that the owner's time is worthless. Some management expense is needed for all real estate investments. Even though management expenses can be very small in some cases, they still need to be recognized.

Replacement Allowance

If only one year's income and expenses are being analyzed, replacement allowances compensate for large expenditures in the future. Replacement allowances are typically calculated as the annual charge for replacing an item at the end of its life. For example, a roof covering that needs to be replaced every 20 years would have a replacement allowance of 1/20 of the cost of the roof in an annual expense analysis. Some appraisers insist that a current cost estimate of a replacement item should be forecast as of the date of replacement and then discounted at a savings account rate to accumulate the money for that future expense.

Many appraisers and many buyers just use the contemporary estimate and divide it by the total economic life, not the remaining economic life. If the item is near the end of its economic life, the reserve amount should still be based on total economic life. However, another adjustment should be made to compensate for the short remaining life of the current item, or a lump-sum adjustment should be made to the value conclusion. If you use the remaining economic life, you are overcharging for this item. For example, you could be deducting an amount that reflects that you replaced the roof shingles every two years rather than every 20 years.

Clearly, the correct procedure for estimating reserves for capital replacements is to follow the same process for the subject as for the comparable sales. In other words, if you are consistent in the extraction and application process, your analysis will be correct. In many cases, appraisers may not include these reserves at all because the comparables used to extract the income rate did not include the reserves.

Rates of Return

The rate of return on a real estate investment competes with the rates of return on other investments, not just other real estate. Real estate investments compete for capital with stocks, bonds, and other investments. Real estate is only one of many options available to investors. If the returns on real estate fall in comparison to mortgages (as an investment), stocks, bonds, or other business opportunities of similar risk, the money will flow

---

operating expenses
The amount of money the property owner would have to pay annually to operate the property; the cost of maintaining the income stream. These are not expenses for improvements or betterments but rather the cost of maintaining the "status quo."

Capital Expense and Replacement Allowance

Capital expenses are the amount required to satisfy the interest on and amortization of an investment, or the expenses a property owner occasionally incurs that are required to upgrade the property or make capital replacements. Examples include replacing roof coverings every few years, repaving a parking lot, or replacing HVAC units. Capital expenses cost the owner a lot of money, but owners and brokers seldom include them in their operating statements.

A *replacement allowance* provides for the periodic replacement of building components that wear out more rapidly than the building itself and must be replaced during the building's economic life; replacement allowances are also referred to as *reserves for replacement*. Keep in mind that if the owner of the subject property does not include a replacement allowance in the reported expense amounts, then any capitalization rates extracted from sales of comparable properties have to be adjusted to reflect similar expenses as the subject property. In other words, the treatment of replacement allowances must be consistent.

---

to the investment with the best return. Real estate must satisfy the requirements of the investor or lose the cash to other investments. If real estate cannot satisfy those requirements, the prices will fall until the price relative to the return is more favorable and new investors are attracted.

Return on and Return of Capital

To calculate an investment's rate of return, all of the invested income must be returned in one way or another. Sometimes the return *of* the investment is accomplished with each payment (like the principal returned through mortgage payments), and at other times it is accomplished by repayment of the capital amount in a lump sum at the time of resale (like the proceeds of the sale of a retail center in a good location at the end of a holding period). Return *on* the investment is like the interest on a mortgage. Real estate investments can be structured in many different ways, so it is important to understand this concept. Investors need to get the investment back along with a fair return on the investment while their money is extended.

Income Rates

The overall capitalization rate (R_O) is the relationship of one year's net operating income to the lump-sum value or sale price. To calculate R_O, appraisers research the relationships of cash flows to the sale prices of comparable properties and then apply that ratio to the income expectancy of the subject. If a sale property has a net income of $25,000 next year and comparable properties have shown a relationship of income to value near 10%, the value can be estimated by dividing the net income by the capitalization rate. (The calculations are based on the IRV relationships described in Chapter 17 and reviewed later in this chapter.)

If a property sells for 10 times its net income, its income is 10% of the price (i.e., the ratios are reciprocals). The accuracy of this relational model is based on research that uncovers properties with similar upside potential and lease terms, with improvements of similar age, and in areas with similar risk.

The direct calculation of R_O is a very old technique that relies little on technology; a handheld calculator is all that is needed. It is used often but sometimes applied erroneously. Appraisers may fail to recognize the differences in upside potential between the subject and the comparables and therefore misapply the technique. Direct capitalization does not allow appraisers to isolate the income attributable to the investment from the income that may be used to repay the diminishing asset value, such as principal and interest payments in a mortgage. Return *on* and return *of* the investment are reflected in this ratio but are not identifiable; that is, the calculations do not show them individually as in a mortgage amortization schedule.

The net income multiplier is the reciprocal of the capitalization rate. The multiplier is not widely used even though it reflects the same ratio of income to value. In other words, the capitalization rate and net income multiplier are the same fraction with the numerator and denominator reversed. In the stock market, this ratio is known as the *price-earnings* (PE) *ratio*.

Exhibit 21.4 illustrates how some appraisers extract and apply the direct capitalization technique. Appraisers estimate and list the income and expenses associated with the subject and some recent sales on the worksheet. Remember that the comparables should reflect similar upside potential as the subject, or the analysis will be misleading. Based on the extraction of the obvious 9% capitalization rate (R_O), the value of the subject is

$$\$273,925/0.09 = \$3,043,611$$

rounded to $3,050,000

Exhibit 21.4 **Capitalization Rate Extraction Worksheet**

	Subject	Sale 1	Sale 2	Sale 3
Reported sale price		$1,985,000	$1,458,000	$3,258,000
PGI for next year	$510,000	$369,000	$253,680	$601,000
Vacancy and collection loss	− 25,500	− 25,830	− 15,221	− 48,080
EGI for next year	$484,500	$343,170	$238,459	$552,920
Operating expense for next year				
Taxes	$56,000	$44,258	$26,000	$72,000
Insurance	10,600	9,600	4,500	14,500
Management (5%)	24,225	17,159	11,923	27,646
Maintenance—building	22,050	16,055	10,700	26,500
Maintenance—grounds	11,000	8,000	4,900	13,800
Utilities	67,000	55,000	34,000	76,800
Reserve fund—roof covering	5,000	4,200	2,600	4,200
Reserve fund—parking lot	4,500	3,900	2,500	7,500
Reserve fund—HVAC	3,200	2,500	2,900	6,200
Reserve fund—elevator	1,500	1,200	1,800	3,600
Tenant improvements	5,500	4,400	3,500	12,600
Total expenses	$210,575	$166,272	$105,323	$265,346
Net operating income	$273,925	$176,898	$133,136	$287,574
Extracted capitalization rates		8.9%	9.1%	8.8%

Discount Rates

Discount rates, yield rates, interest rates, and internal rates of return all belong to the same general category. The overall capitalization rate is the simple ratio of income to sale price (or value), but the yield rate or discount rate is the rate of return on the investment assuming that the investors get all their money back at the end of the holding period. In other words, the yield rate that an investment achieves is a function of the amount invested and the amount returned each year, which has to include a return of the amount invested.

A discount rate is used to convert several future cash flows to a lump-sum value today. If a $100 investment with an interest rate of 10% will grow to $259.37 in 10 years, then the $259.37 that a property yields 10 years from now is only worth $100 today. In a discounted cash flow analysis, several years' income estimates are discounted to a present value using a financial discounting calculation.

Exhibit 21.5 illustrates a cash flow projection for a six-unit retail center. The rental projections show flat lease rates until the rollover date, which is when the rates change. All of the expenses have been totaled on one line. This example is a simplified version of how a property can be valued using a discount rate applied to the net income estimates for several years in the future. The more complex the property, the more likely the discount rate will be the valuation technique of choice.

With end-of-year accounting, the investor has to wait 12 months to receive the net income from the first year. Rent may be paid monthly, but in most markets the analysis is still done on an annual basis. At a 9% discount rate, the first year's income of $195,295, which is received 12 months from now, is only worth $179,164 today. The second year's income of $193,837 is only worth $163,153 today because it would be received 24 months from now. Note that the last year's income (Year 5) includes a relatively large cash flow of $2,158,366, which is the resale value of the property. After discounting the last year's cash flow for the time value of money, the cash flow of $2,375,558 was discounted to $1,543,875.

After discounting all of the future cash flows to present worth, the final step is summing up the present values to calculate the value of the subject property today. The property value shown by this analysis is $2,202,891, which would be rounded to $2.2 million.

Yield rates are rates of return. In a real estate investment, the yield rate is the ratio of the net in-

Exhibit 21.5   Cash Flow Projection

	Year 1	Year 2	Year 3	Year 4	Year 5	
Tenant 1	$72,000	$72,000	$72,000	$84,000	$84,000	
Tenant 2	66,144	66,144	66,144	66,144	66,144	
Tenant 3	51,600	53,000	60,000	60,000	60,000	
Tenant 4	14,400	18,000	19,200	19,200	19,200	
Tenant 5	27,780	27,780	27,780	27,780	27,780	
Tenant 6	28,800	24,000	33,600	33,600	33,600	
Potential gross income	$260,724	$260,924	$278,724	$290,724	$290,724	
Vacancy and collection (4%)	− 10,429	− 10,437	− 11,149	− 11,629	− 11,629	
Effective gross income	$250,295	$250,487	$267,575	$279,095	$279,095	
All expenses	− 55,000	− 56,650	− 58,350	− 60,100	− 61,903	
Net operating income	$195,295	$193,837	$209,225	$218,995	$217,192	
Reversion (10%)	Last year's income divided by the capitalization rate				$2,158,366	
Cash flow	$195,295	$193,837	$209,225	$218,995	$2,375,558	
Discounted at 9%	× 91.74%	× 84.17%	× 77.22%	× 70.84%	× 64.99%	**Total**
Present values	$179,164	$163,153	$161,564	$155,136	$1,543,875	$2,202,892

come to the purchase price, assuming that the investment returns all of the initial amount invested and no more. For example, if an investor pays $1 million for a property and the annual income for 10 years is $100,000 but the investor does not get any additional cash flow at the end of the holding period (i.e., the resale value is $0), the yield on this investment is 0%. However, if the property owner can sell the same asset for $1 million at the end of the holding period, the yield is 10%.

A yield rate can also be called an *internal rate of return (IRR)*. The yield rate is the annualized yield rate or rate of return on capital that is generated or capable of being generated within an investment or portfolio over a period of ownership. The *IRR* is the discount rate that makes the net present value of the investment equal to zero. The *IRR* discounts all returns from the investment, including returns from its reversion, to equal the original capital outlay.

The *overall yield* rate (or *property yield rate*) is the rate of return on the total capital invested, including debt and equity. The overall yield rate takes into consideration changes in net income over the investment period and net reversion at the end of the holding period. It is applied to cash flow before debt service. For an investor, the overall yield rate is the rate of return required to attract money to the deal. If other competing property's rates are high and the yield on the subject property is low, the price will have to fall until it attracts buyers and the yield increases because the price is lower.

The equity yield rate functions in the same way as other yield rates. It measures the relationship between the investment income after the debt has been satisfied and the amount invested in the deal, assuming the investors get their money back at the end. In other words, the equity yield rate is the ratio of equity income and the initial equity cash outlay, which assumes a level income as well as a return of the equity input and no more. This rate can be calculated on most handheld financial calculators for both level and irregular equity cash flows. The reversion is usually the projected sale price of the real estate less the selling costs and the payoff amount of the mortgage loan.

Estimating Rates
Selecting the correct rate can be difficult. The process is related to other similar investment analyses, and the rate cannot be fully estimated without looking at the stock and bond market, the return on mutual funds, and other investments that would be equally attractive to an investor.

Risk
Risk is often the difference between a high yield or capitalization rate and a low yield or capitalization rate. Properties with a higher possibility of losing the income or the principal invested are generally required to have a higher yield or capitalization rate to attract an investor. The higher

the yield or capitalization rate, the lower the value or sale price. Risky investments often appeal to only a very small group of investors. Property type can have a significant effect on risk levels. For example, subdivisions are much riskier investments than land leases with buildings on them, and properties with long-term leases and Grade A tenants are much less risky than properties under month-to-month leases with start-up companies. There is also risk associated with location. A property in a very desirable neighborhood has much less risk of losing the invested capital than a property in a blighted area.

> Risk may mean the difference between a property being marketable or not. A high-risk property may only appeal to the "speculators" of the real estate industry, which means a high return is required to satisfy their investment requirements.

Inflation and Value
Inflation is a loss in the buying power of currency. For example, goods or services that cost $100 today will cost $103 next year if the annual inflation rate is 3%. Deflation occurs when the currency buys more than it did before. It is common for the cost of building real estate improvements to go up every year because of inflation in building costs. Most buildings lose value due to wear and tear each year, so the increase in value of real estate is due to an inflation rate higher than the depreciation rate. For example, if the rate of inflation in building costs is 3% per year but the loss in value due to wear and tear on the improvements is only 2% per year, the increase in building value should be about 1% per year. This does not mean that all properties appreciate at a rate of 1%, only that the building values are limited in this way. Land values could also increase at a much higher or lower rate than the building costs.

Putting money in an investment today in current dollars and retrieving that money some time in the future at future inflated dollars (which are worth less) is a factor in all investments. Any long-term asset will be affected by inflation, and the longer the life of the asset, the more the inflation rate will cause appreciation in the overall value. Real estate investors may be willing to accept lower yields in times of high inflation because they can leverage their positions (using borrowed money) and enjoy the increase in value on both the equity and mortgage portions of the investment.

Procedure
The income capitalization approach to value is a method of converting periodic and reversionary income streams into a current lump-sum capital amount. Of course, the timing of the cash flows makes a big difference. Cash in hand today is worth a lot more than the same amount in the future because you could reinvest the money you get today and earn more on that investment. The time value of money is an important factor in this type of property valuation.

> How much would an investor pay today for the right to receive $X in income in the future?

There are two basic methods of converting future cash flows into a value indication today—*direct capitalization* of a single year's income and *yield capitalization* of multiple years' cash flows (periodic and reversionary).

Direct Capitalization
Direct capitalization is a simple method of converting a single year's *periodic* income into a lump-sum capital amount by establishing a ratio of income to value. The math is simple but appraisers must ensure that the comparable sales used to extract the capitalization rate have the same prospective increase in value over time. The pattern of income rates for many properties in the market is then used to estimate an income rate (i.e., a capitalization rate) for the subject property. You find recent sales of similar properties that were leased or will be leased and compare the sale price with the expected income from the property. This is done by dividing the net operating income (I_O) by the capitalization rate (the ratio of income to value, R_O). This is an easy technique to apply, but it is often misused because brokers and appraisers do not recognize that two properties can have the same income amounts but much different capitalization rates because one is in a much riskier location and has less potential for upside appreciation.

Yield Capitalization
Yield capitalization is a more comprehensive approach to valuing real estate than the direct capitalization of a single year's income. New technology has enabled appraisers to calculate the present value of any future cash flows using a discounting process. The discounting process is a

method of estimating the present value of future cash flows. This technique for capitalizing an income stream provides much more flexibility and allows for analysis no matter how irregular the cash flows are. It works even if the cash flows are negative for a few years.

Direct Capitalization, Yield Capitalization, and Discounting

Direct capitalization, yield capitalization, and discounting each have benefits and liabilities in different situations. The direct capitalization of a single year's income is usually fine for simple applications, but yield capitalization is often a better technique for more complicated problems. Either method can have errors, but in both cases appraisers are responsible for using these techniques in conjunction with the other approaches to value. Many appraisers use both techniques to ensure they are doing and explaining what buyers and brokers may or may not be doing in the market.

> The ratio of a single year's income to the property's sale price is the most commonly used technique in less sophisticated markets but is often avoided in complicated valuation problems.

IRV Review

The IRV formula was devised as a learning technique. If the variable you want to solve for is covered up (use your finger) on the IRV graphic, the relationship of the remaining elements shows the correct process to use. For example, to find the capitalization rate (R), put your finger over the R in the graphic. You can now see that the income is divided by the sale price (or value) to solve for the capitalization rate ($R = I/V$). Similarly, to solve for the income, the value can be multiplied by the rate. To find the value, the income can be divided by the rate.

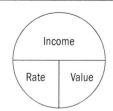

$$Income = Rate \times Value$$
$$Rate = Income / Value$$
$$Value = Income / Rate$$

This capitalization process can also be applied by multiplying the net operating income by the reciprocal ($1/x$) of the capitalization rate, which is called the *net income multiplier*. In other words, instead of dividing the net operating income by 0.10, you can multiply it by 10 to get the same answer.

---

1. The principle of _____ is the basis of the income capitalization approach.

   a) Change

   b) Substitution

   c) Modification

   d) Anticipation

2. Value can be estimated in the income capitalization approach by

   a) Dividing the overall capitalization rate by the net operating income

   b) Multiplying the net operating income by the overall capitalization rate

   c) Dividing the net operating income by the overall capitalization rate

   d) Dividing the base by the multiplier

3. Suppose a lease contract called for a rent of $10 per square foot. However, similar space in the market rented for $15 per square foot. The amount specified in the lease is known as the _____ rent.

   a) Contract

   b) Market

   c) Economic

   d) Overage

4. In a gross lease, who pays the utility costs?

   a) The landlord

   b) The tenant

   c) A subtenant, if there is one

   d) Either the tenant or the landlord

5. *Market rent* is

   a) The amount of rental income a property would command in the open market

   b) The amount of rental income stipulated in the lease

   c) The amount of rental income that reflects the contract rent adjusted for concessions

   d) The amount of rental income that is in excess of the market rate

6. A property has a net income of $36,000 per year. The operating expense ratio is 36%. The vacancy and collection loss is estimated to be 4%. What is the effective gross income?

   a) $12,960

   b) $13,478

   c) $48,960

   d) $56,250

7. A local investor recently purchased a small strip center for $1,235,000. She obtained a 75% mortgage at 7% with a 25-year amortization. The payments are $6,546.54 per month. The buyer expected the first year's net operating income to be $96,000. What is the equity dividend rate (R_E)?

   a) 0.0565

   b) 0.0636

   c) 0.0777

   d) 0.0848

8. A tenant has a lease that states the base rent is $5,000 per month plus 3% of the sales above $50,000 in gross sales per month. The tenant's sales last year were $850,000. How much rent was paid last year?

   a) $25,500

   b) $60,000

   c) $67,500

   d) $75,000

9. In a soft market, a landlord accepted a new tenant with a 60-month lease at $5,000 per month but gave the new tenant six months of free rent. Using the average rent method, what is the effective monthly rent?

   a) $3,000

   b) $4,545

   c) $5,000

   d) $5,555

10. A multitenant building has four tenants described as follows:

    · Suite 1 has 5,000 square feet and is under lease for five more years at $12 per square foot per year.

    · Suite 2 has 5,000 square feet and is vacant. The market for this space is $15 per square foot per year.

    · Suite 3 has 5,000 square feet and is under lease for two more years at $13 per square foot per year.

    · Suite 4 has 5,000 square feet and is on a month-to-month tenancy at $15 per square foot per year.

    Expenses for this building are $5 per square foot per year. Vacancy and collection loss is estimated at 5% of *PGI*. All the leased spaces are the same.

    What is the net operating income? (Round your answer to the nearest $10,000.)

    a) $150,000

    b) $160,000

    c) $170,000

    d) $180,000

Note: Unless otherwise noted, italicized references indicate the pages in *The Appraisal of Real Estate*, 14th edition, that readers should consult for additional discussion of these topics.

Interests to Be Valued Worksheet

1. The value of the leased fee interest is $40,000/0.10 = $400,000.

2. The value of the leasehold interest is $1,800,000 because the tenant paid a market rate for the land lease and invested that amount in the property. This assumes the tenant can lease the land and building to subtenants at a rate equal to the land lease plus the cost of the improvements, which may or may not be true. It is assumed here but should not be assumed in an appraisal.

3. The building will fall into disrepair because the tenant knows the leasehold interest runs out at the end of the lease. Buildings often have to be razed at the end of the lease because of long-term deferred maintenance.

4. The reversion 75 years later discounted at 10% equals only 0.079% (0.00079), which is less than one-tenth of one percent of the total value. Therefore, it doesn't matter whether the value of the fee simple interest at the end of the lease is $1,000 or $1 million. The difference between the value today if the resale value in 75 years is $1 million ($1,000,000 × 0.00079 = $790) and the value today if the resale value is $1,000 ($1,000 × 0.00079 = $0.79) is only $789 ($790 − $0.79).

    Compound growth is based on the formula

    $$\$X \times (1 + i)^n$$

    where i is the interest rate. This means if the interest rate is 5%, the formula would be

    $$\$X \times 1.05^n$$

    For example, $1,000 that is deposited in the bank at a compound interest rate of 5% for 25 years would be $1,000 × 1.05^{25}, or $3,386.35. Conversely, $1,000 that is not payable for 25 years at 5% would be $X × 1/1.05^{25}, or $1,000 × 0.2953028. In others words, $1,000 payable in 25 years at a 5% compound interest rate is only worth $295.30 payable today, which is the same principle applied in this exercise. A dollar in the distant future is worth a lot less than a dollar today.

---

1. **d) Anticipation**
   Page 440

2. **c) Dividing the net operating income by the overall capitalization rate**
   Pages 459-460

3. **a) Contract**
   Page 448

4. **a) The landlord**
   Page 445

5. **a) The amount of rental income a property would command in the open market**
   Page 447

6. **d) $56,250**
   Page 451

   Keep in mind that the complement of the operating expense ratio is the net income ratio. In this case, 100% − 36% = 64%. This means that the net income is 64% of the effective gross income:

   $$EGI \times 0.64 = \$36,000$$
   $$\$36,000 / 0.64 = \$56,250$$

7. **a) 0.0565**
   Page 451

   $$V_M = 1,235,000 \times 0.75 = 926,250$$
   $$V_E = 1,235,000 - 926,250 = 308,750$$
   $$I_M = 6,546.54 \times 12 = 78,558$$
   $$I_E = 96,000 - 78,558 = 17,442$$
   $$R_E = 17,442/308,750 = 0.0565$$

8. **c) $67,500**

$$850,000 - 600,000 = 250,000$$
$$250,000 \times 0.03 = 7,500$$
$$7,500 + 60,000 = 67,500$$

9. **b) $4,545**

Pages 448-449

$$(60 \times 5,000)/66 = \$4,545$$

10. **b) $160,000**

Page 451

Tenant	*PGI*
1	$60,000
2	$75,000
3	$65,000
4	+ $75,000
PGI	$275,000
Vacancy and collection loss	− $13,750
EGI	$261,250
Expenses	− $100,000
NOI	$161,250

22

Income and Expense Analysis

Investors are primarily concerned with net income rather than gross income, so accurately estimating income and expenses is an important appraisal task. Most investors, brokers, and appraisers focus on the property's economic history, but this should only be used as a guide for projections of the future.

When converting periodic income (monthly or annual payments to the owner) into a lump-sum value estimate, appraisers can estimate value from the following:

1. Potential gross income using a potential gross income multiplier
2. Effective gross income using an effective gross income multiplier
3. Net operating income using a capitalization rate
4. Equity income using an equity capitalization rate and adding back the value of the mortgage
5. Analysis of income estimates for several years using a discounted cash flow model

Estimating and Adjusting Market Rent

Market rent is very similar to market value. Instead of selling the property, though, think of what happens when an owner puts a "for rent" sign in front of the property. Buyers use a variety of techniques to estimate how much a property will rent for, so appraisers must do the same. Many types of leases are possible, and appraisers must be able to analyze these leases in the same manner investors do.

As formally defined, *market rent* is

The most probable rent that a property should bring in a competitive and open market reflecting all conditions and restrictions of the lease agreement, including permitted uses, use restrictions, expense obligations, term, concessions, renewal and purchase options, and tenant improvements (TIs).

In other words, market rent is the amount of money an owner would expect to receive if the property were put up for lease with a knowledgeable owner or agent and an informed tenant under no duress to rent by either party.

Income and Expense Data

In estimating income and expenses, appraisers should have some support for their opinions. Like most appraisal issues, support can come from more than one source. If the assignment involves a leased fee interest, the first place you should look for data to support an estimate of market rent is to the leases that are in place on the property. The following sections discuss the information to consider in income and expense analysis.

Lease Data

Rent

As explained in the previous chapter, the term *rent* commonly refers to the amount of money a tenant pays the landlord for the right to use a specific property for a specific time period. On its

KEY TERMS	
above-the-line expense	market rent
below-the-line expense	net income ratio (*NIR*)
continued occupancy clause	operating expense ratio (*OER*)
escalation clause	operating expenses
escape clause	replacement allowance
exclusive use clause	tenant improvement allowance
expense cap	tenant improvements (TIs)
expense stop	vacancy and collection loss
fixed expenses	variable expenses

own, rent is often used to describe a monthly payment, but some real estate professionals also use the term for annual amounts.

Rent Concessions

The term *rent concession* refers to an offsetting factor used to entice a tenant to rent a property when the other lease terms are inadequate. Typical rent concessions include early occupancy, finish upgrades, free rent for the first or last month of the lease, or some sort of upgrade or rebate to a CEO, managing partner, or other high official in the company.

Division of Expenses between the Lessor and Lessee

For tenants and landlords, the answer to the question "Who pays what?" is as important as the rental. A tenant who pays the taxes and maintenance is in an altogether different position than the tenant of a landlord who pays those expenses. An appraiser cannot proceed with the expense analysis without knowing exactly who pays what.

Renewal Options

A tenant's option to renew a lease at a specified rent can be devastating to a property's value. A renewal option allows the tenant to decide whether to stay or go. The lessor may not have the opportunity to replace a tenant who has a below-market rate if that tenant exercises a renewal option. If the rent is lower than the market rate, a tenant will probably stay, but if the rent is too high, the tenant will leave or renegotiate. A tenant might defy logic and renew a lease at a higher-than-market rate because of the high cost of moving a business, and tenants may move despite a favorable lease rate if the space no longer fits their needs. Sometimes tenants move just because they want to move. Sometimes tenants move because they have problems with a landlord. Sometimes tenants move because of unknown and unrelated factors. For example, a tenant in an office building moved the subsidiary of a larger company because he did not

like having his boss in the same building, which allowed her to drop in on the manager of the subsidiary. A landlord cannot anticipate and plan for the effect of this sort of reasoning.

Expense Stop and Expense Cap Clauses

Many leases stipulate that the landlord pays the expenses up to a predetermined point. If expenses exceed this point, the tenant pays the difference. This allows landlords to offer long-term leases without the fear that increases in taxes, insurance, and other expenses will erode their profit margins. The reverse situation can also be stipulated in a lease, so that the landlord pays expenses above a certain point.

An *expense stop* clause protects the landlord while an *expense cap* clause is used to protect the tenant. Expense stops are common in office leases. In industrial and retail leases, tenants generally pay most of the expenses anyway, so an expense stop is less applicable.

Escalation Clauses and Expense Recovery Clauses

An escalation clause allows the landlord to increase the rental rate based on some predetermined criteria. Escalation clauses are often based on the Consumer Price Index (CPI), but sometimes a lease stipulates a real estate index from the National Association of Realtors or some other trade association.

Expense recovery clauses are common in retail leases. The tenant is often responsible for reimbursing the landlord for all property expenses. Shopping center owners often bill tenants periodically, usually monthly, for their share of all the operating expenses incurred, which can amount to a lot of money. An expense recovery clause makes a retail lease more similar to a net industrial lease, meaning that the landlord has few expenses. Remember that there is no tenant to pay for the pro rata share of expenses on vacant space, so that is an expense to the ownership.

Purchase Options

A "right of first refusal on sale" or an "option to purchase" clause may be included in a lease. The right of first refusal on sale is usually the tenant's right to match any proposed purchase price offered for the leased property. This ensures that the tenant has a little control over who the landlord is in case of sale. A purchase option like this does not usually significantly affect income analysis, and appraisal because a buyer can only match a proposed price rather than establish the price.

Options to renew do not indicate if the option rental price is at the market rate, but they do indicate if the option rental rate is less than or close to market rental value. If a tenant renews at an option rate, it is logical that the tenant would not have done so if better options were available. When an appraiser is developing an opinion of market rent, it would not be a good idea to use rollover rates (prenegotiated several years before) as indications of market rent. Rollover rates are indications of what the landlord and tenant thought the rates would be in the future, not what the market actually supports at the rollover date.

However, an option to buy at a specific price can be a significant factor in the appraisal. An option to purchase at a specified price is significant in appraisal because it is illogical to value the property as higher than the option price without giving consideration to the option of others to purchase the property at the contractual amount (i.e., $X). These options are not always exercised, but an appraiser cannot ignore them.

For example, an option to buy a property was given at the start of a lease with the price set at $1.5 million, but the value of the property grew unexpectedly to $2 million as a result of external economic factors. In this situation, the tenant is likely to buy the property to protect the interest. In the appraisal analysis, the option to buy the property at $1.5 million requires the appraiser to consider that price as a ceiling of value, unless there are other reasons the tenant would not or could not buy the property at the below-market value price. This is another example of why an appraiser should read every lease that affects the subject property. An appraiser should not just rely on a lease synopsis, rent rolls, or a property manager's income estimate.

Escape, Kick-Out, Cotenancy, and Buyout Clauses

Escape or kick-out clauses (also called *cancellation clauses*) allow tenants to leave before the end of the lease period. If the landlord spent considerable amounts of money in the form of commissions, remodeling, or incentives to bring the tenant in, the cancellation of the lease can have significant penalties. These clauses are put in leases for the landlord's protection when a tenant's future is not certain and an early departure is anticipated. Landlords sometimes put in a cash penalty when a tenant exercises this option. A buyout clause allows the landlord or the tenant to cancel a lease through a payment to the other party set either in the original lease or negotiated at the time of cancellation, which is another reason to read all the leases.

Continued Occupancy Clauses

Continued occupancy clauses are common in retail leases. Most often, smaller tenants stipulate that they will stay in the shopping center only as long as the anchor store remains. For example, a shoe store in a shopping mall may not survive if a big department store leaves the mall, taking the traffic that the larger tenant attracts with it. Tenants ask for these clauses in leases to protect themselves from external factors.

Tenant Improvements

Leased space generally requires some build out to meet the requirements of a new tenant, and the landlord's responsibilities for the tenant improve-

---

Lease Data

Certain information in the lease contract is essential for income and expense analysis.

Date of Lease
A lease might be dated in June even though the tenant moved in January. In a weak market, brokers may choose not to discount the rental rate but instead give tenants several months of free rent. This may lead appraisers to conclude that the rent is higher than it really is, which can explain why one tenant has a much higher lease rate than other tenants are paying for similar space.

Description of the Leased Premises
What the property manager thinks and what is written in the lease could be very different. In some cases, the size of the leased premises shown in the lease could be different from the actual size of the occupied space.

Lease Terms, Rental Rate, and Payment
Lease terms can be as important as rent. A lease with two weeks to run is entirely different than one with 10 years to run.

Tenant-Installed Trade Fixtures
If a tenant installs anything in a leased property, it becomes the property of the landlord unless the item is used in the tenant's trade. Items that are installed by the tenant in a permanent way for use in the tenant's specific business are called *trade fixtures*. Trade fixtures should generally not be included in the appraisal because the items will not transfer with the real estate. A common example of trade fixtures is large medical equipment installed by a medical group in a leased office.

Revaluation Clauses
Revaluation clauses allow the landlord to change the rent based on the value of the asset as established by a third party, usually an appraiser. These clauses usually generate some income for appraisers and assure landlords that they are getting a fair return on their assets.

Signage
Some leases stipulate that signs with the names of larger tenants can be installed on the building's exterior. Signage can generate income for the owners, but it may also be an incentive for a tenant to sign a lease.

ments (TIs) are usually specified in the lease. TIs are a significant issue in nearly all office and retail properties. In some markets, landlords are forced to build out tenant spaces. The expenses paid by the lessor can be a small amount, or the cost of tenant improvements can be high enough to double the lease rate because of the amortization expense. A landlord paying for tenant improvements usually tries to amortize the expenses over the original term of the lease. Therefore, if the tenant leaves when the lease expires, the landlord has recovered all those expenses.

Capital improvements paid by the landlord will normally be reflected in the lease rate, but capital improvements paid by the tenant will not. When a tenant pays to improve a leased property, there is often a large difference in the market rent for the improved space and the contract rent, which is based on the unimproved space.

Noncompete, Dark Store, and Exclusive Use Clauses

A tenant in a retail center may demand that the landlord avoid renting space that center to other companies that compete directly with the current tenant's business. Noncompete clauses are not usually significantly restrictive because the landlords do not want to cause any of the tenants to lose business. The landlord is in fact "in business" with the tenants because the landlord gets paid out of the receipts of the tenants' business.

The tenant mix is important to the performance of shopping centers. Landlords can protect their investment in a shopping center and its tenant mix by including a dark store clause in a lease, requiring the tenant to occupy the store until the end of the lease term (so that the store does not "go dark") and also prohibiting the tenant from opening a competitive store within a certain distance and within a certain length of time after the end of the lease. This is because it is not unusual in retail properties for a tenant to outgrow a space, not have any expansion options, and then move into larger space nearby but not within the subject property. The tenant still pays the rent, but the anchor tenant is now effectively gone.

Developing Reconstructed Operating Statements

To develop a reconstructed operating statement, appraisers usually start from the top of the income and expense list and move down until an estimate of net operating income is calculated.

Potential Gross Income

Estimating Potential Gross Income from the Comparable Leases

A straightforward way of estimating the market rental rate of a fee simple interest in a property or a rollover rate for a leased fee interest is to research and compare recently signed leases of properties that compete with the subject. Rental rate adjustments may have to be made to compensate for one or more items of dissimilarity. These adjustments are sometimes made in the analysis of the recent leases on the subject property. All real estate investors base purchase decisions on the present worth of future benefits, so estimates of the subject's rental income should reflect the market rate for the year immediately after the effective date. This means if the value estimate is as of today, the income estimate should be for the next 12 months.

A comparable property with a 10-year lease signed on January 1, 2008, is a good comparable for an appraisal with an effective date in 2008 and possibly in 2009, but it is not a good comparable for an appraisal dated 2014 even though the lease is still running. The effective date of the lease is the date of "the meeting of the minds," not 10 years later. To further support this, think about how well the terms of a 99-year land lease reflect the current market.

Exhibit 22.1 provides an example of a lease comparison grid used to estimate the market rental rate based on comparable leases. Remember that only a closed lease agreement can indicate what the subject will bring on the market. This doesn't mean that asking rents (i.e., listings) cannot be used as comparables, just that they only show conclusively how much the subject will not bring. It is possible to ask for a lot but accept a little. If the market for leased space is oversupplied, the asking prices will eventually be lowered to compensate or large concessions will be given. If the market is undersupplied, the properties will lease for the full list price in a short time.

Keep in mind that in Exhibit 22.1 rent is analyzed on the basis of price per square foot of building area. An adjustment for the size of the building is already accounted for by the unit of comparison.

Estimating Potential Gross Income from the Current Subject Property Leases

Another way to estimate the market lease rate of a fee simple interest in a property or the potential gross income or rollover rate of a leased fee

Exhibit 22.1   Lease Comparison Grid

	Subject	Comparable 1	Comparable 2	Comparable 3	Comparable 4
Annual rent		$145,000	$155,000	$75,866	$52,500
Rate per sq. ft.		$9.67	$7.75	$10.12	$9.55
Expenses included	net lease	net lease	net lease	net lease	taxes and insurance
Conditions of sale	arm's-length	arm's-length	arm's-length	arm's-length	arm's-length
Date of lease	now	13 months ago	20 months ago	6 months ago	20 months ago
Lot size (acres)	5.0	3.0	7.0	3.0	3.0
Access/visibility	adequate/interior	superior	equal	equal	equal
Rail siding	no	yes	no	yes	yes
Design	1-story/detached	1-story/detached	1-story/detached	1-story/detached	2-story/detached
Construction quality	masonry/avg.	masonry	masonry	steel	masonry
Improvement age	31	12	22	15	25
Improvement condition	fair	superior	superior	superior	superior
Total AGLA	14,628	15,000	20,000	7,500	5,500
Finished %	6%	5%	5%	10%	20%
Basement area	0	0	0	0	0
Wall height	16-ft. ceilings	18-ft. ceilings	20-ft. ceilings	20-ft. ceilings	20-ft. ceilings

interest is to analyze recently signed leases for the subject property. These rental rates usually require little or no adjustment, and this analysis is required in the appraisal of leased fee interests. If the property being appraised is subject to a lease, the market value of the property is limited by its income rate. In almost all cases, the buyer of an income-producing property inherits the leases in place on the property prior to purchase. Therefore, an income estimate for a leased fee interest must be on par with the income stipulated in the existing leases. As leases roll over, the market rate can be applied. Before then, rates are limited by the terms of the leases in place. Some leases stipulate steps up, steps down, or escalation clauses, so appraisers must read each and every lease for special details to accurately estimate the future income potential.

As an example, consider the following leases in place for a multitenant office building:

Date	Tenant	Size (Sq. Ft.)	Location	Rate per Sq. Ft.
Current	Jones Financial	3,500	Third floor	$24.00
6 months ago	Combs Cable Co.	7,000	Second floor	$23.50
9 months ago	General Electric Inc.	3,500	First floor	$24.50
9 months ago	Zema Marketing Group	3,500	First floor	$23.50
18 months ago	Lassiter Limb Co.	3,500	Third floor	$23.00

The fourth floor of this building has 7,000 square feet of vacant space. To determine how much the space would rent for, think about the premium a first-floor tenant pays and the possible premium the top-floor tenant would pay. Also, think about a size adjustment because smaller spaces usually rent for more per square foot than larger ones.

The first floor appears to be leasing for $23.50 to $24.50 per square foot. This rent difference on the floor could be the result of different tenant improvements or longer or shorter leases. Perhaps one tenant could be a renewal tenant and the other a new tenant. The second-floor tenant has a much larger area, which would normally bring a lower rate, but it appears that the second-floor tenant paid a similar amount ($23.50 per square foot) as the first-floor tenants. This could be due to tenant improvements or longer lease terms. The top floor should have a higher rate than the other floors, but it could also rent for less because the larger size keeps the unit price lower. All things considered, it would appear a rate of $24.00 to $24.50 per square foot is reasonable depending on the TIs, terms, and other expenses associated with the lease.

Estimating Potential Gross Income from the Subject Property History

For some property types, a review of historical (non-current) leases for the subject property can support estimates of the potential gross income. This usually works best for properties with short-term leases like apartments. Office or retail property leases that are not current are usually too old to mean anything in the current market, but an "old" apartment lease could be only 13 months past the inception date. Keep in mind that the date of the "meeting of the minds" of the lessor and lessee is relevant in the estimation of market rent.

Other sources of income should also be considered at this point. If an income stream is attributable to the real estate, it will typically be included in the calculation of *PGI*. Examples include billboard signs, income from laundry or vending operations (in which a commission is usually paid), parking income, and the like.

Vacancy and Collection Loss

After an appraiser estimates the potential gross income of the subject property, the amount of money that will be lost due to vacancy and problems collecting rent from tenants must be estimated. This amount can be small, as is the case with a property in a high-demand area with a waiting list, or very large for a property in a depressed market with few current tenants. It is probably even correct to estimate a small vacancy and collection deduction for properties under long-term leases to compensate for the extended vacancy when the long-term lease ends. Long-term land leases with many years remaining may not require a deduction, but most others do.

Estimating Vacancy and Collection Loss from Comparable Properties
Researching and comparing the historical amounts of vacancy and collection loss reported by competing property owners is an excellent way to substantiate an estimate for the subject. To get a good vacancy and collection loss estimate for the subject property, be sure to use comparable properties with equal occupancy rates, supply and demand factors, and, if applicable, the same lease conditions in place. Estimating vacancy and collection rates is not typically difficult, and the conclusions can be supported with a simple discussion of local and regional economic factors.

Estimating Vacancy and Collection Loss from History
For improved properties that have been stabilized (i.e., properties that are not in the lease-up phase or in a state of falling occupancy), estimating the vacancy and collection loss is only a matter of reviewing the subject's historical losses in the last three years and comparing those amounts to the potential gross income estimate over the same time period. Sometimes this estimate can be made simply by obtaining and reviewing the average occupancy reports. Remember that this estimate looks forward to future vacancy and collection loss, so the historical vacancy and collection loss data may not be definitive evidence.

Appraisers will never find vacancy and collection loss on the owner's operating statement because it is solely a paper deduction from the potential gross income. Owners never deal with potential gross income because they do not ever see that amount. Owners only see the effective gross income, which is the amount of money that they actually receive on a gross basis.

Effective Gross Income

Effective gross income is calculated as the potential gross income minus the vacancy and collection loss allowance. This is the amount the landlord would expect to deposit in his or her account.

Operating Expenses

Next on the subject's reconstructed operating statement are the estimated operating expenses. These payments are required to keep the subject property in an "earning" condition. If the expenses are too low, the property condition might fall and the income would suffer because of poor maintenance. If the expenses are in line with other properties but much of the money is wasted, the property condition could also suffer. Sometimes operating expenses are very high due to inefficiencies. On-site or off-site management can make a big difference because off-site managers tend to be unaware of problems at an early stage when they are correctable at a much lower cost. Some properties have high expenses because the structure of the leases encourages ownership to pass the higher expenses on to the tenants instead of spending money on capital items that may lower expenses. Sometimes a temporary "band-aid" cure is in the owner's best interest, but it usually leads to deferred maintenance, which may snowball into a "pay now or pay later" philosophy.

Estimating Leasing Commissions

In some markets, leasing commissions are an upfront payment based on the entire amount of the lease. Leasing commission rates can be broken down into original and renewal amounts. Sometimes the property manager negotiates a commission on lease renewals because the commission could be a big factor in a tenant's decision to stay or go. You will need to research the appropriate amount for leasing commissions in a given market.

Estimating Operating Expenses Using Comparable Properties

Operating expenses can be estimated like *PGI* and vacancy and collection loss using the operating expense ratios of comparable properties as an analytical benchmark. These estimates can also be supplemented by using industry ratios published in industry magazines and from talking to suppliers of some expense items. This works well for estimating utility expenses in some markets.

Estimating Operating Expenses Using the Subject Property History

Obviously, it is possible to estimate a property's operating expenses by reviewing the expenses incurred over the last three years. Historical expense data is probably the best support for this estimate as long as no unusual changes are anticipated in the future. There is seldom a reason to ignore the historical expenses of a property, but there are often reasons to adjust them up or down. An anticipated capital expenditure made to lower the expenses, such as replacing a roof or HVAC unit, will have to be reflected in the appraisal by deducting the cost of the repair from the final value opinion in "as is" condition.

Estimating Reserves for Replacement Using Contractors' Estimates

Reserves for replacement are commonly estimated by obtaining contractors' estimates for the work needed. Some appraisers divide the current cost of the item by the total economic life. Other appraisers adjust the cost to future amounts (usually higher) and then discount that amount back to current dollars using an appropriate discount rate. Since this expense in the cash flow estimate for the years before the expense is incurred is theoretical, the discount rate should be equal to a "safe" rate or a savings account rate. The future expenditure should be projected out only until the expense is incurred. In yield capitalization, the capital improvements are expensed in the years they occur, but in direct capitalization some investors set up accounts to save for that expense. Each market is different in this regard.

Estimating Tenant Improvement Expenses

The cost of tenant improvements can also be estimated using contractors' forecasts. If an appraiser is developing an opinion of market value using a single year's income ratio, the cost of tenant improvements will have to be stabilized in the first year to reflect the future irregular expense.

This expense is typically significant for multitenant office and retail properties, which are generally valued with a discounted cash flow model, in which case the expense is just scheduled in the year it occurs. If a single year's income analysis is used, the net income from the comparables used to extract the capitalization rate must include a TI expense. Again, it is important to make the extraction and application processes the same for the comparables and the subject.

Net Operating Income

Net operating income is simply the difference between effective gross income and total operating expenses, or the amount of the effective gross income that is left after expenses and can be used for debt service and equity cash flow.

Additional Calculations

"Below-the-line" calculations get their name from their place below the net operating income line in the reconstructed operating statement. These items often include capital expenses that the Internal Revenue Service will not allow the property owner to expense and are often the same items that would be reserved for in many appraisals. On the balance sheet, below-the-line items are considered depreciating assets and a portion of their cost, including leasing commissions, will be deducted by the accountant each year. Below-the-line items can also include mortgage debt service and equity income in some markets. Confusion arises when some owners include below-the-line items in their expenses and others do not. In income and expense analysis, it is important to deal with these items consistently to ensure "apples-to-apples" comparisons between the subject and comparable properties.

Mortgage Debt Service

Financing as an expense is usually not accounted for in the net operating income figure, but the annual total of all mortgage payments made–i.e., the mortgage debt service–can be deducted from net operating income to give a figure that is used in some capitalization procedures. The net income after deducting debt service is commonly called the *cash flow to mortgage* (I_M). The financing terms used in the estimation of mortgage debt service should be typical of the market, as implied by the definition of *market value.*

Equity Income

The equity income is simply the difference between the net operating income and the mortgage debt service, or what's left after deducting for mortgage payments. Analysis of a property at this level is difficult because of the variety of mortgage terms and conditions available from various institutions. Always be conscious of the variety of available alternatives to ensure that the cash flows from the property are adequate to pay the debt services for the typical sale. This is a check of reasonableness because most buyers finance their purchases. In highly leveraged investments, there is higher risk of default on a mortgage because a small loss in income (e.g., one tenant leaves) will cause a decline in net income sufficient to cause the owner to have to input funds from outside the investment, i.e., to "feed the investment."

Expense and Income Ratios

The net income ratio is the ratio of net operating income to the effective gross income (I_O/EGI). The net income ratio is the complement of the operating expense ratio ($1 - OER$). A property that has an EGI of \$100,000 and expenses of \$33,000 has an expense ratio of 33.3% and an NIR of 66.6%. This can be a good tool to use to confirm consistency in the market.

1. What are the operating expense ratios of the following properties?

Property	I_o	Fixed Expenses	Variable Expenses	Total Expenses	Expense Ratio
1	$555,666	$111,000	$125,898	_____	_____
2	$535,000	$107,000	$124,589	_____	_____
3	$505,000	$100,000	$120,000	_____	_____
4	$443,598	$95,000	$100,000	_____	_____
5	$425,657	$85,000	$95,000	_____	_____
6	$398,756	$78,900	$90,000	_____	_____

2. The income and expense history of this property for the last five years is available. What is the net operating income and the operating expense ratio for each year?

9568 S. Greenway Street	5 years ago	4 years ago	3 years ago	2 years ago	1 year ago
Income					
Apartment rental income	$228,800	$230,880	$227,200	$227,040	$221,760
Laundry income	720	619	740	611	576
Carport income	1,800	1,800	1,800	1,800	1,800
Total income	$231,320	$233,299	$229,740	$229,451	$224,136
Expenses					
Management expense	$13,879	$13,998	$13,784	$13,767	$13,448
Real estate taxes	21,258	22,555	23,001	23,456	23,698
Insurance (for the real estate)	1,850	1,900	1,900	1,900	2,900
Electricity (common areas)	1,500	1,538	1,576	1,615	1,656
Water and sewer (incl. in rent)	8,064	8,266	8,472	8,684	8,901
Bad check (loss in income and fee)	800	1,650	1,650	1,640	2,460
Bank service charge	197	368	98	491	29
Mowing service	2,880	2,880	3,040	3,040	3,040
Site maintenance: parking lot	-	3,900	-	-	3,900
Site maintenance: lawn care	1,225	1,350	1,350	1,450	1,600
Bldg: apt. cleaning	916	1,016	916	450	1,112
Bldg: apt. painting	2,550	2,125	1,700	2,550	2,975
Bldg: maintenance (HVAC)	1,320	2,565	1,895	2,966	3,654
Bldg: maintenance (other)	7,895	8,855	8,658	4,500	3,800
Bldg: plumbing/electrical	555	1,750	598	985	2,588
Misc. expenses	3,900	1,000	708	210	989
Total expenses	$68,789	$75,716	$69,346	$67,704	$76,750
Net operating income	_____	_____	_____	_____	_____
Expense ratio	_____	_____	_____	_____	_____

Note: Unless otherwise noted, italicized references indicate the pages in *The Appraisal of Real Estate*, 14th edition, that readers should consult for additional discussion of these topics.

1.

Property	I_o	Fixed Expenses	Variable Expenses	Total Expenses	Expense Ratio
1	$555,666	$111,000	$125,898	$236,898	42.63%
2	$535,000	$107,000	$124,589	$231,589	43.29%
3	$505,000	$100,000	$120,000	$220,000	43.56%
4	$443,598	$95,000	$100,000	$195,000	43.96%
5	$425,657	$85,000	$95,000	$180,000	42.29%
6	$398,756	$78,900	$90,000	$168,900	42.36%

Page 488

2.

9568 S. Greenway Street	5 years ago	4 years ago	3 years ago	2 years ago	1 year ago
Income					
Apartment rental income	$228,800	$230,880	$227,200	$227,040	$221,760
Laundry income	720	619	740	611	576
Carport income	1,800	1,800	1,800	1,800	1,800
Total income	$231,320	$233,299	$229,740	$229,451	$224,136
Expenses					
Management expense	$13,879	$13,998	$13,784	$13,767	$13,448
Real estate taxes	21,258	22,555	23,001	23,456	23,698
Insurance (for the real estate)	1,850	1,900	1,900	1,900	2,900
Electricity (common areas)	1,500	1,538	1,576	1,615	1,656
Water and sewer (incl. in rent)	8,064	8,266	8,472	8,684	8,901
Bad check (loss in income and fee)	800	1,650	1,650	1,640	2,460
Bank service charge	197	368	98	491	29
Mowing service	2,880	2,880	3,040	3,040	3,040
Site maintenance: parking lot	-	3,900	-	-	3,900
Site maintenance: lawn care	1,225	1,350	1,350	1,450	1,600
Bldg: apt. cleaning	916	1,016	916	450	1,112
Bldg: apt. painting	2,550	2,125	1,700	2,550	2,975
Bldg: maintenance (HVAC)	1,320	2,565	1,895	2,966	3,654
Bldg: maintenance (other)	7,895	8,855	8,658	4,500	3,800
Bldg: plumbing/electrical	555	1,750	598	985	2,588
Misc. expenses	3,900	1,000	708	210	989
Total expenses	$68,789	$75,716	$69,346	$67,704	$76,750
Net operating income	$162,531	$157,583	$160,394	$161,747	$147,386
Expense ratio	29.7%	32.5%	30.2%	29.5%	34.2%

Pages 485-488

23

Direct Capitalization

Direct capitalization is widely used to value non-residential properties that have stabilized income streams and predictable expenses. This technique allows appraisers to develop a lump-sum indication of value based on an estimate of a single year's net operating income. Direct capitalization is an old tool still used in many markets. It requires minimal calculations after the net income estimate is developed. Even with the sophisticated software for the estimation of cash flows and value available today, many nonresidential brokers still quote "the cap rate" of a sale property as a criterion for investors.

To convert the subject property's annual income expectancy into a value estimate, the annual income is divided by an appropriate capitalization rate. The capitalization rate is extracted from comparable sales by dividing the annual net operating income of each property by its gross sale price—i.e., a simple ratio of what the property earns to what it sold for, which can then be applied to the subject's earnings to convert the ratio back to a current lump-sum value. This ratio is calculated on a net income basis, so small differences in expense ratios should not undermine the validity of the analysis. Note that the expenses included in the income and expense analysis of the subject should also be included in the expense estimate of the comparables.

The most common problem in the application of direct capitalization is how to account for reserves for replacement and tenant improvement expenses. If the list of expenses for the compa-rables includes line items for reserves and tenant improvement expenses, the same items should be included in the calculation of the subject property's expenses. The reverse is also true. Remember that this analysis is a ratio model that uses only the next year's income as an indication of the subject's potential. The income level that the property actually achieves may be very similar to the forecast amount or it could be very different, which would significantly affect the results of the direct capitalization process.

As a simple example of the analysis of a single year's income using direct capitalization, consider a market in which a small single-tenant industrial building on Main Street sold last month for $555,000. The property's net operating income estimate for next year is $55,000. A small single-tenant industrial building on Adams Street in the same market sold three months ago for $625,000 with a net operating income of $62,500. The subject property, another small single-tenant industrial building, has an annual net operating income of $75,000. The comparable properties had capitalization rates around 10% ($55,000/$555,000 = 9.91% and $62,500/$625,000 = 10%). Applying this rate to the forecast income of the subject property gives a value of

$$\$75,000/0.10 = \$750,000$$

The actual sales and income data that appraisers collect seldom result in ratios that are so consis-

KEY TERMS	
band of investment	land capitalization rate (R_L)
building capitalization rate (R_B)	land residual technique
building residual technique	loan-to-value ratio (M)
debt coverage ratio (DCR)	mortgage capitalization rate
debt service (I_M)	(R_M)
direct capitalization	overall capitalization rate (R_O)
equity capitalization rate (R_E)	residual techniques
equity ratio (E)	

tent. Appraisers are usually required to reconcile various capitalization rates found in the market.

Derivation of Overall Capitalization Rates

Derivation of R_0 from Comparable Sales

The easiest method for estimating the ratio of income to value is to go directly to the market to find sales of properties that are typically rented. If you can research the sale price and the estimated net operating income for the year following the sale, you can then establish a ratio of income to value for comparable properties by applying the IRV formula as shown in Exhibit 23.1.

The problem with the direct extraction of an overall capitalization rate (R_0) from market data is that any difference in the future income potential of the comparables should be very similar to that of the subject property. If the subject's upside potential is much greater than the potential of the comparables, the extracted overall rate will be skewed. If the comparable has a different income pattern than the subject, the ratio of income to value will also be skewed.

For example, suppose a comparable property has a level income due to a lease, but the subject property's rent is increasing by 4% per year. These two properties are not comparable without an adjustment for the difference in future earnings. Finding comparable properties with the same upside potential and income patterns as the subject is often difficult.

In addition to using sales extracted from the market to calculate the overall capitalization rate, you can use a variation of the IRV formula if the effective gross income multiplier ($EGIM$) and the net income ratio (NIR) are known. The formula is

$$R_0 = \frac{NIR}{EGIM}$$

As an example, assume a property has an $EGIM$ of 5.5 and an expense ratio of 52%. The net in-come ratio is 48%. The capitalization rate would be calculated as follows:

$$\frac{0.48}{5.5} = 0.087273$$

Although this technique is a possible alternative to direct extraction from market data, it is seldom used in practice because if you have the net income ratio, you usually already have enough income and expense data to easily calculate net operating income.

Derivation of R_0 by Band of Investment—Mortgage and Equity

The primary alternative to extracting a capitalization rate from comparable market data is the band-of-investment technique, which is based on partitioning the overall capitalization rate into components. The most common method of partitioning the overall capitalization rate is into mortgage and equity components. Weighting the mortgage and equity components at market ratios should resemble market logic. The formula for calculating an overall capitalization rate is

$$\begin{array}{rl} M^* \times R_M = & \text{Weighted Amount} \\ (1-M) \times R_E = + & \underline{\text{Weighted Amount}} \\ & R_0 \end{array}$$

* Mortgage ratio

The mortgage constant, R_M, can be calculated by dividing the annual debt service (ADS) by the initial amount of the mortgage. It can also be calculated on a financial calculator as follows:

Keystrokes	Output
25 [g] [n]	300.000000
10 [g] [i]	0.833333
1 [PV]	1.000000
0 [FV]	0.000000
[PMT]	-0.009087
R_M = PMT × 12:	
[CHS] 12 [X]	0.10904

As an example, consider a sale for which the lender quoted a 10% annual rate with monthly payments for 25 years, which results in a monthly mortgage constant of 0.10904 as shown above. The equity capitalization rate (R_E) was 13%, and the loan-to-value ratio (M) was 75%. The band-of-investment technique can be used to calculate the overall rate as follows:

$$\begin{array}{rl} 0.75 \times 0.10904 = & 0.08178 \\ 0.25 \times 0.13000 = + & \underline{0.03250} \\ & 0.11428 \text{ or } 11.428\% \end{array}$$

Exhibit 23.1	IRV Relationships

Income = Rate × Value

Rate = Income / Value

Value = Income / Rate

This technique is exceptionally user-friendly because it puts much of the emphasis on the market mortgage rate (in the example above, 75%) and much less on the equity component (only 25%). Also, appraisers only need to estimate or extract the equity capitalization rate (R_E) because the lender will quote the mortgage constant (R_M). The only difficulty with this analysis is that the equity capitalization rate can vary, going from a large percentage to even a negative number (such as -15% to -20%), which can affect the overall capitalization rate significantly despite the smaller emphasis on the equity component. Like the overall capitalization rates (R_O), this capitalization rate is just the ratio of the first year's income to the capital amount paid (i.e., the down payment). If there are substantial changes in the future, the equity capitalization rate (R_E) will be affected significantly.

Derivation of R_O by Band of Investment— Land and Building

If the land-to-building ratio and land and building capitalization rates are known, appraisers can also use the band-of-investment technique to estimate an overall capitalization rate. For example, a property was reported to have a 25:75 land-to-building ratio. The land capitalization rate (R_L) is 9% and the building capitalization rate (R_B) is 13%. The overall capitalization rate is calculated as follows:

$$0.75 \times 0.1300 = \quad 0.0975$$
$$0.25 \times 0.0900 = + \underline{0.0225}$$
$$0.1200 \text{ or } 12\%$$

It is recognized that buyers and sellers transfer and appraisers value the rights in realty, not land and buildings, so this is a theoretical analysis. It is a common way to look at real estate and is also the basis of the cost approach.

Debt Coverage Formula

Some appraisers believe it is possible to estimate an overall capitalization rate from data obtained directly from the mortgage lender. Most property sales require financing, so the technique of using the debt coverage formula to analyze capitalization rates, also known as the *mortgage underwriters method*, gives direct consideration to the terms available in the mortgage market. The formula used in the mortgage underwriters method is

$$DCR = \frac{I_O}{I_M}$$

$$R_O = M \times R_M \times DCR$$

> The debt-coverage ratio (*DCR*) is a ratio of net income to the mortgage payments on an annual basis. It is a lender's tool used to gauge how much excess cash flow there is above the loan payments. If there is any problem when there is little or no extra cash flow, the mortgage payments may cease.

where R_O is the capitalization rate, M is the mortgage ratio, R_M is the mortgage constant, and DCR is the debt coverage ratio. The debt coverage ratio can also be calculated using the following formula:

$$DCR = I_O / ADS$$

In other words, the capitalization rate can be estimated by calling the lender and asking for the best terms available for a specific property and then converting those loan parameters to a capitalization rate using the debt coverage formula.

This technique requires minimal research, but if the lender is reluctant to make loans on a particular class of properties, the value estimate may be affected. If rates are not favorable, the buyers have to accept a smaller loan or not purchase the property. If the lender is conservative and gives unfavorable terms, the equity investor must factor these unfavorable terms into the decision to buy. If the mortgage lender is liberal, the requirements on the equity portion of the investment should be liberal as well. Thus, reported debt coverage ratios are driven by individual banks and may not be consistent within a market.

Some appraisers consider the mortgage underwriters method to be market-oriented because most real estate involves mortgage funds, but many do not because there are no buyer's inputs. The lender's interest may represent 80% or more of the property value, so using their parameters is probably valid. At the very least, the mortgage underwriters method is an excellent technique to affirm a capitalization rate obtained from another source.

As an example, suppose the property being appraised has an estimated income of $100,000. The lender quotes a 75% loan-to-value ratio and a 9% monthly mortgage with full amortization over 20 years if the debt coverage ratio is 1.2. The annual mortgage constant for a 20-year loan at 9% can be calculated using a financial calculator or a computer as 0.10797. The overall capitalization rate is calculated as follows:

$$R_O = M \times R_M \times DCR$$

$$R_0 = 0.75 \times 0.10797 \times 1.2$$
$$R_0 = 0.09717 \text{ or } 9.717\%$$

The capitalization rate (R_M) can be calculated as follows:

9 [g] [i]		
20 [g] [n]		
1 [CHS] [PV]		
0 [FV]		
Solve for [PMT] =		0.008997
[ENTER] 12 [X] =		0.107967

This calculation uses 100% (1.0) as the basis for calculation, not actual dollars.

The overall capitalization rate can then be used in direct capitalization of the estimated net operating income as follows:

$$\$100,000/0.09717 = \$1,029,124$$

Surveys

Appraisers have long used the capitalization rates reported by real estate research firms as support for their estimates of rates applicable to particular properties. These surveys of institutional investors provide a picture of a portion of the real estate market, with some caveats related to the source of the survey data, the precise method of derivation of the reported rates, and the relevance of national data to a local real estate market. Asking real estate brokers about the capitalization rates they see in sales of income-producing property in a specific market is another source of information commonly used by appraisers.

Residual Techniques

Residual techniques allow appraisers to estimate the value of property if, for example, the net income, land value, and land and building capitalization rates are known. This technique can be applied to mortgage and equity or different configurations of land values and building ratios as well.

As an example of applying this alternative technique, suppose the subject has a net operating income of $45,000 per year. The value attributable to the land (V_L) is $95,000. The land capitalization rate (R_L) is 9%, and the building capitalization rate (R_B) is 12%. The property value is calculated as shown in Exhibit 23.2.

While residual techniques appear to be good for estimating value when an overall capitalization rate (R_O) is not known, they are usually not feasible options because they require so much other data that can be difficult to obtain.

Leased Fee and Leasehold Residuals

In theory, leased fee and leasehold interests can be analyzed using residual techniques, although in practice the sum of the values of leased fee and leasehold interests cannot be assumed to equal the value of the fee simple estate. As a result, leased fee and leasehold residuals are even more difficult to work with than land and building or mortgage and equity residuals.

The most clear-cut application of a leasehold residual calculation is the case of a below-market lease, where the tenant has a financial advantage over a prospective tenant renting the same space at the market rent. That rent loss can be calculated at an appropriate rate (if that rate can be supported with other data) and capitalized to give a value of the leasehold interest. In a lease-up situation, where the property is expected to achieve stabilized occupancy at market rates at some future date, discounted cash flow analysis is often a more convincing technique for valuing the leased fee and leasehold interests.

Gross Income Multipliers and Gross Rent Multipliers

The analysis of gross income multipliers is a simple direct capitalization technique used by buyers and brokers in some markets, usually

Exhibit 23.2	Mortgage Underwriters Method

Formula	Numbers	Rationale
$V_L \times R_L = I_L$	$\$95,000 \times 0.09 = \$8,550$	This is a simple IRV calculation to derive the income to the land.
$I_O - I_L = I_B$	$\$45,000 - \$8,550 = \$36,450$	The income to the building is equal to the income overall less the income to the land.
$I_B / R_B = V_B$	$\$36,450 / 0.12 = \$303,750$	The value of the building is calculated by dividing the building income by the building capitalization rate.
$V_B + V_L = V_O$	$\$303,750 + \$95,000 = \$398,750$	Adding the value of the land and building components together yields the overall property value.

with small, simple properties such as one-unit homes, duplexes, and small offices. The sale price is divided by the potential gross income or effective gross income to calculate the respective multipliers. For example, a comparable property that sells for $500,000 and has an effective gross income of $50,000 has an effective gross income multiplier (*EGIM*) of 10.0 ($500,000/$50,000). If the subject property also has an effective gross income of $50,000, its indicated value would also be $500,000 based on this analysis. Gross income multipliers are good techniques when

- Buyers think this way and use this as a decision-making technique.
- The properties compared have similar operating expense ratios.
- The properties have similar upside potential for appreciation or depreciation.

> Most appraisers use the term *gross income multiplier* (GIM) to describe a ratio of sale price to annual gross income. Most appraisers use the term *gross rent multiplier* (GRM) to describe the sale price divided by the monthly income.

The problem with the use of potential and effective gross income multipliers is that if the comparable used for extracting the ratio has a different expense ratio, the conversion to a lump-sum value estimate would be skewed because the gross income multiplier would not reflect the difference in expenses and their effect on net income. The persuasiveness of this technique is also weakened by the absence of any consideration of reversion value. This is like the capitalization of a single year's income in which the appreciation or depreciation is implicitly accounted for in the capitalization rate but is not specified in the analysis.

As an example of *EGIM* analysis, consider a small single-tenant industrial building on Main Street that sold last month for $555,000. The effective gross income estimate for next year is $70,000. Another small single-tenant industrial building on Adams Street in the same market sold three months ago for $625,000 with an effective gross income estimate for next year of $80,000. The subject property, another small single-tenant industrial building in the market, has an annual effective gross income of $90,000. The comparable properties have *EGIM*s of roughly 7.9 ($555,000 / $70,000 = 7.93 and $625,000 / $80,000 = 7.81). Ap-

plying the extracted *EGIM* to the income stream of the subject gives a value of

$$\$90,000 \times 7.9 = \$711,000$$

Note that this calculation is similar to the simple use of a capitalization rate to convert an income stream into value, but rather than divide the net operating income by a rate (as in the IRV formula) the I_O is multiplied by *EGIM* or *PGIM*.

Estimation of Gross Income Multipliers

The same standards for selection of comparable sales in the sales comparison approach should be applied in the estimation of a gross income multiplier. Sale properties should be similar in terms of unit counts, locations, sizes, functional utility, condition, time of sale (i.e., market conditions), and neighborhood influences. Also, the future income potential of the property should be similar for both the subject and comparable properties.

Sales prices need not be adjusted if the comparable sales are truly comparable with the subject property. Remember that the goal of the analysis is to extract a ratio of sale price to income that can be applied to the estimated gross income of the subject, not to adjust the price of the comparable sale for differences from the subject property as in the sales comparison approach. While some transactional adjustments would be appropriate, you should not adjust the sale price for market conditions (i.e., the "time" adjustment) because they are not making a corresponding adjustment in rent. A ratio of price to income (i.e., the *GIM*) should reflect the ratio of both the sale price and the gross income at the time of sale. A price that includes concessions would give a multiplier with concessions, so the effect of any concession should be adjusted for first.

As an example of the application of a gross rent multiplier, suppose you are appraising a one-unit residential home and you have found 10 recent sales of rented properties that are similar to the subject. These sales are shown in the Sale and Rent Comparable Worksheet.

When several gross rent multipliers have been obtained from comparable sales, a pattern should emerge. Appraisers then select an appropriate gross rent multiplier based on the data presented. This multiplier will be applied to the estimated market rent of the subject property to derive an estimate of the defined value.

Using the data in the example, calculate the gross rent multipliers for the comparables, and then reconcile the data to estimate a *GRM* for the subject property's market. The subject property is currently renting for $2,750 per month, which is considered to be its market rental rate. Determine the market value of the subject property, and check your answer with that presented in the Suggested Solutions at the end of this chapter.

	Sale and Rent Comparable Worksheet		
	Sale Price	Gross Rent Estimate	GRM
1	$280,000	$2,500	_____
2	$320,000	$2,900	_____
3	$305,000	$2,750	_____
4	$275,000	$2,500	_____
5	$330,000	$2,900	_____
6	$325,000	$2,900	_____
7	$300,000	$2,700	_____
8	$298,000	$2,700	_____
9	$285,000	$2,500	_____
10	$290,000	$2,750	_____
Average	_____	_____	_____

Note: Check the Suggested Solutions at the end of this chapter for answers.

1. The subject property has an annual net income expectancy of $75,000, and recent comparable sales have the following characteristics:

   · Sale 1 sold for $1,000,000 and has an annual net income expectancy of $98,000.

   · Sale 2 sold for $750,000 and has an annual net income expectancy of $75,000.

   · Sale 3 sold for $650,000 and has an annual net income expectancy of $62,500.

   · Sale 4 sold for $500,000 and has an annual net income expectancy of $49,500.

   What is the market value of the subject property (rounded to the nearest $50,000)?

   a) $800,000

   b) $750,000

   c) $700,000

   d) $650,000

2. What is the expected annual income of a property that recently sold for $100,000 and for which the buyers indicated that they used an overall capitalization rate (R_O) of 9.25%?

   a) $925 per year

   b) $9,250 per year

   c) $92,500 per year

   d) Cannot be determined with this data

3. The subject property has a potential gross income (*PGI*) of $100,000, a vacancy and collection loss of 7%, fixed expenses of $35,000, variable expenses of $25,000, and reserves for replacement of $7,000. Recent sales of very similar properties in this market suggest that a capitalization rate of 12.0% is appropriate. The capitalization rates were extracted from sales in which the price was divided into the estimate of net operating income from the broker without reserves. What is the market value of the subject property?

   a) $300,000

   b) $275,000

   c) $250,000

   d) $225,000

4. What is the value of a property with an effective gross income (*EGI*) of $423,000, an operating expense ratio (*OER*) of 32%, and an overall capitalization rate (R_O) of 0.11?

   a) $2,250,000

   b) $2,500,000

   c) $3,850,000

   d) $4,230,000

5. The subject property has a level income of $30,000. In the mortgage market for this type of property, the best rate available is 9.0% per year with monthly payments, a 25-year amortization, and a maximum 75% loan-to-value. The equity capitalization rate is 15%. What is the market value? (Use the band-of-investment technique and round your answer to the nearest $1,000. You will need a financial calculator to answer this question.)

   a) $325,000

   b) $300,000

   c) $275,000

   d) $265,000

6. What is the market value of a property with a net operating income (I_O) of $75,000, an annual debt service of $60,000, a loan-to-value ratio of 75%, and a mortgage constant of 0.1281? (Use the debt coverage formula.)

   a) $500,000

   b) $600,000

   c) $700,000

   d) $800,000

7. What is the indicated equity capitalization rate (R_E) of a property with a sale price of $400,000, a net operating income (I_O) of $35,000, mortgage terms of 9.75% for 25 years, fully amortized with monthly payments, and a loan-to-value ratio of 65%? (You will need a financial calculator to answer this question.)

   a) 0.0514

   b) 0.0650

   c) 0.0875

   d) 0.0975

8. What is the indicated property value of a property that has a net operating income of $150,000 per year? The value of the land (V_L) is $550,000. The land capitalization rate (R_L) is 9.75%, and the building capitalization rate (R_B) is 12.25%. What is the property value (to the nearest $100,000)?

   a) $1,300,000

   b) $1,400,000

   c) $1,500,000

   d) $1,600,000

9. An investment has a net operating income (I_O) of $140,000. Market rate mortgage financing is available at 75% of value at 9.5% per year with monthly payments, amortization over 25 years, and an equity dividend (R_E) rate of 5.5%. What is the market value? (Use the band of investment technique. You will need a financial calculator to answer this question.)

a) $1,200,000

b) $1,300,000

c) $1,400,000

d) $1,500,000

10. The subject property is a four-family residence. Prepare a reconstructed operating statement and estimate the value of the property using direct capitalization.

Subject address	815 N. 6th Avenue
Property rights appraised	fee simple
Vacancy last year	4%
Vacancy two years ago	5%
Vacancy three years ago	4%
Collection loss	one month's rent each year for the last three years (one unit per year)
Taxes	$2,727 per year
Insurance expense	$2,200 per year
Variable expenses	$2,000 three years ago, $2,300 two years ago, $2,100 last year
Improvements	
Improvement type	attached, four-unit apartment building (2-story)
Improvement age	built in 1980—effective age = actual age
Foundation	concrete blocks
Roof type	4/12 pitch, asphalt shingles over plywood underlayer
Construction	wood frame, concrete block foundation
Veneer	aluminum siding
Gutters and downspouts	continuous aluminum
Window type	wood double-hung with aluminum storm windows
Site size	0.5 acre

	Unit 1	Unit 2	Unit 3	Unit 4
Current rental rate	$485	$475	$450	$425
Lease date	last week	24 months earlier	2 months ago	6 months ago
Lease term (remaining)	12 months	month to month	10 months	6 months
Estimated potential rent				
Furnishings included	unfurnished	unfurnished	unfurnished	unfurnished
Utilities included	water/sewer	water/sewer	water/sewer	water/sewer
Construction quality	average	average	average	average
Improvement condition	average	average	average	average
Story	first floor	first floor	second floor	second floor
Room count	5/2/1	5/2/1	5/2/1	5/2/1
Above-grade area	700 sq. ft.	700 sq. ft.	700 sq. ft.	700 sq. ft.
Basement area	none	none	none	none
Garage	none included	none included	none included	none included
HVAC	GFA/central AC	GFA/central AC	GFA/central AC	GFA/central AC
Appliances	R/O, refrig., dish.	R/O, refrig., dish.	R/O, refrig., dish.	R/O, refrig., dish.
Walls	painted drywall	painted drywall	painted drywall	painted drywall
Trim/finish	wood/average	wood/average	wood/average	wood/average
Other	patio	patio	balcony	balcony

Comparable Sale 1

Address	744 N. 19th Street	
Sale price	$175,000	
Date closed	3 months ago	
Financing	new mortgage with no concessions	
Vacancy and collection loss	5% of *PGI* per year	
All expenses	$7,400 (includes fixed and variable)	
Lot size	0.5 acre	

Item	Unit 1	Unit 2	Unit 3	Unit 4
Current rental rate	$450/month	$475/month	$450/month	$450/month
Lease date	15 months ago	12 months ago	8 months ago	4 months ago
Lease remaining	month to month	month to month	4 months remaining	8 months remaining
Estimated potential rent	$485	$485	$475	$475
Furnishings included	unfurnished	unfurnished	unfurnished	unfurnished
Utilities included	none	none	none	none
Age of improvement	1980	1980	1980	1980
Construction quality	average	average	average	average
Improvement condition	average	average	average	average
Story	upper level	upper level	first floor	first floor
Room count	5/2/1	5/2/1	4/1/1	4/1/1
Above-grade area	800 sq. ft.	800 sq. ft.	700 sq. ft.	700 sq. ft.
Basement area	none	none	none	none
Garage	none	none	none	none
Appliances	R/O, refrig., dish.	R/O, refrig., dish.	R/O, refrig., dish.	R/O, refrig., dish.
Other	balcony	balcony	porch	porch

Comparable Sale 2

Address	242 N. 9th Street	
Sale price	$150,000	
Date closed	12 months ago	
Financing	new mortgage with no concessions	
Vacancy and collection loss	5% of *PGI* per year	
All expenses	$6,750	
Lot size	0.5 acre	

Item	Unit 1	Unit 2	Unit 3	Unit 4
Current rental rate	$415/month	$425/month	$405/month	$425/month
Lease date	5 months ago	2 months ago	16 months ago	4 months ago
Lease remaining	5 months	10 months	month to month	8 months remaining
Estimated potential rent	$415	$425	$425	$425
Furnishings included	unfurnished	unfurnished	unfurnished	unfurnished
Utilities included	none	none	none	none
Age of improvement	1978	1978	1978	1978
Construction quality	average	average	average	average
Improvement condition	needs remodeling	needs remodeling	needs remodeling	needs remodeling
Story	upper level	upper level	first floor	first floor
Room count	5/2/1	5/2/1	4/1/1	4/1/1
Above-grade area	750 sq. ft.	750 sq. ft.	650 sq. ft.	650 sq. ft.
Basement area	none	none	none	none
Garage	none	none	none	none
Appliances	R/O, refrig., dish.	R/O, refrig., dish.	none	none
Other	balcony	balcony	10 x 10 porch	10 x 10 porch

Comparable Sale 3

Address   435 N. 28th Street
Sale price $145,000
Date closed   15 months ago
Financing   new mortgage with no concessions
Vacancy and collection loss   5% of *PGI* per year
All expenses $6,600
Lot size   0.5 acre

Item	Unit 1	Unit 2	Unit 3	Unit 4
Current rental rate	$400/month	$405/month	$400/month	$415/month
Lease date	5 months ago	2 months ago	9 months ago	8 months ago
Lease remaining	month to month	month to month	4 months remaining	8 months remaining
Estimated potential rent	$425	$425	$400	$415
Furnishings included	unfurnished	unfurnished	unfurnished	unfurnished
Utilities included	none	none	none	none
Age of improvement	1975	1975	1975	1975
Construction quality	average	average	average	average
Improvement condition	average	average	average	average
Story	upper level	upper level	first floor	first floor
Room count	5/2/1	5/2/1	4/1/1	4/1/1
Above-grade area	650 sq. ft.	650 sq. ft.	600 sq. ft.	600 sq. ft.
Basement area	none	none	none	none
Garage	none	none	none	none
Appliances	R/O, refrig., dish.	R/O, refrig., dish.	none	none
Other	balcony	balcony	porch	porch

Comparable Sale 4

Address   567 7th Street
Sale price $155,000
Date closed   18 months ago
Financing   new mortgage with no concessions
Vacancy and collection loss   5% of *PGI* per year
All expenses $6,450
Lot size   0.5 acre

Item	Unit 1	Unit 2	Unit 3	Unit 4
Current rental rate	$415/month	$405/month	$400/month	$415/month
Lease date	7 months ago	2 months ago	16 months ago	14 months ago
Lease remaining	5 months	10 months	month to month	month to month
Estimated potential rent	$415	$405	$415	$415
Furnishings included	unfurnished	unfurnished	unfurnished	unfurnished
Age of improvement	1970	1970	1970	1970
Utilities included	none	none	none	none
Construction quality	average	average	average	average
Improvement condition	average	average	average	average
Story	upper level	upper level	first floor	first floor
Room count	5/2/1	5/2/1	5/1/1	5/1/1
Above-grade area	700 sq. ft.	700 sq. ft.	700 sq. ft.	700 sq. ft.
Basement area	none	none	none	none
Garage	none	none	none	none
Appliances	R/O, refrig., dish.	R/O, refrig., dish.	none	none
Other	porch	porch	10 x 10 porch	10 x 10 porch

Reconstructed Operating Statement

Estimated *PGI*

    Unit 1 _____   _____

    Unit 2 _____   _____

    Unit 3 _____   _____

    Unit 4 _____   _____

    Monthly estimated rent _____   _____

    Annual potential gross income _____   _____

    Vacancy and collection loss _____   _____

    Effective gross income _____   _____

Expenses

    Taxes _____   _____

    Insurance _____   _____

    Variable expenses _____   _____

    Reserves for replacement _____   _____

Total expenses _____   _____

Net operating income _____   _____

Capitalized value _____   _____

Note: Unless otherwise noted, italicized references indicate the pages in *The Appraisal of Real Estate*, 14th edition, that readers should consult for additional discussion of these topics.

Sale and Rent Comparable Worksheet Solution

	Sale Price	Gross Rent Estimate	GRM
1	$280,000	$2,500	112.00
2	$320,000	$2,900	110.34
3	$305,000	$2,750	110.91
4	$275,000	$2,500	110.00
5	$330,000	$2,900	113.79
6	$325,000	$2,900	112.07
7	$300,000	$2,700	111.11
8	$290,000	$2,700	107.41
9	$285,000	$2,500	114.00
10	$290,000	$2,750	105.45
Average	$300,800	$2,710	110.71

The market value of the subject property is

$$\$2,750 \times 110.71 = \$304,452.50$$

1. **b) $750,000**
   - Sale 1 sold for $1,000,000 and has an annual net income expectancy of $98,000 = 0.098
   - Sale 2 sold for $750,000 and has an annual net income expectancy of $75,000 = 0.10
   - Sale 3 sold for $650,000 and has an annual net income expectancy of $62,500 = 0.09615
   - Sale 4 sold for $500,000 and has an annual net income expectancy of $49,500 = 0.099

   75,000/0.10 = $750,000

2. **b) $9,250 per year**
   Page 492

3. **b) $275,000**

PGI	$100,000
Vacancy and collection loss	− 7,000
EGI	$93,000
Fixed expenses	$35,000
Net income	$33,000
$33,000/0.12 =	$275,000

4. **b) $2,500,000**

423,000 × 0.68 =	287,640
287,640/0.11 =	2,614,909

   (rounded down to $2,500,000)

5. **d) $265,000**
   Page 505

$R_o = 0.75 \times 0.1007 =$	0.0755
$0.25 \times 0.1500 =$	+ 0.0375
	0.1130
30,000/0.1130 =	265,487

6. **b) 600,000**
   Page 508

   $R_o = DCR \times M \times R_M$
   $R_o = 1.25 \times 0.75 \times 0.1281$
   $R_o = 0.12009$
   75,000/0.12009 = 624,532

7. **a) 0.0514**

    Page 506

    $R_O = 35,000/400,000 = 0.0875$

    $R_M = PMT \times 12$

Term:	25 $\boxed{g}$ $\boxed{n}$
Mortgage rate:	9.75 $\boxed{g}$ $\boxed{i}$
Present value of $1	1 $\boxed{CHS}$ $\boxed{PV}$
Future value of $0	0 $\boxed{FV}$
Solve for $\boxed{PMT}$ =	0.008908

    $R_M = PMT \times 12 = 0.1069$

    $R_E = [R_O - (M \times R_M)]/(1 - M)$
    $= [0.0875 - (0.65 \times 0.1069)]/(1 - 0.65)$
    $= 0.0514$

8. **a) $1,300,000**

    Pages 502-503

$NOI =$	150,000
550,000 $(V_L) \times 0.0975 = -$	153,625 (I_L)
	96,375 (I_B)
96,375/0.1225 =	786,735 (V_B)
786,735 + 550,000 =	1,336,735

9. **d) $1,500,000**

    Pages 496-497

$0.75 \times 0.10484 =$	0.07863
$0.25 \times 0.055 =$	0.01375
	0.09238
140,000/0.09238 =	1,515,479

10. **Comparable Sale 1**

$PGI =$	$23,040
$EGI =$	$21,888
$NOI =$	$14,488
$R_O =$	0.0827886

    Comparable Sale 2

$PGI =$	$20,280
$EGI =$	$19,266
$NOI =$	$12,516
$R_O =$	0.0834

    Comparable Sale 3

$PGI =$	$19,980
$EGI =$	$18,981
$NOI =$	$12,381
$R_O =$	0.08539

    Comparable Sale 4

$PGI =$	$19,800
$EGI =$	$18,810
$NOI =$	$12,360
$R_O =$	0.07974

    Again, this is one solution, not the only solution. There is some room for interpretation in the income and expense estimates. Students should have an answer similar to this, but there will be some variations due to judgment calls.

Reconstructed Operating Statement		
Estimated *PGI*		
Unit 1	$485	
Unit 2	485	
Unit 3	450	
Unit 4	+ 435	
Monthly estimated rent	$1,855	
Annual potential gross income		$22,260
Vacancy and collection loss	6.00%	− 1,336
Effective gross income		$20,924
Expenses		
Taxes	$2,800	
Insurance	$2,200	
Variable expenses	$2,200	
Reserves for replacement	+ —	
Total expenses	$7,200	− 7,200
Net operating income		$13,724
Capitalized value	$13,724/0.08 =	$171,550

24

Yield Capitalization

As discussed in the previous chapter, the simplest way of converting the annual income expectancy of a property into a value estimate is to establish a ratio of how much properties sell for to how much net income they produce. This technique is called *direct capitalization* of a single year's income. It works well when there is enough data to support the extraction and application process. The problem with this procedure is that it fails to recognize substantial changes in future cash flows or property values unless the comparable sales that the capitalization rates are extracted from have the same potential for change as the subject property. Also, direct capitalization is almost unusable when the building is new construction or has been recently remodeled because the property's net income in the first year is likely to be a negative number or not yet stabilized. You cannot assume a rental property is full on the date of completion of construction; this practice was discredited a long time ago.

The development of the modern computer and financial calculator have greatly enhanced the ability to perform complex analyses of a property's income potential and feasibility as an investment using *yield capitalization* techniques. In other words, before buyers purchase a property, they can project what their yield will be based on periodic cash flows and the reversion of the property. Investors can then compare and choose among various investments based on their proposed yields.

Any investment can be analyzed by calculating the present worth of future benefits. How much an investor will put into a property depends on the projected cash flows and the timing of the cash flows. A dollar today is worth a lot more than that same dollar in the future. For example, the grid in Exhibit 24.1 shows how much $1 will grow to with compound interest–i.e., the investor earns interest on the original amount of capital put into the investment and also on the interest earned but not paid out.

Exhibit 24.1 shows the growth of $1 deposited in an account earning 10% interest per year for 10 years. That is, the dollar was deposited at the beginning of the projection period or at the end of Year 0, and the interest was left in the account. The formula to calculate the compound interest is

$$FV = (1 + I)^N$$

where I is the interest rate and N is the number of periods.

Exhibit 24.1 shows that money left in an investment can grow substantially over time. It is also possible to do the opposite calculation to find out how much $1 received in the future is worth today. If $1 (or any multiple) will grow over time with interest, then $1 in the future cannot be worth as much as $1 today. The dollar used here is a substitute for 100%, meaning that the calculations are a tool to get percentages of the growth of the investment.

KEY TERMS	
annuity payable in advance	level annuity
balloon payment	net proceeds of resale
cash flow	ordinary annuity
conversion factor (*a*)	projection period
discounted cash flow (DCF) analysis	property model
	step-up or step-down annuity
exponential curve (constant-ratio) change per period	straight-line change per period
	terminal capitalization rate (R_N)
holding period	variable annuity
increasing annuity	

Exhibit 24.1	Future Value of One

Yield rate = 10.0%

Amount of original deposit = $1.00

	1 + Interest Rate	×	Previous Balance	=	New Balance
End of Year 1	1.1000	×	$1.0000	=	$1.1000
End of Year 2	1.1000	×	$1.1000	=	$1.2100
End of Year 3	1.1000	×	$1.2100	=	$1.3310
End of Year 4	1.1000	×	$1.3310	=	$1.4641
End of Year 5	1.1000	×	$1.4641	=	$1.6105
End of Year 6	1.1000	×	$1.6105	=	$1.7716
End of Year 7	1.1000	×	$1.7716	=	$1.9487
End of Year 8	1.1000	×	$1.9487	=	$2.1436
End of Year 9	1.1000	×	$2.1436	=	$2.3579
End of Year 10	1.1000	×	$2.3579	=	$2.5937

On a financial calculator, the keystrokes for the calculation of the future value of $1 in 10 years at a yield rate of 10% are

Keystrokes	Output
10 [n]	10.00
10 [i]	10.00
1 [PV]	1.00
0 [PMT]	0.00
Solve for [FV] =	-2.59

Discounting

Exhibit 24.2 shows how compound interest diminishes the present value of the dollar received in the future. To calculate compound interest, the original number is multiplied by one plus the interest rate, which is 1.10 in this case. To calculate the loss, or discount, in value due to timing, the amount must be divided by one plus the interest rate, or 1.10. Exhibit 24.2 shows how much $1 (or any multiple of $1) is worth if the investor has to wait the indicated number of years to get it. Each year represents the present value of $1 if it was deposited into an account in the future or how much $1 received in the future is worth today. For example, the Year 5 row reveals that $1 received five years from now is worth only $0.6209 today. In other words, any amount of money paid at the end of Year 5 is worth 62.09% of that amount today.

Exhibit 24.2 indicates that the value of $1 (or any multiple of $1) is worth less and less the longer the investor has to wait. Note that while $1 is used as the base in the table, any multiple of $1 (or one unit of any other currency) can be represented by these ratios. For example, a return of $100 ($1 × 100) expected in five years with a yield of 10% is only worth $62.09 ($0.6209 × 100) today.

Exhibit 24.2	Present Value of One

Yield rate = 10%

Year					Present Worth
1	$1.00	/	110.0%	=	$0.9091
2	$0.9091	/	110.0%	=	$0.8264
3	$0.8264	/	110.0%	=	$0.7513
4	$0.7513	/	110.0%	=	$0.6830
5	$0.6830	/	110.0%	=	$0.6209
6	$0.6209	/	110.0%	=	$0.5645
7	$0.5645	/	110.0%	=	$0.5132
8	$0.5132	/	110.0%	=	$0.4665
9	$0.4665	/	110.0%	=	$0.4241
10	$0.4241	/	110.0%	=	$0.3855

On a financial calculator, the keystrokes for the calculation of the present value of $1 received in 10 years at a yield rate of 10% are

Keystrokes	Output
10 [n]	10.00
10 [i]	10.00
1 [FV]	1.00
0 [PMT]	0.00
Solve for [PV] =	-0.39

The yield capitalization technique is based on the premise that the value of property is equal to the sum of the "present values" of the future cash flows. The process of adding up the present worth of each future cash flow and the reversion is called *discounted cash flow analysis*, which is the modern technique of income capitalization analysis used in many sophisticated markets in the United States.

As an example of the procedure, consider a group of investors who bought a property for $1 million, received $100,000 per year for 10 years, and resold the property for $1 million after 10 years. In this example, it is clear that the investors have received a 10% yield on their investment. The ratio of the first year's income to the price holds true throughout the length of the investment, and the investors got all their money back in the end. Calculating the yield on this investment is a simple matter. In this case, $R_O = Y_O$.

Exhibit 24.3 illustrates this point in more detail. If the group invested $1 million at the start of Year 1 and received the cash flows shown in the table, the present value of these flows would be equal to the amount invested when discounted at the yield rate of 10%. The cash flow in Year 10 is the same $100,000 periodic cash flow plus the

Exhibit 24.3   Discounted Cash Flows—Level Annuity

Discount rate = 10%

Year	Cash Flow		Discount Factor*		Present Value
1	$100,000	×	0.9091	=	$90,909
2	$100,000	×	0.8264	=	$82,645
3	$100,000	×	0.7513	=	$75,131
4	$100,000	×	0.6830	=	$68,301
5	$100,000	×	0.6209	=	$62,092
6	$100,000	×	0.5645	=	$56,447
7	$100,000	×	0.5132	=	$51,316
8	$100,000	×	0.4665	=	$46,651
9	$100,000	×	0.4241	=	$42,410
10	$1,100,000	×	0.3855	=	$424,098
Total					$1,000,000

* Figures in column rounded to four significant digits for display.

The present value of the income stream for each year can be calculated using the following algorithm (shown for Year 2):

	Keystrokes	Output	
1.	10 [i]	10.00	
2.	2 [n]	2.00	
3.	100,000 [CHS] [PMT]	-100,000.00	
4.	Solve for [PV] =	173,553.72	Present value for Year 1 + Year 2
5.	1 [n]	1.00	Change period to previous year
6.	Solve for [PV] =	90,909.09	
7.	[-]	82,644.63	Subtract present value for previous year

Note that in the calculation for Year 10, an additional step will be required between Steps 5 and 6, changing the Year 10 payment of $1,100,000 to the Year 9 payment of $100,000.

reversion of $1 million. Note that the total of the present value column is $1 million, as anticipated.

Estimation of a Yield Rate for Discounting

Unlike a capitalization rate, which can be extracted from market data, the yield rate that investors require cannot be mathematically extracted from compiled market data. An appraiser who knows what a group of investors paid for a property, how much income they received each year, and what the property sold for can calculate the yield on the investment. Researching comparable properties when that information is known might seem like the best way to support a yield rate. However, the following reasons explain why it is not:

1. The data is too old. If the investment has been bought, held for several years, and then sold, the amount of time that has passed precludes the transaction from use as a comparable of a current sale. In fact, if a property was purchased five years earlier at a price indicative of the future cash flows, the market would have to have stagnated for five years for this comparable to be useful.

2. The goal of the analysis is not how well the investment did but how well the investors thought it would do, which is what influenced their decision to put down the cash. Investors often project several different cash flow scenarios before buying a property. They usually ask "what if" several times, and eventually they decide based on their best projections. What actually does happen is usually different. Appraisers analyzing what current buyers would do must know what the investors think, not how lucky they were in their previous investments.

Different Rates

Sometimes the location and design of a property may make it a risky investment, but the tenant is not risky at all. In this situation, the rate used to discount the cash flows may need to be different for the periodic cash flows (usually from rent) and the reversion (resale). Using one discount rate for the cash flows and another for the reversion is not difficult. The calculations are straightforward and can even be done on a handheld calculator.

For example, a major US drugstore corporation arranged a "build-to-suit and leaseback" deal 10 years ago for a new drugstore building in an area of the city that has seen very little development or redevelopment. The properties in this area are not usually in great condition, but the chain still wanted a new building in this market. The corporation bought 1.5 acres of land in the area on a corner of two busy streets. The property cost $2.06 million to develop, including the land acquisition. The lease payments were based on a capitalization rate of 9.256%. Therefore, the rent was $190,673.60 per year ($2,060,000 × 0.09256) or $15,889 per month. The lease was written for 20 years with three 10-year renewal options. There are 10 years left on the initial lease.

Brokers and appraisers in this area have mixed opinions about the resale possibilities of this property. The store is not doing well, and some think a new buyer will be found quickly while others think the property will be boarded up for a long time. An appraiser who uses a high discount rate because of the neighborhood may be overcompensating for the risk because the cash flows for the next 10 years are fairly risk-free. The reversion is risky, but the cash flows are not. The investment analysis shown in Exhibit 24.4 assumes no appreciation in the value of the property since it was built.

The periodic cash flows are low risk because of the guarantees from the major corporation, so they were discounted at only 8%. The reversion/resale is very risky due to the neighborhood and was discounted at 14%. The present value of the cash flows was added to the present value of the reversion to get the indicated property value of $1.8 million.

Income Stream Patterns

Real estate deals are structured in many ways, so appraisers need to be able to read, interpret, and value many different patterns of cash flow streams. Several labels are used to describe these cash flow patterns, as shown in Exhibit 24.5.

Reversion

A reversion is the resale value of the property or the balloon payment of the mortgage. For investors, the reversion is the last cash flow they receive from the asset. Although it is treated like any other cash flow in the analysis, it is usually a much different amount than the periodic cash flows. The reversion of a real estate investment is often much more or much less than the going-in purchase price. If this amount is less than the amount of investment, the periodic payments must subsidize the reversion to recoup the initial investment. If the reversion is much more than the purchase price, part of the increase in the reversion is used to increase the yield over the term of the investment. In real estate, the reversion can be the difference between a good investment and a bad one. Investments in wasting assets like mining operations usually have low reversionary values. Properties like retail centers in developing areas are usually expected to have high appreciation rates.

In most discounted cash flow analyses, the reversion is calculated by the direct capitalization of the last year's income or by extending the analysis one more year and using that as the basis of capitalization. This is logical because the reversion would probably result from a sale to an investor based on the last year's cash flows or one year extended past the end of the projection period—i.e., the first year's income to the new owner. Once the gross sale price at the end of the projection period has been estimated, most appraisers discount this price to compensate for selling expenses. The reversion can also be estimated by sales comparison and cost analysis, but if the value is dated contemporaneously, they must be adjusted to the date of reversion.

If the subject property is a leased fee interest, the reversion will often be the fee simple interest at the end of the lease. Sometimes the property will still be subject to a lengthy lease, and the reversion will be a reflection of the lease income.

Discounting Models

Today, most appraisers simply enter projected cash flows into a spreadsheet program that calculates the present worth, but the process was not always so easy. To make this somewhat tedious task more manageable, certain techniques were developed that allowed appraisers to use algebra

Exhibit 24.4	Investment Analysis of Drugstore

Discount rate for the periodic cash flows = 8%

Year	Cash Flow		Discount Factor		Present Value
1	$190,674	×	0.925926	=	$176,550
2	$190,674	×	0.857339	=	163,472
3	$190,674	×	0.793832	=	151,363
4	$190,674	×	0.735030	=	140,151
5	$190,674	×	0.680583	=	129,769
6	$190,674	×	0.630170	=	120,157
7	$190,674	×	0.583490	=	111,256
8	$190,674	×	0.540269	=	103,015
9	$190,674	×	0.500249	=	95,384
10	$190,674	×	0.463193	= +	88,319

Present value of the periodic cash flows only $1,279,436

Discount rate for the reversion = 14%

10	$2,060,000	×	0.269744	= +	555,673
Total					$1,835,109

Keystrokes	Output	
8 [i]	8.00	
10 [n]	1.00	
190,674 [PMT]	190,674.00	
0 [FV]	0.00	
Solve for [PV] [CHS] =	1,279,438.06	Total present value of periodic cash flows
14 [i]	14.00	
10 [n]	10.00	
0 [PMT]	0.00	
2,060,000 [FV]	2,060,000.00	
Solve for [PV] =	-555,672.25	Reversion
Add PV of cash flows		
[CHS] [+] =	1,835,110.31	

Exhibit 24.5   Income Stream Patterns

Pattern	Characteristics	Valuation Techniques Used
Variable annuity—nonsystematic change	An income stream that is not regular or predictable.	It is very difficult to analyze with any technique except discounted cash flow (DCF) analysis.
Level annuity	An income stream that is the same each period, like a mortgage payment.	This income can be valued by DCF analysis or direct capitalization depending on the reversion value
Ordinary annuity	Payments are in arrears, like a mortgage.	Most real estate investments are valued as if in arrears.
Annuity payable in advance	Payments are made in advance of the period; annuity in advance is like a lease contract that indicates that payments are made in advance.	The present value of an ordinary annuity with payments in arrears can be converted to the present value in advance by multiplying the arrears number by $1 + I$. For example, if the present value of $15,000 per year for 10 years discounted at 8% in arrears is $100,651, the present value in advance would be $100,651 $\times$ 1.08 or $108,703.08. This can be confirmed on any handheld calculator by changing it from "End" to "Begin" mode.
Increasing or Decreasing Annuities		
Step-up or step-down annuities	Usually leases have steps up or down for a variety of reasons; these can be a result of expense increases or amortization of tenant improvements.	The only practical technique to value these income streams is the DCF model
Straight-line (constant-amount) change per period annuity	A cash flow that is increasing or decreasing on a straight-line basis (not compounded); the amount of change is the same dollar amount each period; this is like a lease that calls for the rent to go up $500 per year every year over the life of the lease.	These income streams can be valued by direct capitalization but are more easily valued by discounted cash flow analysis.
Exponential-curve (constant-ratio) change per period annuity	A cash flow that is going up or down on a compound basis; this is like a lease agreement that states the rent goes up 3% each year compounded annually.	This income stream can be valued by direct capitalization or using the DCF model.

and other statistical tools to estimate the value without discounting the cash flows individually. These techniques are classified into two types:

1. Income models, for investments that include only cash flows
2. Property models, for investments that include cash flows and property reversions

Keep in mind that these techniques were developed before modern computers were widely available, and what may seem like cumbersome techniques today actually made life easier for appraisers at the time.

Income Models

Variable or Irregular Income
The variable income model is the simple process of calculating the present value of future cash flows by applying the discount rate for the year that the cash flow occurred. In this case, there is

no formula or shortcut, so the cash flows for each year and the reversion must be calculated individually and added up. This can be done easily, though, with a number of spreadsheet programs and also on most financial calculators.

Level Income
If an investor can reasonably expect an unchanging stream of income over the projection period, that income stream can be capitalized by dividing the amount of income by a discount rate.

Straight-Line (Constant-Amount) Change per Period in Income
The present value of an investment with an income stream (but no reversion) that increases or decreases at a constant dollar amount each period can be calculated using the following formula:

$$\text{Present Value} = (d + h\,n)\,a_{\overline{n}|} - \frac{h(n - a_{\overline{n}|})}{i}$$

where d is the starting income at the end of the first period, h is the amount of change per period, and n is the number of periods. The symbol $a_{\overline{n}\rceil}$ stands for the present worth of a periodic payment, or $(1 - 1/S^n)/I$.

As an example, consider the present value of \$1 received each period for 27 years with a discount rate of 9%. In this example, the income increases \$0.05 per year, and the present worth of the periodic payment, $a_{\overline{n}\rceil}$, is 10.026580. The present value is calculated as follows:

$$PV = (1 - 0.05 \times 27)\,10.026580 - \frac{0.05\,(27 - 10.026580)}{0.09}$$

$$PV = 23.562463 - 9.429678$$

$$PV = 14.132785$$

Exhibit 24.6 shows the calculation of the individual cash flows that together add up to the value given by the present value formula.

Exhibit 24.6	Straight-Line Change

Discount rate = 9.00%

Year	Cash Flow		Discount Factor		Present Value
1	\$1.00	×	0.9174	=	\$0.91743
2	\$1.05	×	0.8417	=	\$0.88376
3	\$1.10	×	0.7722	=	\$0.84940
4	\$1.15	×	0.7084	=	\$0.81469
5	\$1.20	×	0.6499	=	\$0.77992
6	\$1.25	×	0.5963	=	\$0.74533
7	\$1.30	×	0.5470	=	\$0.71114
8	\$1.35	×	0.5019	=	\$0.67752
9	\$1.40	×	0.4604	=	\$0.64460
10	\$1.45	×	0.4224	=	\$0.61250
11	\$1.50	×	0.3875	=	\$0.58130
12	\$1.55	×	0.3555	=	\$0.55108
13	\$1.60	×	0.3262	=	\$0.52189
14	\$1.65	×	0.2992	=	\$0.49376
15	\$1.70	×	0.2745	=	\$0.46671
16	\$1.75	×	0.2519	=	\$0.44077
17	\$1.80	×	0.2311	=	\$0.41593
18	\$1.85	×	0.2120	=	\$0.39219
19	\$1.90	×	0.1945	=	\$0.36953
20	\$1.95	×	0.1784	=	\$0.34794
21	\$2.00	×	0.1637	=	\$0.32740
22	\$2.05	×	0.1502	=	\$0.30787
23	\$2.10	×	0.1378	=	\$0.28934
24	\$2.15	×	0.1264	=	\$0.27177
25	\$2.20	×	0.1160	=	\$0.25513
26	\$2.25	×	0.1064	=	\$0.23938
27	\$2.30	×	0.0976	=	\$0.22450
Total				=	\$14.13278

Exponential-Curve (Constant-Ratio) Change per Period in Income

The exponential-curve income model is used for assets that only have an income stream that increases or decreases at a compound rate each period. The formula is

$$\text{Present Value} = \frac{1 - \dfrac{(1 + x)^n}{(1 + i)^n}}{i - x}$$

where x represents the ratio of change in the income for any period.

Using the same discount rate of 9% for 27 years but with an increase per period of 4%, the calculations are as follows:

$$PV = \frac{1 - \dfrac{(1 + 0.04)^{27}}{(1 + 0.09)^{27}}}{0.09 - 0.04}$$

$$PV = \frac{1 - \dfrac{2.883369}{10.245082}}{0.05}$$

$$PV = \frac{1 - 0.281439}{0.05}$$

$$PV = 14.371213$$

Again, the individual cash flows are illustrated in Exhibit 24.7. And, again, this process is more easily performed with spreadsheet software than by calculating the individual cash flows.

Level-Equivalent Income

On occasion, appraisers need to estimate market rent on a level-equivalent basis. Any non-level income stream can be converted into a level-equivalent income by calculating the present value of the non-level income stream and then converting that amount into a level payment with the same present value. This calculation is also easily accomplished with any pattern of income using either a financial calculator or a computer.

Property Models

Income models are designed to allow appraisers to calculate the present value of a series of cash flows regardless of the reversion. Most real estate investments include some sort of reversion, so a more useful and realistic formula would have to include the reversion in the calculations. Property models were designed for several purposes:

- to value property when certain patterns of income and value change could be recognized
- to value property using direct capitalization if the appraiser knows the required yield and the pattern of income and value

Exhibit 24.7   Exponential-Curve Change

Discount rate = 9.00%

Year	Cash Flow		Discount Factor		Present Value
1	$1.00	×	0.9174	=	$0.91743
2	$1.04	×	0.8417	=	$0.87535
3	$1.08	×	0.7722	=	$0.83519
4	$1.12	×	0.7084	=	$0.79688
5	$1.17	×	0.6499	=	$0.76033
6	$1.22	×	0.5963	=	$0.72545
7	$1.27	×	0.5470	=	$0.69217
8	$1.32	×	0.5019	=	$0.66042
9	$1.37	×	0.4604	=	$0.63013
10	$1.42	×	0.4224	=	$0.60122
11	$1.48	×	0.3875	=	$0.57364
12	$1.54	×	0.3555	=	$0.54733
13	$1.60	×	0.3262	=	$0.52222
14	$1.67	×	0.2992	=	$0.49827
15	$1.73	×	0.2745	=	$0.47541
16	$1.80	×	0.2519	=	$0.45360
17	$1.87	×	0.2311	=	$0.43280
18	$1.95	×	0.2120	=	$0.41294
19	$2.03	×	0.1945	=	$0.39400
20	$2.11	×	0.1784	=	$0.37593
21	$2.19	×	0.1637	=	$0.35868
22	$2.28	×	0.1502	=	$0.34223
23	$2.37	×	0.1378	=	$0.32653
24	$2.46	×	0.1264	=	$0.31155
25	$2.56	×	0.1160	=	$0.29726
26	$2.67	×	0.1064	=	$0.28363
27	$2.77	×	0.0976	=	$0.27061
Total				=	$14.37121

- to estimate the yield rate of a property based on the extracted capitalization rate, R_O, if the pattern of income and property value is known

Again, these techniques have been largely replaced in the market with the computer-assisted spreadsheet analysis of cash flows.

Sometimes, income and property values increase or decrease at predictable rates. If these

> Income and property models were great techniques before computers and handheld financial calculators were available, but now this information is much easier to analyze by just entering the cash flows into a spreadsheet program and automatically discounting to present value.

factors can be projected, a capitalization or yield rate can be calculated based on those assumptions. In the direct capitalization of a single year's income, the overall capitalization rate is extracted from comparable sales that have projected income. This ratio is applied to the projected net operating income for the subject's next year.

The capitalization rate can also be estimated by adjusting the yield rate (Y_O) for the change in income or value. The general formula for calculating the capitalization rate (R_O) is

$$R = Y - \Delta a$$

where R stands for the capitalization rate, Y stands for the yield rate, and the symbol Δ stands for the change in income or value. The a represents a conversion factor known as the *annualizer* because the capitalization rate is an annual rate.

Remember that the capitalization rate (R) is a ratio of the first year's income to the value or sale price. The yield rate (Y) is the rate of return on the investment considering the price paid, the interim cash flows, and the reversion or resale of the asset. Therefore, this formula is saying that the ratio of one year's income to value can be calculated if you know the required yield in the market and the market's perception of what is going to happen to the income and property value reversion over time. The formula $R = Y - \Delta a$ is a general formula that is modified depending on the situation it is applied to.

Level Income
Capitalization in Perpetuity
If the income and property value are projected to remain unchanged, the capitalization rate is equal to the yield rate, therefore

$$R_0 = Y_0 - \Delta a$$

Assume the subject property is in a market where the yield required to attract investors is 10% and the annual income and property values are stable. The capitalization rate would then be calculated as follows:

$$R_0 = 0.10 - 0$$
$$R_0 = 0.10 \text{ or } 10\%$$

If there is no change in value (i.e., the investors get all of their money back at the end of the projection period) and there is no change in income levels (i.e., the first year's income is indicative of all future years), then the income divided by the amount of the investment equals the yield. If there is no change in property value or income, the capitalization rate is clearly equal to the yield rate. If the income or value is increasing, the yield rate is adjusted downward, which means the capitalization rate will be lower and the property will be worth more than if its income or value were not increasing.

Level Income with Change in Value

If the income of a property is level but the property value is increasing, it is still possible to calculate the capitalization rate based on the required yield rate. The following formula applies:

$$R_0 = Y_0 - (\Delta \times \text{Sinking Fund Factor})$$

This is the same formula as set for the earlier example, except that the annualizer is the *sinking fund factor* $(1/S_{\overline{n}})$. The sinking fund factor is the amount of money it takes to accumulate to $1 over the projection period with compound interest. It is easily calculated with a financial calculator.

If the yield rate is 10% and the property value change is +10% over five years, then

---

Exhibit 24.8   Level Income in Perpetuity

Analysis of property with level income and no change in value at 8%

Direct capitalization = $25,000/0.08 = $312,500

Year	Income	Discount Factor		Present Value
1	$25,000	×	0.925926 =	$23,148
2	$25,000	×	0.857339 =	$21,433
3	$25,000	×	0.793832 =	$19,846
4	$25,000	×	0.735030 =	$18,376
5	$25,000	×	0.680583 =	$17,015
6	$25,000	×	0.630170 =	$15,754
7	$25,000	×	0.583490 =	$14,587
8	$25,000	×	0.540269 =	$13,507
9	$25,000	×	0.500249 =	$12,506
10	$25,000	×	0.463193 =	$11,580
11	$25,000	×	0.428883 =	$10,722
12	$25,000	×	0.397114 =	$9,928
13	$25,000	×	0.367698 =	$9,192
13*	$312,500	×	0.367698 =	$114,906
Net present value				$312,500

* Reversion

Keystrokes	Output
8 [i]	8.00
13 [n]	13.00
25,000 [PMT]	25,000.00
312,500 [FV]	312,500.00
Solve for [PV] [CHS] =	312,500

$$R_0 = Y_0 - (\Delta \times 1/S_{\overline{n}})$$
$$R_0 = 0.10 - (0.10 \times 0.16380)$$
$$R_0 = 0.10 - 0.01638$$
$$R_0 = 0.08362$$

Algebraically, it has to be true that $Y_0 = R_0 - (\Delta \times 1/S_{\overline{n}})$, which means an appraiser who knows the capitalization rate and the income and value pattern could also calculate the yield to the investment. Exhibit 24.9 shows the calculations using the level income with change in value formula and the sum of the present value in each individual year.

Assume now that the overall capitalization rate is 0.08362. The formula could be rewritten as follows:

$$Y_0 = 0.08362 + (0.10 \times 0.16380)$$
$$Y_0 = 0.08362 + 0.01638$$
$$Y_0 = 0.1000$$

Exhibit 24.9   Analysis of Property with Level Income and Change in Value

$\Delta = 10\%$

$Y = 0.10$

$N = 5$ years

$R = Y - (\Delta \times 1/S_{\overline{n}})$

$R = 0.10 - (0.10 \times 0.16380)$

$R = 0.083620$

Direct capitalization: $25,000 / 0.083620 = $298,972

Year	Cash Flow	Discount Factor		Present Value (rounded)
1	$25,000	×	0.909090909 =	$22,727
2	$25,000	×	0.826446281 =	$20,661
3	$25,000	×	0.751314801 =	$18,783
4	$25,000	×	0.683013455 =	$17,075
5	$25,000	×	0.620921323 =	$15,523
5*	$328,869	×	0.620921323 =	$204,202
Net present value				$298,972

* The reversion was calculated as 125% of the present value or $298,972 × 1.10 = $328,869

Keystrokes	Output
10 [i]	10.00
5 [n]	5.00
25,000 [PMT]	25,000.00
Solve for [PV] [CHS] =	94,769.67
328,869 [FV]	328,869.00
0 [PMT]	0.00
Solve for [PV] =	-204,201.77
Add cash flows	
[CHS] [+]	298,971.44

This result clearly verifies the accuracy of the formula. However, an astute observer would recognize that to perform the second calculation, one would already have to know the answer because the sinking fund factor used (0.16380) is based on the yield rate. This calculation can be done without knowing the sinking fund factor, but it would be based on trial and error rather than a precise calculation. You would have to try several rates until you could narrow down the number, which is done automatically on most handheld calculators.

Also, if the yield rate was 10% and the capitalization rate was 12%, the formula could be used to determine the amount of change occurring each year:

$$\Delta = \frac{Y - R}{1/S_{\overline{n}}}$$

$$\Delta = \frac{0.10 - 0.12}{0.16380}$$

$$\Delta = \frac{-0.02}{0.1638}$$

$$\Delta = -0.1221 \text{ or } -12.21\%$$

There is a financial calculator shortcut for the above problem. The following keystrokes will calculate the capitalization rate:

Keystrokes	Output
f 5	0.00000
10 i	10.00000
5 n	5.00000
1 CHS PV	-1.00000
1.10 FV	1.10000
Solve for PMT =	0.08362

The capitalization rate can always be calculated using the PMT key with -1.00000 as the present value and 1.10000 (10% increase) as the future value.

Straight-Line (Constant-Amount) Changes in Income and Value

If the income and property value are increasing equally on a straight-line basis, it is still possible to calculate the capitalization rate based on the required yield rate. In this situation, the formula becomes

$$R_0 = Y_0 - (\Delta \times 1/n)$$

> The property model formulas are great tools for maintaining consistency within appraisal reports.

If the yield rate is 10% and the property value and income change is 10% over 10 years, then

$$R_0 = 0.10 - (0.10 \times 1/10)$$
$$R_0 = 0.10 - 0.01$$
$$R_0 = 0.09 \text{ or } 9\%$$

Also

$$Y_0 = 0.09 + (0.10 \times 1/10)$$
$$Y_0 = 0.09 + 0.01$$
$$R_0 = 0.10 \text{ or } 10\%$$

This technique is applicable in fewer situations because appraisers do not often anticipate that a property's income and value will increase on a linear (i.e., not compound) basis. If a property were under lease with step-up or step-down changes in the rental rate and the rental rate was the basis of the reversion as well, this scenario could apply. Exhibit 24.10 illustrates the analysis of a property with constant change in income and value.

The net present value of the cash flows and the reversion equals the calculation using the formula, confirming the accuracy of the formula. This analysis is not used often because most real estate investments do not have cash flows like this.

Exponential-Curve (Constant-Ratio) Changes in Income and Value

If the income and property value are increasing on a compound or constant-ratio basis, calculating the capitalization rate on the basis of the required yield rate is a very straightforward process. The formula is as follows:

$$R_0 = Y_0 - CR$$

where CR represents the constant ratio. If the yield rate is 10% and the property value and income change is 2% per year over the length of the investment, then

$$R_0 = 0.10 - 0.02$$
$$R_0 = 0.08 \text{ or } 8\%$$

Also

$$Y_0 = 0.08 + 0.02$$
$$Y_0 = 0.10 \text{ or } 10\%$$

This formula is easy to use, applicable in many situations, and can be much faster than applying discounted cash flow analysis. This is an excellent tool for evaluating capitalization (R_0) or yield rates (Y_0). If an appraiser states in a report that prices are increasing by 3% per year ($\Delta = 0.03$) and the yield rate is 8%, then the review

Exhibit 24.10   Constant Change in Income and Value

Increase in income and value = 35.00%

Income = $35,000

Projection period = 10 years

$Y = 0.08$

$R = Y - (\Delta \times 1/n)$

$R = 0.08 - (0.35 \times 0.10)$

$R = 0.08 - 0.035$

$R = 0.045$

Direct capitalization: $35,000 / 0.045 = $777,777

To calculate the amount of cash flow change each period, the following formula applies:

$$V \times (\Delta \times 1/n) \times Y = \text{the increase in cash flows}$$

$$\$777,777 \times (0.35 \times 0.10) \times 0.08 = \text{the increase in cash flows}$$

$$\$777,777 \times 0.035 \times 0.08 = \$2,177.78$$

Year	Initial Income		Income Change		Adjusted Income		Discount Factor		Present Value
1	$35,000				$35,000	×	0.9259259	=	$32,407
2	$35,000	+	$2,178	=	$37,178	×	0.8573388	=	$31,874
3	$35,000	+	$4,356	=	$39,356	×	0.7938322	=	$31,242
4	$35,000	+	$6,533	=	$41,533	×	0.7350299	=	$30,528
5	$35,000	+	$8,711	=	$43,711	×	0.6805832	=	$29,749
6	$35,000	+	$10,889	=	$45,889	×	0.6301696	=	$28,918
7	$35,000	+	$13,067	=	$48,067	×	0.5834904	=	$28,046
8	$35,000	+	$15,244	=	$50,244	×	0.5402689	=	$27,146
9	$35,000	+	$17,422	=	$52,422	×	0.5002490	=	$26,224
10	$35,000	+	$19,600	=	$54,600	×	0.4631935	=	$25,290
10	$1,050,000					×	0.4631935	=	$486,353
Net present value								=	$777,777

appraiser can expect to see a capitalization rate of around 5% because $R = Y - CR$, which means R = 8% − 3% = 5%.

As an example, assume the subject property is in an area where 8% yields are required. Properties are appreciating by 3% per year. Income is $35,000 per year, and it is also increasing at 3% per year. Exhibit 24.11 clearly shows that the constant-ratio formula works. The estimated value of the subject property is $700,000, and the sum of the present values of all of the cash flows is exactly $700,000 to the penny.

Note that with a projection period of 16 years, the reversion is calculated to be $1,123,294.51, or $700,000 × 1.03^{16}. If a shorter projection period was used, the cash flows would have less value, but the reversion ($940,741.47) arrives sooner and is therefore worth more in current dollars ($435,745.32), as shown in Exhibit 24.12. The value still works out to be the same number despite the shortened projection period.

Variable or Irregular Income and Value Changes

Discounted cash flow analysis, which is discussed in the following chapter, is usually necessary to account for income and expenses that do not follow a regular pattern.

Level-Equivalent Income

The level income property models (capitalization in perpetuity, etc.) work the same if the income stream is converted into a level-equivalent income stream from some other pattern. Suppose an industrial building's income is expected to increase at 3% over the next five years:

Year	Income	Present Value (@ 10%)
1	$50,000	$45,454.55
2	$52,500	$43,388.43
3	$55,125	$41,416.23
4	$57,881	$39,533.50
5	$60,775	$37,736.49

Exhibit 24.11 Constant-Ratio Change in Income and Value

$R = Y - CR$

$R = 0.08 - 0.03$

$R = 0.05$

Direct capitalization: $35,000/0.05 = $700,000

Year	Income	Reversion			Total Cash Flow		Discount Factor	Net Present Value
1	$35,000.00				$35,000.00	×	0.92592593	$32,407.41
2	$36,050.00				$36,050.00	×	0.85733882	$30,907.06
3	$37,131.50				$37,131.50	×	0.79383224	$29,476.18
4	$38,245.45				$38,245.45	×	0.73502985	$28,111.55
5	$39,392.81				$39,392.81	×	0.68058320	$26,810.08
6	$40,574.59				$40,575.59	×	0.63016963	$25,568.88
7	$41,791.83				$41,791.83	×	0.58349040	$24,385.13
8	$43,045.59				$43,045.59	×	0.54026888	$23,256.19
9	$44,336.95				$44,336.95	×	0.50024897	$22,179.51
10	$45,667.06				$45,667.06	×	0.46319349	$21,152.68
11	$47,037.07				$47,037.07	×	0.42888286	$20,173.39
12	$48,448.19				$48,448.19	×	0.39711376	$19,239.44
13	$49,901.63				$49,901.63	×	0.36769792	$18,348.73
14	$51,398.68				$51,398.68	×	0.34046104	$17,499.25
15	$52,940.64				$52,940.64	×	0.31524170	$16,689.10
16	$54,528.86	+	$1,123,294.51	=	$1,177,823.37	×	0.29189047	$343,795.42
Total =								$700,000.00

Exhibit 24.12 Constant-Ratio Change in Income and Value

Year	Income	Reversion			Total Cash Flow		Discount Factor	Net Present Value
1	$35,000.00				$35,000.00	×	0.92592593	$32,407.41
2	$36,050.00				$36,050.00	×	0.85733882	$30,907.06
3	$37,131.50				$37,131.50	×	0.79383224	$29,476.18
4	$38,245.45				$38,245.45	×	0.73502985	$28,111.55
5	$39,392.81				$39,393.81	×	0.68058320	$26,810.08
6	$40,574.59				$40,574.59	×	0.63016963	$25,568.88
7	$41,791.83				$41,791.83	×	0.58349040	$24,385.13
8	$43,045.59				$43,044.59	×	0.54026888	$23,256.19
9	$44,336.95				$44,336.95	×	0.50024897	$22,179.51
10	$45,667.06	×	$940,741.47*	=	$986,408.53	×	0.46319349	$456,898.01
								$700,000.00

* $700,000 × 1.0310 = $940,741.47

If the yield rate is 10%, the present value of the income stream is $207,529.20. Essentially, amortizing that amount over five years gives a level-equivalent income of $54,745.68. An overall capitalization rate can then be calculated using the level income property model, $R = Y - \Delta a$. Suppose the property value is expected to increase 8% over the five-year projection period. The capitalization rate is then calculated as follows:

$R = 0.12 - 0.08(0.15741) = 0.1074072$

The value of the property at a level-equivalent rate of 10.74% and level-equivalent income of $207,530 then becomes

$$V = \frac{I}{R} = \frac{207,530}{0.1074} = \$1,932,309$$

You will need a financial calculator to solve these review exercises.

1. An apartment complex has a net operating income (I_o) of $100,000. Both income and value are expected to increase gradually over the next 10 years at a compound rate of 2% per year. What is the market value if the yield rate necessary to attract investors is 10%? (Round to the nearest $50,000.)
   a) $1,100,000
   b) $1,150,000
   c) $1,200,000
   d) $1,250,000

2. What resale price is necessary to achieve a yield rate of 11% on the investment, given the following information:
   · Sale price = $150,000
   · Net operating income (level) = $7,000
   · Projection period = 5 years
   a) $200,000
   b) $210,000
   c) $220,000
   d) $230,000

Use the following information to solve Review Exercises 3 and 4.
The subject property has the following cash flows:
· $5,000 per year for the first three years
· $6,000 per year for the next five years
· $9,000 per year for the next five years
· $1.2 million reversion at the end of the lease

3. What is the market value of a leased fee interest in the subject if it is valued at a 9% yield as an ordinary annuity with annual accounting? (Round to the nearest $5,000.)
   a) $435,000
   b) $440,000
   c) $445,000
   d) $450,000

4. What is the market value if the cash flows are paid in advance? (Round to the nearest $5,000.)
   a) $435,000
   b) $440,000
   c) $445,000
   d) $450,000

5. The subject property has a projected level income of $30,000 for the next five years. The property value is expected to increase by 10% over the projection period of five years. The yield rate is 8%. What is the market value of the property? (Round to the nearest $50,000.)
   a) $450,000
   b) $500,000
   c) $550,000
   d) $600,000

6. A property was just sold for 25% more than its purchase price nine years ago. If the seller originally paid $750,000 and there was a level net operating income (I_o) of $59,000 over this period, what yield did the seller realize?
   a) 8%
   b) 9%
   c) 10%
   d) 11%

7. A property was purchased for $1,250,000. The net operating income (I_o) is $100,000. Both net operating income and value are expected to increase at a compound rate of 1% per year. What yield will be achieved if the property is held for 10 years?
   a) 9%
   b) 10%
   c) 11%
   d) 12%

8. What is the yield on the purchase of a leasehold position paying $25,000 per year for the next 25 years with payments at the end of the period if the purchase price is $175,300? (Round to the nearest full percentage point.)
   a) 13%
   b) 14%
   c) 15%
   d) 16%

9. A coal mine produces about $100,000 a year in net income. The consulting geologist indicated that the mine will produce that amount of money each year for 11 more years. At the end of the mining operation, the land will have no value except as a landfill. The value for that use should be about $100,000. Investors in this type of property require a yield of 9% on the investment. What is the value of the coal mine?
   a) $600,000
   b) $650,000
   c) $700,000
   d) $750,000

Note: Unless otherwise noted, italicized references indicate the pages in *The Appraisal of Real Estate*, 14th edition, that readers should consult for additional discussion of these topics.

1. **d) $1,250,000**

    Page 516

    $R_0 = Y_0 - CR$

    $R_0 = 0.10 - 0.02$

    $V = I/R = \$100,000 - 0.08 = \$1,250,000$

    Verification Using Cash Flow Analysis
    Based on Present Value of $1,250,000

Cash Flow	Amount Increasing 2% Annually	Financial Calculator Keystrokes
CF_0	0	0 [g] [CFo]
CF_1	100,000	100,000 [g] [CFj]
CF_2	102,000	102,000 [g] [CFj]
CF_3	104,040	104,040 [g] [CFj]
CF_4	106,121	106,121 [g] [CFj]
CF_5	108,243	108,243 [g] [CFj]
CF_6	110,408	110,408 [g] [CFj]
CF_7	112,618	112,618 [g] [CFj]
CF_8	114,869	114,869 [g] [CFj]
CF_9	117,166	117,166 [g] [CFj]
CF_{10}	119,509 + 1,523,743*	1,643,252 [g] [CFj]
Yield rate	10%	10 [i]
Solve for	$NPV =$	[f] [NPV] = 1,250,000

    * Reversion calculation based on original market value of $1,250,000 increasing at 2% per year:

    10 [n]
    2 [i]
    0 [PMT]
    1,250,000 [PV]
    Solve for [FV] = -1,523,743

2. **b) $210,000**

    This is easiest to solve on a financial calculator but can be done with formulas.

Formulas	Financial Calculator
$R_0 = I/V$	5 [n]
$R_0 = \$7,000/\$150,000$	11 [i]
$R_0 = 0.04667$	150,000 [CHS] [PV]
	7,000 [PMT]
$\Delta = (Y - R)/(1/S_n)$	Solve for [FV] = 209,164
$= (0.11 - 0.04667)/0.16057*$	
$\Delta = 0.06333/0.16057$	
$\Delta = 0.39441$	
$FV = \$150,000 \times (1 + \Delta)$	
$FV = \$150,000 \times 1.39441$	
$= \$209,162$	

    * Sinking fund factor for $n = 5$, $i = 11\%$

3. **b) $440,000**

Clear registers:	[f] [REG]
Set for end of period:	[g] [END]
	0 [CFo]
First three years:	5,000 [CFj]
	3 [Nj]
Next five years:	6,000 [CFj]
	5 [Nj]
Next four years:	9,000 [CFj]
	4 [Nj]
Last year's income (with reversion):	1,209,000 [CFj]
Yield rate:	9 [i]
Solve for [NPV] =	$439,660, rounded to $440,000

4. **c) $445,000**

Clear registers:	f REG
Set for beginning of period:	g BEG
First year:	5000 CFo
Second and third years:	5000 CFj
	2 Nj
Next five years:	6,000 CFj
	5 Nj
Next five years:	9,000 CFj
	5 Nj
Reversion:	1,200,000 CFj
Yield rate:	9 i
Solve for NPV =	$444,003, rounded to $445,000

5. **b) $500,000**

Calculate present value using income model:

$R_o = Y_o - \Delta\, 1/S_{\overline{n}}$

$= 0.08 - (0.10 \times 0.170456^*)$

$= 0.062954$

$V = I/R$

$= 30,000/0.062954$

$= 476,538$

$FV = PV + (PV \times 0.1) = PV \times (1 + 0.1)$

$= 476,538 \times 1.1$

$= 524,192$

Calculate future value using income stream and present value of property:

5 n

8 i

476,538 CHS PV

30,000 PMT

Solve for FV = 524,189

* Sinking fund factor for $n = 5$, $i = 8$

6. **c) 10%**

Term:	9 n
Original purchase price:	750,000 CHS PV
Level net operating income:	59,000 PMT
Current purchase price:	
750,000 × 1.25 =	937,500 FV
Solve for i =	9.7288, rounded to 10%

7. **a) 9%**

$R_o = 100,000/1,250,000$

$CR = 0.01$

$Y_o = R_o + CR$

$Y_o = 0.08 + 0.01$

$Y_o = 0.09$

8. **b) 14%**

Purchase price:	175,300 CHS PV
Payments to leasehold position:	25,000 PMT
Holding period:	25 n
Future value (no reversion of leasehold position):	0 FV
Calculate i =	13.68, rounded to 14%

9. **c) $700,000**

Annual net income:	100,000 PMT
Projection period for income stream:	11 n
Value of depleted mine as landfill:	100,000 FV
Yield rate:	9 i
Solve for PV =	-719,272, rounded to $700,000

25

Discounted Cash Flow Analysis and Investment Analysis

Applicability of DCF Analysis

Discounted cash flow (DCF) analysis requires appraisers to follow certain procedures, and these procedures have certain strengths and weaknesses.

- The current and future *potential gross income levels* of the property must be estimated. Both direct capitalization and the DCF model require first-year income and expense projections, but projections into the future are also required for the DCF model. As with any forecast, but especially in DCF analysis, these projections vary from one appraiser to another. In the direct capitalization procedure, only one year's income and expenses are estimated, but the appraiser puts all the emphasis of the analysis on that single year, which means a small error in that projection will become a large error in the conclusion. Multiple years are used in the DCF model, so any single year's projections have much less effect on the overall result. However, the fact that projections of changes in the income and expenses are needed leads to a divergence of opinions.

- Appraisers must project *vacancy and collection losses* for several years in discounted cash flow analysis. In the DCF model, the vacancy estimate may be correct for the first year but not for the second, third, or following years. If a new multitenant property is currently vacant, the first year's income may be negative, and the property may not become profitable for several years. Direct capitalization is worthless in this scenario because the negative cash flows in the beginning would imply a negative value for the property when in fact it is just

a normal lease-up period. The DCF model enables appraisers to put real numbers in for vacancy and derive a much more precise answer. For complicated properties or properties in transition, the estimation of vacancy and collection loss is the point at which the DCF analysis takes over as the technique of choice.

- Appraisers also have to estimate *expenses.* Again, this is the point at which DCF analysis is the superior technique because it allows appraisers to account for larger projected expenses in the years in which they will occur. In the direct capitalization calculation, appraisers have to anticipate the future expenses and then, in the case of capital items, create a reserve account to save money for the eventual expenditure. If a new roof covering will be needed in four years, the entire expense for that item can be put on that year's line in the DCF model. The property income may fall below zero that year as a result, but the DCF technique can accommodate that also. If the property has level income and predictable expenses, the direct capitalization calculation can work well; if the property has irregular cash flows or expenses, the DCF model is probably the only technique that can effectively handle that sort of input.

- In DCF analysis, appraisers must also convert the future net income estimates to a current lump-sum value by *discounting* each cash flow at the market rate. This process is almost all mathematical, and the calculations are simple except for the estimate and support of the correct discount rate. But the amount of

KEY TERMS	
discounted cash flow (DCF) analysis	payback period (*PB*)
	profitability index (*PI*)
internal rate of return (*IRR*)	time-weighted rate
net present value (*NPV*)	

numbers on a page is sometimes disconcerting to clients. The discount rate is difficult to obtain from comparable sales, so appraisers usually survey buyers in the market to see what yield rates are appropriate as of the date of appraisal. An estimate of a discount rate can be difficult to support, so many appraisers prepare cash flow projections using several rates to show the reader how much influence different rates have on the final value.

Investment Analysis

In addition to using discounted cash flow analysis to estimate the market value of a property, the technique can be used to help investors evaluate the income potential of investments they are thinking about making, investments they are already involved in, or investments they have held for a period of time and then liquidated.

Net Present Value and the Internal Rate of Return

The net present value of an investment is the sum of the present values of all the positive and negative cash flows associated with an investment. If investment analysis includes the purchase price, the amount of money (present value) that exceeds the sale price is the net present value of the investment at the specified discount rate, as shown in Exhibit 25.1.

The -$550,000 represents the purchase price and the $625,000 represents the cash flow from the resale of the asset. Because the sale price represents the cash flow at the beginning of the projection period, it was not discounted. In other words, $1 received today is worth $1 today. The first cash flow is shown at the end of the first year, which means the investors have to wait a year to receive that income. Since these calculations were made at an 8% discount rate, the results show how much more ($85,162) the buyers could have paid for the property and still received an 8% yield.

Exhibit 25.2 shows how, if the cash flows are known, the yield rate can be raised or lowered until the net present value is 0. When the net

Exhibit 25.1	Calculating Net Present Value

Discount rate = 8%

Year	Cash Flow		Discount Factor		Present Value
0	-$550,000*	×	1.000000	=	-$550,000
1	$35,000	×	0.925926	=	$32,407
2	$40,000	×	0.857339	=	$34,294
3	$45,000	×	0.793832	=	$35,722
4	$50,000	×	0.735030	=	$36,752
5	$51,000	×	0.680583	=	$34,710
6	$56,000	×	0.630170	=	$35,290
7	$60,000	×	0.583490	=	$35,009
8	$61,000	×	0.540269	=	$32,956
9	$64,000	×	0.500249	=	$32,016
10	$65,000	×	0.463193	=	$30,108
11	$49,000	×	0.428883	=	$21,015
12	$54,000	×	0.397114	=	$21,444
13	$55,000	×	0.367698	=	$20,223
14	$60,000	×	0.340461	=	$20,428
14	$625,000†	×	0.340461	=	$212,788
Net present value of the investment					$85,162

* Acquisition price

† Reversion

Exhibit 25.2	Calculating Net Present Value

IRR = 0.0973208

Year	Cash Flow		Discount Factor		Present Value
0	-$550,000	×	1.000000	=	-$550,000
1	$35,000	×	0.911311	=	$31,896
2	$40,000	×	0.830487	=	$33,219
3	$45,000	×	0.756831	=	$34,057
4	$50,000	×	0.689708	=	$34,485
5	$51,000	×	0.628539	=	$32,055
6	$56,000	×	0.572794	=	$32,076
7	$60,000	×	0.521993	=	$31,320
8	$61,000	×	0.475698	=	$29,018
9	$64,000	×	0.433508	=	$27,745
10	$65,000	×	0.395061	=	$25,679
11	$49,000	×	0.360023	=	$17,641
12	$54,000	×	0.328093	=	$17,717
13	$55,000	×	0.298994	=	$16,445
14	$60,000	×	0.272477	=	$16,349
14	$625,000	×	0.272477	=	$170,298
Net present value of the investment					$0

present value is 0, the discount rate is equal to the yield rate. After trying different discount rates and refining the model, the internal rate of return was set at 0.0973208 or 9.73208%, which is the discount rate at which the present value of the positive and negative cash flows equals 0.

Limitations and Pitfalls of the IRR

Appraisers usually do not have problems if the internal rate of return is used to value real estate with standard cash flows, but when the cash flows are both positive and negative and the absolute value of the cash flows is 0, the calculations may be misleading.

Reinvestment Concepts

If an investor receives a return on an investment (i.e., the yield), it is assumed that when the investor is given the cash then that investor is free to reinvest it in any other investment. All yields are calculated this way (e.g., stocks, bonds, and so on). In real estate, as in some other investments, there is another issue. If a property is a diminishing asset (such as coal or gravel mines or a residential subdivision development), part of the principal amount of the investment is returned during the "periods" as opposed to at the end. This raises the question of what an investor should do with a very small increment of the investment returned each period. Small investments seldom receive good yields, and the increments received each period may be too small to reinvest.

Discounted cash flow analysis also assumes that as the investors receive income from the investment, they can reinvest those funds at a fair rate or the money remains in the investment and continues to grow at the same rate. This factor is significant for real estate in which the cash flows are paid out and the investors must find another investment vehicle in which to put the return of the investment. For some investments, the amount of money paid to the investor can be left in the investment to earn compound interest, while other investments may not allow that reinvestment.

IRR with Investment

This variant of investment analysis assumes that certain reinvestment rates are applicable. This calculation allows appraisers to adjust for the partial payment of the yield during the projection period.

IRR with a Specified Borrowing Rate

When the cash flows of an investment are all positive, investors receive their money and do with it what they will. When the investment yields are negative, money must be borrowed to cover the shortfall. This analysis adjusts for that situation, which is common in new construction when a negative cash flow is normal for a while. This technique is not used often because cash flows do not stay negative for long in most real estate investments.

Other Measures of Performance

Payback Period

The payback period of an investment disregards the time value of money, which is the amount of time it takes to get the investment amount back. If an investor puts $100,000 into a property and the cash flows to equity are $10,000 per year, the payback period is 10 years. One investor may put a small down payment into a deal while another investor may contribute a lot more, and the payback period for each investor will be affected by that ratio.

In some markets, the payback period is a popular way of measuring investment performance. If buyers think this way, appraisers must give some consideration to this process even though it is not the best measure. An appraiser's job is to read the market behavior, not to establish it or adjust it. An example of payback period analysis is shown in Exhibit 25.3.

Profitability Index

The profitability index compares the present value of the future cash flows to the cost of acquiring the investment (see Exhibit 25.4). The formula most commonly used is

$$PI = \frac{\dfrac{CF_1}{(1+I)^1} + \dfrac{CF_2}{(1+I)^2} + \dfrac{CF_3}{(1+I)^3} + \dfrac{CF_4}{(1+I)^4} + \cdots}{CF_0}$$

Exhibit 25.3	Payback Period	

Amount invested = $1,250,000

Year	Annual Cash Flows	Running Total	
1	$142,589	$142,589	⎫
2	$146,268	$288,857	
3	$150,042	$438,899	
4	$153,913	$592,812	⎬ — Payback period
5	$157,884	$750,696	
6	$161,957	$912,653	
7	$166,135	$1,078,788	⎭
8	$170,422	$1,249,210	← Payback point
9	$174,819	$1,424,029	
10	$179,329	$1,603,358	

Exhibit 25.4   Profitability Index

Discount rate = 8.0%

Purchase price = $1,250,000

Year 1	Cash flow	$89,000	× 0.9259259	=	$82,407
Year 2	Cash flow	$97,500	× 0.8573388	=	$83,591
Year 3	Cash flow	$103,300	× 0.7938322	=	$82,003
Year 4	Cash flow	$109,800	× 0.7350299	=	$80,706
Year 5	Cash flow	$114,000	× 0.6805832	=	$77,586
Year 6	Cash flow	$116,300	× 0.6301696	=	$73,289
Year 7	Cash flow	$118,650	× 0.5834904	=	$69,231
Year 8	Cash flow	$119,850	× 0.5402689	=	$64,751
Year 9	Cash flow	$121,350	× 0.5002490	=	$60,705
Year 10	Cash flow	$123,850	× 0.4631935	=	$57,367
10	Reversion	$1,548,125	× 0.4631935	=	$717,081
Sum of the present values of the *CFs*					$1,448,717

Profitability index = $1,448,717/$1,250,000 = 1.16

Time-Weighted Rate

The time-weighted rate measures the performance of an investment assuming that the investment was paid for in full at the time of acquisition and no other funds were added later. This technique also assumes that all of the dividends are reinvested rather than taken out by the investor. This means that there are only two cash flows—the first being the initial cost of the investment and the second being at the end of the investment and including the resale. Reducing the number of cash flows in this way can make investment performance analysis less complicated.

The time-weighted rate is often used to measure the performance of mutual funds, but it is used less often for real estate investments.

1. What are primary uses of discounted cash flow (DCF) analysis?

    a) To calculate the future value and payment

    b) To calculate the present value and historical value

    c) To calculate the rate of return and future value

    d) To calculate the present value and rate of return

2. A property recently sold for $587,000, and the buyer indicated that he anticipated a 10-year holding period and used a 7% discount rate and a level net income of $64,000. What should have been the expected reversion at the time of resale?

    a) $270,465

    b) $587,000

    c) $1,000,000

    d) $1,155,000

3. A property earning $10,000 per year was purchased for $150,000 seven years ago. In this market, investors require a 7% annual yield rate. What will the property have to resell for in order to achieve this rate of return?

    a) $142,857

    b) $148,269

    c) $154,327

    d) $305,768

4. What is the internal rate of return on a real estate investment paying $10,000 per year for the next 20 years with payments at the end of the period if the purchase price is $71,306? There is no reversion on this investment.

    a) 12.75%

    b) 15.20%

    c) 16.24%

    d) 17.39%

5. What is the value of an investment that generates no periodic income but has a reversion of $456,000 in 12 years at a discount rate of 6%? Use end-of-year, annual calculations.

    a) $226,618

    b) $456,000

    c) $512,036

    d) $917,561

6. The subject property is a four-acre site that was leased 22 years ago for $1,000 per month, absolute net for 99 years. There were no improvements at that time, but there is a 35,000-sq.-ft. office building on it now that was built by the tenant. This area is quite popular now and probably will be in the future. The typical holding period for a leased property like this is 20 years. The value of the property would be based on a terminal capitalization rate of 8%. What is the value of the leased fee using a 6% discount rate? Assume that there are no sales costs on the reversion.

    a) $150,000

    b) $184,000

    c) $186,000

    d) $200,000

7. What is the internal rate of return for a property that was purchased for $450,000; had net operating incomes of $45,000, $52,000, $56,000, $56,000, $56,000 and $60,000 per year; and was sold for $407,000 at the end of the sixth year? The periodic cash flows are payable in arrears. Round your answer to the nearest percent.

    a) 9%

    b) 10%

    c) 11%

    d) 12%

8. Calculate the value of a property with the following cash flows and reversion:

    · $5,000 per year for the first three years

    · $6,000 per year for the next five years

    · $9,000 per year for the next five years

    · $1.2 million reversion at the end of the lease

    The required yield rate is 11%.

    a) $321,261

    b) $351,884

    c) $1,137,703

    d) $1,290,000

9. Calculate the value of the subject property based on the following cash flows: The cash flows start at $34,000 per year for two years but then increase by $5,000 for five years, and again by $5,000 for five years. There is an option to purchase at the end of the lease for $500,000, which is expected to be exercised because the tenant has invested $500,000 in tenant improvements. This is a low-risk investment because of the lease and almost guaranteed reversion, so the discount rate is 7.0%.

    a) $486,000

    b) $492,000

    c) $535,500

    d) $983,000

Note: Unless otherwise noted, italicized references indicate the pages in *The Appraisal of Real Estate*, 14th edition, that readers should consult for additional discussion of these topics.

1. **d) To calculate the present value and rate of return**
   Page 529

2. **a) $270,465**
   The correct keystrokes for the HP-12C are:
   10 [n]
   7 [i]
   587,000 [CHS] [PV]
   64,000 [PMT]
   Solve for [FV] = 270,465

3. **c) $154,327**
   The correct keystrokes for the HP-12C are:
   10,000 [PMT]
   150,000 [CHS] [PV]
   7 [n]
   7 [i]
   Solve for [FV] = 154,327

4. **a) 12.75%**
   The correct keystrokes for the HP-12C are:
   10,000 [PMT]
   20 [n]
   71,306 [CHS] [PV]
   0 [FV]
   Solve for [i] = 12.7525

5. **a) $226,618**
   The correct keystrokes for the HP-12C are:
   12 [n]
   6 [i]
   0 [PMT]
   456,000 [FV]
   Solve for [PV] = -226,618

6. **b) $184,000**
   The correct keystrokes for the HP-12C are:
   12,000/0.08 = 150,000 (resale value)
   20 [n]
   6 [i]
   12,000 [PMT]
   150,000 [FV]
   Solve for [PV] = 184,410

7. **c) 11%**
   The correct keystrokes for the HP-12C are:
   450,000 [CHS] [g] [CFo]
   45,000 [g] [CFj]
   52,000 [g] [CFj]
   56,000 [g] [CFj]
   3 [g] [Nj]
   467,000 [g] [CFj]
   Solve for [IRR] = 10.65

8. **b) $351,884**

The correct keystrokes for the HP-12C are:

[f] [CLx]

5,000 [g] [CFⱼ]

3 [g] [Nⱼ]

6,000 [g] [CFⱼ]

5 [g] [Nⱼ]

9000 [g] [CFⱼ]

4 [g] [Nⱼ]

9,000 + 1,200,000 = 1,209,000 [g] [CFⱼ]

11 [i], solve for [NPV] = 351,884

9. **c) $535,500**

The correct keystrokes for the HP-12C are:

[f] [CLx] 34,000 [g] [CFⱼ]

2 [g] [Nⱼ]

39,000 [g] [CFⱼ]

5 [g] [Nⱼ]

44,000 [g] [CFⱼ]

4 [g] [Nⱼ]

544,000 [g] [CFⱼ]

7 [i]

Solve for [f] [NPV] = 535,497.64 (This is the answer if the income is capitalized at 7%.)

26

Applications of the Income Capitalization Approach

Example of Reconstructed Operating Statement

To analyze the eight-unit apartment property represented by the reconstructed operating statement in Exhibit 26.1, a ratio model analysis (i.e., capitalization of a single year's income) is used.

Several large expenditures are anticipated. To accommodate these future capital expenses in each year of the reconstructed operating statement, an annual deduction can be made. This deduction will equal the amount that, if deposited in a savings account, will grow to the replacement cost of the item by the time it is scheduled to be replaced. The annual expense can be estimated with most standard financial calculators.

Property owners rarely set aside reserves for replacement, so an appraiser must make sure that the overall capitalization rate derived from the market reflects the same operating expenses—including similar allotments for reserves. That is, if the reconstructed operating statement of the subject property includes line items for certain replacement allowances, then the comparable properties analyzed to develop an overall capitalization rate for similar properties in the market should also include those reserve expenses in the net operating income data used in the calculation of capitalization rates. The 9% capitalization rate used in Exhibit 26.1 was derived from income and expense data for properties with the same listed operating expenses, including

Exhibit 26.1	Income Capitalization Approach Calculations for an Eight-Unit Property

Reconstructed Operating Statement

Rental income	8 units @ $650 × 12 =	$62,400
Other income (vending)		+ 1,200
Potential gross income (*PGI*)		$63,600
Vacancy and collection loss	5% of *PGI*	− 3,180
Effective gross income (*EGI*)		**$60,420**
Expenses		
Taxes		$4,500.00
Insurance		1,800.00
Utilities (water, sewer, electricity)		3,400.00
Maintenance (scheduled)		3,600.00
Maintenance (miscellaneous repairs)		2,500.00
Management (5% of *EGI*)		2,166.00
Reserve for roof shingles and gutters—15 years	$5,600 × 1/15 =	373.33
Reserve for parking lot resurfacing—12 years	$4,600 × 1/12 =	383.33
Reserve for HVAC system—15 years	$6,500 × 1/15 =	+ 433.33
Total expenses		$19,156.00 = − 19,156
Net operating income (I_o)		**= $41,264**
	I_o/capitalization rate = value	
Value conclusion	$41,264/0.09 = $458,489	

reserves for roof replacement, parking lot repair, and HVAC system replacement.

Forecasting in DCF Analysis

Exhibit 26.2 illustrates how DCF analysis can work. Notice that the vacancy loss for the retail center is very high in the first year and decreases in later years. This situation is similar to a new building or a building that has lost a major tenant. Consider the difficulty of capitalizing a single year's income in this situation.

The cells in the grid shown in red font are the properties under lease during that year. The line at the top labeled "rollover rate" is used to calculate and track the market rent per square foot over time. This is needed in a spreadsheet so that the analyst has a cell with the market rate each year for use in calculations of the rent when the leases end and a new lease is assumed. Of course, options within a lease will often establish a rollover rate. Appraisers will often also have to estimate the probability of renewal. If a tenant renews at a previously negotiated rate, that rate may be much different than the market rate at that time. For example, a lease says the tenant can renew for five more years at $22 per square foot, but the market rate is only $19 per square foot. What should the appraiser assume will happen? This is a difficult question with multiple scenarios: tenants may accept higher rates because they do not want to move, they may renegotiate the rate with a threat to move, or they may just move.

The reversion was based on the sixth year's income, which was used to calculate the reversion but not included as a cash flow. In other words, to estimate the resale of the property, the analyst assimilated the buyer's actions at that time and capitalized a single year's income for the following year. Most appraisers avoid putting one-time capital expenses in the resale year because it falsely overstates expenses as a reflection of the future income.

As can easily be seen in Exhibit 26.2, there are projections on nearly every line. The ability to support the amount forecast is important, but the ability to support the estimate of increases is also important. In this case, most of the increases have been calculated at 3%, which is very close to the rate of inflation in building costs in this area. If the appraiser stays close to these numbers, few people will challenge the estimates. However, if the appraiser projects 5% increases in rents but only

a 1% increase in expenses in a market with 3% inflation, eyebrows will be raised. Forecasts must be consistent and well explained. This situation is possible if the property was undervalued, poorly managed, and overcharged for expenses, but a long discussion of the market and property conditions would be needed to squelch the skeptics.

Potential Gross Income

In Exhibit 26.2, the first projections refer to the potential gross income estimate. In this case, there were seven tenants with four suites currently leased and occupied, leaving three vacant. In this market, it is common for a retail tenant to sign a five-year lease with a renewal option based on a CPI adjustment. It is not difficult to project that the tenant's lease rate will be flat and then will increase to the market rate, which assumes a 3% increase per year compounded. The years in which the current tenants in the subject property are subject to leases appear in red in the grid to show the lease term. Because it is not known which suite will lease when, the rents are increased each year. This may overstate the income a little if a flat five-year lease was assumed in each new lease. This projection does not assume one suite each year but an average of 735 square feet each year. Different markets mean different practices, and the analysis must be adapted to the situation. The discounted cash flow analysis is very adaptable to nearly every situation.

Vacancy and Collection Loss

The forecast of vacancy and collection (V&C) loss is the point at which the DCF analysis gives appraisers an easy and reasonable answer. Direct capitalization is limited here because an estimate of one year's vacancy and collection loss is not usually indicative of several future years. The estimate is best supported by the subject's recent history or the losses incurred by comparable properties in this area. Vacancy and collection losses can start as a large amount that slowly diminishes over the following years. This estimate is going to be a combination of data research, the appraiser's knowledge of the local market, and some experience in the market.

Effective Gross Income

Of course, the effective gross income estimate is simply a calculation based on the appraiser's estimate of potential gross income and vacancy and collection loss.

Exhibit 26.2 Discounted Cash Flow Analysis of a Small Retail Center

Tenant	Sq. Ft.	Leased	Rate	Year 1	Year 2	Year 3	Year 4	Year 5	Year 6
Estimated market (rollover) rate =			2.0%	$20.00	$20.40	$20.81	$21.22	$21.65	$22.08
Tenant A	1,500	1,500	$19.00	28,500	28,500	28,500	31,836	32,473	33,122
Tenant B	1,500	0	vacant	30,000	30,600	31,212	31,836	32,473	33,122
Tenant C	1,500	1,500	$19.50	29,250	30,600	31,212	31,836	32,473	33,122
Tenant D	1,500	1,500	$19.25	28,875	30,600	31,212	31,836	32,473	33,122
Tenant E	1,500	0	vacant	30,000	30,600	31,212	31,836	32,473	33,122
Tenant F	1,500	0	vacant	30,000	30,600	31,212	31,836	32,473	33,122
Tenant G	1,500	1,500	$18.50	27,750	27,750	27,750	31,386	32,473	33,122
Totals	10,500	6,000	57%						
Other income and pass-throughs =				10,000	10,200	10,404	10,162	10,824	11,041
Potential gross income =				$214,375	$219,450	$222,714	$233,014	$238,135	$242,898
Vacancy loss		Decrease	7.00%	-42.9%	-35.9%	-28.9%	-21.9%	-14.9%	-7.9%
Collection loss				-1.0%	-1.0%	-1.0%	-1.0%	-1.0%	-1.0%
Total vacancy and collection loss				-43.9%	-36.9%	-29.9%	-22.9%	-15.9%	-8.9%
Effective gross income				**$120,356**	**$138,567**	**$156,218**	**$180,102**	**$200,374**	**$221,384**
Expense Items Rate of increase in expenses =			3.00%						
Administrative			$0.02	$210	$216	$223	$229	$236	$243
All utilities (adjusted for occupancy)			$1.50	9,000	10,406	11,877	13,415	15,019	16,689
Management expense			5.0% of *EGI*	6,018	6,928	7,811	9,005	10,019	11,069
Advertising, promotion			$0.04	420	433	446	459	473	487
Salaries and commissions			$0.25	2,625	2,704	2,785	2,868	2,954	3,043
Insurance			$0.25	2,625	2,704	2,785	2,868	2,954	3,043
Taxes and licenses			$1.25	13,125	13,519	13,924	14,342	14,772	15,215
Maintenance			$1.35	14,175	14,600	15,038	15,489	15,954	16,433
Contract cleaning (adj. for occupancy)			$1.00	6,000	6,937	7,918	8,943	10,013	11,126
Total operating expenses				**$54,198**	**$58,446**	**$62,807**	**$67,620**	**$72,395**	**$77,350**
Operating expenses per square foot				$5.16	$5.57	$5.98	$6.44	$6.89	$7.37
Buildout and leasing expenses	**Sq. Ft.**		**Rate**	**Year 1**	**Year 2**	**Year 3**	**Year 4**	**Year 5**	**Year 6**
Repainting/carpets (existing)	1,000		$4.00	$4,000	$4,000	$4,000	$4,000	$4,000	$0
New space buildout	735		$20.00	14,700	14,700	10,000	10,000	10,000	0
Leasing commissions	735		$4.00	2,940	2,940	2,000	2,000	2,000	0
Reserves for HVAC, etc.			2.50% of *EGI*	3,009	3,464	3,905	4,503	5,009	0
Total capital items				**$24,649**	**$25,104**	**$19,905**	**$20,503**	**$21,009**	**$0**
Capital items total per square foot				$2.35	$2.39	$1.90	$1.95	$2.00	$0.00
Total all expenses				**$78,847**	**$83,551**	**$82,713**	**$88,123**	**$93,404**	**$77,350**
Net operating income				**$41,510**	**$55,016**	**$73,505**	**$91,979**	**$106,969**	**$144,034**

The reversion of the property is estimated via a terminal capitalization rate of: 10.00% of the last year's income less selling expenses (7%)

Reversion of property =									$1,339,520
Cash flow with reversion				$41,510	$55,016	$73,505	$91,979	$1,446,490	
Discounted @			10.0%	0.909091	0.826446	0.751315	0.683013	0.620921	**Value**
Present value of cash flow				$37,736	$45,468	$55,226	$62,823	$898,156	$1,099,409

Note: Columns may not sum due to rounding.

Expenses

The estimation of expenses is also a strength of the DCF model. This technique allows appraisers to estimate and place large, unusual, or one-time charges in the years in which they occur or to reserve uncertain charges, as in direct capitalization. Overall expenses usually increase at a similar rate as the income, but sometimes expenses may increase more than income. For example, if occupancy is low but expected to increase, this increase in occupancy would be at odds with increasing rental rates.

Fixed expenses usually run with the rate of inflation, but they can be affected by the local environment. A property may have stiff increases in taxes or insurance while other expenses are much less volatile. The DCF model allows appraisers the most flexibility to account for increases or decreases in variable expenses. The DCF technique also allows appraisers to tie expenses such as janitorial, utilities, and maintenance expenses to future occupancy amounts. Expenses for tenant improvements, the build-out of new space, commissions, and capital improvements are often tied to the absorption rate of vacant space. In Exhibit 26.2, most of the expenses increased at a rate of 3% per year except for management, which is usually tied to collected rents and other income.

Discounting

The discount rate should represent the required yield for investors in the subject's market. Since the discount rate can vary depending on who you talk to, it is advisable to run through the DCF model with two or more discount rates, which shows the reader what the variance would be if the rate were higher or lower.

Case Study: Analysis of an Office Building Investment

The subject is a small, multitenant office building with six tenants and one vacant suite. Leases in this market are typically written for five years at a flat rate, with the tenant paying the increases in expenses over a base year. The base year is established within the first year of the lease based on a percentage of total expenses divided by the tenant's percentage of space. These are all full-service leases. The market rents are increasing by 3% compounded annually.

- Suite 100, comprising 2,500 square feet, is leased to a computer hardware distributor on a five-year lease with two years left. The flat rate is $62,500 per year ($25 per square foot per year). There is a high likelihood of a renewal for another five years. If the tenant renews, the market rate should be applicable because the tenant improvements (TIs) would be amortized with little up-front expense. This space has better-than-average finish and features and is right off the lobby, which generally commands a slightly higher rent. Considering the lack of tenant improvement expenses, the space should be renewed at the market rate.

- Suite 101, comprising 3,900 square feet, is leased to an electronic reproduction firm on a seven-year lease at a flat rate of $103,350 per year ($26.50 per square foot per year). This lease has seven years left to run. This space also has better-than-average finish and features. This space is nicer and off the lobby as well, but if the tenant renews, the TIs have been amortized so there will be few up-front expenses with the lease.

- Suite 112 has 4,600 square feet and is vacant. It should lease within a year at or near $25.00 per square foot per year with standard finishing. This space is assumed to be of average finish at that rate. TIs with average finish cost about $20.00, all things considered. A new lease can be assumed to be for five years, and it will roll over at the market rate.

- Suite 114, comprising 4,000 square feet, is leased to a consumer products manufacturer on a five-year lease with only one year left to run. The lease rate is $21.00 per square foot per year, but with only one year to go a big increase in rent and probably some TI expenses are anticipated. This company may or may not stay. The probability of renewal is about 25%.

- Suite 205, comprising 5,000 square feet on the second floor, is leased to an auto manufacturer on a five-year lease with four years remaining at a flat rate of $24.00 per square foot per year. This

company may stay or go when its lease runs out. The landlord thinks there is only a 25% chance of a renewal because the tenant already says it does not need all the space it has. The finish is standard.

- Suite 210, comprising 5,000 square feet on the second floor, is leased to a real estate investment company for five years with four years left. This space also has standard finish and features, and there is an estimated 25% probability of lease renewal because the company just bought an office building site nearby. This lease is at $23.50 per square foot.

- Suite 215 comprises 5,000 square feet on the second floor, and it is leased to a soft drink distributor for five years with only two years left. This space has standard finish. The tenant is fairly happy in the building but not happy with the configuration of the space. There is a high likelihood the tenant will stay, but major expenditures to reconfigure the suite will be needed.

Because the leases are flat rate for several years, there is a fairly large amount of pass-through income. The first year it should equal about $49,000 and increase by about 3% compounded each year. Vacancy should be 5% for Years 1, 2, and 6, and 10% for Years 3, 4, and 5 due to rollovers. The collection loss is estimated at only 1% per year because of the quality of the tenants. The suites with leases in place during the lease period are shown in red in the reconstructed operating statement.

Expenses are listed in the grid. Most are increasing by 3% per year. Tenant improvements are a function of the leases, rollovers, and probability of renewal. Leasing commissions are generally 4% of the total lease amount, and the leases are usually five years. No one in this market pays leasing commissions on renewals. The building will need $25,000 for a new roof in the second year, $35,000 for new HVAC units in the third year, and $42,000 for parking lot resurfacing in the sixth year.

Discount rates on properties like this are generally between 8% and 9%. The terminal capitalization rate (used to estimate the reversion in the fifth year) is 9%. The mathematical formula to find the appropriate discount factor is $1/(1+i)^N$. The holding period for this type of investment is five to eight years with some periods as short as three years. A review of recent sales found that 60% were held for nearly five years.

All the blank spaces in the reconstructed operating statement shown on the following page can be filled in using the information provided above. The Year 1 figures are provided as a starting point.

	Sq. Ft.	Leased	Rate	Year 1	Year 2	Year 3	Year 4	Year 5	Year 6*
Suite 100	2,500	2,500	25.00	62,500	_____	_____	_____	_____	_____
Suite 101	3,900	3,900	26.50	103,350	_____	_____	_____	_____	_____
Suite 112	4,600	0	25.00	115,000	_____	_____	_____	_____	_____
Suite 114	4,000	4,000	21.00	84,000	_____	_____	_____	_____	_____
Suite 205	5,000	5,000	24.00	120,000	_____	_____	_____	_____	_____
Suite 210	5,000	5,000	23.50	125,000	_____	_____	_____	_____	_____
Suite 215	5,000	5,000	22.00	110,000	_____	_____	_____	_____	_____
Total >>>	30,000	25,400	84.67%						

			Year 1	Year 2	Year 3	Year 4	Year 5	Year 6*
Pass-through =			$49,000	_____	_____	_____	_____	_____
Potential gross income =			768,850	_____	_____	_____	_____	_____
Estimated market (roll over) rate =			$25.00	_____	_____	_____	_____	_____
Vacancy loss			-6%	_____	_____	_____	_____	_____
Effective gross income			$722,719	_____	_____	_____	_____	_____

Expense items (Rate of increase in expenses = 3.00%)

		Year 1	Year 2	Year 3	Year 4	Year 5	Year 6*
All utilities	$1.50/occupied sq. ft.	42,750	_____	_____	_____	_____	_____
Management expense	5.00% of *EGI*	36,136	_____	_____	_____	_____	_____
Maintenance salary	$0.50/sq. ft.	15,000	_____	_____	_____	_____	_____
Taxes, insurance, and licenses	$1.25/sq. ft.	37,500	_____	_____	_____	_____	_____
Maintenance (snow, trash, etc.)	$0.75/sq. ft.	22,500	_____	_____	_____	_____	_____
Contract cleaning, etc.	$1.50/occupied sq. ft.	42,750	_____	_____	_____	_____	_____
Supplies (HVAC, janitorial, etc.)	$0.50/sq. ft.	15,000	_____	_____	_____	_____	_____
Total expenses from operations		$211,636	_____	_____	_____	_____	_____
Operating expenses per sq. ft.		$7.05	_____	_____	_____	_____	_____

Build-out and leasing expenses

	Year 1	Year 2	Year 3	Year 4	Year 5	Year 6*
New space build-out	$92,000	_____	_____	_____	_____	_____
Leasing commissions	$23,000	_____	_____	_____	_____	_____
Capital replacements (HVAC, roof)	_____	_____	_____	_____	_____	_____
Total build-out/reserves expense	$115,000	_____	_____	_____	_____	_____
Build-out per sq. ft. GFA	$3.83	_____	_____	_____	_____	_____
Total all expenses	$326,636	_____	_____	_____	_____	_____
All expenses per sq. ft.	$10.89	_____	_____	_____	_____	_____
Income overall (I_o)	$396,083	_____	_____	_____	_____	_____

The reversion of the property is estimated by applying a terminal cap rate of 9% to the last year's income less selling expenses

Reversion of property = _____

Cash flows with reversion

	Year 1	Year 2	Year 3	Year 4	Year 5	Year 6*
	$396,083	_____	_____	_____	_____	_____
Discounted at 8.0%	0.925926	0.857339	0.793832	0.735030	0.680583	**Value**
Present value	$366,744	_____	_____	_____	_____	_____
Discounted at 9.0%	0.917431	0.841680	0.772183	0.708425	0.649931	**Value**
Present value	$363,379	_____	_____	_____	_____	_____

* Year 6 *NOI* is used to calculate the reversion at the end of Year 5.

Case Study

The reconstructed operating statement that follows is one possible solution; it is not the only solution.

	Sq. Ft.	Leased	Rate	Year 1	Year 2	Year 3	Year 4	Year 5	Year 6*
Suite 100	2,500	2,500	25.00	62,500	62,500	66,307	66,307	66,307	66,307
Suite 101	3,900	3,900	26.50	103,350	103,350	103,350	103,350	103,350	103,350
Suite 112	4,600	0	25.00	115,000	115,000	115,000	115,000	115,000	133,317
Suite 114	4,000	4,000	21.00	84,000	100,000	100,000	100,000	100,000	100,000
Suite 205	5,000	5,000	24.00	120,000	120,000	120,000	120,000	140,689	140,689
Suite 210	5,000	5,000	23.50	125,000	125,000	125,000	125,000	140,689	140,689
Suite 215	5,000	5,000	22.00	110,000	110,000	132,613	132,613	132,613	132,613
Total >>>	30,000	25,400	84.67%						
Pass-through =				$49,000	$50,470	$51,984	$53,544	$55,150	$56,804
Potential gross income =				$768,850	$786,320	$814,253	$815,813	$853,796	$873,767
Estimated market (roll over) rate =				**$25.00**	**$25.75**	**$26.52**	**$27.32**	**$28.14**	**$28.98**
Vacancy loss				-6%	-6%	-11%	-11%	-11%	-6%
Effective gross income				$722,719	$739,141	$724,685	$726,073	$759,879	$821,341
Expense items (Rate of increase in expenses = 3.00%)									
All utilities		$1.50/occupied sq. ft.		$42,750	$44,033	$42,966	$44,255	$45,583	$49,559
Management expense		5.00% of *EGI*		$36,136	$36,957	$36,234	$36,304	$37,994	$41,067
Maintenance salary		$0.50/sq. ft.		$15,000	$15,450	$15,914	$16,391	$16,883	$17,389
Taxes, insurance, and licenses		$1.25/sq. ft.		$37,500	$38,625	$39,784	$40,977	$42,207	$43,473
Maintenance (snow, trash, etc.)		$0.75/sq. ft.		$22,500	$23,175	$23,870	$24,586	$25,324	$26,084
Contract cleaning, etc.		$1.50/occupied sq. ft.		$42,750	$44,033	$42,966	$44,255	$45,583	$49,559
Supplies (HVAC, janitorial, etc.)		$0.50/sq. ft.		$15,000	$15,450	$15,914	$16,391	$16,883	$17,389
Total expenses from operations				$211,636	$217,723	$27,648	$223,160	$230,457	$244,520
Operating expenses per sq. ft.				$7.05	$7.26	$7.25	$7.44	$7.68	$8.15
Build-out and leasing expenses									
New space build-out				$92,000	$60,000	$112,500	$0	$150,000	$46,000
Leasing commissions				$23,000	$20,000	$39,784	$0	$56,275	$0
Capital replacements (HVAC, roof)				$0	$25,000	$35,000	$0	$42,000	$0
Total build-out/reserves expense				$115,000	$105,000	$187,284	$0	$248,275	$46,000
Build-out per sq. ft. GLA				$3.83	$3.50	$6.24	$0.00	$8.28	$1.53
Total all expenses				$326,636	$322,722	$404,932	$223,160	$478,731	$290,520
All expenses per sq. ft.				$10.89	$10.76	$13.50	$7.44	$15.96	$9.68
Income overall (I_o)				$396,083	$416,419	$319,753	$502,913	$281,147	$530,822

The reversion of the property is estimated by applying a terminal cap rate of 9% to the last year's income less selling expenses

		Year 1	Year 2	Year 3	Year 4	Year 5	
Reversion of property =							$5,485,157
Cash flows with reversion		$396,083	$416,419	$319,753	$502,913	$5,766,305	
Discounted at 8.0%		0.925926	0.857339	0.793832	0.735030	0.680583	**Value**
Present value		$366,744	$357,012	$253,831	$369,656	$3,924,450	$5,271,693
Discounted at 9.0%		0.917431	0.841680	0.772183	0.708425	0.649931	**Value**
Present value		$363,379	$350,491	$246,908	$356,277	$3,747,703	$5,064,758

* Year 6 *NOI* is used to calculate the reversion at the end of Year 5.

Issues for further thought and discussion involve the following areas of the reconstructed operating statement:

1. First year's projection of income
   - How to make the estimate on a "per square foot of GBA" basis, percentages, etc.
2. First year's projection of expenses
   - How to make the estimate on a "per square foot of GBA" basis, percentages, etc.
3. First year's projection of tenant improvements and capital expenses
   - How to make the estimate on a "per square foot of GBA" basis, percentages, etc.
4. Following years' projections of income
   - Rate of increase as a function of inflation
   - Rate of increase tied to other items like *EGI*, occupancy, etc.
5. Following years' projections of expenses
   - Rate of increase as a function of inflation
   - Rate of increase tied to other items like *EGI*, occupancy, etc.
6. Following years' projections of tenant improvement expenses
   - Rate of increase as a function of inflation
   - Rate of increase tied to other items like *EGI*, occupancy, etc.
7. Operating expense ratios for all years
8. Discount rate and terminal capitalization rate estimation

27

The Cost Approach

Relation to Appraisal Principles

The cost approach is the valuation technique in which appraisers add land value to the depreciated value of the improvements to estimate the subject's value. It is important to recognize that the cost approach is the only approach in which land and building are theoretically separated, which brings up a myriad of issues that do not affect the sales comparison and income capitalization approaches.

In market value appraisals, the cost approach is most applicable to properties with newer improvements that represent the highest and best use of the site as though vacant. This approach is based on the logic that a buyer would consider purchasing a parcel of land and constructing a new building instead of buying an existing building.

Common mistakes in the application of the cost approach include

- poorly supported depreciation estimates
- overestimating or underestimating land value
- overstating the quality of construction
- ignoring reconfiguration costs (i.e., functional obsolescence) on properties with special designs but that have no resale market as designed

Many appraisers do not use the cost approach regularly because it requires current knowledge of construction techniques and costs, and it can be difficult to apply. In some appraisal assignments, a value estimate by the cost approach can be easily manipulated using subjective data. On the other hand, many appraisers use this technique frequently because they believe that, with so few techniques available, they cannot afford to discard one of them in all situations.

Many appraisers believe that the cost approach becomes less relevant, less reliable, and less convincing when the improvements are older or in substandard condition, or when they do not represent the highest and best use of the site as though vacant. Some appraisers who carefully track costs and depreciation rates feel that the cost approach is still relevant in properties with older improvements.

Substitution

The cost approach is based on the principle of substitution, which assumes that no one would pay more for a property than the cost of buying a similar parcel of land and building a new improvement on it. This principle also assumes that no one would buy or rent an old building when they could build a new one with more efficient and cost-effective systems at the same price. The cost approach is an attempt to simulate the thinking of buyers using a new building as an alternative to buying an existing building.

In many situations, the amount of time required to construct a new building inhibits a buyer from building a new improvement when existing improvements are available at slightly higher prices. In other words, buyers may pay premiums to buy existing buildings if they are in a hurry or do not have the time to dedicate to the construction process.

Supply and Demand

When the demand for real estate increases, the supply will increase in the long run as new units are added. However, the supply will not change and prices will increase with the higher demand in the short run. If too many new units are built to meet the increase in demand, the supply will outstrip demand and prices will fall.

KEY TERMS	
cost approach	indirect costs
direct costs	replacement cost
entrepreneurial incentive	reproduction cost
entrepreneurial profit	

Balance

The principle of balance states that the cost of an improvement must be in proportion to the value of the site. Consider the following situations involving market activity as examples:

- A residential builder buys a lot in a subdivision for $80,000 and invests $400,000 in the improvements, representing a ratio of $5 invested in the building to each $1 of investment in the land (land = 17% of the property value).

- A second residential builder pays $80,000 for a vacant lot and invests $360,000, representing an investment of $4.50 in the building to each $1 paid for the land (land = 18.18% of the property value).

- A third residential builder puts a $400,000 house on a $100,000 site, representing a ratio of $4 in the building to each $1 for the land (land = 20% of the property value).

- A fourth residential builder puts a $375,000 house on an $80,000 lot for a ratio of $4.68 of building investment for each $1 invested in the land (land = 17.58% of the property value).

The subject property is a proposed residence and garage (described from blueprints) that will cost $700,000 on a $80,000 lot. The subject improvements will represent $8.75 of investment for each $1 of land value (land = 10.26% of the property value). Most appraisers would consider the subject an overimprovement for the land value, and there will be a substantial loss when the property is resold.

Many appraisers misread this phenomenon and attribute it to a lack of support for the property from surrounding homes—i.e., an overimprovement is a property that is not supported by the neighborhood or district. In this example, the proposed house is an overimprovement because the investment in the building is out of proportion with the investment in the land.

A good illustration of the principle of balance is a waterfront lot on a lake or river that is improved with a 5,000-sq.-ft. home of good quality that would sell for a premium because of its location. Across the street is a very similar 5,000-sq.-ft. house on a lot lacking waterfront access. The high value of the improvements on the first property is supported by the high value of the waterfront lot, but the high value of the improvements on the second property is not supported by the less expensive lot without waterfront access.

The optimum ratio of land value to building value often varies from market to market, so it is important to research the most common ratio in any given market. In one market, land may most often represent 25% of total property value, but in other markets land may commonly account for 50% of property value. Research into land value-to-property value ratios provides good information for residential and nonresidential appraisers alike. For some property types such as fast food restaurants, branch banks, and drugstore chains, the percentage ratio of land value-to-total property value provides an interesting perspective and may lead to more supportable value conclusions.

According to the related concept of *contribution*, various components are valued based on their contribution to the land. The value of a building is based on how much the value of the property would be without the building. The contributory value of an item will be the cost of the item less *all* forms of depreciation. A superadequate item will contribute less than the cost of building or installing the item. Sometimes the buildings do not add anything to value, and if the land value exceeds the improved value by the cost of demolition, the buildings will likely be removed.

Externalities

External factors, ranging from shortages of labor to increasing prices of building material, can increase the construction costs of building improvements but may not always have an equal effect on market value. Likewise, an external event such as the completion of a utility line by the municipal authority may add value to a property without costing the property owner a penny.

Highest and Best Use

Highest and best use considerations are very important in all three approaches to value, but problems related to highest and best use can be more significant in the cost approach. In the sales comparison and income capitalization approaches, losses due to improper improvements on the site, overimprovement, or other highest and best use problems are often reflected in the market data for comparable properties, but these losses have to be identified and adjusted for in the cost approach.

For example, if the subject property is a residence with only two bedrooms in a market where a floor plan with three or four bedrooms is the norm, you may still find comparable properties with two bedrooms and therefore not have to estimate the amount of the loss when applying the sales comparison approach. However, in the cost approach, no such market recognition is possible, and the amount of the loss must be estimated from other sources to make a line item adjustment for functional obsolescence. Note that depreciation will be discussed in detail in Chapter 29.

Stabilization
The term *stabilization* describes the point at which a property reaches a profitable and sustainable level of occupancy. When income-producing properties are built new or substantially remodeled, occupancy levels are much less than 100%. A property that is capable of 100% occupancy but is at 50% occupancy is much less valuable to an investor than a building that is already fully occupied. In other words, a buyer for an empty building will factor in the cost (construction, broker fees, debt service, taxes, etc.) to bring the building up to stabilized occupancy. That cost should be accounted for in the calculation of reproduction cost in the cost approach.

Applicability and Limitations
The cost approach has fallen in and out of favor several times since the Great Depression and the beginning of the appraisal profession. The most recent versions of the standard residential appraisal forms do not require inclusion of the cost approach, which would imply that this approach is currently out of favor with that segment of the profession. Historically, the cost approach has been seen as a way to determine the maximum price market participants would pay. If appraisers misread comparable sales, the cost approach will keep their feet on the ground and bring the value estimate back in line in the reconciliation of the three approaches to value.

The cost approach is more persuasive than other approaches to value when market comparisons are difficult to make. In other words, when sales data does not provide convincing evidence of value, the cost approach may be an appraiser's best friend as well as the only alternative.

The cost approach is easy to develop when the improvements are new or nearly new and represent the highest and best use of the site. Applying the cost approach to properties with older improvements or improvements with functional problems can be more difficult because of the difficulty in estimating total depreciation.

Since the cost approach is designed to reflect the fee simple interest in a property, it must be adjusted to reflect the rights in realty included with the subject property. In some appraisals, an adjustment to the value indicated by the cost approach must be made to reflect the leased fee or leasehold interest.

The cost approach is a favorite tool of some appraisers because it provides more consistency in some markets. That is, when the sales comparison data is confusing, the cost approach can show where the problem lies.

The cost approach is mistakenly used by some appraisers to value special-purpose properties that have no active market with effective demand. If there is no market for a special-purpose property, the appraiser must develop an opinion based on a use that does have market demand. The cost approach can be used to estimate the market value of special-purpose properties, but if there is no demand for that design, reconfiguration costs must be considered. For example, a fire station normally has no demand because the only buyer for that use already owns the property. Reconfiguring the property for a use with demand is required, and the expense of the reconfiguration must be reflected in the cost approach (normally through an estimate of the functional obsolescence of the current use).

Procedure
Exhibit 27.1 illustrates the application of the cost approach to a small improved property.

Land Value
Land value is always estimated as if the land were vacant and available to be put to its highest and best use. This does not mean that every appraisal report must include a separate discussion of land value, but rather that every highest and best use analysis must consider the possibility that the land alone is worth more than the improved property. This analysis helps appraisers judge when buildings should be torn down and the site redeveloped. Land valuation is the first step in the process. It is usually done by sales comparison analysis, but other techniques can be used.

Reproduction Cost versus Replacement Cost
Reproduction cost is the cost of building an exact replica of the subject buildings as of the effective date of appraisal. While building such a replica

> Reproduction cost would include plaster walls, while replacement cost would be priced with drywall.

Exhibit 27.1   Cost Approach Procedure

The procedure for estimating market value using the cost approach is

1. Estimate the hard and soft costs of the improvements

If reproduction cost is estimated, then losses due to changing building standards and efficiencies will need to be reflected in the depreciation estimate. If replacement cost is used, some losses from changing building techniques will not be addressed in the depreciation estimate. The value of the site improvements is also estimated and added here as a hard cost. Typical items include driveways, trees, shrubs, sidewalks, and landscaping.   **$500,000**

2. Estimate and add entrepreneurial incentive

Entrepreneurial incentive is a market-derived figure representing the amount an entrepreneur expects to receive for his or her contribution to a project and risk. In the case of a shopping center, the costs of construction (hard and soft) do not include any profit for the developer who takes the risk of buying the land, building the building, and renting out the property. Compensation for this risk must be added here.   **+ $50,000**

Reproduction or replacement cost of construction $550,000

3. Subtract depreciation

After the cost new with entrepreneurial incentive is estimated, deductions are made to compensate for physical wear and tear, functional losses for superadequacies and inadequacies, and external losses due to economic conditions or locational problems.   **− $50,000**

Depreciated reproduction or replacement cost $500,000

4. Add land value

The land value must always be estimated at the highest and best use of the land as though vacant (ignoring any improvements).   **$100,000**

5. Adjust the indicated value for the rights in realty included with the subject

Again, the cost approach has no inherent way to recognize this adjustment.   **+ $0**

Indicated value via the cost approach $600,000

---

may sound like an easy thing to do, it can sometimes be impossible. Building features or components that were available 30 years ago may not be available today, and estimating reproduction cost may not be possible in this type of situation. Reproduction cost also includes any cost for superadequate items such as plaster walls found in older buildings in which drywall (gypsum board) is currently used. Plaster walls would be superadequate because they cost a lot but add no more to value than the less-expensive drywall. Reproduction cost would also include the cost of installing old knob-and-tube wiring if the subject has it. Note that knob-and-tube wiring is prohibited by most current building codes and therefore cannot actually be reproduced.

Replacement cost is an estimate of the cost of producing an improvement similar to the subject as of the effective date of appraisal using modern building materials and replacing some superadequacies with standard building features. For example, the replacement cost of an older office building with plaster walls would include the cost of drywall, which is less expensive but more acceptable to the market.

A replacement cost estimate does not cure all functional obsolescence nor negate the need to compensate for it. If the subject has plaster walls, using replacement cost instead of reproduction cost would remove that issue. However, if a building has a poor floor plan, estimating replacement cost does not remove the need to calculate the loss due to functional obsolescence.

Cost Estimates

Building costs can be classified as direct or indirect costs. Direct costs, which are typically in the builder's contract, include expenses for all typical materials, labor, fees, and charges. Direct costs are also referred to as *hard costs*. Most appraisers have no problem including all these expenses in their cost new estimates.

Indirect costs are also incurred in building an improvement, but they are not typically included in the builder's contract. The owner or developer usually pays these expenses, which include architectural fees, appraisal fees, insurance during construction, the cost of changing the title, and the

---

Direct costs and *indirect costs* are only labels, and misclassifying items should not affect the quality of the value estimate because all direct and indirect costs are accounted for in the cost approach.

---

cost of marketing the property or initially leasing the space. Indirect costs are commonly referred to as *soft costs*. Appraisers often forget to include some of these expenses in their cost estimates.

Entrepreneurial Incentive and Entrepreneurial Profit

The terms *entrepreneurial incentive* and *entrepreneurial profit* describe the required compensation the market must pay for the management of construction as well as the risk taken by the developer and sometimes the builder when constructing a new building. For example, the cost of building a shopping center does not include the risk of lease up or construction management. This amount will be reflected in the price obtained when the property is sold, so the cost approach needs to reflect that risk and reward as well. The anticipated profit a developer plans to receive is known as *entrepreneurial incentive*. The amount of profit the developer actually receives is called *entrepreneurial profit*.

Depreciation

Depreciation is the difference between what an improvement costs and the value of the improvement on the effective date of appraisal. Depreciation can be estimated by comparing the cost new of an improvement and the value of the improvement on a sale property. When preparing the cost approach, you will need to estimate the total depreciation that has accrued to the improvement as of the date of appraisal.

Depreciation can be broken down into three types:

- physical deterioration
- functional obsolescence
- external obsolescence

It is not necessary to segregate and label the various types of depreciation if the data used to estimate depreciation is accurate, similar, and indicative of the attitudes of the typical buyer. However, segregating and labeling the different types of depreciation can be of considerable benefit in some situations, particularly when one type of depreciation is significant and another is not. It is important for appraisers to speak a common language so they can identify various types of depreciation and readers of their reports will understand the jargon.

Physical Deterioration

Physical deterioration is the loss in the value of an improvement due to wear and tear or the passage of time. This type of depreciation is found in all properties with improvements that are not new. Physical deterioration is not considered to be obsolescence because that would imply a problem with the use of an improvement rather than with its condition.

Functional Obsolescence

Functional obsolescence is the result of incompatibility with current market requirements. In other words, this type of depreciation is the loss in value due to a problem with the utility of certain property improvements. Nearly all improved properties have some functional obsolescence after a few years. Changing decorating styles, construction techniques, and standard features are all sources of functional obsolescence. Be sure to exercise caution when stating that there is no functional obsolescence when appraising properties with older improvements, because most older buildings have typical levels of functional obsolescence.

External Obsolescence

External obsolescence is the loss in value of the improvements due to outside sources, such as a house located next to a busy interstate highway or an office building located next to a contaminated site. This loss in value due to external forces will usually also cause the property to have a lower land value, which requires special treatment when the building and land are segregated in the cost approach. The loss in value to the land due to an external problem simply results in a lower land value rather than obsolescence. The loss in value to the improvement from the same cause is called *external obsolescence*. Only the building portion of a property can have obsolescence.

Property Rights Adjustments

The value indication from the cost approach is of the fee simple interest in the real property at stabilized occupancy and at market rent. Often the market value of the leased fee interest in a property leased at the market rate is the same as the market value of the fee simple interest (i.e., the leasehold interest does not have value). However, if the contract rent is higher or lower than the market rate, the value of the leased fee interest in the property will be different from the value of the fee simple interest, so a property rights adjustment will need to be made to the value indication of the cost approach if the fee simple interest in that leased property is the interest being appraised in the assignment. A property rights adjustment

Depreciation in Appraising and Accounting

The following table shows the difference between changes in market value in an inflationary environment and the losses in value calculated from book depreciation rates. This calculation is the basis of the favorable tax treatment sought by many investors. In other words, an owner can make money but not pay taxes on that money for several years. While an accountant (with the approval of the IRS) would consider the building's value to be declining, the market is actually pushing the value up due to price increases in the cost of building the improvements. The depreciation rate is based on a life of 39 years; however, not all buildings are depreciated at the same rate.

Book Depreciation vs. Market Value

With a 2% Increase in Market Value per Year		Book Value	Market Value
Purchase price of land and buildings		$1,250,000	$1,250,000
Estimated land value		− $250,000	− $250,000
Estimated building value		$1,000,000	$1,000,000
Annual depreciation rate = 1/39 = 2.56%		− $25,641	
Annual appreciation rate = 2%			+ $20,000
Values at the end of Year 1	Subtotal	$974,359	$1,020,000
Annual depreciation rate = 1/39 = 2.56%		− $25,641	
Annual appreciation rate = 2%			+ $20,400
Values at the end of Year 2	Subtotal	$948,718	$1,040,400
Annual depreciation rate = 1/39 = 2.56%		− $25,641	
Annual appreciation rate = 2%			+ $20,808
Values at the end of Year 3	Subtotal	$923,077	$1,061,208
Annual depreciation rate = 1/39 = 2.56%		− $25,641	
Annual appreciation rate = 2%			+ $21,224
Values at the end of Year 4	Subtotal	$897,436	$1,082,432
Annual depreciation rate = 1/39 = 2.56%		− $25,641	
Annual appreciation rate = 2%			+ $21,649
Values at the end of Year 5	Subtotal	$871,795	$1,104,081
Annual depreciation rate = 1/39 = 2.56%		− $25,641	
Annual appreciation rate = 2%			+ $22,082
Values at the end of Year 6	Subtotal	$846,154	$1,126,163
Annual depreciation rate = 1/39 = 2.56%		− $25,641	
Annual appreciation rate = 2%			+ $22,523
Values at the end of Year 7	Subtotal	$820,513	$1,148,686
Annual depreciation rate = 1/39 = 2.56%		− $25,641	
Annual appreciation rate = 2%			+ $22,974
Values at the end of Year 8	Subtotal	$794,872	$1,171,660
Assume a resale at the end of Year 8			
Add the land value back in		+ $250,000	+ $292,915
		$1,044,872	$1,464,575

Capital gains income = $419,702

In this table, the column on the right illustrates the increase in market value based on a 2% compound appreciation rate. The column on the left indicates the property's worth as listed by the owner on the balance sheet. Taxes on capital gains will be assessed at different rates than earned income, and taxes are deferred at least until the property is sold and could be deferred even longer if the property is traded in a like-kind exchange. The table shows that the $1,250,000 purchase price increases to $1,464,575 over the holding period. Because the owner is claiming $25,641 each year in depreciation, the owner is actually making money that is tax-exempt in the year it is earned. This depreciation accumulates to the point that the property is worth only $1,044,872 on the books. The annual non-cash depreciation deduction against income is not tax-free but is tax-deferred and probably will be taxed at a lower rate.

The difference between what the asset (i.e., the real estate) is worth on the books and what it is worth in the market can be taxed at different rates by the IRS. The calculations for tax savings are complicated and are usually done by a competent CPA, but in principle this is the way it works. In other words, do not file your tax return based on this information, and be sure to ask an accountant about current tax benefits and issues.

would also be necessary when a speculative development is being leased up because the occupancy level would not be stabilized during the lease-up period. Estimating the shortfall from a below-market lease or occupancy during the lease-up period usually involves the application of sales comparison or income capitalization techniques.

An example of this issue would be in leased property where the landlord builds a new shell building and the tenant pays for all interior finishing. The appraiser looks at the improved property and sees a well-finished building but looks at the rent and sees what appears to be a below-market rent that is actually proportionate to the investment. If the cost approach reflects what is in place on the date of inspection, the landlord's interest is likely overstated unless a property rights adjustment is made.

1. *Reproduction cost* is defined as the cost of
   a) Building the improvements exactly as they are on the date of the appraisal
   b) Building the improvements exactly as they are on the *effective* date of appraisal
   c) Building the improvements exactly as they would appear if they were new on the effective date of appraisal
   d) Building the improvements with similar quality and utility as of the date of construction

2. *Replacement cost* is defined as the cost of
   a) Building the subject improvements with the same utility as of the date of the report
   b) Building the subject improvements exactly as they stand on the effective date of appraisal
   c) Building the improvements exactly as they would appear if they were new as of the date of the report
   d) Building the improvements with a structure of like utility but new as of the effective date of valuation

3. Indirect construction costs do not include
   a) Architect's fees
   b) Builder's overhead
   c) Selling and leasing fees
   d) Financing fees

4. Site improvements may be valued at
   a) Actual cost plus 10%
   b) Historic cost
   c) Depreciated historic cost
   d) Depreciated reproduction cost

5. Replacement cost is best used
   a) To eliminate some functional obsolescence from the cost approach
   b) To eliminate all functional obsolescence from the cost approach
   c) For non-residential properties only
   d) For residential properties

6. The cost approach is based on the
   a) Theory of substitution
   b) Cost of acquisition
   c) Cost of production
   d) Assessed value

7. The cost approach is
   a) Never a relevant approach for estimating market value
   b) Always a relevant approach for estimating market value
   c) Most applicable when the subject improvements represent the highest and best use of the site as though vacant and are relatively new
   d) Not required, regardless of the property

Note: Unless otherwise noted, italicized references indicate the pages in *The Appraisal of Real Estate*, 14th edition, that readers should consult for additional discussion of these topics.

1. c) Building the improvements exactly as they would appear if they were new on the effective date of appraisal
   Page 570

2. d) Building the improvements with a structure of like utility but new as of the effective date of valuation
   Page 570

3. b) Builder's overhead
   Pages 571-572

4. d) Depreciated reproduction cost
   Pages 568-570

5. a) To eliminate some functional obsolescence from the cost approach
   Pages 569-570

6. a) Theory of substitution
   Page 561

7. c) Most applicable when the subject improvements represent the highest and best use of the site as though vacant and are relatively new
   Pages 566-568

28

Building Cost Estimates

Sources of Cost Data

Cost-Estimating Services

The most common method of estimating building costs is to use a national cost-estimating service such as Marshall & Swift/Boeckh, RSMeans, or McGraw-Hill Construction Dodge. These services have contracts with builders, architects, and contractors to report the costs of building contracts when bids are accepted. The cost estimates are based on winning bids for actual jobs. These winning bids are converted to national averages, and that information is published. The national averages can then be converted to current local estimates using market-based multipliers. For example, if the national average for industrial space is $50.00 per square foot of gross area, the local multiplier is 1.05, and the current multiplier is 1.03, then the cost estimate would be $54.08 ($50.00 × 1.03 × 1.05). A more detailed example of this type of calculation will be provided later in this chapter.

Cost-estimating services are widely used because they allow appraisers to estimate the construction cost of most buildings quickly and efficiently. Analytical speed is traded for accuracy. This trade is acceptable for most appraisers because the market is not so precisely defined and small differences in costs do not usually significantly change the conclusions.

Cost Index Trending

Cost services also provide data that allows appraisers to update the historical cost of construction. If you can determine the cost of construction of a building when it was built, you can update the historical cost of construction using a multiplier. Cost index trending is a secondary method of estimating cost because construction dates further in the past yield less accurate estimates. In other words, it is accurate for a few years but not for many.

As an example, suppose the cost of building a small retail property in the spring of 2012 was reported by the owner (via contract) to be $189,000. To estimate the cost new using cost index trending, you would multiply the original cost (in 2012) by the differences in the published factors for 2012 and the effective date of appraisal. The cost index (as calculated from the cost manual) is 1.859, so the cost estimate is

$$\$189,000 \times 1.859 = \$351,351$$

In other words, a building that cost $189,000 in 2012 would cost about $351,351 today. In addition to estimating current cost, this technique can be used to estimate the cost of construction for an item when backdating the appraisal report.

Cost-Estimating Methods

The three cost-estimating methods are

- the comparative-unit (or calculator) method
- the unit-in-place method
- the quantity survey (or segregated cost) method

The quantity survey method provides the most detailed results, but the comparative-unit and unit-in-place methods are more commonly used.

> Most appraisers do not use cost index trending as a primary technique for estimating cost new, but it is an excellent technique for additional support or for buildings with unusual features.

KEY TERMS	
comparative-unit method	unit-in-place method
quantity survey method	

Estimating Entrepreneurial Incentive

Cost services base their numbers on national averages of "winning bids" for construction projects around the country. Cost estimate figures include entrepreneurial profit on residential properties but do not include entrepreneurial profit on nonresidential properties. The builder is the risk taker in residential development, so the profit is included. In the construction of a nonresidential property, the builder is often not the risk taker. Instead, the risk is carried by the developer who is responsible for making the project work.

Because the cost services do not include entrepreneurial incentive in their cost figures for nonresidential property, appraisers have to add this amount to cost service estimates to determine what the market will pay. To estimate entrepreneurial incentive accurately, research the market for the subject property type and determine how much profit will attract a risk taker to the deal. If buyers recognize that there will be high levels of risk or management involved in putting a property together, the entrepreneurial incentive will have to be higher to compensate. Estimating this amount can be difficult because developers often do not know or cannot quantify the risk. It is very difficult to extract this amount from sales comparables. Many appraisers believe it is inappropriate to include entrepreneurial incentive in the cost analysis of certain property types because owner-occupants do not realize a profit, nor do they expect this amount at resale. Their risks are in the operation of the business rather than in ownership of the real estate.

The most common way to estimate entrepreneurial incentive is to ask participants in the market how much profit they require. It is also possible to extract entrepreneurial profit (not the expected incentive) from the sale of a property with a new improvement that was sold soon after construction. For example, if a developer builds and leases up a new apartment complex and then sells it immediately after it is stabilized, you can compare the construction cost new with the price less the land value.

Entrepreneurial incentive can be estimated as a percentage of hard costs, a percentage of hard costs plus soft costs, or a percentage of hard and soft costs plus land value. There is no standard of measure when discussing entrepreneurial incentive with market participants. When asking developers how much compensation they require, you must also specify on which set of costs the percentage is based. A simple percentage is not meaningful information if the cost basis is unclear.

Comparative-Unit Method

The comparative-unit method is the most commonly used method of estimating the cost of construction. Most appraisers subscribe to a cost service to help them estimate the cost of construction. Assessors and insurance agents also use these cost services. One of the ways the cost services provide data is in written form based on price per square foot of building area. The dollar-per-square-foot estimates are designed to be multiplied by the amount of square feet in each section of the building.

Online and computer subscription services are also popular with appraisers. Computer-based services are much easier to use because they do not require manual adjustment for differences in location and date of appraisal. The appraiser types in the date of valuation and the zip code of the property, and the computer program adjusts for locational and market condition (time) differences.

Unit-in-Place Method

The unit-in-place method segregates the building into units of construction. This technique may involve estimating the cost of a wall including all components. Most appraisers do not use this method to estimate cost because it is too complicated and time-consuming. If a client asks for this level of detail in a cost analysis, the appraiser will commonly hire a professional cost estimator. Exhibit 28.1 illustrates a typical application of the unit-in-place method.

Quantity Survey Method

The quantity survey method is the most detailed way to estimate the cost of construction. With this technique, appraisers estimate the cost of every component of a building. This method is used even less than the unit-in-place method because of the time and cost involved. With the advent of computerized cost estimation, however, the quantity survey method may be more feasible than it once was, but appraisers still tend not to use it unless it is specifically requested by the client. The quantity survey method is more commonly used by contractors who bid jobs by distributing blueprints to subcontractors who factor in the small details. General contractors tend to just add up the cost estimates provided by the subcontractors.

Item	Quantity	Unit Cost		Cost
Foundation	1,912 sq. ft.	$6.00	=	$11,472.00
Framing	1,912 sq. ft.	$13.80	=	$26,385.60
Exterior walls			=	$15,250.00
Roof covering			=	$7,480.00
Interior construction	1,912 sq. ft.	$9.50	=	$18,164.00
Trim/finish	1,912 sq. ft.	$5.50	=	$10,516.00
Painting	1,912 sq. ft.	$3.30	=	$6,309.60
Carpeting	126 sq. ft.	$19.00	=	$2,394.00
Vinyl	84 sq. ft.	$19.00	=	$1,596.00
Insulation	1,912 sq. ft.	$3.00	=	$5,736.00
HVAC			=	$9,000.00
Plumbing	1,912 sq. ft.	$6.70	=	$12,810.40
Electrical/lighting	1,912 sq. ft.	$4.90	=	$9,368.80
Site improvements	1,824 sq. ft.	$5.30	=	$9,667.20
Estimated hard costs				$146,149.60
Estimated soft costs	15% of hard costs			$21,922.44
Estimated overhead and profit	15% of hard costs			$21,922.44
				$189,994.48

Measurement

Most cost services are based on building measurements in gross square feet. If the cost service uses the outside measurements of a building, you must also. It is always important to compare "apples to apples" and use the system of building measurement that is consistent with the data sources. If the sales data is based on assessor's estimates, the possible errors in this data source should be reconciled.

Buildings should be measured with the most accurate technique available, which is usually a tape measure or laser. Other measuring devices may be faster but rarely give more precise results.

Basements

Many buildings have below-grade areas, and appraisers may be tempted to include a well-finished basement area in the above-grade area measurement. While this may work for office buildings, apartments, or other types of income-producing properties, it is not appropriate for one-unit housing because cost services include the cost to build the *foundation* in the cost estimate of the first floor. Therefore, the costs of the foundation of a crawl space or slab concrete foundation walls are already included in the above-grade estimate. For other types of properties, the below-grade area generally generates less income or sells for less because of the lack of or a smaller number of windows.

1. A convenience store building contains 3,100 square feet of building area and has an attached canopy measuring 42 by 24 feet. The per-square-foot reproduction cost is estimated at $94.00 for the building area and $27.00 for the canopy. The total reproduction cost new of the entire structure is _____ . (Round your answer.)

    a) $200,000

    b) $300,000

    c) $400,000

    d) $500,000

2. The most detailed method of estimating the cost new of a structure is the

    a) Quantity survey method

    b) Unit-in-place method

    c) Trade breakdown or builder's method

    d) Segregated cost method

3. The unit-in-place cost-estimating method is

    a) Based on historical cost

    b) Based on the market-extracted costs per square foot of the building

    c) Based on the cost of each component of the building, including all labor and materials

    d) Based on a computerized printout of all labor, materials, and extras

4. A cost-estimating method in which appraisers estimate the current cost of construction based on the amount paid for the building when it was built is called

    a) Cost index trending

    b) Segregated cost

    c) Cost engineered services

    d) Unit-in-place method

5. When appraising an improved property with substantial functional losses, you should

    a) Be conservative in the cost new estimate to accommodate those losses

    b) Accurately estimate the cost and deal with the obsolescence in the depreciation estimate

    c) Not apply the cost approach because it is too hard

    d) Apply the cost approach because it is the only method you have that will give an accurate indication of value

    Note: Questions 6 and 7 are problems for consideration or discussion. No definitive solutions are given. Solutions depend on subjective input and judgement.

6. The subject residence is shown in the accompanying photo and has the following characteristics and features:

- 2,855 square feet
- Two stories
- 1,200-sq.-ft. basement with 900-sq.-ft. (minimal) finishing, 8-in. concrete floor, and all subterranean area (not walkout)
- 726-sq.-ft., three-car attached garage
- 466-sq.-ft., glass-enclosed porch with wood ceiling and wood walls
- Wood siding
- Asphalt shingle roof
- 10 rooms, four bedrooms, and 2½ baths
- One masonry fireplace
- Trim and finish commensurate with market
- Typical kitchen and bath finishes
- 90% carpeted and 10% ceramic floor coverings
- Built-in kitchen appliances including range/oven, dishwasher, disposal unit, and microwave
- Gas forced-air furnace and central air-conditioning

Use the following cost-estimating data to estimate the reproduction cost of the house:

Two-Story, Above-Grade Residence Cost per Square Foot of Area (Frame Residence)						
Area	**Stucco or Siding**	**Shingle or Shake**	**Rustic Log**	**Brick Veneer**	**Stone Veneer**	**Synthetic Plaster (EFIS)**
2,000 sq. ft.	72.65	72.68	88.96	78.33	86.39	74.77
2,200 sq. ft.	70.96	70.99	86.80	76.44	84.20	73.01
2,400 sq. ft.	69.46	69.49	84.88	74.75	82.24	71.44
2,600 sq. ft.	68.10	68.13	83.14	73.23	80.48	70.02
2,700 sq. ft.	67.47	67.50	82.34	72.53	79.67	69.36
2,800 sq. ft.	66.87	66.90	81.57	71.86	78.89	68.73
2,900 sq. ft.	66.30	66.32	80.84	71.21	78.15	68.13
3,000 sq. ft.	65.75	65.77	80.13	70.59	77.43	67.55
3,100 sq. ft.	65.22	65.24	79.46	70.00	76.75	67.00
3,200 sq. ft.	64.71	64.73	78.81	69.44	76.10	66.47
3,300 sq. ft.	64.22	64.25	78.19	68.89	75.47	65.96

Refinements	Add for	Add ons	
Wood shakes	Included in base	Fireplace—one-story	$3,900–4,800
Asphalt shingles	(−) $.78	Fireplace—two-story	$4,700–6,000
Wood shingles	(−) $.12	Fireplace—flueless	$2,100–3,000
Clay or slate	(+) $3.40 per sq. ft.		
Floor covering	(+) $4.92 for carpet/pad	**Appliances**	
	(+) $12.21 per sq. ft. for hard wood	Garbage disposal	$389
	(+) $13 per sq. ft. for ceramic	Oven/microwave	$1,800
	(−) $5 per sq. ft. for vinyl	Refrigerator	$2,100
Plaster walls	(+) $1.50 per sq. ft.	Trash compactor	$325
HVAC	Forced-air system in basement	Central vacuum	$1,900
Central A/C	(+) $1.70 per sq. ft.	Dishwasher	$850
Heat pump	(+) $2.18 per sq. ft.		
Energy efficiency	Mild climate (−) $1.00		
	Severe climate (+) $1.00		

Basement Area	400 sq. ft.	800 sq. ft.	1,200 sq. ft.	1,600 sq. ft.	2,000 sq. ft.
Unfinished 8-in. poured concrete	$24.00	$19.00	$17.65	$14.78	$12.55
Unfinished 12-in. poured concrete	27.25	21.60	18.15	16.95	16.55
Minimal finishing	8.88	7.59	7.05	6.85	6.50
Extensive finishing	32.05	31.50	29.88	29.01	28.55

Garage Area		400 sq. ft.	600 sq. ft.	800 sq. ft.	1,000 sq. ft.
Attached garage	Stucco	$29.50	27.38	26.00	24.67
	Wood siding	29.38	26.68	24.98	23.82
	Masonry	31.99	28.47	26.55	25.18
	Add for interior finish	5.23	4.64	4.41	4.03

Porch Areas	100 sq. ft.	200 sq. ft.	300 sq. ft.	400 sq. ft.	500 sq. ft.
Slab—open	$5.05	4.58	4.23	4.05	3.95
Wood deck	18.08	14.64	11.16	10.85	10.25
Screened porch	13.00	12.50	11.00	10.50	10.01
Enclosed w/wood and glass	41.55	31.58	31.22	29.68	28.55
Enclosed w/masonry and glass	45.85	37.85	34.55	33.00	31.08
Add for ceiling	5.00	4.58	4.25	4.15	4.01

Current cost multiplier = 1.08

Local cost multiplier = 1.03

Worksheet for Cost-Estimating Problem

Fill in the blanks:

House	2,855 sq. ft. @	_____	=	_____
Roof		_____	=	_____
Fireplace		_____	=	_____
Appliances		_____	=	_____
HVAC		_____	=	_____
Basement	1,200 sq. ft. @	_____	=	_____
Basement finish	900 sq. ft. @	_____	=	_____
Garage	726 sq. ft. @	_____	=	_____
Garage finish		_____	=	_____
Enclosed porch	466 sq. ft. @	_____	=	_____
Porch ceiling	466 sq. ft. @	_____	=	_____
Multipliers		_____	=	_____

7. The subject office building is shown in the accompanying photo and has the following characteristics and features:

  · 60,000 square feet of gross area with 51,026 square feet of rentable area

  · Three floors with about 17,000 square feet of rentable space on each floor; nine-foot ceilings on each floor with a total floor height of 12 feet

  · Flat roof with rubberized covering

  · Steel frame with concrete block curtain walls and brick veneer

  · Fixed and lightly tinted windows

  · Built in 1978

  · 20 rooftop package heating and air-conditioning units that service the entire building; these units have standard sheet metal ducts leading to sections of the building; six units serve the first floor, another six serve the second floor, and eight units serve the third floor because of the heat load present there

  · One elevator in the center of the building and two staircases—one on each end of the building

  · Wet fire suppression system that services each floor

- Two canopies—one in the front of the building constructed of metal and exterior-grade plaster and another on the south end of the building made of canvas
- Finished interior with walls of drywall over metal studs, acoustical tile ceilings, and carpeted floors
- Two common restrooms on each floor—five fixtures in each of the women's restrooms and six fixtures in each of the men's restrooms
- One water heater for the entire building
- Electrical service with 277 volts for fluorescent lighting and 110 volts for power
- Eight tenants on the first floor, 11 tenants on the second floor, and three tenants on the third floor. All spaces are used for general office with standard partitioning.

Example of Cost-Estimating Services Similar to Marshall & Swift/Boeckh

Class	Type	Exterior Walls	Interior Finish	Lighting, Plumbing, and Mechanical	Heat	Cost per Sq. Ft.
A	Excellent	· Best metal or stone · Brick or block backup · Solar glass	· Plaster · Best veneers · Vinyl wall coverings · Vinyl · Terrazzo · Carpet	· Luminous ceilings · Many outlets · Many private bathrooms	Hot and chilled water (zoned)	$164.02
	Good	· Good metal and solar glass · Face brick · Precast concrete panels	· Drywall or plaster · Some wall cover · Acoustic tile · Vinyl tile · Carpet	· Good fluorescent, high-intensity lighting · Good restrooms	Hot and chilled water (zoned)	$129.06
	Average	· Brick · Concrete or metal and glass panels · Little trim	· Average partitions · Acoustic tile · Vinyl composition · Some extras	· Average intensity fluorescent lighting · Average restrooms	Warm and cool air (zoned)	$98.72
	Low Cost	· Minimum-cost walls and fenestration · Little trim	· Drywall · Acoustic ceilings · Asphalt tile · Few partitions	· Minimum office lighting · Minimum plumbing	Warm and cool air	$79.65

Multistory buildings: Add 0.5% for each above-ground story over three to all base costs, including basements but excluding mezzanines, for up to 30 stories; over 30 stories, add 0.4% for each additional story

Sprinklers: Wet systems $1.66–$2.58 per square foot

Elevators: This cost is included in all Class A buildings; if the subject has no elevator, deduct $3.45 per square foot

Canopy cost = $8,000 each

Perimeter multiplier = 1.00

Story-height multiplier = 1.00 for 12-foot story height

Local multiplier = 1.02

Current cost multiplier = 1.03

Entrepreneurial incentive is estimated at 20% of the hard and soft costs

Estimate the reproduction cost of the office building using the following grid:

	Reproduction Cost Estimate via Marshall Valuation Service	
Date of survey/page #	current date	
Subject property	9247 N. Meridian Street, Indianapolis	
Occupancy class	commercial—office	
Building class	A	
Building quality	average	
Gross building area	60,000	
Rentable area	51,026	
Floors	3	
Perimeter	110 × 182 × 584 linear feet	
Base square foot cost		
HVAC adjustment		
Sprinklers		
Subtotal		
Number of stories adjustment		
Story height adjustment		
Perimeter floor area adjustment		
Refined square foot costs		×
Subject's sq. ft. area GBA		
Elevator		
Canopies		
Misc. and other buildings	None	=
Subtotal		
Current cost adjustment		
Local cost adjustment		
Subtotal		
Entrepreneurial incentive		
Reproduction cost		

Note: Unless otherwise noted, italicized references indicate the pages in *The Appraisal of Real Estate*, 14th edition, that readers should consult for additional discussion of these topics.

1. **b) $300,000**
   291,400 + 27,216 = 318,616

2. **a) Quantity survey method**
   Page 584

3. **c) Based on the cost of each component of the building, including all labor and materials**
   Pages 590-593

4. **a) Cost index trending**
   Pages 583-584

5. **b) Accurately estimate the cost and deal with the obsolescence in the depreciation estimate**
   Page 581

6. There is no set answer because of interpolation and other quality discussions. Some inputs will have to be subjective or educated guesses.

7. There is no set answer because of some judgment inputs.

29

Depreciation Estimates

Depreciation is the difference between the cost new of the improvements and their value as of the effective date of appraisal. Depreciation can be classified as physical, functional, or external.

Wear and tear or the effects of the passage of time usually cause physical deterioration. Improvements that are not consistent with the demands of the market suffer functional losses. These losses indicate that the market wants something other than what the subject offers. Losses attributed to external obsolescence are caused by factors outside the subject property. These can be categorized further as locational and economic losses. Locational losses are caused by the proximity of adverse factors, such as a noisy railroad track next to a residential property. The noise will affect the land and building values negatively. Economic losses are related to market supply and demand. For example, when mortgage interest rates rise and demand falls off rapidly, the prices paid for real estate will be affected. The loss in value would be reflected as external obsolescence in the cost approach. This loss in value would also be reflected in the sales comparison approach in the prices of properties subject to the same economic conditions.

Estimating an appropriate amount for depreciation in the cost approach can be difficult. There are typically three recognized methods of estimating depreciation:

- the market extraction method
- the economic age-life method
- the breakdown method

Age and Life Relationships

Actual Age and Effective Age

Actual age is the difference between the date of construction and the effective date of the appraisal. Effective age is a numerical age estimate of the improvement based on the conditions of the improved property and comparison with competitive properties of the same actual age. An improved property that is 20 years old but has deferred maintenance may have an effective age of 30 years. A property with a 30-year-old improvement that has been substantially remodeled may have an effective age of only 20 years. The effective age rating is always measured in relation to competitive properties in the market.

If a property is in average (i.e., typical) condition, its effective age and chronological age are the same. If a 30-year-old home has had similar maintenance as other homes in its market, its effective age and chronological age would be the same and the condition rating should be "average." A 75-year-old home that has been continuously maintained or recently remodeled does not compete with 10- to 20-year-old homes; rather, it competes with other 75-year-old remodeled

Curable or Incurable?
Depreciation may be curable or incurable. The simple test for "curability" is the financial feasibility of the cost to repair the item in question, which can be anything from fixing a broken window to repairing a cracked foundation wall. If the item costs less to replace or repair than the increase in value as a result of that action, the item is considered curable.

KEY TERMS	
economic life	property rights adjustment
equilibrium rent	short-lived items
long-lived items	useful life

If one building is better maintained than other buildings in a market area, the *effective age* of that building may be less than its *actual age*. If a building is poorly maintained, its effective age may be greater than its actual age. If a building has received typical maintenance, its effective age and actual age may be the same.

Examples of Long-Lived Items	Examples of Short-Lived Items
· Structural framing	· Floor coverings
· Roof structure	· Roof coverings
· Floor systems	· Windows
· Foundation	· Plumbing
· Nearly all soft costs associated with construction	· Electrical fixtures
	· Furnaces
	· Air-conditioners

homes. This 75-year-old home would be rated as in "average" condition in a market where the standard is to be remodeled and as in "good" condition in a market where standards are lower.

The terms *poor, fair, average,* and *good* are still commonly used in nonresidential appraisal work to describe the quality of construction and condition of improvements. In most cases, these are standards applied against properties that the subject property competes with to answer the question "*Average* compared to what?" It is quite possible to have an 80-year-old improvement be in *average* to *good* condition when compared with the competition.

Recently, Fannie Mae and Freddie Mac revised their standard condition ratings so that comparisons are made between the subject property and all housing, not just the competition. The condition ratings have been revised to a scale from C1 to C6, where *C1* denotes a new house and *C6* denotes a property that is or is close to being uninhabitable. In this case, the answer to the question "Compared to what?" would be "Compared to all housing within the specific definitions." At the same time that Fannie Mae and Freddie Mac revised the condition ratings, they also revised the quality rating system to a scale from Q1 to Q6, as discussed in Chapter 13.

Total Economic Life and Useful Life

In their analyses, appraisers do not really care how long improvements stand. They only care about how long the improvements contribute to property value. The total economic life of a building will be affected greatly by the location

economic life
The period over which improvements to real property contribute to property value.

useful life
The period of time over which a structure or a component of a property may reasonably be expected to perform the function for which it was designed.

of the property and the amount of maintenance and renovation that is done to it. An office building, if maintained properly, may function as an office building indefinitely, but when the income falls off and does not support all the expenses, the property will fall into disrepair. A property that falls into disrepair due to a lack of maintenance can deteriorate to a point at which it is more costly to repair than it is worth. If a property is in a viable area where owners expect to get a good return on their investment, they will put money into their buildings and keep the maintenance up. If the location is not good, investors will not be motivated to keep up their buildings, which will fall into disrepair and eventually be razed.

The economic life of a structure depends on its location and market. For example, a commercial building configured for use as a fast food restaurant will not normally have an economic life as long as an office building. Also, an office building in an area of high demand will usually have maintenance dollars invested in it and will be in good condition, but a similar office building built on the same day in a less desirable market area will not rent for enough for the owner to invest a similar amount to maintain the property. Thus, the improvements will contribute to the property value for a much shorter period than the office building in the area of high demand.

Components of a building can be classified as either long- or short-lived. The long-lived components are usually removed only when the entire building is razed. Short-lived components have economic lives that are shorter than the entire building. These items will be replaced at least once over the life of the property. Short-lived items depreciate much more rapidly than long-lived items for obvious reasons. Most of the condition adjustments made in appraisals reflect short-lived items. Both short- and long-lived items can suffer losses from functional and economic conditions.

Remaining Economic Life and Remaining Useful Life

Remaining economic life is the amount of time left for the improvements to add value to the site:

Effective Age + Remaining Economic Life = Total Economic Life

Total Economic Life − Effective Age = Remaining Economic Life

An improvement's remaining useful life depends on the design, the durability of the item, and its utility. An I-beam in the superstructure of an office building will have a very long useful life. However, if the I-beam is in an office building in an undesirable neighborhood, that I-beam may not be around very long because the owner will not be able to maintain the rest of the property enough to keep it viable.

To calculate the amount of depreciation in a property, use a fraction with the effective age as the numerator and the total economic life as the denominator:

$$Depreciation = \frac{Effective\ Age}{Total\ Economic\ Life}$$

For example, if the roof is 10 years old and typically has a total economic life of 20 years, the depreciation can be calculated by using the simple fraction of 10/20, which can be restated as a 50% depreciation rate. Some appraisers try to estimate the remaining economic life of the entire building using the same technique, but the denominator is a subjective measurement when the age-life procedure is used for the entire building. This can lead to poorly supported results. While it is easy to find out how long a furnace will last, it is not possible to obtain supporting data to estimate the economic life of a building when so many dynamic economic forces affect the life of the structure.

In other words, the lifespan of the entire building depends greatly on its location. Buildings are generally removed for two reasons.

1. The location is so bad that the owner will not or cannot invest money to maintain it, the depreciation accelerates, and soon the property becomes too expensive to repair.
2. The location is so good that redevelopers will buy the lowest-priced property in a redevelopment area and then remove the improvements.

A combination of these two reasons is also possible, such as in a situation in which the property condition is poor, the redevelopment opportunities are fairly good, and the condition allows for removing the improvements.

Market Extraction Method

The market extraction method is the most direct and probably the most accurate method of estimating depreciation. It does not segregate the depreciation estimate into categories. Instead, it deals only with the total amount of depreciation. This technique requires appraisers to find improved comparable sales with similar losses as the subject to ensure that the extracted depreciation rates are applicable to the subject. If the subject property has a poorly designed floor plan but the comparable properties analyzed do not have that problem, the depreciation rate extracted from the comparable sales will not include the loss due to the poor floor plan, and the amount of depreciation present in the subject will be underestimated.

The market extraction procedure follows seven simple steps:

1. Find and verify sales of improved properties that reflect the same losses as the subject. Since depreciation can have physical, functional, or external causes, the comparables should reflect improvements of similar quality and age, an equally desirable location, and similar supply and demand factors. The comparables can be from outside the subject's market area but should reflect similar losses. If the comparable sales do not suffer from the same losses, adjustments may have to be made to compensate. For example, if the subject has floor plan problems but the comparables do not, the extracted depreciation will not be correct without an adjustment.

2. Make adjustments to the sale prices of the comparable properties for property rights conveyed, seller financing assistance, and conditions of sale. Adjustments for expenditures immediately after sale can and should be made if there are atypical problems that will skew the depreciation percentages. This doesn't mean that other condition adjustments should be made; only adjustments for those repairs needed to make the property functional should be made. Consistency is always important. Market condition adjustments are not needed because the goal is to measure the loss as of a specific date rather than from one date to the next. Making market conditions adjustments will skew the depreciation rates. If a comparable sale occurred at a poor time

in the market cycle but the current market is much healthier, the extracted depreciation may reflect external losses that may not be present at a later date. If there are obvious losses in the comparables that are not present in the subject property, adjustments can be made to calculate an estimate of physical depreciation only.

3. Subtract the value of the land (V_L) at the time of sale from the sale price of each comparable. Because land value is always estimated at its highest and best use, additional depreciation may be caused by an improper improvement (see the discussion of consistent use in Chapter 16). If the improvement does not represent the highest and best use of the land, the extracted amount of depreciation reflects functional obsolescence. If the improvements suffer from a great deal of functional obsolescence, large adjustments to the extracted rate would be necessary.

4. Estimate the reproduction or replacement cost of the improvements as of the effective date of appraisal. If reproduction cost is used as the cost basis in the cost approach, it must also be used as the basis of the market extraction method and vice versa.

5. Subtract the calculated value of the building from the estimated reproduction or replacement cost of the improvements to determine the amount of depreciation.

6. Convert this amount of depreciation to a percentage by dividing the dollar amount of depreciation by the cost new of the structure.

7. Develop an annual depreciation rate if there is a difference between the ages of the comparable properties and the subject.

The market extraction method does not segregate the types of depreciation. As a result, a property could appear to be in inferior condition when in fact it is suffering depreciation from other functional or external problems. Many appraisers consider this technique a way to establish the maximum amount of depreciation—i.e., if the overall depreciation is known, the total of all other forms of depreciation must fit under this ceiling. Other losses can be estimated and then incorporated into the subject's cost estimate using paired data analysis and other techniques for estimating depreciation.

Exhibit 29.1 lists three comparable sales of newly improved properties used to estimate depreciation rates. In most markets, newer improvements have a lower amount of total depreciation but a higher annual depreciation rate.

The total economic life can be extracted from this data by dividing the annual depreciation rate into 1.00 (i.e., 100%). The percentage of depreciation per year is the important information gained from this analysis. Calculating total economic life to estimate depreciation using the age-life method is unnecessary if the amount of depreciation is al-

Exhibit 29.1	Depreciation of Newer Improvements (Estimated Using Sales Comparison)		
	Sale 1	Sale 2	Sale 3
Address	143 Goldenrod Dr.	201 Jasmine Dr.	831 E. 13th St.
Sale price	$595,000	$565,000	$540,000
Rights conveyed	0	0	0
Seller concessions	0	(15,000)	0
Conditions of sale	0	0	0
Net sale price	$595,000	$550,000	$540,000
Estimated land value	(135,000)	(160,000)	(160,000)
Site improvement value	(15,000)	(13,000)	(15,600)
Depreciated value of buildings	$445,000	$377,000	$364,400
Reproduction cost	$495,000	$404,000	$395,000
Less building value	(445,000)	(377,000)	(364,400)
Total depreciation	$50,000	$27,000	$30,600
Percentage depreciation	10.10%	6.68%	7.75%
Actual age	8	5	6
Percentage depreciation per year	1.26%	1.34%	1.29%

ready known through market extraction. In other words, extracting a denominator for the fraction in the age-life ratio is possible but not needed because the percentage depreciation is sought; this is shown in Exhibit 29.2. Note that the rate of depreciation per year is higher for the newer improvement. This would imply that annual depreciation rates are higher in the early years of an improvement's life and lower as the improvements get older. This limited amount of data could not give a conclusive answer but implies this conclusion with this data alone.

To illustrate the process of estimating the depreciation of older improvements, consider the properties described in Exhibit 29.2. In this market, maintenance levels are high and owners tend to invest in their properties regularly. The properties in the table are one-unit homes, but the same process works for nonresidential properties. The extracted depreciation rate is often higher for nonresidential properties than one-unit homes. Remember that the extraction method includes all forms of depreciation, and some property types are prone to more or less physical deterioration or functional obsolescence. The improvements in this case are depreciating at an annual rate of less than 1%.

Because the depreciation of short-lived items is accelerated in the early years and the normal replacements occur after the first 10 years, annual depreciation in later years tends to decrease. For example, one-unit homes in this market may

depreciate at an average rate of nearly 1.43% per year in the first years after completion, but they will depreciate at an average rate of less than one-half of 1% per year after 50 or 60 years of age. Note that the percentages of depreciation indicated in older homes are larger than the percentages for the newer homes shown in Exhibit 29.1, but the annual rates are much lower because the higher total amount of depreciation is spread over many more years.

The overall depreciation rate can be divided by the age of the improvements to produce a straight-line estimate of overall depreciation. This does not imply that the depreciation rate remains fixed over the life of the improvement. In most markets, the annual depreciation rate diminishes as the improvements get older. The total economic life would be much longer at a lower annual depreciation rate, which implies that mathematically the total economic life increases as the improvements age. This seems counterintuitive, but the important information in this analysis is the amount of depreciation rather than the economic life. You do not need to calculate economic life if you already have the answer to the larger appraisal question, which is how much the property has depreciated.

The depreciation of an office building can also be estimated using market extraction, as shown in Exhibit 29.3. The depreciation rate is likely to be location-specific. In one market, the depreciation may be very high, but a similar building in a

Exhibit 29.2	Depreciation of Older Improvements		
	Sale 1	**Sale 2**	**Sale 3**
Address	477 Pennsylvania	478 New Jersey	420 Washington
Sale price	$655,000	$590,000	$650,000
Rights conveyed	0	0	0
Seller concessions	0	0	0
Conditions of sale	0	0	0
Net sale price	$655,000	$590,000	$650,000
Estimated land value	(135,000)	(165,000)	(145,000)
Site improvement value	(8,500)	(9,500)	(12,500)
Depreciated value of buildings	$511,500	$415,500	$492,500
Reproduction cost	$685,800	$555,000	$660,000
Less building value	(511,500)	(415,500)	(492,500)
Total depreciation	$174,300	$139,500	$167,500
Percentage depreciation	25.42%	25.14%	25.38%
Actual age	60	62	59
Percentage depreciation per year	0.42%	0.41%	0.43%

Exhibit 29.3   Depreciation of an Office Building

	Sale 1	Sale 2	Sale 3
Address	9999 N. Meridian	8809 N. Pennsylvania	7765 N. Andrews
Sale price	$3,100,000	$1,250,000	$4,050,000
Rights conveyed	(50,000)	0	0
Seller concessions	0	0	(35,000)
Conditions of sale	0	0	0
Net sale price	$3,050,000	$1,250,000	$4,015,000
Estimated land value	(215,000)	(75,000)	(325,000)
Site improvement value	(35,000)	(22,000)	(55,000)
Depreciated value of buildings	$2,800,000	$1,153,000	$3,635,000
Reproduction cost	$6,600,000	$3,000,000	$7,500,000
Less building value	(2,800,000)	(1,153,000)	(3,635,000)
Total depreciation	$3,800,000	$1,847,000	$3,865,000
Percentage depreciation	57.58%	61.57%	51.53%
Actual age	27	31	25
Percentage depreciation per year	2.13%	1.99%	2.06%

better area might suffer much less depreciation. Owners of properties with high rents should have excess money to invest in replacing worn items, updating the condition, and remodeling when needed. If a property does not rent for much, the owners typically cannot afford to or are unwilling to invest in the same items of repair or remodeling, and the properties will fall into disrepair and eventually be razed when they no longer contribute any value.

Applicability and Limitations
Many appraisers prefer the market extraction method of estimating depreciation over the other methods because it eliminates the problem of estimating the denominator of the age-life ratio. It also eliminates the problem of over- or underestimating overall depreciation that is commonly encountered when using the breakdown method, which will be covered later in this chapter. The direct extraction of information from market data is usually the best available indication of market behavior. It is easy to understand and hard to refute.

The market extraction method does not segregate the losses by classification, making adjustments for dissimilar improvements more difficult to gauge accurately. Because the calculations of overall depreciation are based on estimates of land value and reproduction or replacement cost, any errors in those analytical steps may often be repeated in the later analysis. That is, if the land

value is underestimated in the extraction technique, the same underestimation will commonly appear in the subject's cost approach.

Economic Age-Life Method
The economic age-life method of estimating depreciation is based on two assumptions:

1. Any improvement has a life span that can be estimated.
2. Depreciation can be estimated by dividing the age of the improvement by the total length of its life.

Actual age is usually an easily obtained fact, but effective age is estimated by the appraiser. Effective age is higher than the actual age when the improvements have had poorer-than-average maintenance, and it is adjusted below the actual age when the improvements have had better-than-average maintenance. The effective age rating relates more to the condition rating of the improvement than the actual age.

Age-life techniques for estimating depreciation are best illustrated and applied to building components rather than to the entire improve-

> The economic age-life method is best used as a primary technique of estimating component depreciation and as a secondary technique in the estimation of overall building depreciation.

ment. For example, a 10-year-old roof covering that typically has a useful life of 20 years can be said to have depreciated by 50%. This depreciation rate could not be applied to the entire property when some components in the building have short lives and others have long lives. The total economic life of roof shingles can be obtained from a survey of roofing companies who can tell you how long the roof shingles typically last. Some appraisers use the date of demolition of comparable buildings as an indication of the total economic life of the building, but that logic can be flawed because buildings are often razed as a result of external factors or economic considerations, such as when an improvement is razed to make room for a new building with another use.

Estimating the economic life of short-lived components is easy, but estimating the economic life of the entire structure is more difficult and harder to support. The market extraction method discussed earlier can be used for this purpose. Remember that the total economic life of an improvement is location-specific, and the rate of depreciation varies throughout the term. Therefore, extraction of the economic life for one property type in one market cannot be automatically extended to another property in another market.

Applicability and Limitations
The age-life ratio is a favorite analytical tool of appraisers because it supports an easy and consistent method of estimating depreciation. However, estimating the total life of a structure can be difficult because of locational restraints and the complex relationship of the various building improvements that make up a functional property. While it is easy to estimate the life of a water heater, it can be hard to judge how long a retail center will last. Overall depreciation is best extracted directly from the market using the market extraction method.

The economic age-life method of estimating depreciation is easy to understand but does not work well when the property has an excessively high land value. In certain situations, the age-life method may not recognize external losses or deferred maintenance. This method requires the appraiser to estimate the economic life of the improvement, which is often more affected by the location and property type than by the construction or typical property lives. In other words, the appraiser has little support for the denominator in the equation (total economic life). It tends to be difficult to explain and to use as the improvements get older or if the improvements have substantial obsolescence.

Variations of the Economic Age-Life Method
In some situations, the standard method of dividing the effective age by the total economic life produces an inaccurate result. If a property has substantial deferred maintenance or short-lived items with extra depreciation, the age-life ratio can be modified by subtracting the cost of the deferred maintenance items or short-lived items from the estimate of cost new and then applying the depreciation percentage. This procedure allows the appraiser to "zero out" those short-lived items or items that are worthless without affecting the age-life percentages. Many appraisers call this the *modified economic age-life method*. While this technique removes the danger that excessive deferred maintenance will skew the depreciation estimate, it still does not solve the problem of finding support for the denominator of the age-life ratio.

Breakdown Method
In the breakdown method, appraisers identify and estimate the different kinds of losses due to depreciation of the improvements. This technique is limited by the difficulty of estimating losses to

Exhibit 29.4	Methods of Calculating Depreciation in the Breakdown Method

Method	Use
Estimation of the cost to cure the problem	Used primarily for functional obsolescence and physical deterioration
Application of the estimated age-life ratio	Used primarily for physical deterioration
Application of the functional obsolescence procedure	Used for functional problems only
Analysis of market data, usually using paired sales and income capitalization	Used for physical, functional, or external losses
Capitalization of the income loss	Used for physical, functional, or external losses; capitalization of income loss applies to property types for which the typical buyer is primarily concerned with the potential income

long-lived improvements and external obsolescence, but it is appropriate and accurate when coupled with the market extraction method.

The breakdown method can be used to segregate and label particular types of depreciation if the overall depreciation is known. Once isolated by extraction, the segregated depreciation can be applied to a property that has similar losses. Working the other way, the breakdown method can be used to develop an overall estimate of depreciation by estimating and adding up all the separate forms of depreciation found in a market. This requires appraisers to identify and measure each form of depreciation for all components of a building.

Applicability and Limitations

The breakdown method is not commonly used because it is laborious and difficult to support when many calculations are necessary. In most market value appraisals, depreciation can be estimated using the sales comparison (market comparison) or age-life techniques, so the more time-consuming breakdown method is not popular. Also, this method requires appraisers to know what types of depreciation exist and to measure each one. Finally, the breakdown method is not usually more accurate despite the extra time and effort involved.

Physical Deterioration

Curable Physical Deterioration—Deferred Maintenance
Curable physical deterioration is commonly known as *deferred maintenance*. Curable items may be broken or may have lived beyond their useful lives, and the depreciation attributable to these items is equal to or greater than the cost of the item. Nearly all problems can be physically cured, but not all items are financially feasible to cure. The benefit of curing the problem must outweigh the cost.

The method applied to estimate the depreciation due to deferred maintenance is usually the cost to cure, such as the cost of repainting a house. If the exterior of the house was painted nine years earlier and that is the average life of exterior paint in this market, a prudent buyer would factor the need for new paint into the purchase price. The cost of repainting the house is likely to be less than the additional amount the seller could expect to ask for the property, so a shrewd seller would probably have the house repainted. Note that the paint job is completely depreciated (i.e., it has an age of nine years and a total life of nine years) and the benefit of curing the problem exceeds the cost to cure.

Incurable Physical Deterioration—Short-lived Items
Short-lived items with incurable physical deterioration have shorter lives than the entire property and will be replaced at least once over the life of the building. As of the date of appraisal, however, they are not worn out completely. Examples include roof shingles that are 10 years old but have a life of 20 years or a furnace that is five years old but should have an efficient service life of 20 years. Depreciation is usually estimated based on the age-life ratio of the components. The denominator is easily and logically obtained from the manufacturer or the installation person.

Incurable Physical Deterioration—Long-lived Items
Some long-lived items suffer from incurable depreciation because the cost of replacement exceeds the amount the item contributes to value. Examples are the framing, foundation, and roof structure of the building. The amount of depreciation is estimated most effectively by applying the sales comparison method to determine the overall losses and then subtracting the estimated losses due to short-lived items and other losses. The remainder is attributable to the long-lived items.

Damage/Vandalism

Losses due to damage or vandalism are treated separately from other items for two reasons.

1. Curing these problems will not usually improve or change the property, and
2. The cost to cure damage or vandalism is usually not a standard operating expense that owners make room for in their budgets.

Repairing a leaking roof will not usually significantly increase the property value. If a new roof is installed, a typical buyer should pay more for the property. If a roof is only repaired because it is leaking, it is doubtful that the repair will change the amount paid for the property. Some appraisers argue that not making a critical repair will inhibit a sale much more than the cost of the repair because a different class of buyer is now going to be the typical buyer. In other words, if you do not fix a leaking roof, the buyer shifts from a retail buyer to a wholesale buyer, and the loss is greater.

The problem with this classification is that it often includes some functional losses due to outdated designs, which are hard to identify, isolate, and estimate. The age-life and market extraction methods give estimates of total depreciation (of short- and long-lived items) that can be used as a basis for extracting the incurable physical deterioration.

Estimating All Forms of Physical Deterioration Using the Age-Life Procedure

Total physical deterioration can be estimated by dividing the effective age by the total useful life of components with similar life spans. The logic behind this technique is that some items last 10 years, others 20 years, and still others 50 years. The long-lived items will function until the wrecking ball comes. Again, this technique assumes that appraisers know the total useful life of the item, which can be difficult to determine. If you can support the isolated depreciation by extraction from sales, you already know the total depreciation amount, which eliminates the need for interim steps involving age-life calculations. The obvious benefit of using this technique is that you will isolate depreciation in certain improvements and then use those conclusions in later assignments.

Functional Obsolescence

When a property is at odds with the market, it loses value as a result of functional obsolescence. The losses can be classified as deficiencies or superadequacies. Functional obsolescence can be caused by problems like a poor floor plan, a house too large or small for the lot, or an ugly color scheme. A three-story office building lacking an elevator is an example of functional obsolescence in most markets.

Problem-Solving for Functional Obsolescence

When estimating functional obsolescence, appraisers follow a series of problem-solving steps:

1. Identify the functional problem. This step can be performed by interviewing typical buyers in the market or by interviewing brokers who work in the market, which is the next best thing.
2. Identify the component of the property that is causing the problem.
3. Identify possible corrective actions and the cost to cure.
4. Select the most appropriate corrective measure from the possible actions.

5. Quantify the loss caused by the functional problem, which adds to the value when corrected.
6. Determine if the item is curable or incurable.
7. Apply the functional obsolescence procedure.

Using the Functional Obsolescence Procedure

Exhibit 29.5 illustrates the process of estimating functional obsolescence.

Examples of a Deficiency

Suppose that the subject property is a three-story office building that has no elevator in a market that demands an elevator for a multistory office building. The cost of the elevator if installed new when built was $75,000, but the cost to install it today is $200,000 because of the additional cost of retrofitting the space. Similar properties with the same problem in this market generally sell for $210,000 less than properties with elevators. The improvement is 14 years old, and the physical depreciation would be 2% per year. The functional obsolescence is calculated in Exhibit 29.6.

As a second example, consider a small retail center that was built on a five-acre site near the center of the acreage. The market and legal requirements for parking only required this site to be three acres. The building's location on the front of the site precluded selling off any outlots. This property has too much parking and the excess could not be sold off. The highest and best use of the site as though vacant included the retail center site and two outlots. The indicated value of the site is $200,000. The outlots added $50,000 each to the $200,000 value. The cost of moving the building would be $400,000. The functional obsolescence is calculated as shown in Exhibit 29.7.

The third subject is a small office building that was built 30 years ago. It was lighted with four-tube, fluorescent 2-by-4-ft. ceiling light fixtures with magnetic ballasts. The lighting industry is now marketing more efficient "electronic ballast" fixtures that use a smaller light bulb with

> As the process of estimating losses from physical, functional, and external factors becomes more complicated, many appraisers discount or completely eliminate the use of the cost approach. It is easy for appraisers to argue about the correct techniques for estimating depreciation. However, most appraisers agree that when the process of estimating these losses becomes too complicated, the cost approach is less useful. One thing is certain: when the process becomes very complicated, the appraiser's actions no longer reflect typical behavior in most markets.

Exhibit 29.5   The Functional Obsolescence Procedure

Step	$	Item	Explanation
1	$	Estimate the cost of the item	Represents the cost of the item that is causing the problem. In the case of a missing item that is causing a loss, this amount would be $0.
2	−	Less the depreciation already charged	Usually the appraiser's estimate of the loss due to physical deterioration. This has to be subtracted from the cost of the item to prevent double-counting of the item for both physical and functional losses. If there is a missing item, this amount would be $0.
3	+	Plus the cost to cure or the present value of the loss (in many cases, this includes the cost of retrofitting an item)	The main adjustment. If the item is curable, the estimate of depreciation would be the cost to cure; if the item is incurable, the depreciation amount would be the present value of the future additional expenses. Adding these amounts reveals the amount of depreciation that will be subtracted from the cost new to reduce the value estimate derived via the cost approach.
4	−	Less the cost, if curable, or depreciated cost, if incurable, of the proper item if included in new construction	It the item is curable, the contribution of the proper item to the replacement (or reproduction) cost if it had been part of the original design is deducted from the cost to cure to determine the excess cost to cure. If the item is incurable, the depreciated cost is deducted from the value of the loss to indicate the value of the loss over and above the cost of the item if installed in new construction.
5	=	Equals the depreciation attributable to functional obsolescence	The amount the appraiser subtracts from reproduction cost for functional obsolescence. This amount lowers the value of the property.

Step	$	Item	Explanation
1	$0	Estimate the cost of the item	There is no item on site now, so this amount is $0.
2	$0	Less the depreciation already charged	Again, since there is no elevator, this amount is also $0
3	+ $200,000	Plus the cost to cure or the present value of the loss	This is curable because the owner can spend $200,000 and return $210,000 in value. The cost of curing the problem is the cost of installing a new elevator.
4	− $75,000	Less the cost, if curable, or depreciated cost, if incurable, of the proper item if included in new construction	This has to be subtracted because the market is recognizing only a $210,000 difference in the value with and without the item, and the cost for this building is already starting out $75,000 less than a property that has an elevator. If you do not subtract this amount, the value of the property would be diminished twice for the cost of the item ($75,000) because the cost at the time of completion is already $75,000 less than a property with the item in place.
5	= $125,000	Equals the depreciation attributable to functional obsolescence	This amount is correct because a buyer would think he or she could buy this property for $200,000 less (75,000 + 125,000) and then install an elevator. The $75,000 represents the lower cost of the subject improvement without an elevator.

more lumens per bulb. The newer ballasts and light tubes will lower the light and power bill by 25% ($40,000 per year). Replacing the old light ballasts and tubes with the more efficient units will cost $29,000 (materials and labor). The cost of the existing units if purchased today would be $20,000. The cost of the more efficient units if installed originally is estimated at $25,000. The capitalization rate in this market is 9%. The units in place are estimated to have 50% physical depreciation, and the old units have no salvage value. The functional obsolescence is calculated in Exhibit 29.8.

Examples of a Superadequacy

Suppose a one-story building was built as a sit-down restaurant 10 years ago. It included a 300-gallon, 277-volt electric water heater that was designed for dishwasher use in the restaurant. The water heater costs $5,000 today. After several years of operation, the building was no longer marketable as a restaurant due to excess competition from other restaurants in the area, so it was retrofitted as a shoe store five years ago. The shoe store only has two bathrooms with a total of four hand-washing sinks and one dump sink for the janitor. A 50-gallon, 120-volt water heater costing only $1,000 would

Exhibit 29.7

Exhibit 29.7   Incurable Functional Obsolescence Caused by a Deficiency

Step	$	Item	Explanation
1	$0	Estimate the cost of the item	There is no item.
2	$0	Less the depreciation already charged	There is no item.
3	+ $100,000	Plus the cost to cure or the present value of the loss (in many cases, this includes the cost of retrofitting an item)	The owner lost $100,000 in land value due to the inability to sell off the two outlots. This is incurable because of the high cost of moving the building.
4	$0	Less the cost, if curable, or depreciated cost, if incurable, of the proper item if included in new construction	There is no correct item here, so the cost and value should be $0.
5	$100,000	Equals the depreciation attributable to functional obsolescence	This loss is equal to the lost revenue from the sale of the outlots.

Exhibit 29.8   Curable Functional Obsolescence Caused by a Deficiency Requiring Substitution or Modernization

Step	$	Item	Explanation
1	$20,000	Estimate the cost of the item	The cost of the existing fixtures with magnetic ballasts. Since this is an estimate of depreciation rather than value, this dollar amount is subtracted from the cost of construction.
2	− $10,000	Less the depreciation already charged	The existing units were not new. This adjustment prevents double-counting the physical deterioration of the light fixtures. Note that this amount is subtracted to reduce the amount of depreciation attributable to the functional obsolescence of the item by the amount of depreciation attributable to the physical deterioration.
3	+ $29,000	Plus the cost to cure or the present value of the loss (in many cases, this includes the cost of retrofitting an item)	The cost to replace the ballasts with the correct item now. This is curable because the capital amount of the loss was $10,000/0.09 − $111,111, which is a lot more than the cost of the modernization at $29,000. This adds to the amount of depreciation.
4	− $25,000	Less the cost, if curable, or depreciated cost, if incurable, of the proper item if included in new construction	The cost of installing the more efficient units today during original construction. This lowers the depreciation amount. The difference between the cost to cure and the cost of the correct item if installed new (i.e., Steps 3 and 4) is the excess cost to cure.
5	$14,000	Equals the depreciation attributable to functional obsolescence	This amount will be deducted from the estimate of cost new.

be adequate for the shoe store, but the owners did not replace the oversized heater when they remodeled. The water heater has an economic life of 15 years and is 66% depreciated (10/15). The extra cost of operating this unit is $200 per year. The capitalization rate for this property is 10%. The functional obsolescence is calculated as shown in Exhibit 29.9.

As a second example, consider a subject property that is a recently completed $175,000 residential property in International Falls, Minnesota, with a new $45,000 in-ground swimming pool. The market in this climatic area will generally not pay anything for an in-ground pool in a home of this price. The functional obsolescence is calculated as shown in Exhibit 29.10.

External Obsolescence

External obsolescence is the loss in value due to factors outside the property. These problems can be locational problems, like proximity to railroad tracks, or economic problems, like increases in mortgage interest rates that diminish demand and lower resale prices.

To estimate the loss attributable to external obsolescence, most appraisers use paired data analysis or capitalized income loss. Locational losses are simple to estimate using paired data analysis because sales with and without the locational problems can usually be found. If the loss is due to economic conditions, using paired sales is more difficult because most comparable sales in

Exhibit 29.9   Curable Functional Obsolescence Caused by a Superadequacy

Step	$	Item	Explanation
1	$5,000	Estimate the cost of the item	The cost of the existing oversized water heater.
2	– $3,333	Less the depreciation already charged	The existing units were not new. This adjustment prevents double-counting the physical depreciation.
3	+ $1,000	Plus the cost to cure or the present value of the loss (in many cases, this includes the cost of retrofitting an item)	This is curable because it only cost $1,000 to put in the correct unit and the capitalized cost of the extra expense was $2,000. A prudent owner would replace it.
4	– $1,000	Less the cost, if curable, or depreciated cost, if incurable, of the proper item if included in new construction	The cost of installing the more efficient units today during original construction.
5	$1,667	Equals the depreciation attributable to functional obsolescence	

Exhibit 29.10   Incurable Functional Obsolescence Caused by a Superadequacy

Step	$	Item	Explanation
1	$45,000	Estimate the cost of the item	There is an item here and this is what it costs.
2	$0	Less the depreciation already charged	The pool is new.
3	$0	Plus the cost to cure or the present value of the loss (in many cases, this includes the cost of retrofitting an item)	This is not curable unless the market actually deducts something for having the item. There is no additional cost because of the pool.
4	$0	Less the cost, if curable, or depreciated cost, if incurable, of the proper item if included in new construction	There is no correct item here. This should be $0.
5	$45,000	Equals the depreciation attributable to functional obsolescence	This is clearly the answer and the procedure shows it. The cost of the superadequate item is included in the cost, and subtracting all of the cost should resemble the thought processes of market participants.

the subject's market would be subject to the same problem. Estimating losses using capitalized rent losses works well for income-producing properties when the typical buyer is an investor, but it does not work at all for houses or owner-occupied commercial properties.

An important factor in the calculation of external obsolescence is that the loss is usually extracted from the market. The extracted rate includes losses to the land and building, but in the cost approach the loss is only applied to the building. The appraiser must allocate the loss found in the market to the land and building values. For example, assume the paired sales analysis shows a loss of $50,000 because of the proximity to a negative influence (railroad tracks for a residen-

tial property or a noisy plant for an office building). If the building represents 80% of the value of the property, it would be appropriate but not necessarily required that the loss of $50,000 be allocated to the building and land at an 80%:20% ratio. Therefore, the loss to the building value would be only $40,000, and it can be assumed that the land value was $10,000.

External obsolescence always results from factors outside the property, which means the source will usually affect land and buildings. External obsolescence is different than functional obsolescence, which usually only affects the improvements. Allocation of a measured loss to the land and building is necessary in most cases.

Property Rights Adjustments

In the application of the cost approach, a property that is not at market occupancy or not at market rent may require a property rights adjustment because the value indication of the cost approach is of the fee simple estate at market rent and stabilized occupancy. The most common occurrences of a property rights adjustment are for properties that require a lease-up period and therefore would not be at stabilized occupancy at the time of completion of construction or properties that are leased at a below- or above-market rate. In the latter case, the leased fee interest would not be equal to the value of the fee simple interest because contract rent does not equal market rent.

The techniques used to determine the amount of a property rights adjustment include discounting the excess rent (or deficit rent) at a supportable rate of return, direct comparison of prices of leased fee interests and fee simple interests when comparable data is available, and discounted cash flow analysis of the values of the complete bundle of rights and the leased fee estate.

Cost Approach Examples

Exhibit 29.11 shows a fairly detailed application of the cost approach to a residential property. This example includes more details of depreciation than most residential appraisers would report. More detail than this could also be required. The total depreciation of 8.33% was extracted from comparable sales, which are not shown here. The extracted depreciation rate is from all causes, so the total depreciation is known. This exercise is for allocation and labeling purposes.

If you review the cost figures in Exhibit 29.11 carefully, you will find some inconsistencies due to rounding. In the rounding process, it is pos-

sible to round each calculation on each line (to the nearest dollar) and come to a different answer than if you round to a higher number of significant digits (say, two points past the decimal or to the nearest cent). When the numbers do not add up, the report looks wrong. This is a common problem for appraisers who seek the correct level of rounding.

Exhibit 29.12 shows how residential appraisers typically apply the cost approach. This presents a very simplistic view of the cost approach, which tends to ignore the details of the process. It is a fair analysis and is probably adequate for most properties in markets where the sales comparison data is very good.

Many people believe that all depreciation is physical unless a specific problem is found in exceptional cases. This is not true. Functional obsolescence exists in nearly all improvements after a short time. If typical depreciation rates were only physical losses, then decorating would never change, building designs would never go out of style, and modern conveniences would not be required to meet market demands. Actually, most depreciation is physical, but "typical" functional depreciation nearly always occurs. These losses do not need to be adjusted for because they occur in nearly all properties found in the same market. Examples include the following:

- *Decorating changes.* These are not physical losses but changes that occur on a regular basis. An adjustment for outdated decorating (i.e., a deficiency) is usually not necessary unless all the comparables have been redecorated to current standards.

- *Technological changes* like upgrading furnaces, air conditioners, or plumbing and electrical services. When the market indicates that

Exhibit 29.11   Cost Approach

Type of space	Area (sq. ft.)		Rate		Amount
Residence	2,200	@	$85.00	=	$187,000
Basement (base)	1,000	@	$23.00	=	$23,000
Basement finishing	800	@	$22.00	=	$17,600
Garage	750	@	$22.00	=	$16,500
Screened porch	400	@	$19.00	=	$7,600
Site improvements	1,300	@	$5.00	=	+ $6,500
Estimated cost all items					$258,200

Short-lived items	Cost	Age/Life		% Depreciation	$ Depreciation
Heating and air-conditioning	$6,500	5/25	=	20.00%	$1,300
Plumbing fixtures	$11,439	5/30	=	16.67%	$1,907
Lighting fixtures	$9,975	5/30	=	16.67%	$1,663
Roof covering, etc.	$7,500	5/25	=	20.00%	$1,500
Gutters and downspouts	$2,300	5/35	=	14.29%	$329
Carpet/vinyl	$9,500	5/15	=	33.33%	$3,167
Interior/exterior paint	$7,500	5/25	=	20.00%	$1,500
Garage door and opener	$3,400	5/15	=	33.33%	+ $1,133
Total	$58,114				− $12,499

Reproduction cost of improvements (from above)		
		$258,200
Less the cost of short-lived items	− $58,114	
Cost new of long-lived items only	$200,086	
Depreciation extracted from sales comparison (not included here) (0.08333)		
Total estimated depreciation from all causes (8.33% × 258,200 = $21,517)		
Short-lived physical depreciation (from above)		− $12,499
Estimated depreciation for long-lived items ($21,517 − 12,499)		− $9,018
Subtotal		$236,683
Functional losses (floor plan problem)		− $10,000
External losses (none)		$0
Depreciated value of improvements		$226,683
Estimated land value at highest and best use as though vacant		+ $65,000
Estimated value of the building and site		$291,683
Adjustment for property rights		$0
Final value estimate		$291,683
Rounded to		$290,000

its buyers want a new type of furnace, the old furnaces suffer some functional loss. However, the loss in value is included in all the comparables, so an additional adjustment is not needed.

- *Design differences.* If the subject has low ceilings and the market requires high ceilings, the subject will suffer a functional loss. Adjustment is not needed unless the comparables used do not have this problem.

If the appraiser is listing the depreciation by classification, there are many items that are functional losses but do not require additional adjustment in the sales comparison approach.

Exhibit 29.12   Residential Cost Approach

Estimated land value							$45,000
Estimated reproduction cost of improvements							
Dwelling			2,000 sq. ft. @ $95.00		=	$190,000	
Basement			1,000 sq. ft. @ $25.00		=	$25,000	
Fireplace, porches, patio, pool					=	$35,000	
Garage/carport			750 sq. ft. @ $20.00		=	$15,000	
"As is" value of the site improvements					=	+ $6,500	
Total estimated cost new						$271,500	
	Physical		**Functional**		**External**		
Less depreciation	$13,250	+	$2,500	+	$1,500	=	$17,250
Depreciated value of improvements							+ $254,250
Indicated value of cost approach					=		$299,250

1. An *incurable functional problem* is best defined as

   a) An item that cannot be physically cured

   b) An item that will not return as much in value as it costs to fix

   c) An item that is already cured

   d) An item that is scheduled to be cured but has not yet been cured

2. If a window has an effective age of 10 years and a remaining economic life of 25, the percentage of depreciation (rounded) is

   a) 20%

   b) 30%

   c) 40%

   d) 50%

3. A property has an overhead garage door that is 13 years old and costs $1,900 to replace. Because the inclement weather comes out of the northwest, these doors typically last 15 years if they face west and 25 years if they face east. This door faces east. What is the amount of value left in this item?

   a) $253

   b) $912

   c) $988

   d) $1,647

4. *Effective age* is

   a) The actual age of properties with better-than-normal maintenance

   b) Total economic life minus remaining economic life

   c) Total utility minus diminished utility

   d) Total economic life minus actual age

5. An item of depreciation is curable if

   a) The cost to cure is less than the expected increase in value

   b) The cost to cure is no greater than the reproduction cost

   c) The cost to cure is no greater than the replacement cost

   d) It has any remaining economic life

6. A property has a poor floor plan because it has only 1½ bathrooms in a market that clearly requires 2 or 2½ bathrooms. This problem could be corrected for about $5,500 by moving some interior walls around. The floor plan problem is fairly common in this market, and there is enough data to show that homes with this problem sell for $160,000 and homes without the problem (i.e., with 2 baths) sell for $170,000. This house is 30 years old. Adding the half bath during construction would have cost $1,000. This problem is best identified as

   a) Physical curable depreciation

   b) Functional curable obsolescence

   c) External curable obsolescence

   d) Functional incurable obsolescence

Use the following data to solve Review Exercises 7 through 10.

Assume you are appraising a 10-year-old residence. You estimate reproduction cost at $128,700. Your inspection of the property found only one item needing immediate repair. The garage door opener is broken, which would cost $450 to repair. The short-lived items are scheduled as follows:

Item	Age	Life	Cost New	Depreciation
Roof shingles	10	25	$6,500	$2,600
Furnace	10	20	3,500	1,750
Carpets	4	8	8,500	4,250
Vinyl floor covers	0	8	5,500	0
Kitchen and bathroom finishes	10	30	15,000	5,000
Exterior doors	10	25	4,400	1,760
Windows	10	35	2,900	828
Total			$46,300	$16,188

This home has only 1½ baths, which is clearly deficient. A number of homes in the subdivision have had the half bath converted to a full bath by removing a closet and installing a shower. This conversion costs about $2,000. Adding this shower during the initial construction of the rest of the house would have cost only $1,000.

Comparable sales (with the same bathroom problem) indicate the following depreciation overall:

	Sale 1	Sale 2	Sale 3	Sale 4
Sale price	$89,000	$99,000	$78,000	$88,000
Estimated land value	− 17,000	− 19,000	− 16,000	− 17,000
Calculated building value	$72,000	$80,000	$62,000	$71,000
Estimated reproduction cost	$99,500	$90,000	$80,000	$77,000
Less calculated building value	− 72,000	− 80,000	− 62,000	− 71,000
Calculated depreciation	$27,500	$10,000	$18,000	$6,000
Percentage depreciation	27.64%	11.11%	22.50%	7.79%
Age of improvement	18	7	15	5
Percentage depreciation per year	1.5356	1.5871	1.5000	1.5580

7. Estimate the depreciation for curable physical deterioration.

8. Estimate the depreciation for functional obsolescence.

9. Estimate the depreciation for short-lived items.

10. Estimate the depreciation for long-lived items.

Note: Unless otherwise noted, italicized references indicate the pages in *The Appraisal of Real Estate*, 14th edition, that readers should consult for additional discussion of these topics.

1. **b) An item that will not return as much in value as it costs to fix**
    Pages 599-600

2. **b) 30%**
    10/35

3. **b) $912**
    12/25 × 1,900
    Note that the numerator is 12 rather than 13 because the garage door has a remaining life of 12 (25 − 13).

4. **b) Total economic life minus remaining economic life**
    Pages 600-601

5. **a) The cost to cure is less than the expected increase in value**
    Pages 599-600

6. **b) Functional curable obsolescence**
    Pages 623-624

7. **$450 for the garage door opener**

8. **$1,000 for the excess cost to cure the floor plan problem**

9. **$16,188**

10. **The estimated rate of depreciation is 1.5% per year for all forms per the extraction table; therefore, total depreciation is**

0.015 × 10 × $128,700 =	$19,305
Less the functional curable item =	− $1,000
Less the short-lived depreciation =	− $16,188
Long-lived depreciation =	$2,117

    The garage door opener problem was not in the overall depreciation extraction, therefore the cost to repair it should not be subtracted from the $19,305 cost estimate. The bathroom problem was included in the $19,305 estimate, and the cost of the shower should be subtracted.

30

Reconciling Value Indications

In the second-to-last step of the appraisal process, appraisers reconcile their analyses into a final opinion of value. This is an important step in the appraisal process because at this point appraisers find that either they have a conclusive and convincing opinion of the value of the property or the appraisal has flaws causing the conclusion to be poorly supported. The reconciliation process is when the appraiser finds out what went well and what went wrong in the assignment and how to fix or at least explain any problems. This is usually a qualitative analysis.

The reconciled opinion of value is seldom an average of the data. If that were the case, the appraiser could easily soften the effect of the most significant data by watering it down with inferior data. Instead, the best quality data should be emphasized and the weaker data deemphasized.

Final Reconciliation

The objective of most appraisals is to estimate a defined value (usually market value) of specified rights in realty (usually the fee simple interest) as of a given date. Appraisers reconcile the several differing indications of value derived from the applicable approaches to value into a single, final opinion of value as of the valuation date. In the process of selecting the final opinion of market value from among the indications developed in the analysis, you must apply two important, distinct procedures:

1. Review all the previous work and analysis, checking and verifying the data, logic, and techniques used.
2. Apply logic and judgment in the procedure known as *reconciliation* to arrive at the final opinion of value

Most appraisals include a great deal of research and usually a similar amount of reporting. There are many opportunities for typos and other inadvertent mistakes. Reconciliation is the time when the appraiser should find those mistakes.

Consistency of Items and Findings

Internal consistency is essential if the value indications derived from the different approaches and procedures employed are to be reconciled with one another. Each approach to value is interrelated and should be consistent with the other. For example, it would be illogical to claim that an in-ground pool is worthless but also to say that there is no apparent functional obsolescence. It is inconsistent to adjust the cost approach for a functional problem like a poor floor plan but neglect to compensate for it in the sales comparison approach. For consistency's sake, some appraisers prepare a handwritten "summary of facts" that they fill out as they read the first draft of an appraisal report. This enables them to quickly look to what was said previously in the report.

Single Value Opinion vs. Range of Indicated Values

Most appraisal assignments require appraisers to develop a single, most probable opinion of market value. It is sometimes useful and helpful to provide an indication of the range in which the market value falls. The range of indicated values is generally determined by the upper and lower indications of value from the different approaches used in the appraisal.

Reevaluation

The first task appraisers should do in the reconciliation process is read what they have written in the report. This may seem odd, but it is the single

KEY TERMS	
confidence interval	probability range
final opinion of value	range of value
point estimate	rounding

most important thing the author of the report can do. Writing a report but never reading it on paper is the easiest way to find yourself in a lawsuit or an ethics case, or you may just lose a good client because of the lack of quality control. It is imperative that appraisers write the report, print it out, and then ideally wait a day to read what was written. A review of a draft report is probably the best tool for catching errors. Once the report is out the door and the weighty decisions are made, it may be very difficult to correct any errors that are found.

> It is amazing how much even the most knowledgeable appraisers can do wrong in an appraisal report if they do not read the finished product before sending it to the client.

The second most important task is to read your field notes. Some appraisers take excellent notes but never refer to them, which leads to errors in the property description area. Even if you are not required to do so, try to draw a plan of the improvement to ensure consistency with the property description. Try to take extra pictures of the improvement and print them out (assuming you are taking digital photos) so you can compare the photos with the report. It is common for appraisers to review photos, drawings, and maps and find things they forgot. Again, it is much easier to review your notes, photographs, and maps before you write the report than it is to amend the report after it is out the door.

Another common mistake that gets appraisers into trouble is the practice of "cloning" reports. That is, appraisers will make a computer copy of

---

Reconciliation Checklist

☐ Check *procedures* and *mechanics*—i.e., techniques, calculations, and adjustments. Appraisers sometimes make adjustments the wrong way, adding when they should be subtracting and vice versa. Sometimes appraisers research data well but list it in the analysis incorrectly. For example, a sale price of $434,000 could be typed in as $443,000, or even worse, $343,000.

☐ Check for *consistency* within the approaches to value. It is not unusual for an appraiser to decide that the subject property has a problem and adjust for it in the cost approach but forget to make an adjustment in the sales comparison approach. In some cases, however, the adjustment for an item in the cost approach is not needed in the sales comparison approach.

☐ Check the analysis in each approach for *logic* and consistency with the *highest and best use* as though vacant and as improved. Appraisers sometimes choose data that is not consistent with their opinion of the highest and best use of a property. Appraisers violate the consistent use rule when they value the land under one use and the building improvements under another use.

☐ Check the *applicability* of the principles of each approach or procedure to the appraisal problem and the property being appraised. Appraisers sometimes use a technique that buyers and sellers in that market do not. For example, many buyers and sellers of single-tenant, owner-occupied industrial properties focus on condition, size, age, location, and access, but they are not particularly concerned about what the property will rent for or its net operating income. It is not unusual for appraisers to think that all buyers of nonresidential properties are concerned primarily with income potential, but often they are not.

☐ Check market data for *reliability* and *accuracy*. This is probably the area that causes the largest number of problems for ethical appraisers. In many markets, data can be researched readily, but misstatements can be made if it is not confirmed. Reporting inaccurate market data is usually a mistake made by appraisers who are working too quickly or suffer from unreasonable time constraints. If you do not confirm your data, you must use enough data that one or two pieces of bad data will not affect the conclusion. In other words, a misreported sale price of a comparable property would not be as significant if there were seven comparables than it would be if there were only three. A minimal amount of data requires a higher level of verification. Surplus data allows a lower level of verification because less emphasis is given to any one piece of data.

Consistency Checklist

☐ Is the building area listed in the description of improvements the same as the amount used in the three approaches to value?

☐ Are the property features listed in the description of improvements the same as in the three approaches to value?

☐ Is every item of condition, functional inutility, or locational influence listed in the neighborhood analysis or property description included in the applicable approaches?

☐ Is the effective date of appraisal consistent with the data presented? If you are backdating the appraisal, do the sales or cost data reflect the market on the effective date?

☐ Are the limiting conditions consistent with the remainder of the document? Who inspected the property, and who is signing the report?

the last file they prepared (sometimes including the pictures) and then type over the top of the old report and intend to enter the new data. The problem is that appraisers receive phone calls, people come into the office, or they go out to lunch, and then they return to a file and cannot remember where they left off. It is much better to create a template with macro-level data already in place but no micro-level data. Then, you can complete the appraisal without including data carried over from a previous report. Again, regardless of the techniques used, always read the report on paper after it is completed.

Do not clone an old report—it nearly always leads to mistakes, some of which may be significant.

Reconciliation Criteria

Appropriateness

The three approaches to value rarely have equal relevance in a specific assignment. The income capitalization approach is less significant in the valuation of one-unit homes, but it is probably the most significant approach in the valuation of a multitenant office building. The cost approach means very little in an appraisal of a 40-year-old home in an urban setting, but it may be the best approach available in the valuation of a 40-year-old office building in an urban setting. The sales comparison approach is usually applicable in all markets, but it may suffer in some markets where data is hard to find or commonly misreported or where details are not reported at all.

Appraisers have only a few techniques to work with in the appraisal process, therefore it is important to use the available techniques to the fullest. The emphasis in the report and the approaches used should mirror the thoughts and behavior of market participants. If the market relies on comparable listings as the determinant of value, the comparable sales will be the most important data. If the market relies on cash flow analysis, the income capitalization approach will be most significant. If the market compares the existing properties with new construction costs, the cost approach is the most significant.

Accuracy

If only three comparable sales are available and significant adjustments were made for property differences, the sales comparison approach may not be as accurate as it should be. If the subject improvements are old or have many functional problems, the cost approach may have so many deductions that it is rendered useless as an indication of value. The income capitalization approach can be weakened by the lack of suitable support for the income, expenses, or capitalization rates.

Quantity of Evidence

Do not assume that you need only three comparable sales because that is all the client requires. When you minimize the inputs, you run the risk of reporting data that is skewed or misleading. More market evidence is almost always preferable to less. If you present five or six comparable sales in most appraisal reports, the likelihood of an error due to incorrect reporting or misleading data decreases substantially. It is probably easier to present more data in the report than it is to explain later why your value opinion is correct when an appraisal reviewer disagrees with it.

Final Opinion of Value

A single point estimate is not required by professional valuation standards, but most clients want or need one. Therefore, most appraisers are required to give a single, best opinion of value, even when it would be much wiser to give a range of indicated

---

Rounding
The final value opinion should be rounded appropriately to eliminate any implication or unwarranted claim of precision or excessive accuracy. Rounding brings the estimate to a reasonable degree of accuracy consistent with the standards of the local market, the price level or range within which the value estimate falls, and the type of property involved. The degree of rounding implies the level of accuracy of the analysis. If the final opinion of value is reported as · $108,653, then the appraiser knows value to the $1 level or the difference between $108,653 and $108,654. · $108,660, then the appraiser knows value to the $10 level or the difference between $108,660 and $108,670. · $108,700, then the appraiser knows value to the $100 level or the difference between $108,700 and $108,800, and so on.

values. Appraisers are not required to be advocates for their value opinions. If the value opinion is marginalized by a lack of comparable data, say so in the report and tell your client that the value opinion is your best possible estimate but the complexity of the appraisal problem resulted in a value opinion with less support than is typical. Do not try to sell a weak value opinion as a well-supported one.

1. The final value opinion should
   a) Be very precise
   b) Be rounded to allow the lender to make the loan
   c) Be rounded to show that the number is an opinion, not a precise calculation
   d) Never be rounded

2. The process by which the appraiser evaluates, chooses, and selects a final value opinion is known as
   a) Review
   b) Reconciliation
   c) Recalculation
   d) Data manipulation

3. Giving a client a range of values rather than a single value opinion
   a) Is not allowed by standards rules
   b) Implies that you are open to suggestion
   c) Allows for a greater probability of correctness
   d) Implies that you do not know what you are doing

4. In an appraisal of a property using the three approaches to value, each approach resulted in a different value indication. The indicated value by the cost approach was $100,000, the indicated value by the sales comparison approach was $93,500, and the indicated value by the income capitalization approach was $95,000. Are you forced to choose one of these value indications?
   a) Yes, always. It is only logical that you use the value estimates that you have developed.
   b) Yes, if one equals the sale price.
   c) No, you can give the clients any value they want regardless of the data.
   d) No, you can choose any one of the numbers or any number between and, in some cases, slightly above or below the range.

5. If the three approaches to value provide three different value indications, the appraiser should
   a) Average the three numbers
   b) Choose the highest number to bring in more business
   c) Choose the lowest number to limit liability
   d) Choose a value opinion that best represents the market for the subject based on all data available as of the date of the appraisal

6. How significant is the reported open market sale price of the subject property if the sale has not closed yet?
   a) Insignificant
   b) Insignificant because it is only pending
   c) Significant because after the deal closes, it will be a comparable sale
   d) Significant because the buyers have made a statement with their checkbook

7. A residence has been listed for sale in the MLS for the last six months at a price of $124,900, and it has not sold. In this market, the average marketing period is 45 days for this type of property.
   a) The subject property's market value could be higher or lower than the list price.
   b) The subject property's market value could be higher than the list price.
   c) The subject property's market value could be lower than the list price.
   d) The subject property's market value is less than the list price.

8. If the subject is a special-purpose property and the value indication by the cost approach is much higher than the value indication by the sales comparison approach, what is the typical problem?
   a) The cost approach needs to be adjusted (or adjusted more) for the loss in value due to functional obsolescence.
   b) The cost approach needs to be adjusted for external obsolescence.
   c) The sales comparison approach needs to be adjusted down to make it the same.
   d) The income capitalization approach needs to be developed to average the two value indications out.

9. The appraiser researched several sales of residential development land as shown in the table. Reconcile the data in the following sales comparison grid. What are the strengths and weaknesses of this analysis? Should the adjustments be larger or smaller? Should the more recent sales be emphasized over the properties that are more similar in size?

	Subject	Comparable 1		Comparable 2		Comparable 3	
Address	1125 Rookery Road	SR 44 at Rookery Road		SEC Hadley and Smallson Road		Bridge Street west of SR76	
Data source	Site visit	Co-op # 29601		Co-op # 2586		Co-op # 2586	
Sale price	n/a		$859,654		$1,556,987		$1,066,000
Price per acre	n/a		$13,225		$14,551		$14,806
Rights transferred	fee simple	fee simple	0.0%	fee simple	0.0%	fee simple	0.0%
Subtotal			$13,225		$14,551		$14,806
Financing	assume cash	cash sale	0.0%	cash sale	0.0%	cash sale	0.0%
Subtotal			$13,225		$14,551		$14,806
Conditions of sale	arm's-length	arm's-length	0.0%	arm's-length	0.0%	arm's-length	0.0%
Subtotal			$13,225		$14,551		$14,806
Market conditions	current	6 months	1.5%	12 months	3.0%	18 months	4.5%
Subtotal			$13,423		$14,988		$15,472
Topography	rolling/wooded	equal	0.0%	equal	0.0%	equal	0.0%
Location	Rookery Road	equal	0.0%	superior	-5.0%	superior	-5.0%
Access	limited—2 points	equal	0.0%	superior	-5.0%	equal	0.0%
Visibility	fair—no major road	equal	0.0%	superior	-5.0%	equal	0.0%
Flood area	0.00%	0.00%	0.0%	0.00%	0.0%	0.00%	0.0%
Road frontage	200	1,000	0.0%	1,200	0.0%	900	0.0%
Average depth	1,720	1,720	0.0%	1,720	0.0%	2,640	0.0%
Size (acres)	100.0	65.0	-3.5%	107.0	0.7%	72.0	-2.8%
Zoning	Residential R-3	Residential R-2	5.0%	Residential R-3	0.0%	Residential R-4	-5.0%
Utilities	water/sewer/gas	water/sewer/gas	0.0%	water/sewer/gas	0.0%	water/sewer/gas	0.0%
Other factors	none	none	0.0%	none	0.0%	none	0.0%
Net adjustment			1.5%		-14.3%		-12.8%
Indicated value per acre			$13,624		$12,845		$13,491

10. The subject is a small industrial property in a small town. Reconcile the data in the following sales comparison grid. Are the adjustments correct? If you made the adjustment for age of improvement larger, what would be the effect? If the market conditions (time) adjustment were larger, would it influence the analysis?

	Subject	Comparable 1		Comparable 2		Comparable 3		Comparable 4	
Address	1258 S. Meridian	2120 S. Meridian		125 W. Maryland Street		351 W. Georgia Street		137 E. Maryland	
Price			$1,035,000		$925,000		$1,315,000		$654,321
Property rights conveyed	fee simple	fee simple	0.0%	fee simple	0.0%	fee simple	0.0%	fee simple	0.0%
Subtotal			$1,035,000		$925,000		$1,315,000		$654,321
Financing terms	cash to seller	cash to seller	0.0%	cash to seller	0.0%	cash to seller	0.0%	cash to seller	0.0%
Subtotal			$1,035,000		$925,000		$1,315,000		$654,321
Conditions of sale	arm's-length	arm's-length	0.0%	arm's-length	0.0%	arm's-length	0.0%	arm's-length	0.0%
Subtotal			$1,035,000		$925,000		$1,315,000		$654,321
Expenditures after sale	assume none	none	0.0%	none	0.0%	$55,000 repairs	4.2%	none	0.0%
Subtotal			$1,035,000		$925,000		$1,370,230		$654,321
Market conditions (time)	now	6 mos.	1.5%	12 mos.	3.0%	18 mos.	4.5%	24 mos.	6.0%
Cash-equivalent price			$1,050,525		$952,820		$1,374,487		$693,679
Price/sq. ft. of GBA			$23.88		$28.02		$35.24		$31.53
Site size (sq. ft.)	82,000	95,000	-5.0%	82,000	0.0%	135,000	-10.0%	75,000	0.0%
Location	Merrill-West	S. Meridian	10.0%	Merrill-West	0.0%	Englers Addn.	0.0%	Merrill-West	0.0%
Access/visibility	average	average	0.0%	average	0.0%	average	0.0%	average	0.0%
Building design	1-story/avg.	1-story/avg.	0.0%	1-story/avg.	0.0%	1-story/avg.	0.0%	1-story/avg.	0.0%
Construction quality	masonry/avg.	masonry/avg.	0.0%	masonry/avg.	0.0%	masonry/avg.	0.0%	masonry/avg.	0.0%
Improvement age (years)	15	24	4.5%	22	3.5%	22	3.5%	10	-2.5%
Improvement condition	excellent	average	5.0%	average	5.0%	average	5.0%	average	5.0%
Above-ground building area	37,777	44,000		34,000		39,000		22,000	
Finished area	9%	18%	-3.2%	10%	-0.4%	35%	-9.1%	25%	-5.6%
Basement area (sq. ft.)	0	0	0.0%	0	0.0%	0	0.0%	0	0.0%
Zoning	Industrial I-4	Industrial I-3	5.0%	Industrial I-5	-5.0%	Industrial I-5	-5.0%	Industrial I-5	-5.0%
Other		none	0.0%	none	0.0%	none	0.0%	none	0.0%
Net adjustment			16.3%		3.1%		-15.6%		-8.1%
Indicated value per sq. ft. building w/land			**$27.77**		**$28.89**		**$29.74**		**$28.98**

11. Reconcile the data in the following sales comparison grid. Remember to consider the quality of the data as well as the amount of adjustment.

	Subject	Comparable 1		Comparable 2		Comparable 3	
Address	360 N. Kenwood	361 N. Kenwood Avenue		134 W. 3rd Street		236 W. 3rd Street	
Sale price			$29,850		$28,325		$39,950
Sale price/GLA		$18.29		$19.75		$24.97	
Data source	Site visit	MLS 832464		MLS 924985		MLS 922356	
Value adjustments							
Financing concessions	assume none	no concessions		no concessions		$1,200 CC	-1,200
Date of sale	Jan-14	1-Jul-13	300	1-Jan-13	600	1-Jul-12	1,200
Location	Longacre	Longacre	—	Green Acres	—	Green Acres	—
Leasehold/fee simple	fee simple	fee simple	—	fee simple	—	fee simple	—
Site	59 x 92	59 x 92	—	45 x 145	—	66 x 34	—
View	residential	residential	—	residential	—	residential	—
Design and appeal	2-story/avg.	2-story/avg.	—	2-story/avg.	—	1-story/avg.	—
Quality of construction	frame/avg.	frame/avg.	—	frame/avg.	—	frame/avg.	—
Age	90	85	—	80	—	80	—
Condition	average	average	—	inferior	5,000	superior	-4,000
A/G room count	8/4/1½	6/3/1½	—	6/3/1	500	6/3/1½	—
Gross living area	1,800	1,632	700	1,434	1,500	1,600	800
Basement area	896	816	200	597	600	744	300
Basement fin. area	0	0	—	0	—	0	—
Functional utility	average	average	—	average	—	average	—
Heating and cooling	GFA/cent. AC	GFA/no AC	500	GFA/cent. AC	—	GFA/cent. AC	—
Energy-efficient items	standard	equal	—	equal	—	equal	—
Garage/carport	none	none	—	2-car det. garage	-1,500	2-car det. garage	-1,500
Porches, patios, etc.	porch	porch	—	enclosed porch	-500	porch	—
Fence, pool, etc.	none	none	—		—		—
Other			—		—		—
Net adjustment			1,700		6,200		-4,400
Adjusted sale price of comparable			$31,550		$34,525		$35,550

Gross living area adjustment = $4.00

Basement area adjustment rate = $2.00

Date of sale adjustment rate = 2.0% per year

Note: Unless otherwise noted, italicized references indicate the pages in *The Appraisal of Real Estate*, 14th edition, that readers should consult for additional discussion of these topics.

1. **c) Be rounded to show that the number is an opinion, not a precise calculation**
   Page 647

2. **b) Reconciliation**
   Page 641

3. **c) Allows for a greater probability of correctness**
   Pages 646-647 and this student handbook

4. **d) No, you can choose any one of the numbers or any number between and, in some cases, slightly above or below the range.**
   Page 642

5. **d) Choose a value opinion that best represents the market for the subject based on all data available as of the date of the appraisal**
   Page 642

6. **d) Significant because the buyers have made a statement with their checkbook**
   This student handbook

7. **d) The subject property's market value is less than the list price.**
   This student handbook

8. **a) The cost approach needs to be adjusted (or adjusted more) for the loss in value due to functional obsolescence.**
   Pages 642-643

9. As shown, this analysis is based on the price per acre, which removes size as an item of dissimilarity that needs to be adjusted for. Some appraisers will adjust for a "quantity discount"—i.e., if the analysis is based on a price per acre, the price per acre is lower the more acres you buy.

   The adjustments for topography, location, access, and other property characteristics are all subjective and will vary from one appraiser to another, but care should be taken to avoid making adjustments that cannot be supported. A 5% adjustment for an item of dissimilarity is quite believable to most people, but if an adjustment is estimated at 30%-50% for a single item, an experienced reader begins to doubt the comparability of the sales presented. Appraisers should explain any very large adjustments to ensure they have credibility in the eyes of the reader.

   The market conditions adjustments will often be tied to the rate of appreciation in the subject's market. The adjustment for zoning may be based on market-extracted rates showing the differences in the sale prices of various land sales. Since much of an appraiser's work will have a subjective element, it is important to provide support for adjustments or at least the rationale for adjustments whenever possible.

   In this analysis, the rate of adjustment for Comparable 1 is much less than for Sales 2 and 3, and as a result most appraisers would give much more credibility to that indication of value. Sale 1 is also the most recent sale, which means it is a better indication of the current market. Sale 2 has the same zoning but has substantial adjustments for location, access, and visibility.

10. In this analysis, the appraiser has made the adjustments for the related items first and subtotaled after each one. The adjustment for expenditures immediately after the sale of Comparable 3 compensates for $55,000 of repairs that the buyer had to pay to bring this property to a usable condition. This increased the price for that cost, and subsequent adjustments were based on the higher amount.

    The site adjustment was not very large because the unit of comparison—square foot of building area including land—obviously includes a land component. This means the price per square foot of a small building includes a smaller site and the price per square foot of a larger building includes a larger site. Similarly, no adjustment for the size of the building was made because of the unit of comparison, which presumably compensates for differences in building size.

    Sales 1, 2, and 3 are all older buildings. Only Sale 4 is newer than the subject property. It would be preferable to have a few more comparables that were newer than the subject to bracket the subject and ensure the adjustment rates were accurate. By bracketing the subject's age with the age of the comparables, the range in indicated values would obviously widen rather than get narrower.

    The quality of construction adjustments were made to compensate for the subject's superior quality. This is, of course, very subjective, but in many markets these adjustments are necessary and appropriate.

    The adjustments for zoning were made to compensate for the higher utility of an otherwise identical property simply because of a higher zoning classification. In the case of industrial properties, a higher zoning classification might allow outside storage of inventory that is not allowed under a lesser zoning classification.

Comparable 1 is the most recent, but it was adjusted the most (16.3%). Sale 2 is the second most recent and was adjusted only a little (3.1%). Comparable 2 is probably the best comparable and should be given the most consideration. Note that the indicated value of Comparable 2 is bracketed by the indicated values of the comparables with much larger net adjustments (Comparables 1 and 3) and is close to the indicated value of the other comparable.

11. Again, this sales comparison grid is presented for discussion purposes. The single largest adjustment is made for the differences in the condition of the improvements. The inferior condition of Comparable 2 accounts for 17.7% (5,000/28,325) of the total price of that property, and the adjustment to Comparable 3 for its superior condition is more than twice as large as any other adjustment made to that comparable. Note that the condition of Comparable 2 is inferior to that of the subject property even though the subject is 10 years older than the comparable. For older homes like this, the age of the improvement is probably less important to a buyer than the actual physical condition of the structure. Since the condition rating is based on comparison with competing properties, rather than all properties, condition adjustments are not needed if the properties are different ages but are in average condition for their age and market.

The adjustments for condition may seem excessive to some appraisers, but remember that buildings of this age will often have a large amount of deferred maintenance and buyers may have to invest a lot of money to bring the property up to a marketable condition. These adjustments can go both ways because it is also possible for a comparable to have had much remodeling and updating work done.

All three comparable properties are smaller than the subject property, and the subject has one more bedroom and two more rooms in total than any of the comparables. As discussed previously, by making an adjustment for size and room count, the appraiser can be accused of double-counting for the same item. Some appraisers seldom make adjustments for size and room count, while others will make a smaller adjustment for the amount of building area and then make room count adjustments as well. Most appraisers will make adjustments for a greater or smaller number of bathrooms in a dwelling. Bathrooms are very expensive to build, so logically adjustment is needed to compensate for these costs. The area included in a bathroom is already reflected in the gross living area line.

Comparable 2 has a much deeper site than the subject property and Comparable 3 has a much smaller site. In this analysis, adjustments were not made for those differences because it was believed that the site size did not have a significant effect on the price of those properties as compared to the subject. The lack of adjustment for this line item could be controversial if another appraiser argued that any differences in land size are significant and worthy of an adjustment.

All three comparable sales occurred within 18 months of the date of sale of the subject property. The calculation of an adjustment for changing market conditions is straightforward based on an observed annual appreciation rate of 2% in that market. A 2% annual appreciation rate equates to a 0.17% monthly rate (0.0017), which is then multiplied by the number of months that have elapsed from the date of sale of the comparable to the effective date of appraisal. In some markets, this adjustment is not needed because of low rates of change and the availability of recent comparable sales, but in many markets a conditions of sale adjustment is used in every appraisal. All appraisers must know how to make these adjustments.

Overall, Comparable 1 appears to be most similar to the subject property because it has so few adjustments, is the most recent, and is located in the same subdivision. Its address even suggests that it is across the street from the subject property. The only significant differences are the size of the house and the lack of central air-conditioning.

31

The Appraisal Report

An *appraisal* is an action, not a thing. It is the act or process of developing an opinion of value. An *appraisal report* is the method of delivering the conclusions of the appraisal process. Because an appraisal report can be used for many reasons, it is important for appraisers to follow reporting standards. If an appraiser wants to deceive a reader, it can be done easily. The average reader of an appraisal report may never see the subject property or the comparables and therefore cannot spot deception readily. The professional standards for appraisers include both the act and process of estimating value and the reporting of the value conclusion (in both oral and written forms).

Professional Standards for Appraisal Reporting

Professional standards like the Uniform Standards of Professional Appraisal Practice (USPAP) define what has to be in an appraisal report. These sets of rules are revised and updated regularly–every year or two for USPAP–so appraisers must keep abreast of the changes.

The USPAP document is divided into standards, statements, and advisory opinions. The standards and accompanying standards rules are the most significant portion. Of this portion, the most important regulations pertaining to real estate appraisal reports are

- Standard 2, which gives appraisers guidance on what must be included in appraisal reports
- Standard 3, which includes requirements for appraisers who review appraisal reports

Other standards provide guidance and rules on the development and reporting of value opinions relating to personal property, business valuation, and mass appraisal.

An appraiser is required to state certain things in an appraisal report to ensure that the reader is not misled. More importantly, these statements require appraisers to certify that certain minimum standards of practice have been met (see Standards Rule 2-3 of USPAP and the Certification Standard of the Appraisal Institute). You must sign your name to a statement in the appraisal report that explains the specific minimum requirements you have met.

Although not all states require all appraisers to follow USPAP in all appraisals and reports, the USPAP rules must be followed when the report is done for a federal lending institution, for a client who requests it, or if required by state law. In many states, compliance with USPAP is mandatory in all assignments, and USPAP is a good guide even when compliance is not required.

Appraisal Reporting Options

Form reports and narrative appraisal reports are the most commonly used reporting formats. Most appraisal reports for one- to four-unit residential properties are prepared on government-approved forms. Most appraisal reports for nonresidential property types are prepared in a narrative format.

Appraisal reports do not always have to be written, however. An appraiser's testimony as an expert witness in a court proceeding is considered an oral report. The professional standards for developing an opinion of value that will be delivered

> Reviewing appraisal reports is a function in which appraisers read and prepare a critical review of another appraiser's work. This process is somewhat similar to what an accountant does in an audit and is a great tool used by most clients for quality control and in some situations for dispute resolution.

KEY TERMS

oral report	written appraisal report

Note that discussion of schools and the personal information, attitudes, and preferences of buyers in an appraisal report may violate state and federal fair housing laws. While it is important for you to know about the attitudes of buyers, you cannot report certain information in most residential appraisals used for lending. It is not your job to lead the reader of an appraisal report to a conclusion that one type or class of buyer should or should not buy a particular residential property.

The Conduct section of the Ethics Rule of USPAP states explicitly that

> An appraiser... must not use or rely on unsupported conclusions relating to characteristics such as race, color, religion, national origin, gender, marital status, familial status, age, receipt of public assistance income, handicap, or an **unsupported** conclusion that homogeneity of such characteristics is necessary to maximize value [emphasis added]

In some cases, you cannot even use supported conclusions in assignments relating to those characteristics because they are precluded by applicable law.

through an oral report are no different from the standards that apply when delivering the conclusions through a written report.

Oral Reports

The most common form of oral reporting is done directly to clients when appraisers are asked for their opinion of value only. USPAP states that the appraiser must report certain minimum data in an oral appraisal report, but most clients will ask the appraiser to "cut to the chase." Appraisers are sometimes asked to testify in court about property values. This type of testimony can be considered an oral appraisal report, but in most cases the appraiser is testifying about the content of a written appraisal report that is put into evidence in the case.

Oral appraisal reports can be a great tool, but they also can be misleading to some people because the appraiser's words can be misquoted later to others. Appraisers must take very good notes about verbal conversations that include value opinions to ensure that they are not misquoted later.

Written Reports

The format and level of detail in written appraisal reports varies from the form reports used in many appraisals of one-unit residential properties to the long narrative document that may need to be

created in the appraisal of a complex commercial property.

Form appraisals are highly structured, and nearly all forms have the same data in the same places. This consistency of presentation allows clients to find the data easily. Form reports are also compatible with computer programs and electronic data interchange (EDI) systems. In some cases, form reports do not provide enough detail to adequately explain or clarify significant problems or issues, and you may have to prepare additional pages to address specific questions lenders have about a property.

Narrative appraisal reports can have many different formats, depending on the property type, the client's needs, and issues that need to be dealt with. Narrative appraisal reports offer the most flexibility but require the most work. A complete narrative appraisal report may be as short as 10 pages or as long as 200 pages or more.

Form Reports

A form appraisal report is also a type of checklist. Using a form is a way to standardize the presentation of data, which facilitates electronic data

---

The Record Keeping Rule of USPAP (2014-2015 ed.) says

> A workfile must be in existence prior to the issuance of any report. A written summary of an oral report must be added to the workfile within a reasonable time after the issuance of the oral report.

The FAQ section of USPAP adds

> If an appraiser testifies in court to the opinions provided in a written report, the appraiser must also have a summary of the testimony in the file.

---

oral report
An appraisal report that is transmitted orally rather than in written form. An unwritten appraisal report should include a property description as well as all facts, assumptions, conditions, and reasoning on which the value conclusion is based. The reporting requirements for oral reports are the same as those applied to written reports, according to professional valuation standards.

written appraisal report
Any written communication of an appraisal, appraisal review, or consulting service that is transmitted to the client upon completion of an assignment.

interchange and other methods of transferring data from computer to computer. Forms reports also eliminate the possibility of skipping important steps because the steps in the process are enumerated on the form itself. Lenders, attorneys, and other clients all use some sort of form report for the reasons described above as well as to allow them to compare prices for appraisal services.

For all their strengths, form reports can also serve as an excuse for bad appraisal habits. It is never satisfactory for an appraiser to say, "There was not enough room on the form to explain." Nor is it ever appropriate to say, "The form does not ask that question, so I do not have to research or report that." Professional standards like USPAP do not differentiate between form and narrative reports, so requirements for appraisals do not change depending on the written format used. The scope of work of the appraisal assignment dictates the format of the appraisal report, not the other way around.

Not all government forms comply with the current edition of USPAP, so appraisers must review these forms for compliance when they are used. The standards are revised every two years, but some appraisal forms have not been changed in two decades. It is the appraiser's responsibility to comply with the current professional standards relating to reporting.

Narrative Appraisal Reports

Narrative appraisal reports vary substantially in content, format, and length. A narrative report can be 10 pages or 200 pages long, and in some cases even more than 200 pages. The size of the document depends on the complexity of the appraisal problem. Although most narrative reports are written on a computer using a base or template report, they are much more flexible than a form report that has a specific number of pages and sections.

A narrative appraisal report may be similar to a form appraisal in that much of the data can be put in standard-sized tables and grids and organized in standard sections and analysis pages. With standardized tables, these reports can be as easy to complete as a form appraisal report. However, most appraisers vary the content to suit the perceived requirements of the assignment.

Effective as of the 2014-2015 edition, USPAP allows for two types of appraisal reports: (1) what is called simply an *appraisal report* and (2) a *restricted appraisal report*, distinguished by the content and level of information provided. The latter option is intended for use by the client only and must contain a notice to any reader that the conclusions and opinions expressed in the report may not be understood properly without information in the appraiser's workfile that was not included in the restricted appraisal report. In the determination of the scope of work of the assignment, the appraiser and the client must discuss who the intended users of the appraisal are, and this in turn largely determines which reporting option under USPAP is appropriate.

A narrative appraisal report is typically organized into a few major sections that echo the sequence of the valuation process:

- *Introduction.* The introduction to the appraisal report often includes a table of contents and executive summary of the conclusions of the report to help the intended user navigate the document. It also can include a title page and letter of transmittal, and it must include a signed certification. The certification will be discussed later in this chapter.

- *Identification of the appraisal problem and scope of work.* This portion of the report states the client, the intended use and user, the subject real estate, the property rights appraised, the type and definition of value, and the effective date of the value opinion.

Uniform Residential Appraisal Report and AI Reports Forms

The Uniform Residential Appraisal Report (URAR) form is used in countless appraisals every year. Fannie Mae and Freddie Mac developed the URAR form for their own purposes, but many other lenders use the form as well. The URAR form is used for appraisals of one-unit attached and detached homes that include both exterior and interior inspections. Other standard Fannie-Freddie forms are used for small residential income properties, individual condominium units, and other special assignments.

For non-mortgage lending situations, the AI Reports AI-100 Summary Appraisal Report—Residential form is an option. Examples of purposes for which the AI-100 form can be used include valuation for insurance, probate, litigation, and estate and financial planning purposes. It is not a good idea to use a secondary market lending form to report an appraisal with an intended use for non-lending purposes. These forms include many statements and certifications that apply to lender work but not to appraisals for non-lending purposes.

Any extraordinary assumptions, hypothetical conditions, jurisdictional exceptions, general assumptions, or limiting conditions are also stated here.

- *Presentation of data.* The data presented includes the legal description of the subject, any personal property or other items that are not real property, the subject's listing and sale history, a description of the subject's location and market area, descriptions of the land and improvements, and tax information.
- *Analysis of data and conclusions.* This portion of the report describes the market analysis, the highest and best use analysis, the land value, the application of one or more of the approaches to value, the reconciliation and final value opinion, the exposure time estimate, and the appraiser's qualifications.
- *Addenda.* Addenda to the report may include photographs, a detailed legal description of the subject, detailed statistical data, leases or lease summaries, or exhibits.

Delivering the report document itself fulfills the final step of the valuation process.

Appraiser Liability

While many appraisers will never be sued for their work, it is becoming more common for appraisers to be held responsible for errors in appraisal reports such as failing to report perceived deficiencies in the property—e.g., a leaky roof or a failed heating plant—or poor reporting of items like flood hazard areas or zoning problems. To insure against losses due to mistakes, you can obtain errors and omission insurance. Education focused on physical real estate and buildings can also help minimize your exposure to this type of lawsuit.

The public at large often perceives appraisers as building inspectors more than valuation professionals. Therefore, in the eyes of buyers and their attorneys, you are responsible for knowing what the repairs or maintenance problems of a property are.

Helpful Hint

To review the certification required by the Uniform Standards of Professional Appraisal Practice, see Standards Rule 2-3. To review the certification statement required of members of the Appraisal Institute, see the Certification Standard of the Appraisal Institute.

In recent cases, appraisers have been sued for their value opinions or conclusions when their clients have lost a lot of money on property investments. The greater the losses, the more likely the investor will look for a way to shift financial responsibility.

The requirements of professional appraisal standards stipulate the steps that appraisers must take to achieve competency. Under the certification requirements of relevant professional standards, appraisers give written notice of compliance by signing their names to documents in which they make certain warranties and claims. You should review the certification statement carefully before signing an appraisal report. Most appraisers do not read these certifications very often, if at all. This can put them at risk of being sued if the clients can prove that the appraisers who signed the report did not perform all the required steps in the appraisal.

Another problem related to the certification required by professional standards is the "ghost appraiser." It is common in some markets for trainees to perform appraisals and the boss to sign the appraisal report as if the boss had done the work. Clearly, appraisers who engage in these practices are misleading their clients, which is unethical. The certification statements included in form reports were designed to make appraisers swear that they are the parties who inspected the property and collected and analyzed comparable sales and other relevant data. Statements like the following make an appraiser who signs the report responsible for the reported conclusions:

- I have (or have not) made a personal inspection of the property that is the subject of this report. (If more than one person signs this certification, the certification must clearly specify which individuals did and which individuals did not make a personal inspection of the appraised property.)
- No one provided significant real property appraisal assistance to the person signing this certification. (If there are exceptions, the name of each individual providing significant real property appraisal assistance must be stated.)

It is never acceptable for you to say you inspected the subject property or comparable sales when you did not. Lying to the client and the intended users of an appraisal report cannot be good for anyone involved in the transaction.

1. The type of appraisal report

   a) Has no influence on the appraisal process

   b) Is always the same, regardless of the problem

   c) Is determined by the amount of the fee

   d) Is determined by the property owner and the loan amount

2. A narrative appraisal report

   a) Is no more than 10 pages long

   b) Is always a self-contained appraisal report

   c) Cannot include the types of grids used in form reports

   d) Gives the appraiser the freedom to design the report in the manner that is most efficient

3. Residential appraisal reports always involve

   a) A Uniform Residential Appraisal Report (URAR) form

   b) A summary report

   c) A condominium form

   d) Various forms and report types, depending on the assignment

4. In an appraisal report, the appraiser must include

   a) The effective date of the appraisal and the date of the invoice

   b) The effective date of the appraisal and the date of the report

   c) The date the report was written and the date it was ordered

   d) The date of report, the effective date of the report, and the date the invoice was paid

5. A client ordered an appraisal of his property at 2134 Roberts Road in Smallburg. The local appraiser developed an opinion of value. Before she could get finish the job, the client cancelled the order. The appraiser never provided any of her findings to the client orally or in writing. This appraiser completed an

   a) Appraisal only

   b) Appraisal report only

   c) Appraisal and appraisal report

   d) Appraisal review

6. An attorney is reading a document prepared by an appraiser on a vacant lot. The document states and supports a value of $1,000,000 on the property. This document is called a(n)

   a) Appraisal

   b) Appraisal report

   c) Market analysis

   d) Market value letter

Note: Unless otherwise noted, italicized references indicate the pages in *The Appraisal of Real Estate*, 14th edition, that readers should consult for additional discussion of these topics.

1. a) Has no influence on the appraisal process
    USPAP and this student handbook

2. d) Gives the appraiser the freedom to design the report in the manner that is most efficient
    Page 654

3. d) Various forms and report types, depending on the assignment
    Page 649

4. b) The effective date of the appraisal and the date of the report
    Page 658

5. a) Appraisal only

6. b) Appraisal report

32

Appraisal Review

The appraisal profession encompasses much more than appraising real property for a fee. The real estate business offers many areas of specialty, as does the appraisal field. Residential mortgage appraisers make good money when mortgage interest rates are declining, but they suffer when rates increase and the volume of sales decreases. Right of way and condemnation appraisers do very well when public works projects are fully funded but are not very busy when they are not. Litigation appraisers do well most of the time because litigation work (such as divorce, partnership dissolution, and similar assignments) is ongoing regardless of the economic climate. Tax appeal appraisers are very, very busy immediately after reassessment notices are mailed, but their workload is flat the rest of the time. Most appraisers take the work as it comes, but the smart ones seek a diverse clientele and do not let one type of client take over their practices.

One of the common ways appraisers diversify is through providing appraisal review services to the variety of clients who would want to confirm the correctness of an appraisal prepared by another person and sometimes to provide a second opinion about the value relating to real property. *Appraisal review* is a process in which one appraiser develops an opinion about the quality of another appraiser's work.

Appraisal review may require appraisal reviewers to present their own opinions of the subject property value. Many clients request that appraisal reviewers indicate their value opinion if they disagree with the conclusion presented in the appraisal report under review. When appraisal reviewers present their opinions of value, the

> Wise appraisers diversify their practices as much as possible. It is usually inadvisable to "put all your eggs in one basket."

product is also an appraisal and must meet the minimum criteria for an appraisal, but it can be reported within the review appraisal document.

It is very important for appraisal reviewers to indicate what the assignment includes. The scope of work of an appraisal review may include only a desk review of the document and confirmation of the data but not include an actual inspection of the subject property. Reviewers commonly do only curbside inspections of properties.

> Appraisal review is similar to what an accounting auditor would do to check the books of another accountant. Appraisal review is a common tool in the quality control process.

Why Appraisal Reviews Are Needed

Clients request appraisal reviews for many reasons, but the most common ones include the following:

- Some lenders and investors do not approve large loans until the appraisal reports are reviewed, at least in a desk review. These clients usually require fast turnaround because the loan approval is waiting on the appraisal reviewer's opinion. This preapproval review can be required if the lender has not worked with the appraiser before and would not be comfortable extending a large loan based on an appraisal from a stranger. A third-party review provides assurance to investors because they hire the appraisal reviewer directly. It is important to remember that the scope of work in a review must be adequate to produce credible results within the context of the intended use.

- Some lenders require a curbside or desk review on all loan packages under consideration for purchase. A large investor in mortgage loans may find it necessary to review all the loans in a package offered for sale. More often, though, appraisal reviewers will review a portion of the loans, and then, if the reviews are negative, they will review more loans in the package.

- Some lenders spot-check their portfolio of loans as a quality control measure to satisfy bank regulators who are always concerned about the quality of a loan portfolio. The bank regulators should be much more comfortable with a loan if they have a competent third-party review of the appraisal report.

- Many government agencies require a review appraisal on all appraisals done for litigation in condemnation proceedings. This type of review appraisal may involve no communication between the two appraisers, or the reviewer and appraiser may communicate regularly.

Who Can Prepare Appraisal Reviews?

Professional standards apply to appraisal review assignments just as they do to appraisal assignments. There are state laws and regulations that apply to appraisers doing review work for any client, but there are also some federal rules that apply to appraisers doing work for federally related transactions (FRTs). Appraisers should be clear on what regulations apply to them before accepting an assignment with unusual conditions. For each appraisal review assignment, the reviewer must be

- competent in the applicable valuation methods and techniques
- independent
- objective
- impartial

A reviewer's level of competency depends on the scope of work of the individual review assignment. Generally, the reviewer must be competent in terms of

- the property type involved in the work being reviewed

- the applicable valuation methods
- the market area and geographic area of the involved property

Before accepting a review assignment, you must be able to understand the level of competency required and objectively decide if you qualify to perform such an assignment. It is also important to remember that appraisers cannot so limit their scope of work as to render the assignment not credible when considering the intended use.

Applicability of Professional Standards

An appraisal reviewer must initially identify the professional standards or specific regulations that apply to each review assignment. These may include

- the Uniform Standards of Professional Appraisal Practice (specifically Standard 3)
- the Uniform Appraisal Standards for Federal Land Acquisition (i.e., the "Yellow Book")
- FHA or VA regulations
- Fannie Mae and Freddie Mac regulations

For example, the use of Fannie Mae Form 2000/ Freddie Mac Form 1032 is required for review assignments performed for these two entities. In order to complete this form, you must indicate an agreement or disagreement with the original value opinion. As a result, the scope of work of every review assignment performed for Fannie Mae or Freddie Mac must include this information.

Structuring the Appraisal Review Assignment

The extent of research and analysis required in an appraisal review depends on the scope of work of the specific assignment, although appraisal reviews are commonly divided into two categories—desk reviews and field reviews. A desk review requires an appraisal reviewer to assume that much of the physical description of the property is true. This does not mean that you cannot check the appraisal

---

Appraisal Review Used in Litigation

Attorneys preparing for litigation hire appraisers to prepare analyses of the properties in litigation, and the attorneys on the other side may hire their own appraiser to do the same thing. Sometimes the results of these two appraisals are significantly different, and the attorneys will order a third appraisal, which can confuse the issue even more. However, one or both sides may request that the other side provide a list of acceptable appraisers to prepare a review of the two appraisal reports that indicates where the fault lies. Using an appraisal reviewer as an arbiter is often better than ordering a third appraisal because it provides the judge, jury, or arbiter with the reasoning of an appraisal expert regarding the difference in the two values. When both sides agree on an appraisal review, they are more or less agreeing to arbitrate the valuation part of the case. This is a great technique in many situations.

report against old listing sheets (from a broker) or the assessor's office, but in the absence of other data you have to assume that the physical description is correct as listed. To perform a field review, you must at least go to the site, which allows you to compare the building and site description in the report under review with the property itself. Be careful to avoid comparing a property inspected in June with an appraisal prepared in September of the year before. Properties change and sometimes the property will be different when inspected at a later date.

The scope of work of a review appraisal can be more or less than these common assignment types. Depending on the client, the scope of work could require much more work than the original appraisal and appraisal report. If the client asks for a scope of work that is very limited, the appraiser must decide if the scope of work will still allow credible results considering the intended use. There are two important issues in reporting the results of a review assignment:

1. A review appraisal report, like any appraisal report, cannot be misleading.
2. A review report must contain sufficient information to enable the intended users to understand the report.

Notice that the first item does *not* state that a review report cannot be misleading to the intended users. Instead, the item states that a review report cannot be misleading, which means it cannot be misleading to anyone. The second item states that the report should be understood by the intended users. If the intended user is a bank underwriter, the report can be written to a higher level of understanding than if the report was written with a homeowner as the intended user.

Developing the Appraisal Review Opinion

When a reviewer develops an appraisal review opinion, the appraisal is evaluated considering only the market conditions in place as of the effective date of that appraisal. However, information on transactions dated after the effective date of the appraisal is not considered. The reviewer also judges the quantity and quality of the appraisal's data and analyses, looking for areas where additional data or analyses may have been needed. Depending on the specific assignment, the reviewer may read the appraisal report from front to back or may initially skim the report for the main points presented and then focus in on the key

data and analyses. Regardless of the appraiser's approach or the situation of the specific assignment, the reviewer's main goal should be to communicate the quality of the appraisal to the client so that the client can then decide if the appraisal serves its intended use.

Providing an Opinion of Value as a Reviewer

If the scope of work of a review assignment calls for the reviewer to either agree or disagree with the value opinion in the appraisal under review, a reviewer who agrees with the value conclusion in the appraisal is taking on responsbility for that value opinion as well, subject to certain assignment conditions. These sorts of conditions may include an extraordinary assumption of the appraisal review assignment that some of the information provided in the appraisal report is accurate if verification of that information was not part of the scope of work of the review assignment. When accepting an assignment with an assumption that certain information is correct, the appraiser must decide if that scope of work is sufficient to produce credible results considering the intended use and the resulting review appraisal report is not misleading. If the reviewer disagrees with the value conclusion, that reviewer is, as a result, providing another appraisal that contradicts the results of the appraisal being reviewed.

If the reviewer disagrees with the value conclusion, it is not enough to merely state this disagreement in the report. Because the reviewer is in effect providing another appraisal, he or she must provide support for the new value opinion. However, the reviewer does not have to create an entirely new report or start over from square one. The reviewer may only need to remove the part of the original data and analyses that is deemed to be insufficient or unacceptable and replace it with appropriate data and analysis. The new data and analyses must be included in the review report.

Review appraisers should avoid using certain terms if they do not intend to convey an opinion of value. For example, statements that do not imply a new value in a review include

- The value opinion is or is not adequately supported.
- The value opinion is or is not reasonable.
- The value opinion is well supported.

Statements that do imply a new value opinion are

- I concur with the value.

Components of an Appraisal Review Report

A review report must include the following minimum components to comply with professional standards:

1. The client and intended users of the review
2. The intended use of the review
3. The objective of the review
4. The subject of the review assignment
5. The ownership interest of the subject property of the work under review
6. The date of the work under review
7. The effective date of the conclusions of the work under review
8. The name of the appraiser
9. The effective date of the review
10. Extraordinary assumptions and hypothetical conditions used by the reviewer (and a statement that their use might affect the conclusions)
11. The reviewer's scope of work
12. The reviewer's opinions and conclusions
13. The reviewer's opinion of value, the reasoning behind this opinion, and a statement explaining which segments of the appraisal were considered credible and what additional information was used in the review (if part of the review assignment's scope of work)
14. The reviewer's signed certification

- I think the value is correct at $xx.
- I think the value is too high.

Reporting the Appraisal Review Opinion

The main goal of an appraisal review report is providing a clear and supported opinion of the appraisal under review. Repeating or summarizing the appraisal is not necessary because the client already has access to the appraisal report under review. Communicating the appraisal review may take the form of an oral report, a written report using a standardized format, or a written report using a format created by the reviewer.

In an oral report, the reviewer and client discuss the appraisal under review in person or over the phone. Reviewers may also provide oral reports in court. In either case, the review opinion must be developed prior to delivery of the report. Due diligence and a workfile are both required for oral reports.

Clients may require a form review or the use of a predetermined format. Fannie Mae Form 2000/ Freddie Mac Form 1032 is most commonly used in reviews involving one- to four-unit residential properties. Regardless of the format used, relevant professional standards of appraisal practice may also require additional detail. If you are using a nonstandardized written format, you should ensure that the report meets the needs of the client and intended user, complies with the applicable professional standards, and is not misleading.

The Reviewer's Workfile

According to professional standards such as USPAP and the Code of Professional Ethics of the Appraisal Institute, reviewers must maintain workfiles for each review assignment. Each workfile must be kept for either five years or two years after the final disposition of any related court proceedings in which the reviewer provided testimony, whichever is longer. The reviewer must keep the workfile or have a working agreement in place with the keeper of the workfile.

The workfile for a written review report must include

- an exact copy of the review report provided to the client
- any additional information supporting the reviewer's findings (usually including a copy of the work under review) or an indication of where that information can be found

The workfile for an oral review report must include

- an indication of who the client and intended users are
- adequate data to support the reviewer's conclusions
- any additional information supporting the reviewer's findings (usually including a copy of the work under review) or an indication of where that information can be found

- the reviewer's signed certification
- a summary of the oral report or transcript of the reviewer's court testimony

Common Issues Found in Appraisal Reviews

The issues that are most commonly uncovered in appraisal reports during the review process include

- the appraiser lacking the necessary training, experience, or competency to adequately complete the assignment
- inadequacies in the report due to unrealistic assignment time frames or deadlines
- reports with missing pages or a missing appraiser signature
- failure on the part of the appraiser to
  - meet the client's requirements for the assignment
  - comply with FIRREA or USPAP when required
  - provide effective "when completed" or "at stabilization" dates for proposed projects
  - provide meaningful analysis and a highest and best use conclusion
  - explicitly state hypothetical conditions
  - discuss market trends
  - independently verify comparable data
- reports that contain
  - flawed data
  - excessive limiting conditions, meaningless statements, repetition, or irrelevant data
  - outdated source references
  - inadequate exhibits
  - improperly recycled material from other appraisal reports
  - overuse of boilerplate material from textbooks
  - typos, inconsistencies, and math errors
  - non-market-oriented units of comparison

1. An appraisal review assignment
   a) Must include the reviewer's opinion of the value of the subject property of the report under review, as of the date of the first appraisal
   b) Must not include the reviewer's opinion of the value of the subject property of the report under review, as of the date of the first appraisal
   c) Can include the reviewer's opinion of the value of the subject property of the report under review, as of the date of the first appraisal
   d) Must include the reviewer's opinion of the value of the subject property of the report under review, as of the date of the review appraisal

2. An appraiser who specializes in review appraisal work
   a) Can do a review of any property type providing the appraiser has read a similar report before
   b) Must be competent to do the review or follow the required steps to become competent
   c) Should always be very critical of the report because that is why the appraisal reviewer is hired
   d) Cannot review a report if it is in litigation

3. An appraiser was asked to look at an appraisal report of the subject property prepared by another appraiser. The client wanted a report that included the appraiser's opinion of the first report and also an independent opinion of value (if different than that of the first report). This client is asking for a(n)
   a) Appraisal assignment only
   b) Appraisal report only
   c) Appraisal review and an appraisal by the reviewer
   d) Consulting assignment

4. An appraiser prepared an appraisal report on a small commercial property. A reviewer found that there were many small errors in the report. Which of the following statements is correct?
   a) This is not a significant problem under any circumstances and therefore is not an ethics violation.
   b) This may be a problem if all the errors are pointing in the same direction.
   c) Small errors are common in nearly all appraisals and therefore are only human. This is not a lapse in ethics in any situation.
   d) If the errors were about the subject it would indicate an ethical lapse, but if the errors are regarding the comparable it would be considered normal.

5. In an appraisal review assignment, the subject
   a) Is the real estate that was appraised by the appraiser under review
   b) Is the real property that was appraised by the appraiser under review
   c) May be all or part of a report, a workfile, or a combination of these and may be related to appraisal, appraisal review, or consulting
   d) Is the person who wrote the report under review

6. If a reviewer does a poor job of reviewing an appraisal assignment and report,
   a) No one will ever or could ever know
   b) This may be revealed by a review of the review
   c) There is no standard for this work, so USPAP does not apply
   d) The standard for review work is a combination of USPAP Standards 1 and 2

7. In a review assignment, the scope of work
   a) Must be the same as the appraisal work under review
   b) Can be different than the appraisal work under review
   c) Must be different than the appraisal work under review
   d) Is always limited to drive-by, exterior-only inspections

8. In an appraisal review assignment, the reviewer
   a) Cannot offer an opinion of value of the real property shown as the subject in the appraisal report under review
   b) Must give an opinion of value of the real property shown as the subject in the appraisal report under review if he or she disagrees with the first value opinion
   c) May offer an opinion of value for the real property shown as the subject in the appraisal report under review if the scope of work includes this
   d) Must always be prepared to offer an opinion of value for the property listed as the subject in the appraisal report under review; the reviewer does not have to express this in the report, but it must be developed and not reported

Note: Unless otherwise noted, italicized references indicate the pages in *The Appraisal of Real Estate*, 14th edition, that readers should consult for additional discussion of these topics.

1. c) Can include the reviewer's opinion of the value of the subject property of the report under review, as of the date of the first appraisal
   Pages 671-672

2. b) Must be competent to do the review or follow the required steps to become competent
   Pages 673-675

3. c) Appraisal review and an appraisal by the reviewer

4. b) This may be a problem if all the errors are pointing in the same direction.

5. c) May be all or part of a report, a workfile, or a combination of these and may be related to appraisal, appraisal review, or consulting
   Page 671

6. b) This may be revealed by a review of the review

7. b) Can be different than the appraisal work under review
   Page 676

8. c) May offer an opinion of value for the real property shown as the subject in the appraisal report under review if the scope of work includes this
   Page 676

33

Consulting

Appraisers who want to diversify their practices can look beyond the typical appraisal and appraisal review assignments to the much broader range of services under the umbrella of *consulting*, which is a generic term that must be used with care. An appraisal-related consulting assignment may involve an opinion of value, but developing the opinion of value is not the sole purpose of the assignment. A consulting assignment may involve a service in which the consultant is considered to be "acting as an appraiser" and thus is subject to professional standards. The important thing to remember about consulting is that when the consultant is acting as an appraiser (that is, when the client expects the consultant to have valuation expertise and to maintain an unbiased and objective role), professional standards such as the Uniform Standards of Professional Appraisal Practice apply, and the consultant cannot be paid a fee that is contingent on or subject to a subsequent event. In that case, the consulting assignment must be performed without advocacy.

Consulting assignments involve the appraiser's training, research skills, and analytical techniques. For example, imagine you are hired to testify about the effect of asphalt plants on nearby residential properties. You have studied the effect of proximity of residential property to asphalt plants in other areas by comparing the prices of houses upwind of asphalt plants before and after the construction of the plants and can testify about those findings. That information, which does involve considerations of value, could be used in court to support or refute the general assertion that proximity of an asphalt plant to a residential area affects the values of homes in a certain way. Now suppose you are asked to use the information you have gathered about the effect of asphalt plants on residential property values in other areas to forecast the effect on the value of a particular property or properties that would be affected by the construction of the proposed plant. That service would be an appraisal. In either case, you are acting as an appraiser because you have been hired because of your valuation expertise and unbiased and objective perspective.

Types of Consulting Assignments

Clients hire appraisers for consulting assignments to help them with financial planning and decision-making as well as developing strategies regarding the purchase, sale, marketing, and managing of real estate—in other words, to evaluate choices and make recommendations about which choice is best. Examples of appraisal-related consulting assignments include

- feasibility studies
- cost-benefit studies
- pricing and rent projection studies
- property tax services
- litigation consulting

Feasibility studies usually involve developing a value opinion for a proposed land use and testing that use's feasibility by comparing its costs and benefits and considering alternative uses. The appraiser can develop the value of the proposed use as part of the consulting assignment, but the value itself is not the information needed by the client to make an informed business decision.

Public bodies, community leaders, and developers hire appraisers to conduct cost-benefit studies on proposed projects, such as developing infrastructure. Cost-benefit studies involve determining risk and considering various scenarios to help clients decide whether or not to implement these sorts of projects.

A pricing and rent projection study may be part of a marketability study or may stand on its own. These studies help clients develop sales and marketing strategies for their real estate projects as well as make decisions regarding property management or investment.

Property owners also hire appraisers as consultants when disputing, or deciding whether or not to dispute, property tax assessments. Appraisers may develop an opinion of value for the property (and this valuation must comply with applicable professional standards, e.g., Standards 1 and 2 of USPAP), perform research that may reveal unclaimed tax exemptions for the property owner, or provide some other information that the property owner may base a dispute of the assessed value on, such as the correct property size or classification. When working on these types of assignments, appraisers must remain unbiased. The appraiser cannot act as an advocate for the property owner, nor can the property owner base the fee paid on the amount of tax money saved.

Litigation work is a favorite assignment type for some appraisers. It is not unusual for some appraisers to spend a good deal of time researching special situations and problems to be resolved with litigation and providing court testimony.

An appraiser's services may also be needed for other types of consulting assignments, such as

- land use studies
- market and marketability studies
- due diligence for a client's acquisition or sale decision
- operations audits
- absorption analysis
- adaptive reuse analyses
- property inspections
- capital market analysis

- risk analysis
- portfolio analysis
- arbitration

The services provided by the appraiser depend on the specific circumstances of the assignment. The last three types of assignment in the list usually involve a valuation.

Competency Issues

As in any typical appraisal assignment that a practitioner may be offered, an appraiser acting as a consultant must be competent to do the job required. If you have no experience in a particular type of consulting assignment, the Uniform Standards of Professional Appraisal Practice require three things:

1. You must notify the client that you have little or no experience in this type of assignment.
2. You must do whatever is necessary to become competent, which may include research, reading instructional materials, taking a class, or, more commonly, joining forces with another appraiser who does have the experience and training to do the relevant portion of the job competently.
3. You must tell the reader of the report of your limited experience and the steps you have taken to become competent.

The competency issue can be critical in consulting assignments because these types of assignments are usually not mainstream. Instead, they are more often one-of-a-kind and require appraisers to use a wide range of analytical techniques.

1. Professional standards apply

   a) To appraisal assignments only and not appraisal review or consulting assignments

   b) To any service in which the individual is "acting as an appraiser"

   c) To appraisal, appraisal review, and consulting assignments, regardless of whether the service includes a valuation

   d) To appraisal, appraisal review, and only those consulting assignments that include a valuation

2. Assignments that fall under the category of consulting services include

   a) Land use studies, risk analysis, and portfolio analysis

   b) Risk analysis, portfolio analysis, and discounted cash flow (DCF) analysis

   c) Highest and best use analysis, land use studies, and risk analysis

   d) All of the above

Note: Unless otherwise noted, italicized references indicate the pages in *The Appraisal of Real Estate*, 14th edition, that readers should consult for additional discussion of these topics.

1. b) To any service in which the individual is "acting as an appraiser"
    Page 683

2. d) All of the above
    Page 687

34

Valuation for Financial Reporting

Just as a family's house is usually its largest financial investment, the real property holdings of corporate America are often significant assets (or liabilities) for companies large and small. Since the collapse of Enron, the increased scrutiny of the accounting of assets in the financial reports filed by publicly traded companies is having an effect on how real estate is accounted for on corporate balance sheets. At the same time, the shift in who is able to perform the valuation of those assets presents real estate appraisers with a growing opportunity.

Why Is Fair Value Important and What Is VFR?

The discipline known as *valuation for financial reporting* (VFR) has been around for a long time, but changes to the Financial Accounting Standards Board's (FASB's) definition of *fair value* along with standards relating to financial reporting from the FASB and the International Accounting Standards Board have opened up the playing field to appraisers more than ever. So far, the International Valuation Standards Council (IVSC) has gone further than the Appraisal Standards Board in incorporating fair value into real estate appraisal standards, but the convergence of the concepts of *fair value* and *market value* is well on its way.

Current generally accepted accounting principles have moved away from book value and toward fair value as the standard measure of asset value for financial reporting. Recording "current" values in financial reporting rather than book values involves the analysis of the depreciated cost of long-lived and short-lived items along with analysis of the estimated sale price of assets in the current market, all of which real estate appraisers are familiar with.

The most commonly cited definitions of *market value* are in line with the current FASB definition of *fair value*, as stated in Accounting Standards Codification Topic 820:

> The price that would be received to sell an asset or paid to transfer a liability in an orderly transaction between market participants at the measurement date.

The concept of an "orderly transaction between market participants" mirrors the requirements of most market value definitions that buyers and sellers be typically motivated and act prudently and knowledgeably. Likewise, the requirement in most market value definitions that the property receive reasonable exposure time in the marketplace also echoes the "orderly transaction" statement in the fair value definition.

The term *valuation for financial reporting* seems to be replacing the concept of *mark to market*, at least in appraisal. The latter term referred to the practice of adjusting rental income to current market levels to accurately project property income and property value in a financial report. Again, valuation for financial reporting is not a new idea—it simply has increasing relevance to real property appraisers as their profession intersects more and more with the world of accounting.

Acronyms in Valuation for Financial Reporting	
VFR	valuation for financial reporting
FASB	Financial Accounting Standards Board
IASB	International Accounting Standards Board
IVSC	International Valuation Standards Council
IVS	International Valuation Standards
GAAP	generally accepted accounting principles

KEY TERMS	
fair value	mark to market

Historical Context

To perform an assignment involving valuation for financial reporting, an appraiser needs to understand how the market value and book value of the shareholder's interests in corporately owned real estate have traditionally been defined and treated in financial reports. Market value is the value of the property in the market area in which the property competes. If a share of stock in a corporation is sold from one owner to another, the market price can be said to represent the market value of that stock. This analysis is done every day for all stocks that are openly traded. The price of stock is not necessarily the value of the underlying assets, but in many cases it is a reflection of the upside potential of that corporation and, to some degree, its asset valuation.

Financial reporting of the value of corporately held real estate has traditionally focused on the book value of the real estate–i.e., the asset value after subtracting tax depreciation. If an appraiser received a number that represented the book value of the asset, it was usually just the acquisition cost less the scheduled amount of depreciation allowed by the Internal Revenue Service. The analysis of book value rarely included the sort of market and highest and best use analysis familiar to real estate appraisers. As a result, an asset could have a market value much higher or lower than book value.

As an example, assume a corporation bought a small parcel of land for $100,000 and built a customized 2,000-sq.-ft. building at a cost of $400,000. This building is so customized to the corporation's specific needs that there is no resale potential. The market value of the real estate would probably be less than the land value of $100,000 because of the cost of removing the unmarketable building. The book value of this asset would be the value of the land plus the cost of construction of the building less the scheduled depreciation amount.

Hierarchy of Inputs

In corporate financial reporting, the source of information about an entity's financial performance and pricing assumptions related to assets can be issues because some "inputs" are more objective and reliable than others. Quoted stock prices are an example of a Level 1 input at the top of the scale because the uniformity of the assets is clear and the reliability of the information source is verifiable. Level 2 inputs might include quoted prices for similar assets (rather than identical assets) or for assets in an inactive market. Further down the scale, Level 3 inputs are unobservable and more subjective than inputs at higher levels. Much of the information appraisers collect about real estate markets would qualify as Level 2 inputs because the data is observable, but any real property asset is unique by virtue of its location and thus not identical to some other asset.

What Services Can Appraisers Provide?

The shift from book value to fair value opens the door for real estate appraisers to perform work that was once considered to be within the exclusive domain of accountants. In fact, accountants may become the clients of appraisers in situations that require the services of a "valuation specialist." Common VFR assignments for appraisers include the valuation of corporate real estate assets as part of a corporate merger or acquisition, corporate debt valuation, portfolio review, or property tax assistance.

Impairment of Fixed Assets

When a fixed asset is considered to be "impaired" based on the test prescribed by accounting standards, appraisers may be called in for the revaluation of those assets. The impairment test is a comparison of the carrying amount of an asset recorded in a company's financial statement and the amount that could be recovered through the use or sale of the asset. Impairment tests involve a discounted cash flow analysis of the income attributable to the use of the existing fixed assets, although certain expenses are not included in the net operating income estimate.

Professional Auditing, Accounting, and Valuation Standards

Professional standards relating to valuation for financial reporting were developed many years ago by the International Valuation Standards Council, and the 2011 edition of the International Valuation Standards added material specifically addressing VFR assignments. "Valuers" in the United Kingdom, much of Europe, and elsewhere have been involved in this sort of appraisal work even before the inception of the IVSC's predecessor organiza-

> Note that the concept of book value in accounting can change based on rulings of the FASB, and the amount of depreciation for taxation purposes can change based on tax law revisions.

tion in 1981 because of the accounting standards in force in those countries. Globalization, the unification of Europe, and the rapid growth of emerging markets have all put new pressure on standards-setting bodies to work toward consistent international standards that will improve the efficiency and transparency of financial markets.

Since the Norwalk Agreement between the Financial Accounting Standards Board and the International Accounting Standards Board in 2002, FASB has included more statements in the accounting standards that recognize the importance of market inputs when valuing corporate assets for financial reporting purposes. The development of professional standards for auditing professionals has also followed a similar pattern as international accounting and valuation standards in recent years, furthering the convergence.

1. *Book value* is equal to
   a) The sum of the value of inventory for a publishing company
   b) The value of the assets after the scheduled depreciation has been subtracted from the original cost plus any improvements
   c) The current market value of the property
   d) The cost new of the asset less physical and functional depreciation

2. *Fair value* is
   a) The price on the New York Stock Exchange of stock in the company holding the real estate assets
   b) The value of the assets after the scheduled depreciation has been subtracted from the original cost plus any improvements
   c) The current value of the property in its market
   d) The value of the assets to a specific investor

3. The practice of valuation for financial reporting has been informed by which set of professional standards?
   a) International Accounting Standards
   b) Financial Accounting Standards
   c) International Valuation Standards
   d) All of the above

4. How long have accounting and valuation professionals been developing standards and techniques related to valuation for financial reporting?
   a) Since 1989 and the passage of FIRREA
   b) For more than 30 years
   c) Since the Enron accounting scandal
   d) Since the establishment of the Appraisal Institute

5. The impairment of fixed assets
   a) Is a type of environmental contamination
   b) Results from a lack of access to a site
   c) Is tested through a comparison of the carrying amount of the asset on the company's books and the recoverable amount through use or sale of the asset
   d) Results from the influence of external obsolescence on the book value of real property

6. The hierarchy of inputs
   a) Refers to the order of operations in income capitalization calculations
   b) Has five defined levels
   c) Is a system of categorizing the accounts receivable for an operating business
   d) Gives more weight to quoted prices of similar assets than to the property owner's subjective assumptions

Note: Unless otherwise noted, italicized references indicate the pages in *The Appraisal of Real Estate*, 14th edition, that readers should consult for additional discussion of these topics.

1. b) The value of the assets after the scheduled depreciation has been subtracted from the original cost plus any improvements
    This student handbook

2. c) The current value of the property in its market
    Pages 691-692

3. d) All of the above
    Pages 689-690, 698-699

4. b) For more than 30 years
    Pages 690-691

5. c) Is tested through a comparison of the carrying amount of the asset on the company's books and the recoverable amount through use or sale of the asset
    This student handbook

6. d) Gives more weight to quoted prices of similar assets than to the property owner's subjective assumptions
    This student handbook

35

Valuation of Real Property with Related Personal Property or Intangible Property

Real estate appraisers primarily deal with rights in realty, but they may also be asked to value personal property or other intangible property related to real estate or allocate the value of real property assets from a group of diverse assets. Those assignments involve specialized valuation considerations, and practitioners continue to debate the proper methodologies–some of which are borrowed from the discipline of business valuation–to apply in those situations.

Certain types of real estate, such as car wash, restaurant, or hotel properties, can have value tied to the business conducted on the site. In those situations, allocating value among different asset classes (such as the real property and any intangible assets related to the business operations) can be a challenge. Real estate appraisers may need to work with accountants or business valuers for assistance in allocating value to the non-realty assets, or they may be hired as experts to help specialists in other fields allocate value attributable to real property. Various types of appraisal assignments can entail an allocation of real property value, including some appraisals for ad valorem taxation, eminent domain, financial reporting, and mortgage lending.

Asset Classes, Transaction Types, and Sales Premises

The three general classes of property are straightforward:

1. Real property
2. Personal property } —— Tangible property
3. Intangible property

When a sale involves other asset classes in addition to the rights in real property, things can get complicated for real estate appraisers. The non-physical assets of a business, such as contracts, franchises, trademarks, and copyrights, can have

value in the marketplace that may be included in the sale price of the business and real estate.

Businesses are commonly sold either as entities or assets. That is, either the operating business is sold under the assumption that the business will continue to exist as a going concern, or the individual assets are partitioned off and sold individually, often under a liquidation premise. It can be assumed that a business will continue to operate as a going concern under the going-concern premise, which is often used in the valuation of real estate-intensive businesses along with a liquidation premise.

A comparison of the value of the assets under both premises may influence conclusions of highest and best use of the real property. For example, if the value of the total collection of assets under the liquidation premise is higher than the value under the going-concern premise, some sort of modification or even demolition and conversion of the existing improvements to a different use may be warranted to achieve the highest and best use of the real property.

Under the going-concern premise, it is generally agreed that the sum of the values in exchange for the individual assets might not be equal to the value of the entire combination of assets. This concept can complicate the analysis and allocation of values of individual assets, particularly when different classes of assets are involved.

Application of the Approaches to Value

In the valuation of business properties in which real estate is a significant component, the three approaches to value can still be applicable, but certain approaches are less applicable in valuing some asset classes and in allocating an opinion of value between assets. For example, the cost approach is well suited to the valuation of tangible property but less so to intangible property, unless the replacement cost of certain intangible assets such as an assembled workforce can be reliably estimated.

"Apples-to-apples" comparisons of sales and rentals of similar asset types can be difficult to find, which affects the applicability of the sales comparison and income capitalization approaches. When real property, personal property, and intangible assets are sold together (as they often are in the sale of an operating business) but are not allocated into value for individual assets, the sales comparison approach may only be useful in the analysis of the market value of the total assets of the business. Similarly, the usefulness of income stream analysis is constrained by the reliability of the information on income allocation to different asset classes. Again, the capitalized value of the income stream attributable to all assets may serve as a credible indication of value for the total assets of the business, but more information than may be available would be needed to allocate value between the individual assets.

The Ongoing Debate over Valuation Techniques

Various specialized appraisal techniques have been used to value interests in non-realty assets. All the techniques have both proponents and critics, and the debate continues to this day in appraisal literature and forums of public opinion.

The Cost Approach

The cost approach is a straightforward and useful tool in the valuation of real property with associated non-realty assets because the value indication of the real estate using the cost approach can be used to allocate a portion of a purchase price or other value indication of the total assets of the business to the tangible real property alone.

The Management Fee Approach

For some property types such as hotels, deducting a management fee (and sometimes a franchise fee) from net operating income and capitalizing the remainder is a residual technique used to estimate the value of certain intangible assets.

Market Participant Survey Approach

Surveying the opinions of market participants and researching regulatory filings are considered to be direct engagement with the parties that make up a market. Interviewing market participants gives an appraiser the best understanding of how these participants value various asset classes.

Parsing Income Method

The income streams associated with various property interests can be capitalized to estimate the value of, for example, the income attributable to an intangible asset. However, finding support for capitalization and yield rates for income streams attributable to specific property interests can be extremely difficult.

Communicating Value Opinions

When non-realty interests are involved in an appraisal assignment, the precise use of technical language is especially important. A variety of imprecise jargon is commonly used by market participants in discussions of businesses as going concerns. Ambiguous terms such as *business value*, *business enterprise value*, *going-concern value*, and *dark value* are often incorrectly used to describe different types of value.

The type of value being reported is a basic element of an appraisal assignment that should be determined in the scope of work and communicated to the client without confusion. If assets other than real property are included in an appraisal assignment, you must make sure you understand what precisely is being valued and are able to communicate that to the intended users of the appraisal.

1. The three general classes of property are
   a) Real property, personal property, and public property
   b) Tangible property, intangible property, and taxable property
   c) Real property, intangible property, and personal property
   d) Real estate, trade fixtures, and goodwill

2. Which of the following is *not* a specialized technique for valuing non-realty interests?
   a) The parsing income method
   b) The market participant survey approach
   c) The management fee approach
   d) The subdivision development method

3. Which of the following property types is the most likely to involve consideration of non-realty assets?
   a) Newly developed one-unit homes
   b) National chain hotel properties
   c) Multitenant suburban office buildings
   d) Flex office/warehouse buildings

Note: Unless otherwise noted, italicized references indicate the pages in *The Appraisal of Real Estate*, 14th edition, that readers should consult for additional discussion of these topics.

1. **c) Real property, intangible property, and personal property**
    Page 704

2. **d) The subdivision development method**
    Pages 710-714

3. **b) National chain hotel properties**
    This student handbook